MANUAL OF CLINICAL PROBLEMS IN DERMATOLOGY
WITH ANNOTATED REFERENCES

MANUAL OF
CLINICAL PROBLEMS
IN DERMATOLOGY
WITH ANNOTATED
REFERENCES

Edited by

Suzanne M. Olbricht, M.D.
Instructor in Dermatology, Harvard Medical
School; Dermatologist and Director,
Dermatologic Surgery Unit, Beth Israel
Hospital, Boston

Michael E. Bigby, M.D.
Assistant Professor of Dermatology, Harvard
Medical School; Associate Dermatologist, Beth
Israel Hospital, Boston

Kenneth A. Arndt, M.D.
Professor of Dermatology, Harvard Medical
School; Dermatologist-in-Chief, Beth Israel
Hospital, Boston

Little, Brown and Company
Boston/Toronto/London

Library of Congress Cataloging-in-Publication Data

Manual of clinical problems in dermatology : with annotated references / edited by Suzanne M. Olbricht, Michael E. Bigby, Kenneth A. Arndt.
    p. cm.
  Includes bibliographical references and index.
  ISBN 0-316-09425-0
    1. Dermatology—Handbooks, manuals, etc. 2. Skin—diseases—Handbooks, manuals, etc. I. Olbricht, Suzanne M. II. Bigby, Michael E. III. Arndt, Kenneth A.
  [DNLM: 1. Skin Diseases. WR 140 M294]
RL74.M35 1992
616.5—dc20
DNLM/DLC
for Library of Congress   91-45992
                                              CIP

Printed in the United States of America

SEM

To those who have taught us
and those who continue to teach us

CONTENTS

PREFACE

For more than 20 years, weekly literature conferences in dermatology have been a tradition for trainees in the departments of dermatology at Beth Israel Hospital and Harvard Medical School. The format of these conferences has varied over the years, but the objectives have always remained the same: thorough, in-depth review of the dermatologic and medical literature about disorders pertinent to the field of cutaneous biology, medicine, and surgery. Topics covering all aspects of dermatology and related disciplines are planned on a 2- to 3-year cycle, and trainees choose or are assigned topics. At the conference, trainees deliver 30- to 60-minute talks and hand out 6- to 12-page papers including annotated bibliographies. Landmark articles from the literature and sections from texts are assigned and read by all prior to the conference. It is expected that the literature is carefully and critically reviewed and that the pertinent points and new information about the subject at hand are skillfully elucidated.

Manual of Clinical Problems in Dermatology primarily represents the efforts of dermatology, dermatopathology, and other departmental trainees during a recent 3-year cycle. The topics discussed were chosen by the editors, the material to be covered was initially reviewed and discussed by the trainees and their editor-preceptors, and all manuscripts were then reviewed, revised, updated, and put into publication format by the editors. The editors would like to gratefully acknowledge the expert editorial and secretarial assistance of Patricia Novak, Jean DePasquale, Lisa Feldman, and Carolyn Guiod.

The Beth Israel dermatology conferences have helped educate generations of dermatologists, dermatopathologists, medical students, nurses, and rotating house officers; and the editors hope this manual will be useful for all who read these pages.

S.M.O.
M.E.B.
K.A.A.

CONTRIBUTING AUTHORS

R. Rox Anderson, M.D.
Associate Professor of Dermatology, Harvard Medical School; Assistant in Dermatology, Massachusetts General Hospital, Boston

Kenneth A. Arndt, M.D.
Professor of Dermatology, Harvard Medical School; Dermatologist-in-Chief, Beth Israel Hospital, Boston

Lynn A. Baden, M.D., M.P.H.
Instructor in Dermatology, Harvard Medical School; Dermatologist, Brigham and Women's Hospital, Boston

Mark S. Bernhardt, M.D.
Consultant, Department of Dermatology, Holy Cross Hospital, Fort Lauderdale, Florida

Michael E. Bigby, M.D.
Assistant Professor of Dermatology, Harvard Medical School; Associate Dermatologist, Beth Israel Hospital, Boston

Paul S. Birnbaum, M.D.
Attending Dermatologist, Newton-Wellesley Hospital, Newton, Massachusetts

Paul A. Bleicher, M.D., Ph.D.
Assistant Professor of Dermatology, Harvard Medical School; Cutaneous Biology Research Center, Department of Dermatology, Massachusetts General Hospital, Boston

Clarence E. Boudreaux, M.D.
Clinical Assistant Professor of Dermatology, University of Florida College of Medicine, Gainesville

Serge A. Coopman, M.D.
Department of Dermatology, University of Leuven; Department of Dermatology, University Hospitals of Leuven, Belgium

Thomas G. Cropley, M.D.
Assistant Professor of Medicine, Division of Dermatology, University of Massachusetts Medical Center, Worcester

Susan D. DeCoste, M.D.
Instructor in Dermatology, Harvard Medical School; Clinical Associate in Dermatology, Massachusetts General Hospital, Boston

Jeffrey S. Dover, M.D., F.R.C.P.C.
Assistant Professor of Dermatology, Harvard Medical School; Chief, Division of Dermatology, New England Deaconess Hospital, Boston

Jerome D. Fallon, M.D.
Dermatologist, Racine Medical Center, Racine, Wisconsin

William Frank, M.D.
Clinical Fellow, Department of Dermatology, Harvard Medical School; Clinical Instructor, Department of Dermatology, Massachusetts General Hospital, Boston

Richard L. Gallo, M.D., Ph.D.
Instructor in Dermatology, Harvard Medical School; Assistant in Dermatology, Massachusetts General Hospital, Boston

Richard Gold, M.D.
Clinical Fellow, Department of Radiology, Harvard Medical School; House Staff, Department of Radiology, Beth Israel Hospital, Boston

Paul B. Googe, M.D.
Assistant Professor of Pathology, University of Tennessee Graduate School of Medicine; Dermatopathologist, University of Tennessee Medical Center, Knoxville

Anita M. Grassi, M.D.
Instructor in Dermatology, Harvard Medical School; Clinical Associate in Dermatology, Beth Israel Hospital and Massachusetts General Hospital, Boston

Joop M. Grevelink, M.D.
Instructor in Dermatology, Harvard Medical School; Assistant Dermatologist and Director of the Dermatology Laser Center, Massachusetts General Hospital, Boston

Andree A. Haas, M.D.
Instructor in Dermatology, Harvard Medical School, Boston; Courtesy Staff, Department of Medicine, Mt. Auburn Hospital, Harvard Community Health Plan, Cambridge, Massachusetts

Richard F. Horan, M.D.
Assistant Clinical Professor of Dermatology, Harvard Medical School; Associate Physician (Dermatology) and Consultant in Allergy, Brigham and Women's Hospital; Physician, Section of Allergy, New England Deaconess Hospital, Boston

Sewon Kang, M.D.
Resident in Dermatology, Harvard Medical School; Clinical Research Fellow, Department of Dermatology, Massachusetts General Hospital, Boston

Joseph C. Kvedar, M.D.
Instructor in Dermatology, Harvard Medical School, Boston; Chief of Dermatology, Cambridge Hospital, Cambridge, Massachusetts

David A. Laub, M.D.
Assistant Clinical Professor, University of California, Davis, School of Medicine; Clinical Instructor, University of California, San Francisco, School of Medicine; Attending Dermatologist, Marin General Hospital, Greenbrae

Ethan A. Lerner, M.D., Ph.D.
Assistant Professor in Dermatology, Harvard Medical School; Associate Physician in Dermatology, Brigham and Women's Hospital, Boston

Jay A. Levin, M.D.
Clinical Instructor in Dermatology, Emory University School of Medicine, Atlanta; Clinical Instructor in Dermatology, Medical College of Georgia Hospital and Clinics, Augusta

Sharon J. Littzi, M.D.
Attending Physician, Division of Dermatology, Hartford Hospital and St. Francis Hospital, Hartford, Connecticut

Edward V. Maytin, M.D., Ph.D.
Instructor in Dermatology, Harvard Medical School; Assistant in Dermatology, Massachusetts General Hospital, Boston

Suzanne M. Olbricht, M.D.
Instructor in Dermatology, Harvard Medical School; Dermatologist and Director, Dermatologic Surgery Unit, Beth Israel Hospital, Boston

Scott B. Phillips, M.D.
Instructor in Dermatology, Harvard Medical School; Chief, Dermatology Clinical Investigations Unit, Massachusetts General Hospital, Boston

Deborah A. Scott, M.D.
Clinical Instructor in Dermatology, Boston University School of Medicine; Chief of Dermatology, Massachusetts Institute of Technology, Cambridge

Richard J. Sharpe, M.D.
Instructor in Dermatology, Harvard Medical School; Associate in Dermatology, Department of Dermatology, Beth Israel Hospital, Boston

Christopher R. Shea, M.D.
Assistant Professor of Medicine and Pathology, Cornell University Medical College; Assistant Attending Physician, The New York Hospital, New York

Robert H. Shmerling, M.D.
Instructor in Medicine, Harvard Medical School; Associate Physician, Department of Medicine, Beth Israel Hospital, Boston

Arthur K. F. Tong, M.B., B.S. (Lond.)
Staff Dermatologist, Quincy City Hospital, Quincy, Massachusetts

Martin A. Weinstock, M.D., Ph.D.
Director, Dermatoepidemiology Unit, Department of Medicine, Brown University Program in Medicine; Chief of Dermatology, Veterans Administration Medical Center; Director, Rhode Island Moles and Melanoma Unit, and Director of Photomedicine, Roger Williams Medical Center, Providence, Rhode Island

I. ESTABLISHING A DIAGNOSIS

1. OFFICE EVALUATION
Thomas G. Cropley

Dermatologic diagnosis is approached in the same fashion as the diagnosis of disease of any other organ system. The conventional method is one of orderly progression from the patient's history to physical examination and, ultimately, to the performance of laboratory tests or other special diagnostic tests that together reduce the number of diagnoses from many to one. This chapter outlines some of the techniques of history taking, physical examination, and ancillary testing that are especially important in dermatology.

As in medical history-taking in general, the **dermatologic history** begins with the patient's chief complaint, which is fully delineated by careful questioning by the interviewer regarding the time of onset of symptoms, factors that exacerbate or relieve the problem, and response to previous therapies. A general medical systems review serves to fill in missing and often important bits of information that otherwise may have been minimized or forgotten by the patient.

In taking a history from a patient whose complaint is referable to the skin, the interviewer may need to emphasize several areas, depending on the circumstances:

1. Are the lesions related to the patient's work environment (occupational eczema, for example), to contact exposure to plants or chemicals, or to medications?
2. Are lesions induced or exacerbated by sun exposure (e.g., lupus erythematosus, polymorphous light eruption), cold (chilblains), heat (cholinergic urticaria), excessive dryness (asteatotic eczema), or excessive hydration of the skin (immersion foot)?
3. Is the skin disease associated with fever? Febrile illnesses are, by definition, systemic. A useful rule of thumb is that all skin diseases associated with fever should be considered serious and potentially life-threatening until proven otherwise.
4. Has a previously stable lesion begun to change in size, shape, color, or symmetry? Such a change may indicate malignant transformation of a previously benign lesion (e.g., malignant melanoma).

The mucocutaneous integument is unique among the organ systems of the body in being entirely accessible to the eyes and fingers of the examiner. The **physical examination** is designed to allow skin lesions to be characterized in a systematic fashion, as an aid to differential diagnosis. One morphologic schema that is commonly employed is the "T.S.A.D." system proposed by Fitzpatrick:

1. **Type** of lesion: primary lesions (macule, papule, plaque, wheal, nodule, tumor, cyst, vesicle, bulla, pustule, erosion, ulcer, atrophy); secondary lesions (scale, crust, lichenification); color of lesion should be noted.
2. **Shape** of individual lesion: dome-shaped, flat-topped, polygonal, linear, annular, serpiginous.
3. **Arrangement** of lesions with respect to one another: annular grouping, linear grouping, serpiginous grouping, herpetiform grouping, diffuse.
4. **Distribution** of lesions on the body: symmetrical, dermatomal, segmental, random, localized, generalized.

Ideally, the patient should be completely undressed, with every effort made to preserve the patient's modesty. A brief explanation of the need to examine all areas, including the scalp, buttocks, and perineum in order to detect lesions of which the patient might not be aware, will usually allay the patient's anxiety regarding the examination. Boyce and Bernhard found that only 5% of patients in a busy dermatology clinic objected to total skin examination.

The examination should be conducted in a well-lit room. Natural sunlight generally provides the best combination of neutral white color and even illumination but, of course, its intensity varies with weather conditions. Most modern examination rooms are illuminated with fluorescent tubes, which cast a shadowless light with a slightly greenish tone, usually of low intensity. Unfortunately, this type of lighting tends to

3

render surface textures less visible, and the greenish cast often mutes subtle erythema. Probably the best artificial light source for examining the skin is high-intensity incandescent lighting, as is used in operating rooms. Surgical lights reproduce the color mix of natural sunlight, and cast enough shadow to reveal surface textures.

Examination should proceed in an orderly fashion. Individual methods vary, but a commonly used approach is as follows:

1. With the patient seated, examine the scalp and hair. A blow dryer may be needed if the hair is thick.
2. Examine the face, ears, and neck, directing attention particularly to areas in shadow, such as the alar folds, the external auditory meatus, the medial canthi, and the postauricular folds, where lesions may easily be missed.
3. Examine the conjunctivae, lips, and oropharynx.
4. Turn next to the trunk and extremities. At this point, the patient should lie down. The anterior and posterior aspects of the body are examined in turn. Examining one quadrant at a time, leaving other areas draped, avoids uncovering the patient unnecessarily. As each quadrant is examined, pay particular attention to the palm or sole and to the nails.
5. Examine the gluteal cleft, perianal skin, and the external genitalia each as a separate region.

Special physical diagnostic tools may facilitate diagnosis. On occasion, the minute details of skin lesions must be examined. **Magnification** using a hand lens allows the pattern of melanin pigment deposition in nevi, lentigines, and melanomas to be seen, as an aid to differential diagnosis. Dilated nailfold capillaries in connective tissue diseases are easily discerned only with magnification. Hand lenses are available with magnification ranging from $2\times$ to $10\times$. For most purposes, a $5\times$ to $7\times$ lens provides effective magnification while remaining relatively easy to use. An ophthalmoscope set at $+20$ diopters may be used for extreme magnification, which is sometimes necessary when one is examining nailfold capillaries.

Applying **mineral oil** to certain skin lesions evens out the refractive index of the surface, allowing the underlying pattern of colors to be seen. This procedure is analogous to applying varnish to a piece of wood to reveal the grain. Pigmented lesions, nailfold capillaries, and the Wickham's striae of lichen planus are all highlighted with this technique.

Low-angle incident lighting, or **sidelighting,** causes even very small elevations, depressions, and other textural changes of the skin's surface to cast shadows, thus becoming more visible. Sidelighting is often used to detect atrophy of the epidermis, which may present as a subtle sheen and loss of skin markings; to distinguish lentigines, which are truly flat, from junctional nevi, which are slightly elevated; and to detect elevation of purpuric lesions in vasculitis. A penlight or a small gooseneck lamp is used for sidelighting.

The term **diascopy** refers to pressing a flat, transparent glass or plastic plate against the skin to blanch away any redness, allowing the underlying color of the lesion (golden tan in granulomas and lymphocytic infiltrates, purple in the purpuras) to be seen. Commonly, two glass microscope slides are used for diascopy, but care must be taken to avoid snapping the slides when pressure is applied. A $2\times$ folding pocket hand lens may work well as a diascope, or a specially designed shoehorn-shaped plastic diascope can be purchased for a few dollars.

The **Wood's lamp** is a hand-held lamp that emits long-wavelength ultraviolet light ("black light"). Examination is carried out in a completely dark room. Over the years, the Wood's lamp has found several uses in dermatology:

1. Assessment of the amount and location of pigment in the skin. Depigmented areas fluoresce bright white; hypopigmented areas also become more visible but do not fluoresce brightly. Hyperpigmented areas appear darker in contrast to surrounding skin when the pigmentation is in the epidermis; dermal pigmentation is not enhanced under Wood's lamp.
2. Erythrasma fluoresces coral red.
3. Tinea capitis caused by *Microsporum canis* or *audouini* fluoresces green.

4. Acidified urine from a patient with porphyria cutanea tarda fluoresces orange-pink.

A variety of simple techniques are used for the rapid bedside or office diagnosis of cutaneous infections and infestations. The **Gram stain** is a technique used to detect pathogenic bacteria:

1. Use heat or methyl alcohol to fix an air-dried smear of pus, crust, or similar material on a glass slide.
2. Flood the slide with crystal violet stain and rinse with tap water after 15 seconds.
3. Flood with Gram's iodine and rinse after 15 seconds.
4. Dribble alcohol decolorizer onto the stained smear until the blue color has almost entirely faded. Then quickly rinse with tap water.
5. Flood with alcoholic safranin; rinse after 20 seconds and gently blot dry with bibulous paper.

Candida albicans, Pityrosporum orbiculare, and members of the dermatophyte genera *Trichophyton, Microsporum,* and *Epidermophyton* cause superficial fungal infections of the skin. These organisms grow in the stratum corneum, and thus are easily removed for microscopic examination or culture. Direct microscopic examination of skin scrapings is rapidly performed, but requires a certain amount of experience to achieve uniformly good results. Fungal culture, especially on an indicator medium (Dermatophyte Test Medium), takes days to weeks to yield a positive result, but requires little prior skill or experience. Culture also allows species identification, which cannot be done with direct microscopy of skin scrapings.

The basic principle of **fungal scrapings** is that a strong alkali, potassium hydroxide (KOH), is used to dissolve the keratinaceous stratum corneum so that hyphae are revealed, or, alternatively, a dye is used that selectively stains the hyphae. The Shwartz-Lamkin stain does both:

1. Using a No. 15 scalpel blade or the edge of a microscope slide, scrape across the leading edge of the skin lesion, collecting the fragments of scale on a clean microscope slide. If the lesions are blisters, scrape the underside of the blister roof. If examining a nail, collect the debris under the nail plate.
2. Cover these with a coverslip. Apply one or two drops of stain adjacent to the coverslip so that the stain is drawn under the coverslip by capillary action.
3. Gently heat over an alcohol burner. Do not boil.
4. Press firmly on the coverslip to expel air bubbles and flatten the hyphae.
5. Examine under low power and high dry magnification, with the condenser turned down to enhance contrast.

Alternative methods for preparation and staining of exfoliative fungal specimens are listed in the references.

Sabouraud's modified dextrose agar and Dermatophyte Test Medium (D.T.M.) are selective **fungal culture** media used to grow dermatophytes and *Candida.* D.T.M. is similar to Sabouraud's medium except it contains a color indicator that turns from yellow to red if a dermatophyte is growing. Scrapings of stratum corneum, pieces of nails, or hair may be planted on test agar. The cap of the vial should be loose enough to allow air to enter, and the vial should be incubated at room temperature for 2 to 3 weeks.

The **Tzanck smear** is a cytologic method for diagnosis of herpesvirus infections. In this technique, virus-infected multinucleated giant cells are identified. The yield of Tzanck smears is reportedly higher than that of viral culture in varicella-zoster virus infections, but slightly lower than that of culture in herpes simplex.

One of many variations of the method, which is rapid and effective, is as follows:

1. Unroof the vesicle or pustule with a No. 15 scalpel blade. Brushing aside the fluid, scrape the jellylike material from the base of the vesicle and smear it on a clean microscope slide.
2. Air dry the smear, then gently heat fix.
3. Flood the slide with undiluted Giemsa stain for 30 seconds, then rinse with tap water. (A Wright stain may also be used.)

4. Drain the slide until dry.
5. Apply a drop of immersion oil, then a coverslip, and examine under medium and high power.

Scabies is a superficial infestation of the skin caused by *Sarcoptes scabiei*, a nearly microscopic mite. Female mites burrow into the stratum corneum, where they lay their eggs. Demonstration of the adult mite, eggs, nymphae, or fecal pellets (called scybalae) is diagnostic of scabies:

1. Select one or several of the largest papules available. Excoriated papules do not have high yields. The end of a burrow is often productive.
2. Dip a No. 15 scalpel blade in sterile mineral oil and scrape or superficially shave the papule repeatedly, until slight bleeding begins.
3. Smear the epidermal shavings from the blade onto a microscope slide.
4. Apply a drop of mineral oil or immersion oil, then a coverslip, and examine under low power.

Boyce JA, Bernhard JD: Total skin examination: patient reactions (letter). *J Am Acad Dermatol.* 1986;14:280.
Patients really do not mind getting undressed when they understand why it is necessary.

Fitzpatrick TB, Polano MK, Suurmond D: Outline of an approach to dermatologic diagnosis. In: *Color Atlas and Synopsis of Clinical Dermatology.* New York, NY: McGraw-Hill Book Co.; 1983: 2–4.
Discusses T.S.A.D. system.

Ganczarczyk ML, Lee P, Armstrong SK: Nailfold capillary microscopy in polymyositis and dermatomyositis. *Arthritis Rheum.* 1988;31:116–119.
The authors were able to distinguish different morphologies of dilated nailfold capillaries in dermatomyositis and polymyositis, pointing out the utility of magnification.

Katz HI, Prawer SE, Hien NT: Skin-surface touch print for diagnosing fungal infections. *Am Fam Physician.* 1985;31:189–194.
Put one drop of cyanoacrylate adhesive (Krazy Glue) on microscope slide. Slide is pressed against skin for 20 seconds, then rocked free. Stain with a toluidine blue/ basic fuchsin stain for 60 seconds, apply Permount and coverslip. Excellent results with tinea capitis; poor results with palms, soles, folds. Ninety-four percent concordance with KOH preparation.

Austin VH: Mineral oil versus KOH for Sarcoptes (letter). *J Am Acad Dermatol.* 1982;7:555–556.
One can detect telltale movement of mites in mineral oil preps, whereas KOH kills them. However, mites can survive on oil slides for prolonged periods, thus posing some risk to personnel. Unlike mineral oil, KOH also dissolves fecal pellets of mites.

Motyl MR, Bottone EJ, Janda JM: Diagnosis of herpesvirus infections: correlation of Tzanck preparations with viral isolation. *Diagn Microbiol Infect Dis.* 1984;157–160.
Eighty-six percent of culture-proven herpes simplex lesions were Tzanck positive.

Pehamberger H, Steiner A, Wolff K: In vivo epiluminescence microscopy of pigmented skin lesions. I. Pattern analysis of pigmented skin lesions. *J Am Acad Dermatol.* 1987;17:571–583.
Subtle patterns of pigment deposition in benign and malignant lesions were easily seen with high magnification and mineral oil.

Rockoff AS: Fungus cultures in a pediatric outpatient clinic. *Pediatrics.* 1979;63:276–278.
Pediatric house officers with no mycologic experience were able to diagnose dermatophyte infections as accurately as their hospital's mycology lab staff, using DTM cultures.

Sadick NS, Swenson PD, Kaufman RL, et al: Comparison of detection of varicellazoster virus by Tzanck smear, direct immunofluorescence with a monoclonal antibody, and virus isolation. *J Am Acad Dermatol.* 1987;17:64–69.
Tzanck was positive in 64%, immunofluorescence in 55%, and culture in 26% of

patients with herpes zoster. Similar concordance between Tzanck smear and direct immunofluorescence has been seen with herpes simplex in other studies.

Shwartz JH, Lamkin BE: A rapid, simple stain for fungi in skin, nail scrapings, and hairs. *Arch Dermatol.* 1964;89:89–94.
The original, and most successful modification of the basic 10% plain KOH method: 2.5% KOH plus a surfactant (docusate) plus Parker's "Super Quink" permanent blue-black ink.

Solomon AR, Rasmussen JE, Weiss JS, et al: A comparison of the Tzanck smear and viral isolation in varicella and herpes zoster. *Arch Dermatol.* 1986;122:282–285.
Tzanck prep was clearly more sensitive than viral culture in varicella (100% vs. 64%) and herpes zoster (80% vs. 60%).

Solomon AR, Rasmussen JE, Varani J: The Tzanck smear in the diagnosis of cutaneous herpes simplex. *JAMA.* 1984;251:633–635.
Culture positive in 78%. Tzanck positive in 66.7% of vesicles, 54.5% of pustules, and 16% of crusted lesions.

Woodley D, Saurat JH: The burrow ink test and the scabies mite. *J Am Acad Dermatol.* 1981;4:715–722.
Suspected burrows are rubbed with a fountain pen, and excess ink is wiped away. Burrows are easily seen as serpiginous lines. Ink-test–positive lesions were scraping positive 100% of the time, but the ink test yielded false-negative results 36% of the time.

---

2. PRURITUS
Mark S. Bernhardt

Itching is the cardinal symptom of most inflammatory diseases of the skin. Pruritus may also be of diagnostic and prognostic significance for several internal maladies. While neurophysiologists debate the distinction between pain and itch, poets recognize that the former is tragic and the latter is merely pathetic. No mythic hero is glorified in his stoic struggle against scratching. Without his martyrdom therein, it is highly unlikely that Marat's tub would have become an icon of the French Revolution. Indeed, the incessantly scratching sufferer is as often an object of ridicule as of sympathy. Yet only to an impartial observer is pruritus a trivial problem. No matter how gratifying the scratch, itching is almost always an unpleasant sensation that may even lead to suicidal despair.

Itch sensation begins at free, unmyelinated, penicillate nerve endings serving as receptors in the skin for noxious stimuli. The afferent pathway is along unmyelinated C fibers that enter the spinal cord via the dorsal root ganglia and ascend in the spinothalamic tracts. Itch and pain sensation are carried along similar pathways: itching does not occur in an area insensitive to pain, nor can it be elicited in patients with congenital absence of cutaneous pain sensation. However, experimental as well as experiential evidence supports the clinical distinction between pain and itch as two closely related but distinct sensory modalities. That there is CNS processing of pruritus is undeniable. The premorbid psychology of a patient will influence the perception of pruritus to a constant pruritogenic stimulus. Itching of any cause usually seems worse at bedtime, when there are fewer distractions. The occurrence of unilateral or segmental pruritus following CNS tumors, infections, and strokes also implies central processing, though the sites of involvement are too inconsistent to support the concept of a single "itch center." There is no conclusive evidence demonstrating efferent, modulatory pathways analogous to those for pain sensation.

Histamine is the classic mediator of pruritus. It cannot be the only mediator, however, since most itchy conditions are not accompanied by the other signs of histamine release (i.e., wheal and flare). Various proteases, peptides, and prostaglandins potentiate histamine's effect without being directly pruritogenic. Substance

P, a peripheral neurotransmitter involved in pain sensation, may also have a role in pruritus. Serotonin is another possible mediator of itch. Enkephalins ("endogenous opiates") are apparently involved in the central processing of pruritus: opiate antagonists can temporarily diminish the perception of itch.

A **methodical approach** to the itchy patient obviously must determine the proximate cause of the pruritus. In the case of most acute dermatitides, specific therapy for the rash will produce relief from the itch, and any antipruritic treatment may be considered secondary, though hardly unappreciated. For dermatoses such as atopic dermatitis, psoriasis, and lichen planus, itching may need to be treated aggressively, as scratching per se tends to aggravate the underlying condition. Those patients who present with pruritus without rash are certainly the most vexing. A meticulous examination may reveal subtle clues indicating scabies, asteatosis, or other occult skin disease. In their absence, an internal cause of the pruritus must be sought systematically. A specific diagnosis may not dictate the antipruritic therapy when itch is due to a skin disease, but certainly will when itch is secondary to an internal disorder. For this reason, we will now discuss general treatment principles and then specific internal conditions in which pruritus is a particularly common complaint.

Topical antipruritics act by either anesthesia of cutaneous nerve endings or a counterirritant effect. The latter is a poorly understood phenomenon in which another sensation (e.g., coolness, heat) "drowns out" the itch. It is conceivable that scratching itself, by producing pain, has a counterirritant effect. Though present in numerous over-the-counter preparations, topical anesthetics will not penetrate intact skin, will have minimal antipruritic effect even when applied to inflamed permeable skin, and are notorious potential allergic sensitizers. Those ingredients that may relieve pruritus by topical anesthesia include camphor, phenol, pramoxine hydrochloride (Prax), and triethanolamine. Topical capsaicin depletes and prevents reaccumulation of substance P in peripheral neurons. It has been shown to reduce histamine-induced pruritus, but otherwise its usefulness as an antipruritic is unknown. Compounds that act as counterirritants include menthol, methyl salicylate, and turpentine oil. Camphor is a counterirritant as well as an anesthetic. Salicylic acid and tar compounds are often incorporated into antipruritic preparations; their mode of action is unknown. Many topical antipruritics contain a combination of active ingredients, such as Sarna lotion (menthol, camphor, and phenol) and Pamscol (phenol and salicylic acid).

Oral antihistamines are often prescribed as "itch pills." They may be no more effective than a placebo for relief of nonhistamine-related itching (i.e., eczematous eruptions as opposed to urticaria), although their sedative effects may be clinically useful, especially when pruritus interferes with sleep. Certainly, antihistamines are the drugs of choice for treating histamine-related disorders such as urticaria or systemic hypersensitivity reactions. In these cases, hydroxyzine or chlorpheniramine is most effective, although one of the nonsedating antihistamines such as terfenadine or astemizole may be better tolerated. Antihistamines should be gradually increased until either clinical remission occurs or side effects such as sedation, gastrointestinal complaints, excitation, dry mouth, blurred vision, or urinary retention become significant. Combined use of a classic H_1-blocking antihistamine and an H_2 blocker (cimetidine, ranitidine) may have an additive effect for certain patients. There may be an enormous placebo effect when antihistamines are prescribed for pruritus, and the magnitude of this beneficial phenomenon (and the paucity of proven alternatives) should not be overlooked. Table 2-1 gives starting dosages for several oral antihistamines. For patients who tolerate sedation poorly or who have particular difficulty with itch at bedtime, a useful regimen may be hydroxyzine 50 mg PO with supper, repeated at bedtime.

Given the multiplicity of **internal disorders** that may manifest as or produce itch, the evaluation of pruritus without rash must be open-minded yet orderly. Complaints of pruritus are common for patients with uremia, obstructive biliary disease (e.g., primary biliary cirrhosis), myeloproliferative disorders (especially polycythemia vera and Hodgkin's disease), iron deficiency, endocrine disorders (most commonly thyrotoxicosis), visceral malignancies, and neurologic disorders (e.g., brain abscess, stroke). Once the proper diagnosis has been made, relief of pruritus can still be elusive. Treatment of the specific underlying condition alone may be sufficient or necessary.

Table 2-1 Oral antihistamines

Drug	Trade name	Dosage
H$_1$ BLOCKERS		
Diphenhydramine	Benadryl	50 mg PO q4h
Tripelennamine	Pyribenzamine	50 mg PO q4h
Hydroxyzine	Atarax	25 gm PO q4h
Brompheniramine	Dimetane	4 mg PO q4h
Chlorpheniramine	ChlorTrimetron	4 mg PO q4h
Promethazine	Phenergan	12.5 mg PO qid
Cyproheptadine	Periactin	4 mg PO q4h
Terfenadine	Seldane	60 mg PO bid
Astemizole	Hismanal	10 mg PO every day
H$_2$ BLOCKERS		
Cimetidine	Tagamet	300 mg PO qid
Ranitidine	Zantac	150 mg PO bid

This is the case for intracranial masses, iron deficiency, thyrotoxicosis, and Hodgkin's disease. Otherwise, pruritus must be considered a separate issue demanding its own therapeutic resolution.

Chronic renal failure is the most common internal disorder associated with pruritus. Whether the greater prevalence of pruritus since the advent of dialysis therapy is due to dialysis itself or to increased patient longevity is unclear. Abnormalities in calcium and phosphorous metabolisms are common in uremia, and efforts aimed at correcting these disturbances, especially parathyroidectomy for secondary hyperparathyroidism, may alleviate pruritus. UVB phototherapy is very effective in uremic pruritus; usually a response is seen after 8 to 10 suberythemogenic doses. Its mode of action is unknown, though general improvement following treatment to only one side of the body suggests a systemic effect. Activated charcoal (6 gm PO daily for 8 weeks) is useful but often impractical, as it will nonspecifically bind any other oral medications the patient might be receiving. Cholestyramine, an ion exchange resin, may relieve uremic and cholestatic pruritus (vide infra). Presumably both cholestyramine and charcoal therapy act by absorbing or sequestering an unidentified, nondialyzable pruritogen. Low-protein diets also help alleviate uremic pruritus.

Itching is frequently produced by cholestatic liver disease, but rarely encountered in hepatitis without biliary obstruction. Purified bile salts applied to the skin are pruritogenic, and lowering serum bile concentration usually ameliorates itching. No direct link has been established, however, between the presence of pruritus and the level of total or individual circulating or cutaneous bile salts. Cholestyramine (4 gm PO 1–3 times daily) apparently relieves cholestatic pruritus by mechanisms unrelated to its ability to sequester and reduce serum bile salts. Like activated charcoal, cholestyramine will bind other oral medications and can also be quite constipating. Oral vitamin K supplements (10 mg/wk) should be given concurrently. Phenobarbital (3–4 mg/kg/d PO) reduces pruritus by unknown mechanisms. Phenobarbital is sedating and interferes with the metabolism of many other drugs. Phototherapy may alleviate pruritus, though not as predictably as in uremia. Plasma perfusion has also been found effective. Itching can rarely be alleviated by dietary supplementation with polyunsaturated fatty acids. Most recently, rifampin (150 mg PO bid-tid) has been found effective in cholestatic pruritus, presumably because it reduces intrahepatic bile acids or detoxifies unidentified nonbile salt pruritogenins.

The pruritus of polycythemia vera often has a prickling sensation and is provoked by a sudden decrease in temperature, as when a person gets out of a hot shower. Though elevated plasma and urine histamine levels, correlating with an increased number of basophils, have been found in the majority of patients with polycythemia vera, antihistamines are not uniformly effective for controlling their pruritus. Cyproheptadine, an antihistamine with antiserotonin activity, and the H$_2$ blocker cimetidine may be of value in select patients.

Denman ST: A review of pruritus. *J Am Acad Dermatol.* 1986;14:375–392.
Thorough review that concludes with an approach to the evaluation and treatment of a patient with pruritus.
Fransway AF, Winkelmann RK: Treatment of Pruritus. *Seminars in Dermatology.* 1988;7:310–325.
Recent review of topical and systemic antipruritic agents.
Ghent CN, Carruthers SG: Treatment of pruritus in primary biliary cirrhosis with rifampin. *Gastroenterology* 1988;94:488–493.
Double-blind, controlled, crossover clinical trial of rifampin in nine patients with primary biliary cirrhosis and pruritus with significant improvement in itch within the first week of treatment.
Gilchrest BA: Pruritus: Pathogenesis, therapy, and significance in systemic disease states. *Arch Int Med.* 1982;142:101–105.
Generalized pruritus may be associated with systemic disease in 10% to 50% of patients. Renal, hepatic, hematopoietic, endocrine, or neoplastic disorders presenting with itch are reviewed.
Hanifin JM: The role of antihistamines in atopic dermatitis. *J Allergy Clin Immunol.* 1990;86:666–669.
In this disease, which may not be primarily mediated by histamine, the efficacy of the classic antihistamines has been severely limited by sedative effects. Multifunctional, newer antihistamines may provide greater relief of pruritus by a variety of mechanisms.
Kantor G, Lookingbill DP: Generalized pruritus and systemic disease. *J Am Acad Dermatol.* 1983;9:375–382.
Retrospective study of 44 patients with generalized pruritus compared to 44 psoriatic controls. Recommendations for outpatient evaluation are discussed.
Shapiro PE, Braun CW: Unilateral pruritus after a stroke. *Arch Dermatol.* 1987;123:1527–1530.
Case description followed by discussion of the neural pathways of pruritus and the role of the CNS in the initiation and modulation of the itch sensation.
Tan JKL, Haberman HF, Coldman AJ: Identifying effective treatments for uremic pruritus. *J Am Acad Dermatol.* 1991;25:811–818.
Authors identify and critically review the literature concerning treatment of uremic pruritus and conclude that phototherapy with ultraviolet B light is most effective.
Toth-Kasa I, Janeso G, Bognar A, et al: Capsaicin prevents histamine-induced itching. *Int J Clin Pharmacol Res.* 1986;6:163–169.
In human subjects, capsaicin pretreatment reduced flare and itch but did not influence wheal formation.

3. BIOPSY TECHNIQUES
Thomas G. Cropley

Skin biopsy is the most commonly performed procedure in dermatology. Samples of skin are most frequently taken for histopathologic examination by routine light microscopy. Special studies, such as immunofluorescence microscopy or electron microscopy, may be performed on biopsied material. Tissue obtained by biopsy may also be processed for bacterial, viral, or fungal culture, or, rarely, for cell culture.

Four biopsy techniques are commonly employed: punch biopsy, shave biopsy, excisional biopsy, and wedge (incisional) biopsy. The specimens are placed in formalin for routine histopathology, Michel's medium for immunofluorescence study, or a sterile cup or culture tube for microbiological tests. Laboratories performing specialized tests such as electron microscopic examination and cell cultures usually participate in the handling of a freshly obtained specimen.

The **punch, or trephine, biopsy** (Table 3-1) is the technique most commonly employed by dermatologists for routine diagnostic biopsy. The biopsy punch is a cylindrical knife with a short screwdriver-like handle. Biopsy punches are available with diameters ranging from 2 mm to 8 mm; most routine biopsies are done with 3- or 4-mm punches. Modern biopsy punches are disposable and intended for one-time use only.

Punch biopsy is an appropriate technique for sampling a representative area of a widespread disease process, for removing small lesions in toto, or for removing a portion of a larger lesion. Care must be taken to biopsy the part of a large lesion that will be the most likely to yield an adequate pathologic examination. In general, tumors are biopsied at their thickest parts, and annular plaques and expanding lesions are biopsied at their leading edges. Blisters present a particular problem; unless the entire blister can be excised, it is preferable to sample the skin immediately adjacent to the blister edge, where diagnostic changes are most likely to be found.

Shave biopsy (Table 3-2) is a simple technique that allows removal of lesions or portions of lesions projecting above the surrounding skin surface. Its principal advantages are the ease and rapidity with which it can be done, and the good cosmetic result usually obtained. The primary problem with the shave biopsy technique is that it does not sample the dermis. Shave biopsy is often used to rule out malignancy

Table 3-1 Punch biopsy*

1. Obtain informed consent. Risks to the patient include allergic reaction to Xylocaine, bleeding, infection, and a small scar.
2. Select area to be biopsied.
3. Clean with alcohol.
4. Slowly infiltrate the dermis and subcutis with 1 cc of Xylocaine until a wheal is raised. Xylocaine with epinephrine may be used except on fingers, toes, penis, and in patients with coronary artery disease, tachyarrhythmias, or patients taking beta blockers.
5. With one hand, stretch skin perpendicular to natural skin tension (skin fold) lines.
6. With other hand, twist the punch to-and-fro between the fingers while slowly pushing it into the skin. Except in areas with little subcutaneous fat, such as the dorsa of the hands, eyelids, and external ears, push the punch in to the hub.
7. Pull the punch straight out. Usually, the plug of skin will remain in place in the wound because it is still attached to the fat.
8. Gently grasp one edge of the specimen with toothed forceps, taking care not to crush it. Snip the specimen free with scissors. Include some fat in the lower portion of the specimen.
9. Place one or two interrupted sutures, closing the defect in such a way that its long axis lies parallel to the skin tension lines.
10. Apply pressure to obtain hemostasis, if necessary.
11. Dress with antibiotic ointment and a small adhesive bandage.

The patient should be instructed to keep the site clean and dry and covered with antibiotic ointment and an adhesive bandage. Sutures may be removed 5 to 14 days after the procedure, depending on the site of the biopsy (5 days for face, 10 days for arms and trunk, 14 days for legs).

*The equipment needed to perform this procedure includes sterile gloves, protective eyewear, and mask; a biopsy punch (2, 3, or 4 mm); sharp pointed scissors, such as iris scissors; small toothed forceps; a needle holder; a monofilament nylon suture (e.g., Ethilon, Dermalon) with a reverse cutting needle (6-0 for face, 5-0 or 4-0 elsewhere); a jar of buffered formalin or appropriate carrier medium; 1% Xylocaine, plain or with epinephrine 1:10,000; a 1.0-cc syringe with a 30-gauge needle; alcohol sponges; 4- × 4-in. sterile gauze sponges; antibiotic ointment; and a small adhesive bandage.

Table 3-2 Shave biopsy*

1. Obtain informed consent. Risks to the patient include allergic reaction to the Xylocaine, bleeding, infection, and a small atrophic or hypertrophic scar.
2. Clean lesion and surrounding skin with alcohol.
3. Insert needle almost parallel to skin surface and inject 1 cc of Xylocaine, so that a wheal forms beneath the lesion. Xylocaine with epinephrine may be used except on fingers, toes, penis, and in patients with coronary artery disease, tachyarrhythmias, or patients taking beta blockers.
4. Keeping the blade horizontal to the surrounding skin surface, carefully cut the lesion free from the skin. Make the cut as smooth as possible to avoid a jagged bottom. A forceps may aid in grasping one edge of the tissue.
5. Use Monsel's solution or 20% aluminum chloride solution to obtain hemostasis. Good results are acquired by alternately blotting with a dry cotton-tipped swab and rolling a cotton-tipped swab saturated with the hemostatic agent across the wound.
6. Apply antibiotic ointment and small adhesive bandage.

Most shave sites will heal within 7 to 10 days. The area should be vigorously cleansed with diluted hydrogen peroxide or soap and water twice daily, after which an antibiotic ointment and adhesive bandage should be applied.

*The equipment needed to perform this procedure includes sterile gloves, protective eyewear, and mask; a No. 15 scalpel blade on handle; small toothed forceps; Monsel's solution or 20% aluminum chloride solution (Drysol); a jar of buffered formalin or appropriate carrier medium; sterile cotton-tipped swabs; 1% Xylocaine, plain or with epinephrine 1:10,000; a 1.0-cc syringe with a 30-gauge needle; alcohol sponges; 4- × 4-in. sterile gauze sponges; antibiotic ointment; and a small adhesive bandage.

in sessile or pedunculated lesions such as seborrheic keratoses and cutaneous horns. It is seldom of use in diagnosing inflammatory skin diseases.

Sometimes, an **excisional biopsy** (Table 3-3), i.e., excising an entire lesion, is the most appropriate biopsy technique. This is especially true in the case of malignant melanoma and dysplastic nevi, since the degree of cellular atypism may vary widely within a single lesion. Excision also provides a much greater volume of tissue than punch biopsy, giving the pathologist more material to review or allowing some tissue to be sent for culture for microorganisms or other special tests. Unfortunately, because excisional biopsy sites are larger, the degree of scarring and the relative risks of bleeding or infection are greater.

The **wedge biopsy** or incisional biopsy is essentially a very narrow elliptical biopsy that extends deeply into a nodule or subcutaneous process. It is used when it is important to sample the subcutis, as when large vessel vasculitis, panniculitis, or deep fungal infection is suspected. The technique is similar to that described for excisional biopsy, although generally the ellipse is narrower (with a length-width ratio of about 4:1 or 5:1) and extends more deeply in the subcutaneous fat.

Ackerman BA: Biopsy: why, where, when, how. *J Dermatol Surg.* 1975;1:21–23.
   Not so much a surgical article as a discussion by a renowned dermatopathologist of the proper types of specimens to obtain in different situations.
Braunstein BL, Greer KE: Skin biopsy. In: Suratt PM and Gibson RS, eds. *Manual of Medical Procedures.* St. Louis, MO: CV Mosby; 1982: 143–149.
   Well illustrated; covers all four techniques.

Table 3-3 Excisional biopsy*

1. Obtain informed consent. Risks to the patient include allergic reaction to Xylocaine, bleeding, infection, and a scar as long as the wound necessary to obtain the appropriate specimen.
2. Prepare skin with alcohol followed by povidone-iodine.
3. Infiltrate the lesion and surrounding skin with 3 to 12 cc of Xylocaine. Xylocaine with epinephrine may be used except on fingers, toes, penis, and in patients with coronary artery disease, tachyarrhythmias, or patients taking beta blockers.
4. Orienting the long axis of the incision parallel to skin tension lines, make an elliptical incision around the lesion into the superficial dermis. The ratio of length to width should be about 3:1. Repeat incising perpendicular to the skin surface until the subcutaneous fat is seen at the base and the ellipse sits like an island in the center of the wound.
5. Lift one point of the ellipse with the forceps and carefully dissect the base of the specimen free with a scissor, taking care to include some subcutaneous fat with the specimen.
6. Venous oozing is best controlled with pressure using a gauze sponge. Electrocautery may also be used for hemostasis. Small arterial bleeders should be clamped with a hemostat and ligated with absorbable suture material.
7. Close the wound with simple interrupted nylon sutures or with vertical mattress sutures. A layered closure may be necessary if the wound is large or in a cosmetically important area.
8. Apply an antibiotic ointment and pressure dressing.

The patient should keep the pressure dressing in place and take care not to get the wound wet for 48 hours. After 48 hours, the wound should be kept clean and dry, covered with antibiotic ointment and an adhesive bandage. Remove sutures on the face in 7 days, 10 to 14 days elsewhere.

---

*The equipment needed to perform this procedure includes sterile gloves, protective eyewear, and mask; a No. 15 scalpel blade on handle; small toothed forceps; a needle holder; a mosquito or other hemostat (optional); absorbable suture material (e.g., 4-0 Dexon or Vicryl); a monofilament nylon suture (e.g., 4-0 or 5-0 Ethilon or Dermalon); a jar of buffered formalin or appropriate carrier medium; 1% Xylocaine, plain or with epinephrine 1:10,000; a 3.0-cc to 6.0-cc syringe with a 30-gauge needle; alcohol sponges; povidone-iodine swabs; 4- × 4-in. sterile gauze sponges; antibiotic ointment; and a pressure bandage.

II. ACUTE PROBLEMS

4. ERYTHEMA MULTIFORME AND TOXIC EPIDERMAL NECROLYSIS
Lynn A. Baden

Erythema multiforme (EM) is an acute, self-limited inflammatory disorder, involving both skin and mucous membranes, that presents with a distinctive cutaneous lesion, called the target, or iris, lesion. It has a peak age of incidence from 20 to 30 years with 20% of cases occurring in children and adolescents and a male-female ratio of 6:4. Recurrences develop in 22% to 37% of cases and are most frequently associated with recurrent herpes simplex virus (HSV). Traditionally, EM has been divided into minor and major forms, the latter also known as Stevens-Johnson syndrome.

EM minor usually presents with a mild 7 to 10 day prodrome of malaise, fever, headache, rhinorrhea, and cough. Target lesions then appear on extensor surfaces, palms and soles, most often symmetrically. After the initial acral eruption, there may be centripetal spread with a few oral lesions. New lesions occur over 3 to 5 days and last for 1 to 2 weeks. The characteristic lesion of EM, the target lesion, may appear abruptly or develop over 24 to 48 hours. It begins as an erythematous macule that becomes raised and evolves concentrically to result in a central dusky erythema or vesicle within a pale edematous ring that in turn is surrounded by a darker band of erythema. With progression, central necrosis may be seen and lesions may coalesce into polycyclic or annular plaques. Lesions generally heal with scarring, although postinflammatory hyperpigmentation can be seen. Sometimes EM presents without typical target lesions but with urticarial plaques that, unlike true urticaria, are not transient. EM may also present with vesicles and bullae that form in preexisting macules, papules, and wheals.

EM major is a more severe clinical variant. The prodrome consists of fever, malaise, and prostration followed by an explosive widespread eruption of target lesions and mucosal bullae. Any mucosal surface may be involved, commonly the oral mucosa, respiratory tree, and conjunctivae. Mucosal surfaces may be extensively involved even in the presence of very few skin lesions. Secondary infection is common. In 20% of cases, severe mucosal erosions lead to significant morbidity with pain, difficulty maintaining adequate oral fluid intake, ocular complications, respiratory compromise, and dysuria. Mortality, reflecting infection and respiratory compromise, ranges from 3% to 15%.

The **histopathology** of EM, like the clinical picture, is variable. The gross morphology of the lesion is determined by the pattern of the inflammatory cell infiltrate and associated epidermal changes seen histologically. Pathologists recognize three histologic patterns: dermal, epidermal, and mixed dermal and epidermal EM. All three are associated with varying degrees of acute epidermal injury manifested by individually necrotic keratinocytes surrounded by lymphocytes. Lymphocytes are also seen along the dermal-epidermal junction ("tagging" infiltrate) and around superficial dermal blood vessels. Extensive papillary dermal edema may be present. Bullae form subepidermally because of hydropic degeneration of the basal cell layer as well as full thickness epidermal necrosis. The histologic pattern varies among rings of the target lesion, correlating with the clinical picture. Immunoreactants, including complement and immunoglobulins, are found in the microvasculature of 75% of lesions less than 24 hours old. Most commonly found are IgM and C3 in the walls of the superficial dermal vessels.

The **pathogenesis** of EM is not well understood, although it is presumed to be a hypersensitivity reaction to a variety of antigens. The histologic findings suggest that cell-mediated immune mechanisms are responsible for tissue damage. The immunohistochemical findings may reflect the presence of circulating immune complexes, which have been demonstrated in some cases of EM. Multiple precipitating factors are cited in the literature; however, in 50% of cases no etiologic factor is found. Well-documented precipitants include bacterial or viral infections, and drugs. Historically, the first association described was with *Mycoplasma pneumoniae,* which causes a 1- to 3-week respiratory illness in children, adolescents, and young adults, followed by the classic clinical picture of EM major. Bullae are often noted as well as high fevers and systemic complications. Recurrences are uncommon. HSV-associated EM occurs most often in adolescents and young adults, representing 15% to 65% of cases of EM. EM minor usually occurs 10 days after an acute eruption with either type 1 or type 2 HSV. Fifteen percent of patients with recurrent EM have concomitant HSV infection. The list of drugs associated with EM is long but the usual agents incriminated are sulfonamides, penicillins, hydantoins, and phenobarbitals. Drug-associated EM occurs at any age and is usually seen 1 to 3 weeks after initial ingestion. Unfortunately, confusion commonly occurs when a preceding upper respiratory illness has been treated with antibiotics, making it unclear whether the infectious agent, the drug, or the interaction of both precipitated the EM.

Evaluation of the patient with suspected EM includes documenting preceding prodromes and drug exposures. In addition to looking for characteristic target lesions, examination of the cutaneous surface may find evidence of acute HSV infection, which can then be documented by a Tzanck preparation or culture. The rest of the physical examination may reveal evidence of other infections, generally respiratory. Tests such as CBC, chest x ray, cold agglutinins, and complement fixation tests for *M. pneumoniae* may be done to complete the evaluation.

When a fully developed target lesion is present, the diagnosis is not a dilemma; however, less characteristic presentations may merit further evaluation with a skin biopsy. The **differential diagnosis** includes chronic urticaria, serum sickness, figurate erythema, toxic erythemas associated with viral infection or drug exposure, graft-versus-host disease, necrotizing vasculitis, and systemic lupus erythematosus. When blisters are present, bullous pemphigoid, pemphigus vulgaris, impetigo, toxic epidermal necrolysis, dermatitis herpetiformis, and mucocutaneous syndromes such as Behçet's and Reiter's must be considered. Lesions limited to the mucosa may resemble cicatricial pemphigoid, pemphigus vulgaris, lichen planus, acute herpetic mucositis, and recurrent aphthae. A biopsy specimen prepared for direct immunofluorescence allows the differentiation of EM from pemphigoid, dermatitis herpetiformis, and pemphigus.

Treatment options are limited, and controlled studies have not been performed to evaluate efficacy. Elimination of suspected precipitating factors and treatment of underlying infection are essential. In patients with *M. pneumoniae,* appropriate antibiotics include tetracycline derivatives and erythromycin. In patients with recurrent HSV-associated EM, oral acyclovir, taken daily in a prophylactic fashion, has resulted in fewer episodes of acute eruptions of HSV and concomitant EM. Most cases of EM minor resolve in 2 to 3 weeks without specific treatment. Supportive care includes wet dressings or soaks, and analgesics. The use of topical steroids is debatable, but may reduce erythema and edema via their vasoconstrictive effects. For EM minor, common practice is to employ short, rapidly tapering courses of systemic steroids, although there is no support in the literature for this treatment. In EM major, systemic steroids have been the treatment of choice, although controlled studies have not been performed. Retrospective studies report that use of systemic steroids results in a prolonged recovery, with longer hospital stays and increased rates of complications including infection and gastrointestinal bleeding. Oral lesions are symptomatically improved with the use of saline mouth washes and topical anesthetics. Eye involvement should prompt ophthalmologic consultation. Rigorous observation for secondary infection and appropriate treatment are essential. Newer experimental therapies include thalidomide and azathioprine, both effective in small groups of patients.

Toxic epidermal necrolysis (TEN), Lyell's syndrome, is a true dermatologic emergency characterized by generalized erythema that rapidly develops full thickness epidermal necrosis and exfoliation associated with mucosal involvement and serious secondary complications. Often a prodrome of conjunctival burning, mild cutaneous tenderness, fever, headache, and malaise for 24 to 48 hours precedes a morbilliform or generalized erythema of the face and extremities. Within 12 to 48 hours, the widespread erythema is followed by blister formation, with subsequent confluence into large flaccid bullae that are easily ruptured, resulting in sloughing of large sheets of epidermis. Lateral pressure moves existing blisters into adjacent skin, inducing further sloughing (positive Nikolsky sign). Target lesions are notably absent in many cases of TEN. Some patients, however, progress more slowly, first with typical target lesions of EM, then bullous EM, and finally a TEN-like process with denuding of the epidermis. Mucous membranes are usually severely affected, including oral mucosa, conjunctivae, trachea, bronchus, and anogenital region. Loss of all nails often occurs. Systemic involvement is reflected by fever, leukocytosis, elevation in liver transaminases, and electrolyte imbalance.

The **histology** of TEN reveals a subepidermal blister with full thickness epidermal necrosis. Dermal infiltrates are minimal to absent. A Tzanck preparation of the base of the blister reveals rounded cells with large nuclei and a few inflammatory cells. Immunofluorescent studies are not specific.

The **pathogenesis** of TEN is poorly understood and many factors have been implicated, although a specific mechanism has not been elucidated. Drugs presumed to cause an adverse reaction can be identified in up to 75% of cases. The mean onset of exposure prior to the development of the eruption is 7 to 14 days. Although the list is extensive, the drugs most frequently implicated include sulfonamides, hydantoins, nonsteroidal anti-inflammatory drugs, allopurinol, and penicillins. Other less-commonly implicated factors include vaccination; graft-versus-host disease; lymphoma; leukemia; and viral, bacterial, and fungal infections. An immunologic process with circulating immune complexes is postulated because of the association of TEN with drug-dependent antiepidermal antigens and altered lymphocytes in peripheral blood. Alternatively, the process may be mediated by circulating toxins, since inflammation in the epidermis and dermis is sparse and other organ systems are not involved. Some authors believe that cytotoxic T lymphocytes may be directed against antigenic sites on the keratinocyte cell surface.

The relationship between TEN and EM is controversial. Some authors support the hypothesis that the two are related as points along a disease spectrum with similar pathogenesis, while others suggest that the two syndromes are different processes. Those favoring the former argue that both are often related to similar drug exposure or infection. They also note that in some patients target lesions appear first, then evolve into an exfoliative, TEN-like process with concomitant mucous membrane lesions. In addition, TEN and EM may be similar histologically, although EM is usually associated with a dermal inflammatory response not seen in TEN. Authors who suggest these are entirely different disease processes argue that most patients with TEN have a rapidly progressive course without the target lesions typical of EM. They note that EM, not TEN, is commonly associated with acute HSV eruption or *M. pneumoniae* infection. Although the controversy will not be readily resolved, TEN is generally defined arbitrarily for study purposes as those processes in which more than 10% of the total cutaneous surface is involved with epidermal necrosis.

The **differential diagnosis** of TEN depends on whether the patient is first seen early in the course of the disease or later, after exfoliation has developed. The morphology of the early eruption may resemble a morbilliform drug eruption, EM minor or major, Kawasaki's disease, or staphylococcal scalded skin syndrome (SSSS). When exfoliation is obvious, diagnoses often considered include a generalized bullous drug eruption, acute pustular psoriasis, and thermal injury from scalding or kerosene or paraffin burns.

In the past, the use of the term TEN also included SSSS (Ritter's disease); however, it is now widely recognized that these two entities are distinct. The cause of SSSS is a staphylococcal phage group 2 exotoxin. Features distinguishing TEN from SSSS include the association of the former with drug ingestion, age greater than 40, severely affected mucous membranes, and a high mortality rate. In SSSS, the patients are either young children or immunosuppressed adults, and identification of a suspect drug is difficult. In addition, mucous membranes are not usually involved, concurrent impetigo is often seen, and the patient responds to antistaphylococcal antibiotic therapy. TEN and SSSS can be rapidly differentiated by histologic examination of a fresh frozen section of epidermis obtained by rolling the wooden end of a cotton swab over an area of active exfoliation. In TEN, full thickness epidermal necrosis is seen. In SSSS, necrosis is limited to the upper portion of the epidermis, and the basal layer is not present in the specimen.

TEN is associated with a **mortality** rate of 30% to 100%. Widespread loss of epidermis destroys the body's primary barrier to infection and fluid loss. Fifty percent of deaths are due to infection, most commonly with *Staphylococcus aureus* or *Pseudomonas*. Hypovolemia may also be life-threatening. Nearly one-half of deaths occur within 4 days of onset of the illness. Survivors can expect a hospital stay of at least 1 month. Sequelae are significant and include corneal ulceration and blindness, scarring alopecia, sicca syndrome, hyper- and hypopigmented scars, anonychia, and renal complications.

The most effective **treatment** for TEN is in the setting of a burn intensive care unit where constant nursing care with specialized skills can be provided. Fluid replacement, with careful electrolyte management, is essential. Compulsive wound care and careful monitoring for early signs of infection may prevent sepsis. Broad spectrum antibiotics are sometimes initiated on admission to an ICU, but it is probably preferable to withhold drugs until evidence of infection is indicated by fever, hypothermia, or changes in consciousness, and after cultures have been obtained. Antibiotic therapy may then be directed against specific organisms. Topical antiseptics and silver nitrate are used frequently; however, silver sulfadiazine (Silvadene) is usually avoided because it may cause neutropenia. In some centers, temporary cadaveric or porcine dressings are applied to protect exposed dermis. Meticulous eye care is indicated to prevent symblepharon and blindness. Important adjuvants to care include low-dose heparin to prevent thrombophlebitis, antacids and H_2 blockers to prevent gastrointestinal ulcers or bleeding, and tranquilizers and analgesics to relieve pain.

The use of systemic corticosteroids has been reappraised and is currently in disfavor. The rationale for use was based on an assumption that corticosteroids would halt necrolysis by aborting inflammatory response and other immunologic processes; however, immunologic factors in the pathogenesis of the syndrome have not been satisfactorily documented, and, in fact, dermal inflammation is usually absent. Recent studies conclude that patients treated without corticosteroids have an improved survival rate compared to that of patients on steroids. The former group has a decreased incidence of gastrointestinal bleeding, candidal sepsis, and an improved survival rate after septic complications. Corticosteroids mask early signs of infection, decrease a patient's ability to fight infection if it occurs, and impair and delay wound healing.

Other approaches used for treatment of TEN include plasmapheresis and high-dose pulse corticosteroids. Plasma exchange has been postulated to be effective by removing an offending drug or metabolite, or a "necrolytic" factor. Recently cyclophosphamide has been reported to dramatically alter the course of the disease. These treatments have not been used for large numbers of patients. In general, it is thought that recent improvements in survival have been due to advances in infection control and supportive care, allowing the patient to survive until reepithelization can occur.

Goldstein SM, Wintroub BW, Elias PM: Toxic epidermal necrolysis: Unmuddying the waters. *Arch Dermatol.* 1987;123:1153–1155.
This editorial summarizes recent studies and discussions regarding TEN.

Halbein PH, Madden MR, Finklestein JL, et al: Improved burn center survival of patients with toxic epidermal necrolysis managed without corticosteroids. *Ann Surg.* 1986;204:503–512.
A decreased mortality is found in patients treated without corticosteroids.

Heng MCY, Allen SG: Efficacy of cyclophosphamide in toxic epidermal necrolysis. *J Am Acad Dermatol.* 1991;25:778–786.
Report of four cases of drug induced TEN whom the authors feel responded dramatically to cyclophosphamide and oral corticosteroids.

Huff JC, Weston WL, Tonnesen MG: Erythema multiforme: A critical review of characteristics, diagnostic criteria, and causes. *J Am Acad Dermatol.* 1983;8:763–775.
This review gives a historical perspective of the evolution of the definition of EM, describes the clinical characteristics of EM major and minor, gives criteria for diagnosis, and describes some of the well-known associated precipitating factors.

Lemak MA, Duvic M, Bean SF: Oral acyclovir for the prevention of herpes-associated erythema multiforme. *J Am Acad Dermatol.* 1986;15:50–54.
The use of acyclovir for HSV-associated EM is described.

Peters W, Zaidi J, Douglas L: Toxic epidermal necrolysis: a burn-centre challenge. *Can Med Assoc J.* 1991;144:1477–1480.
A burn center in Toronto reports the treatment and course of 10 patients, 2 of whom died. Biobrane was used as a dressing. Antibiotics were prescribed for evidence of infection.

Rasmussen JE: Erythema multiforme in children. Response to treatment with systemic corticosteroids. *Br J Dermatol.* 1976;95:181–186.
Review of 32 cases of SJS treated with either systemic corticosteroids or supportive care reveals not only that the patients on steroids did not recover sooner but that they had more medical complications.

Roujeau JC, Guillaume JC, Fabre JP, et al. Toxic epidermal necrolysis. Incidence and drug etiology in France, 1981–1985. *Arch Dermatol.* 1990;126:37–42.
Nationwide, 253 cases of TEN were validated and the incidence estimated to be 1.2 cases per million. Antibacterial sulfonamides and nonsteroidal antiinflammatory agents were the drugs incriminated most often.

Stern RS, Chan HL: Usefulness of case report literature in determining drugs responsible for toxic epidermal necrolysis. *J Am Acad Dermatol.* 1989;21:317–322.
Authors review case reports of TEN and propose specific diagnostic criteria.

Tonnesen MG, Harrist TJ, Wintroub BU, et al: Erythema multiforme: Microvascular damage and infiltration of lymphocytes and basophils. *J Invest Dermatol.* 1983;80:282–286.
The various histologic patterns seen in EM and related immunologic findings are discussed.

5. STAPHYLOCOCCAL SCALDED SKIN SYNDROME
Sharon J. Littzi

Staphylococcal scalded skin syndrome (SSSS) was recognized as a distinct clinical entity in the mid 1800s, and has been called a confusing number of names including pemphigus neonatorum, Ritter's disease, and toxic epidermal necrolysis. It was only very recently appreciated that a toxin-producing strain of *Staphylococcus aureus* is the etiologic agent in the disease, and for a time SSSS was also called staphylococcal toxic epidermal necrolysis. SSSS is primarily a disease of neonates and young children, with a fatality rate of less than 4%. Epidemics have occurred in contaminated nurseries and the strain may be transmitted by an asymptomatic carrier. SSSS has also been reported in adults, most of whom were immunocompromised or had renal failure, in addition to having a staphylococcal abscess, septicemia, or pneumonia.

The **clinical manifestations** of SSSS are often preceded by evidence of primary infection with *S. aureus,* such as impetigo, purulent conjunctivitis, otitis media, or nasopharyngeal infection. The child may have fever, malaise, and irritability. The center of the face becomes tender and erythematous. Around the mouth, the erythema may weep and crust, with a distinctive appearance often referred to as "potato chip scales." The flexural areas and trunk may also become involved. In some patients, the rash then stabilizes. In others, widespread flaccid blisters develop within the next 24 to 48 hours. Nikolsky's sign is present (blisters may be moved into adjacent normal skin with lateral pressure), and large areas of skin slough, giving the appearance of a thermal burn. Hair and nails may be shed. Pustules rarely develop. Mucous membrane involvement is not prominent. Because of the distinctive appearance of the eruption, the diagnosis is generally easy to make clinically. If needed, a skin biopsy can be done. Histologic examination reveals noninflammatory keratinocyte necrosis in the superficial epidermis with bullous separation in the granular cell layer, beneath which there is normal basilar epidermis and dermis.

The **evaluation** of the patient must include a search for the source of *S. aureus* infection. Staphylococci may be cultured from pyogenic foci on the skin, conjunctivae, ala nasi, nasopharynx, and stools. They are rarely isolated from blisters, exfoliated surfaces, or blood since the entire entity is mediated by an epidermolytic toxin called exfoliatin, which is usually produced by *S. aureus* belonging to phage group 2. In this regard SSSS resembles toxic shock syndrome, since both are produced by toxins released from either frank infection or occult colonization with *S. aureus*. The epidermolytic toxin is directly responsible for the superficial epidermal necrosis in SSSS and may be identified by a newborn mouse bioassay or slide latex agglutination.

The **differential diagnosis** of this disease in infants usually includes Kawasaki's disease, erythema multiforme, toxic epidermal necrolysis, toxic shock syndrome, and scarlet fever. Leiner's disease, a rare exfoliative erythroderma thought to be related to generalized seborrheic dermatitis, must be considered in very young infants. Blistering can also be seen in children, secondary to generalized cutaneous mastocytosis or primary bullous dermatoses such as immunoglobulin A–associated bullous dermatosis of childhood, pemphigus vulgaris, and pemphigus foliaceous. In adults, SSSS is rare, generally occurring only in immunocompromised hosts with renal failure. Healthy adults are presumed to have specific antistaphylococcal antibodies and are able to excrete the toxin quickly through the kidneys. The clinical picture can be confused with erythema multiforme, toxic shock syndrome, and scarlet fever. Recently SSSS has been reported to resemble graft-versus-host disease in an adult patient. The most common dilemma, however, is whether the adult patient has SSSS or toxic epidermal necrolysis (TEN). Histologically SSSS is easily differentiated from TEN, most rapidly with microscopic evaluation of a frozen section of a specimen obtained by peeling a small portion of new blister roof from an exfoliating site. In TEN or severe erythema multiforme, the entire epidermis is obtained with full thickness necrosis, whereas in SSSS, only the uppermost portion of the epidermis is detached.

Treatment requires prompt administration of antistaphylococcal antibiotics appropriate to the organism's antibiotic sensitivities, generally a beta-lactamase–resistant antibiotic. Antibiotics are given to eliminate a subclinical infection and decrease the number of toxin-producing staphylococci, as well as to decrease the risk of contagion. Care is generally initiated in an inpatient setting since the patients often appear very ill and have poor oral intake of fluids. Fluid balance must be rigorously controlled. Secondary infection may occur. Topical care of the involved skin includes wet dressings for exudative, crusted sites and antibiotic ointments such as bacitracin for denuded areas. Only relatively inert dressings are recommended for neonates. Response to antibiotics is rapid and the patients heal uneventfully and without scarring in less than 1 week.

Amon RB, Dimond RL: Toxic epidermal necrolysis. Rapid differentiation between staphylococcal and drug-induced disease. *Arch Dermatol.* 1975;111:1433–1437.
Given the differences in the level of the epidermal split, SSSS (with a cleavage plane high in the malphigian layer) can be rapidly differentiated from drug-induced TEN (subepidermal split).

Curran JP, Al-Salihi FL: Neonatal staphylococcal scalded skin syndrome. Massive outbreak due to an unusual phage type. *Pediatrics.* 1980;66:285–288.
An epidemic of SSSS due to an organism with an unusual phage pattern lasted 115 days and involved 68 newborns. The illness was mild in all patients.

Dancer SJ, Simmons NA, Poston SM, et al: Outbreak of staphylococcal scalded skin syndrome among neonates. *J Infect Dis.* 1988;16:87–103.
Two distinct outbreaks of SSSS over a 2-month period in a maternity unit are described. All neonates responded rapidly to a short course of intravenous antibiotics. The outbreak ceased after appropriate treatment of all carriers and implementation of an extensive disinfection procedure within the unit.

Diem E, Konrad K, Graninger W: Staphylococcal scalded skin syndrome in an adult with fatal disseminated staphylococcal sepsis. *Acta Dermatol Venereol.* 1982;62:295–299.
A case of a 63-year-old male with SSSS as the first clinical manifestation of dis-

seminated staphylococcal sepsis is reported. Possible explanations for the fatal outcome are discussed.

Gentilhomme E, Faure M, Piemont Y, et al: Action of staphylococcal exfoliative toxins on epidermal cell cultures and organotypic skin. *J Dermatol.* 1990;17:526–532.
This study compared the effects of exfoliative toxins A or B on human keratinocyte cell cultures to those on human and mouse organotypic skin cultures.

Goldberg NS, Ahmed T, Robinson B, et al: Staphylococcal scalded skin syndrome mimicking acute graft vs. host disease in a bone marrow transplant recipient. *Arch Dermatol.* 1989;125:85–87.
A necrolytic eruption developed 90 days after an allogenic bone marrow transplant for chronic myelogenous leukemia. Diagnosis was made by skin biopsy, and phage group 2, type 71 S. aureus was cultured from the blood.

Lyell A: The staphylococcal scalded skin syndrome in historical perspective: Emergence of dermopathic strains of *S. aureus* and discovery of the epidermolytic toxin. *J Am Acad Dermatol.* 1983;9:285–290.
This article is a historical review of the events establishing SSSS as a distinct disease.

Melish ME, Glasgow LA: The staphylococcal scalded skin syndrome—development of an experimental model. *New Engl J Med.* 1970;282:1114–1116.
Phage group 2 coagulase positive staphylococci were isolated from 17 children with generalized scarlatiniform erythema with or without exfoliation. These organisms were found to produce exfoliation in newborn mice, confirming their role as the etiologic agent in this syndrome.

Neife LI, Tuazon CU, Cardella TA, et al: Staphylococcal scalded skin syndrome in adults: Case report and review of the literature. *Am J Med Sci.* 1979;277:99–107.
Most adults in whom SSSS has been reported are immunosuppressed and have renal failure. Prognosis is generally good if sepsis does not intervene.

6. TOXIC SHOCK SYNDROME
Sharon J. Littzi

Toxic shock syndrome (TSS) was first described by Todd et al in 1978 as a constellation of high fever, headache, confusion, conjunctival hyperemia, scarlatiniform rash, subcutaneous edema, vomiting, diarrhea, oliguria, acute renal failure, liver abnormalities, disseminated intravascular coagulation, and severe prolonged shock in seven children. A marked desquamation of the hands and feet as well as a fine desquamation of the trunk and extremities was observed during convalescence. In 1979 and 1980, a dramatic increase in the number of cases of TSS was reported in the United States. In this epidemic, TSS seemed to be closely related to continuous use of high-absorbency tampons during menses, but it is now known that the same full-blown syndrome can occur in nonmenstruating females and males with a variety of medical and surgical conditions ranging from an infected insect bite, lung abscess, recent inguinal hernia repair, and after nasal packing. Interestingly, of the first cases reported, none were associated with menses or tampon use, although *Staphylococcus aureus* was cultured from the vagina of one patient.

Fewer cases have been reported each year since 1980, but the yearly reported incidence is still 304 per 100,000 females of menstrual age, with the actual incidence probably being even higher. Nonmenstrual cases of TSS have been reported with increasing frequency. In initial studies, mortality was greater than 10%, but current mortality is closer to 2%. Recurrent TSS, usually occurring in menstruating women, has been reported with an incidence as high as 30%.

The **etiology** of TSS is not entirely understood, but it is believed to be mediated by a toxin produced by *S. aureus*. The term *toxic shock syndrome toxin-1* (TSST-1) is used for the toxin believed to be the causative agent, which is probably identical to other reported toxins: pyrogenic exotoxin-C (PE-C) or enterotoxin F (EF). Bergdoll and associates have shown that TSS patients have an increased sensitivity to EF as well as an absence of antibodies to TSST-1. In 1985, it was reported that TSST-1 production rates were profoundly affected by magnesium ion concentrations in the media in which the toxin-producing *S. aureus* was growing. A low concentration of magnesium ion resulted in significantly greater production of TSST-1. The materials formulating the Rely tampon, in particular, were responsible for magnesium ion concentrations that markedly increased total TSST-1 production. Other toxins, such as staphylococcal enterotoxin B, may also play a role in TSS.

Investigators at the Centers for Disease Control have proposed a detailed **case definition** with at least three organ systems involved, including the skin (see Table 6-1). These strict clinical criteria may exclude many cases of TSS, so that a lower incidence is probably reported than actually occurs. Dermatologic criteria include a diffuse macular sheetlike erythema at the time of diagnosis and desquamation 1 to 2 weeks after the onset of illness, particularly involving palms and soles. Mucous membrane involvement is characterized by conjunctival injection and a strawberry tongue. Other morphological features that have been reported include bullae, petechiae, and a maculopapular morbilliform erythema, all of which have been followed by significant desquamation of the hands and feet. Edema of the hands and feet has also been stressed by Fischer. Of note, there have been no reports of a large group of patients who were examined by dermatologists.

None of the cutaneous findings are pathognomonic for TSS. The **differential diagnosis** includes Kawasaki's disease, Rocky Mountain spotted fever, leptospirosis, rubeola, and other viral exanthems, as well as staphylococcal or streptococcal scarlet fever, staphylococcal scalded skin syndrome and early drug reactions including toxic epidermal necrosis (TEN). Other bacterial infections must also be excluded, including gram-negative septicemia and acute meningococcemia. Kawasaki's disease (mucocutaneous lymph node syndrome) usually occurs in younger persons and is associated

Table 6-1 Case definition of toxic shock syndrome

MAJOR CRITERIA (ALL 4 MUST BE MET)
1. Fever: temperature $\geq$ 38.9°C (102°F)
2. Rash: diffuse macular erythroderma
3. Hypotension: systolic blood pressure $\leq$ 90 mm Hg for adults or below fifth percentile by age for children under 16, orthostatic drop in diastolic blood pressure $\geq$ 15 mm Hg from lying to sitting position, orthostatic syncope, or orthostatic dizziness
4. Desquamation: 1–2 wk after onset of illness, particularly affecting palms and soles

MULTISYSTEM INVOLVEMENT (3 OR MORE MUST BE MET)
1. Gastrointestinal: vomiting or diarrhea at onset of illness
2. Muscular: severe myalgia or creatine kinase level at least twice upper limit of normal for laboratory
3. Mucous membrane: vaginal, oropharyngeal, or conjunctival hyperemia
4. Renal: BUN or creatinine level at least twice upper limit of normal for laboratory or urinary sediment with pyuria ($\geq$ 5 leukocytes per high-power field) in absence of urinary tract infection
5. Hepatic: total bilirubin, SGOT, SGPT at least twice upper limit of normal for laboratory
6. Hematologic: platelets $\leq$ 100,000/mm³
7. CNS: disorientation or alterations in consciousness without focal neurologic signs when fever and hypotension are absent

NORMAL RESULTS ON THE FOLLOWING TESTS (IF PERFORMED)
1. Blood, throat, or cerebrospinal fluid cultures (blood culture may be positive for *Staphylococcus aureus*)
2. Antibody titer tests for Rocky Mountain spotted fever, leptospirosis, or rubeola

with lymph node enlargement without notable hypotension. The rash of Rocky Mountain spotted fever usually begins peripherally, extends centrally after 6 to 18 hours, and becomes petechial within 2 to 4 days. Fewer than one-half of the cases of leptospirosis have cutaneous involvement, which varies from nonspecific macules and wheals to purpura. Scarlet fever may mimic TSS, but rarely has multisystem involvement. A drug rash or viral illness may be suspected by history, and the erythema is generally morbilliform with discrete and confluent 2- to 4-mm blanching erythematous papules. TEN is identified by red painful skin with sloughing of full thickness epidermis when it's rubbed (Nikolsky's sign).

The **histology** of TSS is variable, depending on the morphologic appearance of the eruption. Hurwitz and Ackerman studied five patients in whom erythematous papules were biopsied, and all had the classic sunburn reaction with a superficial perivascular and interstitial mixed cell infiltrate that contained neutrophils and sometimes eosinophils, foci of spongiosis that contained neutrophils and scattered necrotic keratinocytes that sometimes were arranged in clusters within the epidermis. For these five patients, the authors felt that their findings were consistent and specific.

The **treatment** of TSS is most successful with early recognition and elimination of the presumed site of staphylococcal infection. All patients should have, in addition to a thorough history, a thorough skin exam, not only for an evaluation of the rash associated with toxin release but also for a search for sites of staphylococcal colonization, such as infected insect bites, which may be the initiating event in cases of nonmenstrual TSS. Once TSS is diagnosed or suspected, antistaphylococcal antibiotics should be immediately started intravenously. Hospitalization is usually necessary for close monitoring of vital signs and general cardiovascular support.

Bach MC: Dermatologic signs in TSS—clues to diagnosis. *J Am Acad Dermatol.* 1983;8(3):343–347.
A brief overview of some important dermatologic findings in TSS and differential diagnosis.

Bergdoll MS, Crass BA, Reiser RF, et al.: A new staphylococcal enterotoxin, enterotoxin F (EF) associated with toxic shock syndrome, *S. aureus. Lancet.* 1981;1: 1017.
A discussion of identification and properties of EF, which is probably identical to TSST-1 and PE-C.

Case records of Massachusetts General Hospital. *N Engl J Med.* 1986;314:302–310.
A case presentation and brief review of TSS.

Davis JP, Chesney PJ, Wand PJ, et al.: Toxic shock syndrome: Epidemiologic features, recurrence, risk factors and prevention. *N Engl J Med.* 1980;303:1429–1434.
Surveillance of TSS in Wisconsin from September 1975 through January 1979. Thirty-five patients were matched for age and menstruation to 105 controls to evaluate potential risk factors for TSS associated with menses.

Elbaum DJ, Wood C, Abuabara F, et al.: Bullae in a patient with TSS. *J Am Acad Dermatol.* 1984;10:267–272.
In this case presentation, subepidermal bullae were present along with macular erythema.

Hurwitz RM, Ackerman AB: Cutaneous pathology of TSS. *Am J Dermatopathol.* 1985;7(6):563–578.
Histologic findings in TSS are presented with a review and critique of the dermpath literature.

Reingold AL, Hargrett NT, Dan BB, et al.: Nonmenstrual toxic shock syndrome: a review of 130 cases. *Ann Intern Med.* 1982;95(Pt 2):871–874.
This report shows that the syndrome occurs in a wide range of clinical settings and is associated with S. aureus infections at a variety of sites. Although the chemical features of nonmenstrual TSS are similar to the menstrual cases, the epidemiologic and demographic features are different.

Resnick SD: Toxic shock syndrome: recent developments in pathogenesis. *J Pediatr.* 1990;116:321–328.
An editorial reviewing currently known research data, placing it in clinical perspective.

Schlievert PM, Shands KN, Dan BB, et al.: Identification and characterization of

exotoxin from *S. aureus* associated with toxic shock syndrome. *J Infect Dis.* 1981;143:509–516.
This study examines a protein exotoxin released from patients with TSS. The protein was purified and its biologic properties are discussed.

7. SEPSIS, ENDOCARDITIS, AND RELATED SERIOUS INFECTIONS
Richard J. Sharpe

The intact, undiseased cutaneous surface represents the body's first line of defense against infection. It is therefore not surprising that conditions compromising this barrier can result in an increased risk of systemic infection; this risk is further magnified if second-line defense mechanisms are impaired by corticosteroids, chemotherapeutic agents, or immunosuppressive disease. The skin also provides a window through which clinical clues of serious systemic infection are seen. In addition, skin biopsy specimens provide material that can result in identification of an offending organism. Proper interpretation of these cutaneous clues and appropriate biopsies can result in the institution of life-saving therapy. In all serious infections, a complete history and physical examination, coupled with a complete blood count with differential, form the core of the evaluation. An elevated white blood count and a left shift occur in serious bacterial infections in hosts capable of mounting such a response. A complete urinalysis, urine culture, sputum Gram stain and culture, multiple blood cultures, chest x ray, and Gram stain and culture of purulent material from suspicious skin lesions are also usually performed when a source of infection is not obvious. Considering the clinical differential diagnosis, skin biopsy and other special procedures may be necessary to obtain material for a microbiological diagnosis.

Staphylococcal bacteremia may be a sequela of any localized staphylococcal infection, even a minor-appearing skin infection. Examination of the patient may reveal an infected site of trauma, cellulitis, or a primary skin disease such as eczema that favors bacterial colonization or compromises the barrier function of the skin. Pustules, subcutaneous abscesses, and purpuric papules or plaques with purulent centers from metastatic abscess formation are relatively common with any protracted *Staphylococcus aureus* bacteremia. The disease may progress slowly, causing low to moderate fever and metastatic abscess formation in other organs. Meningitis or endocarditis can occur with prolonged bacteremia. Rarely, patients with bacteremia die in less than 24 hours with high fever and a septic shocklike state. Multiple blood cultures from different sites over time, plus cultures and Gram stains of specimens from other possible primary or secondary sites of infection, should be carried out. Aspiration of skin lesions for Gram stain and culture can occasionally help the clinician make a rapid diagnosis. Patients with extensive psoriasis, erythroderma, atopic eczema, or other generalized skin conditions who require evaluation for suspected sepsis or bacteremia pose a special problem. Blood cultures drawn through diseased skin that is simply colonized with *S. aureus* may result in falsely positive blood cultures despite careful technique.

Prior to the availability of antibiotics, over 80% of patients with staphylococcal bacteremia died. With the development of antibiotics and appropriate surgical treatment of local sites of infection, the mortality rate has been reduced to roughly 30%. For nonmethicillin-resistant strains, high-dose intravenous oxacillin or nafcillin is the treatment of choice in individuals not allergic to penicillin. Intravenous first-generation cephalosporins can be substituted in many penicillin-allergic patients. For the treatment of methicillin-resistant strains, vancomycin should be used. Rifampin and gentamycin are synergistic with penicillins in killing *S. aureus* and might be useful adjuncts, especially during the first several days of treatment. Given the seriousness of untreated *S. aureus* bacteremia, the clinician should treat a patient with suspected bacteremia without delay, using systemic antibiotics even before culture results are known.

Acute bacterial endocarditis is commonly caused by highly pathogenic organisms such as *S. aureus,* pneumococcus, group A streptococcus, and gonococcus. Either a normal or a diseased heart may be involved. The patient may exhibit evidence of primary infection with the organism. Secondary skin findings include petechiae and embolic purpuric or purulent lesions. Roth spots, small flame-shaped hemorrhages, may be seen on a retinal exam. Osler nodes are erythematous, purpuric, or pustular tender papules located on the digital tufts and are rare in this disease. Janeway lesions, similar in color but not tender, are located on palmar and plantar surfaces, and are also uncommon. The diagnosis of acute bacterial endocarditis is based on the constellation of clinical findings as well as the results of multiple blood cultures drawn from different sites over time.

Suspected acute bacterial endocarditis should be treated quickly and aggressively with appropriate intravenous antibiotics. Vancomycin is often the first choice for *S. aureus,* but can be replaced with oxacillin or nafcillin if the organism is sensitive. Penicillin G remains the drug of choice for serious group A streptococcus and pneumococcus infections, including endocarditis. Ceftriaxone is used to treat gonococcal endocarditis unless in vitro susceptibility testing shows that the organism is sensitive to penicillin.

Subacute bacterial endocarditis (SBE) is most commonly seen in individuals with congenital cardiac defects or rheumatic valvular disease. Other risk factors include arteriovenous fistulas, aneurysms, foreign bodies such as cardiac valve prostheses, and repeated bacteremia, as is seen in intravenous drug abusers. Viridans streptococci, part of the normal oral flora, are the organisms most often cultured. Enterococci, which inhabit the gastrointestinal tract and perineal areas, are another important cause of SBE. *Streptococcus bovis* endocarditis should alert the clinician to an intestinal portal of entry, such as colon carcinoma. Although *S. aureus* more often produces acute endocarditis, SBE due to this organism has been reported.

Cutaneous manifestations of SBE include Osler nodes, Janeway lesions, subungual splinter hemorrhages, petechiae, and purpura. Osler nodes and Janeway lesions are much more common in SBE than in acute bacterial endocarditis; however, they may also be seen in other conditions, including gonococcemia, systemic lupus erythematosus, hemolytic anemia, and typhoid fever. Splinter hemorrhages are nonspecific and common in the general population, probably secondary to minor trauma. A clinical suspicion of SBE should be evaluated with multiple sets of blood cultures drawn over several days and appropriate cardiac examination.

Treatment is the administration of long-term systemic antibiotics, depending on the in vitro sensitivities of the organism cultured. Surveillance blood cultures are often collected during and after antibiotic treatment. Antibiotic prophylaxis against organisms commonly incriminated in SBE, usually with penicillin, should be administered for any high-risk patient prior to oral surgery, including biopsy of the oral mucosa, and even minor surgery of the perineal area or other mucosal surfaces.

Prosthetic valve endocarditis occurs in 2% or greater of patients with prosthetic valves. Early infections, occurring less than 2 months after valve replacement, are commonly caused by *S. aureus, S. epidermidis,* colliform bacteria, diphtheroids, *Candida* species, and *Aspergillus* species. Organisms causing late infections include viridans streptococci, enterococci, *S. aureus,* and *S. epidermidis.* The cutaneous manifestations seen in acute or subacute infectious endocarditis can be seen in prosthetic valve endocarditis. Prevention of endocarditis by prophylaxis with antibiotics is of primary importance in patients with prosthetic valves. They should be treated with antibiotics before undergoing elective surgical procedures involving mucous membranes or the perineal area. Some authorities argue that these patients should be prophylaxed even when normal skin is incised. The combination of 500 mg of ciprofloxacin and 1 g of amoxicillin PO 1 hour before surgery and then again 8 hours later will provide coverage against commonly encountered organisms in prosthetic valve endocarditis.

Right-sided endocarditis is almost always secondary to intravenous drug abuse or to contaminated transvenous pacing wires or other intravenous appliances. The most commonly encountered organisms include such skin flora as *S. aureus* and *Candida* species and such organisms as *Pseudomonas* species or *Serratia marcescens,* which are often found in contaminated injected materials. Cutaneous lesions are not frequently seen, but may be similar to those of acute infectious endocarditis. Evaluation of the patient proceeds as in acute infectious endocarditis, and antibiotics or antifungal drugs should be tailored to the offending organism.

Pseudomonas species are ubiquitous aerobic gram-negative rods that cause a variety of infections ranging from trivial nail or skin conditions to sepsis and death. Certain hosts have an increased probability of developing a life-threatening pseudomonas infection. Hospitalization itself is a risk factor, particularly in patients with a compromised cutaneous barrier, indwelling catheters, neutropenia or immunosuppression of any cause, corticosteroid therapy, or chemotherapy. *Pseudomonas aeruginosa* and occasionally *P. maltophilia* are the most common species that cause life-threatening systemic infection. Patients with pseudomonas septicemia are usually very ill and often develop septic shock. As with other forms of sepsis, if patients are on moderate to high doses of systemic corticosteroids, many of the early features of sepsis can be masked. In patients whose bone marrow is capable of responding, leukocytosis is typically one of the first hallmarks of pseudomonas bacteremia along with high spiking fevers.

The skin lesions of pseudomonas infection have characteristic features and can provide diagnostic clues that allow early intervention and the institution of possibly life-saving therapy. Characteristic findings are small, painless macules or slightly elevated papules on the trunk, randomly distributed hemorrhagic vesicles and bullae, ecthyma gangrenosum, and gangrenous cellulitis. The lesions of ecthyma gangrenosum are composed of an indurated, painless ulcer with a central necrotic region and gray-black eschar surrounded by erythema. Gangrenous cellulitis appears as a painless, sharply demarcated, necrotic lesion resembling a decubitus ulcer. It is, however, relatively acute in onset and does not necessarily involve pressure areas. In addition to the history which may reveal a hospitalization, a debilitated state, or neutropenia, and physical examination, appropriate cultures of blood, sputum, urine, and suspected metastatic lesions should be performed when one is evaluating patients with pseudomonas sepsis. Aspiration or biopsy specimens of skin lesions are particularly valuable since the organism is usually abundant in these samples. Histologic evaluation of a biopsy specimen from a metastatic lesion reveals a necrotizing vasculitis, with the walls of small arteries and veins invaded by abundant bacteria.

Treatment of suspected pseudomonas sepsis includes the immediate institution of two intravenous antipseudomonas antibiotics with different modes of action. An aminoglycoside is usually chosen as one of these agents. The optimal aminoglycoside depends on the particular resistance patterns known to the hospital, but in the absence of such information the use of tobramycin or amikacin is appropriate. The aminoglycoside is supplemented with an antipseudomonas penicillin such as ticarcillin. In penicillin-allergic patients, ceftriaxone or a monobactam such as aztreonam can be substituted. Orally administered quinolones should not be relied on to treat pseudomonas sepsis. When the culture results are available, two-agent antibiotic therapy may be modified to reflect the results of in vitro sensitivity assays. Aminoglycoside doses should be adjusted according to serum peak and trough levels. Renal toxicity is an ever present danger with aminoglycosides, particularly if serum levels are not closely monitored.

The gram-negative diplococcus *Neisseria meningitidis* can cause a variety of infections, most notably meningitis, bacteremia, and endocarditis. Acute **meningococcemia** is frequently preceded by a mild upper respiratory infection associated with headache, nausea, vomiting, and myalgias. These symptoms, however, do not always occur and the patient may present with fever, obtundation, and other findings of meningitis. In fulminant meningococcemia, vomiting, stupor, hemorrhagic rash, and septic shock may be evident within a few hours of the onset of symptoms. The cutaneous findings associated with classic acute meningococcal disease are petechiae and purpura, but transient urticarial, macular or papular lesions have been described. The petechiae are small, irregular, and often raised with pale, grayish centers. They are common on the extremities, but may also be found on the head, palms, soles, and mucous membranes. Extensive bullous and hemorrhagic lesions with central necrosis can also develop. Fulminant meningococcemia, or the Waterhouse-Friderichsen syndrome, is a rapidly progressive infection associated with life-threatening septic shock. Purpura fulminans, hemorrhagic necrosis of the skin with irregular geographic margins, is often seen in this rapidly fatal variant, secondary to both the infection and the associated fulminant disseminated intravascular coagulation. Infarction of internal organs, including the adrenal glands, is frequent.

If meningococcemia is suspected on clinical grounds, cerebrospinal fluid should be gram-stained, cultured, and sent for protein, glucose, and latex agglutination tests. If a cutaneous lesion is aspirated or biopsied, gram-negative diplococci can be demonstrated by Gram stain or culture 40% to 90% of the time. Blood should also be cultured. Therapy must be instituted immediately, even before the results of these tests are known. The treatment of choice for meningococcemia and meningitis is high-dose intravenous penicillin G. Chloramphenicol can be used in penicillin-allergic patients. Untreated meningococcemia or meningitis is almost always fatal. Treatment is life-saving in 90% of patients, although even with aggressive treatment, mortality of the Waterhouse-Friderichsen syndrome remains close to 100%.

Neisseria gonorrhoeae is a gram-negative diplococcus that commonly causes acute urethritis in both males and females as well as inflammation of the pharynx, eye, rectum, and other parts of the genitourinary tract, especially the fallopian tubes. From these sites, **gonococcemia** can result, rarely complicated by meningitis, pericarditis, or endocarditis. The bacteremia usually results in a characteristic clinical syndrome of fever, chills, arthralgias, arthritis, and tenosynovitis. Skin lesions, petechial or erythematous papules, occur early and evolve into vesicles or pustules surmounting an erythematous or hemorrhagic base. These lesions are usually few in number and are most frequently distributed distally around the joints of the arms and legs. Although organisms can sometimes be isolated from skin lesions, the diagnosis is usually made after a thorough physical examination supplemented by appropriate cultures of the pharynx, rectum, urethra, and cervix. Patients may have simultaneous infection with other sexually transmitted organisms such as *Treponema pallidum*, chlamydia, and human immunodeficiency virus. Treatment should be instituted promptly to prevent further metastatic spread of the infection and joint destruction. Intravenous ceftriaxone is the treatment of choice because of the increasing emergence of penicillin-resistant strains. Concurrent treatment for occult chlamydia infection is prudent because of the high false-negative rate of currently available diagnostic tests for this organism.

Occurring in both normal and immunocompromised patients, **gram-negative sepsis** is a manifestation of serious infection with bacteria such as *Pseudomonas, Escherichia coli, Klebsiella, Salmonella,* and *Enterobacter* species. Noncholera *Vibrio* species can cause serious soft tissue infection by direct inoculation through the skin while a person is wading in estuaries, occasionally resulting in sepsis. The urinary tract is a common initial source of infection, but almost any portal of entry, including the skin, can serve as a source. Metastatic skin lesions ranging from papules to pustules to cellulitis and necrosis can occur. Characteristically, gram-negative sepsis is accompanied by vasomotor collapse, a result of endotoxin release (and possibly exotoxin release when associated with infection by gram-positive bacteria), which induces mediators such as tumor necrosis factor (TNF), also called cachectin. Vasomotor collapse is managed with variable success by aggressive intravenous fluid therapy and vasopressors. The use of corticosteroids in sepsis remains controversial. Experimentally, anti-endotoxin (lipopolysaccharide) antibodies or anti-TNF antibodies have suppressed the septic shock response.

Disseminated intravascular coagulation (DIC) occurs in the setting of various infections, the most frequent of which is gram-negative sepsis. Less commonly DIC is associated with gram-positive sepsis, viremia, miliary tuberculosis, Rocky Mountain spotted fever, subacute bacterial endocarditis, and malaria. In these infections, as well as in some noninfectious disorders such as the Kasabach-Merritt syndrome, the clotting cascade is activated. Clotting factors and platelets are actively consumed, and their depletion results in abnormal bleeding tendencies that can be rapidly fatal. Fibrin thrombi occlude capillaries and small arterioles, and, in the presence of few platelets and abnormal clotting parameters, cause petechiae, purpura, and massive ecchymoses. **Purpura fulminans,** associated with fulminant DIC, refers to large, sharply demarcated geographic purpuric lesions that commonly become necrotic in the center and are often surrounded by a narrow rim of erythema. If the patient lives long enough, the cutaneous necrosis becomes widespread. Histologic examination of a biopsy specimen taken from the border of a necrotic lesion will document the presence of fibrin emboli.

Treatment of DIC and accompanying purpura fulminans is difficult. Therapy is directed toward treatment of the trigger for the DIC, such as empiric broad-spectrum antibiotics for suspected infection. Replacement of coagulation factors and platelets, fresh frozen plasma, and cryoprecipitate may be futile since they will also be consumed and produce more fibrin thrombi. Heparinization prior to replacement therapy has been successful in a small number of cases. Supportive therapy with maintenance of fluid and electrolyte balance is essential. Despite aggressive and sophisticated treatment, fatalities are common.

Disseminated candidiasis due to such organisms as *Candida albicans, C. tropicalis,* and *C. pseudotropicalis* rarely occurs in the normal host. Factors that predispose patients to disseminated candidiasis include immunosuppression, indwelling catheters, hyperalimentation, intravenous drug abuse, recent abdominal surgery, high-dose systemic corticosteroid treatment, and recent broad-spectrum antibiotic therapy. Frequently patients will have more than one risk factor. The skin, lungs, spleen, kidneys, liver, heart, and brain are commonly involved. Eye findings include an endophthalmitis that correlates well with multiple organ involvement. Skin lesions occur in up to 15% of patients with disseminated candidiasis. The recognition of skin lesions is particularly important since blood cultures are negative in many cases. The characteristic skin lesion is a papulonodule, 0.5 to 1.0 cm in diameter, that is often hemorrhagic. Lesions may be numerous to few in number and usually occur on the trunk and extremities. The differential diagnosis includes other disseminated infections such as pseudomonas sepsis.

Suspect skin lesions may be scraped and a KOH preparation evaluated microscopically, or biopsied and evaluated microscopically by a touch preparation stained with Shwartz-Lamkin stain or other appropriate fungal stain as well as a Gram stain. Any purulent material that is obtained on biopsy or aspiration may be similarly processed. Cultures for fungi and bacteria should also be performed, and the histopathology laboratory should be alerted to process a tissue Gram stain and fungal stains on formalin-fixed biopsy specimens. Treatment consists of removal of potentially contaminated indwelling lines and administration of an appropriate systemic antifungal agent. Amphotericin B remains the treatment of choice, but ketoconazole, itraconazole, and some of the other newer agents may also be effective.

Ahmed AR, Moy R: Death in pemphigus. *J Am Acad Dermatol.* 1982;7:221–228.
  This study concludes that infection, in particular, and sepsis are the most common cause of death in pemphigus. Corticosteroid therapy is considered a major risk factor for such deaths, stressing the need for a high index of suspicion for life-threatening infection, rapid and complete evaluation, and early administration of adequate broad-spectrum antibiotic therapy in patients on high-dose systemic corticosteroids.
Craven DE, Googe PB: Case records of Massachusetts General Hospital: Weekly clinicopathological exercises. Case 41-1989: A 65-year-old man with fever, bullae, erythema, and edema of the leg after wading in brackish water. *N Engl J Med.* 1989;321:1029–1038.
  A case of noncholera vibrio cellulitis with an excellent discussion of differential diagnosis.
Fanning WL, Aronson M: Osler nodes, Janeway lesions, and splinter hemorrhages. *Arch Dermatol.* 1977;113:648–649.
  A concise review of these lesions commonly associated with endocarditis.
Fine JD, Miller JA, Harrist TJ, et al.: Cutaneous lesions in disseminated candidiasis mimicking ecthyma gangrenosum. *Am J Med.* 1981;70:1133–1135.
  As these authors clearly document, skin lesions that appear identical to ecthyma gangrenosum can be caused by emboli containing Candida organisms. The importance of skin biopsy in evaluating septic immunocompromised patients is stressed.
Greene SL, Su WP, Muller SA: Ecthyma gangrenosum: report of clinical, histopath-

ologic, and bacteriologic aspects of eight cases. *J Am Acad Dermatol.* 1984;11:781–787.
   This paper, with excellent clinical photographs, stresses the need for rapid diagnosis and early, aggressive intervention in this disease.
Plaut ME: Staphylococcal septicemia and pustular purpura. Report of cases. *Arch Dermatol.* 1969;99:82–85.
   This report highlights the cutaneous findings in staphylococcal septicemia.
Tracy KJ, Beutler B, Lowry SF, et al.: Shock and tissue injury induced by recombinant human cachectin. *Science.* 1986;234:470–474.
   Intravenous administration of cachectin (TNF) in an animal model can induce a septic shocklike response.
Wagner RF, Grande DJ, Feingold DS: Antibiotic prophylaxis against bacterial endocarditis in patients undergoing dermatologic surgery. *Arch Dermatol.* 1986;122:799–801.
   This commentary suggests that endocarditis prophylaxis be carried out in high-risk individuals even when the clinician will be incising normal skin.

8. VIRAL EXANTHEMS
Joseph C. Kvedar

Exanthem is the term used to describe a generalized, symmetric, usually monomorphous cutaneous eruption. The most common morphology is a widespread blotchy erythema composed of discrete and confluent pinkish red or reddish purple macules and papules, often referred to as a "maculopapular" eruption. Some exanthems may also have vesicular, urticarial, and petechial components. An enanthem is a similar eruption of mucosal surfaces, most commonly the oral mucosa. Exanthems and enanthems have a variety of etiologies and associations, of which the most common is viral infection. The pathogenesis of viral exanthems is believed to be related to one of two mechanisms. Actual deposition of viral particles in the skin (either free-floating or via diapedesis of infected leukocytes) might produce vasodilatation (erythema), edema, perivascular infiltration of mononuclear cells (papules), and hemorrhage and vesicle formation. Isolation of viral particles from skin lesions in numerous instances substantiates this hypothesis. Alternatively, the immune response to a viral illness might have, as part of its manifestation, a "hypersensitivity" reaction in the skin, producing an exanthem. Support for this theory comes from the observation that different viruses as well as drug reactions and graft-versus-host disease can cause very similar skin eruptions.

Historically, the common exanthems were labeled First disease (measles), Second disease (scarlet fever), Third disease (rubella), Fourth disease (not a clinically recognized disease today), Fifth disease (erythema infectiosum), and Sixth disease (roseola infantum). After the advent of widespread vaccination against measles and rubella in the 1960s, many clinicians began to think of these diseases as of historic interest only. In fact, epidemics as well as sporadic cases have occurred. Familiarity with these clinical syndromes is imperative not only for prompt diagnosis and isolation of the patient but also for avoidance of laborious and expensive investigation.

Measles, caused by a paramyxovirus, is spread by the respiratory route, and has an incubation period of about 10 days. A prodrome precedes the appearance of the exanthem by 3 to 4 days. The first symptom is generally fever, followed by dry cough, coryza, headache, conjunctivitis, and photophobia. During this phase, Koplik spots, a pathognomonic feature, appear in the mouth. They are white, 1- to 2-mm papules on an intensely red base, usually found on the buccal and lower labial mucosa. The exanthem develops with remarkable regularity on the fourteenth day after exposure. Erythematous papules and blotchy macular erythema begin on the back of the neck and hairline and spread to the trunk and extremities in a centrifugal and symmetric fashion over 3 to 4 days. The eruption often becomes confluent over the trunk, then fades in 3 to 4 days, leaving a fine scale in its wake. An exanthem with these clinical features is termed morbilliform.

Typical measles is confused with little else by those familiar with this syndrome. The disease is normally self-limited and of no consequence, but occasional complications such as encephalitis (1:1000 cases), otitis media, and bacterial infections occur. In the postvaccine era, two additional clinical syndromes have been recognized in individuals who developed partial immunity after vaccination. Mild modified measles differs from typical measles in that the prodrome is shorter and milder, Koplik spots are often absent, and the eruption tends to be papular and discrete. In atypical measles, the prodrome consists of 2 to 3 days of high fever and myalgias. The exanthem starts peripherally and either remains stationary or spreads centripetally. Vesicles and petechiae may occur. Koplik spots are not usually seen. This illness is most often confused with Rocky Mountain spotted fever. These two clinical syndromes make the diagnosis of measles in teenagers and adults a challenge.

Scarlet fever, not a viral process, is often considered in the differential diagnosis of exanthems. The disease has a 24-day incubation period and is characterized by 1 to 3 days of fever and sore throat followed by a generalized sheetlike bright red, finely papular, sandpaperlike exanthem often called a scarlatiniform erythema. Circumoral pallor is usually observed. The face may not be involved. Other manifestations include palatal petechiae and strawberry tongue, present in 50% and 75% of cases, respectively. Pastia's lines, linear petechial lesions in the axillary, anticubital, and inguinal folds, may also be seen. Scarlet fever is the result of infection with subtypes of group A streptococci that produce an erythemogenic toxin. A similar clinical picture may be seen in patients with a toxin-producing staphylococcal infection or a cytomegaloviral infection.

Rubella has become a rarity in the United States since the licensure of the rubella vaccine in 1969. After an incubation period of 12 to 25 days, the classic syndrome begins with a 4- to 5-day prodrome of fever, headache, and symptoms of mild upper respiratory tract infection. Conjunctivitis is notably absent. The exanthem, in contrast to measles, begins on the face. It then spreads centrifugally to involve the entire cutaneous surface within 24 to 36 hours, with distinctive, discrete pink macules and papules. Resolution of the eruption occurs within 3 to 4 days. Lymphadenopathy is characteristic, particularly of the suboccipital chain.

Erythema infectiosum has been recently identified as a manifestation of parvovirus infection. This common illness is most easily identified in the 2- to 6-year-old age group. The incubation period is 5 to 10 days and a prodrome is rare. The exanthem starts on the cheeks as a fiery red erythema, giving a characteristic "slapped cheek" appearance. In 2 to 3 days this fades, but is followed by discrete erythematous papules and macules in a lacy pattern seen primarily in an acral distribution, particularly on the buttocks and over the knees. The duration of the illness is highly variable. Disease in adults may be a flulike illness without rash or with only an acral reticular papular exanthem. Its complications include arthritis, typically costochondral, and hydrops fetalis.

Roseola infantum, common in the first 2 to 3 years of life, is believed to be a hypersensitivity response to a number of different viruses. The incubation period is 5 to 15 days, and the first symptom is sudden onset of high fever that persists for 3 to 5 days. The child is alert, active, and has few other symptoms. Coincident with defervescence, the eruption, which consists of transient, discrete and confluent macules and papules, appears suddenly and travels from neck to trunk to extremities, usually disappearing within 1 to 2 days.

Hand-foot-and-mouth disease is most often associated with infection with Coxsackie A16 virus, but other enteroviruses (Coxsackie and echoviruses) may be causative as well. The incubation period is 4 to 6 days, and the illness begins with fever and vague constitutional symptoms. Oral lesions appear in 1 to 2 days as vesicles that quickly erode and become ulcerations. With size varying from 4 mm to 2 cm, they are most commonly located on the tongue and buccal mucosae. Painful vesicular lesions, typically discrete ovoid 2- to 10-mm blisters, appear on the palms, soles, and dorsae of the hands and feet shortly after the enanthem. These lesions generally heal without crusting, an important point differentiating the illness from varicella.

Herpangina, also associated with a variety of Coxsackie and echovirus infections, has an incubation period of 4 to 7 days. The onset of the illness is sudden, with fever, vomiting, headache, sore throat, and malaise. The diagnostic feature is a painful enanthem consisting of circular, punched-out ulcers with fibrinous exudate and hyperemic borders, occurring on the tonsillar pillars and soft palate. The fever lasts 3 to 4 days. The illness differs from herpetic gingivostomatitis in that the latter also involves the gingival mucosa and the lips. Herpangina may be confused with aphthous stomatitis.

Papular acrodermatitis (Gianotti-Crosti syndrome) is characterized by a 1-week prodrome of fever, malaise, and symptoms of upper respiratory tract infection, followed by an eruption of monomorphous, flat-topped, erythematous papules with a collarette of scale, distributed symmetrically on the face, buttocks, and extremities. The lesions are not pruritic and they last 15 to 20 days. Lymphadenopathy and hepatomegaly may develop. If papular acrodermatitis is associated with hepatitis B virus infection, acute hepatitis usually follows within 1 to 2 weeks. Epstein-Barr virus, cytomegalovirus, and Coxsackie viruses have also been incriminated in this syndrome.

Other viral infections may be associated with exanthems. **Echovirus 9** infection causes a syndrome that resembles meningococcal disease, with headache, photophobia, nausea, vomiting, and nuccal rigidity. The eruption often has a petechial component. Infection with **echovirus 16** has been associated with a roseolalike illness (Boston exanthem). **Adenoviruses** can cause morbilliform eruptions and usually have respiratory illness as a common clinical feature. While the enteroviruses, e.g., echoviruses 9 and 16, tend to cause epidemics in the summer and fall months, the adenoviruses are often diagnosed in the winter and spring. Rhinoviruses, influenza viruses, reoviruses, and parainfluenza viruses are only very rarely associated with an exanthem.

The **diagnosis** of viral illness is usually made by thorough evaluation of the history; the clinician should pay particular attention to the prodrome and time course of the eruption and to any past history of viral illnesses and immunizations. Examination of the skin and mucous membranes reveals characteristic lesions. Physical examination of family members or playmates who are also ill may be essential. A knowledge of what viruses are active in the community at the time is also often very helpful. Serologic testing, including both acute and convalescent titers, is frequently employed. Viral culture is routinely done in situations where the herpes simplex virus is considered in the differential diagnosis. Most virology laboratories also culture adenoviruses and echoviruses. If the clinical situation requires exact identification of these viruses, consultation with a virology laboratory is advised, so that appropriate specimens can be obtained.

The most common problem in the **differential diagnosis** of an exanthem is to distinguish a viral infection from a drug eruption, and this task is often complicated by the fact that many patients with a febrile illness have taken antibiotics. Information obtained from the history and examination may help differentiate these entities. Fever, symptoms of a viral prodrome, and history of exposure to an individual with a similar eruption may be significant. The presence of an enanthem in association with an exanthem strongly suggests a viral etiology. In addition, drug eruptions often begin on the trunk and spread centrifugally, whereas viral exanthems often begin on the face or neck and spread distally. The presence of lymphadenopathy is more common in viral illness. Finally, while most drug eruptions run a course of 10 to 21 days, most viral exanthems disappear within 7 to 10 days. Pruritus and palm and sole involvement are not helpful findings, as they may occur in either process.

Other diagnoses to be considered in the differential diagnosis of an exanthem include Kawasaki's disease, with the characteristic findings of conjunctivitis, fissured lips, fever, lymphadenopathy, scarlatiniform eruption with acral desquamation, and strawberry tongue. Likewise, toxic shock syndrome is accompanied by fever, hypotension, and a scarlatiniform eruption with desquamation of the palms and soles. Strawberry tongue may also be seen in this disorder. In the appropriate patient, early graft-versus-host disease must be considered as it is often indistinguishable from the exanthems previously mentioned. Rocky Mountain spotted fever is a rickettsial illness that begins as erythematous macules on the wrists and ankles. In 24 hours the palms and soles become involved, and the spread is then cephalad. The rash eventually becomes hemorrhagic, typically resembling a petechial exanthem. Meningococcemia, in its very early phase, may be associated with generalized erythema before the development of a purpuric eruption.

Histopathologic evaluation of a skin biopsy specimen taken from an active area of exanthem has limited utility for the clinician refining the differential diagnosis. Most of the viral infections cannot be distinguished, nor can they be reliably differentiated from a morbilliform drug eruption, scarlet fever, toxic shock syndrome, Kawasaki's disease, or early graft-versus-host disease. All of these disorders are characterized by a superficial perivascular infiltrate composed of lymphocytes. On rare occasions, specific intranuclear inclusion bodies may be seen, allowing the definitive diagnosis of measles. Herpesvirus infections can usually be identified by multinucleated giant cells and intranuclear inclusion bodies. According to some authors, the presence of eosinophils in the infiltrate may favor a drug eruption, but is not definitive. Clinical expertise, therefore, remains the dominant factor in diagnosis.

Bialecki C, Feder HM Jr, Grant-Kels JM: The six classic childhood exanthems. *J Am Acad Dermatol.* 1989;21:891–903.
A thorough review of the classic exanthems, including tabulated data and color photographs.
Bligard CA, Millikan LE: Acute exanthems in children. *Postgrad Med.* 1986;79:150–167.
Written by dermatologists for primary care physicians, this review stresses morphology and has several useful tables.
Cherry JD: Viral exanthems. *Disease a Month.* 1982;28:1–56.
The "compleat" reference on viral exanthems by one of the foremost authorities. A copy should be in everyone's files.
Feder HM Jr, Anderson L: Fifth disease. *Arch Intern Med.* 1989;149:2176–2178.
This report reviews in a concise manner all aspects of Fifth disease, including the viral pathogenesis.
Goodyear HM, Laidler PW, Price EH, et al.: Acute infectious erythema in children: A clinical microbiological study. *Br J Dermatol.* 1991;124:433–437.
In 100 children presenting with widespread exanthem and fever, specific infectious agents were identified in 65. Authors discuss patterns of eruptions.
Peterson PK, Dahl MV: *Dermatologic Manifestations of Infectious Diseases.* Kalamazoo, MI: Upjohn Co; 1982.
This Scope monograph has concise text and high-quality photographs.
Woolf AD, Campion GV, Chishiek A, et al.: Clinical manifestations of human parvovirus B19 in adults. *Arch Intern Med.* 1989;149:1153–1156.
A controlled epidemiologic investigation of human parvovirus infection and its manifestations. The variability of signs and symptoms is quite interesting.

9. DRUG ERUPTIONS
Michael E. Bigby

Drug eruptions are both extremely common and diverse. A practical approach to a patient with a suspected drug eruption includes recognition that the rash is a drug eruption, identification of the drug causing the eruption, and management of the eruption. **Recognition** requires knowledge of the wide spectrum of drug-induced skin diseases. A thorough discussion of the clinical features of all adverse cutaneous reactions to drugs and their differential diagnoses would require a textbook of several hundred pages. Fortunately such a book exists (Bork, K. *Cutaneous Side Effects of Drugs*. Philadelphia, PA: WB Saunders; 1988).

The methods available for **identifying** the particular drug responsible for an eruption are limited. They include an assessment of the patient's history and a review of the suspected drug's association with rashes; intentional or inadvertent rechallenging of the patient with the suspected drug; and in vivo and in vitro tests. The first method, using historical features and knowledge about the propensity of drugs to cause rashes, is currently the most commonly utilized method. The degree of causality between drugs and observed cutaneous reactions is judged according to a group of historical observations that include whether other causes have been excluded and whether the rash resolves when the drug is discontinued and reappears when the drug is reinstituted. This method also relies on existing data regarding the propensity of drugs to induce rashes.

Intentional drug rechallenging to detect the causative agent of a drug eruption is rarely performed in the United States today, although oral provocation testing as a method for detecting the causative agent of a drug eruption has its advocates. The aim of provocation tests is to elicit the reappearance of a drug eruption in a mild form. The testing is usually done after the original eruption has faded, and the test dose is often significantly lower than the therapeutic dose. If an eruption or fever occurs, the test is considered positive and prima facie evidence that the test agent was the cause of the eruption. Provocative testing is not recommended for patients who have had anaphylaxis, toxic epidermal necrolysis (TEN), Stevens-Johnson syndrome, or systemic lupus erythematosus. In a recent study, oral provocation confirmed the etiologic agent in 128 out of 225 patients with drug eruptions (57%). The majority of the test reactions were mild (only five were described as "intense"). A negative provocation test is of no value and provides no assurance that the patient will not develop an eruption if given therapeutic doses of the drug. Accurate assessments of the sensitivity and specificity of provocation tests are not available.

In vivo and in vitro tests to determine the etiologic agents of drug eruptions have been investigated for at least half a century. The methods tested have included scratch testing, patch testing, lymphocyte proliferation in the presence of suspected agents, cytokine secretion provoked by suspected agents, a lymphocytoxicity assay, and evaluation of enzyme defects. While all of these techniques have shown promise at various times, none have yet been proven to be consistently helpful in determining the etiologic agent in drug eruptions, and none are commonly used in clinical practice. In addition, few investigators have determined whether patients who take rash-producing drugs but do not develop rashes have similar results when tested.

The **management** of a patient with a drug eruption includes identification and withdrawal of the etiologic agent, treatment (if any is available) of the eruption, and substitution of another therapeutic agent to treat the illness for which the rash-producing drug was given. The withdrawal of the causative agent is usually followed by the disappearance of the eruption within 2 to 3 weeks. The efficacy of treatments of drug eruptions has generally not been critically evaluated.

The **drug exanthem** is the most common adverse cutaneous reaction to drugs and occurs in 2% to 3% of patients. The drug exanthem presents as a fine, erythematous papular eruption that commonly becomes confluent. Drug exanthems generally appear within the first 2 to 3 days after the offending agent is begun. Antibiotics and allopurinol may induce rashes 2 or more weeks after they are started. Drug exanthems often begin in areas of trauma or pressure, such as on the backs of bedridden patients and on the extremities of ambulatory patients. The pathogenesis of drug exanthems is unknown, although deposition of antigen-antibody complexes is highly suspected. Antimicrobial agents, blood products, nonsteroidal anti-inflammatory drugs (NSAIDs), and CNS drugs are the agents most frequently found to cause drug exanthems. The incidence of drug exanthems and reaction rates for more than 60 drugs has been determined from data collected by the Boston Collaborative Drug Surveillance Program on over 37,000 medical inpatients who were prospectively monitored between 1966 and 1982. Drugs with reaction rates greater than 1% include trimethoprim-sulfamethoxazole, ampicillin, amoxicillin, semisynthetic penicillins, penicillin, red blood cells, and cephalosporins.

The risk of developing a drug exanthem is increased in certain populations. The incidence of drug exanthems is 35% to 50% higher in women than in men. Fifty percent to 80% of patients with infectious mononucleosis who take ampicillin develop a drug exanthem. The incidence of drug exanthems is much higher in patients taking ampicillin and allopurinol together than in patients who take either drug alone. Explanations for these unusually high reaction rates and for the discrepancy between the sexes are lacking.

There are no good data available to indicate the best method for handling the situation in which a patient develops an exanthematous reaction to a drug that is deemed essential for his or her recovery or survival. The fear in such instances is that continued use of the medication will induce a life-threatening eruption such as TEN or an exfoliative erythroderma. Accurate assessment of the frequency with which life-threatening eruptions are provoked by continued use of a drug that causes an exanthem is lacking. Equally lacking are data to support the notion that patients can be treated "through" a drug-induced exanthem by continued use of a suspected agent. Patients who have developed exanthematous eruptions due to sulfonamides, penicillin, or carbamazine have been successfully desensitized by withdrawing the drug until the rash resolves and then receiving gradually increasing doses until therapeutic doses were reachieved. The utility of systemic corticosteroids as adjunctive therapy during a drug exanthem is also unproven. One special situation in which there appears to be unanimity of opinion about the use of corticosteroids in drug eruptions is the phenytoin hypersensitivity syndrome, a drug exanthem with hepatitis and fever associated with a high mortality rate. In this syndrome, prompt withdrawal of phenytoin and high-dose systemic corticosteroid therapy are considered essential for survival.

Urticaria is the second most common allergic cutaneous reaction to drugs. The frequency with which drugs cause urticaria has not been accurately determined. The agents most commonly implicated as the cause of urticaria include antibiotics, blood products, radiocontrast agents, NSAIDs, and opiates.

Urticaria appears as firm, erythematous plaques that have normal overlying epidermis and no scaling. Lesions characteristically last for less than 24 hours and are replaced by new lesions in new locations. Round or oval plaques of varying sizes are most commonly seen. Less-common variants, including giant, papular, arcuate, and annular lesions, may be encountered. Urticaria may occur in conjunction with other signs and symptoms of immediate type hypersensitivity including pruritus, bronchospasm, diaphoresis, hypotension, and eosinophilia. **Angioedema** is manifested by large areas of swelling, often lacking erythema and frequently involving mucous membranes. Persistence of urticarial lesions for more than 24 hours or the appearance of hyperpigmentation, purpura, or scarring in areas where lesions have faded should suggest another diagnosis (e.g., urticarial vasculitis or erythema multiforme). The predominant pathologic feature of urticaria is edema of the reticular dermis. A sparse lymphocytic, perivascular infiltrate may be seen. Eosinophils may be present. In angioedema, edema and lymphocytic infiltration extend into the subcutaneous tissue.

Some cases of drug-induced urticaria and angioedema are caused by immunoglobulin E–mediated, immediate type hypersensitivity. The drug acts as a hapten, combining with a host protein to form a complete antigen. Antigen-specific IgE antibodies are generated and bind by their Fc portions to basophils and mast cells. Subsequent exposure to the antigen leads to mast cell and basophil degranulation, mediator release, edema, and cellular infiltration. Patients with this type of urticaria may have antigen-specific IgE antibodies detectable by a radioallergosorbent test (RAST) or an enzyme-linked immunosorbent assay (ELISA), or they may have positive scratch tests with the responsible drug. The most completely studied example of IgE-mediated urticaria is that induced by penicillin.

Many cases of drug-induced urticaria are not IgE mediated but are due to direct mediator release from mast cells and basophils. This pseudoallergic urticaria may be accompanied by anaphylactoid symptoms such as bronchospasm and hypotension. Well-documented causes of pseudoallergic urticaria include radiocontrast agents and opiates. Urticaria and anaphylactoid reaction induced by aspirin and other NSAIDs may also result from this mechanism.

Urticaria usually resolves quickly when the offending drug is recognized and discontinued; however, persistence of episodes of urticaria for a few weeks after drug discontinuation is not uncommon. A few caveats are worth remembering. First, even when the offending drug is recognized, the patient may not realize that the same or a cross-reacting medication is still being taken. Second, patients with urticaria may have more than one concomitant cause for their urticaria. Third, although drugs are the most commonly recognized cause of acute and chronic urticaria, in many cases the causes remain undetermined.

The most important therapeutic intervention for patients with acute anaphylactic or anaphylactoid reactions accompanied by hypotension is to provide adequate amounts of volume intravenously. If drug therapy is required, parenteral epinephrine is the drug of choice. Antihistamines, aminophylline, and corticosteroids may also be indicated.

The clinician should manage urticaria unaccompanied by systemic complaints by identifying and eliminating the underlying causes, by relaxing and reassuring the patient, and by providing symptomatic relief of pruritus with antihistamines or small doses of doxepin. Systemic corticosteroids and subcutaneous epinephrine are rarely indicated.

Allergic **contact dermatitis** to topical medications is common. Accurate incidence figures are not readily available. The hallmark of allergic contact dermatitis is the presence of an eczematous dermatitis in a configuration and distribution consistent with contact from an outside source. Initially, the lesions consist of erythematous plaques made up of papules, vesicles, and, in severe cases, bullae. With time, vesicles and bullae break, leading to exudation and crusting. In the chronic stages, plaques may become lichenified secondary to scratching. The rash may begin from 12 to 72 hours after application of the medication, depending on the immunogenicity of the medication and the thickness of the stratum corneum of the area to which it is applied. The rash will slowly resolve over a 2- to 4-week period after exposure has been discontinued.

Patch testing may be used to demonstrate contact hypersensitivity to a suspected topical medication. A nonirritating concentration of the medication in an appropriate vehicle (usually petrolatum) is placed on clinically normal skin for 48 hours and then removed. The development of edema and vesicles indicates contact hypersensitivity to the tested agent.

The principal pathologic features of allergic contact dermatitis are the presence of spongiosis (intercellular edema of the epidermis), papillary dermal edema, and a mononuclear cell perivascular infiltrate. Eosinophils may be present. Allergic contact dermatitis is an example of helper T cell–mediated delayed type hypersensitivity.

Some cases of contact dermatitis due to topical preparations result, however, from irritation rather than allergy. In these instances, antigen-specific delayed type hypersensitivity to nonirritating concentrations of the substance cannot be demonstrated. It is often impossible to distinguish allergic versus irritant contact dermatitis using clinical or pathologic criteria.

Agents found in topical medications that are commonly associated with allergic contact dermatitis include neomycin, benzocaine, ethylenediamine, diphenhydramine (present in Caladryl), and parabens (preservatives found in many topical preparations including some topical corticosteroids). Neomycin is the most sensitizing of currently used topical antibiotics. Approximately 5% of patients patch tested with neomycin have positive reactions to it. The prevalence of reactivity is even higher in patients with stasis dermatitis (30%) and otitis externa (15%). Since several alternative topical antibiotics are available (e.g., polymyxin and bacitracin ointment, bacitracin ointment, and mupirocin cream), topical preparations containing neomycin can easily be avoided.

Ethylenediamine is a stabilizer found in many topical preparations. It cross-reacts with aminophylline and with several of the antihistamines (e.g., tripelennamine and hydroxyzine). Patients who are topically sensitized to ethylenediamine may develop systemic allergic contact dermatitis if they are systemically exposed to aminophylline or to cross-reacting antihistamines. Systemic contact dermatitis is manifested by the development of a generalized eczematous dermatitis, dyshidrotic eczema of the hands, or a localized dermatitis at the site of previous contact with the sensitizing medication. Systemic contact dermatitis is quite rare.

Several reports of allergic reactions to nitroglycerin ointment have been published. Interestingly, most patients tolerate sublingual nitroglycerin even after having been sensitized to the use of ointment.

Contact dermatitis occurs in sites where transdermal patches are applied. The incidence of contact dermatitis with transdermal nitroglycerin products is low, most commonly due to an irritant mechanism. Allergic contact dermatitis develops in approximately 15% to 20% of patients using transdermal clonidine. Adverse cutaneous reactions to transdermal scopolamine have also occurred. Dermatitis due to transdermal therapeutics systems has been thoroughly reviewed by Fisher (see references).

Identifying the responsible topical inciting agent is essential for successful therapy of drug-induced contact dermatitis. In confusing cases, patch testing may provide invaluable information. In the acute stages allergic contact dermatitis is treated with warm compresses (e.g., aluminum acetate, normal saline, or water) and a topical corticosteroid lotion or cream. In chronic stages, especially if lichenification is present, hydration and the use of a topical corticosteroid ointment are indicated. It is important to inform the patient that 3 weeks or more is often required for the rash to resolve completely. In severe cases when both eyes are swollen shut or when large areas are involved, a short course of prednisone (approximately 1 mg/kg/d for 7 days followed by a rapid taper over the next 7 to 10 days) can significantly shorten the duration and lessen the severity of the disease.

TEN and **erythema multiforme** are thoroughly discussed elsewhere in this volume. Only a few salient points will be made in this chapter. TEN is a catastrophic illness with significant morbidity and mortality rates between 15% and 60%. Drugs are most often implicated as the cause of TEN and severe erythema multiforme. In two recent studies the annual incidence of TEN was estimated to be approximately 0.5 to 1 per million. TEN is thus, fortunately, a rare complication of drug therapy. The drugs most often implicated are the NSAIDs (especially phenylbutazone, oxyphenbutazone, sulindac, and piroxicam), antibiotics (especially trimethoprim-sulfamethoxazole), barbiturates, phenytoin, and allopurinol.

Fixed drug eruptions characteristically develop in fixed locations on repeated exposure to the offending agent. Typical lesions in fixed drug eruptions are erythematous or dusky plaques. Bullae also occur frequently. Postinflammatory hyperpigmentation is commonly observed. The pathogenesis of fixed drug eruptions is unknown. The most commonly implicated drugs are phenolphthalein, tetracycline, and oxyphenbutazone. Patch testing with the suspected agent in previously involved sites may produce positive reactions. Patch testing on uninvolved skin most commonly gives negative results. Neither the specificity nor the sensitivity of patch testing for fixed drug eruptions has been determined.

Photoinduced drug eruptions are either photoallergic or phototoxic in origin. Photoinduced drug eruptions have been thoroughly reviewed recently (see references). Photoallergic drug reactions require the interaction of the drug, ultraviolet (UV) irradiation, and the immune system. The morphology of the eruption is variable. Erythematous plaques with or without scale, eczematous dermatitis, vesicles, and bullae all occur. The distribution is characteristically in sun-exposed areas, including the face, the V of the neck, and the backs of the hands and arms. The upper lids, behind the ears, and below the chin are often spared. In severe cases, the eruption may spill over into sun-protected areas or may become generalized. Pathologic features resemble those of allergic contact dermatitis. In an animal model, a photoallergic reaction was demonstrated to be a T cell–mediated, delayed type hypersensitivity reaction to a drug that became immunogenic after exposure to UVA in the skin. Clinically encountered photoallergic drug reactions may have a similar pathogenesis.

Photoallergic drug reactions must be distinguished from phototoxic eruptions, which are much more common. Phototoxic eruptions will occur in all patients given adequate amounts of the drug and adequate UV exposure. Photoallergic reactions occur in only a small percentage of exposed patients. Phototoxic reactions present as exaggerated sunburns and may occur after the first exposure to the drug. The rash appears within 24 hours of exposure, peaks within 48 to 72 hours, and resolves, often with desquamation, within 1 week. Resolution of photoallergic eruptions may take weeks after drug discontinuation and avoidance of UV exposure.

Drugs implicated in causing photoallergic reactions include thiazide diuretics, sulfonamides, and phenothiazine. Drugs that cause phototoxic eruptions include demeclocycline, psoralens, amiodarone, and nalidixic acid. Patients with amiodarone-induced photosensitivity often develop a blue-gray discoloration in sun-exposed areas. Some drugs produce both phototoxic and photoallergic reactions.

Drug eruptions are disproportionately frequent in patients with **acquired immunodeficiency syndrome** (AIDS). Fifteen percent to seventy percent of AIDS patients with *Pneumocystis carinii* pneumonia who were treated with trimethoprim-sulfamethoxazole developed rashes. These rates are more than five times the rates seen in other populations of hospitalized patients. The drug exanthem occurs most commonly, but the incidences of erythema multiforme and TEN are also increased. Many patients were successfully desensitized, and therapy was continued. AIDS patients treated with azidovudine (AZT) developed nail pigmentation. The hyperpigmentation characteristically affects the proximal fingernails but may spread distally. Toenails are sometimes affected. The incidence of drug eruptions induced by antituberculosis drugs is also higher in AIDS patients.

A wide variety of **chemotherapeutic agents** are used to treat malignant or inflammatory diseases. Chemotherapeutic agents cause a large number of adverse mucocutaneous reactions. Some occur commonly and may be induced by all drugs of a particular class. Other reactions are rare and occur only with specific drugs.

Stomatitis occurs in association with many chemotherapeutic agents when they are used in high enough doses. Methotrexate, fluorouracil, doxorubicin, and daunorubicin are among the drugs most likely to cause stomatitis. Alopecia is, similarly, produced by many agents, especially doxorubicin, the nitrosoureas, and cyclophosphamide. Hyperpigmentation of the skin, nails, mucous membranes, or hair has occurred in association with chemotherapeutic agents. The wide variety of drug-specific pigmentary reactions have been reviewed by Bonner and Hood (see references). Finally, exanthems, urticaria, erythema multiforme, TEN, and photosensitivity have all been induced by chemotherapeutic agents.

Pemphigus vulgaris and pemphigus foliaceus are autoimmune bullous diseases in which intraepidermal blisters form in association with autoantibodies directed against intercellular adherence molecules. Bullous diseases similar to pemphigus foliaceous and vulgaris have occurred in patients taking penicillamine or captopril. Penicillamine-induced pemphigus is almost always of the foliaceous type and occurs in up to 7% of patients taking the drug. Captopril-associated pemphigus is usually of the vulgaris type. Interestingly, patients with drug-induced pemphigus often do not have circulating autoantibodies. The response to withdrawing the drug in patients with penicillamine- or captopril-induced pemphigus is variable. In some patients the disease resolves within several weeks. Other patients, however, have persistent disease that, like idiopathic pemphigus, requires high-dose systemic corticosteroid or immunosuppressive therapy.

Bigby M, Stern RS, Arndt KA: Allergic cutaneous reactions to drugs. *Primary Care.* 1989;16:713–727.
   Recent, thorough review of allergic cutaneous reactions to drugs. Large sections of the review were incorporated into this chapter with permission.
Bonner AK, Hood AF: Cutaneous complications of chemotherapeutic agents. *J Am Acad Dermatol.* 1984;9:645–663.
   Thorough review of adverse cutaneous reactions to chemotherapeutic agents.
Bork K: *Cutaneous Side Effects of Drugs.* Philadelphia, PA: WB Saunders; 1988.
   Excellent clinical descriptions of the whole spectrum of adverse cutaneous reactions to drugs with a thorough discussion of the differential diagnoses. The photography is excellent.

Bruinsma W: *A Guide to Drug Eruptions: The file of side effects to the skin (1987)*. Oosthuizen, the Netherlands: The File of Medicine; 1987.
Excellent compilation of adverse cutaneous reactions seen with nearly every drug, updated every four to five years.

Chan HL, Stern RS, Arndt KA, et al.: The incidence of erythema multiforme, Stevens-Johnson syndrome, and toxic epidermal necrolysis: A population-based study with particular reference to reactions caused by drugs among outpatients. *Arch Dermatol.* 1990;126:43–47.
The annual incidence of TEN was estimated to be approximately 1 per million. Antibiotics and antiseizure medications were the most common causes of TEN and SJS.

DeSwarte RD: Drug allergy. In: Patterson R, ed. *Allergic Diseases: Diagnosis and Management.* Philadelphia, PA: JB Lippincott Company; 1985:505–661.
In my opinion, the best chapter on drug eruptions ever written. If you want to read only one thing about drug eruptions, read this chapter.

Fisher AA: Dermatitis due to transdermal therapeutics systems. *Cutis.* 1984;34:526–531.
Review of contact dermatitis caused by transdermal patches.

Halevy S, Grunwald MH, Sandbank M, et al.: Macrophage migration inhibition factor in drug eruption. *Arch Dermatol.* 1990;126:48–51.
Macrophage migration inhibition factor was detected more commonly among patients with drug rashes, but its detection was not specific for the drug most likely to have caused the rash.

Penneys NS: *Skin Manifestations of AIDS.* Philadelphia, PA: JB Lippincott Company; 1989:183–192.
Review of eruptions in AIDS patients, including drug eruptions. Rashes in AIDS patients are more common and more severe.

Roujeau JC, Guillaume JC, Fabre JP, et al.: Toxic epidermal necrolysis (Lyell syndrome): Incidence and drug etiology in France, 1981–1985. *Arch Dermatol.* 1990;126:37–42.
The annual incidence of TEN was estimated to be 0.5 per million. NSAIDs and antibiotics were most commonly implicated.

Shear NH: Diagnosing cutaneous adverse reactions to drugs. *Arch Dermatol.* 1990;126:94–100.
Currently available in vitro tests for drug eruptions can only play an adjunctive role in determining which drug is responsible for the eruption.

Shear NH, ed.: Adverse reactions to drugs. *Seminars in Dermatology.* 1990;8:135–225.
This volume contains sections on systemic contact dermatitis due to drugs, photoinduced drug eruptions, drug-induced pemphigus, chemotherapy-induced cutaneous reactions, reactions to NSAIDs, oral provocation tests, and patch testing in drug eruptions.

Torgovnick J, Arsura E: Desensitization to sulfonamides in patients with HIV infection. *Am J Med.* 1990;88:548–549.
Eleven of 13 patients with sulfonamide eruptions were successfully desensitized.

10. KAWASAKI'S DISEASE
Richard L. Gallo

Kawasaki's disease (KD), also known as mucocutaneous lymph node syndrome, is an acute febrile disease that is characterized by fever, rash, conjunctival injection, and lymphadenopathy. Physicians worldwide have become increasingly aware of the acute features of this syndrome. As a result, the interval from onset of symptoms to diagnosis and treatment has shortened. The significance of rapid diagnosis and treatment is highlighted by recent reports of sudden death in up to 2% of patients with

KD, and cardiovascular sequelae ranging from asymptomatic coronary artery ectasia to coronary aneurysm formation in approximately 20% of KD patients. Currently, KD is considered the leading cause of acquired cardiovascular disease in the pediatric age group.

The original description of the characteristic **clinical features** of this disease was made in 1967 by Dr. Tomisaku Kawasaki in a cohort of 50 Japanese children. In the U.S. population, a similar illness was first reported by Melish and coworkers in 1976. Since these original descriptions, more than 80,000 cases have been recognized in Japan. In the United States, the Centers for Disease Control has recorded more than 2300 cases. Current epidemiologic evidence suggests that these values represent an underestimate of the actual number of cases, and the incidence of KD appears to be increasing in both Japan and the United States.

Currently there is no diagnostic test for KD; thus the establishment of a diagnosis rests on identification of characteristic clinical criteria. The Centers for Disease Control has established the following epidemiologic case definitions for diagnosis:

1. fever lasting 5 days or more without another, more reasonable explanation
2. bilateral conjunctival injection
3. mucous membrane changes consisting of injected or fissured lips, injected pharynx, or strawberry tongue
4. extremity changes consisting of erythema of the palms or soles, edema of hands and feet, or generalized or periungual desquamation
5. rash
6. cervical lymphadenopathy

The diagnosis of KD is established by the presence of fever and four of the five remaining criteria without an alternative explanation for the illness.

The affected patient is generally under 8 years of age with 80% under 4 years old. Rare cases have been reported in adults, although it is currently controversial whether these cases represent undetected cases of toxic shock syndrome. All races are affected, with Asians at highest risk, blacks intermediate, and whites at lowest risk.

Fever in patients with KD is typically high (104°F), spiking, and remittent. The duration is prolonged (1 to 2 weeks) without aspirin therapy, but typically resolves in 2 to 3 days following institution of treatment.

Conjunctival injection in the patient with KD usually begins shortly after onset of fever and lasts 1 to 2 weeks. It is characterized by greater involvement of the bulbar than the palpebral conjunctiva and is not usually associated with an exudate.

Mucous membrane changes of KD are characterized by erythema, dryness, fissuring, peeling, and bleeding of the lips. A bright red erythema of the vermilion border has been described as reminiscent of that accompanying carbon monoxide poisoning. Crusting and fissuring of the lips follows within days of the original erythematous eruption. Intraoral changes include a diffuse mucositis and strawberry tongue with diffuse erythema and prominent papillae. Oral and lingual ulcerations do not occur.

Extremity involvement in KD is impressive. Erythema of the palms and a firm nonpitting edema of the hands and feet are classic and occur in over 90% of patients. Induration of the hands and feet is painful and typically limits movement as well as resulting in a refusal to bear weight. Edema in the extremities is occasionally accompanied by similar findings in the face and eyelids. Later in the course of this disease (after the first week) desquamation of the fingers and toes occurs. This begins in the periungual region and may extend to involve the palms and soles. Following resolution of the illness, Beau's lines can be seen in the nail plate.

The generalized skin rash seen with KD is variable. Widespread erythematous eruptions have been described as urticarial, scarlatiniform erythroderma, morbilliform, and multiform with target lesions reminiscent of erythema multiforme. Accentuation in the perineal region may occur, as may pustular lesions. Vesicles or bullae are not seen. Desquamation, usually limited to the hands and feet, can occur at other sites in approximately 10% of patients.

Cervical lymphadenopathy is the least common of the diagnostic criteria and occurs in only 50% to 75% of patients. The incidence of lymphadenopathy appears to be higher in Asians than in others. Nodes are greater than 1.5 cm in diameter and may be unilateral or bilateral. On palpation these nodes are firm and tender, nonfluctuant, and culture negative.

In addition to the major diagnostic criteria for KD, several associated clinical criteria have been reported: pyuria (sterile urethritis), arthralgia and arthritis, aseptic meningitis, diarrhea, abdominal pain, pericardial effusion, jaundice, hydrops of gallbladder, myocarditis, myocardial infarction, mitral insufficiency, pericarditis, uveitis, and hemolytic uremic syndrome. Laboratory tests that may be abnormal include an increased erythrocyte sedimentation rate and C-reactive protein, mild anemia, and albuminuria. Thrombocytosis often occurs in the second week of illness.

The typical course of KD can be divided into an acute febrile phase lasting 7 to 14 days, a subacute phase in which irritability and conjunctival injection persist, and a convalescent phase lasting 6 to 10 weeks during which clinical signs have disappeared but the sedimentation rate remains elevated. Atypical cases are not rare, and recurrence has been reported in 0.8% of cases.

Histopathologic findings in KD vary with the severity of the illness. Early dermatopathologic findings from skin biopsies taken during the first week of illness include (1) edema of the papillary dermis, (2) perivascular granulocytic and monohistiocytic infiltrates, (3) endothelial cell swelling, (4) immunoglobulin G deposition on the vascular wall, (5) activated Langerhans cells, and (6) liquefaction of basal squamous cells. During the second week of illness, a diffuse interstitial pancarditis has been noted in some patients. The inflammatory patterns in the arterial wall at this stage are predominantly granulocytes gathered on the intima. In the third to fifth week, vascular changes take on a distinctive pattern with predominant monocyte invasion. A dissociation of medial smooth muscle cells is seen, as is a distinctive fibrocellular intimal thickening. Arteries thus injured are susceptible to aneurysmal dilatation. When these changes occur within the cardiovascular system, they lead to the most significant risk to the patients, which is sudden fatality. In addition, 10% to 20% of patients with KD will develop coronary artery aneurysms, which may be detectable only by echocardiographic analysis. Peripheral vascular compromise, although rare, has also been reported.

The **etiology** of KD is currently unknown. Epidemiologic clues strongly point to an infectious cause for this disease. Strongest among the arguments for an infectious etiology are observations of clustered epidemic outbreaks of KD. Interestingly, these outbreaks usually occur in late winter and spring. In addition, rare households with more than one affected child have been reported, although little evidence of person-to-person transmission exists. The male-female ratio for KD is 1.5:1, and appears most commonly in Asian individuals of middle to upper socioeconomic class. Numerous attempts have been made to identify other more specific epidemiologic risk factors in order to better describe a possible etiologic agent. However, most of these associations have proved inconsistent. Among these associations are an apparent higher incidence of antecedent respiratory illness in KD patients than in controls, a statistically higher rate of rug shampooing or spot-cleaning within 30 days of the onset of KD, and a higher incidence of KD patients living near a body of water. All of these observations have been controversial, inconsistent, and require further investigation.

No etiologic agent has been identified. Retroviruses have been implicated as a possible etiologic agent as have other infectious agents, including human parvovirus, leptospires, *Ehrlichia*, and *Borrelia burgdorferi*, and a variant strain of the anaerobic bacterium *Propionibacterium acnes*. However, demonstration of these associations remains controversial. Other investigations continue to pursue a hypersensitivity phenomenon to environmental allergens in KD patients.

Therapy for the patient with KD is aimed at reducing myocardial and coronary artery inflammation and preventing thrombosis. Several studies have suggested that a combination regimen of IV gamma globulin and high doses of acetylsalicylic acid is the therapy of choice. Aspirin doses of 80 to 100 mg/kg/d are recommended in conjunction with careful monitoring of serum levels. High-dose aspirin therapy is suggested immediately on diagnosis of KD and should be continued during the first 10 days of illness. Gamma globulin therapy has been effective in conjunction with aspirin when given as a single dose of 2 gm/kg. After the acute phase, current recommendations are that the aspirin dose be reduced to 3 to 5 mg/kg/d, given as a single dose beginning on the fourteenth day of illness. Aspirin may be stopped 6 weeks after onset of KD if there is no evidence of coronary artery abnormalities by echocardiography. Dipyridamole has also been used in addition to the above treatments for patients with documented coronary aneurysms and elevated platelet counts or the suggestion of early thrombus formation. Careful cardiac evaluation is imperative in all KD patients and should include serial echocardiograms performed in both the acute and the convalescent phases of the disease. Patients with documented coronary aneurysm formation may require prolonged low-dose maintenance aspirin therapy.

Bierman FZ, Gersony WM: Kawasaki disease: Clinical perspective. *J Pediatr.* 1987;111:789–793.
Thoughtful discussion of therapeutic options.
Bitter JJ, Friedman SA, Paltzik RL, Mofenson HC: Kawasaki's disease appearing as erythema multiforme. *Arch Dermatol.* 1979;115:71–72.
Case description of variant presentations of the rash in KD.
Committee on Infectious Disease 1987–1988. Intravenous gamma-globulin use in children with Kawasaki disease. *Pediatrics.* 1988;82:122.
Current recommendations of gamma globulin treatment of KD.
Golitz LE: The vasculitides and their significance in the pediatric age group. *Dermatology Clinics.* 1986;4:117–123.
Brief discussion of KD for the dermatologist in the setting of other pediatric vasculitides.
Hausen RC: Staphylococcal scalded skin syndrome, toxic shock syndrome, and Kawasaki disease. *Pediatr Clin North Am.* 1983;30:533–544.
An excellent review that compares and contrasts these three entities.
Kawasaki T: Historical background and current issues. *Prog Clin Biol Res.* 1987;250:1–4.
Historical perspective from Kawasaki himself.
Kyogoku M: A pathological analysis of Kawasaki Disease with some suggestions of its etio-pathogenesis. *Prog Clin Biol Res.* 1987;250:257–273.
Review and discussion of the pathology in KD.
Rauch AM: Kawasaki syndrome: review of new epidemiologic and laboratory developments. *Pediatr Infect Dis.* 1987;6:1016–1021.
Epidemiologic clues suggest infectious etiology of KD.
Rowley AH, Gonzalez-Cruzzi F, Shulman, ST: Kawasaki syndrome. *Rev Infect Dis.* 1988;10:1–15.
Excellent overall review and discussion of recent evidence for a retroviral etiology of KD.
Rowley AH, Shulman ST: Current therapy for acute Kawasaki syndrome. *J Pediatrics.* 1991;118:987–991.
Current recommendations for therapy of KD.

11. ERYTHRODERMA
Jerome D. Fallon

Erythroderma, also known as exfoliative dermatitis, is a severe and extensive inflammatory condition manifesting as redness and scaling of essentially the entire cutaneous surface. It is a specific term describing a nonspecific pattern with a variety of etiologies. Erythroderma is an uncommon disorder and occurs in males three times more often than in females. The average age in several large case series has been approximately 50 years with a broad range.

A useful classification of the **etiologies** of erythroderma includes drug reactions, preexisting dermatoses, malignancies, and indeterminate causes. In recent years, drugs have been incriminated in about 40% of cases of erythroderma. The most frequently associated drugs are sulfonamides, antimalarials, and penicillin. Other drugs that are well-known causes of erythroderma include barbiturates, allopurinol, aspirin and other nonsteroidals, diphenylhydantoin, and gold. Another 30% of cases occur in patients with preexisting skin conditions, including psoriasis, atopic dermatitis, allergic contact dermatitis, stasis dermatitis, lichen planus, Reiter's syndrome, pityriasis rubra pilaris, and pemphigus foliaceus. Of these, psoriasis and atopic dermatitis are the most common; the others are rare causes of erythroderma. Malignancies cause up to 20% of erythrodermas and are almost strictly limited to lymphomas and leukemias. Primary cutaneous T cell lymphoma (CTCL), or mycosis fungoides, and its leukemic variant, the Sézary syndrome, predominate. Of extracutaneous lymphomas, Hodgkin's disease occurs most often. Finally, about 10% of cases do not have an apparent cause.

Though the etiologies for erythroderma may vary, they all result in a common **clinical appearance** of generalized erythema, warmth, edema, pruritus, increased skin thickness, and scaling. The process usually begins in a limited area, extending to the entire skin in days to weeks. Erythema precedes scaling. Mucous membranes are normally spared, but palms, soles, scalp (leading to alopecia), and nails are frequently involved. Dystrophic nails are primarily seen in patients with psoriasis. If erythroderma is prolonged, skin may become thickened and lichenified, and palms and soles may display keratoderma. The underlying cause for erythroderma may only be recognizable in the early stages; remnant diagnostic lesions are often missing in established disease.

Among other physical findings in erythroderma are thermoregulatory disturbances, presenting with fever or hypothermia. Chills are a common patient complaint. The skin's ability to act as a water barrier may be impaired, leading to orthostatic hypotension or other signs of dehydration. Lymphadenopathy is found in the majority of cases. Most lymph node enlargement is a secondary response to severe skin inflammation; however, it may suggest lymphoma. Hepatosplenomegaly (not always referable to lymphoma), tachycardia, and extremity edema are other frequent features.

The **metabolic effects** of erythroderma may be profound. The basal metabolic rate is elevated as high as 50% above normal; this change is believed to be due to the demands of increased peripheral blood flow and exfoliation. The increased epidermal proliferation may be remarkable, transforming the normal 27-day transition from basal cell to exfoliated keratinocyte into a four-day whirlwind. Exfoliation is vast in quantity compared to normal: up to 20 g of scale per day in erythroderma as opposed to 0.5 to 1.0 g per day in normal skin. Since most of the exfoliated material is protein, features of malnutrition such as weight loss, a negative nitrogen balance, and decreased serum total protein and albumin are often observed. Other common laboratory abnormalities include anemia (usually anemia of chronic disease), leukocytosis, eosinophilia, and an elevated erythrocyte sedimentation rate.

Just as the clinical pattern of erythroderma often reveals little concerning etiology, so the **histologic findings** often specify no diagnosis. Histologic examination commonly reveals a chronic or subacute dermatitis. A psoriasiform dermatitis is probably the most common coherent pattern, but that does not imply psoriasis as the etiology. Even in patients with known psoriasis, the diagnostic pathology is not often retained in the erythrodermic phase. The biopsy is helpful only in CTCL when typical histology with atypical lymphocytes, epidermotropism and occasional Pautrier microabscesses is demonstrated. Multiple biopsies over many months may be required before a diagnostic section is found.

Given the diagnostic difficulty, the **approach** to the erythrodermic patient must be methodical. A history with compulsive attention to medications and hints of previous dermatoses can be fruitful. Physical examination should include a diligent search for cutaneous clues such as a single characteristic plaque of psoriasis, a papule of lichen planus, an island of sparing of pityriasis rubra pilaris, or a nodule within a plaque of CTCL. The evaluation should also include an examination of lymph nodes, liver, and spleen.

After this initial evaluation, all medicines should be discontinued if possible. Two to three or more skin biopsies, particularly of areas involved with thick skin or nodules, should be obtained. The diagnosis of CTCL may require five to ten biopsies distributed over weeks to months. An examination of the peripheral blood buffy coat for Sézary cells, immunophenotyping of the infiltrates on biopsy specimens, and T cell gene rearrangement studies of cultured cells may corroborate the diagnosis of CTCL but are not generally useful as primary diagnostic tests. A lymph node biopsy of cervical or axillary chains may be considered.

Treatment of patients with erythroderma frequently requires hospital admission for stabilizing measures such as fluid volume replacement and temperature control. Antipruritic therapy and nutritional supplements should be instituted. Essentially all patients can be made more comfortable with intensive use of moisturizing baths and emollients. Certainly a trial of topical steroids is warranted. Many eruptions will resolve spontaneously, suggesting that the offending agent has been eliminated. Failing these supportive measures, systemic therapies such as methotrexate and retinoids may be tried. Ultraviolet light therapy is relatively contraindicated (with the exception of CTCL) during the frank erythrodermic phase, because of the potential for increased phototoxicity. Systemic corticosteroid use is controversial, but should probably be avoided because of the likelihood of erythrodermic flare on withdrawal.

The **course** of erythroderma is obviously dependent on the underlying cause. The death rate is significant and ranges from 11% to 30%. The most common cause of death is pneumonia, followed by sepsis, high output cardiac failure and other cardiac complications, and lymphoma. Some patients die without evidence of any organ failure other than the skin.

Though the duration of illness may range from weeks to years, several large series have determined 5 years to be an average. The unfortunate CTCL patient may be destined to have chronic erythroderma or, at best, a remitting and relapsing course. The outlook for the patient with erythroderma from other causes is quite good, with complete resolution in up to 50%. Drug eruptions will often clear within days to weeks. Patients with preexisting dermatoses will gradually return to their baseline state or better in weeks to months, although recurrence of the erythroderma is possible.

Boyd AS, Menter A: Erythrodermic psoriasis. *J Am Acad Dermatol.* 1989;21:985–991.
Careful analysis of 50 cases of erythroderma beginning as psoriasis at one center. Includes insights in treatment.

Freedberg IM, Baden HP: The metabolic response to exfoliation. *J Inves Dermatol.* 1962;38:277–284.
Meticulous study of metabolism during erythroderma, with special attention to scale collection and analysis, and nitrogen and water balance.

King LE Jr, Dufresne RG Jr, Lovett GL, et al.: Erythroderma: Review of 82 cases. *South Med J.* 1986;79:1210–1215.
Straightforward, well-written review similar in style and viewpoint to Nicolis and Helwig's review.

Nicolis GE, Helwig EB: Exfoliative dermatitis: a clinicopathologic study of 135 cases. *Arch Dermatol.* 1973;108:788–797.
Authoritative and largest published review. Dedicated to histology and autopsy in the search for the cause of erythroderma in a mostly military population. May be too far reaching in its conclusions.

Shuster S: Systemic effects of skin disease. *Lancet.* 1967;1:907–912.
Opinionated and entertaining review of the thermoregulatory, metabolic, and hemodynamic effects of severe skin disease.

Thestrup-Pedersen K, Halkier-Sorensen L, Sogaard H, et al.: The red man syndrome. Exfoliative dermatitis of unknown etiology: a description and follow-up of 38 patients. *J Am Acad Dermatol.* 1988;18:1307–1312.
Thirty-eight patients with erythroderma of unknown etiology were evaluated over a 15-year period and represented 19% of all patients admitted for erythroderma. The male-female ratio was over 6:1. Four patients were diagnosed with mycosis fungoides and one-third of the patients achieved complete remission during the observation period.

12. TENDER RED NODULES ON THE LEGS
Joseph C. Kvedar

The group of cutaneous disorders classified as "panniculitis" are quite different pathogenetically but share the common clinical finding of deep-seated nodules in the skin, usually erythematous to brown in color, quite firm, barely elevated, and variably tender. The patient may or may not appear systemically ill. Even the dermatologic novice can identify the site of pathology in the skin in these cases as the subcutaneous fat, but the most experienced clinician can seldom go further. This difficulty arises because many cases do not fit clearly into any well-defined clinical entity. Understanding these disorders is further complicated by our poor knowledge of their pathogenesis. Little meaningful investigative literature about these disorders has been published. Thus we are left with an abundance of case reports and repeated attempts to rework the classification of already poorly defined disorders. As a result, patients with subcutaneous lower extremity nodules are among the most difficult to diagnose accurately and to treat appropriately.

A deep elliptical skin biopsy including a generous sampling of fat is almost always required to direct the **differential diagnosis,** organizing these processes on the basis of histopathologic rather than clinical characteristics. Panniculitis is generally separated into disorders primarily involving the connective tissue septa (septal panniculitis) and those primarily involving the fat lobules (lobular panniculitis). The presence or absence of vasculitis further divides the disorders. Although the septal panniculitides are fairly well described entities, the lobular panniculitides have a confusing nosology.

Erythema nodosum, a septal panniculitis, is the most common and best-defined disease, presenting as nodules on the legs. It is best considered a cutaneous reaction pattern, a hypersensitivity response to an often-unknown antigen. The onset of the disease may be abrupt or preceded by fever, arthralgia, or other symptoms of the acute phase response. The lesions arrive as a crop of deep, warm, erythematous nodules that are exquisitely tender and may be painful when the legs are in dependent position. The most common site of involvement is the anterior shins. The nodules can vary in size from two to several centimeters and are usually found on both legs. The lesions evolve from red to purple to brown and typically fade without scarring in a few weeks. They do not ulcerate.

The histopathology of erythema nodosum is confined to the subcutaneous fat and is the prototype of septal panniculitis. In acute lesions, there is septal widening as a result of edema and lymphohistiocytic infiltration. The septal blood vessels show involvement with vessel wall edema and infiltration with inflammatory cells. Vasculitis is not present and lobular involvement is minimal. As the lesions become older, the histiocytic component of the infiltrate becomes more prominent and giant cells as well as granuloma formation can be seen.

If the diagnosis is clinically obvious, a biopsy is sometimes not performed out of respect for the difficulties inherent in wound healing on lower extremities. Once the diagnosis of erythema nodosum is established, the clinician must then initiate the search for a triggering factor. The most common triggers of erythema nodosum include infectious disease (in decreasing order of importance: streptococcal infection, tuberculosis, coccidioidomycosis, histoplasmosis, and *Yersinia* enterocolitis), drugs (halides, sulfonamides, gold, and oral contraceptives), and other processes, such as sarcoidosis, pregnancy, and inflammatory bowel disease. If the etiology is not apparent on history or physical examination, a standard laboratory investigation is warranted: CBC, erythrocyte sedimentation rate, tuberculin skin test, chest radiography, and antistreptolysin-0 titer. Other work-up may be tailored to the clinical setting in which the eruption occurs.

A chronic form of erythema nodosum, described under the rubric of **subacute nodular migratory panniculitis** or erythema nodosum migrans, differs from erythema nodosum in that lesions are typically fewer and larger than those of acute erythema nodosum and often occur on only one leg. Most of these cases have no obvious triggering agent. The disease can last from months to years, and there is a tendency for the shape of the lesions to change over time and leave depressed scars in their wake. The histology does not differ from that of erythema nodosum, and even more of these cases have no obvious triggering agent.

The treatment of erythema nodosum is often not satisfactory. Nonsteroidal anti-inflammatory agents have been used with limited success. Bed rest and leg elevation, as well as support stockings, are also helpful for the symptoms of pain and tenderness. Potassium iodide is perhaps the most successful of treatments to date (the conventional dose is 300–900mg/d). Gastrointestinal upset is a common side effect and may necessitate discontinuation of the medication. Intralesional injections of corticosteroids will induce individual lesions to subside. Administration of oral corticosteroids is largely unwarranted but usually will cause remission of clinical signs and symptoms.

Septal panniculitis can also be caused by both **necrobiosis lipoidica** and **scleroderma**. Other clinical and histologic features of these diseases aid in diagnosis in most cases.

Superficial migratory thrombophlebitis is a septal panniculitis with vasculitis. The clinical hallmark of this disease is the appearance of multiple, tender, dusky-colored nodules, most commonly on the lower extremities, that form obvious cords after several days. The initial lesions tend to occur in linear array. Histopathology reveals a thrombosed vein at the dermal-subcutaneous interface with inflammation of the vessel wall. These changes are very focal and highly diagnostic. Although usually no underlying disease is present, an underlying malignancy, especially of the lung or pancreas, may occasionally be found. The treatment is with thrombolytics and anticoagulants and the prognosis is usually good.

Pancreatic fat necrosis is a lobular panniculitis associated with pancreatic disease of various etiologies. The pathogenesis is thought to be related to the resultant release of pancreatic enzymes into the circulation and subsequent fat necrosis. Patients have fever, arthritis, abdominal pain, and crops of tender subcutaneous nodules. Laboratory evaluation shows elevated serum amylase and lipase. The histopathology is quite characteristic and consists of multiple foci of fat necrosis with ghostlike adipocytes having thick, shadowy walls without nuclei. A polymorphous infiltrate and foreign body giant cells are also present. All types of pancreatic disease have been associated with this syndrome, including alcoholic, traumatic, cholelithiasis, and pancreatic cysts. If pancreatic cancer is involved, the syndrome can be much more subtle, with only cutaneous findings.

Cutaneous lesions of **lupus erythematosus profundus** can extend into the subcutaneous fat and present a somewhat characteristic clinical and histopathologic picture. Lesions most commonly occur on the face or arms but can be seen anywhere, and generally appear as firm, dusky-colored plaques that are nontender and few in number. The overlying skin may appear normal or may be involved with typical cutaneous lupus. The histopathology shows a lobular panniculitis with a lymphohistiocytic and plasma cell infiltrate. Mucinous and eosinophilic degeneration of the strands that separate adipocytes is also seen. Other dermal and epidermal features of lupus erythematosus help make the diagnosis. Healing usually results in a prominent depression. Treatment is similar to that of refractory discoid lupus, with intralesional corticosteroid injection or administration of antimalarial drugs.

Physical panniculitides are a group of disorders with lobular panniculitis on biopsy that results from either physical injury to the skin or injection of substances into the subcutaneous fat. Traumatic fat necrosis may result at the site of any trauma, and is most commonly seen in the pendulous breasts of obese women following incidental injury. Injection of any substance into fat, either as a medication or for other reasons, can result in local panniculitis. The best-defined of these reactions is the "paraffinoma" that results from the injection of paraffin oil into the skin as a filling agent for scars or wrinkles, giving rise to the histologic appearance of oil-filled vacuoles with a "swiss cheese" appearance in the fat lobules. In cold-induced panniculitis, actual chilling of the tissue results in fat necrosis and inflammation. Such panniculitis occurs most commonly in infants, and it is hypothesized that the higher saturated fat content of infant fat allows it to solidify at higher temperatures. A common history with lesions located on the cheeks is that a popsicle was left in the child's mouth for a long time.

Poststeroid panniculitis has been reported exclusively in children and is characterized by nodular lesions on the cheeks, arms, and trunk in patients who have received high-dose glucocorticoids, usually for several weeks, as treatment for rheumatic fever. Most commonly the eruption is seen in children who gained weight during treatment. It is hypothesized that the rapid loss of fat stores on cessation of steroid therapy somehow triggers the panniculitis. The histopathology shows areas of fat necrosis surrounded by inflammatory cells and foreign body giant cells. Needle-like clefts can also be seen in this disorder.

Two diseases involving the subcutaneous fat are unique to the neonate. **Sclerema neonatorum** is a rapidly progressive disease with symmetric, spreading hardening of the skin during the first few days of life. The thighs are usually involved initially, and the disease rapidly progresses in a centrifugal manner. It is almost universally fatal. The histopathology characteristically shows increased size of adipocytes, and wide intersecting fibrous bands between adipocytes, many of which are filled with rosettes of tiny clefts. There is relatively little inflammatory cell infiltrate. By contrast, **subcutaneous fat necrosis of the newborn** is a benign disorder with a good prognosis. Discrete nodules and plaques appear within a few days of birth, most often on the cheeks, back, buttocks, arms, and thighs. They remain localized and generally resolve spontaneously in a few weeks without scarring. The histopathology is similar to that of poststeroid panniculitis.

Weber-Christian panniculitis is the term used to describe a group of idiopathic disorders lumped together because of a common clinical-pathologic reaction pattern of nodular panniculitis associated with fever and recurrent crops of skin nodules. The involvement of mesenteric and other fat beds has also been described. Clinically, patients have recurrent crops of tender, warm, red nodules accompanied by fever. New waves of lesions typically appear at intervals of weeks to months. There are frequent systemic complaints of arthralgia, malaise, fatigue, and abdominal pain. Occasionally the skin lesions ulcerate and drain an oily material. An elevated erythrocyte sedimentation rate is common. Many types of therapy have been tried without success. It is unlikely this syndrome represents a single disease entity.

The histopathology may represent as a three-stage process. The first two correspond to clinical induration and the third to atrophy and hyperpigmentation. Examination of early lesions reveals degeneration of adipocytes and a lobular inflammatory infiltrate composed of neutrophils, lymphocytes, and histiocytes in which neutrophils may predominate. Later lesions have a similar lobular pattern with an infiltrate composed mainly of foamy histiocytes with a few lymphocytes and plasma cells. In late lesions, fibroblasts intermingle with, and gradually replace, the foam cells, leading to fibrosis.

Several patients have been described recently with clinical and histopathologic findings similar to those of Weber-Christian disease in association with severe **alpha-1-antitrypsin deficiency.** Many researchers feel that as more etiologies and associations are uncovered, fewer and fewer cases will be idiopathic and thus appropriately labeled Weber-Christian disease.

Nodular vasculitis, also called erythema induratum, is a clinical-pathologic syndrome with lobular panniculitis and vasculitis found on biopsy. This syndrome presents as indurated, subcutaneous nodules that are usually no warmer than the surrounding skin, minimally tender, dusky colored, and tend to suppurate and scar. The most common site is the posterior calf. Middle-aged women with thick, edematous legs and an associated livido pattern are prone to this disease. The lesions may persist as ragged ulcers for long periods before healing. The histopathology is characteristic, with tuberculoid granuloma formation, caseous necrosis, and vasculitis of small- and medium-sized vessels. The granulomas are disposed in fat lobules and are composed of epithelioid cells and giant cells. Both tuberculoid and nonspecific inflammation extends beyond these areas, largely obliterating the fat lobule. The vasculitis is neutrophil mediated and has characteristic features of necrotizing vasculitis with thrombosis, fibrinoid necrosis, edema, and endothelial cell swelling.

Nodular vasculitis was originally described by Bazin as erythema induratum and was felt to be a manifestation of tuberculosis because of the occasional association with active tuberculosis and the granulomatous inflammation seen on biopsy. Some modern cases have been described in which the tuberculin skin test was positive and the eruption resolved with antituberculous therapy. There is, however, no convincing evidence that tuberculosis plays a role in the process, and this entity appears to be a hypersensitivity vasculitis of the subcutaneous vessels to unknown antigens.

Treatment options include antituberculosis therapy in cases in which there may be an association with tuberculosis, prednisone, nonsteroidal anti-inflammatory agents, minocycline, and potassium iodide administration.

Black MM: Panniculitis. *J Cutan Pathol.* 1985;12:366–380.
This article focuses on the histopathology of these disorders.
Forstrom J, Winklemann RK: Acute panniculitis; a clinical and histopathologic study. *Arch Dermatol.* 1977;113:909–917.
These authors grouped patients by clinical features and correlated these with the histologic findings.
Jorizzo JL, White WL, Zanolli MD, et al.: Sclerosing panniculitis: A clinicopathologic assessment. *Arch Dermatol.* 1991;127:554–558.
A report of six patients with lower leg inflammatory plaques in which biopsy reveals fat necrosis, sclerosis, and a lobular panniculitis. Venous stasis may have a role in pathogenesis. Treatments have not been clinically effective.
Patterson JW: Panniculitis: new findings in the "third compartment." *Arch Dermatol.* 1987;123:1617–1618.
This editorial is the most up-to-date review of panniculitis and has many references.
Soderstrom RM, Krull EA: Erythema nodosum, a review. *Cutis.* 1978;21:806–810.
A thorough review on erythema nodosum that is reasonably up-to-date.
Smith KC, Pittlekow MR, Sun WPD: Panniculitis associated with severe alpha-1-antitrypsin deficiency: treatment and review of the literature. *Arch Dermatol.* 1987;123:1655–1661.
Thorough discussion of this subset of patients previously thought to have Weber-Christian disease.
Winkelmann RK: Panniculitis in connective tissue disease. *Arch Dermatol.* 1983;119:336–344.
The author reviews the histopathology and clinical courses of both specific syndromes and nonspecific associations that occur with panniculitis.

III. BLISTERING DISORDERS

The pemphigoid group of disorders is a spectrum of chronic bullous diseases affecting the skin or mucous membranes, all of which are characterized by subepidermal bulla formation and deposition of immunoglobulin G and complement at the dermoepidermal junction. They differ in their severity and distribution.

Bullous pemphigoid (BP) is the most common variant of generalized cutaneous pemphigoid. It typically presents with large tense bullae, which may occur on erythematous or nonerythematous skin or on urticarial plaques. The bullae show a predilection for flexor aspects of extremities, lower abdomen, groin, inner thighs, and axillae. The size of the bullae range from less than 1 cm to up to 8 cm. Erythematous papules, plaques, and urticaria may also be present. The bullae are not easily ruptured, and patients have a negative Nikolsky sign. After the bullae rupture, erosions heal without scarring unless secondarily infected. Pruritus is variable. Oral cavity involvement has been reported to occur in 8% to 39% of patients, usually involving the palate, tongue, and buccal mucosa while sparing the gingiva. These bullae also tend to heal without scarring. Involvement of other mucous membranes is uncommon.

Bullous pemphigoid is usually a self-limited disease, occurring most commonly in the 60 to 70 age group with a less common variant occurring in childhood. In general, remission with therapy occurs in 3 to 6 years in 75% of patients. A mortality rate of 10% to 20% is reported and is most often related to therapy with systemic steroids. There appears to be a female predominance in those younger than 60 with disease; otherwise the sexes are affected equally. There is no association of BP with any human leukocyte antigen (HLA) haplotype nor any increased susceptibility for any racial group.

The association of BP with malignancy is controversial but has been described for cancers of the lung, breast, gastrointestinal tract, pancreas, lymphoreticular system, and others. These associations are not well substantiated. Several autoimmune disorders and other systemic diseases have been associated with BP, including rheumatoid arthritis, pernicious anemia, systemic lupus erythematosus, thyroiditis, primary biliary cirrhosis, ulcerative colitis, psoriasis, diabetes, and lichen planus as well as other bullous disease. Critical review of the literature does not support more than chance associations except for rheumatoid arthritis. Certain drugs have been implicated in the development of BP, including phenacetin, furosemide, penicillamine, salicylazosulfapyridine, and sulfasalazine. There are also reports of BP associated with PUVA, UVB, anthralin, coal tar, and the use of topical 5-fluorouracil.

Clinical variants of generalized cutaneous bullous pemphigoid occur. The primary clinical morphology may be urticaria, vesicles, vegetations, nodules, seborrheiclike lesions or generalized erythroderma. While urticarial lesions do not have the same transient time course as true urticaria, the lesions are similar with large edematous, gyrate or annular plaques. Vesicular lesions in BP resemble dermatitis herpetiformis clinically and histopathologically; however, the immunofluorescence is that of BP. Pemphigoid vegetans presents as massive verrucous vegetations in the intertriginous areas. The nodular variant resembles prurigo nodularis, persisting as hypertrophic scars, and may be a variant of localized scarring pemphigoid. The nodular and seborrheic types of BP are rarely reported.

Bullous pemphigoid occurs occasionally in childhood and infancy. The clinical, histologic, and immunofluorescent findings are the same; however, there is a predilection for lesions over the face, thighs, lower trunk, and genitalia. Unlike adult BP, childhood BP commonly includes oral involvement and blistering of palms and soles. The course is unpredictable with remissions and exacerbations, yet usually resolves within 2 years. Differential diagnosis includes the acute blistering disease of childhood and the chronic hereditary and nonhereditary blistering disorders of childhood. Immunofluorescent studies will be diagnostic even if the clinical picture is not.

Localized cutaneous pemphigoid may be divided into nonscarring or scarring types (Brunsting-Perry variant). Mucosal surfaces are not involved in either. Nonscarring types may be further divided into a pretibial form and dyshidrosiform variant, the latter characterized by palmar or plantar vesicles that heal without scarring. These forms are often easier to control than generalized disease, and usually resolve within several months, although 15% to 30% of patients who present with a localized nonscarring form of BP proceed to generalized BP. The scarring variety presents as persistent and recurrent blistering plaques of the head and neck, and is most likely a cutaneous variant of cicatricial pemphigoid (see below).

Mucosal pemphigoid is often considered in the differential diagnosis of BP. As with cutaneous pemphigoid, the mucosal group can be divided into single mucous membrane or generalized involvement. Cicatricial pemphigoid, which has also been inappropriately termed benign mucous membrane pemphigoid, is a chronic blistering disorder of multiple mucosal epithelia that heal with scarring, It most often affects oral mucosa but also affects conjunctivae, larynx, genitalia, and esophagus in descending order of frequency. Resultant scarring may be severe and may cause blindness, ulceration, and strictures. Approximately 25% of those with the generalized form also have cutaneous involvement presenting either as tense bullae around the affected mucous membrane surface that heal with scarring, or a generalized eruption identical to BP that heals without scars. The localized variant involves only one mucosal surface and the name reflects the location. Mucosal pemphigoid has the same histopathology and immunofluorescent patterns as BP; however, immunoglobulins and complement are located at a lower level in the lamina lucida.

The **differential diagnosis** of BP includes pemphigus vulgaris, dermatitis herpetiformis, epidermolysis bullosa acquisita, bullous drug eruption, bullous erythema multiforme, linear IgA bullous dermatosis, cicatricial pemphigoid, and herpes gestationis. In addition to clinical features, diagnosis is made by biopsy of perilesional skin near a recently formed intact bulla and studied for specific histology and immunofluorescence patterns. Serum antibodies may also be tested.

Routine **histopathology** of BP reveals several characteristic patterns, depending on whether the biopsy was from erythematous or nonerythematous skin. Two constant features are subepidermal bullae with a normal overlying epidermis and dermal inflammation. Biopsies from noninflamed skin adjacent to the bulla are infiltrate-poor with a sparse perivascular infiltrate consisting of eosinophils and monocytes. In inflammatory bullae, a rich infiltrate is found around the upper- and middermal vessels as well as scattered in the mid to upper dermis and along the basement membrane zone (BMZ). The infiltrate is composed mostly of eosinophils with fewer numbers of lymphocytes, histiocytes, and polymorphonuclear cells. Occasionally, the biopsy will reveal a predominance of polymorphonuclear cells.

Immunofluorescent studies are required for the definitive diagnosis of BP. Characteristic findings of direct immunofluorescence are linear subepidermal BMZ deposits of IgG in 45% to 90% of cases and C3 in 80% to 100% of cases. Other immunoglobulin classes seen include IgA, IgM, IgE, and IgD but are found only in conjunction with IgG. Indirect immunofluorescence reveals circulating anti-BMZ IgG in 70% of cases. Antibody titers may not reflect clinical activity. Electron microscopy has localized the IgG deposition in the upper lamina lucida where the BP antigen is found. The BP antigen is produced by basal keratinocytes and has been characterized as a 220–240 kD protein that is thought to stabilize the interaction of epidermal basal cells in the BMZ. Other immunoreactants in the BMZ of perilesional skin include components of both the classical and the alternate complement pathways. Blister fluid has been shown to contain active complement fragments as well as chemotactic factors for PMNs and eosinophils. Rare false-positive immunofluorescent patterns occur in burn victims, psoriasis, and leg ulcers. In order to differentiate bullous pemphigoid from epidermolysis bullosa acquisita, direct immunofluorescence must be performed on saline split-skin specimens. When a skin biopsy specimen is incubated in saline, the BMZ splits in the lamina lucida, and immunofluorescent techniques document the immunoglobulin on the epidermal side in BP and the dermal side in epidermolysis bullosa acquisita.

Researchers have defined an orderly sequence of events leading to the **pathogenesis** of BP by correlating histologic, ultrastructural, and immunopathologic findings as the lesion progresses from normal-appearing skin to blisters. These histologic changes likely reflect the following stages: an undefined initiating event results in the development of autoantibodies that upon binding with BP antigen, lead to complement fixation and activation. Complement activation, in turn, results in cellular infiltration and degranulation of mast cells, producing factors chemotactic for PMNs and eosinophils and products of anaphylaxis. The eosinophils and PMNs then elaborate enzymes at the dermoepidermal junction, which, in conjunction with complement-mediated cytotoxicity, cause keratinocyte death and bullae formation.

Management of BP depends on whether disease is localized or generalized, and attempts are made to tailor treatment to an individual's presentation and changed according to the course of the disease.

Systemic glucocorticosteroids have been the mainstay therapy of generalized BP. Dosages depend on severity of involvement, and the age and general health of the patient. Mild disease (20 lesions or less) may be effectively controlled by topical steroids alone. Moderate to moderately severe disease (21–60 lesions) may require oral prednisone (1 mg/kg/d). Severe disease (60 + lesions) may require 100 mg per day or more. Divided daily doses are recommended during acute disease. Control of disease, defined as no new blisters for 5 to 7 days, may take 2 to 4 weeks. If disease progresses beyond this time, then increasing the prednisone by 10 to 20 mg per day is suggested. If a patient is unresponsive to 60 mg per day of prednisone, an immunosuppressive agent such as azathioprine may be added. Sometimes dapsone is also useful. With control, switching to daily or alternate-day doses and slowly tapering the dose is recommended. Most patients require 6 to 12 months of treatment with systemic steroids. Side effects of systemic corticosteroids are many, especially in the elderly.

Immunosuppressive agents are used both for their primary effects and for their steroid-sparing effects. Indications include unresponsiveness to 80 to 100 mg of prednisone daily, patients in whom corticosteroids are contraindicated or who develop significant corticosteroid side effects, those younger than 60 with widespread disease, those with a nodular or vesicular variant, and patients with cicatricial pemphigoid unresponsive to prednisone or dapsone. Azathioprine is most often used, and its concomitant use with steroids reduces steroid dose and duration of use. Azathioprine is begun at 50 mg per day and may be increased to 50 mg 3 times a day. Cyclophosphamide and methotrexate are also used. Recently cyclosporine has been used in a small number of patients.

Dapsone and sulfapyridine appear to be most effective in patients whose biopsies reveal greater numbers of PMNs and fewer eosinophils; such biopsies are seen in vesicular pemphigoid, the Brunsting-Perry variant, and cicatricial pemphigoid. The dose of dapsone used is increased slowly over 3 weeks, starting at 25 to 50 mg per day and reaching a dose of 150 to 200 mg per day. Screening for G6PD deficiency is a prerequisite to use of the drug. Periodic monitoring of the blood count is suggested because methemoglobinemia and hemolytic anemia are common side effects.

Intralesional steroids are of significant benefit in localized scarring and nonscarring pemphigoid and may be used for mucous membrane disease. Triamcinolone diacetate injections of 5 mg/ml initially and up to 10 mg/ml for resistant lesions may be used.

Topical therapy is an important adjunct to prevent superinfection which can lead to scarring. Baths or wet-to-dry dressings with Burow's solution are beneficial to healing by debriding without trauma. Potent topical steroid creams are useful adjuncts for patients on systemic therapy or as therapy for patients with mild disease. Mucosal therapy includes topical steroids, viscous lidocaine, and oral rinses containing hydrogen peroxide, dexamethasone, and diphenhydramine.

Newer **experimental therapies** tested on small groups of patients may be useful in an unresponsive patient. Among these is the use of high-dose pulse steroid therapy for patients with severe generalized disease unresponsive to other treatment. Deaths from electrolyte imbalance and sepsis have been reported with this treatment. Plasma exchange has been effective in decreasing steroid doses required to control disease; however, the rate of recurrence and the incidence of steroid side effects were unaffected. Finally, oral tetracycline, erythromycin, and niacinamide have been used successfully alone or in combination with each other or with an immunosuppressive agent.

Ahmed AR, Maize JC, Provost TT: Bullous pemphigoid. Clinical and immunologic follow-up after successful therapy. *Arch Dermatol.* 1977;113:1043–1116.
A description of the general features of bullous pemphigoid as well as a discussion of treatment with systemic steroids. The study compares therapeutic response in patients treated with systemic steroids with or without concomitant azathioprine and finds that the addition of the immunosuppressant decreased the length of treatment and amount of steroid needed for control of disease.
Ahmed AR, Newcomer VD: Clinical features (of BP). *Clinics in Dermatology (Bullous Pemphigoid).* 1987;5(1):6–12.
The authors clearly classify the clinical variants of bullous pemphigoid, describe each, and include color photographs.
Ahmed AR, Rogers RS III: Therapy and management (of BP). *Clinics in Dermatology (Bullous Pemphigoid).* 1987;5(1):146–153.
This monograph is a review of the various treatments of bullous pemphigoid and an outline for practical management. Newer experimental practices are described. The extensive list of references provides information for seeking primary sources.
Dvorak AM, Mihm MC Jr., Osage JE, et al.: Bullous pemphigoid, an ultrastructural study of the inflammatory response: eosinophil, basophil and mast cell granule changes in multiple biopsies from one patient. *J Invest Dermatol.* 1982;78:91–101.
This study clearly describes the sequence of histopathologic events in the pathogenesis of bullous pemphigoid by describing the histology and electron microscopy of the evolution of clinical lesions in one patient.
Imber MJ, Murphy GF, Jordan RE: The immunopathology of bullous pemphigoid. *Clinics in Dermatology.* 1987;5(1):81–92.
A review of the immunopathologic features of bullous pemphigoid, including a table showing the different findings in several subepidermal bullous disorders.
Jordan RE, Kawana S, Fritz KA: Immunopathologic mechanisms in pemphigus and bullous pemphigoid. *J Invest Dermatol.* 1985;85:72s–78s.
An excellent description of the role of immunoreactants in bullous pemphigoid, including a proposed model of bulla formation.
Korman N: Bullous Pemphigoid. *J Am Acad Dermatol.* 1987;16:907–924.
This review is an excellent summary of the clinical manifestations of bullous pemphigoid and its variants, including pathology, immunofluorescence, pathophysiology, and the differential diagnosis. Therapeutic management is described.
Lindelof B, Islam N, Eklund G, et al.: Pemphigoid and cancer. *Arch Dermatol.* 1990;126:66–68.
An epidemiologic study in Sweden concluding that pemphigoid is not statistically associated with malignancy.
Nemeth AJ, Klein AD, Gould EW, Schachner LA: Childhood bullous pemphigoid. Clinical and immunologic features, treatment, and prognosis. *Arch Dermatol.* 1991;127:378–386.
This report describes a 2½-month-old infant with BP and reviews childhood pemphigoid and other rare immunobullous disorders of infancy.

14. PEMPHIGUS
Richard J. Sharpe

The family of diseases known as pemphigus is manifested by the loss of intercellular adhesion between keratinocytes with resultant bulla formation. The site of the blister formation within the epidermis broadly divides pemphigus into two main categories. In pemphigus vulgaris, pemphigus vegetans, and benign familial pemphigus, the blisters form above the basal layer. Pemphigus foliaceus, pemphigus erythematosus (Senear-Usher syndrome), and folgo selvagem (Brazilian pemphigus) are characterized by blister formation just below the stratum corneum. All forms of pemphigus except benign familial pemphigus are characterized by autoantibodies that have specificity for the surface of stratified squamous epithelial cells. These antibodies may cause the loss of cellular cohesion and subsequent blister formation. One possible mechanism of injury involves the induction of proteases secondary to binding of pemphigus antibodies to the surface of stratified squamous epithelia. In addition, complement may play an additive role in the pathogenesis of this disease.

The blisters of pemphigus are flaccid and can be extended laterally with gentle pressure. This phenomenon is known as the Nikolsky sign and is relatively specific for pemphigus but is not pathognomonic. Other blistering diseases, such as staphylococcal scalded skin syndrome and toxic epidermal necrolysis, can also be associated with a positive Nikolsky sign. At presentation, some patients may not have clinically evident blisters due to spontaneous rupture or erosion. This feature is particularly true in the superficial forms of pemphigus.

When clinicians obtain a biopsy specimen in any blistering disease, it should be taken from the edge of an intact blister, including a margin of normal skin. Routine histologic examination of formalin-fixed sections as well as immunofluorescence testing on specimens fresh frozen or fixed in Michel's medium should be routinely obtained. Routine examination will define the site of blister formation. Direct immunofluorescence shows immunoglobulin G deposited in the intercellular spaces between keratinocytes in involved skin. Complement, properdin, properdin factor B, and fibrin can also be seen. Indirect immunofluorescence using the patient's sera on a suitable substrate, commonly monkey esophagus, shows similar findings. The titer of pemphigus antibody often correlates with the severity of the disease and can be used to follow the patient's response to treatment.

Pemphigus vulgaris can affect all age groups but its onset is more common in the fourth or fifth decade of life. Lesions can involve the entire body surface but are usually seen on the chest, scalp, periumbilical and intertriginous areas. Oral lesions are common in pemphigus vulgaris. They frequently antedate the lesions on nonmucosal skin and may be the sole manifestation of the disease. Pemphigus vulgaris can involve the oropharynx and other mucosal surfaces, sometimes extending into the esophagus and cardia of the stomach. Nasal, laryngeal, and vaginal mucosal involvement have also been described. Pemphigus vulgaris may be more common in patients of Mediterranean and Jewish heritage. It is also associated with certain class 1 histocompatibility antigens. Whether this association represents close linkage with a gene responsible for an increased susceptibility to pemphigus or a direct immunoregulatory effect is unknown.

Histologically, pemphigus vulgaris is characterized by intraepidermal blister formation due to acantholysis (loss of intercellular adhesions) in the superbasilar epidermis and intact basal cells that resemble rows of tombstones ("tombstoning"). Inflammation is not a prominent feature, although eosinophilic spongiosis may be present in the epidermis.

Pemphigus vegetans is clinically manifested by vegetating lesions and sometimes pustules. The latter may represent superinfection at the edges of broken bullae. The intertriginous areas are more commonly affected. The histology of this variant commonly shows abscess formation within the epidermis, and eosinophils are frequently present in moderate numbers. Hyperkeratosis, pseudoepitheliomatous hyperplasia, and papillomatosis also occur.

In **pemphigus foliaceus,** blister formation is much more superficial. The blisters are easily ruptured and the patient may have only crusting, scales, erosion, and excoriations on presentation. Given the lack of bullae at presentation, the diagnosis may be missed. Patients with this disease sometimes complain of a burning pruritus. The age distribution and ethnic predilections for this disease are similar to those for pemphigus vulgaris.

Drug-induced pemphigus in association with D-penicillamine has been described by a number of investigators. Most of the patients described with this entity were clinically diagnosed as having pemphigus foliaceus, although several carried the diagnosis of pemphigus vulgaris or pemphigus erythematosus. In almost all cases, the disease resolved with the cessation of D-penicillamine therapy. A small number of case reports also exist that link captopril or rifampicin and other drugs to pemphigus-like eruptions. In the case of D-penicillamine–induced pemphigus, the mean time to onset of the disease is 12 months.

Pemphigus erythematosus is similar to pemphigus foliaceus histologically and represents a localized form of pemphigus. The lesions of pemphigus erythematosus can result in a lupus-like butterfly rash as well as bullous and seborrheic-like lesions. There may be an association between pemphigus erythematosus and other autoimmune diseases, including rheumatoid arthritis, thymoma, myasthenia gravis, and systemic lupus erythematosus.

Brazilian pemphigus (folgo selvagem) is a form of pemphigus endemic to certain regions of Brazil. Clinically and histologically, it is similar to pemphigus foliaceus. It has a wide spectrum of severity, from localized bullae to diffuse desquamation. Even now, the fatality rate is in the range of 40% or greater. This high mortality rate, which is similar to the mortality rate in pemphigus vulgaris in the precorticosteroid era, might be due to the lack of aggressive medical care in the regions where this disease is endemic, or be inherent to the disease itself. There is an increasing body of literature suggesting that Brazilian pemphigus might be associated with infection by a yet-unknown agent that triggers the host to mount an autoimmune response. An attractive hypothesis along these lines is that the immune response to the putative infectious agent may break the host's natural humoral tolerance to the pemphigus antigen.

Benign familial pemphigus (Hailey-Hailey disease) is characterized by localized vesicles that usually occur in a recurrent fashion in the second or third decade of life. The lesions typically arise on an erythematous base and are very fragile, breaking easily and leaving behind denuded areas of skin that usually become crusted. The initial lesions tend to heal, sometimes with residual hyperpigmentation. The lesions tend to recur at the same sites; however, dissemination occasionally occurs. All parts of the skin surface can be affected. Mucosal involvement is rare. The disease, although a considerable nuisance to the patient, does not generally compromise the general health of the patient. Maceration and fissures of intertriginous areas and burning with pruritus are common complaints.

Histologically, blister formation occurs largely above the suprabasal cleft. Elongated papillae with a single layer of basal cells commonly protrude upward into the blister cavity. Many of the detached cells in the stratum corneum show loss of intercellular bridges. The cells of the detached epidermis in many places show only slight separation from one another because of a few intact intercellular bridges holding them loosely together. This phenomenon gives the lesion the typical histologic picture of a "dilapidated brick wall." In benign familial pemphigus, unlike other forms of pemphigus, autoantibodies against the surface of stratified squamous epithelia are not found. A primary defect of cellular adhesion may be responsible for the disease.

The mainstay of the **treatment** of pemphigus involves the use of systemic corticosteroids. Because of the potential for severe morbidity and mortality in this disease, hospitalization may be necessary in the case of extensive disease. Pemphigus vulgaris, the most serious and the most common form of pemphigus, was associated with a mortality rate of about 50% in the precorticosteroid era. The mechanisms of death in the untreated pemphigus patient and in patients unresponsive to treatment are usually similar to those of burn patients. Sepsis, cachexia, and major fluid and electrolyte imbalances predominate.

Numerous treatment regimens have been advocated. However, the risks of immunosuppressive therapy must be carefully balanced against the benefit in any given patient. Most clinicians favor high initial doses of prednisone or prednisolone, on the order of 80 to 160 mg/d. Oral prednisone is commonly used. Equivalent doses of intravenous or intramuscular adrenocorticoids may also be used. Once lesions begin to clear, the dose can usually be tapered to 40 to 60 mg/d, and then slowly tapered to a maintenance dosage of 5 to 10 mg/d. The patient should be closely monitored for the development of adrenocorticoid side effects including hyperglycemia, electrolyte imbalances, infection, vertebral fractures, mood disturbances, and gastric ulcers. In addition, given the potential for long hospitalizations, prophylaxis for deep venous thrombosis should be considered. Prophylactic antacids, carafate, or H_2 blockers should be considered because of the potential for peptic ulcer disease. Stools should be monitored for occult blood.

Other immunosuppressive agents may be useful in pemphigus. Cyclophosphamide and azathioprine, in doses of 100 to 200 mg/d, have been used and may also have steroid-sparing effects. Bone marrow suppression, hemorrhagic cystitis, and the potential for malignancy exist. Methotrexate has also been used in pemphigus. With methotrexate, bone marrow suppression and hepatotoxicity should be monitored. Fifteen to thirty mg of methotrexate is given weekly. Cyclosporine-A has shown some effectiveness in controlling recalcitrant pemphigus, but more data are needed to assess its risk to benefit ratio.

As a single agent or in conjunction with other drugs, gold may have efficacy in selected patients and is considered first-line therapy for mucous membrane pemphigus by some investigators. Gold sodium thiomalate should be started with an initial test dose of 10 mg IM followed by 25 mg the second and third weeks, then 25 to 50 mg weekly until the disease is controlled. Maintenance therapy is usually 50 mg IM every 3 to 4 weeks. Oral gold preparations are now available. As experience with oral gold preparations increases, they may become a first- or second-line drug for the treatment of this disease. Side effects of gold therapy include leukopenia, dermatitis, and proteinuria.

Plasmapheresis can be used to rapidly lower autoantibody titers, but this form of therapy is complicated by a rebound of autoantibody formation and an increased risk of sepsis. The rebound effect can be minimized with the adjunctive use of an alkylating agent such as cyclophosphamide. Replacement of lost immunoglobulin with pooled preparations may help protect patients receiving plasmapheresis from infections.

Extracorporeal immunoabsorption of autoantibodies is a new and promising approach to the treatment of autoimmune disease. By passing plasma over a column coated with protein A or recombinant protein A, one can selectively remove immunoglobulin from the plasma. This approach is presently being tested in several antibody-mediated autoimmune diseases.

Topical antimicrobial agents or wet to dry dressings may be useful. Potent topical steroids can be applied to individual lesions. Electrolytes and fluid balance should be carefully monitored and maintained. Aggressive nutritional support is important in the treatment of pemphigus. The patients must be evaluated often, so that superinfection is identified early, and the clinician should be aware of the real possibility of life-threatening septicemia in these patients.

Pemphigus foliaceus and pemphigus erythematosus may respond to lower doses of steroids. The lower morbidity and mortality rates for these disorders are probably due to the superficial location of bulla formation. Pemphigus vegetans should be managed as aggressively as pemphigus vulgaris. The high mortality associated with Brazilian pemphigus also necessitates aggressive treatment. However, adequate medical care may not always be available to patients where this disease is endemic.

Unlike other forms of pemphigus, benign familial pemphigus responds moderately well to antibiotics. Tetracycline, given initially at a dosage of 2 g/d, has been reported to be effective, and most clinicians begin tapering the drug once the lesions clear. Dicloxacillin, first-generation cephalosporins, erythromycin, and minocycline may also be effective. Treatment of bacterial superinfection may be the mechanism by which antibiotics are useful in treating this disease; thus, antibiotic therapy should be guided by appropriate cultures. Dapsone in doses of 200 to 300 mg daily may also be beneficial. Systemic corticosteroids commonly suppress the disease, but a rebound phenomenon sometimes occurs. Topical corticosteroids are of limited usefulness.

Aberer W, Wolff-Schreiner EC, Stingl G, Wolff K: Azathioprine in the treatment of pemphigus vulgaris. A long-term follow-up. *J Am Acad Dermatol.* 1987;16:527–533.

Describes a prospective study of 37 patients treated with a corticosteroid-azathioprine regimen. This study demonstrates the utility of both of these agents in combination for treating severe, generalized pemphigus vulgaris.

Anhalt GJ, Patel H, Diaz LA: Mechanisms of immunologic injury: pemphigus and bullous pemphigoid. *Arch Dermatol.* 1983;119:711–714.

In this editorial, models of immunologic injury are reviewed. The bibliography is complete and historically traces the major studies that have led to our present understanding of these diseases.

Lever W: Pemphigus and pemphigoid: review of the advances made since 1964. *J Am Acad Dermatol.* 1979;1:2–31.

This article summarizes treatment recommendations using steroids alone or in combination with methotrexate, cyclophosphamide, or azathioprine. Several treatment protocols are outlined, depending upon the extent of the disease and initial response to corticosteroids.

Murdock DK, Lookingbill DP: Immunosuppressive therapy of pemphigus vulgaris complicated by nocardia pneumonia. Gold as an alternate therapy. *Arch Dermatol.* 1990;126:27–28.

The dangers of conventional immunosuppressive therapy in pemphigus are described, and an alternative therapy (gold) is discussed.

Penneys N, Eaglestein W, Frost P: Management of pemphigus with gold compounds. *Arch Dermatol.* 1976;112:185–187.

Gold thiomalate was effective in 4 of 15 patients treated with this drug. Toxicities included erythema nodosum, agranulocytosis (two patients), and pruritic eczematous dermatitis. The authors conclude that gold may be the treatment of choice for pemphigus, following initial treatment with steroids in certain cases.

Pisani W, Rvocco V: Drug-induced pemphigus. *Clin Dermatol.* 1986;4:118–132.

This article reviews the literature on drug-induced pemphigus. The histology and natural history of drug-induced pemphigus are also reviewed and several hypotheses are presented as to how drugs may induce pemphigus.

Rougeau JC: Plasmapheresis therapy of pemphigus and bullous pemphigoid. *Seminars in Dermatol.* 1988;7:195–200.

Discusses the use of plasmapheresis and techniques for overcoming the rebound effect.

Salomon D, Saurat JH: Oral gold therapy (auranofin) in pemphigus vulgaris. *Dermatologica.* 1986;172:310–314.

In a small study of three patients with pemphigus vulgaris treated with the oral gold salt auranofin for 9 to 18 months, slight relief with significant oral pain relief was seen in two patients and one patient went into complete remission. All patients showed subsequent flares. This study suggests that oral gold may have some efficacy in pemphigus vulgaris, but a larger controlled study is obviously needed.

Trattner A, Lurie R, Leiser A, et al.: Esophageal involvement in pemphigus vulgaris: a clinical, histologic, and immunopathologic study. *J Am Acad Dermatol.* 1991;24:223–226.

Patients with pemphigus are potentially at risk for involvement of the upper gastrointestinal tract. The clinical implications of these observations await elucidation.

Yung CW, Hanbrick GW: D-penicillamine-induced pemphigus syndrome. *J Am Acad Dermatol.* 1982;6:317–324.

This paper describes the side effects of D-penicillamine, its uses, and its association with the induction of autoimmune diseases, including pemphigus.

15. EPIDERMOLYSIS BULLOSA

Clarence E. Boudreaux

Epidermolysis bullosa (EB) is a group of hereditary diseases whose common feature is the development of blisters following minimal mechanical trauma. These diseases are divided into three subgroups, EB simplex, junctional EB, and dystrophic EB, depending on the site of the blister cleavage plane. Currently, more than 13 distinct syndromes have been well described, in addition to numerous case reports of isolated variants. The individual diseases are diagnosed according to their subgroup, inheritance pattern, family history, course and severity of disease, and associated clinical findings. Although many clinicians find it useful to classify EB by the presence or absence of dystrophy, atrophy, scarring, or milia, this morphologic classification is inadequate in separating the distinct EB syndromes. The diagnosis is most precise when based on light and electron microscopic location of blister separation.

Knowledge of the anatomical terminology describing blister cleavage plane is therefore important in understanding both classification and pathogenesis. The cell membrane of the basal keratinocyte, the proliferating bottom layer of the epidermis, is attached by hemidesmosomes to a specialized structure referred to as the basement membrane zone (BMZ). The BMZ secures the epidermis to the dermis. By electron microscopy the BMZ can be divided into two regions. The lamina lucida is an electron-lucent linear band immediately beneath the plasma membrane of the basal keratinocyte. Adjacent to, and immediately below, the lamina lucida is an electron-dense collagen-rich band referred to as the lamina densa. Fibers extending from the lamina densa into the upper levels of the dermis are called anchoring fibrils and partially fill the zone just below the lamina densa; this zone is known as the sublamina densa zone. An inherent defect in any of these structures may result in an increased susceptibility to the forces of shear and stress such that the epidermis separates from the dermis and a blister forms.

In anatomical terms, EB simplex represents true epidermolysis with cytolysis of basal cells and intraepidermal separation. The blistering generally heals without sequelae. The cleavage plane in junctional EB is in the lamina lucida, and healing of blisters at this site usually results in atrophic scarring. Dermolytic (or dystrophic) EB, usually the most severe form of EB, has a separation plane just below the BMZ in the sublamina densa zone. Healing of these blisters produces dystrophy, scarring, and milia (0.5- to 1.0-mm white keratin-filled cysts), indicating the deep level of disruption. Most of these inherited conditions appear at, or soon after, birth; and there's a characteristic appearance to the blisters. However, the differential diagnosis of blistering in the neonate is long and includes herpes simplex or varicella infection, congenital syphilis, bullous impetigo, staphylococcal scalded skin syndrome, toxic epidermal necrolysis, bullous ichthyosiform erythroderma, herpes gestationis, incontinentia pigmenti, contact dermatitis, miliaria, transient neonatal pustulosis, and, rarely, the primary blistering eruptions of pemphigus, bullous pemphigoid, or chronic bullous disease of childhood. Appropriate diagnosis of a bullous eruption in a neonate therefore can be difficult and requires rigorous assimilation of historical, clinical, and investigational data.

There are four forms of **EB simplex,** all of which are inherited as an autosomal dominant trait. The two most commonly encountered forms are the generalized type and the localized type. Recent studies with fibroblast cultures reveal a sevenfold increase in activity of the enzyme gelatinase in patients with generalized EB simplex and similar results in about half of the patients with localized EB simplex. The cause and effect of this finding are unknown.

Generalized EB simplex, also known as the Koebner variant, presents at birth or in infancy with generalized blistering, especially marked on the feet, hands, and extremities. Blisters and erosions heal without atrophy, scarring, or milia. Nails and teeth are normal and mucosal erosions are rare. Increased environmental temperature results in a lowered threshold to trauma such that blistering is increased in the summer. Histologically, blister formation occurs within the basal keratinocyte layer. This disorder is not life-threatening and is treated symptomatically. Prophylactic care includes a cool environment and avoidance of trauma, especially friction. Properly fitted, soft footwear is essential.

Localized EB simplex, the Weber-Cockayne variant, causes recurrent bullae limited to hands and feet. It presents in late childhood or occasionally in adult life in conditions of excessive mechanical stress. The disease is relatively mild but at times may cause painful blisters and erosions and prevent ambulation, precluding sports or military field duty. Blistering increases during summer months because of hot humid weather, compounded by a high incidence of hyperhidrosis in these patients. Intraepidermal blistering occurs in the upper levels of the epidermis or within the basal cell layer. Treatment is similar to that used for generalized EB simplex. In addition, treatment of hyperhidrosis, with 10% glutaraldehyde or 20% aluminum chloride in anhydrous alcohol (Drysol) applied once a day, may be helpful.

Uncommon forms of EB simplex include **EB herpetiformis** (also known as the Dowling-Meara variant) and **EB simplex-Ogna.** The former presents with nonscarring generalized blistering at birth, frequently with a herpetiform appearance especially around the mouth. As the child grows older, the tendency to blister may diminish such that disease-free periods of months at a time occur. By the age of 6 to 8 years, the child has palms and soles that have become hyperkeratotic. Although EB herpetiformis is included in the simplex group of EB, healing of blistered sites results in milia formation and nail dystrophy. Death due to extensive disease has been reported. Histology reveals intraepidermal blister formation similar to that caused by the other forms of EB simplex. EB herpetiformis is distinguished on electron microscopy when tonofilaments clumped to hemidesmosomes are noted. The Ogna variant of EB simplex has been described in kindreds of a Norwegian village. Characterized by nonscarring blisters of the extremities, it is unique because of its association with easy bruisability and a genetic linkage to the erythrocyte glutamic pyruvic transaminase locus.

There are five types of **junctional EB,** all inherited in an autosomal recessive pattern. Although scarring does not generally occur, atrophy of blister-prone areas is a prominent feature, and the term epidermolysis bullosa atrophicans is often used. The two most common forms of EB atrophicans are the gravis and mitis types.

EB atrophicans-gravis is also known as the Herlitz syndrome, after the original describer, or as EB letalis, because many infants deteriorate rapidly and die within the first few months of life. The condition appears at birth with generalized cutaneous, oral, and esophageal blisters and erosions that heal with atrophy. Nails are almost always dystrophic, and dentition dysplastic. Complications include failure to thrive, anemia, and sepsis. Congenital pyloric atresia is an associated finding and requires early surgical intervention. If the patient survives to 3 to 6 months of age, nonhealing beefy granulation tissue develops around the mouth, nose, and sites of trauma. Light microscopy reveals a subepidermal blister, and electron microscopy demonstrates cleavage through the lamina lucida associated with a reduction in number and size of hemidesmosomes. The prognosis is poor; most patients die within 2 years of life. Aggressive supportive therapy should be carried out early in the course of the disease because the benign mitis type may mimic the fatal gravis type in the first few months of life. No definitive treatments have been reported. Genetic counseling of the family is warranted.

EB atrophicans-mitis, also called generalized atrophic benign epidermolysis bullosa, similarly begins with blistering at birth. The blisters tend to be large and generalized, and occur spontaneously. Extensive erosions develop that heal with atrophy. The nails are markedly dystrophic and palmoplantar hyperkeratosis is common. Enamel defects result in dysplastic dentition. Mucous membrane involvement is usually mild; however, esophageal stricture has been reported. Atrophic alopecia of the scalp and absence of pubic and axillary hair are prominent features. Histologically the mitis type of EB atrophicans is indistinguishable from the more lethal gravis type. Both have blister cleavage planes that occur at the lamina lucida and a decrease in hemidesmosomes. Improvement as the patient with EB atrophicans-mitis ages is expected. Exuberant granulation tissue, anemia, and failure to thrive do not develop. Although patients suffer significant morbidity, the prognosis is good with a normal life span. Treatment consists of rigorous topical care of erosions and avoidance of trauma and hot environments. Recently cultures of keratinocytes harvested from the patient's uninvolved skin have been used to successfully graft areas of chronic erosion. In at least one trial, the use of phenytoin resulted in decreasing bulla formation.

The other three forms of junctional EB are uncommon. **EB atrophicans localisata** presents in early school-aged children with localized blisters occurring primarily on the soles of the feet. Usually the nails have been dystrophic since birth. Examination of the teeth reveals enamel dysplasia and caries. Oral mucosa is spared. **EB atrophicans inversa** occurs in the neonatal period with blistering on the trunk and proximal extremities and in intertriginous areas. The hands and feet are spared. Nails and teeth are dysplastic, and oral and corneal mucosal surfaces are occasionally involved. **EB atrophicans progressiva** has been described in several Norwegian and Swedish families. Trauma causes dystrophy and loss of nails beginning at ages 5 to 8. Later blistering of the hands and feet develops. As the name implies, this disease is progressive into adult life, with increasing frequency, severity, and extent of blister formation. A distinguishing feature of this variant is an associated hypoacusis.

Dystrophic EB, also referred to as **dermolytic EB,** is best classified on the basis of inheritance pattern. Two distinct syndromes in this group are inherited in an autosomal dominant pattern and are less severe and less life-threatening than the two forms inherited by recessive traits. All dystrophic EB variants heal with milia and scarring, and patients are at increased risk for developing skin cancer in the areas of chronic blistering.

The milder of the two dominantly inherited forms is the **Cockayne-Touraine syndrome.** Blisters begin in infancy or early childhood and are often limited to the elbows and knees and the dorsal aspects of the hands and feet. The lesions heal with scarring that becomes hypertrophic and often hyperkeratotic. Oral mucosal lesions occur in 20% of patients but are generally without sequelae. Nails are dystrophic but teeth are normal. Histologically, the cleavage plane of the blister is below the BMZ in the upper dermis, associated with decreased numbers of anchoring fibrils on electron microscopy. Interestingly, uninvolved skin has normal numbers of anchoring fibrils. These patients have a normal life expectancy and their condition may improve with age.

The **Pasini variant** of dominant dystrophic EB tends to be more severe than the Cockayne-Touraine variant. Blisters are usually present at birth and primarily involve the extremities. Healing occurs with atrophic scarring and milia formation. At puberty small white or skin-colored papules, called albopapuloid lesions, develop on the trunk independent of blisters. Prior to the development of these papules, it may not be possible to distinguish between the Pasini and the Cockayne-Touraine variants by clinical presentation; however, electron microscopy demonstrates a decreased number of anchoring fibrils in both blister-prone areas and uninvolved skin. Patients with the Pasini variant have a normal life expectancy.

There is a wide variation of clinical severity in recessive dystrophic EB, which is also known as the **Hallopeau-Siemens variant.** The mild end of the spectrum presents with a localized blistering process beginning at birth or in infancy, limited primarily to the extremities, and may clinically be indistinguishable from the Cockayne-Touraine variant of dominant dystrophic EB. Nail dystrophy is common. Although oral blisters and erosions occur, they tend to be mild and heal without sequelae. Teeth are usually normal. The severe end of the spectrum results in terribly disfiguring disease. Widespread cutaneous, oral, esophageal, and anal involvement with scarring begins at birth. Because of repeated blistering and scarring, the fingers and toes fuse, forming an encasement of scar tissue that results in nonfunctional mittenlike deformities and subsequent bone resorption of the digits. Scarring around major joints causes contractures that further decrease the patient's functional capabilities. The oral mucosa is rarely without painful erosions, resulting in dysphagia and poor nutritional intake. Maintenance of adequate oral hygiene by brushing the teeth may cause devastating trauma to the oral mucosa. Esophageal mucosal involvement commonly results in stricture formation requiring mechanical bougienage or surgical intervention. Anal strictures cause painful defecation and frequent fecal impactions. Cutaneous and mucosal areas of chronic blister formation and erosions may develop squamous cell carcinomas, most of which are metastatic at the time of diagnosis. Any progressive nonhealing ulcerating lesion is suspicious for the development of a carcinoma. In addition to the profound morbidity of the disease, death often occurs within the first three decades of life.

As in dominant dystrophic EB, the blister cleavage plane in the Hallopeau-Siemens variant is subepidermal, beneath the BMZ, and associated with decreased numbers of anchoring fibrils. Unique to recessive dystrophic EB is a marked degeneration of collagen in the papillary dermis. Collagenase activity is increased sevenfold, because of an increase in the rate of synthesis as well as production of a collagenase that is structurally abnormal and may not respond to normal physiologic control mechanisms. Phenytoin has been shown to inhibit collagenase activity. Used in therapeutic trials, it has successfully decreased the severity of disease in a majority of patients with recessive dystrophic EB. Blood levels of 8 to 10 µg/ml are recommended. The mainstay of treatment, however, includes strict avoidance of trauma and adequate topical care of erosions and ulcers. In addition, genetic counseling plays an important role in the care of the family of an affected individual. Prenatal diagnosis has been made by in utero skin biopsy, allowing early termination of pregnancy.

Recessive dystrophic EB inversa is a rare variant that appears at birth or in early infancy with bullae and erosions of the axillae, neck, and groin. Early in the neonatal period, blisters may occur on the extremities; however, later in life blisters usually become limited to the intertriginous areas. Oral and esophageal involvement is common and may lead to shortening of the frenulum of the tongue and to esophageal stricture. The prognosis may be somewhat better than in the Hallopeau-Siemens variant, but the morbidity is often similar.

Epidermolysis bullosa acquisita (EBA) is an acquired syndrome of mechanobullous disease that is unrelated to any inherited form of EB. Blistering begins in adulthood and there is no family history of similar disease. Light microscopic examination of a skin biopsy specimen reveals a cleavage plane in the BMZ. Direct immunofluorescence studies identify a linear deposition of immunoglobulin G along the BMZ. Using immunoelectron microscopy, one can find these immunoreactants in the sublamina densa zone. The pathogenesis of EBA therefore appears to be related to some sort of immunologic dysfunction.

Classically, bullae are produced by mild trauma. The hands and feet are the most prominent areas involved, with hemorrhagic bullae, atrophic scarring, and milia occurring over the extensor aspects. The nails are frequently dystrophic. The eruption is most often misdiagnosed as porphyria cutanea tarda; however, hirsutism, liver abnormalities, and elevated urine porphyrins do not occur in EBA. Recent studies indicate that as many as 50% of patients will present with recalcitrant generalized blistering disease, which is indistinguishable from bullous pemphigoid other than by localization of immunoreactants with immunoelectron microscopy or with an indirect immunofluorescence technique using the patient's serum and normal human skin split by a hypertonic sodium bromide solution. In EBA, immunoreactants are found in the sublamina densa zone, directed against anchoring fibrils, whereas those of bullous pemphigoid are located in the lamina lucida.

EBA may be associated with myeloma, lymphoma, ulcerative colitis, Crohn's disease, or amyloidosis. Once the diagnosis is established, a search for these systemic processes is warranted. Treatment has been generally unsatisfactory. Administration of dapsone, azathioprine, or cyclophosphamide may be attempted. Trauma should be avoided.

Anton-Lamprecht I, Rauskolb R, Jovanovic V: Prenatal diagnosis of epidermolysis bullosa dystrophica Hallopeau-Siemens with electron microscopy of fetal skin. *Lancet.* 1981;2(8255):1077–1079.
Prenatal diagnosis allowed early termination of pregnancy.
Cooper TW, Bauer EA: Therapeutic efficacy of phenytoin in recessive dystrophic epidermolysis bullosa. *Arch Dermatol.* 1984;120:490–495.
Twenty-two patients with recessive dystrophic EB were treated with phenytoin (blood

level 8–10 μg/ml). *Sixty-four percent of patients had a greater than 40% decrease in blister formation.*

Didolkar MS, Gerner RE, Moore GE: Epidermolysis bullosa dystrophica and epithelioma of the skin. *Cancer.* 1974;33:198–202.
Review of 19 cases of EB dystrophica with skin cancer developing in blister-prone areas. Most patients had metastatic disease.

Fine J-D: Epidermolysis bullosa. *Int J Dermatol.* 1986;25:143–157.
An easy-to-read review of EB, with current discussion of investigational findings and therapeutic trials.

Fine JD, Bauer EA, Briggaman RA, et al.: Revised clinical and laboratory criteria for subtypes of inherited epidermolysis bullosa. A consensus report by the Subcommittee on Diagnosis and Classification of the National Epidermolysis Bullosa Registry. *J Am Acad Dermatol.* 1991;24:119–135.
This report summarizes the clinical literature and makes recommendations concerning clinical and laboratory criteria for the diagnosis and subclassification of patients with EB.

Gammon WR, Briggaman RA, Woodley DT, et al.: Epidermolysis bullosa acquisita— A pemphigoid-like disease. *J Amer Acad Dermatol.* 1984;11:820–832.
Perhaps as many as 50% of EBA patients present with clinical, histologic, and immunofluorescent findings indistinguishable from those of bullous pemphigoid.

Gedde-Dahl T: Epidermolysis syndromes. *Curr Prob Dermatol.* 1987;16:129–145.
This review article is written by one of the foremost experts in the field of epidermolysis bullosa. It contains many good photographs and an excellent text.

Haber RM, Hanna W, Ramsay CA, et al.: Hereditary epidermolysis bullosa. *J Am Acad Dermatol.* 1985;13:252–278.
A comprehensive and well-written review article.

Katz SI: The epidermal basement membrane zone—structure, ontogeny, and role in disease. *J Amer Acad Dermatol.* 1984;11:1025–1037.
A detailed look at the anatomy and constituents of the BMZ and how they relate to known disease processes.

16. DERMATITIS HERPETIFORMIS
Christopher R. Shea

Dermatitis herpetiformis (DH) is an uncommon, chronic, pruritic, papulovesicular disorder characterized by granular immunoglobulin A deposits in the dermis along the papillary dermoepidermal junction (DEJ) and by an association with a gluten-sensitive enteropathy (GSE). Because both skin and gut lesions clear on a strict gluten-free diet, DH is now considered a multisystem disease of altered immune reactivity to dietary gluten. In most reported series, there is a predominance of male patients with onset generally between the second and fourth decades of life, although children can be affected. DH is more common in persons of Scandinavian (annual incidence of about 1:100,000 persons), Irish, or British descent, and is rare in blacks and Japanese. Familial cases of DH are extremely rare, a curious finding in view of the strong association of DH with certain histocompatibility-antigen haplotypes: HLA-A1, HLA-B8, and HLA-DRw3 are all significantly increased compared to their frequency in the general population. Untreated, DH tends to run a relentlessly chronic course, marked by temporary remissions and recurrences at intervals of weeks to months; recurrences in some cases appear to be provoked by illness or other stress. Prolonged spontaneous remissions are the exception, occurring in less than 20% of patients followed for many years.

The **primary cutaneous lesions** are vesicles, erythematous papules, urticarial plaques, or, rarely, bullae; these lesions are often grouped (hence, "herpetiform").

Intense pruritus or pain may precede and usually accompany the eruption of primary lesions, leading to rapid excoriation with formation of erosions and crusted papules that may heal with hypopigmentation or, less commonly, hyperpigmentation. The lesions of DH are usually strikingly symmetrical in distribution and favor the extensor surfaces of the extremities (elbows, knees, and buttocks) as well as the sacrum, face, scalp, shoulders, and nape of the neck. When biopsied, early lesions are most diagnostic of DH and show accumulations of neutrophils at the tips of the dermal papillae. Later lesions reveal papillary microabscesses containing greater numbers of eosinophils and deposits of fibrin, and subepidermal blisters. Dermal changes include a subpapillary acute inflammatory infiltrate with nuclear dust, and acute and chronic inflammation around subpapillary blood vessels.

The **diagnosis** of DH is made by direct immunofluorescence of a biopsy specimen from clinically uninvolved skin; this study will document IgA deposition at the DEJ, such deposition classically forming a granular pattern accentuated at the subepidermal papillae. Direct immunofluorescence of blistered skin is usually fruitless, as the inflammatory response (phagocytosis, proteolytic enzymes) destroys the characteristic findings. About 10% of all patients with IgA at the DEJ demonstrate a smooth, linear distribution of IgA, which may reflect a distinct disorder, linear IgA disease (see below). In association with IgA, C_3 is usually demonstrable on direct immunofluorescence; occasionally IgG or IgM is also present. By immunoelectron microscopy, the granular deposits are present in the region of anchoring fibrils, beneath the basement membrane.

DH is associated with a number of other conditions. As noted previously, the most common is GSE, which occurs in greater than 90% of cases of DH. Although pathologically indistinguishable qualitatively from the changes seen in celiac disease (CD), the changes in DH are less quantitatively severe than in CD, with changes often limited to lymphocytic infiltration and mild villous atrophy. In accordance with pathologic evidence of less severe bowel disease in DH, patients usually do not have abdominal complaints or symptomatic malabsorption, even though sophisticated testing may reveal disturbance of intestinal permeability. In addition, several studies have reported a significantly increased incidence of lymphoma in DH patients, an association also noted with CD. Frequently, these lymphomas arise in the gastrointestinal tract, especially the jejunum. Several other case reports have also documented the coexistence of DH and other malignancies (leukemia, carcinoma), although this association may be by chance. There does appear to be a true association of DH with autoimmune diseases such as thyroiditis, diabetes mellitus, pernicious anemia, and glomerulonephritis. Clinical serologic thyroid abnormalities have been noted in as many as 26 of 50 patients with DH.

The **pathogenesis** of DH is related to the genetic susceptibility of patients, their ingestion of gluten, and an abnormal response of humoral immunity to the gluten. To explain these factors, the following account is often given. Patients with a genetic predisposition (apparently indicated by HLA-B8/DRw3) in concert with an unclear initiating factor develop an abnormal immune response to ingested gluten via the gut-associated lymphoid tissue. Resulting antibody-mediated reactions cause lymphocytic infiltration and villous atrophy of the small intestine, and lead to circulating immune complexes. Patients with DH have been documented to have circulating antibodies to gluten, of both the IgA and the IgG classes, as well as circulating IgA-class antiendomysial antibodies. The IgA is then thought to deposit in the subpapillary dermis, perhaps cross-reacting with normal tissue antigens such as reticulin, leading to complement fixation. The resultant cascade of events is held to include chemotaxis of neutrophils, liberation of mediators causing pruritus, and enzymatic separation of dermis and epidermis to form vesicles. Evidence to confirm parts of this hypothesis is either lacking or contradictory, but ongoing research may clarify the issues.

The **treatment** of choice for DH is strict adherence to a gluten-free diet, which will clear the clinical manifestations of DH in most patients gradually over several months. Any rechallenge with even minimal gluten will lead to clinical relapse. Maintenance of a gluten-free diet for several years is also the only therapy known to resolve the GSE and the cutaneous IgA deposits. Although it is not clearly established whether adherence can reduce the risk of lymphoma, an attempt to resolve gut-associated lymphoid proliferation seems an appropriate beginning. The pharmacologic agent used most commonly for treating DH is dapsone, a sulfone. Response to the drug is usually dramatic and rapid, with clearing of pruritus and skin lesions within 1 week in most cases. GSE and cutaneous IgA deposits, however, are not affected, even after years of therapy, so that dapsone should be considered as an agent affording quick, symptomatic relief without affecting the basic process. Dapsone is generally started at 100 mg PO every day; occasional patients require up to 400 mg PO every day. Lowering the dose of dapsone should be possible in patients following a strict gluten-free diet. The most important side effects of dapsone are hematologic. In order to avoid dramatic hemolysis, clinicians should screen patients for glucose-6-phosphate dehydrogenase (G6PD) deficiency. Mild hemolytic anemia will also occur in most patients with normal G6PD levels receiving 50 mg or more per day. The anemia may be more severe in patients rendered iron- or folate-deficient by intestinal malabsorption. Other side effects of dapsone are noted in Chapter 83. PUVA photochemotherapy has recently been reported to improve DH.

As noted previously, some patients (about 10% in most series) with vesiculo-bullous lesions and IgA in the skin show a smooth, linear pattern of IgA deposition along the DEJ. Histopathology can usually distinguish between linear IgA disease (LAD) and classic DH. Several other features also distinguish LAD from classic DH. Lesions may be bullous rather than vesicular and located in mucous membranes. There is no significant increase in the haplotypes HLA-A1, B8, and DRw3, as is typical of DH. There is no circulating antibody to gluten, no apparent clinical gluten sensitivity, and rarely any jejunal pathology suggestive of GSE. The cutaneous IgA deposits do not contain J chains and therefore are not dimeric, as in DH. LAD is often relatively resistant to dapsone. Treatment may require systemic steroids and immunosuppressive agents. A gluten-free diet is not effective. Because of these numerous differences, many authorities consider classic DH and LAD to be different entities.

Buckley DB, English J, Molly W, et al.: Dermatitis herpetiformis: a review of 119 cases. *Clin Exp Dermatol*. 1983;8:477–487.
   Large case series demonstrating association with various HLA haplotypes and autoantibodies, and discussing management by diet and drugs.
Fry L: The treatment of dermatitis herpetiformis. *Clin Exp Dermatol*. 1982;7:633–642.
   Authoritative review of therapy of DH, emphasizing dapsone and gluten-free diet.
Fry L, Leonard JN, Swain F, et al.: Long term follow-up of dermatitis herpetiformis with and without dietary gluten withdrawal. *Br J Dermatol*. 1982;107:631–640.
   Adherence to a gluten-free diet allowed 71% of DH patients to discontinue drug therapy, but mean time between dietary change and discontinuation of drugs was 29 months.
Hall RP: The pathogenesis of dermatitis herpetiformis: recent advances. *J Am Acad Dermatol*. 1987;16:1129–1144.
   Excellent review with 130 references.
Harrington CI, Read NW: Dermatitis herpetiformis: effect of gluten-free diet on skin IgA and jejunal structure and function. *Br Med J*. 1977;1:872–875.
   Institution of a gluten-free diet led to decreased IgA deposits in skin, improvement of jejunal histology, decreased malabsorption, and reduced dapsone requirement.
Huff JC: The immunopathogenesis of dermatitis herpetiformis. *J Invest Dermatol*. 1985;84:237–238.
   Editorial review that summarizes current understanding of pathogenesis of DH and provides a useful bibliography.
Kalis JB, Malkinson FD: Dermatitis herpetiformis: a commentary. *JAMA*. 1983;250:217–221.
   Good brief review of clinical, pathogenic, and therapeutic considerations.
Katz SI, Hall RP 3rd, Lawley TJ, et al.: Dermatitis herpetiformis: the skin and the gut. *Ann Intern Med*. 1980;93:857–874.
   Indispensable review article summarizing a National Institutes of Health conference.

Leonard J, Haffernden G, Tucker W, et al.: Gluten challenge in dermatitis herpe-tiformis. *N Eng J Med.* 1983;308:816–819.

Gluten challenge in patients who were clear on a gluten-free diet led to reappearance of rash in 11 of 12, and worsened jejunal pathology in 7 of these 11.

Smith SB, Harrist TJ, Murphy GF, et al.: Linear IgA bullous dermatosis v dermatitis herpetiformis. *Arch Dermatol.* 1984;120:324–328.

Histopathologic features of the two entities permit correct diagnosis with a high degree of probability.

Ward MM, Pisetsky DS, Hall RP: Soluble interleukin-2 receptor levels in patients with dermatitis herpetiformis. *J Invest Dermatol.* 1991;97:568–572.

Fifteen of thirty (50%) dermatitis herpetiformis patients had elevated levels of IL-2R compared to one out of thirty-one (3%) healthy control subjects. It was determined that the soluble IL-2R levels were related to a mucosal immune response, suggesting that some of the T-cell activation present in DH reflects ongoing immune response in the gastrointestinal tract.

IV. SCALY OR THICKENED SKIN

17. DRY SKIN
Suzanne M. Olbricht

Dry skin (xerosis) is a frequent complaint, sometimes beginning in the third decade and increasing in prevalence with age. Objective evidence of dryness has been found in 77% of 163 persons older than 64 years, and in 100% of patients over the age of 80. This dryness and the accompanying pruritus is of much concern and discomfort, and accounts for many visits to physicians and for a significant portion of the energies and income of the cosmetic industry.

The **diagnosis** of dry skin is generally easy to make: it has a rough and finely flaking or scaly surface. In darkly pigmented people, dry skin may be slightly hypopigmented or gray (ashy) in color. These changes are most evident on the upper back and extremities, especially the shins, but may also occur on the trunk and face. Dry skin tends to wax and wane, especially exacerbated by cold weather. Frank dermatitis, an inflammatory eczematous process, may occur if the dry skin becomes irritated, as evidenced by erythema and fissures. Asteatotic dermatitis (winter itch) appears in areas of dry skin as poorly demarcated, scaling, round, faintly erythematous macules or thin plaques. Another manifestation of dry skin complicated by dermatitis is eczema craquelé, which has the distinctive appearance of red scaly fissures in an irregular netlike pattern resembling cracked porcelain. Dry skin associated with even mild dermatitis may become hyperpigmented in some skin types. It may also be complicated by superficial bacterial infection (impetiginization), especially in cracked or fissured areas.

Pruritus accompanying dry skin is particularly annoying. Paroxysms of itching can be stimulated by mild tactile sensations such as the friction of clothing or the pressure of bedclothes. Some patients report worsening of itch during periods of mild stress. A peculiar burning sensation may also be ascribed to areas of dry skin, seemingly unrelated to the paucity of skin findings or the good general health of the patient. Often the patient decides to seek medical attention because the itch or burning sensation prevents comfortable sleep, especially in the early evening.

Not only does dry skin look dry but it measures dry, i.e., there is less water in the stratum corneum. Aged skin has a lower water content than skin of younger individuals, documented by using propagation velocities of shear waves in the epidermis in vivo. Evidence and theories abound concerning the **etiology** of dry skin in the elderly. Water in the epidermis depends on diffusion from three sources: dermal vasculature, surface sweat, and the environment. Hydration is determined by the rate of diffusion from these sources and the rate of evaporation from the epidermal surface. Normally, surface sebum and other endogenous oils in the stratum corneum retard the rate of evaporation. Aged skin has thinned microvasculature walls, and changes in connective tissue proteins have reduced their solubility; both of these factors probably account for the measurably decreased dermal water content in the elderly. It is unclear why diffusion does not keep the epidermis moist, but one possible explanation is that the aged atrophic epidermis, which lacks rete ridges, presents much less surface area to the dermis for water passage. Certainly, sweating is greatly diminished in aged skin. Within eccrine sweat glands, the secretory cells flatten, become atrophic, and accumulate lipofuscin. The rate of sweat production, the amount produced, and the sodium content of sweat are greatly decreased in older individuals. This reduced sweat gland function may be related to low levels of outdoor activity. In addition, the rate of evaporation of water is less controlled by surface lipids in aged skin. Several studies document a decrease in measurable surface lipids. Sebaceous glands atrophy with age, presumably secondary to a decrease in production of endogenous androgens. Also, membrane coating granules are formed irregularly by aged keratinocytes, which may lead to the disappearance of the lipid film normally surrounding the stratum corneum cells.

The **evaluation** of an elderly patient with dry skin and pruritus includes a review of previous dermatologic history and current medical condition. Dry skin due to aging may exacerbate other skin conditions such as atopic eczema, irritant dermatitis, and congenital ichthyosis. Diabetes mellitus probably accelerates aging of many organs, including the skin. Some patients report the advent or exacerbation of dry skin with the use of diuretics. Cimetidine has been reported to cause dryness, probably secondary to its antiandrogenic properties and subsequent reduction in sebum secretion. Severe dryness with large scales may represent an acquired ichthyosis, the causes of which include chronic malnutrition, vitamin A deficiency, hypothyroidism, lymphomas, multiple myeloma, solid tumors, sarcoidosis, borderline or lepromatous leprosy, systemic lupus erythematosus, and the use of drugs such as triparanol, nicotinic acid, phenothiazines, lithium, and butyrophenones. If an elderly patient complains of severe itch without accompanying visible skin changes, the physician should look for systemic causes of pruritus, including renal and hepatic disease. The presence of prominent excoriations, crusts, and nodules without dryness may lead the physician to suspect scabies, dermatitis herpetiformis, or neurodermatitis.

The principles of **treatment** of dry skin involve altering the factors affecting hydration. The physician can promote rehydration of the epidermis by encouraging physical activity as tolerated, which will increase sweat production. External sources of water such as daily baths or showers in lukewarm water and cool mist humidifiers are helpful. Retardation of evaporation of water from the surface may be accomplished by having the patient apply an emollient. While some emollients, appropriately called moisturizers, are oil-in-water emulsions (creams) and supply an immediate softening of the skin from the water in the emulsion, they generally lack enough oil to seal this added water into the epidermis for a prolonged period of time. The most effective compounds are often the least cosmetically acceptable—notably, semisolid insoluble oils that work best when applied to freshly rehydrated skin and probably act as an occlusive covering, preventing evaporation. For example, one well-controlled study showed that petrolatum almost abolished signs of dryness after 10 daily applications over a 2-week period and that the beneficial effect was still observable for about 2 weeks after the last application. Lanolin was nearly as effective as petrolatum. Only limited efficacy was demonstrated with the use of mineral oil or cold cream. Eucerin cream, containing lanolin and petrolatum in a water-in-oil emulsion, was effective and may be cosmetically appealing because it has a less greasy feel. Eucerin lotion, with the same ingredients as Eucerin cream but compounded as an oil-in-water emulsion, was less effective. Other creams and lotions used for dry skin may contain glycerin, lactic acid, urea, and propylene glycol, substances usually classified as humectants and purported to be absorbed between the lamellae of the stratum corneum to replace missing hygroscopic substances, thereby attracting water from the atmosphere. The addition of humectants, however, may not improve the efficacy of moisturizing emulsions, and emollients containing humectants are probably less effective than petrolatum applied to wet skin. When recommending an emollient to a patient, it is also helpful to remember that with the exception of petrolatum and hydrolated petrolatum, all emollients contain additives (usually preservatives, detergents, stabilizers, and humectants), any of which may increase irritation or produce contact dermatitis. Bath oils are not advised in the elderly, since a slippery surface can cause a damaging fall.

Prevention of dry skin involves environmental manipulation. Baths in hot water are not recommended. Although hot water temporarily stuns the nerves relaying the itch sensation, it strips surface lipids and allows increased evaporation of epidermal water. Soaps also defat the epidermal surface as well as irritate it. The inherent irritant properties of various soaps have been measured with a chamber method. Dove soap, available without fragrance, is the single least irritating soap, at a level at which it has no competition. Aveenobar, Neutrogena, and Emulave are commonly recommended "mild" soaps but are more irritating than Dove soap. Ivory, Basis, Irish Spring, and Zest are moderately to strongly irritating. After soaps (including shampoos) are used, the skin should be rinsed well to remove irritating residues.

Dry skin conditions are also generally exacerbated in the winter because the relatively low humidity of cold air outdoors and artificially heated cold air indoors increases evaporation of water from the epidermal surface. Clothing designed for protection, including that for the hands, legs, and face, should be worn for any outdoor exposure. A humidifier may increase the comfort of heated indoor space. Dry heating pads and sitting in front of an open fire should be avoided because of their drying potential. Aging of the skin is accelerated by chronic cumulative sun exposure, and the development of dry skin may be delayed by the use of adequate sunscreens during younger years.

Beauregard S, Gilchrest BA: A survey of skin problems and skin care regimens in the elderly. *Arch Dermatol.* 1987;123:1638–1643.
  Elderly patients frequently complain of itch and "rashes," and their routine skin care regimens are often limited by physical disabilities.
Dotz W, Berman B: The facts about treatment of dry skin. *Geriatrics.* 1983;38:93–100.
  A practical review.
Frosch PJ: Irritancy of soaps and detergent bars. In: Frost P, Horwitz SN, eds. *Principles of Cosmetics for the Dermatologist.* St. Louis, MO: C.V. Mosby Co.; 1982:5–12.
  In-depth description of studies of irritancy using the soap chamber method.
Garwood M, Engel BT, Kusterer JP: Skin potential level: age and epidermal hydration effects. *J Gerontol.* 1981;36:7–13.
  Reduced sweat gland potential in elderly males is related to low levels of outdoor activity.
Greist MC, Epinette WW: Cimetidine-induced xerosis and asteatotic dermatitis. *Arch Dermatol.* 1982;118:253–254.
  Two patients developed generalized skin changes while on cimetidine, possibly related to the antiandrogenic properties of the drug and its effect on sebum production.
Kligman AM, Lavher RM, Grove GL, et al.: Some aspects of dry skin and its treatment. In: Kligman AM, Leyden JJ, eds. *Safety and Efficacy of Topical Drugs and Cosmetics.* New York, NY: Grune & Stratton; 1982:221–238.
  Review of studies on effectiveness of various emollients and moisturizers.
Potts RO, Buras EM Jr, Chrisman DA Jr: Changes with age in the moisture content of human skin. *J Invest Dermatol.* 1984;82:97–100.
  Aged skin has a lower water content than younger skin, as tested in men by propagation and attenuation of shear waves in skin tissue.
Saint-Leger D, Francois AM, Leveque JL, et al.: Stratum corneum lipids in skin xeroxis. *Dermatologica.* 1989;178:151–155.
  The severity of dry skin was found to be related to a decreased proportion of neutral lipids and an increased proportion of free fatty acids in the lipids on the skin surface.

18. ICHTHYOSES
Sharon J. Littzi

The ichthyoses are a heterogeneous group of hereditary disorders of keratinization, characterized by the accumulation of scale on the cutaneous surface. Although sometimes confusing, the various disorders in the group can often be distinguished by mode of inheritance, age of onset, clinical appearance, distribution, histologic findings and associated clinical features. There are four major, relatively common types of ichthyoses: ichthyosis vulgaris, recessive X-linked ichthyosis, lamellar ichthyosis, and epidermolytic hyperkeratosis. There are several rarely occurring types as well.

Ichthyosis vulgaris is the most common of the ichthyoses, with an estimated prevalence of 1:250 to 1:1000 persons. The disease is transmitted as an autosomal dominant trait and rarely has its onset before the third month of life. Ninety-five percent of cases manifest themselves prior to age 5, and the course is lifelong. There is seasonal variation in the severity of the disease and there may be some improvement of this dermatosis with age. The patient often gives a family history of "dry skin," and clinical findings may be misdiagnosed as xerosis. The disease can be quite mild; however, in dry weather, the hyperkeratosis may be severe enough to resemble that of lamellar ichthyosis.

In its classic presentation, ichthyosis vulgaris has fine scales that are white to translucent with turned-up edges, accounting for the rough nature of the skin. The scaling is most prominent over the extremities, sparing the antecubital, axillary, and popliteal fossae. Scaling of the neck is uncommon. Palmar markings are frequently accentuated in ichthyosis vulgaris, and keratosis pilaris may be apparent. Up to one-half of patients with ichthyosis vulgaris have a personal or family history of atopy. Eczema herpeticum has also been known to occur with ichthyosis vulgaris.

Histologically, ichthyosis vulgaris has mild to moderate hyperkeratosis with occasional parakeratosis. The granular cell layer is usually absent or very thin, but may also be normal. A slight dermal perivascular and periappendageal lymphocytic infiltrate may be present. With electron microscopic examination, abnormalities of tonofilament orientation and keratohyaline structure have been noted. At the current time, it is thought that the scale in this disorder occurs because of an epidermal hyperproliferative state.

X-linked ichthyosis affects males and is usually more severe than ichthyosis vulgaris. Occurring with a prevalence of 1:6000 males, it usually begins in the first few months of life and is appreciable in affected individuals by age 1. The scaling is most severe on the extensor surfaces, but also commonly affects flexural regions. The ears, neck, and scalp are frequently affected. Palms and soles are normal. The scales tend to be large and dark because of the oxidation of keratin. Atopy occurs rarely and keratosis pilaris is not associated. Posterior corneal opacities may be seen on slit lamp examination in affected males and, less often, in female carriers. Light microscopy reveals a thickened stratum corneum, a normal to slightly thickened granular layer, acanthosis with prominent rete ridges, and a slight perivascular lymphocytic infiltrate. Electron microscopic studies reveal a normal or slightly increased number of keratohyaline granules.

The disease is closely linked to the Xg blood type and affected males have a deficiency in arylsulfatase C and steroid sulfatase. Steroid sulfatase is an enzyme that removes the sulfate group from the 3-position of steroids and sterols. Reduced levels have been found in cultured fibroblasts and peripheral leukocytes in patients with X-linked ichthyosis. Cholesterol sulfate is one of the natural substrates for steroid sulfatase and has been noted to be increased in patients with the disease. Because cholesterol sulfate is found primarily in the low-density lipoprotein fraction of plasma, a rapidly migrating LDL band on serum protein electrophoresis is a diagnostic test for X-linked ichthyosis. Steroid sulfatase has also been shown to be deficient in cultured amniotic fluid cells from fetuses with X-linked ichthyosis; testing for this deficiency may aid in prenatal diagnosis, in addition to fetoscopy and fetal skin biopsy. The functional importance of cholesterol sulfate and steroid sulfatase in the physiology of the skin is unknown. There have been suggestions that in X-linked ichthyosis, increased amounts of cholesterol sulfate may act as a glue, holding the stratum corneum together so that excessive scale is retained.

Lamellar ichthyosis, or nonbullous ichthyosiform erythroderma, usually manifests itself at birth. Affected infants may be born encased in a collodion membrane, a tight, nonpliable film of stratum corneum that may evert the lower eyelids and lips, causing ectropion and eclabion, respectively. Most collodion babies have lamellar ichthyosis, but a collodion membrane may precede X-linked ichthyosis or, rarely, ichthyosis vulgaris. In lamellar ichthyosis, the membrane usually desquamates in 10 to 14 days and is replaced by generalized, large, parchmentlike scales, with associated erythema of the skin and fissuring of the hands and feet. Flexural creases are not spared. Hair is sparse and bound down by scale. Occasionally the scalp develops a scarring alopecia secondary to recurrent infection. Nails have ridges and grooves. Heat intolerance is often a problem for these patients and results from obstruction of sweat glands. An abnormal odor may occur because of excessive scale. Nutritional requirements are high in early childhood. The process is lifelong, remaining relatively constant or worsening with age.

Histologically, this skin has hyperkeratosis with focal parakeratosis, a normal to slightly thickened granular layer, acanthosis, and follicular plugging. There may be a patchy inflammatory infiltrate in the upper dermis. Electron microscopy shows increased numbers of keratinosomes and an increase in intercellular substance. Reportedly, there is also a decreased number of Langerhans cells. The defect in this disorder is unclear but appears to be in the epidermis, as demonstrated by graft studies on nude mice. Studies of epidermal kinetics suggest a hyperproliferative state.

Epidermolytic hyperkeratosis, also called bullous congenital ichthyosiform erythroderma, is inherited as an autosomal dominant trait and starts at or shortly after birth, with erythematous, moist skin that blisters easily. Bullae present at birth are due to shearing of the superficial epidermis as the infant passes through the birth canal. As the stratum corneum reforms, the skin becomes scaly and dry. A verrucous appearance with furrowed hyperkeratosis is characteristic in the flexural areas and on the elbows and knees, or the entire cutaneous surface may be involved. The scales are usually dark and patients may have an unpleasant odor. Blistering occurs most commonly in childhood and may recur in adult life in approximately 20% of patients. Healing of the bullae results in temporarily normal-appearing skin. Hair is usually normal, but nails may be ridged. Bacterial infection is a common problem for these patients.

The histology of the skin shows variable hyperkeratosis, papillomatosis, and acanthosis with a distinctive vacuolization of the granular and upper spinous cell layers. There may be an increased number of large, irregularly shaped keratohyaline granules in the thickened granular cell layer. Within cells of the granular and upper malpighian layers, electron microscopic studies have shown large areas of perinuclear endoplasmic reticulum associated with abundant ribosomes and mitochondria. Tonofilaments are also increased. Fetal skin biopsy has established this diagnosis by 20 weeks' gestation. Epidermolytic hyperkeratosis is also associated with hyperproliferation of the epidermis. Vacuolization of epidermal cells is due to intracellular edema. Metabolic defects have not yet been identified.

Erythrokeratoderma variabilis is an autosomal dominantly inherited disease in which angular, arcuate, gyrate, and circinate erythematous scaly plaques are noted at birth or shortly thereafter. The plaques may begin as urticarial lesions and migrate slowly over a period of days. The disease tends to persist throughout life, with exacerbations and remissions. Pregnancy, temperature changes, and trauma are common exacerbating factors. The histologic changes are not specific. There is hyperkeratosis, irregular acanthosis, variable dermal edema, and a variable inflammatory infiltrate. Pathogenesis is not known.

Harlequin fetus, inherited by an autosomal recessive trait, is clinically the most severe form of ichthyosis, presenting at birth with thick armorlike scale composed of plaques up to 4 to 5 cm on a side in a diamondlike configuration. It is associated with massive eclabion, ectropion, absent pinnae, and gangrene of the terminal phalanges. Death usually occurs within the first few weeks of life, although one infant has been reported to survive and develop at least to the age of 5 months by treatment with etretinate and general supportive measures. Prenatal diagnosis is possible by skin biopsy, which reveals extreme hyperkeratosis, a grossly deficient or absent granular layer, and plugging of eccrine sweat ducts and sebaceous follicles by hyperkeratotic debris. Biochemical abnormalities in keratin manufacture or epidermal lipid metabolism have been proposed as pathogenic factors.

Several syndromes of ichthyosis occur in association with neurologic disease. **Refsum's disease** is a multisystem disorder inherited as an autosomal recessive trait, and is due to a deficiency of phytanic acid alpha-hydroxylase that results in an accumulation of phytanic acid. The diagnosis may be confirmed by elevated levels of phytanic acid in the triglyceride portion of the serum lipids. The syndrome usually involves mild scaling of the skin, resembling that of ichthyosis vulgaris. Histologically there is hyperkeratosis with a reduced granular cell layer containing normal keratohyaline. Associated features include night blindness secondary to atypical retinitis pigmentosa, peripheral neuropathy, cerebellar ataxia, cataracts, bone abnormalities, and other neurologic defects such as deafness, anosmia, miosis, and poor pupillary reactions. Cerebrospinal fluid protein is elevated without pleocytosis. Therapy consists of avoidance of dietary phytanic acid. **Sjögren-Larsson's syndrome,** inherited by an autosomal recessive trait, consists of lamellar ichthyosis, retinal changes, spastic paralysis, oligophrenia, mental retardation, epilepsy, speech defects, and dental and skeletal abnormalities. Skin biopsy reveals hyperkeratosis and a normal granular cell layer. Pathogenesis is unknown. **Rud's syndrome** is a rare congenital syndrome consisting of mild to moderately severe ichthyosis, acanthosis nigricans, hyperhidrosis of the palms and soles, infantilism, small stature, hypogonadism, epilepsy, alopecia, deformed teeth, polyneuritis, tetany, macrocytic anemia, and variable mental retardation. Skin biopsy shows hyperkeratosis, hypergranulosis, irregular acanthosis, and papillomatosis. A metabolic defect has not been identified.

Ichthyosis may also occur with hair abnormalities. **Netherton's syndrome** is an autosomal recessive disorder presenting with ichthyosis and abnormal hair. Migratory polycyclic and gyrate scaly areas, known as ichthyosis linearis circumflexa, are seen. The degree of skin involvement is variable, with prominent erythema even in nonscaly areas. Lamellar-type ichthyosis has also been described in these patients. Histology shows acanthosis, hyperkeratosis, focal parakeratosis, and amorphous material in the spinous cells. Hair is short and fragile because of hair shaft abnormalities known as trichorrhexis nodosa. Partial remission of skin lesions has been achieved with PUVA. The **IBIDS syndrome** consists of ichthyosis, brittle hair, intellectual impairment, decreased fertility, and short stature. Patients have brawny scales on the trunk with variable erythema, and large polygonal tan-colored scales particulary on the extensor surfaces of the limbs. Small, adherent scales may be present on the palms and soles, as well as on the dorsal surfaces of the hands and feet. Nails are thickened, with subungual keratin accumulation. Hair shafts from these patients reveal disordered cuticular scales on scanning electron microscopy, alternate dark and bright banding on polarizing light microscopy, and low sulfur content on biochemical testing. Photosensitivity may be a further feature of this syndrome, therefore leading to a new acronym: PIBIDS.

Other rare ichthyosiform disorders have been described. The **CHILD syndrome** is an acronym for congenital hemidysplasia, ichthyosiform erythroderma, and limb defects. A sharply delineated unilateral ichthyosiform erythroderma is seen at birth or within the first few weeks of life, associated with ipsilateral limb defects varying from hypoplasia of the fingers to the absence of limbs. The disorder may be caused by an X-linked dominant trait that is lethal in males. The **KID syndrome** is an acronym for keratitis, ichthyosis, and deafness. Mild scaling and exaggerated skin markings with discrete erythematous plaques of the face, extremities, and trunk are present. Scarring alopecia and nail dystrophy are also frequently noted. Patients may develop a keratitis with neovascularization and a variety of neuromuscular abnormalities. Severe combined immunodeficiency associated with micromelic dwarfism and ichthyosis has been described in 10 patients in the literature.

Acquired ichthyosis, with onset in adult life, is clinically and histologically similar to ichthyosis vulgaris. It is frequently associated with lymphomas, especially Hodgkin's disease, but has also been associated with multiple myeloma, carcinoma of the lung, breast, or cervix, Kaposi's sarcoma, and leiomyosarcoma. The ichthyosis often remits with the treatment of the malignancy. Drugs may also produce an acquired ichthyosis, particularly those affecting cholesterol metabolism (such as triparanol, nicotinic acid, dixyrazine, and butyrophenones). Ichthyosis has also been seen with sarcoidosis, leprosy, systemic lupus erythematosus, and chronic malnutrition.

The mainstay of **treatment** of any ichthyosis is hydration of scale, facilitating its mechanical removal. Patients, especially those with ichthyosis vulgaris and X-linked ichthyosis, improve considerably if they regularly apply an ointment such as petrolatum immediately after a daily bath or shower in lukewarm water. Creams containing urea are presumed to bind water and may be helpful for some patients. In addition, keratolytic agents topically applied to the skin can diminish corneocyte adhesion and decrease scaling. The most commonly used keratolytic agents contain propylene glycol, salicylic acid, or lactic acid.

Oral synthetic retinoids have dramatic effects in some ichthyoses. Etretinate has been used in lamellar ichthyosis, X-linked ichthyosis, epidermolytic hyperkeratosis, and erythrokeratoderma variabilis. Isotretinoin has also been used in lamellar ichthyosis and erythrokeratoderma variabilis. Unfortunately, improvement in the ichthyosis is maintained only during administration of the drug, which is associated with many serious acute and chronic adverse affects, such as teratogenicity, night blindness, bone spurs, and premature closure of the epiphyses. The usefulness of oral retinoids in controlling lifelong disease is therefore limited.

Aram H: Acquired ichthyosis and related conditions. *Int J Dermatol.* 1984;23:458–465.
Review of etiologic factors associated with the onset of ichthyosis in adulthood.

Dykes PJ, Marks R: Acquired ichthyosis: Multiple causes for an acquired generalized disturbance in desquamation. *Br J Dermatol.* 1977;97:327–334.
Detailed study of four patients with acquired ichthyosis. Clinically these patients' signs and symptoms resembled those of ichthyosis vulgaris. No single clinical association or biochemical defect was found.

Epstein EH Jr., Krauss RM, Shackleton CH: X-linked ichthyosis: Increased blood cholesterol sulfate and electrophoretic mobility of low density lipoproteins. *Science.* 1981;214:659–660.
Classic study defining a reliable test for the metabolic defect in X-linked ichthyosis.

Epstein EH Jr., Williams ML, Elias PM: Biochemical abnormalities in the ichthyoses. *Curr Probl Dermatol.* 1987;17:32–44.
Most recently published review of the rapidly evolving understanding of the pathogenetic bases for inherited scaling disorders.

Golbus MS, Sagebiel RW, Filly RA, et al.: Prenatal diagnosis of congenital bullous ichthyosiform erythroderma (epidermolytic hyperkeratosis) by fetal skin biopsy. *N Engl J Med.* 1980;302:93–95.
First clinically helpful use of a fetal skin biopsy in utero.

Jorizzo JL, Crounse RG, Wheeler CE Jr.: Lamellar ichthyosis, dwarfism, mental retardation, and hair shaft abnormalities. A link between the ichthyosis-associated and BIDS syndromes. *J Am Acad Dermatol.* 1980;2:309–317.
Report of a case and review of the classification of ichthyoses associated with other neuroectodermal and mesodermal defects. One syndrome in this group may be delineated by the finding of low sulfur content in the hair.

Langer K, Konrad K, Wolff K: Keratitis, ichthyosis and deafness (KID)-syndrome: Report of three cases and a review of the literature. *Br J Dermatol.* 1990;122:689–697.
Etretinate therapy was of little value in any of these patients. Early audiologic, ophthalmologic, and medical evaluation and follow-up are necessary in those with the KID-syndrome.

Lawlor F, Peiris S: Harlequin fetus successfully treated with etretinate. *Br J Dermatol.* 1985;112:585–590.
Etretinate and supportive measures allowed this child to survive through the neonatal period. She was continuing to develop at 5 months, at the time of this report.

Rand RE, Baden HP: The ichthyoses—a review. *J Am Acad Dermatol.* 1983;8:285–305.
Substantive review with extensive reference list.

Rappaport IP, Goldes JA, Goltz RW: Erythrokeratoderma variabilis treated with isotretinoin. *Arch Dermatol.* 1986;122:441–445.
A case report with thorough clinical, histologic, and ultrastructural evaluation, documenting the response to isotretinoin.

19. SEBORRHEIC DERMATITIS
Sewon Kang

Seborrheic dermatitis is a common skin eruption characterized by erythema and scaling with a distinctive distribution over the scalp, face, and upper trunk. More common in males, it occurs after puberty, and the incidence increases with age. It has been observed in varying degrees in patients with Parkinson's disease, mental retardation, and other neurologic disorders. Use of certain medications, particularly neuroleptics, has also been associated with the rash.

The **clinical features** of seborrheic dermatitis include prominent scaling and mild to moderate erythema of the underlying skin. The patient is asymptomatic or complains of mild itching or burning. The scales feel greasy and are slightly yellowish in color. Frank exudation or pustules may be present. In the beard area especially, the eruption frequently involves the hair follicle, and a pustular folliculitis develops, which, when severe, leads to destruction of follicles and scarring. The extent of skin involvement varies widely. Seborrheic dermatitis is usually localized to one or a few sites. It may also involve the entire body surface, and is, therefore, one of the causes of chronic generalized exfoliative dermatitis. Typical areas of involvement include the scalp, face, presternal and interscapular areas, suprapubic skin, inframammary folds, and flexural creases. Paranasal involvement is characteristic. The eyebrows and periauricular skin are also commonly affected. Blepharitis and otitis externa are common complications.

The **pathology** of seborrheic dermatitis is not diagnostic. Histologic features of both psoriasis and chronic dermatitis are usually present. Some acanthosis of the epidermis with mild to moderate elongation of rete ridges is usually noted. Focal parakeratosis in the horny layer may be associated with the presence of pyknotic neutrophils similar to those seen in the Munro microabscesses of psoriasis. Unlike psoriasis, however, slight intracellular edema and spongiosis are often appreciated.

The **etiology** of seborrheic dermatitis is not known. Possible pathogenic factors include abnormal sebaceous gland activity, infection, and neurologic dysfunction. Abnormalities of sebaceous glands have been implicated primarily because of the distribution of the eruption in sites with a predominance of large glands. Although maturation of sebaceous glands or increased gland activity may be a factor in the development of the dermatitis, excessive production of sebum (seborrhea) has not been documented. Quantitative studies of the sebum excretion rate have shown normal to even decreased levels in young individuals with seborrheic dermatitis. In addition, studies of the composition of sebum have not demonstrated significant qualitative abnormalities.

An infectious etiology for seborrheic dermatitis has been postulated since the disease was first described in 1904. Many studies have recovered great quantities of bacteria and yeasts from affected and, in some patients, unaffected skin sites. Isolation from accumulated greasy scale of various microorganisms including *Candida albicans, Staphylococcus aureus,* and *Pityrosporum* species may, however, represent secondary local colonization rather than a primary pathogenic event. Recently, *Pityrosporum ovale,* a lipophilic yeast, has received much attention as a possible etiologic agent. The ability of *P. ovale* to activate the alternate complement pathway in vitro is often cited as its means to induce inflammation and possibly desquamation. Animal and human studies involving topical application of a suspension of *Pityrosporum* species have shown skin changes suggestive of seborrheic dermatitis or psoriasis, and folliculitis. The follicular inflammation was observed only in those with a history of seborrheic dermatitis involving hair follicles, and not in controls or those with seborrheic dermatitis without folliculitis, suggesting a role for host susceptibility. Clinical studies with both oral and topical ketoconazole, an imidazole effective against the organism, have shown treatment successes. A definitive role for *P. ovale* is not clear, however, since its numbers may be decreased by other antiyeast preparations without significant improvement in the eruption.

A number of hypotheses relating neurologic aberration to the development of seborrheic dermatitis have been suggested. Neurotransmitters, such as those produced in the dopaminergic system, may be involved. The hypothalamus may control production or release of sebotrophic hormones. Melanocyte-stimulating hormone has also been hypothesized to be a sebum regulator. To date, none of these theories have been substantiated.

The **differential diagnosis** of seborrheic dermatitis is often directed by the sites of involvement. On hairless skin of the face, scaling and erythema occur predominantly in the malar region. Although seborrheic dermatitis is the most common cause of a butterfly rash, systemic lupus erythematosus and acne rosacea are often suspected. The presence of scales in the eyebrows and periauricular areas and the absence of telangiectasia, atrophy, and pustules are highly suggestive or typical of seborrheic dermatitis. Dermatomyositis, perioral dermatitis, contact dermatitis, pemphigus foliaceus, pemphigus erythematosus, necrotizing migratory erythema of glucagonoma syndrome, acrodermatitis enteropathica, and eruptions associated with photosensitivity can also mimic seborrheic dermatitis in the malar region. In addition, scales may occur in an annular pattern, suggesting tinea faciale, a dermatophyte infection.

Psoriasis is frequently considered in the differential diagnosis of seborrheic dermatitis, especially when the scalp is involved. Psoriatic plaques tend to be thick and well demarcated, with a striking pink-purple color beneath thick micaceous scaling in contrast to the thin, poorly demarcated, and mildly erythematous plaques of seborrheic dermatitis. Features of both disorders may coexist, however, making definitive diagnosis difficult. The clinical appearance of the eruption is generally more useful than the distribution, since both favor the same locations. Even involvement of intertriginous areas can be confusing since psoriasis inversus, which characteristically and by definition is found in those sites, is not uncommon. Erythema and scaling resembling seborrheic dermatitis in the inframammary folds and other intertriginous areas may also be a manifestation of dermatophyte infection, candidiasis, or erythrasma. The diagnosis of seborrheic dermatitis therefore requires a detailed history of personal and familial skin disease, neurologic disease, and medication, as well as an examination of the entire cutaneous surface, a microscopic examination of scrapings of scale prepared with KOH, and a Wood's lamp examination.

A seborrheic-like dermatitis, more or less distinct from typical seborrheic dermatitis, may occur in association with systemic disease. In particular, seborrheic-like dermatitis is one of the most common cutaneous manifestations of **acquired immunodeficiency syndrome**, with a prevalence approaching 85%. The eruption is usually indistinguishable clinically from that of typical seborrheic dermatitis, although it may be more extensive and often severe. However, it differs histologically and may therefore represent a distinct entity. In AIDS patients, spotty keratinocyte necrosis, leukoexocytosis, and a superficial perivascular infiltrate of plasma cells are prominent, a pattern more reminiscent of a graft-versus-host reaction than seborrheic dermatitis. Severity of the eruption in AIDS patients correlated with their prognosis in one study.

Infantile seborrheic dermatitis is a variant most frequently seen in infants about 1 month of age. Whether it is analogous to the seborrheic dermatitis seen in adults is unclear. As in the adult form there is no established relationship with seborrhea or even sebum, although sebaceous glands are active in infancy because of stimulation from maternal androgens. Other proposed pathogenic factors include infectious agents whose etiologic role remains unresolved. Nutritional factors have also been suspected; however, careful studies have not been able to support incrimination of biotin or essential fatty acid deficiencies as causative factors.

Infantile seborrheic dermatitis is characterized by confluent erythematous, scaly patches in the scalp, diaper area, and flexural creases. Diffuse scalp involvement, especially over the vertex, is referred to as cradle cap. The scale is characteristically adherent and greasy with minimal underlying inflammation. Tiny vesicles, milia, and comedones may also be present. The infant is otherwise healthy with no disturbance of feeding or sleep, and little evidence of pruritus. The eruption resolves spontaneously in 1 to 2 months.

Differentiating infantile seborrheic dermatitis from atopic dermatitis according to the morphology of the cutaneous eruption alone may be very difficult. Involvement of skin in the axillae tends to favor seborrheic dermatitis, whereas involvement of the forearms and shins is more common in atopic dermatitis. Eruption solely in the diaper area also favors the diagnosis of seborrheic dermatitis. Although difficult to assess in this age, pruritus is considered unusual in seborrheic dermatitis, but typical in atopic dermatitis. A family history of atopy and the age of onset of skin lesions are of little value. Unlike seborrheic dermatitis, however, atopic dermatitis tends to persist beyond infancy. Although not commonly done, measuring serum immunoglobulin E (total or antigen-specific) may be very useful in differentiating difficult cases. It is generally normal in patients with seborrheic dermatitis but increased with atopic dermatitis. Other diseases to consider in the differential diagnosis include primary irritant diaper dermatitis, psoriasis, scabies, and histiocytosis X. All of these diseases, as well as bullous and nonbullous forms of icthyosis, staphylococcal scalded skin syndrome, Kawasaki's disease, and diffuse mastocytosis, can cause erythroderma in infancy. Seborrheic dermatitis–like eruptions are also noted in infants with congenital immunodeficiency syndromes or AIDS. Making a definitive diagnosis may require months of observation and study.

Fortunately, in only a very few infants does seborrheic dermatitis of the scalp, face, and diaper area progress to a generalized exfoliative dermatitis known as **Leiner's syndrome**. Rarely the syndrome presents abruptly as an erythroderma. Usually seen in infants under 4 months of age, the eruption is accompanied by generalized lymphadenopathy and severe recalcitrant diarrhea. Anemia and hypogammaglobulinemia are frequent concomitant findings. The patients have an unusual susceptibility to infection with a variety of organisms, especially gram-negative bacteria. The etiology remains unknown, although immunodeficiency has been suggested. A similar clinical picture has been described in a familial disorder with a functional defect in the fifth component of complement. The immunodeficient features of Leiner's syndrome have not been definitively linked to C5 deficiency, and an equivocal clinical response is seen with administration of fresh plasma. Although the course of Leiner's syndrome may be relatively benign in some infants, dehydration, fever, and failure to thrive are not infrequent sequelae. Death was not rare in the preantibiotic era.

Numerous **treatment** regimens for seborrheic dermatitis have been described to date. Agents vary in terms of their presumed mechanisms of action. In general, anti-inflammatory, anti-mycotic, and keratolytic agents are used.

For scaly scalp, shampoos containing selenium sulfide and zinc pyrithione are the mainstay of therapy. For maximal effectiveness, lathered shampoo should be left on the scalp for 5 to 10 minutes before rinsing. Treatment 2 or 3 times a week is usually adequate therapy. Shampoos containing tar, chloroxine, and surfactants can also diminish the scaling and erythema. These agents are probably keratolytic and anti-mycotic. Removal of thick, adherent crusts is facilitated by several applications of keratolytic agents such as Baker's P & S liquid or Dermasmoothe under occlusion overnight before shampooing in the morning. Salicylic acid, in Keralyt gel, may also be helpful. Application of topical corticosteroid creams is not effective unless the scale has first been removed.

Topical corticosteroid preparations have assumed a central role in the treatment of seborrheic dermatitis in areas other than the scalp. Very low potency agents such as 0.5% or 1% hydrocortisone cream are effective in most patients. Use of potent corticosteroids is unwarranted both because they are not needed and because they cause atrophy and telangiectasia, especially on the face and in the intertriginous areas. Tar preparations and topical creams containing sulfur have also been used successfully. Clinical studies of ketoconazole have shown efficacy. Oral administration has serious potential adverse effects; however, topical application is safe and is considered by some to be the treatment of choice, especially for dermatitis located in areas prone to develop the adverse effects of corticosteroids.

Variants of seborrheic dermatitis may be difficult to treat. The seborrheic-like dermatitis seen in patients with AIDS responds poorly to conventional therapies. While limited infantile seborrheic dermatitis generally resolves spontaneously, cradle cap can be treated with repeated applications of vegetable oil or petrolatum to a wet scalp, followed in several hours by lathering with a mild shampoo or soap. In generalized erythrodermic seborrheic dermatitis, PUVA therapy has been shown to be beneficial. Patients with Leiner's disease may require systemic corticosteroid therapy (of questionable effectiveness) and in-hospital supportive care.

Arndt KA: Seborrheic dermatitis and dandruff. In: *Manual of Dermatologic Therapeutics*, 4th ed. Boston, MA: Little, Brown & Co.; 1989: Chap. 28.

  A variety of treatment regimens are specified.

Bergbrant IM, Faergemann J: The role of *Pityrosporum ovale* in seborrheic dermatitis. *Semin Dermatol.* 1990;9:262–268.

No significant difference is present in the number of P. ovale *in patients compared with controls, or between healthy and lesional skin.*

Binder RL, Jonelis FJ: Seborrheic dermatitis in neuroleptic-induced parkinsonism. *Arch Dermatol.* 1983;119:473–475.
The association of neuroleptic-induced parkinsonism and seborrheic dermatitis is discussed.

Clift DC, Dodd HJ, Kirby JD, et al.: Seborrheic dermatitis and malignancy. An investigation of the skin flora. *Acta Derm Venereol* (Stockh). 1988;68:48–52.
No significant difference in skin flora, including Pityrosporum *species, was detected among patients with disseminated malignant disease and seborrheic dermatitis, otherwise healthy subjects with seborrheic dermatitis, and controls. Immunosuppression does not appear to provide uninhibited growth of microorganisms.*

Eisenstat BA, Wormser GP: Seborrheic dermatitis and butterfly rash in AIDS. *N Engl J Med.* 1984;311:189.
A letter that first suggested an association of the two diseases.

Farr GP, Schuster S: The response of seborrheic dermatitis to ketoconazole. *Br J Dermatol.* 1984;111:603–607.
Clinical trial using oral ketoconazole for seborrheic dermatitis. Pityrosporum *species suggested as the etiologic organism.*

Goodfield IJD, Saiham EM, Crowley J: Experimental folliculitis with *Pityrosporum orbiculare:* the influence of host response. *Acta Derm Venereol* (Stockh). 1987;67:445–447.
Interesting human study suggesting host factor as a determinant in the pathogenesis of seborrheic dermatitis with folliculitis.

Mathes BM, Douglass MC: Seborrheic dermatitis in patients with acquired immunodeficiency syndrome. *J Am Acad Dermatol.* 1985;13:947–951.
Clinical features of seborrheic dermatitis in this population are discussed. Correlation of severity of the eruption with overall prognosis is suggested.

Perniciaro C, Peters MS: Tinea faciale mimicking seborrheic dermatitis in a patient with AIDS. *N Engl J Med.* 1986;314:315–316.
The need for KOH preparation for complete evaluation of scaly eruption is stressed.

Schuster S: The etiology of dandruff and the mode of action of therapeutic agents. *Br J Dermatol.* 1984;111:235–242.
Commentary from the most outspoken supporter of Pityrosporum *species as the pathogen of seborrheic dermatitis.*

Skinner RB, Noah PW, Taylor RM, et al.: Double blind treatment of seborrheic dermatitis with 2% ketoconazole cream. *J Am Acad Dermatol.* 1985;12:852–856.
Efficacy of the topical imidazole without notable side effects is shown.

Soeprono FF, Schinella RA, Cockerell CJ, et al.: Seborrheic-like dermatitis of acquired immunodeficiency syndrome. A clinicopathologic study. *J Am Acad Dermatol.* 1986;14:242–248.
Convincing study presenting histologic evidence for the unique nature of this eruption in AIDS.

Yates VM, Kerr RE, MacKie RM: Early diagnosis of infantile seborrheic dermatitis and atopic dermatitis—clinical features. *Br J Dermatol.* 1983;108:633–638.
A good discussion describing clinical features that may nor may not help distinguish the two rather similar infantile skin eruptions.

20. PSORIASIS
Christopher R. Shea

Psoriasis is a chronic, scaling, inflammatory dermatosis of unknown etiology. It has a prevalence of about 1% in the United States. The peak age of onset is the second decade, but psoriasis may first appear at any age from infancy to the aged. The extreme variability of the clinical spectrum of psoriasis makes its precise demographic assessment difficult. The term "psoriasis" is derived from the Greek *psora,* meaning "itch." Most patients complain of itch, despite the common statement in textbooks that psoriasis is not pruritic.

Genetic factors play a significant role in the **pathogenesis** of psoriasis, but the mode of inheritance is not simple and the expression of the disease is highly variable. A positive family history can be elicited in about one-third of patients, and there is a high rate of concordance in monozygotic twins. An increased prevalence of the major histocompatibility haplotype HLA-Cw6, as well as of other HLA types, through linkage disequilibrium, has been noted. In addition, patients with psoriatic arthritis have a strong tendency to express HLA-B27. It also occurs sporadically, perhaps because of frequent spontaneous mutations. Extrinsic factors are also important, perhaps as triggers in patients who are genetically susceptible. External trauma can induce local lesions of psoriasis (the Koebner or isomorphic phenomenon). Streptococcal infections such as pharyngitis frequently precede eruptive small-plaque psoriasis, called guttate psoriasis. A variety of drugs such as lithium carbonate and beta-adrenergic antagonists can precipitate or worsen psoriasis. Patients frequently complain that psychological stress causes flares of disease activity. Thus psoriasis is best considered a multifactorial disease with a strong genetic component.

The **primary cutaneous lesion** is a sharply circumscribed, erythematous papule or plaque surmounted by a thick, silvery, or micaceous scale. Removal of scale may lead to the appearance of pinpoint foci of bleeding (positive Auspitz sign), due to the thinness of the epidermis overlying hypervascular dermal papillae. A whitish macular halo may be present at the periphery of lesions (ring of Woronoff). Although characteristically occurring on the scalp, elbows, knees, and buttocks, lesions can be present on any region of the body. Nail involvement including pitting, yellowish-brown discoloration (an "oil stain"), and frank dystrophy with distal onycholysis and subungual debris is frequent. Oral involvement is uncommon, although lingua geographica (geographic tongue) may occur. Patients with psoriasis have a markedly irregular course. Although some patients have a few lesions continuously, most experience long remissions punctuated by exacerbations of widely varying duration and severity.

Psoriasis has many clinical variations. In psoriasis inversa, lesions are localized mainly in flexural areas, such as the groin, axillae, and inframammary skin, rather than in typical extensor regions. The plaques are often macerated, with little scale. In pustular psoriasis, inflammation predominates: small, sterile pustules appear, often at the periphery of active lesions, and tend to coalesce into lakes of pus. Pustular psoriasis can be localized—for example, to the palms and soles (Barber form)—or it may become generalized. Patients with generalized acute pustular psoriasis (von Zumbusch variety) appear toxic, with high fever, leukocytosis, vascular instability, and hypocalcemia, and they can die from metabolic imbalance. Their course may also be complicated by septicemia secondary to impaired cutaneous barrier function. Not rare, but also serious, the generalized erythrodermic form of psoriasis presents with total-body erythema and exfoliation.

Histopathologic examination of a skin biopsy of a typical lesion of psoriasis reveals parakeratosis, hyperkeratosis, absence of the stratum granulosum, acanthosis with regular elongation of rete ridges, thinning of the suprapapillary plates, and tortuous, dilated capillaries within edematous, club-shaped dermal papillae. A sparse, perivascular mixed inflammatory infiltrate is present, and frequently there are focal collections of neutrophils within the stratum corneum and stratum malpighii (the Munro microabscesses and spongiform pustules of Kogoj, respectively). In pustular psoriasis, collections of neutrophils in the epidermis are extensive, and dominate the histologic appearance. Because of its histologic appearance, psoriasis was viewed for many years as a primary disorder of epidermal hyperproliferation; this view was corroborated by studies documenting an increased labeling index in mitotic cells and an increased transit time through the viable epidermis and stratum corneum. More recent work has emphasized the roles of dermal-epidermal interactions and inflammatory cells. In a skin-equivalent model, psoriatic fibroblasts can induce hyperproliferation of normal keratinocytes. Cytokines and lymphocyte-keratinocyte interactions on epidermal hyperproliferation are currently being vigorously investigated. Many effective treatments for psoriasis, such as phototherapy, corticosteroids, methotrexate, and cyclosporine, may work in part by affecting the immunologic and inflammatory components of the disease.

The **differential diagnosis** of psoriasis vulgaris includes eczema, pityriasis rubra pilaris, seborrheic dermatitis, tinea, syphilis, Bowen's disease, lupus erythematosus, cutaneous T cell lymphoma, and parapsoriasis. Psoriasiform drug reactions sometimes represent the unmasking of a true psoriatic diathesis in susceptible patients. Erythrodermic psoriasis may be indistinguishable from Sézary syndrome, widespread seborrheic dermatitis, drug reactions, or extensive eczema. Pustular variants raise the differential diagnosis of Reiter's syndrome, pustular drug eruptions, acrodermatitis continua of Hallopeau, subcorneal pustulosis of Sneddon-Wilkinson, septicemia, and inflammatory candidiasis or tinea. Biopsy can be helpful in diagnosis, particularly to exclude parapsoriasis, cutaneous T cell lymphomas, and lupus erythematosus. Special stains may be done on tissue sections to exclude infection. Nonspecific laboratory abnormalities that may be seen in psoriasis include hyperuricemia in about one-third of patients, anemia correlating with the extent and severity of skin involvement, and elevated acute-phase reactants.

Treatments of psoriasis must be undertaken with the realization that it is a lifelong disease with marked variability. The goal is to control the disease the patient currently exhibits. Education is important so that patients can understand the disease and participate in decisions about treatment, much of which is more troublesome or has greater morbidity than the disease itself. Physical trauma or cutaneous irritation, e.g., from dryness or sunburn, should be avoided as lesions may be precipitated. Mild cases may be controlled with bland emollients, intermittent use of occlusive dressings, and judicious exposure to sunlight. Topical corticosteroids are very helpful in limited, early disease, but are less acceptable in widespread disease because of nuisance and expense, and have significant potential for local and even systemic adverse effects if abused. Intralesional steroids are effective in localized disease. Topical preparations of anthralin (dithranol) cause rapid thinning of thick plaques, but they are messy, tend to stain the skin, and may cause irritation. Topical keratolytics are helpful for densely hyperkeratotic lesions, both alone and for increasing the effectiveness of other topical therapy. Thick scale may also be manually debrided after good hydration. Topical tar treatments were widely used in the presteroid era, and may still be useful for a few patients.

Patients who cannot use topical remedies alone, usually because of widespread disease, are often started on ultraviolet phototherapy. Exposure to broad-spectrum UVB radiation (290–320 nm) is generally administered 2 or 3 times a week until clearance, and then less frequently as required for maintenance. The formerly common combination of UVB and topical tar (Goeckerman regimen) has been abandoned by many centers; the tar is not a photosensitizer at UVB wavelengths and probably works mainly as an emollient. UVB phototherapy is frequently effective, but can cause short-term toxicity from sunburn and has the long-term potential for causing "aging" changes in the skin and cutaneous carcinogenesis. Patients who fail to improve with UVB phototherapy may be candidates for photochemotherapy with PUVA, the combination of orally administered psoralen (methoxsalen) and exposure to UVA radiation (320–400 nm). PUVA is highly effective in clearing the skin and maintaining a lesion-free state. Adverse effects include nausea, pruritus, phototoxic reactions simulating sunburn, and an increased risk of squamous cell carcinoma of the skin. Patients must wear special dark glasses for 24 hours after ingesting methoxsalen, in order to prevent photoactivation of the drug in the eye, which may cause keratitis or early cataract formation. Recently, the use of a topical psoralen bath followed by UVA exposure has been studied.

Patients with severe psoriasis may require systemic therapy. Systemic steroids are almost never indicated: withdrawal of these agents frequently precipitates a flare of psoriasis, sometimes even life-threatening pustular psoriasis. Methotrexate given orally or intramuscularly at weekly intervals in doses of 5 to 25 mg will clear most patients' skin, but hepatic cirrhosis occurs with chronic administration and is dose-related. Serum liver function tests may be normal in early cirrhosis. Liver biopsies are mandatory after a cumulative dose of 1.5 g of methotrexate, and should be performed periodically with each additional gram thereafter, regardless of intervening drug-free intervals. Monitoring for bone marrow toxicity is also required. The synthetic retinoid etretinate is the treatment of choice for pustular and erythrodermic psoriasis. It is not helpful as monotherapy for psoriasis vulgaris; however, the combination of etretinate and PUVA is very effective. The side effects of etretinate include acute idiosyncratic hepatoxicity, soft-tissue calcification, and teratogenicity. Since etretinate is stored in tissue for years, it should not be prescribed for women who plan to become pregnant at any time in the future. Oral cyclosporine is highly effective but causes immunosuppression when used at high doses. The ideal oral dose is still being investigated, and topical formulations and intralesional injection are being studied. Some studies have shown that activated vitamin D and its analogues are useful in both topical and systemic formulations. Omega-3 fish oils improve the inflammation of psoriasis somewhat, but will not suffice as monotherapy for most patients.

Involvement of some sites with psoriasis requires special care. Topical steroids used on the face, flexural areas, and groin must be of low potency to avoid atrophy and stria formation. The treatment of the scalp is frequently problematic. UV phototherapy is usually not effective because the hair reduces optical penetration. Mild keratolytics (Dermasmoothe, Baker's P & S Oil) used under occlusion overnight, and daily shampoos with agents containing tar, salicylic acid, sulfur, or zinc can be helpful. Nail lesions of psoriasis are notoriously refractory to topical treatment; potent topical steroids or local irradiation with PUVA may occasionally work.

About 5% to 10% of psoriatic patients have an associated **arthritis**, which may appear at any age, although commonly in the fourth or fifth decade. Psoriatic arthritis may present with asymmetric, proximal involvement with or without tenosynovitis, symmetric polyarthritis similar to rheumatoid arthritis, predominant inflammatory involvement of distal interphalangeal joints, highly destructive arthritis mutilans with resorption of digits, or ankylosing spondylitis. The rheumatoid factor is usually negative. As with cutaneous psoriasis, the etiology of the arthritis is unknown, but both genetic and environmental factors appear to play a role. Psoriatic arthritis most commonly occurs in patients with severe cutaneous disease, especially with nail involvement. Usually cutaneous psoriasis precedes the development of arthritis. The management of psoriatic arthritis generally relies on the nonsteroidal anti-inflammatory agents. Theoretically there is a risk of worsening associated skin disease with these agents, but it is usually not a practical impediment. Intra-articular steroid injections, oral gold, immunosuppressive therapy, and surgery are used for treatment of difficult cases. Oral steroid therapy generally has no role in the management of psoriatic arthritis. Methotrexate and PUVA may control both arthritis and cutaneous disease, emphasizing the common pathophysiologic role of inflammation in both manifestations.

Bittiner SB, Tucker WFG, Cartwright I, et al.: A double-blind, randomized, placebo-controlled trial of fish oil in psoriasis. *Lancet.* 1988;1:378–380.
Oral use of eicosapentaenoic acid improves psoriasis, implying that arachidonic acid metabolites mediate in part the pathogenesis of the disease.
Bos JD: The pathomechanisms of psoriasis; the skin immune system and cyclosporin. *Br J Dermatol.* 1988;118:141–155.
Masterly review of cellular pathogenesis of psoriasis, with emphasis on the many possible sites of action of cyclosporine.
Elder JT, Fisher GJ, Lindquist PB, et al.: Overexposure of transforming growth factor-alpha in psoriatic epidermis. *Science.* 1989;243:811–814.
TGF-alpha, an analogue of epidermal growth factor, is overexpressed in the epidermis in psoriatic lesions when compared to normal skin or noninvolved skin in patients with psoriasis. It is hypothesized that TGF-alpha may mediate both keratinocytic hyperproliferation and angiogenesis in psoriasis.
Ellis CN, Gorsulowsky DC, Hamilton TA, et al.: Cyclosporine improves psoriasis in a double-blind study. *JAMA.* 1986;256:3110–3116.

Fully immunosuppressive doses (14 mg/kg/d) of oral cyclosporine melt psoriasis away.

Fry L: Psoriasis. *Br J Dermatol.* 1988;119:445–461.
Historical review that also discusses new findings on immunology of psoriasis.

Kragballe K, Beck MI, and Sogaard H: Improvement of psoriasis by a topical vitamin D₃ analogue (MC903) in a double-blind study. *Br J Dermatol.* 1988;119:223–230.
Seven of nine patients using a noncalciotrophic analogue of vitamin D₃ (100 μg/g of MC903 cream bid) showed moderate to excellent improvement.

Saiag P, Coulomb B, Lebreton C, et al.: Psoriatic fibroblasts induce hyperproliferation of normal keratinocytes in a skin equivalent model in vitro. *Science.* 1985;230:669–672.
Elegant experiments show the role of the fibroblast in modulating epidermal proliferation.

Updike J: At war with my skin. *New Yorker.* 2 Sept. 1985;39ff.
A marvelous account of the celebrated author's personal experiences as one afflicted with severe psoriasis.

von Joost T, Bos JD, Henle F, et al.: Low-dose cyclosporin A in severe psoriasis. A double-blind study. *Br J Dermatol.* 1988;118:183–190.
At a mean dose of 5.6 mg/kg/d, oral cyclosporine significantly improves psoriasis. Mild hypertension and reversibly impaired renal function are the most important side effects.

Nickoloff BJ: The cytokine network in psoriasis. *Arch Dermatol.* 1991;127:871–884.
This article reviews the cytokine networks, the genes that produce cytokines and are regulated by cytokines, and suggests how studies can lead to new concepts about putative psoriasis gene mutations in keratinocytes, with induction of autoreactive T-lymphocytes. The author believes that epidermal gene mutations contribute to epidermal hyperplasia and psoriasis.

21. LICHEN PLANUS AND RELATED DISORDERS
Paul A. Bleicher

Lichenoid eruptions are a group of disorders that share similarities in clinical appearance or in histopathology. Lichenoid disorders have primary lesions described as violaceous, flat-topped, polygonal, shiny papules that histologically demonstrate an interface inflammatory cell infiltrate composed of lymphocytes arranged in a bandlike array in the papillary dermis with basal cell liquefaction. The prototype lichenoid dermatitis is lichen planus, which displays both the histologic and the clinical features described here. When used without qualification, the term lichenoid can be ambiguous because it may refer to eruptions with either the clinical or the histologic features of lichen planus.

Lichen planus (LP) was first noted in 1869 by Erasmus Wilson, who described 50 typical cases of the disease. The disease is present throughout the world in all races, with incidence figures of less than 1% in healthy outpatients. The disease is rare at the extremes of ages; most patients are between 30 and 60 years old at the onset of the disease. It occurs in both sexes equally. Sporadic familial clusters of LP (1% to 2% of all cases) have motivated geneticists to evaluate HLA haplotype linkage disequilibriums in LP. The results were mixed, with one group demonstrating a significant increase in HLA-A3 and two other groups failing to show an HLA association. Other groups have shown increased HLA-B7 (10 familial cases) and HLA-A28 (in 22 Jewish patients). A strong and consistent HLA association is not evident.

LP is an immediately recognizable, distinctive, clinical entity that can also demonstrate a wide range of **clinical features**. The disease is manifested by the usually gradual onset of violaceous, polygonal, flat-topped, shiny papules distributed symmetrically on the flexor wrists and forearms, lumbar region, genitalia, and lateral and medial ankles and shins. Some lesions may demonstrate a fine lacy network, known as Wickham's striae, on the surface (made more readily visible when viewed through a film of mineral oil). The papules can be tiny or may coalesce into large plaques of hypertrophic tissue. In 30% to 80% of patients, oral mucous membrane involvement is shown as a characteristic reticulate white network on the buccal mucosa. In 15% to 25% of cases, the oral lesions are the only manifestation of the disease. Other mucous membranes may be similarly involved. Characteristically, a Koebner phenomenon can be seen in areas of trauma, with linear arrays of papules occurring over traumatized skin.

Many variations on LP lesions occur. Hypertrophic lesions are usually verrucous large plaques that can occur especially on the lower legs. The plantar surface is a common site for the development of ulcerative lesions. Acute inflammatory lesions of LP may develop central vesicles or bullae. This unusual manifestation of LP is distinguished from an LP variant, lichen planus pemphigoides, that displays tense bullae on involved and uninvolved skin with histology of LP and indirect immunofluorescence of bullous pemphigoid. Lesions of LP may be atrophic or follicular (as part of the syndrome lichen planopilaris). The individual lesions of LP may be arranged in annular, linear, or zosteriform configurations.

Two other areas of the body affected by LP are the scalp and nails. LP does not produce polygonal papules on the scalp, but rather leads to inflammatory destruction of the follicle with the production of an atrophic scarring alopecia. Nail involvement occurs in 6% to 10% of patients, with changes varying from mild thinning of the nail plate and minor nail disfigurement to severe atrophic destruction of the nails and formation of a pterygium.

The **clinical course** of LP can be as varied as the morphology of the lesions. Commonly, LP begins with the appearance of a small number of discrete lesions on the wrists or ankles followed by the development over 2 to 5 weeks of generalized involvement of the extremities and torso. The lesions usually subside within 9 months (50% of cases) to 18 months (85% of cases). The major symptom is pruritus, especially in hypertrophic lesions. Although this clinical course is characteristic, a significant number of patients either present with or more commonly resolve into a small number of hypertrophic or ulcerative lesions. A characteristic feature of LP is that resolving plaques often leave hyperpigmented macules that slowly resolve.

Other **variants** of LP are uncommon. Lichen planus erythematosus occurs in elderly patients and presents with erythematous papules on the forearms, minimal pruritus, and histologic changes of LP with vascular ectasia and collagen degeneration. Lichen planus actinicus is usually found on areas exposed to sunlight in young patients from tropical climates in the Middle and Far East, consisting of typical lesions of LP without pruritus or scalp or nail involvement. The lichen planus-lupus erythematosus overlap syndrome, or coexistent LP and LE, has been reported with lesions demonstrating both LE and LP histology, clinical appearance, and immunopathology. Lichen planopilaris (Lasseur-Graham-Little-Piccardi syndrome) is distinguished by a scarring alopecia of the scalp; perifollicular scaly lesions on the scalp and on other hair-bearing areas; and, sometimes, typical LP lesions elsewhere.

The typical case of LP is not easily mistaken for other disorders. The **differential diagnosis** includes drug-induced lichenoid eruptions, secondary syphilis, lichen simplex chronicus, psoriasis, lichen amyloidosis, lupus, and, occasionally, cutaneous malignancies. The mucosal lesions are less distinctive; candidiasis, leukoplakia, secondary syphilis, and blistering disorders must also be considered. Isolated lesions on the scalp, nails, penis, or palms and soles each have a separate list of differential diagnoses.

Lichenoid drug eruption is the name given to lesions that are clinically identical to LP lesions and that are produced by the ingestion of a variety of drugs (Table 21-1). Histologically these eruptions may be distinguished from LP lesions by the presence of focal parakeratosis and eosinophils in the dermal infiltrate. This type of drug reaction usually resolves slowly with the discontinuance of the inciting agent.

A special LP-like eruption has occurred as a contact reaction after exposure to color film developer, specifically *p*-phenylenediamine. After exposure to the chemical,

Table 21-1 Causes of lichenoid drug eruption

Cardiovascular	Methyl dopa, captopril, propranolol, labetolol
Antituberculotic	Isoniazid, ethambutol, p-amino salicylic acid
Diuretic	Hydrochlorothiazide, chlorothiazide, spironolactone
Antibiotic	Tetracycline, streptomycin
Antiarthritic	Gold, penicillamine
Hypoglycemic	Chlorpropamide, tolazeamide
Antisyphilitic	Arsenicals, mercury, iodides
Chemotherapeutic	Hydroxyurea, fluorouracil
Antiarrhythmic	Quinidine
Antipsychotic	Metropromazine, levopromazine
Antimalarial	Quinacrine, chloroquine, pyrimethamine
Respiratory stimulant	Amiphenazole

Source: Adapted from: Arndt, KA. Lichen planus-like eruptions. *Cutis.* 1971;8:353–357.

a skin reaction ranging from eczematous dermatitis to LP occurs on the exposed areas and can generalize. Other contactants that may give this type of reaction include tattoo pigments, nickel salt hydroxylamine hydrochloride, and isopropyl aminodiphenylamine. LP has recently been associated with a number of autoimmune diseases such as primary biliary cirrhosis, vitiligo, alopecia areata, myasthenia gravis, bullous pemphigoid, and ulcerative colitis. There is also an association with abnormal glucose tolerance and chronic active hepatitis. An association with hypertension in older patients with LP has been made.

Generalized lichenoid eruptions are frequently seen as one manifestation of **graft-versus-host disease** (GVHD). GVHD can develop when donor immunocompetent T lymphocytes are introduced into a host that is histoincompatible and unable to eliminate the foreign lymphocytes. This disease is most often seen in patients who have had an allogeneic bone marrow transplant. However, it can also be produced by transplacental transfer of maternal lymphocytes into an immunodeficient fetus by nonirradiated blood transfusion into immunoincompetent individuals. Paradoxically, a form of GVHD can be produced by autologous bone marrow replacement. Acute GVHD occurs within 3 months of bone marrow transplantation and is manifested by a generalized morbilliform eruption, often with involvement of the palms and soles. Occasionally, frank toxic epidermal necrolysis may ensue. The cutaneous manifestations are often accompanied by fever, diarrhea, and hepatitis. In contrast, chronic GVHD develops after 3 months. The initial cutaneous features of chronic GVHD often simulate those of LP, with involvement of the skin, oral mucosa, and nails. The lichenoid changes frequently resolve, leaving hyper- and hypopigmentation, localized and generalized sclerotic skin, and poikiloderma. Chronic GVHD can also resemble lupus erythematosus, dermatomyositis, Sjögren's syndrome, vitiligo, and other "autoimmune" diseases. Therapy for GVHD is usually directed at immunosuppression, either by drug therapy or with targeted monoclonal antibodies. Since the introduction of cyclosporine and T cell depletion in bone marrow transplantation, the incidence of GVHD has greatly diminished.

The clinical diagnosis of LP does not require a biopsy in those cases with typical morphology. However, the **histology** is quite characteristic and diagnostic when biopsy is performed. Fully developed lesions demonstrate a hyperkeratotic epidermis with hypergranulosis and acanthosis. The basal layer has liquefactive degeneration with the production of colloid bodies of degenerating epidermal cells. The basal layer may demonstrate early keratinization, and the rete ridges characteristically form a sawtooth pattern. The dermis contains an intense collection of lymphocytes and histiocytes arrayed in a band closely adherent to the dermoepidermal junction. Pigment incontinence is evident as well. The various subtypes of LP each have a somewhat distinctive histology.

The **etiology** of LP is a subject of much speculation. The heavy lymphocytic infiltrate, along with the association with autoimmune diseases, has been viewed as evidence for an immunologic etiology for LP. The mononuclear infiltrate at the dermoepidermal junction is predominantly T lymphocytes of the CD4$^+$ T-helper type. The association of LP with autoimmune diseases is further evidence for an immune-mediated mechanism. Studies with patients have revealed other suggestions of immune mechanisms in LP. Chronic GVHD has several morphologies, one of which appears as an LP-like eruption with clinically indistinguishable oral and cutaneous lesions. The pathologic changes of LP and GVHD can be quite similar as well. Changes in the humoral immunity of some patients have been noted, with depressed immunoglobulin A and M levels noted in some patients.

The earliest changes in LP involve an increase in the numbers of Langerhans cells. It has been hypothesized that these cells present foreign antigens to the epidermotropic T cells, which go on to attract more T lymphocytes and induce keratinocyte damage and apoptotic bodies. This attractive hypothesis has been tested in part in mice: autoreactive T cells directed against class 2 antigens were cloned and injected into mice, where they produced LP-like lesions clinically and histologically.

Other investigative groups have focused on the epidermal changes in LP. Several have demonstrated that rapidly proliferating spindle cells could be found in clusters at the edge of LP lesions. These were felt to be migrating in to replace damaged basal cells. At the same time, the stratum corneum was formed 2.4 times faster in LP than normal perilesional skin. Therefore, the epidermis in LP seemed to be subject to rapid destruction and hyperproliferation.

LP is notoriously resistant to **therapy**. The older literature is filled with a variety of therapies, including antimalarial drugs, heavy metal therapy, vaccines, antituberculotic drugs, irradiation, antibiotics, and other therapies that have not been adequately demonstrated to be efficacious. Elimination of any potential causative agents for LP-like reactions is essential. Once this is done, the major therapeutic agent in the treatment of LP is topical corticosteroids. Therapy should be initiated with only the most potent topical steroids (except in body folds and on the face). Steroids may be injected into hypertrophic lesions as well.

Short courses of systemic corticosteroids can be used to effectively halt the rapid progression of acute LP. Cyclosporine administered orally for severe chronic LP may induce longstanding remission of disease. Griseofulvin has been reported to be of benefit in several patients when given for a 4- to 6-week course. Other studies have suggested a trial of trimethoprim-sulfamethoxazole therapy. Photochemotherapy (PUVA) is another treatment often useful in generalized LP. Ulcerative and erosive LP of the mouth can be treated with topical or injected corticosteroids, cyclosporine mouthrinse, tretinoin 0.1% gel, and oral retinoids such as etretinate.

Ahmed AR, Schreiber P, Abramovits W, et al.: Coexistence of lichen planus and systemic lupus erythematosus. *J Am Acad Dermatol*. 1982;7:478–483.
Three patients with SLE who had typical LP lesions on biopsy.
Bhan AK, Harrist TJ, Murphy GF, et al.: T cell subsets and Langerhans cells in lichen planus: in situ characterization using monoclonal antibodies. *Br J Dermatol*. 1981;105:617–622.
Definition of the infiltrating cells with T cell subset markers.
Eisen D, Ellis CN, Duell EA, et al.: Effect of topical cyclosporine rinse on oral lichen planus: A double-blind analysis. *N Engl J Med*. 1990;323:290–294.
Erosions and erythema were each improved more than 50% in 87% of 16 patients studied, on therapy with 5 ml (100 mg/ml) swished and expectorated three times daily each. Cyclosporine levels in oral mucosa were similar to those in psoriatic lesions after treatment with systemic cyclosporine (14 mg/kg/day).
Giustina TA, Stewart JC, Ellis CN, et al.: Topical application of isotretinoin gel

improves oral lichen planus. A double-blind study. *Arch Dermatol*. 1986;122:534–536.

Topical tretinoin clears plaques but does not change erosions.

Gonzalez E, Momtaz-T K, Freedman SJ: Bilateral comparison of generalized lichen planus treated with psoralens and ultraviolet-A. *J Am Acad Dermatol*. 1984;10:1958–1961.

PUVA is an effective therapy for LP.

Harper JI: Cutaneous graft-versus-host disease. *Br Med J*. 1987;295:401–402.

A succinct editorial summarizing GVHD; its references are an excellent starting point for understanding GVHD.

Laurberg G, Geiger J-M, Hjorth N, et al.: Treatment of lichen planus with acitretin: A double-blind, placebo-controlled study in 65 patients. *J Am Acad Dermatol*. 1991;24:434–437.

Sixty-four percent of retinoid treated patients showed remission or marked improvement compared to 13% of placebo patients after 8 weeks of therapy. During the subsequent 8 week open phase, 83% of previously placebo-treated patients responded favorably to acitretin.

Mahood JM: Familial lichen planus. *Arch Dermatol*. 1983;119:292–294.

A report of nine cases and a brief review of the literature.

Massa MC, Rogers RS: Griseofulvin therapy of lichen planus. *Acta Derm Venereol*. 1981;61:547–550.

A review of patients treated with griseofulvin.

Rebora A, Rongioletti F: Lichen planus and chronic active hepatitis. A retrospective survey. *Acta Derm Venereol*. 1984;64:52–56.

Six of forty-four inpatients with LP had liver disease, five with chronic active hepatitis.

Saito K, Tamura A, Narimatsu H, et al.: Cloned auto Ia-reactive T cells elicit lichen planus-like lesion in the skin of syngeneic mice. *J Immunol*. 1986;137:2485–2495.

A clearly applicable experimental model that may explain the association of LP with GVHD.

Salman SM, Kibbi AG, Zaynoun S: Actinic lichen planus. *J Am Acad Derm*. 1989;20:226–231.

A variant of lichen planus consisting of hyperpigmented annular plaques in sun-exposed sites is described clinically and histologically in 16 patients.

22. KERATODERMA
Richard L. Gallo

A number of disorders are characterized by keratosis of the palms and soles. When one speaks specifically of palmoplantar keratoderma, one refers to a group of uncommon, usually hereditary and idiopathic disorders that tend to overlap by several clinical criteria. The rarity of these disorders has made study of significant populations of individuals extremely difficult, and relatively little convention can be found in the literature regarding terminology and classification. In general, a helpful approach to the diagnosis of keratoderma is through subdivision into hereditary and acquired forms. Of the hereditary forms of keratoderma both dominant and recessive disorders have been described. Table 22-1 lists the primary forms of hereditary keratoderma.

Unna-Thost disease is also known as keratosis palmaris plantaris hereditica, or tylosis, and although rare, is among the most common of the hereditary keratodermas. The exact incidence of Unna-Thost disease has not been determined, although it has been estimated at 1:40,000 in a northern Ireland community and is probably similar worldwide. Inheritance of Unna-Thost disease is typically considered to be autosomal dominant, although reports of recessive and sex-linked or sex-limited cases have been rarely reported. No preponderance of either sex has been described for this disease.

Table 22-1 Hereditary keratoderma of the palms and soles

Dominant inheritance	Recessive inheritance
Unna-Thost disease	Mal de Meleda
Keratosis punctata	Papillon-Lefèvre syndrome
Epidermolytic keratoderma	Richner-Hanhart syndrome
Mutilating keratoderma	
Keratosis striata	
Howel-Evans syndrome	
Progressive keratoderma	
Keratoderma with deafness	

No racial, geographical, or occupational associations have been consistently made. Unna-Thost disease typically has its onset during infancy or shortly thereafter. The classic case has an insidious onset beginning with an increase in erythema, smoothness and tenderness of the infant's palms and soles and progressing to thick hyperkeratosis limited to the palmar and plantar surfaces. Two varieties have been described, including a dry, rough-surfaced variety and a smooth-surfaced, yellowish variety with slight variation in color due to the presence of small black dots that correspond to eccrine sweat pores. In the classic description of Unna-Thost disease there is frequent mention of a particular red-purple band at the periphery of the keratosis, which gradually disappears with time. Erythema, vesicle, or bulla formation is not considered to be part of the classic presentation of Unna-Thost disease, although mechanical irritation and a high incidence of dermatophyte infection have been reported. Patients with Unna-Thost disease often present with additional destructive changes of the nail, skin and bone; these changes lead to a tapering and foreshortening of the fingers. Deep fissuring and cracks, as well as secondary opportunistic bacterial infection, are a frequent occurrence. Patients will occasionally have some limitation in the functional use of hands and feet as a result of these complications. Histologically, the only consistent abnormality reported is an extremely thick stratum corneum. In some cases mild vasodilatation, perivascular infiltrates, or an absent granular cell layer has been reported. Other associated abnormalities present with Unna-Thost disease have included clubbing of the fingers, clinodactyly, arthritis, and a motor-sensory neuropathy. However, these associated findings are generally considered to be fortuitous and not specific to the disease. The general prognosis for patients with Unna-Thost disease is of a chronic unremitting keratoderma that will temporarily respond to any mechanical or chemical method designed to soften the keratosis. Frequent paring with a sharp knife or scalpel in addition to rubbing with a pumice stone or emery board is a common approach with many of the hyperkeratotic plaques. In addition, a number of topical keratolytics have been used with limited success. In more severely affected individuals etretinate and isotretinoin have been somewhat successful in limiting the extent of the hyperkeratosis, although adverse effects secondary to these drugs often limit their usefulness.

Keratosis punctata is also known as Brauer-Bushke disease. This uncommon disorder has been estimated to have an incidence of approximately 1:2,000 dermatologic patients, and is characterized by a regularly autosomal dominant inheritance and a clinical presentation of discrete yellow to dark brown firm papules limited to the palms and soles. Typically, the lesions of keratosis punctata develop during the first decade of life. Palmar and plantar papules seen in these patients are extremely firm, anywhere between 2 and 20 mm or more in diameter, and distributed diffusely over the palms and soles, although not usually in the creases. The keratotic plugs of keratosis punctata frequently are either knocked out accidentally or pulled out deliberately, leaving small well-formed pits. Regrowth of new plugs frequently will begin within these pits within 2 weeks of removal. Few associated abnormalities have been described with this disease with the exception of nail dystrophy. The prognosis and the therapy for keratosis punctata are similar to those for Unna-Thost disease.

Epidermolytic keratoderma is also known as Vörner-type keratoderma. This uncommon form of dominantly inherited palmoplantar keratoderma is described by some as a variant of the Unna-Thost type. Since its original description in 1901 by Vörner, less than two dozen cases have been described, and those are clinically extremely similar to cases of Unna-Thost keratoderma, with the exception of a distinct histologic appearance that demonstrates characteristics of epidermolytic hyperkeratosis (i.e., orthohyperkeratosis, hypergranulosis, and acanthosis). A lack of histologic examination in many of the reported cases of Unna-Thost disease has led some to hypothesize that the true incidence of epidermolytic keratoderma of the Vörner type is higher than previously suspected. The significance of this variation of hereditary keratoderma is unknown, and no additional associated findings have been described in this form of keratoderma. Prognosis and treatment are similar to those of the other forms of keratoderma.

Mutilating keratoderma, also known as Vohwinkle's syndrome, is an extremely rare, autosomal dominant disease characterized by its onset in the first decade of life and by progressive formation of constricting fibrous bands in the hands and feet, leading to strangulation of the digits. This form of destruction of the distal appendages is highly reminiscent of that which occurs in ainhum, and has also rarely been described as a complication of Mal de Meleda, pityriasis rubra pilaris, Olmsted syndrome, and pachyonychia congenita. Untreated mutilating keratoderma is extremely destructive. Successful therapy has been described with oral etretinate administration.

Keratosis striata, also known as Brunauer-Fuhs disease, is a rare, dominantly inherited form of keratoderma characterized by its typical clinical appearance. A pattern of linear streaks of keratoderma on the palms, extending toward the fingers, is found highly conserved within families but varying significantly from one family to the next. The onset of striata keratoderma is typically during the first few weeks of life, but has been reported to occur as late as age 15. Associated abnormalities have included corneal opacities, hypohidrosis, dental abnormalities, hyperextensible joints, and sensory-neural hearing loss. The course, prognosis, and treatment for this form of palmoplantar keratoderma are similar to those for Unna-Thost disease.

Howel-Evans syndrome is characterized by an autosomal dominant inheritance and by carcinoma of the esophagus in association with keratosis of the palms and soles. In its original description by Howel and Evans in 1958, two Liverpool families were shown to have a 70% incidence of carcinoma of the esophagus in affected family members with palmoplantar keratoderma, but no carcinomas were demonstrated in family members without keratoderma. Clinically and histologically this palmoplantar keratoderma associated with carcinoma is not distinct from other forms of keratoderma. More recently, nonfamilial forms of palmoplantar keratoderma associated with internal malignancy have been described. Observations of patients with both squamous cell carcinomas and adenocarcinomas have shown that the prognosis for these patients is extremely poor. In a single case report, curative excision of a primary bronchial carcinoma was accompanied by resolution of the palmoplantar keratoderma. The interrelationship of these two phenomena is currently unknown.

Progressive keratoderma, also known as Greither's syndrome, is a rare, dominantly inherited form of keratoderma characterized by a diffuse keratoderma of the palms and soles that begins in infancy and progresses in severity and extent for several years. Progressive keratoderma appears to be inherited by an autosomal dominant gene. Individuals affected with this disorder demonstrate profuse scaling and erythema that extend from the palms and soles to the sides and dorsa of hands and feet, and occasionally develop patches over the arms and legs. Patients with progressive palmoplantar keratoderma are normal otherwise, which distinguishes it from similarly appearing keratodermas of recessive inheritance that are associated with numerous additional defects. Treatment for progressive palmoplantar keratoderma is similar to that described for Unna-Thost disease.

Keratoderma with deafness has been described in a single family of 38 members. A diffuse palmoplantar keratoderma is associated with progressives sensory-neural hearing loss, and the inheritance of this disorder, traced through three generations, appears to be autosomal dominant. Onset occurs early in childhood, as opposed to the onset in infancy of Unna-Thost disease.

Mal de Meleda is an extremely rare, hereditary keratoderma that is inherited by autosomal recessive transmittance. In its original description in 1826, this disorder was found in the southeast part of the Island of Meleda, off the coast of Yugoslavia. Most reported cases of this disease have appeared only in the Yugoslavian, German, and French literature. Clinically, this condition becomes evident within the first few weeks of life and is persistent and progressive. Palms and soles have been described as yellow-brown and waxy, rough surfaced, and with a significant erythematous and scaly component. Histologically this disorder is most easily distinguished from Unna-Thost disease by the presence of marked acanthosis and irregular hyperkeratosis with some parakeratosis and a perivascular infiltrate of lymphocytes and histiocytes. Several associated abnormalities have been described in Mal de Meleda, including poor physical development, short fingers and nails, a high arched palate, and EEG abnormalities. Occasionally, spontaneous regression has been described in Mal de Meleda. Generally, however, this disease is progressive and therapy is limited to keratolytics.

Papillon-Lefèvre syndrome, also known as hyperkeratosis palmoplantaris with periodontosis, is a rare syndrome inherited by an autosomal recessive gene. Redness and thickening of the palms and soles begin within the first 6 months of life, with development of gingivitis and periostial changes in the alveolar bone. Periostial changes eventually lead to loss of both deciduous and permanent teeth. Histological changes in Papillon-Lefèvre syndrome resemble those seen in Mal de Meleda. Associated findings in this syndrome include dural calcification. In addition to symptomatic treatment for keratoderma, dental extraction and denture construction are recommended for these patients.

Richner-Hanhart syndrome is a recessively inherited disorder that is characterized by a complex of ocular changes, osseous changes, mental abnormalities, and painful punctate palmoplantar keratosis. The clinical presentation of these patients often also includes keratosis of the prepatellar region. Ocular abnormalities in the Richner-Hanhart syndrome are characterized by a herpetiform corneal dystrophy and associated photophobia and epiphora. Treatment for these patients involves symptomatic care of the keratoderma and keratoplasty.

Frequent external trauma to the palms and soles will lead to the development of keratoses in these areas with far greater frequency than is observed in hereditary disorders. The typical callous in **acquired keratoderma** varies widely in its presentation and distribution and is dependent on the particular inciting event. The etiology behind the formation of callouses remains unclear at this time. Occupational history may be a clue to diagnosis. Keratoderma climacterium is a relatively common acquired form of keratoderma and is predominantly seen in women between the ages of 35 and 60. Clinically the keratoses are described as sharply circumscribed plaques with an oval configuration. The degree and extent of keratoderma in this condition vary greatly from patient to patient, but plantar skin is generally more diffusely involved than the palmar surface, which has discrete lesions. Occasionally, some thickening of the skin is seen over the knees. The course of keratoderma climacterium tends to increase in severity over several months following menopause and then reaches a stable phase, which can persist for many years. Although the association with menopause suggests an endocrine etiology, treatment with estrogens is not universally indicated. Weight reduction and salicylic acid treatment are the treatment of choice for these patients. The other forms of acquired keratoderma, which must also be considered in the differential diagnosis, include those associated with arsenic ingestion, gold ingestion, dermatophyte infection, contact dermatitis, syphilis, yaws, lichen planus, and psoriasis. These disorders do not present with a unique keratoderma that can readily establish the diagnosis.

Baden HP, Brownstein BR, Rand RE: Hereditary callosities with blisters. *J Am Acad Dermatol.* 1984;11(3):409–415.
A review with emphasis on a new case presentation of keratoderma with blistering.
Blanchet-Bardon C, Nazzaro V, Rognin C, et al.: Acitretin in the treatment of severe disorders of keratinization. Results of an open study. *J Am Acad Dermatol.* 1991;24:982–986.

This open study of 33 patients revealed that most patients with ichthyosis, palmoplantar keratoderma, or Darier's disease improved or cleared during a four month trial.

Costello MJ, Gibbs RC: *The Palms and Soles of Medicine.* Springfield, IL: Charles Thomas Publishers; 1967:98–155.
A thorough review of the history and clinical presentation of the keratodermas.

Kanitakis J, Tsoitis G, Kanitakis C: Hereditary epidermolytic palmoplantar keratoderma Vorner type. *J Am Acad Dermatol.* 1987;17(3):414–422.
An excellent review of keratoderma in general and particularly on epidermolytic keratoderma.

Murata Y, Jumano K, Tani N: Acquired diffuse keratoderma of the palms and soles with bronchial carcinoma. Report of a case and review of the literature. *Arch Dermatol.* 1988;244:497–498.
A description of the resolution of keratoderma following successful treatment of a bronchial carcinoma.

Nielsen PG: Hereditary palmoplantar keratoderma and dermatophytosis. *Intern J Dermatol.* 1988;27(4):223–231.
A discussion of hereditary keratoderma, with emphasis on the prevalence of dermatophyte infections in this disorder.

Parnell VD, Johnson SAM: Tylosis palmaris et plantaris. *Arch Dermatol.* 1969;100: 7–9.
The classic paper describing association between internal malignancy and keratoderma.

Rook A, Wilkinson DS, Ebling FJG: *Textbook of Dermatology.* Vol. 2, 3rd ed. Oxford: Blackwell; 1979;1452–1461.
A succinct synopsis of the hereditary keratodermas.

Roustad OJ, Vance JC: Punctate keratoses of the palms and soles and keratotic pits of the palmar creases. *J Am Acad Dermatol.* 1990;22S:468–476.
This study of 283 patients revealed a prevalence of 11% and 3% of the lesions, respectively, in a metropolitan county hospital clinic. These keratoses are aggravated by trauma and predominate in men, especially black men.

23. STIFF SKIN DISORDERS
Richard J. Sharpe

A wide range of diseases can result in stiff skin. These diseases are of diverse etiology, but all result from a change in the architecture of the dermis. This alteration can be due to abnormal rearrangement of normal dermal components, increased deposition of normal dermal elements, or infiltration of the dermis by cells or substances not normally present in healthy dermis. In most cases of stiff skin, a combination of these factors occurs, although one or two may predominate.

Many causes of stiff skin are associated with systemic disease. It is therefore important for the clinician to take a thorough history and to perform a complete physical examination. In many cases a skin biopsy will aid in the diagnosis or will verify the clinical diagnosis in these patients. Appropriate laboratory studies are sometimes necessary to aid in diagnosis, to look for systemic involvement, or to evaluate the patient for associated diseases.

Scleredema (scleredema of Buschke) is a connective tissue disorder characterized by woody induration of the skin, easily identified by palpation but associated with only subtle changes in appearance. The plaques are firm or wooden, with a shiny or waxy surface that gradually blends with normal skin. Symmetrical involvement of the upper back and neck is most common, but sometimes the disorder spreads to the face, sides of the neck, shoulders, arms, and remaining thorax. The abdomen, buttocks, and lower extremities are rarely involved.

The cause of scleredema is unknown. It may result from an autoimmune response triggered by antecedent infection, from an aberrant response to cytokines or growth signals, from injury of lymphatics, or from abnormal pituitary function. Whatever the mechanism, the result is a markedly thickened dermis with increased hydroxyproline and hexosamine content.

A self-limited variant of scleredema may occur acutely after group A streptococcal infection or, rarely, after other infections caused by mumps, measles, influenza, and various nonstreptococcal bacterial pathogens. In this variant, peak involvement occurs in 1 to 12 weeks, and then the disorder slowly resolves over a period of a couple of years. The skin lesions are usually painless; however, morbidity secondary to restricted opening of the mouth when facial involvement occurs and the cosmetically displeasing effects of stiff facial skin combine to cause significant suffering in many of these patients.

The evaluation of patients with the acute form of scleredema, particularly children, should include a search for an antecedent infection. Since rheumatic fever may be the trigger, a cardiac exam should be particularly thorough. Cardiac abnormalities have also been associated with acute scleredema even in the absence of a documented group A streptococcal antecedent infection.

A second type of scleredema has been described in adults, strongly associated with diabetes mellitus. These patients are also frequently obese and may be somewhat refractory to treatment. They develop a form of scleredema that lasts for many years or decades and can be slowly progressive. Control of blood sugar does not seem to affect the course of the skin disease in these patients. Every adult who presents with scleredema, especially if obese, should be evaluated for diabetes mellitus. Adults with scleredema should also be evaluated for a monoclonal gammopathy since this has been described in several cases.

Except for laboratory tests performed to identify an infectious trigger, a monoclonal gammopathy, or diabetes mellitus, only a complete history and physical examination are necessary in evaluating these patients. Skin biopsy is almost never necessary to make the diagnosis, and if a skin biopsy is done, the wound can be difficult to close, primarily because of the wooden consistency of the involved skin.

At present, no effective treatment exists for scleredema.

Papular mucinosis is a relatively rare condition that has a range of clinical presentations. At one extreme, patients present with a few lichenoid (flat-topped) papules, while in the more generalized form, large, firm, somewhat erythematous infiltrated plaques may develop. The term **papular mucinosis** is often reserved for the former presentation, and the term **scleromyxedema** is used to describe the more generalized form. The papular variant has some predilection for the face, neck, upper trunk, and upper extremities. The generalized form can result in diffuse thickening and even nodular involvement of these structures as well as the ears, neck, groin, and scrotum.

Although it has long been recognized that dermal mucin and increased fibroblast proliferation are present in both the papular and the generalized forms of the disease, the cause of these changes remains unknown. A paraprotein is present in the sera of many patients with papular mucinosis or scleromyxedema. In addition, the sera of these patients contains a factor that will stimulate fibroblast proliferation in vitro. Removal of the paraprotein from these sera does not abrogate this effect. The paraprotein may be an epiphenomena or may stimulate the production or release of fibroblast stimulatory factor(s) by other cell types.

Both varieties of this disease are chronic and rarely affect adults before the age of 30. In mild papular mucinosis the patients may suffer little more than minor cosmetic defects and occasionally pruritus. In advanced scleromyxedema severe cosmetic disfigurement, particularly of the face, may occur, and reduced mobility of the mouth, arms, hands, and legs can result in significant morbidity. Scleromyxedema is sometimes associated with systemic findings such as acute organic brain syndrome, proximal myopathy, polyarthritis, esophageal motility problems, and hoarseness.

A skin biopsy can be helpful in documenting the diagnosis of papular mucinosis or scleromyxedema. A serum protein electrophoresis and concurrent immunoelectrophoresis are useful for identifying the commonly associated paraprotein. Although a plasmacytosis is sometimes found in the bone marrow of these patients, the extremely rare evolution to frank myeloma makes bone marrow aspiration or biopsy unnecessary in most cases.

Potentially efficacious treatment includes alkylating agents, such as melphalan or cyclophosphamide, used alone or in combination with corticosteroids. However, their use should be reserved for patients in which the potential benefits of reducing significant morbidity outweigh the risks of these therapies.

Scleroderma is a disease characterized by hardening of the skin and, usually, thickening of the dermis. Cutaneous lesions tend to evolve from early edematous plaques to nonpitting indurated persistent plaques and finally to atrophic plaques. In localized forms of scleroderma, there is a sharp demarcation between the plaques and the surrounding normal skin. The plaques themselves may be riddled with telangiectasias and are often waxy or ivory colored. The borders of individual plaques may have a lilac color. In advanced plaques, skin appendages are lost, and hypo- and hyperpigmentation in mottled patterns are common. In the systemic forms of the disease, telangiectasias are frequently found on nail folds, palms, lips, face, tongue, and mucous membranes. The pathogenesis of scleroderma in either localized or generalized disease is unknown, but some data point to increased collagen synthesis as the cause of the sclerosis. Many theories have been advanced to explain this increased collagen synthesis, ranging from a primary defect in fibroblast function to stimulation of these fibroblasts by cytokines from autoreactive lymphocytes. Some recent evidence suggests that localized scleroderma (morphea) may be associated with a spirochete (*Borrelia*) infection in a subset of patients.

Progressive systemic sclerosis (PSS) consists of fibrotic degenerative changes of skin as well as of essentially all other organs. In many patients, disease involving the kidneys, heart, lungs, gastrointestinal tract, and vessel walls is most troublesome. Raynaud's phenomena and osteolysis of the distal phalanges frequently occur. In classic systemic scleroderma, diffuse involvement of the skin of the proximal and distal extremities as well as that of the face and trunk is commonly seen. These patients tend to develop rapid systemic organ involvement. Patients with the CREST syndrome (calcinosis, Raynaud's phenomena, esophageal dysfunction, sclerodactyly, telangiectasia) have a somewhat better prognosis. These patients tend to have cutaneous disease confined to the fingers and face and have delayed visceral involvement.

Morphea (localized scleroderma) and two variants, linear scleroderma and scleroderma en coup de sabre, are not associated with internal organ involvement, although the individual skin lesions of these localized forms are indistinguishable clinically and histologically from the lesions of systemic forms of the disease. The cutaneous fibrosis may include subcutaneous tissues, even muscle, rarely. Morphea can occur at any age and can involve any area of the body. Rarely, morphea can become generalized and resemble PSS, but no internal organ involvement occurs. Morphea can also resemble lichen sclerosis et atrophicus. It is usually self-limited and can spontaneously regress over several years. Linear scleroderma is a localized scleroderma variant characterized by bandlike lesions with a predilection to involve subcutaneous tissue, including bone. If it involves the frontoparietal region of the forehead and scalp, it is given the name "coup de sabre," and may be associated with hemiatrophy of the face.

Systemic scleroderma may be present with other collagen vascular diseases, including lupus erythematosus, polymyositis, and rheumatoid arthritis. It has been postulated that all these syndromes represent different expressions of an autoimmune phenomenon. These patients are frequently designated as suffering from a mixed connective tissue syndrome.

A skin biopsy can be helpful in confirming that a skin lesion is either a plaque of systemic scleroderma or a plaque of one of the localized forms of scleroderma (morphea and its variants). However, a biopsy cannot distinguish between localized or generalized disease. To make a diagnosis, the clinician must look for involvement of other organ systems by taking a complete history, performing a thorough physical examination, and ordering appropriate laboratory studies. In this regard, serologies, including Scl-70 titers, may be helpful.

Present treatment modalities for systemic forms of scleroderma and the localized variants are controversial at best. Except for supportive treatments for organ failure in advanced systemic forms of the disease, no treatment has been proven efficacious. Agents that may have limited utility in treating generalized morphea and systemic scleroderma include d-penicillamine, corticosteroids, colchicine, and immunosuppressive agents. However, at this time no controlled trials have proven the efficacy of any of these agents. Likewise, except for a few reports of patients with morphea improving after a course of systemic antibiotics and some evidence of a spirochete infection in a few of these patients, no good documentation exists for this form of therapy either.

Raynaud's phenomena can, however, be controlled with systemic agents that induce peripheral vasodilatation. Reserpine, methyldopa, prazosin, and calcium channel blockers have utility alone or in combination. Patients must also be very careful to avoid exposure to cold. Topical nitropaste has also been used; however, this agent is systemically absorbed, and reflex cardiac vasospasm with a resultant myocardial infarction is a potentially serious consequence in patients who use the agent intermittently (i.e., only during the cold winter months).

Newer, promising treatment modalities for scleroderma include gamma interferon, which may inhibit collagen synthesis, and extracorporeal photophoresis, which may alter the autoimmune response. Cyclosporine A is also being evaluated in systemic scleroderma and may have several beneficial modes of action, including disruption of fibrosis-inducing cytokine release and suppression of a putative autoimmune response. Hopefully, one of these modalities or a yet-to-be-discovered treatment will provide us with a means of effectively treating both localized and systemic scleroderma.

Eosinophilic fasciitis (Shulman's syndrome) presents with the rapidly progressive onset of erythematous, tender, edematous plaques most often involving the extremities symmetrically. The plaques evolve to shiny, firm, indurated, bound-down lesions, and the pain subsides. In a significant number of patients, flexion contracture of the joints occurs. Significant systemic disease is uncommon, but can include pulmonary disease, aplastic anemia, thrombocytopenia, hemolysis, dysphagia, and cardiac abnormalities.

The etiology of eosinophilic fasciitis is unknown, but the eosinophil has been postulated to be important in the pathogenesis of eosinophilic fasciitis. A similar process has been described with use of L-tryptophan contaminated by production by-products. Eosinophilia and myalgia are predominant clinical signs and symptoms.

If eosinophilic fasciitis is suspected on clinical grounds, it should be confirmed with a deep wedge biopsy that adequately samples subcutaneous tissue including fascia and muscle. Frequently abnormal laboratory studies in these patients include a peripheral blood eosinophilia (present in 90% of patients), an elevated erythrocyte sedimentation rate (present in 50% of patients), and elevated creatinine phosphokinase. A polyclonal hypergammaglobulinemia and the presence of serum immune complexes have been observed. Because of associated hematologic abnormalities, a complete blood count and platelet count should be included in the work-up of these patients.

Patients with eosinophilic fasciitis quickly and dramatically improve with moderate doses of systemic corticosteroids (40 to 60 mg of prednisone per day or equivalent). Once an adequate response is obtained, the prednisone can be reduced to a low maintenance dose and can usually be discontinued within 2 to 4 years of beginning treatment. Hydroxychloroquine and salicylates have also been used with success in several patients, but systemic corticosteroids remain the treatment of choice.

Amyloidosis can be confined to the skin as in lichen amyloidosis, or the skin can be affected in systemic forms of amyloidosis. Both types of amyloidosis can result in stiff skin mimicking that of disorders such as papular mucinosis or scleromyxedema.

Pretibial myxedema is a manifestation of Graves' disease and usually presents with diffuse infiltration of the pretibial skin with mucin. The resultant nonpitting edema can be treated with some success with topical steroids under occlusion and with intralesional steroids.

Sclerema neonatorum is a rare condition affecting premature and low birth weight infants. It occurs within the first 2 weeks of life and is characterized by the development of symmetrical indurated plaques, usually starting on the legs and moving upward. Histologically, crystals are seen within fat cells, thought to produce cell death. The prognosis is poor in the generalized forms, but limited disease can spontaneously resolve.

Progeria is a rare, autosomal recessive disorder usually first noted at 6 to 12 months of age. Patients with this disorder undergo changes that in some ways mimic accelerated aging. Many of these patients develop scleroderma-like changes of the skin, along with atrophy of the subcutaneous tissue and nails. Most patients die during their second decade of life.

Werner's disease is another rare autosomal recessive disorder commonly associated with myriad systemic problems as well as scleroderma-like skin changes.

The list of conditions that can result in stiff skin is almost endless. Any insult that alters the structure of the dermis, results in an increase in normal dermal constituents, or results in infiltration of the dermis by abnormal constituents (cellular or acellular) can cause stiff skin. For example, x-irradiation of the skin alters the structure of dermal collagen, destroys appendages, and perturbs fibroblast growth and function. It is not surprising then that **chronic radiodermatitis** can result in stiff skin. Similarly, chronic exposure of skin to inflammation can cause both nonspecific damage probably secondary to superoxide radicals produced by neutrophils and alteration of collagen synthesis secondary to the myriad cytokines released by mononuclear cells. It is therefore also not surprising that skin in areas of **chronic inflammation**, such as a lower extremity after **recurrent cellulitis**, or chronic stasis dermatitis can become somewhat stiff. **Porphyria cutanea tarda** may eventuate on sclerodactyly by this mechanism. Finally, if **tumor cells** diffusely infiltrate skin, then this can also create a stiff skin syndrome. Evaluation of a patient with stiff skin can therefore be complex.

Asbrink E, Hovmark A: Cutaneous manifestations in Ixodes-borne *Borrelia* spirochetosis. *Int J Dermatol*. 1987;26:215–223.
These authors describe a possible link between certain cases of morphea and a spirochete infection. More data are needed to prove such a link.

Carsons S: Newer laboratory parameters for the diagnosis of rheumatic disease. *Am J Med*. 1988;85:34–38.
An overview of currently available serologic assays useful in evaluating patients with suspected connective tissue disease, including scleroderma and overlap syndromes.

Helfrich DJ, Walker ER, Martinez AJ, Medsger TA: Scleromyxedema myopathy: case report and review of the literature. *Arthritis Rheum*. 1988;31:1437–1441.
This paper describes the rare but important association of scleromyxedema and proximal myopathy and discusses the authors' experience treating this serious entity.

Martin RW, Duffy J, Engel AG, et al.: The clinical spectrum of the eosinophilia-myalgia syndrome associated with L-tryptophan ingestion. Clinical features in 20 patients and aspects of pathophysiology. *Ann Int Med*. 1990;113:124–134.
Patients described had eosinophilia and disabling myalgias. Other manifestations included eosinophilic fasciitis, pneumonitis, myocarditis, neuropathy, encephalopathy, and fibrosis around the gallbladder duct.

Phelps RG, Fleischmajer R: Clinical, pathologic, and immunopathologic manifestations of the toxic oil syndrome. Analysis of fourteen cases. *J Am Acad Dermatol*. 1988;18:313–324.
Fourteen patients from Madrid, Spain, who ingested industrial oil sold as olive oil are described. These patients developed a disorder very similar to systemic sclerosis, and this toxic exposure may have resulted in a "human model" of this devastating disease.

Rocco VK, Hurd ER: Scleroderma and scleroderma-like disorders. *Semin Arthritis*. 1986;16:22–69.
An excellent review of scleroderma, including eosinophilic fasciitis.

Venencie PY, Powell FC, Su WP, Perry HO: Scleredema: a review of thirty-three cases. *J Am Acad Dermatol*. 1984;11:128–134.
This is an excellent review and overview of scleredema.

Young EM, Barr RJ: Sclerosing dermatoses. *J Cutan Pathol.* 1985;12:426–441.
   A review of the histologic differential diagnosis of conditions that result in cutaneous sclerosis.

V. GLANDS, HAIR, AND NAILS

24. ACNE
Jerome D. Fallon

Acne vulgaris is an extremely common disorder whose peak prevalence occurs during adolescence. Since it most commonly affects the face and, in severe cases, can lead to permanent scarring, acne can have profound and long-lasting physical, psychological, and social effects. Fortunately, insights into the pathophysiology of acne have resulted in the development of rational and effective therapy.

The age of onset, the severity, and the duration of acne are quite variable and are influenced by genetic factors. In males, acne most commonly begins in early adolescence, is more severe, and resolves in the early to mid twenties. In females, acne generally begins later (late teens, early twenties), is less severe, and lasts longer (persisting into the late twenties and early thirties). Patients with severe acne often have a family history of severe acne.

Three major **pathogenic factors** are believed to play roles in the development of acne vulgaris. The initial factor is defective keratinization of the follicular infundibulum (above the opening of the sebaceous duct). Keratinocytes lining the infundibulum multiply in increased numbers in acne lesions, and they show enhanced cohesiveness, thereby obstructing follicular channels. Cellular debris and sebum then collect behind the obstruction to form a solid mass known as a comedo.

The second contributor to acne development is sebum accumulation. No qualitative differences in the sebum of acne patients have been substantiated; however, disease severity roughly correlates with quantitative sebum production. Sebaceous gland development and sebum production are primarily controlled by androgenic hormones. In some acne patients, elevated androgen levels have been documented; in others with normal androgen levels, it is presumed that affected skin has increased sensitivity to androgenic stimulation.

Inflammation is the third major factor in acne pathogenesis, and it results from the action of the anaerobic diphtheroid *Propionibacterium acnes* within follicles. The population of *P. acnes* is markedly elevated in acne patients relative to controls. Lipases made by this organism liberate free fatty acids from their normally esterified state in freshly secreted sebum. These fatty acids elicit a perifollicular inflammatory response. In addition, *P. acnes* inflames follicles directly by producing agents chemotactic for polymorphonuclear leukocytes. Complement and the immune response directed against *P. acnes* may also contribute to the inflammation.

The pathognomonic **clinical lesion** of acne is the comedo. It is a small papule, less than 2 mm in diameter, and may be either open with a dilated follicular ostium (blackhead) or closed (whitehead). The black material plugging the open comedo is probably a combination of oxidized lipids, melanin, and keratin. The closed comedo, in which the plug traps sebum and *P. acnes,* is thought to be the precursor of more-severe acne; this lesion may develop into an inflammatory papule or pustule or even into a nodular or cystic lesion. Large inflammatory lesions may resolve, leaving "ice pick" scars, saucerlike depressions, or hypertrophic scars. In some patients, shallow erosions covered with a honey-colored crust from manipulation or excoriation dominate the clinical picture (acne excoriée). Most patients manifest a mixture of lesions distributed predominantly over the face, back, and chest, the areas of highest sebaceous gland density.

The **diagnosis** of acne is normally straightforward, based on characteristic clinical features and the age of the patient. The differential diagnosis includes rosacea and folliculitis (from *Pityrosporum,* gram-negative bacteria, or staphylococci), as well as acne induced by external agents or drugs. Follicular eczema, inflammatory keratosis pilaris, and hidradenitis suppurativa may be diagnosed when acneiform papules occur in unusual locations. Excoriated acne, usually in young women, is often confused with impetigo or factitia.

Endocrinologic disorders associated with excess androgen secretion may need to be excluded in patients with certain clinical features. Women with severe, recalcitrant or late-onset acne, or acne associated with hirsutism or menstrual abnormalities, may have increased androgen levels. Evaluation of these patients most commonly reveals no structural abnormalities. However, polycystic ovarian disease or tumors of the ovaries or adrenal glands may rarely be found. Women with acne, elevated androgen levels, and no structural endocrinologic abnormalities have been reported to respond to therapies aimed at decreasing the androgen levels. These therapies include low-dose systemic corticosteroids, spironolactone, and the use of exogenous estrogen. The utility of extensive screening for elevated androgen levels in all women with acne is controversial, and such testing is generally not performed.

Therapeutic measures against acne are many and varied. The best treatments, however, have specific mechanisms of action directed at one or more of the major pathogenic factors. Many patients present having used multiple regimens of skin care and over-the-counter medications. Basic personal hygiene for acne patients includes washing with mild soap and water once or twice a day (no vigorous scrubbing), allowing full drying, applying recommended medications, and using oil-free makeups if desired.

Benzoyl peroxide is a highly effective medication that is both anticomedonal and antibacterial. In the laboratory, it can be shown to be bacteriocidal and a more potent antibacterial agent than topical antibiotics. Human studies have documented that it is the only antiacne agent that decreases the number of inflammatory papules and pustules within the first week of its use. It is generally used as a 2½%, 5% or 10% cream or gel, applied topically twice a day to the entire acne-prone area. Mild drying and irritation often develop secondary to its use. Very rarely, a type of immediate contact hypersensitivity occurs, manifested by redness, swelling, and a burning sensation in the area to which the medication is applied. Benzoyl peroxide is an excellent first-line drug, and it is commonly included in regimens with other medications, regardless of the severity of the acne.

Topical tretinoin (Retin-A), a vitamin A derivative, has been used for acne therapy since 1960. Unlike its use for aging and wrinkling, its use for acne is well supported by data and is not controversial. It specifically combats the altered keratinization of the acneiform follicle, reversing the enhanced cohesiveness of keratinocytes in the follicular infundibulum. It is the most effective anticomedonal agent available. It has been widely used as first-line therapy in mild to moderate inflammatory acne, but is particularly useful in the patient with numerous comedones. It is sparingly applied once a day to the entire acne-prone area of the face, preferably in the evening, at least 30 minutes after washing the face. Six months or more of therapy may be required to obtain maximal improvement in the acne. Irritation is very common, occurring in almost 90% of patients who use it consistently. However, this effect may be ameliorated by an alternate-night application of a low dose. Retin-A is available as a cream, gel, or solution; while the lowest effective concentration is available in a cream, the gel may be less irritating for some people. The irritation often improves after 4 to 6 weeks of therapy. Oil-free moisturizers and avoidance of sun exposure may diminish the side effects.

Antibiotics are frequently prescribed for acne. Although it is commonly thought that they are effective because of their antibacterial actions, there is some data indicating that antibiotics may also diminish the inflammatory response. They are most useful in inflammatory acne and are not recommended for patients with primarily comedonal acne. Improvement requires 2 to 3 months of full compliance with the recommended agent and dose.

Many patients with mild to moderate inflammatory acne consisting of a few small inflammatory papules and pustules are satisfied with the improvement they obtain with the use of topical erythromycin or clindamycin, equally effective agents. They are commonly administered in solutions applied twice a day to all acne-prone areas of the face. Irritation due to these agents or their vehicles is rare. Benzoyl peroxide is generally applied at the same time as the topical antibiotic, but if Retin-A is also used, it should be applied at a time different from either of the other medications.

Oral antibiotics most commonly used include tetracycline and erythromycin, with most patients responding best to 1 g daily in a divided dose. At this dosage, oral antibiotics are more effective than topical antibiotics, especially in patients with large inflammatory papules or nodules. The dosage may be increased to 2 g daily for unresponsive patients. Tetracycline must be taken on an empty stomach, which sometimes interferes with compliance of active teenagers. Side effects of these agents are few; gastrointestinal intolerance early in the course is relatively common, and approximately 10% of female patients will develop symptomatic vaginal moniliasis. The latter usually can be treated locally with topical anticandidal agents without stopping the antibiotic therapy. Minocycline is an alternative agent that in several studies is the most effective medication, clearing inflammatory acne in up to 90% of patients with inflammatory acne when used for at least 3 months. Its use produces noticeable improvement somewhat earlier than tetracycline or erythromycin, and relapse is often delayed after discontinuation. It is well absorbed, even with meals, and does not give rise to gastrointestinal upset. Because of its increased expense, it is often used only for patients who do not respond to either tetracycline or erythromycin or who cannot tolerate their side effects. A highly effective regimen for moderate to severe inflammatory acne, including nodulocystic acne, is the use of minocycline, 200 mg daily in divided dosage, in conjunction with topical benzoyl peroxide bid and Retin-A at bedtime.

An oral retinoid (vitamin A derivative), isotretinoin (Accutane) is available for the treatment of acne. It has an action similar to that of topical tretinoin, reversing altered keratinization, and has the added benefit of diminishing sebum production, thus producing decreases in *P. acnes* populations and inflammation. In a dose of 0.5 to 1.0 mg/kg for 20 weeks, it is highly effective in inducing long-term remissions in cystic acne. Its use, however, should be limited to severe, recalcitrant, nodulocystic, scarring acne because of its myriad side effects, which include dry skin, cheilitis, alopecia, hypertriglyceridemia, night blindness, and teratogenicity. The drug is known to produce universal serious congenital malformations (of the heart, ears, and nervous system) and fetal death if it is taken during pregnancy, especially in the first trimester. Fortunately, the half-life of the drug is short, and pregnancy may ensue safely 1 month after the drug is discontinued. Any prescribing practitioner, therefore, must make sure his or her patient is not pregnant before starting treatment and will not become pregnant during the administration of the drug. Adequate contraceptive counseling must be provided, and an effective form of contraception must be used during therapy and for at least 1 month after therapy is discontinued. Therapy is instituted on the second or third day of the menstrual cycle after a negative result has been obtained on a pregnancy test. Periodic follow-up visits to reinforce the importance of contraception are essential to avoid unwanted pregnancies.

Chronic administration of isotretinoin has been complicated by the development of bony spurs and other skeletal disorders. In a recent report, calcification of the axial spine was detectable in up to 20% of acne patients who were treated for 20 weeks.

Some patients with acne may respond to other therapeutic interventions. Patients unresponsive to the most commonly used antibiotics may respond to sulfamethoxazole and trimethoprim (Bactrim), oral clindamycin, or other antibiotics. The practitioner can decrease sebum production by instituting estrogenic or antiandrogenic agents, which may be used in conjunction with a low dose of prednisone in women to suppress adrenal production of androgens. Direct anti-inflammatory treatment may also be provided by the use of intralesional corticosteroid injections in patients with a few isolated nodular lesions. Comedones are often markedly improved in a very short period of time by incision and drainage. Irradiation with x rays is not recommended because of the subsequent risk of cutaneous and deep carcinoma.

Infantile acne is an uncommon acne variant, presenting in neonates and infants with inflammatory papules and pustules in a distribution resembling acne in older patients, predominantly the face, back, and chest. It may result from hormonal effects in utero in a predisposed infant. Sebaceous glands develop rapidly and are very active in late fetal life, probably in response to maternal androgens. Infants with persistent acne may have prolongation of this hormonal effect, or they may experience transient increases in circulating androgens. In addition, there may be a familial tendency for acne in infants. If a careful physical examination is normal, particularly without any sign of precocious puberty, a search for androgenic endocrinopathy is probably unwarranted. This disease may persist for several months, but spontaneous resolution is the rule, and treatment is seldom required. Acne in the neonate or infant may be a harbinger of severe acne during adolescence.

Acne conglobata is a severe disease of sebaceous follicular inflammation presenting almost exclusively in adult men. The etiology is not well understood. Clinical lesions consist of a mixture of cysts, abscesses, inflammatory nodules, and scars distributed primarily on the trunk, often avoiding the face. Comedones may have multiple ostia and result in sinus tracts. The disease is frequently associated and confused with hidradenitis suppurativa. *Staphylococcus aureus* is often isolated from active lesions. Because of a relatively older age of onset and different clinical findings, acne conglobata is considered distinct from acne vulgaris. Standard therapies for acne vulgaris are used in treatment; however, they are often less effective. For many of these patients, isotretinoin is the most useful agent. Surgical debridement and excision may also be useful adjuncts.

Other processes may present with severe acne. **Acne necroticans** is an erosive disease, usually of the upper trunk. Inflammation of follicles is so marked that necrosis ensues. Treatment is difficult, and oral corticosteroids or dapsone may be required to diminish the inflammation. An ulcerating acneiform process termed **acne fulminans** may occur explosively and be associated with fever, leukocytosis, and other systemic symptoms. Poorly demarcated osteolytic bone lesions have been seen on x-ray examination in this condition. Systemic glucocorticoids, in conjunction with antibiotics, are generally necessary to change the course of the disease. **Acne edema** may deform the central face permanently. The acne itself appears to be minor, but the associated inflammation scleroses underlying lymphatic vessels, producing lymphedema. **Acne arthropathy** is a destructive arthropathy reminiscent of rheumatoid arthritis and occurs in the setting of markedly inflammatory acne, probably on an immunologic basis.

Acne cosmetica is a term used to describe an acne process, often in adult women, that seems to be associated with the use of heavy, occlusive cosmetics. Many dermatologists therefore routinely advise patients not to use greasy or occlusive cosmetic preparations in order to avoid causing acne or exacerbating acne vulgaris. While this extrapolation seems logical, its true clinical validity has never been proven. Similarly, **pomade acne** occurs most commonly in black patients who use pomades or thick oils for hair care. Numerous closed comedones are found closely packed on the forehead and temples, close to the hairline. Compulsive washing or scrubbing and repetitive rubbing by clothing or helmets may also give rise to acne lesions, often termed **acne detergicans** and **acne mechanica**, respectively.

Steroid acne is an acneiform folliculitis arising in patients after several days to weeks of treatment with oral or topical corticosteroids. The distinctive eruption consists of very small monomorphous red papules and pustules. Lesions are limited to the areas of topical steroid application or most commonly occur in the "cape" areas (chest, back, shoulders) in patients on systemic therapy. Corticosteroids thin the follicular epithelium, making follicles more susceptible to rupture. Since inflammation is often checked by steroids, lesions are generally small or may appear only as the medicine is being withdrawn. After withdrawal of the medication, resolution is spontaneous, though sometimes delayed.

Many **drugs** can cause an acneiform eruption. Phenytoin sodium (Dilantin) and isoniazid are among the most commonly known, primarily causing a monomorphous pustular eruption. Lithium exacerbates acne vulgaris. It may also cause a polymorphous, severe acneiform eruption in patients who previously had no skin complaints. Acne vulgaris may also be induced or exacerbated in women taking oral contraceptives containing an androgenic progestational agent such as norgestrel or norethindrone. This acne may become much more manageable when an alternate contraceptive is substituted. Medications containing iodide (potassium iodide), bromide (particularly cold remedies), and chlorine (chloral hydrate) may induce a folliculitis morphologically resembling steroid acne. Other drugs associated with an acneiform eruption include actinomycin D, adrenocorticotropic hormone, androgens (including androgenic progestins), cod liver oil, halothane, thiouracil, thiourea, trimethadione, and vitamin B_{12}.

Occupational or vocational exposure to a variety of **chemicals** may produce acne or an acneiform syndrome. Chronic exposure to dioxin or Agent Orange produced enormous numbers of comedones, often generalized but characteristically involving the infraorbital rim and helix of the ear. Chlorinated hydrocarbons may induce a severe inflammatory acne on exposed skin, with lesions ranging from inflammatory follicular papules to nodules found on a background of irritant dermatitis. A similar eruption may be caused by coal tar and insoluble metalworking fluids. Mechanics exposed to machine oil, greases, and lubricants also frequently manifest severe acne. As with drug-induced acne, withdrawal of the agent or discontinuation of the exposure improves the eruption, although many months to a few years may be required for noticeable improvement. Patients may be treated with standard medical and surgical approaches to acne; however, the results may not be entirely satisfactory.

American Academy of Dermatology. Guidelines of care for acne vulgaris. *J Am Acad Dermatol.* 1990;22:676–680.
   Staging and treatment of acne vulgaris is reviewed with emphasis placed on risk-benefit ratios and stepwise addition of effective agents.
Fisher AA: *Contact Dermatitis.* 3rd ed. Philadelphia, PA: Lea and Febiger; 1986:368–393, 486–514.
   Contains an excellent review on occupational and cosmetic acne with specifics on incriminated ingredients.
Knutson DD: Ultrastructural observations in acne vulgaris: the normal sebaceous follicle and acne lesions. *J Invest Dermatol.* 1974;62:288–307.
   Thorough histologic study of normal follicles and comedones in different developmental stages. This classic paper helped establish defective keratinization as the primary pathogenic factor in comedogenesis.
Marynick SP, Chakmakjian ZH, McCaffree DL, et al.: Androgen excess in cystic acne. *N Engl J Med.* 1983;308:981–986.
   Men and women with cystic acne were found to have higher levels of androgens than controls. Use of low-dose dexamethasone and oral contraceptives improved acne, but no placebo group was employed.
Pochi PE: Endocrinology of acne. *J Invest Dermatol.* 1983;81:1.
   Editorial which reminds us that there still is no consistent endocrinopathy in, or treatment for, acne patients. Serum levels may not reflect cellular events.
Pochi PE: The pathogenesis and treatment of acne. *Ann Rev Med.* 1990;41:187–198.
   Detailed review of pathogenetic factors and drugs used specifically to ameliorate the abnormalities.
Shalita AR, Smith EB, Bauer E: Topical erythromycin vs. clindamycin therapy for acne. A multicenter, double blind comparison. *Arch Dermatol.* 1984;120:351–355.
   No significant differences in the overall excellent or good response achieved in 166 patients with moderate acne including mixed lesions.
Strauss JS, Rapini RP, Shalita AR, et al.: Isotretinoin therapy for acne: results of a multicenter dose-response study. *J Amer Acad Dermatol.* 1984;10:490–496.
   Recent study of 150 patients with treatment-resistant nodulocystic acne. Significant improvement at all doses, but the group treated with 0.1 mg/kg more often required retreatment.
Vexian P, Husson C, Chivot M, et al.: Androgen excess in women with acne alone compared with women with acne and/or hirsutism. *J Invest Dermatol.* 1990;94:279–283.
   Twenty-five (86%) of 29 women with treatment-resistant acne had elevated androgen levels.
Webster GF, Leyden JJ, McGinley KJ, et al.: Suppression of polymorphonuclear leukocyte chemotactic factor production in *Propionibacterium acnes* by subminimal inhibitory concentrations of tetracycline, ampicillin, minocycline, and erythromycin. *Antimicrob Agents Chemother.* 1982;21:770–772.
   Strains of P. acnes cultured with subminimal inhibitory concentrations of erythromycin, minocycline, and tetracycline showed decreased neutrophil chemotactic activity, while those cultured with ampicillin did not.

25. ROSACEA
Paul A. Bleicher

Rosacea is a common, chronic skin disorder characterized by papules and pustules concentrated on the central face and associated with erythema and telangiectasia. In its most florid manifestations, the disease is associated with a bulbous nose having hypertrophied sebaceous glands that has been incorrectly associated with inebriation and alcohol overindulgence. Because of this association, rosacea imparts to the afflicted an often unwarranted social stigma. In many articles and textbooks the disease is misnamed acne rosacea, which refers to the historical grouping of predominantly facial papular eruptions. The histology and clinical setting of rosacea clearly distinguishes the disease from acne, and the name acne rosacea serves only to confuse.

The typical **clinical setting** of rosacea is characteristic but not exclusive. The disease is most prevalent in the third and fourth decades but can be seen in any group, including in children. Rosacea is more frequently seen by dermatologists in women, but this may reflect a bias of ascertainment in that women may seek therapy more frequently than men. It is most common in patients from northern Europe and is rare in blacks. A family history of easy flushing or a rosy complexion is often elicited.

The **clinical features** of rosacea vary from faint central-facial erythema to myriad papules and pustules on a swollen erythematous face. The onset of the disease is frequently insidious and is characterized by intermittent episodes of facial flushing that resolve with increasingly permanent erythema and telangiectasia. The changes eventually become persistent and are usually localized to the cheeks, forehead, nose, and chin. The distribution is usually symmetric, but can be unilateral. Rarely, the typical lesions of rosacea may be found on the extremities. In more-advanced rosacea there are episodes of facial swelling associated with the eruption of rose-colored, dome-shaped papules and smaller numbers of frank pustules. In addition, the presence of telangiectasia and the absence of comedones are typical and can be used in clinically distinguishing rosacea from acne. The disease is characteristically chronic with frequent fluctuations in disease severity.

Rosacea may be complicated by a variety of severe ocular manifestations in up to 58% of patients. Many patients complain of a gritty or dry discomfort in the eyes that objectively correlates with conjunctival injection. Blepharitis, episcleritis, iritis, hordeolum, and chalazion are all benign conditions commonly associated with rosacea. Rosacea keratitis occurs less commonly but can lead to corneal ulceration and scarring, with discomfort and loss of visual acuity. These ocular lesions may precede the development of cutaneous rosacea in approximately 20% of cases.

Another finding in rosacea is rhinophyma, a bulbous, craggy enlargement of the nose present up to 12 times more commonly in men than in women. The nose in rhinophyma demonstrates follicular prominence and a thickened texture with color ranging from yellow-pink to deep red. Histologically, rhinophyma is characterized by a prominent increase in sebaceous gland size and number. Recurrent episodes of lymphedema can also lead to similar chronic changes on the face, generally persistent lymphedema and firmness related to scarring of lymphatic channels.

The disease spectrum of rosacea is characteristic, and rarely does the **diagnosis** require biopsy. The histology is rather nonspecific in classic rosacea. When rosacea demonstrates merely erythema and telangiectasia, a biopsy will show dilated vessels and a nonspecific dermal inflammatory infiltrate. In papular rosacea, a biopsy of the papules will likewise demonstrate a nonspecific mononuclear dermal infiltrate. In approximately 10% of cases, areas of epithelioid and giant cell granulomas will be demonstrated, leading to a tuberculoid appearance.

Clinically, a variety of facial eruptions must be distinguished from rosacea. Acne can be distinguished by the lack of comedones, the localization to the face, and the usual age of occurrence. Perioral dermatitis is characterized by smaller papules and pustules on the lower face of young women, usually in the absence of underlying erythema. Seborrheic dermatitis may occur simultaneously with rosacea but can be distinguished by the total absence of papules and pustules and the presence of greasy scale. Both lupus erythematosus and dermatomyositis can demonstrate facial flushing and telangiectasia but characteristically do not display discrete papules and, unlike rosacea, do not spare the facial folds.

The **pathophysiology** and **etiology** of rosacea have been the subject of much speculation but are not yet generally agreed on. It is commonly observed that maneuvers that induce flushing will exacerbate rosacea. Such maneuvers include holding hot beverages in the mouth, ingestion of alcohol or spicy foods, exposure to the sun, and emotional blushing. Interestingly, patients with carcinoid syndrome who experience repeated facial flushing will often develop a rosacea-like syndrome. The flushing does not appear to be epinephrine-, acetylcholine-, or histamine-mediated but rather may involve enkephalin-like substances or bradykinin.

Although antibiotics such as tetracycline and metronidazole are effective in the treatment of rosacea, the lesions are not apparently infected with bacteria. The mite *Demodex folliculorum* has been suggested as a causative agent in rosacea. It has been observed that female patients who do not use facial soaps or cleansers occasionally develop clinical rosacea with an associated overabundance of *D. folliculorum* mites. This may only be coincidental in that many patients with rosacea do not have an increased number of such mites, and measures that suppress rosacea often do not affect mite populations.

An association with a variety of gastrointestinal symptoms, such as indigestion, constipation, and diarrhea, has prompted gastroscopic evaluations of those patients with rosacea who demonstrated prominent achlorhydria and gastritis. Subsequent studies have not confirmed this.

The **management** of rosacea is frequently problematic. In those patients in whom flushing is a problem, it is essential to avoid activities, foods, and beverages that lead to flushing. The mainstay of therapy is oral antibiotics, specifically tetracycline and its derivatives. Erythromycin and ampicillin are occasionally effective, as well. Initially, 500 to 1000 mg/d of tetracycline is necessary to control the disease activity. After 4 to 6 weeks, the dosage can be reduced slowly and adjusted for the individual patient. A minimum of 2 to 3 months of therapy is needed for most patients, but often chronic antibiotic therapy is necessary. Tetracycline is particularly effective in controlling the papulopustular and ocular lesions but is ineffective in treating the erythema and telangiectasia. For many patients, long-term oral antibiotic therapy is unacceptable. Patient compliance is often limited by candidal vaginitis; gastrointestinal and other side effects; concern about the reduction in oral contraceptive efficacy; concerns about the effects of long-term oral antibiotic use; and the loss of efficacy with chronic use. Oral 13-cis retinoic acid has been used with excellent clinical results but with a high rate of significant, severe systemic side effects and a high rate of recurrence of rosacea after discontinuation of the drug.

Although topical clindamycin, erythromycin, and tetracycline have been used in the treatment of rosacea, the therapeutic benefit and the outcome are variable and often unsatisfactory with these agents. Patients who refuse oral therapy or who are unable to take oral tetracycline may benefit from therapy with topical agents. Topical precipitated sulfur (2% to 5%) cream is an older, effective therapy. In addition, sodium sulfacetamide and salicylic acid preparations have been effective in the treatment of rosacea prior to the introduction of tetracycline.

Metronidazole is a broad-spectrum antibiotic that when administered orally, has been shown to be as effective as tetracycline in the treatment of rosacea. Concern over long-term oral antibiotic use; the disulfiram-like effect of alcohol-induced headaches; neuropathy; and the possible mutagenicity and carcinogenicity of metronidazole—all of these factors reduce the enthusiasm for the use of oral metronidazole in rosacea. Topical metronidazole as a 1% cream has been used in Europe and has been found to be as effective as a daily dose of 500 mg of oxytetracycline. A metronidazole 0.75% gel formulation, now available in the United States, has been shown to be effective in reducing inflammatory papules, pustules, and erythema within 3 weeks of twice-daily usage.

Low-potency topical corticosteroids are also effective in reducing the erythema of rosacea. However, long courses of these agents and shorter courses of high-potency topical corticosteroids produce rebound erythema, telangiectasia, and, occasionally, a full-blown rosacea picture. Therefore, the use of potent topical steroids in rosacea must be avoided.

Once the inflammatory activity of rosacea is controlled with oral tetracycline, rhinophyma can be adequately treated with surgical excision, heated loop, or dermabrader. Carbon dioxide laser excision and ablation has been used as well. Telangiectasia can be removed by continuous wave argon or dye laser or pulsed dye laser surgery or by electrosurgery.

Increasing knowledge concerning the association of flushing with rosacea may yield new therapies. Systemic therapy with vasoconstrictors and vasodilator blockers has thus far not yielded improvement of rosacea. Once the mechanism of vasodilatation in rosacea is elucidated, a specific pharmacologic intervention can be developed.

Arndt KA: Argon laser therapy of small cutaneous vascular lesions. *Arch Dermatol.* 1982;118:220–224.
An alternative to electrodesiccation for the removal of telangiectatic vessels.

Bernstein JE, Soltani A: Alcohol-induced rosacea flushing blocked by naloxone. *Br J Dermatol.* 1982;107:59–61.
Pretreatment with an antihistamine did not block flushing but a narcotic antagonist did. This may be the path to a new agent for therapy.

Bleicher PA, Charles JH, Sober AJ: Topical metronidazole therapy for rosacea. *Arch Dermatol.* 1987;23:609–614.
This medication is now marked specifically for the treatment of rosacea.

Clark DP, Hanke CW: Electrosurgical treatment of rhinophyma. *J Am Acad Dermatol.* 1990;22:831–837.
Thirteen patients with moderate to severe rhinophyma had excellent cosmetic responses with few complications.

Eisen RF, Katz AE, Bohigan RK, Grande DJ: Surgical treatment of rhinophyma with the Shaw scalpel. *Arch Dermatol.* 1986;122:307–309.
A heated scalpel blade is used to remove tissue, followed by carbon dioxide laser and dermabrasion.

el-Azhary R, Roenigk RK, Wang TD. Spectrum of results after treatment of rhinophyma with the carbon dioxide laser. *Mayo Clin Proc.* 1991;66:899–905.
Good to excellent results were obtained in 30 patients treated for rhinophyma with the CO_2 laser and followed for 1 to 4 years.

Ellis CN, Stawiski MA: The treatment of dermatitis, acne rosacea, and seborrheic dermatitis. *Med Clin North Am.* 1982;66:819–830.
An excellent clinical summary of therapy for these facial dermatoses.

Franco HL, Weston WL: Steroid rosacea in children. *Pediatrics.* 1979;64:36–38.
A rosacea-like picture in children is caused by potent topical steroids.

Gamborg Nielsen P: A double-blind study of 1% metronidazole cream versus systemic oxytetracycline for rosacea. *Br J Dermatol.* 1983;109:63–65.
Well-done study demonstrating the remarkable efficacy of metronidazole local therapy for rosacea.

Mills QH, Kligman AM: Topically applied erythromycin in rosacea. *Arch Dermatol.* 1976;112:553–554.
One of the few studies of topical agents other than metronidazole in rosacea.

Schmadel LK, McEvoy GK: Topical metronidazole: A new therapy for rosacea. *Clin Pharm.* 1990;9:94–101.
Metronidazole may work in rosacea due to its anti-inflammatory or immunosuppressive actions rather than by suppressing skin bacteria.

Starr PA: Oculocutaneous aspects of rosacea. *Proc R Soc Med.* 1969;62:9–11.
Classic summary of the ocular manifestations of rosacea.

26. PERIORAL DERMATITIS
Paul A. Bleicher

Perioral dermatitis is a common facial dermatosis that was unrecognized as a distinct clinical entity until the early 1960s. The disorder consists of a papular and eczematous eruption involving the perioral region and occurs predominantly in young women. Initially described as a photosensitive eruption, perioral dermatitis has been attributed to a wide variety of causes including topical corticosteroids, fluorinated toothpaste, contraceptive usage, *Candida, Demodex,* contact dermatitis to cosmetics, and emotional stress.

The syndrome of perioral dermatitis is usually seen in young women in the childbearing years of 15 to 40, but is occasionally described outside this age range and in men. The disease spectrum and etiologic agents may vary, depending on the geographic location. For example, large numbers of patients from England have perioral dermatitis associated with topical corticosteroid use, whereas this finding has been reported less often in the United States.

Clinically, the eruption of perioral dermatitis is unique and recognizable with minimal difficulty by most dermatologists. The initial manifestations are an eruption of 1- to 2-mm flesh- to tan-colored papules clustered on an erythematous and usually scaly base. The eruption is characteristically located around the mouth, especially in the nasolabial fold, and at the angles of the mouth. A distinguishing feature of the eruption is that the vermilion border of the lips is entirely spared. At times the papules may be mixed with pustules as well. Occasionally, the eruption may be localized to the area around the eyes. A history of topical steroid usage can often be obtained from the patient, with control of the eruption during the period of usage but ever-worsening flares on cessation.

The **histologic changes** of perioral dermatitis are predominantly perifollicular spongiosis with mild edema, vasodilatation, and lymphohistiocytic perivascular and perifollicular infiltrates. The changes are descriptive of a perifollicular eczematous pattern. The **differential diagnosis** of perioral dermatitis is similar to that of rosacea. When presenting with typical features, perioral dermatitis is characteristic. Contact dermatitis to cosmetics or medications can mimic the changes of perioral dermatitis. However, the vermilion border is usually not spared in contact dermatitis, whereas the opposite is true in perioral dermatitis. Acne can also be concentrated around the mouth but is distinguished by the presence of comedones and larger papules and pustules. Rosacea can be distinguished by telangiectasia, a lack of localization, and the larger size of the individual lesions. The rashes of glucagonoma, zinc deficiency, *Candida* infection, and *Demodex* infestation do not respond to antibiotic therapy.

The peculiar age and sex distribution as well as the sudden increase in identified cases in the early 1960s has led to a great deal of speculation about the **etiology** of perioral dermatitis. The at-risk group is one with significant exposure to cosmetics, ultraviolet light, hormonal shifts, topical corticosteroid usage, and, possibly, *Demodex* infestations. It is quite likely that perioral dermatitis eruptions can be caused by a variety of different factors. Perhaps the most controversial provocative factor is the usage of topical corticosteroids. Many authors ascribe the use of topical corticosteroids as the etiologic agent in the majority of cases of perioral dermatitis. Often these preparations had been used on the face by a patient who had previously been prescribed the medication for a dermatitis at a distant site. Other authors find that potent topical steroids in fact are capable of controlling the eruption. Initially, an association was made with the use of fluorinated steroids, eventually leading to the theory that fluoride in water supplies and toothpaste could induce perioral dermatitis.

The initial description of the syndrome of perioral dermatitis suggested that the eruption was the result of ultraviolet radiation exposure. Subsequent studies have failed to confirm this suggestion. The results of studies demonstrating overgrowth with *Candida* and fusobacterium can be explained as superinfection of areas previously treated with topical corticosteroids. Finally, physical contact with chin straps, hands, stubble on the chin of a mate, or handkerchiefs is a possible cause of perioral dermatitis-like eruptions.

A thorough history will sometimes reveal possible etiologies for the eruption. Successful therapy in such cases will be dependent on elimination of these factors. Potent topical corticosteroids should be discontinued gradually to avoid a rebound effect.

The mainstay of **therapy** in perioral dermatitis is oral tetracycline in a dosage of 500 mg/d bid. Unlike rosacea, perioral dermatitis can be cleared with a single 6-week course of therapy. Some patients may require higher dosages and longer treatment periods. Erythromycin is apparently less effective as an oral agent but can be used in those patients who are allergic or intolerant to tetracycline or who are pregnant. Topical erythromycin and clindamycin have been used successfully as well.

Proper elimination of causative factors coupled with appropriate oral therapy leads to elimination of the disorder with little recurrence.

Ellis CN, Stawiski MA: The treatment of perioral dermatitis, acne rosacea, and seborrheic dermatitis. *Med Clin North Am.* 1982;66:819–830.
  An excellent clinical summary of therapy for these facial dermatoses.
Macdonald A, Feiwel M: Perioral dermatitis: aetiology and treatment with tetracycline. *Br J Dermatol.* 1972;87:315–317.
  Documentation of the effectiveness of tetracycline therapy.
Marks R, Black MM: Perioral dermatitis: a histopathological study of 26 cases. *Br J Dermatol.* 1971;84:242–247.
  The largest series of biopsy study of perioral dermatitis.
Mihan R, Ayres S Jr.: Perioral dermatitis. *Arch Dermatol.* 1964;89:803.
  The original description of perioral dermatitis.

27. ABNORMALITIES OF SWEATING AND SWEAT GLANDS
Joop M. Grevelink

Sweat gland disorders are characterized by an extensive, sometimes muddled nomenclature. In Greek, *hidros* means sweat, not to be confused with *hydor* (meaning water). Horses sweat, men perspire, women glow; *hidrosis* is the word that encompasses all these activities. *Hyper-* (excessive), *hyp-* or *hypo-* (decreased), *an-* (absent), *chrom-* (colored), and *brom-* (foul smelling) are prefixes that accompany the root *hidrosis*. Additional adjectives may be used to define *bromhidrosis*: *alliaceous* (garlicky), *butyric* (buttery), *caprylic* (goaty), and *caseous* (cheesy). The term *urhidrosis* is used when renal failure and increased serum urea levels lead to an increase in urea excretion by the sweat glands, sometimes even precipitating on the skin as uremic frost. *Dyshidrosis* is a term used to describe chronic vesiculation of the hands and feet (pompholyx). Although this process was originally thought to be related to sweat retention because of accompanying hyperhidrosis, it is actually a true eczematous dermatitis.

Humans have two types of sweat glands: eccrine and apocrine. The eccrine gland is a true sweat gland, while the apocrine gland is thought to be a vestige of the scent gland found in other mammals. Both glands probably function in heat regulation and hydration of the skin, although these tasks are better substantiated for the eccrine gland than for the apocrine gland. The two glands differ in origin, distribution, size, secretory product, and mode of secretion. In humans, both glands are in abundance in the axillae. It is difficult to isolate the excretion of either gland; disorders are therefore often confused or poorly understood.

Eccrine glands are small, coiled glands of epithelial origin whose ducts empty directly onto the cutaneous surface. They are found everywhere except the vermilion border of the lips, nail beds, labia minora, glans penis and inner aspect of prepuce, and are in abundance on the palms and soles and in the axillae. Eccrine sweat, produced in the gland by merocrine secretion, is colorless and odorless (hypotonic, pH 4.5–5.5, SG 1.005). The temperature control center in the hypothalamus is able to detect a minute change in temperature, and when excited, stimulates the number and the activity of sweat glands via sympathetic nonmyelinated class C nerve fibers. Under normal conditions, approximately 500 ml of sweat are produced daily, but this amount can be increased to 2 liters per hour if necessary. The loss of electrolytes is partially counteracted by aldosterone, which induces reabsorption of sodium in the sweat duct. Substances such as lead, mercury, ethanol, and griseofulvin are also partially excreted by eccrine glands.

Apocrine glands are large, lobulated structures of epithelial hair germ origin that secrete by capitation (apocrine secretion) into ducts usually emptying into pilosebaceous units. They are found in the axillae, anogenital region, external ear canals (ceruminous glands), eyelids (Moll's glands), and breasts, and are sparse on the face, scalp, and periumbilical skin. The precise chemical composition of apocrine secretion is not known. Portions of the cytoplasm that are excreted via decapitation are visible on histologic examination of the duct and appear to contain sialomucin. Unlike eccrine sweat, apocrine sweat is a turbid-white fluid that is formed in globular droplets in small amounts. There may be a refractory period of 24 to 48 hours for each gland to form a new droplet once the gland has been emptied. Larger amounts of apocrine sweat can be observed in blacks than in whites, while Asians are said to produce only minute amounts. Apocrine glands also respond to beta-adrenergic stimuli; these glands increase in size and secretory production at puberty.

Hyperhidrosis is excessive sweating of primarily eccrine origin and is often a subjective complaint. It may be useful to distinguish generalized hyperhidrosis from localized hyperhidrosis; the former is often secondary to internal disorders such as CNS lesions involving the hypothalamus, thyrotoxicosis, tuberculosis (night sweats), lymphoma, AIDS, pheochromocytoma, carcinoid syndrome, systemic administration of cholinergic agents, hypoglycemia, shock, syncope, and the Riley-Day syndrome of familial dysautonomia. Treatment of the underlying disease or systemic anticholinergic agents are needed to suppress the generalized sweating. Localized hyperhidrosis is usually seen on the palms and soles or in the axillae, and it can be socially embarrassing. Chronically anxious patients often complain of excessive sweating in these areas. Localized hyperhidrosis at other sites has been reported, although the pathogenesis is unclear. It has been noted in areas affected by vitiligo. It may also compensate for other areas that are anhidrotic. Treatment is often difficult. Glutaraldehyde solution applied topically 3 times a day for 2 weeks, aluminum chloride hexahydrate in absolute alcohol under occlusion, 10% methenamine solution, iontophoresis, relaxation techniques, and systemic anticholinergics (glycopyrrolate 1 to 2 mg bid) may be tried. Generalized or localized hyperhidrosis associated with an altered sweat composition may be seen in patients with cystic fibrosis, Cushing's syndrome, or hyperaldosteronism.

Anhidrosis and **hypohidrosis** can be diagnosed by several methods. A skin biopsy may detect the absence of eccrine glands. In research centers, dibromfluorescein paper or other color indicators are used to facilitate the counting of pores producing sweat with or without stimulation by cholinergic agents. When large areas of the body are hypo- or anhidrotic, thermoregulation can be affected, resulting in nausea, dizziness, palpitations, tachycardia, and hyperpnea. Anhidrosis and hypohidrosis are associated with a number of disorders including hypothyroidism, hypothalamic lesions, spinal cord lesions, orthostatic hypotension, heat stroke, dehydration, congenital ectodermal dysplasias, ichthyosis, scleroderma, lichen sclerosis et atrophicus, and radiodermatitis.

Apocrine **bromhidrosis** usually presents after puberty with the patient complaining of odoriferous secretions from the axillae. In Asians, apocrine glands are relatively inactive, and less bromhidrosis is noted. Gram-positive microorganisms on the skin metabolically degrade apocrine sweat and may be responsible for the odor. The usual treatment consists of antibacterial soaps and deodorant-antiperspirant preparations containing acidic aluminum or zinc salts. The use of 10% to 20% aluminum chloride solution under occlusion (Drysol) for several consecutive nights may also be effective, suppressing both eccrine and apocrine sweat production.

Apocrine **chromhidrosis**, a rarity, is usually seen on the face and in the axillae.

The colored secretions are probably oxidized lipofuscins. With physical exertion, colored droplets appear and quickly dry on the skin, leaving a bluish green hue, sometimes mistaken for comedones. No satisfactory treatment is available, although it is sometimes possible to express the glands and wash off the secretions, giving the patient a 24- to 72-hour interval free of discoloration.

Miliaria is a papulovesicular eruption caused by local obstruction and inflammation of the eccrine sweat duct with sweat retention. Miliaria crystallina occurs when sweat ducts are obstructed in the superficial epidermis by processes such as keratin plugs or edema following a sunburn. This process is usually asymptomatic and self-limiting. Miliaria rubra, often called prickly heat, is characterized by an itchy papulovesicular eruption caused by obstruction of the sweat duct just below the granular layer of the epidermis. When subjected to excessive heat and humidity, virtually all infants develop miliaria rubra, usually over the face and in skin folds. It is also seen in older, bedridden or hospitalized patients, and in this population, miliaria rubra may overlap with Grover's disease (transient acantholytic dermatosis). Cool baths, air conditioning, and minimization of occlusion by clothing or bedding are helpful. Anhydrous lanolin and medium-strength or potent topical steroids may be required if the patient is uncomfortable. Miliaria profunda (tropical anhidrotic asthenia) occurs in persons exposed to hot, humid environments for prolonged periods. Miliaria rubra may precede the lesions of miliaria profunda. Obstruction of the duct occurs deep in the epidermis or upper dermis, producing inflammatory nodules. It is often associated with anhidrosis.

Fox-Fordyce disease, also called apocrine miliaria, results from keratinous obstruction of the intraepidermal ducts of apocrine glands. Frequently seen in women, it presents with itchy, flesh-colored papules in a follicular pattern in the axillary and pubic regions. Local alopecia and a decrease in apocrine sweat may be associated. Topical tretinoin (Retin-A), topical steroids, intralesional and systemic steroids, x ray therapy, and estrogens have all been tried with moderate success.

Hidradenitis suppurativa presents as a chronic suppurative, cicatricial disease in apocrine gland–bearing areas, usually the axillary, genital, and inferior-lateral breast areas. The disease may accompany a personal or familial history of severe acne, perifolliculitis abscedens et suffodiens of the scalp, or a pilonidal sinus. Keratinous plugging of the apocrine duct leads to dilatation of the gland and rupture into the surrounding tissues, causing marked inflammation. Secondary bacterial infection of the involved structures occurs frequently. The diagnosis erroneously but most frequently made is recurrent staphylococcal abscesses. In the affected areas, extensive cyst formation and scarring produce sinus tracts with purulent secretion. Chronic administration of systemic antibiotics with repeated monitoring of the microbiologic environment, incision and drainage of acute abscesses, or excision in toto of large involved areas can all be used to manage this disease.

Eccrine **hidrocystomas** are cystic tumors of the eccrine gland, seen as 1- to 3-mm translucent nodules on the face. They are usually asymptomatic and decrease in size with local anticholinergic agents. Apocrine hidrocystomas also occur on the face, but can also be seen on the scalp, ears, and chest. They are generally solitary translucent bluish nodules, varying in size from 3 mm to 15 mm. On histologic examination, an eccrine hidrocystoma appears as a single cystic cavity in the dermis. It is distinguished from an apocrine hidrocystoma by the absence of decapitation secretion, PAS positive granules, and myoepithelial cells. Treatment of either type of hidrocystoma is generally surgical excision or incision and drainage.

Syringomas are seen more often in women than in men, usually presenting on the eyelids, axillae, umbilicus, vulva, and pubic area. Although the locations suggest an apocrine origin, syringomas are adenomas of the intraepidermal eccrine duct. They appear as multiple small, skin-colored or yellowish 1- to 2-mm soft papules. On histologic examination, numerous small ducts with a double lining of epithelial cells are embedded in a fibrous stroma, with a typical "tadpole" appearance of outer wall cells bulging into the lumen. Rarely, eruptive syringomas occur in young adults with numerous small lesions on the chest and abdomen. Localized lesions may be treated surgically by excision, electrodesiccation, or laser ablation. The number of lesions seen in patients with eruptive syringomas defies adequate treatment.

Eccrine poromas occur as asymptomatic, solitary tumors usually found on the sole, the side of the foot, or the palm. They are firm, slightly pedunculated tumors, up to 2 cm in diameter. On histologic examination, the poroma appears within the lower portion of the epidermis, extending downward as anastomosing bands. The tumor cells contain glycogen. When the poroma is located entirely in the dermis, it is described as a dermal eccrine duct tumor. Eccrine poromatosis is a variant in which more than 100 papules are seen on palms and soles and in other locations. Treatment of solitary lesions is surgical excision. Although rare, malignant eccrine poromas, or porocarcinomas, can develop with extensive metastatic dissemination.

Hidradenoma papilliferum presents in postpubertal women as a small intradermal nodule on the labia minora, in the perineal/perianal area, or, rarely, on the eyelids or nipples. In the dermis, tubular and cystic structures are surrounded by a fibrous capsule with papillary folds extending into the lumen. Treatment for this benign tumor is surgical excision.

Cylindromas are tumors that present as multiple papules and nodules on the face and as dome-shaped smooth nodules with telangiectasia over the scalp (turban tumor). They are frequently familial, inherited as an autosomal dominant trait. The lesions are first noted in early adulthood and increase in size and number throughout life. Occasionally, malignant degeneration is seen. On histologic examination, islands of epithelial cells are surrounded by cylindric hyaline sheaths. It is often unclear whether they stem from eccrine or apocrine tissue. Trichoepitheliomas may be seen in association with cylindromas, suggesting that these types of tumors arise from a common matrix cell. Surgical excision is the only effective treatment known.

Highet AS, Warren RE, Weekes AJ: Bacteriology and antibiotic treatment of perineal suppurative hidradenitis. *Arch Dermatol.* 1988;124:1047–1051.
Twenty-six of thirty-two patients had a plausible bacterial pathogen isolated at least once. The major pathogen was S. milleri. Treatment correlated with disappearance of that organism and with clinical improvement.

O'Loughlin S, Woods R, Kirke PN, et al.: Hidradenitis suppurativa: Glucose tolerance, clinical, microbiologic and immunologic features and HLA frequencies in 27 patients. *Arch Dermatol.* 1988;124(7):1043–1046.
Description of 27 patients in whom diabetes was not a significant association and T lymphocytes were markedly reduced.

Sato K, Kang WM, Saga K, et al.: Biology of sweat glands and their disorders. I. Normal sweat gland function. *J Am Acad Dermatol.* 1989;20(4):537–563.
Well-written update reviewing morphology, control, secretion, and function of the eccrine sweat gland.

Sato K, Kang WM, Saga K, et al.: Biology of sweat glands and their disorders. II. Disorders of sweat gland function. *J Am Acad Dermatol.* 1989;20(5):713–726.
A discussion of disorders described within the past 10 years with hyper- or hypohydrosis. Extensive reference list.

28. DISORDERS OF HAIR AND SCALP
Paul S. Birnbaum

Hair is a structure unique to mammals, formed by the third month of embryologic development. It is a vestigial structure in humans, performing no vital function, although its psychosocial importance is immense. The mature follicle is an elongate cylindric structure consisting of a dermal papilla at its base; internal and external root sheaths, which contribute to the bulk of the hair; and associated appendageal structures, such as sebaceous glands and arrector pili. The fully formed hair shaft is composed of well-organized keratinized plates, which overlap to form a shingle effect. An inner medulla and outer cortex can be distinguished with microscopy.

Three major types of hair are recognized: lanugo (fetal), vellus (soft and unmedullated), and terminal (coarse). The development of secondary hair at puberty, from vellus to terminal, and the conversion of terminal hair to vellus in male-pattern baldness are both, paradoxically, dependent on androgenic control.

Each hair follicle undergoes a predictable life cycle consisting of three major phases: (1) anagen, the growing phase, lasting approximately 1000 days; (2) catagen, the dying phase; and (3) telogen, the resting phase, lasting approximately 100 days. The human scalp contains about 100,000 follicles. Since 10% of the follicles are normally in telogen, 100 hairs a day are shed on average. New hairs take 3 weeks to reach the scalp surface and grow at a rate of approximately 1 cm per month. Hair length is genetically determined, depending on the duration of anagen and the rate of hair growth.

Numerous **congenital syndromes** that include abnormalities in the quantity and quality of the hair have been described. Among these are the ectodermal dysplasias, Hallermann-Streiff syndrome, and the premature-aging syndromes. In most of the described syndromes, the hair is sparse with occasional structural defects.

The **evaluation** of a patient with a hair disorder requires the physician to take a careful history, perform a directed physical examination, and order or perform appropriate laboratory tests. The history should include the onset of the condition, any association with possible inciting events (stress, hair care products or techniques, diet, medications), associated symptoms and signs (pruritus, acne, masculinization, etc.), and any relevant familial or personal medical history. Examination of the hair must include a determination of the amount and localization of any loss, any changes in the color or texture of the hair, and an evaluation of the scalp, including the presence or absence of erythema, broken hairs, and scale. When the physician is evaluating a patient with alopecia, determining whether follicular scarring is present is fundamental to making a diagnosis. Close examination with a hand lens is often necessary to confirm the presence or absence of intact follicles. Appropriate laboratory tests may include a potassium hydroxide preparation or culture for fungus, CBC, serum iron, serum androgens, antinuclear antibodies, and thyroid function tests.

Alopecia areata (AA), a noncicatricial alopecia, is a common disorder of unknown etiology, causing well-circumscribed areas of total hair loss in any hair-bearing area, but most typically the scalp. The disorder can occur at any age, with 75% of cases occurring before age 25. Patients with atopy, Down's syndrome, or a family history of AA are particularly prone. Psychological trauma is often implicated as a predisposing event in AA. However, in a study of 73 patients with AA, only 23% reported that nervous stress preceded their attacks. Although autoimmune phenomena have been proposed as a possible etiology for the disorder, no HLA genotypes have been consistently associated with AA; and AA, unlike most autoimmune disorders, doesn't cause any permanent destruction of tissue. Supporting the theory of an immunologic cause for AA is (1) the presence of a perifollicular lymphocytic infiltrate composed of helper T cells in biopsy specimens and (2) a slightly increased incidence of other autoimmune diseases such as Hashimoto's thyroiditis, diabetes mellitus, pernicious anemia, and vitiligo in affected patients.

The typical initial lesion appears over a 24-hour period as an asymptomatic, smooth, bald patch measuring 3 to 4 cm. Some patients note a tingling sensation of the affected area. The scalp is most commonly affected, but the beard, eyebrows, and eyelashes are often involved. In early lesions, 3-mm tapered hairs (exclamation-mark hairs) may be seen around the periphery, and this is an important diagnostic sign. Multiple areas may be affected, sometimes coalescing to form large hairless areas. Rarely, the entire scalp (alopecia totalis) or body surface (alopecia universalis) may be involved. A fine stippling of the nails may be seen in 10% of patients.

The course of alopecia areata is variable. Approximately half of all affected patients experience full regrowth within 1 year. However, one-third of patients never recover from their first attack, and recurrences are common. Factors associated with a poor prognosis include onset at an early age, severe involvement, baldness over 1 year, nail dystrophy, ophiasis (a band of alopecia around the peripheral scalp), and atopy.

For most cases of AA, no treatment is necessary, as the condition is often self-resolving. A high-strength topical corticosteroid gel or solution may be prescribed, although the effectiveness of this practice is questionable. Intralesional steroids are somewhat effective, especially for the eyebrows. For patients with limited disease, triamcinolone acetonide (Kenalog) 5 mg/ml may be injected into involved areas monthly without much risk of dermal atrophy. Good results are obtainable with systemic corticosteroids, but their frequent side effects make their use unjustifiable in almost all patients. Psoralen with ultraviolet light is often effective in severe cases of AA; PUVA has been shown to have a slight immunomodulating effect by decreasing peripheral helper T cells and may work for AA in this way. Other therapies include the use of contact sensitizers (such as diphenylcyclopropenone dinitrochlorobenzene, anthralin, and squaric acid dibutyl ester), minoxidil, and cyclosporine. The patient with severe disease should be told that most therapeutic attempts are unsuccessful. The physician must help the patient make the difficult psychological adjustment to not having hair. The Alopecia Areata Foundation is a national information source for patients, and it sponsors local support groups in major cities.

Telogen effluvium, a noncicatricial alopecia, is second only to male-pattern alopecia as the most common cause of hair loss. The disorder is caused by an alteration of the normal hair-growth cycle. A shift of a large number of anagen follicles to telogen results in an increase in shedding. Although over 25% of the scalp hair must be lost before alopecia becomes obvious, patients will notice an increase in the amount of hair found in brushes and shower drains. Physical or emotional stress frequently precedes the disorder. High fever may lead to hair loss 8 to 10 weeks after the event. Postpartum alopecia is quite common and typically starts 1 to 4 months after childbirth, with resolution taking more than 1 year. Many drugs, including beta-blockers and anticoagulants, may also cause a diffuse telogen effluvium. A similar condition to telogen effluvium is seen in patients suffering from iron deficiency anemia or malnutrition. Telogen hairs fail to reenter anagen, and a net loss of hair is noted.

A detailed medical history is essential to determine the etiology of suspected telogen effluvium. The physician should pay particular attention to medications, diet, and physical and psychological stresses. A definitive diagnosis can be made if the physician observes over 25% telogen hairs in a hair-pull examination. The physician performs the test by grabbing 20 to 30 hairs close to the scalp with a rubber-tipped needle holder, pulling briskly, and examining the hair bulbs microscopically. The test is relatively painless when done properly.

Spontaneous regrowth is characteristic in telogen effluvium, often occurring within 6 months, but chronic cases may last over 2 years. Patients should be reassured that the hair loss is never total and, in fact, is rarely noticeable except to the patient and close associates. Medical treatment is ineffective unless the incipient cause is corrected (in the case of iron deficiency, malnutrition, or drug etiologies).

Anagen effluvium is a sudden, profound hair loss due to antimitotic agents used in cancer chemotherapy (especially vincristine, cyclophosphamide, nitrogen mustard, and 6-mercaptopurine), therapeutic radiation therapy, or certain ingested chemicals (lead, arsenic, mercury).

The pathophysiology of anagen effluvium (another noncicatricial alopecia) is a direct antimitotic effect on the dermal papilla of the hair follicle. Use of a scalp tourniquet during vincristine injection will minimize the amount of alopecia. Continuous low-dose cyclophosphamide causes less hair loss than intermittent high-dose administration.

Traumatic alopecia, a noncicatricial alopecia, usually presents as linear, incompletely bald areas, which suggest an artifactual etiology to the clinician. The most common causes are traction of the hair (from vigorous brushing, curlers, or certain hair styles) and trichotillomania (self-induced alopecia due to frequent scratching, twirling, or pulling of the hair). A high index of suspicion and careful questioning may lead the clinician to perform a punch biopsy to confirm the diagnosis. Microscopically, the biopsy specimen shows hemorrhages in the follicles as a result of the traumatic extraction of the hair. Total regrowth of hair is expected once the patient is made aware of the etiology and discontinues the inciting practice. Treatment for trichotillomania is more difficult since many patients will deny or be unaware of the self-manipulation. A close doctor-patient relationship, coupled with reassurance and treatment with mild shampoos, is an important first step toward treating this condition. In children, the condition is sometimes cured with a very short haircut.

Male-pattern (androgenic) alopecia is a genetically determined hair loss that begins as a bitemporal recession of the hairline and thinning of the vertex area. The inheritance pattern appears to be polygenic. A gradual diminution in hair shaft diameters and length of anagen occur and can result, in men, in a near-total replacement of the scalp hair with vellus hair. A band of hair along the peripheral scalp is always retained, which is the reason for using this area as a donor site for hair transplantation. The pattern differs in women, with a diffuse thinning of the parietal and vertex areas being most common. Onset in men can be as early as adolescence, but in women, onset generally occurs after menopause. Early onset heralds a profound, although noncicatricial, alopecia.

Androgens play a major role in pattern alopecia, and women with significant hair loss of this type should be evaluated for an underlying endocrine disturbance. Laboratory values sometimes elevated in affected females are total testosterone, free testosterone, and dehydroepiandrosterone sulfate.

Topical minoxidil (Rogaine) is the only effective medical treatment for slowing and occasionally reversing hair loss of the vertex, but is less effective for treating recession of the hairline. Almost all patients experience a slowing of hair loss. Moderate growth of new hair is seen in 25% of patients at 4 months and in 50% at 12 months. New hair growth tends to stabilize at 18 months. A 2% minoxidil lotion must be applied twice a day to the balding area and continued indefinitely to maintain any new hair. Results correlate with the number of indeterminate hairs present, the duration of baldness, and the size of the balding area. Young patients with a recent onset of a small, incompletely bald area of the vertex have the best results.

The mechanism of minoxidil's action in alopecia is uncertain, but it probably operates by sending a molecular message to stimulate the dermal papilla. Its vasodilatory effect appears to play no role in promoting hair growth, as other vasodilators have no such effect. Although systemic minoxidil is a potent antihypertensive, topical use has no effect on blood pressure because of the subtherapeutic amounts of the drug that are absorbed. Side effects from topical minoxidil are rare and are predominantly dermatologic in nature (i.e., pruritus and irritant dermatitis). Nevertheless, blood pressure monitoring is an important part of patient follow-up.

Dramatic improvement of male-pattern alopecia can be obtained with hair transplantation. The physiologic basis for hair transplantation depends on the concept of "donor dominance," which was proposed by Orentreich in the 1950s. He observed that the hair in full-thickness skin grafts retained the characteristics of the donor site indefinitely. Since a band of hair around the peripheral scalp is always retained even in advanced male-pattern alopecia, this area is used as the donor site. Small plugs of hair-bearing scalp are "harvested" from the donor site. Small plugs of bald skin at the recipient site are then removed and discarded. The resulting holes are filled with donor plugs. Several hundred plugs must be transplanted over several sessions to yield a good result.

Tinea capitis should always be considered in the differential diagnosis of localized alopecia. It is much more common in children than in adults. Early infection appears as a coin-sized bald patch, typically near the vertex. While a peripheral scale is a hallmark of tinea corporis, dermatophyte infections of the scalp may or may not have scale. This is because fungal infections of the scalp involve the hair predominantly, and the skin to a minor degree. A skin sample for potassium hydroxide examination must contain several stubby hairs that can be extracted from the involved area. Microscopy of ectothrix infections reveals hundreds of spores on the hair, while hyphae and spores are seen within the hair shaft in endothrix infections. Although some fungi will fluoresce green under a Wood's light (UVA), *Trichophyton tonsurans*, currently the most common dermatophyte causing tinea capitis, does not fluoresce, thereby minimizing the sensitivity of this previously useful shortcut test. Advanced tinea capitis often becomes crusted and secondarily infected with bacteria forming a kerion. At that point, rapid diagnosis and treatment is necessary to avoid scarring. The treatment of choice for tinea capitis is oral griseofulvin for 4 to 6 weeks.

A wide range of inflammatory conditions involving the follicle result in complete destruction of the pilosebaceous unit with scarring. The most commonly seen disorders causing **cicatricial alopecia** are discoid lupus erythematosus (DLE), lichen planopilaris (LPP), morphea, cicatricial pemphigoid, and follicular mucinosis. The hallmark of DLE is the presence of follicular plugging, typically seen in the active periphery. LPP is the scalp equivalent of lichen planus, which frequently does not occur coincidentally. LPP appears as punctate, pink papules within a balding patch. Cicatricial pemphigoid may appear as crusts resembling artifacta and does not always present with bullae. With all cicatricial alopecias, biopsy from an active area is necessary to confirm one's clinical suspicions.

Neoplasms of the scalp (e.g., basal cell carcinoma), certain infections (e.g., herpes zoster, leprosy), and physical injury (e.g., burns, radiodermatitis) may also result in scarring.

The amount of body hair varies tremendously across races and ethnicities. Women with excessive body hair, without other signs of masculinization, are usually found to be normal physiologic variants within their ethnic group. When other masculinizing signs are present, a complete endocrinologic evaluation is indicated. Initial laboratory investigation should include urinary 17-ketosteroids and plasma testosterone and DHEA-S levels.

Acquired generalized **hirsutism** with lanugo hairs (hypertrichosis lanuginosa acquisita) is strongly associated with internal malignancy.

Defects in the structure of the hair shaft often result in increased hair fragility. **Monilethrix** is an autosomal dominant disorder characterized by hair shafts with a beaded, or nodal, appearance. The hair is commonly normal at birth but changes in the first months of life. Follicular keratosis is often present in the occiput. **Trichorrhexis nodosa** hairs are so fragile that the patient may present with stubble or gross alopecia. Light microscopic examination of longer hairs reveals areas of longitudinal fissuring and breakage, giving the appearance of interlocking brooms. A mild acquired form may occur after repeated trauma. The congenital form is occasionally associated with argininosuccinicaciduria, an enzyme disorder characterized by mental retardation and increased levels of argininosuccinic acid in the body fluids. **Trichorrhexis invaginata** (bamboo hair) is frequently a sign of Netherton's syndrome, an autosomal recessive disorder also characterized by atopy and ichthyosis linearis circumflexa. Nodes along affected hair shafts have the appearance of a ball-and-socket joint under light microscopy. Spontaneous remission may occur in adolescence. The hairs of **pili torti** show periodic 180-degree twists along their shafts at sites where the hair is flattened. Pili torti may be found as an isolated finding in childhood, presenting in a child with brittle hair that has a dry, lusterless appearance. **Menkes' kinky hair syndrome** is an X-linked recessive disorder of copper metabolism and is characterized by pili torti, seizures, characteristic facies, psychomotor retardation, arterial changes, low plasma copper and ceruloplasm, and death by the age of 4. Treatment with intravenous copper is not effective.

Some hair shaft defects do not result in increased hair fragility. The hair of **pili annulati** has alternating light and dark bands due to air-filled spaces in the cortex, giving the scalp hair a ringed appearance that may appear attractive. "Spun-glass" hair (**pili trianguli et canaliculi**) has a triangular appearance in cross-section. The hair stands out from the scalp as if it were electrically charged.

Birnbaum PS, Baden HP: Heritable disorders of hair. *Dermatol Clin.* 1987;5:137–153.
   A concise review of congenital abnormalities of the hair shaft and syndromes with a hair defect as a contributing characteristic. The disorders are arbitrarily grouped into five classes: primary hair shaft disorders, alopecia without associated defects, ectodermal dysplasias, changes in hair color, and ectopic hair.

Katz HI, Hien NT, Prawer SE, et al.: Long-term efficacy of topical minoxidil in male pattern baldness. *J Am Acad Dermatol.* 1987;16:711–718.
   In a 24-month double-blind study of 153 men with vertex androgenic alopecia, there was a statistically significant increase in terminal hair counts of the vertex with minoxidil usage, but few men had cosmetic improvement. A stabilization of the

balding area was noted in most patients. Usage of 2% and 3% minoxidil solutions gave similar results. No serious drug-related adverse reactions were noted.

Kuster W, Happle R: The inheritance of common baldness: two B or not two B? *J Am Acad Dermatol.* 1984;11:921–926.

A discussion of genetic factors influencing male-pattern baldness. Noting the high prevalence, variation of phenotype, and variable risk of acquisition of pattern baldness dependent on the number, severity, and sex of ancestors with the trait, the authors suggest a polygenic inheritance for androgenic alopecia.

Kvedar JC, Gibson M, Krusinski PA: Hirsutism: evaluation and treatment. *J Am Acad Dermatol.* 1985;12:215–225.

A thorough review of the chemical and endocrine causes for hirsutism in females, with guidelines for patient evaluation. The most commonly found organic abnormalities are elevated testosterone production, elevated serum free testosterone, elevated testosterone clearance, decreased sex-hormone–binding globulin, and increased hair follicle sensitivity. The authors discuss treatment with low-dose dexamethasone, oral contraceptives, and spironolactone.

Tosti A, Bardazzi F, Guerra L: Alopecia totalis: Is treating nonresponder patients useful? *J Am Acad Dermatol.* 1991;24(3):455–456.

One hundred fourteen patients with alopecia universalis or totalis were treated with various sensitizing agents. Eighty-three patients responded to treatment with mild to profuse hair growth. Twenty-six of the nonresponders were treated more aggressively with topical cyclosporine, PUVA, or intravenous thymopentin. None of the 26 patients responded to the aggressive treatments. The authors conclude that aggressive treatment is not useful in patients with profound alopecia areata who do not respond to topical sensitizers.

Whiting DA: Structural abnormalities of the hair shaft. *J Am Acad Dermatol.* 1987;16:1–25.

A complete review of the commonly recognized hair shaft defects, with photographs and presumed pathophysiology. The major hair shaft abnormalities are grouped as fractures, irregularities, twists, and extraneous matter on the hair shaft.

29. DISORDERS OF THE NAILS
Joseph C. Kvedar

The nail is an easily visualized, highly structured skin appendage. Most clinicians, even well-trained dermatologists, find evaluation of nail disease difficult. However, like the skin, the nail unit has a limited number of reaction patterns through which it can express disease. This chapter organizes nail diseases by reaction pattern so that the differential diagnosis and pathophysiology may become clear to clinicians evaluating nail disease in the office.

The **nail unit** is composed of the nail plate, nail matrix, nail bed, and nail folds. The nail plate derives its hardness from an increased number of disulfide bonds in nail keratins relative to epidermal keratins and a decreased ability to hold water because of a relative lack of lipid. The nail plate is surrounded on three sides by the proximal and lateral nail folds, which are invaginations of epidermis that provide a guiding groove for nail growth. In addition, the cuticle grows from the proximal nail fold onto the nail plate and seals the matrix and adjacent soft nail from the outside world. At the innermost inferior edge of the proximal nail fold is the specialized epidermis, the matrix, which produces nail. This region can be divided into proximal and distal portions, which make nail of slightly different biochemical character, but they cannot be anatomically distinguished except at the ultrastructural level. As nail matrix cells differentiate, they keratinize, lose their nuclei, and become compact to produce the nail plate. The growth of nail plate is variable but approximates 0.1 mm per day. The nail bed provides a surface for the growing nail to adhere to, but does not contribute directly to the formation of the nail plate.

Acute paronychia is a red, painful, warm swelling of the proximal or lateral nail fold that causes separation of the fold from the nail and is associated with purulent drainage. In a recent series of 33 cases requiring surgical drainage, a variety of aerobic and anaerobic organisms were recovered, including various species of streptococci and staphylococci. Culture and appropriate antibiotic therapy are warranted. Incision and drainage are appropriate if an abscess is present. The differential diagnosis includes herpetic whitlow, which usually has some vesicular component.

Chronic paronychia has a more insidious course. The important diagnostic feature is separation of the cuticle from the nail plate and retraction of the proximal nail fold. Occasionally some swelling, redness, and mild tenderness of the proximal nail fold occur. Patients are often most concerned with secondary nail plate changes, typically ridging, thickening, and onycholysis (separation of the nail plate from the nail bed).

The etiology of chronic paronychia has not been convincingly demonstrated. It often occurs in individuals who have their hands in and out of water frequently as part of their occupation. Intermittent stretching and relaxation of the nail fold due to hydration may play a role. A mixture of organisms can usually be isolated by culture, including *Candida* species, *Streptococcus pyogenes* and *Pseudomonas* species. These organisms may also be seen on smears obtained from scraping underneath the proximal nail fold or from pus expressed by massaging the proximal nail fold. This clinical picture can also occasionally be seen as an accompanying feature of severe inflammatory skin disease such as eczematous dermatitis affecting the nail fold. Treatment of these patients includes an effort to isolate yeast and bacteria by scrapings and cultures, then treatment with appropriate antibiotics. Topical antifungal treatment with one of the imidazole derivatives is appropriate if yeasts are found. Systemic therapy with ketoconazole may be warranted for severe involvement. However, antimicrobial therapy alone is usually not sufficient to rectify the process, and the crucial aspect of therapy is avoidance of water, best accomplished by the patient's wearing cotton glove liners under loose-fitting rubber work gloves. In recalcitrant cases, surgical excision of 2 to 3 mm of nail fold has been used to reduce dead space and allow healing.

Proximal nail fold telangiectasias are not visible in the normal nail unit. They appear in connective tissue diseases, most commonly systemic lupus erythematosus and dermatomyositis, and occasionally scleroderma and rheumatoid arthritis. Their presence should prompt a search for these diseases. Conversely, when connective tissue disease is suspected, proximal nail fold telangiectasias are usually found. In some cases, use of a hand lens and application of mineral oil to the nail fold may aid evaluation. In one study of a small group of patients, it was possible to distinguish between the various connective tissue diseases by the pattern of proximal nail fold telangiectasias.

A variety of **tumors** may involve the nail fold. When the proximal nail fold is involved, the nail plate may secondarily develop longitudinal ridging and hypertrophy. This location is typical for digital myxoid cysts, usually found in patients older than 50, and for periungual fibromas associated with tuberous sclerosis. Digital myxoid cysts appear as soft, round swellings on the dorsa of the fingers between the proximal nail fold and the distal interphalangeal (DIP) joint. Histologic evaluation of an excised lesion does not reveal a true cyst but does show a loosely organized myxoid stroma with large mucin-containing spaces. Treatment is difficult. Methods used include needle aspiration, intralesional steroid injection, cryosurgery, and excision in toto. Recurrence rates of 10% to 20% are common, particularly when a sinus tract communicates the cyst with the DIP joint, as has been documented by at least one group of investigators. Periungual fibromas of tuberous sclerosis appear to grow out from beneath the nail folds. They are smooth, firm, flesh-colored, conical papules. Human papillomavirus infections (warts) and squamous cell carcinomas also commonly cause tumorous processes in the nail fold.

The nail plate is a direct product of the matrix, so all **primary abnormalities of the nail plate** can be thought of as resulting from defects in nail matrix maturation.

Anonychia, the absence of a formed nail plate, usually results either from congenital abnormalities of the matrix or from scarring diseases that ablate the matrix.

The nail-patella syndrome, transmitted by an autosomal dominant trait, consists of nail atrophy or absence and hypoplastic patellas. Nephropathy occurs in one-third of cases, with an examination of the urine sediment suggesting a chronic glomerulonephritis and a renal biopsy revealing a thickened glomerular basement membrane. The DOOR syndrome (deafness, onycho-osteodystrophy, and mental retardation) has the unique finding of triphalangeal thumbs and biphalangeal fingers as well as absent nails. In the Cronkhite-Canada syndrome, dystrophic or absent nails are associated with diffuse hyperpigmentation of the palms and volar aspects of the fingers, macular hyperpigmentation of the dorsa of the fingers, and gastrointestinal polyps. Acquired anonychia may occur secondary to trauma and, rarely, from primary skin disease such as lichen planus or cicatricial pemphigoid. Psoriasis, dermatophytes, and other fungi do not cause permanent loss of the nail without severe secondary bacterial infection that produces scarring. In alopecia areata, nails may be shed similarly to hair because of a lymphocyte-mediated attack of keratinizing skin appendages.

Pterygium is a distinctive abnormality of the nail unit in which there is adherence of the proximal nail fold to the nail bed as a result of disease scarring the matrix, fold, and bed. The proximal nail fold develops the appearance of a wing, giving rise to its descriptive terminology. The differential diagnosis of pterygium is similar to that of processes causing an anonychia secondary to scarring, and they may be seen together in the same patient. Lichen planus is the most common etiology. Two hereditary diseases, dyskeratosis congenita and epidermolysis bullosa, are also typically associated with pterygium. In dyskeratosis congenita, reported to have both X-linked dominant and autosomal dominant transmission, nail abnormalities are accompanied by leukoplakia of the oral mucosa, reticulate hyperpigmentation of the skin, anemia, dental caries, and esophageal web formation. In some types of epidermolysis bullosa, blistering skin lesions develop after minor trauma and heal with scarring. When the process occurs in the nail unit, pterygium can result.

Dyschromia of the nail plate may result from a variety of disorders. White nails (leukonychia), occurring as a result of disordered keratinization producing parakeratosis in the distal nail matrix, are seen in psoriasis, exfoliative dermatitis, and nutritional deficiency. Leukonychia may also be inherited, presenting at birth or later. Dermatophyte infection can result in a chalky white appearance of the nail plate (white superficial onychomycosis), due to microscopic fracture of the nail plate by the invading fungus, typically *Trichophyton mentagrophytes*. The diagnosis is easily made by microscopic examination of a KOH preparation of scrapings from the nail surface.

Yellow nails can result from jaundice, psoriasis, tetracycline ingestion, topical application of yellowing agents such as cosmetics, hidrotic ectodermal dysplasia, and the yellow nail syndrome. They may also be seen as a manifestation of the acquired immunodeficiency syndrome. The yellow nail syndrome is a clinical constellation of yellow nails, lymphedema, and pleural effusions. Of 97 cases recently reviewed, 89% had yellow nails and in 37% this was the initial symptom. Lymphedema was present in 80%. The authors of this review felt that two of three signs were sufficient to make the diagnosis. No clear disease associations were made and the etiology remains obscure. The yellow color of the nail plate has been successfully treated with nail fold injections of glucocorticoids.

Pigmented streaks due to melanin deposition in the nail plate are a normal color variation in blacks. In whites, they are usually produced by a junctional melanocytic nevus within the nail matrix, but can also be a manifestation of melanoma. Although only 2% to 3% of melanomas in whites involve the nail unit, and the vast majority of these arise in the nail bed, melanoma cannot be excluded as a cause for a longitudinal pigmented streak on clinical grounds alone. If the streak is of recent onset or if the nail bed or the nail fold is involved (Hutchinson's sign), a nail matrix biopsy must be performed. Also in the differential diagnosis of a pigmented streak is subungual hemorrhage, which is often associated with a history of trauma. A subungual hemorrhage is usually wide and irregular with a violet-brown color, whereas a pigmented streak within the nail plate is often narrow and regular. Avulsion of the nail may occasionally be necessary to distinguish the source of the pigment. Investigation and close follow-up are warranted for all pigmented streaks.

Abnormal texture of the nail plate may occur in a large variety of processes. In psoriasis, focal parakeratosis (histologic evidence of abnormal maturation of epidermal cells) in the proximal matrix gives rise to a column of parakeratotic cells that adhere poorly and slough as the nail grows out, producing pitting of the surface of nails. Other manifestations of psoriasis in the nail plate include transverse grooves, crumbling, and irregular thickening of the plate resulting from parakeratosis in both the proximal and the distal matrix. Alopecia areata is associated with a wide variety of similar nail plate abnormalities, such as ridging, pitting, and crumbling as well as atrophy and anonychia. Lichen planus is not always a scarring process and can produce isolated plate changes such as ridging and pitting. Keratosis follicularis (Darier-White disease) commonly results in longitudinal ridging and distal notching of the nail.

Twenty-nail dystrophy of childhood is an interesting and controversial disorder that occurs in early childhood as a self-limited, acquired dystrophy of all twenty nails. Excessive longitudinal ridging is characteristic. Nail plates are also thin, dull, fragile, and opalescent. Although originally defined as an idiopathic disorder occurring in the absence of other explanations for the nail changes, some authors suggest it might represent a "nails only" variant of lichen planus, eczema, alopecia areata, or psoriasis. Examination of biopsy specimens of the nail matrix from cases of twenty-nail dystrophy has revealed, almost exclusively, histologic changes suggestive of lichen planus. No useful therapy has been identified.

Manifestations of **nail bed pathology** include pachyonychia and onycholysis.

Pachyonychia is an abnormality of nail bed keratinization that results in hyperkeratosis of the nail bed, causing subungual debris and lifting of the nail plate. The majority of cases of acquired pachyonychia are related to dermatophyte infection or psoriasis. Psoriasis is usually a diagnosis of exclusion, suggested when the patient has other signs of psoriasis and persistently negative fungal cultures. A nail bed biopsy may be necessary to confirm the diagnosis. Rarely, pachyonychia may be caused by squamous cell carcinoma in situ, incontinentia pigmenti, or epidermal nevi. Pachyonychia congenita, a rare autosomal dominant condition, manifests as marked subungual hyperkeratosis in the absence of nail matrix or plate abnormalities, and is associated with natal teeth, oral leukokeratosis, hyperhidrosis, and palmar and plantar keratoderma.

Onychomycosis, a dermatophyte infection of the nail bed, is a common problem, with an incidence of about 20% and is more common in men than in women. It is almost universal in the elderly. Toenails are most often affected alone, but rarely fingernails may also be involved. Species isolated include *Trichophyton rubrum, T. mentagrophytes,* and occasionally *Epidermophyton floccosum.* Pathogenesis is not completely understood, but the fungus allegedly invades the epidermis just under the distal margin of the nail plate and proceeds proximally to involve the bed, producing onycholysis and pachyonychia. To make the diagnosis, onycholytic nail is clipped and subungual debris is scraped from the nail bed. Microscopic examination of a KOH preparation of the debris will reveal hyphae in 50% of cases with clinically suspected onychomycosis. Only 50% of specimens with positive microscopy will yield organisms on culture. The more distal the location of the specimen examined or cultured, the higher the rate of failure to demonstrate the organism. Samples should therefore be taken from as close to adherent nail as possible.

Treatment of onychomycosis is difficult, but may include repeated mechanical debridement of infected subungual debris or removal of the nail plate in toto and use of topical or systemic antimycotics. Nail plates can be chemically removed with an ointment containing 30% salicylic acid and 40% urea in petrolatum USP. After the normal skin is protected with petrolatum, the ointment is applied under an occlusive dressing. After about 3 weeks, the nail plate will be soft and will debride easily. Nails can also be removed surgically. After removal of nail and subungual debris, topical treatment with an imidazole derivative and systemic griseofulvin may be used in conjunction for a duration of 12 to 18 months. Even with heroic efforts, only 12% to 20% of toenail infections clear, with a relapse rate as high as 50% after 6 months. These dismal results lead most practitioners to discourage patients from undergoing treatment. Fingernail infections have a higher response rate, about 60%

and a lower relapse rate. Ketoconazole may be slightly more effective; but its use cannot be justified in most cases, because of the 1:10,000 incidence of hepatitis and the rarer, but more worrisome, occurrence of fatal hepatic disease. Elderly patients are best served by routine podiatric care to cut and shape the nails and the regular use of a topical antifungal cream on the skin of the entire foot and between the toes to prevent tinea pedis and subsequent secondary bacterial infection.

Onycholysis is the separation of the nail plate from the nail bed, and is obvious because the lifted nail takes on a yellowish hue. Onycholysis is distinctive but nonspecific, and may be multifactorial in pathogenesis. Most commonly, it is associated with trauma (either during a manicure or incidental), maceration, exposure to chemicals or use of nail cosmetics, combined with secondary invasion of fungi, yeast, and bacteria. In a recent series of 113 cases of onycholysis of the great toes, 30% had evidence of infection. The most common microbes found in abnormal toenails are dermatophytes, and in fingernails, yeasts and bacteria. Dermatophyte infections can produce isolated onycholysis, but more commonly both onycholysis and pachyonychia are seen. In contrast, yeast species frequently cause patchy and irregular onycholysis without subungual debris. A greenish discoloration may occur when *Pseudomonas* species are present.

Onycholysis has many other, rarer causes. When it is caused by drugs, it is often symmetric and uniform in appearance. Drug reactions may produce onycholysis by phototoxicity, a mechanism implicated for tetracyclines, especially doxycycline, and the phenothiazines. Nonphotosensitizing drugs that produce onycholysis are chiefly cancer chemotherapeutic agents such as doxorubicin and 5-fluorouracil. Skin diseases affecting other parts of the nail unit, such as psoriasis, lichen planus, and eczematous dermatitis, may also produce onycholysis. Pemphigus vegetans, lichen striatus, and hyperhidrosis have been reported. Onycholysis may also be associated with pregnancy and with metabolic diseases such as diabetes mellitus, thyroid disease, porphyria, pellagra, and iron deficiency. In addition, there are reports of familial and congenital onycholysis.

The clinician begins the evaluation for onycholysis, as with onychomycosis, by clipping the nail and testing samples of the nail plate and scrapings of the nail bed microscopically and by culturing for evidence of fungal, yeast, and bacterial infection. Often more than one microbial agent is found. Treatment includes regular clipping of onycholytic nail and application of a topical antifungal such as an imidazole derivative. Successful therapy of fingernail onycholysis due to *Candida* must involve strict avoidance of water. In refractory cases, if a patient has made a successful effort to avoid water, a 6-month course of ketoconazole may be considered. When pathogenic bacteria have been isolated, antibiotics can also be administered. Soaking nails in diluted acetic acid (vinegar) will eradicate *Pseudomonas*. Unfortunately, however, treating associated bacterial infection is rarely sufficient to reverse onycholysis. Any other predisposing factor or skin disease should also be treated as effectively as possible. Published cure rates associated with any regimen are difficult to find.

Color changes in the nail bed may be diagnostic of a number of systemic conditions. A bluish color occurs in carbon monoxide poisoning, argyria, and ochronosis. Brown pigmentation is associated with Addison's disease, and transverse white lines with hypoalbuminemia. In Terry's nails, associated with cirrhosis, the proximal portion of the nail bed is white, while the distal 1 to 2 mm have a reddish color. In half-and-half nails, a manifestation of renal failure, the proximal portion is white and the distal half is brown or reddish brown.

A number of **tumors** primary to the skin can involve the nail bed, but only the glomus tumor occurs with greater frequency in the nail bed than elsewhere. These lesions are discrete, painful papules, bluish in color. Diagnosis is made by biopsy. An acquired digital fibrokeratoma, a firm flesh-colored papule with a hyperkeratotic surface and a surrounding "moat," is usually found on the distal digit, but can involve the nail bed and cause the nail plate to lift. Histologically, these lesions appear to be hamartomatous growths of fibrous tissue with reactive epidermal hyperplasia. The treatment for both of these tumors is excision.

Achten G, Parent D: The normal and pathologic nail. *Int J Dermatol.* 1983;22:556–565.
  A review of pathologic disturbances as they relate to the normal structure, ultrastructure, and biochemistry of the nail unit.
Andre J, Achten G: Onychomycosis. *Int J Dermatol.* 1987;26:481–490.
  The most complete of a number of current reviews on onychomycosis.
Baden HP: *Diseases of the Hair and Nails.* Chicago, IL: Yearbook Medical Publishers; 1987. An authoritative textbook.
Baran R, Dawber RPR (eds.): *Diseases of the Nails and Their Management.* Oxford: Blackwell Scientific Publications; 1984.
  A very thorough and extensively referenced textbook containing excellent photographs and figures.
Kechijian P: Onycholysis of the fingernails: evaluation and management. *J Am Acad Dermatol.* 1985;12:552–560.
  A well-organized and thorough discussion of onycholysis, its causes, and its therapy.
Norton LA: Nail disorders, a review. *J Am Acad Dermatol.* 1980;2:451–467.
  This review is best considered an update to already acquired basic information. Its discussion of genetic disorders and tumors is particularly useful.
Scher RK, Norton LA: Periodic synopsis: Diseases of the nails. *J Am Acad Dermatol.* 1986;15:523–528.
  A useful list of references from 1983 to 1986.
Siegle RJ, Swanson NA: Nail surgery: a review. *J Dermatol Surg Oncol.* 1982;8:659–666.
  Techniques to biopsy nail structures, and remove or ablate nail plates are discussed in detail.

30. FOLLICULAR DISORDERS PECULIAR TO BLACK SKIN
Deborah A. Scott

Blacks may be affected by a variety of cutaneous disorders that are fairly unique to their race. Pigmentary alterations, including normal variants such as mucosal and nail hyperpigmentation and postinflammatory pigmentary disturbances, are more common in blacks than in whites, for example. Blacks have a greater tendency to develop annular lesions as a manifestation of certain diseases, including secondary syphilis, seborrheic dermatitis, and granulomatous diseases such as sarcoidosis. Hypertrophic or fibromatous lesions including keloids, hypertrophic lichen planus, and discoid lupus also occur more commonly in blacks. Another reaction pattern commonly seen in blacks is the tendency of their skin to develop follicular or papular lesions. Diseases manifested by papular or follicular lesions in blacks include papular eczema, disseminated and recurrent infundibulofolliculitis, juxtaclavicular beaded lines, secondary syphilis, and tinea versicolor. In addition to those diseases that present with a follicular or papular pattern in blacks, a number of conditions primarily involving hair follicles are found more commonly among blacks.

Pseudofolliculitis barbae (razor bumps) is a common condition among black men who shave. Perifollicular papules and pustules with postinflammatory hyperpigmentation are localized to the beard area, primarily lower cheeks, chin, mandible, and anterior neck. Grooves caused by hair growth parallel to the skin surface may develop. Interestingly, the mustache area is rarely involved. Although most commonly encountered on the male face, this condition may occur in either sex on any area of the body that is shaved. The pathogenesis of pseudofolliculitis barbae is related to the tightly curled hair and curved hair follicle characteristically found in blacks. It is essentially a foreign body reaction caused by penetration of the pointed tip of the cut hair into the skin adjacent to the follicular orifice or through the wall of the follicle itself.

The differential diagnosis of pseudofolliculitis barbae includes acne vulgaris, sycosis barbae, and traumatic folliculitis. It is differentiated from acne by the absence of comedones and its strict localization to the beard area. In sycosis barbae, chronic deep bacterial or fungal folliculitis of the beard area, the primary lesions are perifollicular pustules that have a tendency to become confluent, in contrast to the predominantly isolated papules seen in pseudofolliculitis barbae. In addition, shaving tends to improve sycosis barbae, whereas it exacerbates pseudofolliculitis barbae. Traumatic folliculitis, or razor burn, is characterized by tender small erythematous perifollicular papules and superficial excoriations. This condition improves within 24 to 48 hours after cessation of shaving, in contrast to the several weeks required to improve pseudofolliculitis barbae.

The most effective treatment of pseudofolliculitis barbae is to cease shaving and allow the growth of a beard. As the beard lengthens, the curved hairs will spontaneously pull their pointed ends from the adjacent skin. Those men who must remain clean shaven should be instructed in the use of various procedures to reduce epidermal and transfollicular penetration by the sharp cut edge of the hair. These procedures include use of hair clippers instead of razors, avoiding close shaves, not shaving "against the grain," and the use of chemical depilatories. Although the primary treatment is directed toward shaving techniques, medical management includes the use of tretinoin cream to decrease follicular hyperkeratosis and "toughen" the skin, very low potency corticosteroid cream to decrease inflammation, and topical or oral antibiotics to control secondary infection.

Acne keloidalis (dermatitis papillaris capillitii) is another condition found frequently in black men. It is characterized by firm, dome-shaped, flesh-colored perifollicular papules and pustules localized primarily to the occipital scalp and posterior neck. Abscesses and sinus tracts may occur, and individual lesions coalesce to form keloidal plaques. Chronic inflammation and scarring destroy the involved hair follicles and result in a patchy scarring alopecia. The etiology of this condition is unknown, but is thought to be related to tightly curled hair as in pseudofolliculitis barbae. It is also thought that friction may be a causative factor since the lesions occur in an area constantly rubbed by collars. Bacteria can usually be cultured from pustular lesions, representing secondary superinfection.

The differential diagnosis of acne keloidalis includes bacterial folliculitis and pseudofolliculitis barbae. The primary lesion in bacterial folliculitis is a perifollicular pustule, in contrast to the firm papules seen in acne keloidalis. In addition, bacterial folliculitis is an acute process, whereas acne keloidalis is a chronic condition. Hairs perforating the papules and pustules of acne keloidalis may be seen, compared to inapparent ingrown or recurved hairs that characterize pseudofolliculitis barbae. There is no clear relationship between acne keloidalis and shaving, as exists in pseudofolliculitis barbae.

A variety of treatments have been advocated, with varying degrees of success. General recommendations include diminishing friction to the area and avoiding close shaving of the posterior neck. A cream composed of a potent corticosteroid and antibiotic is helpful in diminishing early lesions. Isolated small lesions may be destroyed by electrodesiccation or cryotherapy. Intralesional corticosteroids diminish cysts and keloids. Oral antibiotics such as tetracycline are useful in controlling pustular and cystic lesions. Wide excision that removes all the hair follicles in the affected area with healing by primary intention or grafting has been helpful in severe cases. The carbon dioxide laser may be used similarly.

Dissecting cellulitis (perifolliculitis capitis abscedens et suffodiens) is a chronic suppurative scalp disorder that primarily affects young black men. In the early stages it is characterized by perifollicular comedones, pustules, and tender fluctuant nodules involving the vertex and occiput. As the condition progresses, these lesions coalesce to form deep abscesses and sinus tracts. Pain, continuous purulent drainage, scarring alopecia, and keloids are frequent sequelae. The etiology of dissecting cellulitis is unknown, but is thought to be related to abnormal follicular keratinization. Dissecting cellulitis may occur in association with two other conditions associated with abnormal follicular keratinization, acne conglobata and hidradenitis suppurativa, in what is called the follicular occlusion triad.

The differential diagnosis of dissecting cellulitis includes inflammatory tinea capitis and folliculitis decalvans. Tinea capitis usually affects prepubescent children and is characterized by scaling and pustules, in contrast to the abscesses and sinus tracts seen in dissecting folliculitis. Folliculitis decalvans has no apparent racial predilection, and is characterized by follicular pustules that expand centrifugally, leaving a central area of scarring alopecia.

Treatment of dissecting cellulitis is generally disappointing. Acute cases may benefit from oral antibiotics (appropriate repeated cultures are needed to direct therapy), intralesional corticosteroid injections, or incision and drainage of fluctuant lesions. Oral corticosteroids, dapsone, and zinc may be helpful in diminishing inflammation. Isotretinoin administered in doses similar to those used in cystic acne has been successful in controlling dissecting folliculitis. Unfortunately, the condition tends to relapse once the course of isotretinoin has been completed. Wide surgical excision with removal of the hair follicles in the involved areas has been helpful in extensive cases.

Dellon AL, Orlando JC: Perifolliculitis capitis: surgical treatment for the severe case. *Ann Plast Surg.* 1982;9:254–259.
Surgical excision and grafting is preferred over x ray epilation to treat severe cases.
Dinehart SM, Herzberg AJ, Kerns BJ, et al.: Acne keloidalis: A review. *J Dermatol Surg Oncol.* 1989;15:642–647.
Excellent, recent review of pathogenesis, clinical manifestations, and treatment.
Haldir RM: Pseudofolliculitis barbae and related disorders. *Dermatol Clin.* 1988;6:407–412.
Concise and thorough review of pseudofolliculitis barbae and dermatitis papillaris capillitii (acne keloidalis). Pathogenesis, clinical features, and treatment are discussed.
McLaurin CI: Cutaneous reaction patterns in blacks. *Dermatol Clin.* 1988;6:353–362.
The tendency of black skin to develop pigmentary alterations, follicular involvement, and papular features in common dermatoses is discussed. Note: This volume of Dermatol Clin *(Vol. 6, Number 3, July 1988) is devoted to skin disease in black patients.*
Schewach-Millet M, Ziv R, Shapira D: Perifolliculitis capitis abscedens et suffodiens treated with isotretinoin (13-cis-retinoic acid). *J Am Acad Dermatol.* 1986;15:1291–1292.
Isotretinoin was beneficial but relapse occurred when therapy was discontinued.
Scott DA: Disorders of the hair and scalp in blacks. *Dermatol Clin.* 1988;6:387–395.
Thorough review of a wide range of scalp disorders, including traumatic alopecias, hair shaft abnormalities, and dissecting cellulitis.
Williams CN, Cohen M, Ronan SG, et al.: Dissecting cellulitis of the scalp. *Plast Reconstr Surg.* 1986;77:378–381.
Wide surgical excision and grafting of the involved area of the scalp is advocated as the treatment of choice.

VI. INFECTIONS AND INFESTATIONS

The TORCH syndrome consists of a disparate group of congenital infections that have similar clinical features. The mnemonic "TORCH" stands for toxoplasmosis, other (syphilis), rubella, cytomegalovirus, and herpes simplex. Although viral, parasitic, and treponemal in nature, these infections share their chronicity, clinical presentation, and potentially serious consequences.

Toxoplasmosis is caused by infection with the obligate intracellular parasite *Toxoplasma gondii*. This tissue protozoan is ubiquitous, being found in many mammals, especially cats and birds. Humans can acquire the disease from ingestion of contaminated, undercooked meat, raw eggs, unpasteurized milk, or from accidental ingestion of infected cat feces. The prevalence of acquired infection varies but has been estimated to range from 20% to 70% in the United States.

Fetal infection occurs when the mother acquires toxoplasmosis during pregnancy, leading to maternal parasitemia and invasion of trophozoites into fetal tissue. Congenital toxoplasmosis occurs in about 1:1000 live births in the United States. The risk of fetal transmission increases from the first to the third trimester, but the severity of the disease decreases. Overall only about 3% to 5% of all newborns of mothers with active infection during pregnancy will have severe disease.

Congenital toxoplasmosis infections can affect most major organs, including the CNS, gastrointestinal tract, lungs, eyes, and skin. A common clinical manifestation is chorioretinitis, which is often bilateral. CNS involvement can lead to seizures or mental retardation. Other findings include hepatosplenomegaly, interstitial pneumonitis, and myocarditis.

Skin lesions are found in about one-quarter of the symptomatic newborns. So-called blueberry muffin lesions can occur in congenital toxoplasmosis as well as in other TORCH syndrome infections. They appear as bluish, flat or raised lesions that are caused by cutaneous erythropoiesis. Other cutaneous findings in toxoplasmosis include a macular or papular viral exanthem, petechiae, purpura, jaundice, or calcifications. Skin lesions usually appear at birth and fade by 6 weeks of age.

Associated findings include intracranial calcifications, anemia, thrombocytopenia, eosinophilia, hyperbilirubinemia, as well as elevated cerebrospinal fluid protein and leukocytosis. However, these findings are not specific to toxoplasmosis and can be seen in other TORCH syndrome infections. The diagnosis can be made by serologic tests for antitoxoplasma antibodies. Treatment is controversial. Pyrimethamine and sulfonamides can be used after the first trimester. Spiramycin has been used in Canada and Europe.

Congenital syphilis is caused by transplacental transmission of the spirochete *Treponema pallidum* to the fetus. The risk of infection to the fetus depends on when the disease is acquired in the mother. Maternal infection during early pregnancy can lead to abortion or severe neonatal disease. Acquisition of syphilis in late pregnancy may lead to an asymptomatic newborn who develops clinical findings in infancy. In untreated mothers who contract syphilis before pregnancy, the risk of transmission to the fetus varies, and decreases with time. Treatment of the mother before 16 to 18 weeks' gestation carries a high cure rate for the fetus, but treatment after this time may not prevent the disease.

The clinical signs of congenital syphilis are divided into three categories: early manifestations, late manifestations, and residual stigmata. Early congenital syphilis appears before the age of 2 years. Obvious clinical disease present at birth carries a high mortality rate of about 50%. Common clinical findings are mucocutaneous lesions, jaundice, hepatosplenomegaly, prematurity, and osteochondritis. Other signs are pneumonia, nephritis, myocarditis, lymphadenopathy, and hematologic abnormalities.

Rhinitis, or snuffles, is a frequent feature of early congenital syphilis. It consists of profuse rhinorrhea, sometimes bloody, which is highly infectious. If untreated, it can ulcerate the nose, creating a "saddle-nose" deformity. Syphilitic mucous patches are round, moist, raised lesions that may be found on mucosal surfaces. Condylomata lata may be present. All of these lesions harbor *T. pallidum*. A papulosquamous eruption similar to that of adult secondary syphilis can also be present, particularly on the extremities, palms, and soles. These lesions may range in color from pink to copper and usually fade in 1 week. Other skin findings in early congenital syphilis include bullous lesions, petechiae, erosions, and pustules, which can be virtually diagnostic if on the palms and soles. Osteochondritis may also be seen, causing swellings of the long bones and pain with movement (Parrot's pseudoparalysis).

Late congenital syphilitic signs generally are found in children more than 2 years old. Characteristic findings include interstitial keratitis, painless synovitis of the knees (Clutton's joints), periostitis of the long bones (especially the tibiae), and eighth nerve deafness. Residual stigmata of syphilis include conical upper incisor teeth with notching (Hutchinson's teeth) and flattened molars with enamel hypoplasia ("mulberry molars").

Dark-field examination of scrapings from moist lesions with demonstration of spirochetes is perhaps the fastest method of diagnosis. An FTA-ABS with IgM antibody, a VDRL titer on blood and cerebrospinal fluid, and radiographic studies should confirm the diagnosis. Penicillin is the treatment of choice for neonatal syphilis.

Rubella is caused by a single-stranded RNA virus. Congenital rubella is due to transplacental infection during maternal viremia. About 15% of young adult women in the United States have no protective antibodies from prior infection or vaccination and are therefore at risk of contracting rubella. Fetal infection from maternal rubella may occur at any time during pregnancy, but serious congenital abnormalities usually only develop in those fetuses exposed before the sixteenth week of gestation.

Clinical disease is characterized by CNS and cardiac abnormalities, intrauterine growth retardation, cataracts, retinopathy, microophthalmia, and skin lesions. Deafness is the most frequent manifestation of congenital rubella.

Neonatal cutaneous findings include the petechial, purpuric and blueberry muffin lesions seen throughout the TORCH syndrome. A morbilliform erythematous eruption resembling that of rubella in older children can also be seen in newborns. With infants of 3 to 9 months, seborrhea, recurrent urticaria, hyperpigmentation, reticulate erythema, and leukocytoclastic vasculitis have all been reported. Hypoplasia of dental enamel has also been noted.

Laboratory abnormalities include anemia, thrombocytopenia, and hyperglycemia. The best way to confirm the diagnosis is viral culture of the nasopharynx, CSF, urine, or conjunctiva.

There is no specific therapy available. Perhaps the best method of treatment is prevention of infection by early identification of young women who are not immune. Infants continue to shed virus for more than a year and should be considered actively infective for 6 months. Congenital rubella may be as high as 20%. As many as 86% of infected infants will develop some degree of hearing loss and about 50% will have learning difficulties.

Cytomegalovirus (CMV) is a double-stranded DNA virus of the herpes virus family. CMV infection is relatively common. Approximately half of the pregnant women in the United States are already seropositive for CMV antibodies. The incidence of congenital CMV inclusion disease is as high as 2%, but only 10% of these infants show clinical signs of the disease. The risk of severe congenital defects is higher if the fetus is infected early in pregnancy.

Clinical manifestations of CMV resemble those of the other infections of the TORCH syndrome. Hepatosplenomegaly with or without jaundice is the most consistent finding. Neurologic findings such as microcephaly, deafness, and developmental delay are also common. Periventricular calcifications are often associated with microcephaly. Ocular involvement including chorioretinitis can occur. Gastrointestinal abnormalities such as biliary atresia and colonic stenosis are seen. Due to thrombocytopenia, petechiae or purpura occur in up to 80% of patients. The classic blueberry muffin lesions and jaundice also occur. Laboratory findings also resemble those of the other TORCH syndrome infections.

The pathologic hallmark of cells infected with CMV is the presence of large, eosinophilic intranuclear inclusions. Smaller, basophilic inclusions in the cell cytoplasm also help to distinguish CMV from herpes infection. The most specific method of diagnosis of CMV remains culture of the virus from urine, saliva, blood, CSF, or pharyngeal secretions. CMV-specific IgM antibodies are helpful but may yield both false positive or negative results. Currently there is no specific therapy for CMV.

Neonatal **herpes simplex** virus (HSV) infection occurs when a fetus passes through an infected birth canal. It is a serious postpartum disease that occurs in about 1:3500 live births. Congenital HSV infection, however, occurs when there is true intrauterine transmission, and is far more rare. Transmission to the fetus is caused either by maternal viremia or by cervical infection and chorioamnionitis. Since the incubation period for HSV is from 2 to 12 days, herpetic lesions present less than 48 hours after birth represent a congenital infection.

HSV is a double-stranded DNA virus with two subtypes. Type 2 is predominantly associated with genital herpes and therefore is the overwhelming cause of congenital HSV infection. The clinical findings include hepatosplenomegaly, neurologic and ocular abnormalities. Skin manifestations include those previously described for the TORCH syndrome as well as the classic clusters of grouped vesicles seen in herpetic infections.

The diagnosis may be established by demonstration of multinucleate giant cells on a Tzanck preparation or a skin biopsy. In addition, the virus may be cultured from vesicle fluid or CSF. HSV-specific fluorescent antibodies used to examine tissue smears may be helpful. Herpes virus can also be detected using the polymerase chain reaction with herpes-specific primers. Acyclovir and vidarabine have both been effective anitviral agents for neonatal herpetic infections.

Fine JD, Arndt KA: The TORCH syndrome: A clinical review. *J Am Acad Dermatol.* 1985;12:697–706.
   An excellent, comprehensive review of the TORCH syndrome.
Freij BJ, Sever JL: Herpesvirus infections in pregnancy: Risks to embryo, fetus, and neonate. *Clinics in Perinatology.* 1988;15:203–215.
   A comprehensive discussion of CMV and HSV infections in the newborn.
Freij BJ, South MA, Sever JL: Maternal rubella and the congenital rubella syndrome, *Clinics in Perinatology.* 1988;15:247–257.
   A thoughtful presentation of congenital rubella with excellent lists of clinical findings.
Mascola L, Pelosi R, Blount JH, Alexander CE, Cates W: Congenital syphilis revisited. *Am J Dis Child.* 1985;139:575–580.
   A thorough review of 50 cases of congenital syphilis with attention to clinical manifestations.
Stagno S: Diagnosis of viral infections in the newborn infant. *Clin Perinatol.* 1981;8:579–589.
   Emphasis on virologic and serologic methods that can help distinguish the different TORCH infections.
Whitley RJ, Alford CA: Preventive and therapeutic approaches to the newborn infant with perinatal viral and *toxoplasma* infections. *Clin Perinatol.* 1981;8:591–603.
   A good discussion of immunization and treatments available.

32. HERPES SIMPLEX VIRUS INFECTION
Susan D. DeCoste

Herpes simplex virus (HSV) produces primary and recurrent mucocutaneous disease. HSV is a member of the family of herpesviruses and consists of two serotypes, HSV-1 and HSV-2. While HSV-1 is the primary agent in oral-facial herpes, HSV-2 is usually the agent in genital infections. Overlap does occur, however, and HSV-1 is found in about 10% to 50% of genital herpes cases, depending on the population studied. HSV produces primary mucocutaneous infection when exposed to a mucosal surface or abraded skin, then replicates and enters cutaneous neurons. The virus remains dormant in the sensory ganglia until reactivation occurs. Recurrent disease is milder and of shorter duration than primary disease. Events known to trigger reactivation of latent virus include neurosurgical manipulation of the ganglia, immunosuppression, ultraviolet light exposure, and emotional stress.

About one-third of the U.S. population is affected by recurrent oral-facial HSV, or cold sores. There has been an epidemic of genital herpes in the United States, with a 15-fold increase in private physician visits for genital herpes in the last 2 decades. Many infections with HSV-1 or HSV-2 are subclinical, and transmission of infection is asymptomatic in the majority of cases. The rates of recurrence vary, depending on the serotype, location of infection, and host factors. Genital HSV-2 recurs more often than oral-facial HSV-1 on average, and genital HSV-1 recurs more often than oral-facial HSV-2.

Primary **oral-facial HSV infection** is usually seen in children and young adults, with peak incidence between ages 1 and 5. The primary infection can range from almost inapparent disease to fulminant widespread gingivostomatitis, presenting with clustered vesicles in the oropharynx, on the lips, and extending onto facial skin and associated with fever, lymphadenopathy, and sore throat. Recurrent oral-facial HSV may manifest as asymptomatic salivary excretion of virus, as blisters on the vermilion border of the lip or on adjacent facial skin, or as intraoral ulcerations. In primary disease, the incubation period is 5 to 10 days, and viral shedding lasts 1 to 3 weeks, while in recurrent disease viral shedding usually ceases in about 4 days. The differential diagnosis of oral-facial herpes includes Coxsackie viral infection, erythema multiforme, aphthous stomatitis, infectious mononucleosis, and Behçet's disease.

Genital herpes infection is almost always acquired through sexual contact with an affected partner. A primary episode often presents with widespread vesicles on the vulva or penis, urethritis, inguinal adenopathy, fever, malaise, and headache. Females usually have cervicitis, which may be asymptomatic. Recurrent disease is often preceded by a tingling or burning sensation hours to a few days prior to the outbreak of lesions. The area of skin or mucous membrane involved clinically is usually smaller in recurrent disease, and associated symptoms are uncommon. In primary disease, there is an average of 3 to 14 days between exposure and outbreak of lesions, and viral shedding lasts for about 11 days, with healing in 18 to 21 days. In a recurrence, viral shedding lasts an average of 3 to 4 days, with healing in about 9 to 10 days. The differential diagnosis of genital ulcerations includes syphilis, chancroid, lymphogranuloma venereum, granuloma inguinale, trauma, and Behçet's disease.

Inoculation herpes occurs when secretion containing the virus comes in contact with abraded skin on any area of the body. It is most frequently seen on fingers and hands, called herpetic whitlow, and is a common occupational hazard for medical and dental personnel. The infection is manifested by painful vesicles, swelling, erythematous lymphangitic streaking of the affected area, and associated lymphadenopathy. Recurrences are common and may be heralded by a prodrome of itching or burning. Inoculation herpes must be distinguished from bacterial cellulitis with lymphangitis and paronychia, or insect bite reaction.

Cutaneous HSV infections in patients with cutaneous or systemic **immunodeficiency** can result in considerable morbidity and even mortality. Preexisting skin conditions such as atopic dermatitis or Darier's disease predispose patients to developing widespread cutaneous involvement called eczema herpeticum. Either occurring as a primary outbreak or recurrent disease, the infection is first noted in areas where skin is abnormal. Dissemination is via the epidermal surface, so that complications from viremia are rare. The eruption may last 2 to 6 weeks, associated with fever and lymphadenopathy. Clinically, this process may be difficult to distinguish from impetigo or worsening of the primary skin condition. In systemically immunocompromised hosts, especially those with leukemia, lymphoma, AIDS, or those on immunosuppressive agents, HSV is a common infection with significant morbidity. A deep, ragged ulcer on a chronically indurated base can develop and remain present for months. Dissemination may also occur through viremia, leading to esophagitis, hepatitis, and pneumonia.

Neonates represent another significant high-risk group for HSV infection. They have a 40% chance of acquiring HSV at birth if the mother has an acute primary genital herpes infection, and a much lower risk if the mother has recurrent genital herpes. If untreated, neonates have a greater than 70% risk of visceral and CNS involvement, and a mortality rate of over 50%. Intrauterine infection is also reported, with perinatal morbidity highest if primary infection is acquired in the third trimester.

Diagnosis of HSV infection can often be made on clinical grounds, but laboratory confirmation is usually helpful. A rapid method to make a diagnosis of herpes infection is the Tzanck preparation. Cells from the base and sides of a vesicle are smeared on a glass slide and stained with Wright's or Giemsa stain. If HSV is present, multinucleated giant cells can be found. The Tzanck smear yields positive results about 70% of the time with vesicular lesions of herpes infection, while ulcerative lesions have a lower yield. A skin biopsy can be performed, which will demonstrate multinucleated giant cells and intranuclear inclusions. The most sensitive method of diagnosis is viral isolation in tissue culture, with identification possible usually within 24 to 96 hours. Yield is over 90% in early primary lesions, and lower in older, ulcerative, or crusted lesions. Other methods of diagnosis include antigen detection, commonly by immunofluorescence or enzyme-linked immunoadsorbent assays. Immunofluorescence staining with monoclonal antibodies against HSV-1 and HSV-2, performed on smears of tissue debris obtained from the sides and bottom of a vesicle, has been shown to be as sensitive as viral isolation in recurrent genital herpes. HSV can be rapidly detected and typed by the polymerase chain reaction (PCR) technique using one common upstream primer and two type-specific downstream primers. Further studies are needed using the newer, more rapid methods of diagnosis to detect asymptomatic HSV infection. Serologic tests are also available, but serum antibody titers do not have a role in the diagnosis of HSV infections, particularly recurrent disease.

Therapy for mucocutaneous HSV infections includes conservative measures such as adequate analgesia and compresses to hasten drying of lesions. The most effective antiviral agent against HSV is acyclovir. For oral-facial infections, topical acyclovir has not been shown to be of significant benefit, and oral acyclovir produces a clinically significant difference only in primary infections. When acyclovir is administered early in primary genital herpes, controlled studies have demonstrated that the drug decreases viral shedding and shortens the duration of illness significantly, with oral acyclovir noted to be much more effective than the topical preparation. The recommended dosage is 200 mg 5 times daily for 10 days. In recurrent genital herpes, oral acyclovir has been shown to be marginally beneficial, and then only if the patient begins the medication at the onset of a prodrome. The dosage used is 200 mg 5 times daily for 5 days. In patients with eight or more recurrences per year, a 60% reduction in the number of recurrences may be achieved if acyclovir is taken on a daily basis, 400 mg to 1 g per day. In immunosuppressed patients or neonates, intravenous acyclovir may be required for more severe infections. Topical acyclovir is most useful in treating patients with chronic cutaneous ulcerations and AIDS, but must be applied every 3 hours.

The **prevention** of HSV infection is of most importance in the neonatal group. Pregnant women with primary HSV disease at term pose a significant infection risk to their offspring, while those with recurrent disease are less likely to transmit HSV to the neonate. Women are screened by their doctors and if lesions are present at delivery a cesarean section is frequently performed. Patients in other high-risk groups should avoid contact if at all possible with individuals who show evidence of active disease or who shed virus asymptomatically. Genital herpes can be prevented if sexual contact with individuals with active lesions is avoided. The prevention of asymptomatic transmission poses a significant health problem, but use of barrier methods such as condoms may reduce the risk.

Bader C, Crumpacker CS, Schnipper LE, et al.: The natural history of recurrent facial-oral infection with herpes simplex virus. *J Infect Dis.* 1978;138:897–905. *Clinical parameters were assessed in 41 patients with recurrent facial-oral HSV infections.*

Brown ZA, Vontver LA, Benedetti J, et al.: Effects on infants of a first episode of genital herpes during pregnancy. *N Engl J Med.* 1987;317:1246–1251.
In 29 patients who acquired genital herpes during pregnancy, there was a 40% incidence of serious perinatal morbidity.

Bryson YJ, Dillon M, Lovett M, et al.: Treatment of first episodes of genital herpes simplex virus infection with oral acyclovir. A randomized double-blind controlled trial in normal subjects. *N Engl J Med.* 1983;308:916–921.
Oral acyclovir given to patients with first episode genital HSV infection was shown to have significant clinical benefit, compared to a placebo, but had no effect on recurrent disease.

Corey L, Adams HG, Brown ZA, et al.: Genital herpes simplex virus infections: clinical manifestations, course, and complications. *Ann Intern Med.* 1983;98:958–972.
Course and complications of genital herpes infection are reviewed in 268 patients with primary episodes and 362 patients with recurrent episodes.

Corey L, Spear PG: Infections with herpes simplex viruses. *N Engl J Med.* 1986;314:686–691, 749–757.
Review of the molecular biology, pathogenesis, and epidemiology of HSV infections as well as the clinical spectrum, therapy, and prevention of infections.

Douglas JM, Critchlow C, Benedetti J, et al.: A double-blind study of oral acyclovir for suppression of recurrences of genital herpes simplex virus infection. *N Engl J Med.* 1984;310:1551–1556.
Oral acyclovir given for 4 months was shown to reduce the number of recurrences in patients with frequently recurring genital HSV, but no effect on the long-term history of the disease was seen.

Kimura H, Shibata M, Kuzushima K, et al.: Detection and direct typing of herpes simplex virus by polymerase chain reaction. *Med Micro Immunol.* 1990;179:174–184.
The PCR technique was effective at detecting and typing HSV in primary gingivostomatitis and in genital herpes.

Lafferty WE, Coombs RW, Benedetti J, et al.: Recurrences after oral and genital herpes simplex virus infection. Influence of site of infection and viral type. *N Engl J Med.* 1987;316:1144–1149.
Different rates of reactivation of HSV-1 and HSV-2 were found between oral and genital sites in 39 patients with concurrent HSV infection of the oropharynx and genitalia.

Mercey D, Mindel A: Screening pregnant women for genital herpes. *Biomed Pharmacother.* 1990;44:257–262.
Pregnant women with primary HSV pose a significant risk to the offspring; the risk is less for pregnant women with recurrent disease.

Reichman RC, Badger GJ, Mertz GJ, et al.: Treatment of recurrent herpes simplex with oral acyclovir. A controlled trial. *JAMA.* 1983;251:2103–2107.
Oral acyclovir was shown to marginally shorten the duration of lesions in a large trial of patients with recurrent genital HSV. It may be most beneficial in patient-initiated regimens.

33. VARICELLA-ZOSTER VIRUS INFECTION
Susan D. DeCoste

Varicella (chickenpox) and herpes zoster (shingles) are two clinical entities caused by infection with the varicella-zoster virus (VZV). VZV is a member of the family of herpesviruses, and has similarities with herpes simplex virus (HSV). The virus, which consists of a single serotype, enters the upper respiratory tract of a nonimmune host and produces viremia and the skin lesions of chickenpox. VZV then passes from skin to sensory ganglia and establishes latent infection. When host immunity to VZV ebbs, viral replication within the ganglia occurs and results in the dermatomal pain and rash of herpes zoster.

Varicella is an acute, highly contagious exanthematous disease affecting about 3 million individuals yearly in the United States. About 90% of cases occur in children less than 10 years of age, and the highest attack rates are in winter and spring. The primary mode of contagion is via the respiratory tract, with fomites carrying virus several days before the onset of the eruption. The incubation period ranges from 10 to 23 days. The eruption presents as erythematous, pruritic macules and papules, located primarily on the trunk and proximal extremities. These lesions rapidly progress to tense vesicles surrounded by erythema, resembling "dew drops on rose petals"; then they umbilicate, become pustular, and form a crust in 2 to 4 days. Crusts usually separate in 1 to 3 weeks. Lesions at all stages of development are present simultaneously, and crops of new lesions continue to appear for about 1 week. Patients are no longer infectious after all lesions have become crusted. Children may have mild malaise and fever with the rash, while adolescents and adults often have a prodrome similar to that of other upper respiratory tract illnesses and have more-pronounced constitutional symptoms. The differential diagnosis of varicella includes impetigo, vesicular exanthems of Coxsackie and echo viruses, eczema herpeticum, erythema multiforme, multiple insect bites, pityriasis lichenoides et varioliformis acuta, rickettsial pox, and smallpox. Complications of varicella include bacterial superinfection in children and, rarely, Reye's syndrome or varicella encephalitis. Varicella pneumonia is frequently seen in adults. Immunocompromised patients who are susceptible to VZV are at high risk for having severe varicella infections, with widespread visceral dissemination.

Herpes zoster occurs in patients who have latent virus from prior infection with VZV and is characterized by a unilateral vesicular eruption limited to one dermatome or, rarely, two. There are about 300,000 cases in the United States yearly, two-thirds of which are in individuals over 50 years of ages. Factors that predispose an individual to herpes zoster include increasing age; immunosuppression, especially from lymphoproliferative disorders or exogenous agents; surgical manipulation of the ganglia; local trauma; or radiation to the spinal column. Recurrent zoster is seen in a small percentage of patients. Zoster is contagious only through direct contact with cutaneous lesions. Nonimmune individuals may contract varicella. In addition, zoster is thought to be less infectious than varicella.

Herpes zoster begins with segmental pain that can mimic that of cardiac or pleural disease or an acute abdominal or vertebral disease. The rash appears 3 to 5 days later as papules, progressing to vesicles, pustules, and crusts. The lesions are generally tightly grouped and evolve more slowly than those of varicella. Crusting occurs at about 1 week and persists for 2 to 3 weeks. Thoracic dermatomes are involved most often, although trigeminal distribution is seen in about 10% of patients and lumbar and cervical involvement in 10% to 20%. Vesicles on the tip of the nose indicate involvement of the nasociliary branch of the ophthalmic nerve and raise the possibility that keratoconjunctivitis may occur. The differential diagnosis of zoster includes zosteriform herpes simplex, localized bacterial infection, and contact dermatitis. The most common complication of zoster is postherpetic neuralgia, defined as pain persisting after the crusts have separated, and is seen in 10% to 15% of patients. It is uncommon under age 40, and occurs most frequently following trigeminal zoster. Other possible complications include bacterial superinfection, scarring, and motor paralysis. Dissemination, defined as 20 or more lesions outside the affected dermatome and adjacent dermatomes, is a complication seen usually in immunocompromised patients, where it can progress to widespread and fatal visceral infection.

The **diagnosis** of varicella and herpes zoster infections can be made with the same methods that are utilized to document HSV infections (see Chap. 32). In both processes, a Tzanck preparation allows microscopic visualization of multinucleated giant cells. However, a Tzanck preparation or even a skin biopsy cannot distinguish between VZV and HSV, and viral culture is essential. Culture of VZV may take several days to a few weeks, and is more often false-negative than culture of HSV. The role of serologic testing is limited to indicating susceptibility to varicella in high-risk patients.

Therapy for varicella is usually only local and symptomatic, since it is a benign disease in most children. Topical drying agents, soothing baths, and oral antihistamines may help with pruritus, and compresses dry weeping vesicles. Immunosuppressed patients with varicella or patients with visceral disease generally require treatment with intravenous acyclovir. In contrast to HSV, VZV is relatively resistant to acyclovir, and the doses required to treat it effectively are much larger and must be administered intravenously.

Herpes zoster is treated similarly, with cool compresses and topical drying agents. Patients may require narcotic analgesics for comfort. How to limit the duration and extent of the disease and prevent postherpetic neuralgia is unclear. The role of acyclovir in normal hosts with zoster has not been well established. Oral acyclovir at a dosage of 800 mg 5 times daily for 7 days has been shown to hasten healing and decrease acute pain if administered within 48 hours of the onset of the eruption. The incidence of postherpetic neuralgia has not yet been shown to be decreased by this regimen. Intravenous acyclovir is often used in infected immunosuppressed patients or in patients with disseminated zoster. Administration of systemic corticosteroids may prevent or shorten the course of postherpetic neuralgia in patients over 55. While some controlled studies have demonstrated a benefit, others have not, and until larger trials are done the risk-benefit ratio must be weighed for each patient. If used, prednisone is begun within the first 2 or 3 days of the eruption at 1 mg/kg/d for 1 week and then is tapered over 2 weeks. Once developed, postherpetic neuralgia remains a very difficult treatment problem. Tricyclic antidepressants, particularly amitriptyline, have been used to alleviate pain. Carbamazepine may be effective when there is a prominent lancinating quality to the pain, and other anticonvulsants can be tried as well. Studies of neurosurgical intervention lack controlled trials, but subcutaneous steroid injections, local cryosurgery, and sympathetic nerve blocks have been reported to alleviate pain and do not carry major risks. Capsaicin is a topical agent that depletes substance P locally and may provide pain relief in some patients; controlled studies are underway.

The **prevention** of varicella is highly desirable in high-risk, susceptible persons. Passive immunization with varicella-zoster immune globulin (VZIG) can abort or modify clinical infection if administered within 3 days of exposure. A live attenuated VZV vaccine has been developed and is under investigation in the United States, particularly for use in children with leukemia in remission.

Centers for Disease Control: Varicella-zoster immune globulin for the prevention of chickenpox. Recommendations of the Immunization Practices Advisory Committee. *Ann Intern Med.* 1984;100:859–865.
Statement of the criteria for the use of VZIG for the prophylaxis of varicella.
Eaglstein WH, Katz R, Brown JA: The effects of early corticosteroid therapy on the skin eruption and pain of herpes zoster. *JAMA.* 1970;211:1681–1683.
Double-blind trial of oral triamcinolone in healthy patients showed a decreased incidence of postherpetic neuralgia, a more rapid resolution of pain, and no effect on the rate of healing.
Gershon AA, Steinberg SP, Gelb L, et al.: Live attenuated varicella vaccine use in immunocompromised children and adults. *Pediatrics.* 1986;78(suppl):757–762.
Discussion of varicella vaccine trials in immunosuppressed children and healthy adults and the potential role of the vaccine.
McKendrick MW, McGill JI, White JW, Wood MJ: Oral acyclovir in acute herpes zoster. *Brit Med J.* 1986;293:1529–1532.
Oral acyclovir was given to elderly immunocompetent hosts in a randomized double-blind study and was shown to hasten healing and reduce acute pain.
Koropchak CM, Graham G, Palmer J, et al.: Investigation of varicella-zoster virus infection by polymerase chain reaction in the immunocompetent host with acute varicella. *J Infect Dis.* 1991;163:1016–1022.
Seventy-five percent of skin lesions were positive versus only 3 percent of 30 oropharyngeal samples, indicating perhaps that direct contact with cutaneous lesions rather than respiratory secretions may be the most important route of VZV transmission.

Paryani SG, Arvin AM: Intrauterine infection with varicella-zoster virus after maternal varicella. *N Engl J Med.* 1986;314:1542–1546.
Varicella during 43 pregnancies was associated with maternal morbidity and evidence of fetal infection, but herpes zoster in 14 pregnancies was uncomplicated.

Portenoy RK, Duma C, Foley KM: Acute herpetic and post herpetic neuralgia: clinical review and current management. *Ann Neurol.* 1986;20:651–664.
Summary and critical review of the treatments for acute herpetic neuralgia and post herpetic neuralgia with management guidelines suggested.

Weller TH: Varicella and herpes zoster. Changing concepts of the natural history, control, and importance of a not-so-benign virus. *N Engl J Med.* 1983;309:1362–1368, 1434–1440.
Review of the features of VZV, the pathogenesis of infection, and important diagnostic and therapeutic considerations.

34. PYODERMAS
Sewon Kang

Pyoderma literally means pus in the skin. Numerous dermatoses may show suppurative changes and pus may be seen, but the term *pyoderma* specifically refers to purulent infection of the skin. Moreover, many reserve its use for the infections caused by staphylococci and streptococci. Pathogenic species most frequently isolated from human skin are coagulase-positive *Staphylococcus aureus* and group A streptococcus, also referred to as *Streptococcus pyogenes*. In this chapter, primary skin infections caused by these two gram-positive bacteria will be discussed.

Conditions that favor primary skin infection by staphylococci and streptococci have been studied systematically. Moisture is a well-established promoter of microbial proliferation. Markedly greater numbers of bacterial organisms per unit area are found where eccrine sweat glands are abundant and the body surfaces semioccluded, such as the axillae, perineum, and toe-web spaces, as compared to the extremities. For a given area, increasing the moisture level by application of impermeable plastic film leads to an exponential rise in the number of bacteria.

Damage to the skin is not required for initiation of a *Staphylococcus aureus* pyoderma. The organism can survive on normal, intact skin, as evidenced by its frequent recovery there and also by the presence of a carrier state. The resident flora is, however, undoubtedly important in the defense against the infection. Disinfection of the surface of the skin prior to inoculation of *S. aureus* results in more frequent infection in an experimental setting. In the early neonatal period, before the resident flora is fully established, infections with *S. aureus* are more common.

Unlike *S. aureus,* group A streptococci are unable to survive on intact normal skin for any prolonged period of time. The resident flora does not appear to hinder growth, for disinfecting the skin prior to the inoculation has no effect on the organism's survival. However, if the stratum corneum is disrupted, *Streptococcus pyogenes* is quick to colonize the skin, with frequent subsequent infection. The integrity of the stratum corneum, then, is essential in the defense against this infection.

Impetigo is a common communicable superficial infection of the skin that clinically and bacteriologically can be subdivided into two distinct subtypes, impetigo contagiosa and bullous impetigo. The former, also known as nonbullous impetigo, is caused by both group A beta-hemolytic streptococci and *Staphylococcus aureus.* The bullous type is usually caused by group II *S. aureus,* primarily phage type 71.

This pyoderma occurs most frequently in children and young adults. There is an increased prevalence in late summer and early fall and in tropical and subtropical climates. No sex predilection or racial susceptibility has been observed. The mode of transmission of impetigo is not fully understood. Direct contact, environmental contamination and arthropod vectors, especially the Hippelates fly, appear to play a role. It is thought that streptococci initially colonize unbroken skin, and after an average interval of 10 days, lesions of impetigo can be observed. Since streptococci are known to die rapidly on normal skin, the colonization of the epidermis implies repeated exposure. This is likely, given the association between impetigo and low socioeconomic class, poor hygiene, and crowded surroundings. Streptococci can be isolated from the nose and the throat 14 and 20 days after the colonization of the skin, respectively. In staphylococcal impetigo, however, the organism is first isolated in the respiratory tract. Normal skin colonization follows, and then the development of cutaneous lesions.

Impetigo contagiosa begins as small vesicles that rapidly pustulate and readily rupture. With drying of the purulent discharge, characteristic thick, golden-yellow "stuck-on" crusts are formed. Lesions are most commonly located on exposed areas, especially the legs. Pruritus is a common symptom. Scratching often spreads the infection further. The superficial intraepidermal nature of this infection explains scarless healing. Mild regional lymphadenopathy is commonly seen; however, constitutional symptoms and fever are atypical.

Gram-stain and culture results can be obtained from vesicle fluid, pustules, or the exudate beneath an unroofed crust. Gram-positive cocci are readily seen. Pure culture of group A streptococci is usually limited to early lesions, with S. aureus often growing together with the streptococci in older, crusted lesions.

Following group A beta-hemolytic streptococcal pyoderma, the antistreptolysin O titer is usually scant. This is in contrast to a significant rise in the titer seen after streptococcal pharyngitis. Inhibition of streptolysin O by skin lipids at the infection site is believed to be responsible for this observation. Antihyaluronidase and antideoxyribonuclease B titers show marked elevation after the pyoderma, however.

Poststreptococcal acute glomerulonephritis (AGN) is the most serious complication of impetigo. Infections of the skin or pharynx can be followed by this sequela. More common with the former, it occurs in less than 1% of all patients with impetigo. Only certain M-serotypes (2, 49, 55, 57, and 60) are associated with nephritis. In the presence of a nephritogenic strain, the overall attack rate of AGN is approximately 15%. Scarlet fever, erythema multiforme, and urticaria may also follow streptococcal impetigo, but not rheumatic fever.

Bullous impetigo lesions also begin as vesicles, evolving into large bullae (1–5 cm) that can persist for days. The contents are clear at first, but later become cloudy. When a bulla ruptures, it leaves an erythematous base with a varnishlike thin brown crust. The lesions more commonly occur on the face and trunk than on the extremities. Group II S. aureus is regularly cultured from the lesions. Exfoliative toxin elaborated by the organism is responsible for the bullae. Regional lymphadenopathy is not an associated finding. In neonates, this type of impetigo may become widespread, and was once called, not surprisingly, pemphigus neonatorum.

In most settings, systemic antibiotics are superior to topical preparations for the treatment of impetigo. The longer time for healing, the continued development of new lesions, the inability to eradicate concomitant colonization of the organism in the respiratory tract, the practical difficulty of applying medication to large areas, and the lower cure rates are disadvantages attributed to therapy with topical drugs. A number of treatment regimens have been shown to be effective. One-time intramuscular injection of benzathine penicillin (600,000 units if the patient is 6 years or younger and 1.2 million units if 7 years or older) has been associated with the highest cure rate. Ten-day courses of erythromycin or phenoxymethyl penicillin (both 1 g every day) are usually adequate. The sensitivity of the pathogenic organism to antibiotics should certainly guide therapy. With the emergence of erythromycin-resistant S. aureus (approximately 10% to 20%), semisynthetic penicillins such as dicloxicillin (250 mg PO qid) are an appropriate first-choice therapy for bullous impetigo. First-generation cephalosporins also have good staphylococcal and streptococcal coverage.

Mupirocin (pseudomonic acid) is a topical antibiotic effective in treating impetigo and only recently approved for use in the United States. A randomized study of 75 patients with a small number of lesions demonstrated that mupirocin applied 3 times daily produced effects similar to those of oral erythromycin, and was superior to erythromycin in eradicating *S. aureus.* A double-blind placebo-controlled study of 54 children (2 months to 11 years old) confirmed that both drugs are equally effective, both produce side effects, and found that compliance was much better with topical application. Topical mupirocin may therefore have a role in treating superficial pyodermas, especially limited disease. It may also be helpful in preventing streptococcal pyoderma when applied to minor skin trauma, especially in children at increased risk for the infection.

Local care with soaks or wet dressings combined with crust removal performed 3 to 4 times a day is an important part of therapy.

Ecthyma is a pyogenic infection of the skin with certain similarities to impetigo. The lesion begins as a vesicle or vesicopustule with underlying erythema. The formation of a hard, thick, and adherent crust usually quickly ensues. Beneath this crust, which is removed with difficulty, is a purulent "punched-out" ulcer. The margins are raised and violaceous. Culture from the ulcer often yields mixed growth of group A streptococci and *S. aureus.* The former is believed to be the initiating pathogen. Because of ulceration into the dermis, lesions heal with scarring. Children are more commonly affected. Poor hygiene and malnutrition are predisposing factors. Minor skin injuries from trauma, insect bites, or scabies infestation often determine the site of lesions, the lower legs being most frequently involved. The treatment is the same as that for impetigo.

Folliculitis is a pyoderma localized to the hair follicles with surrounding inflammation and small central pustulation. It can be subdivided according to the depth of involvement—superficial or deep. Although *S. aureus* is the most common pathogen, other microorganisms are at times incriminated.

Impetigo of Bockhart is a superficial staphylococcal folliculitis characterized by small dome-shaped pustules located at the opening of the hair follicles. It is most common in childhood. The pustules develop in crops, and the scalp and extremities are often involved. The integrity of hair is not affected.

Superficial folliculitis need not be a pyogenic infection. Contact with mineral oil or exposure to tar products or adhesive dressings can lead to typical lesions with sterile pustules.

Sycosis barbae is a deeper form of folliculitis occurring in the bearded area. *S. aureus* is again the usual etiologic agent. Hair growth is usually not affected, but in the severe chronic form, the follicles can be destroyed. If scarring is present, the infection is called lupoid sycosis.

Minor superficial folliculitis often requires only good local hygiene, washing with antibacterial soap containing chlorhexadine, and application of topical antibiotics. If lesions do not clear, a course of systemic antibiotics is indicated. Folliculitis of the beard commonly is recurrent and may require repeated courses of therapy.

Pseudomonas aeruginosa is the agent responsible for **"hot-tub folliculitis."** A number of outbreaks from swimming pools and whirlpools contaminated with large numbers of these organisms have been well documented. Markedly pruritic, follicular papulopustular lesions usually appear about 48 hours after the exposure (8 hours to 5 days) and have a predilection for the hips, buttocks, axillae, and lateral aspects of the trunk. Otitis externa and mastitis, as well as some constitutional symptoms, often accompany the folliculitis. Healing without scarring is the rule. Spontaneous resolution occurs usually by the fifth day. Inadequate chlorination of water sources has been responsible for many outbreaks.

Extended use of broad-spectrum antibiotics, such as tetracycline, alters the nasal flora to the point that colonization by gram-negative bacteria can occur. **Gram-negative folliculitis** is a superinfection by these organisms, primarily seen in patients with acne vulgaris on long-term systemic antibiotic therapy. There are two clinical types — a superficial pustular type and a deep nodular variety. In the more common superficial type, pustules without comedones extend from the infranasal area to the chin and cheeks. Lactose-fermenting gram-negative rods, such as *Klebsiella, Escherichia,* and *Serratia,* are cultured from the pustules and anterior nares. In the deep nodular type, cystic lesions are seen, often on the neck, with *Proteus* as the recovered agent. Isotretinoin treatment (0.5–1.0 mg/kg/d PO for 5 months) has led to excellent results.

A **furuncle,** or boil, is a perifollicular abscess that progresses to necrosis and destruction of the follicle. It develops most often from a preceding folliculitis. *S. aureus* is invariably the etiologic agent. Furuncles occur in hairy skin areas subject to friction, perspiration, and maceration (buttocks, neck, face, and axillae). Appearing as nodules, furuncles are red and markedly tender. Predisposing factors include malnutrition, poor hygiene, obesity, blood dyscrasias, corticosteroid therapy, and possibly diabetes mellitus. In some patients, this infection may become chronic and recurrent. A nasal or perineal carrier state is usually present in such situations.

A **carbuncle** is a more extensive process, regarded as an aggregation of furuncles that develop in thick inelastic skin. There are multiple points that drain to the surface. The nape of the neck, the back, and the thighs are commonly affected areas.

Treatment of furuncles and carbuncles varies, depending on the extent and chronicity. Isolated furuncles can be treated satisfactorily by the application of moist heat. This promotes localization, allowing the lesion to point, with subsequent spontaneous drainage. Systemic antibiotics, however, are at times indicated, along with local measures, particularly when there is surrounding tissue inflammation and infection. Incision and drainage of fluctuant lesions and more-aggressive surgical intervention with debridement of necrotic tissue may be needed. Lesions on the upper lip and nose deserve special respect, for the infection may spread via facial and angular emissary veins to the cavernous sinus with resultant serious complications.

Erysipelas is a superficial cellulitis of the skin with prominent lymphatic involvement. It is usually caused by group A streptococci or *S. aureus*. The lesion is a sharply demarcated, bright red, hot plaque with edema and induration (peau d'orange). An advancing raised border is a characteristic clinical feature, and central clearing may be present. The lesions are painful, and patients are febrile and acutely ill. The face, especially the cheeks, the bridge of the nose, and the scalp are commonly involved sites. There is a predilection for areas of preexisting lymphatic obstruction or edema, such as in an upper extremity after a radical mastectomy. No obvious portal of entry can be identified in most cases.

A number of clinical entities can present with similar lesions: the "slapped cheek" of erythema infectiosum (fifth disease), early herpes zoster involving the second division of the fifth cranial nerve, contact dermatitis, giant urticaria and malar rash of systemic lupus erythematosus may all be in the differential diagnosis.

Erysipeloid is a cellulitis induced by *Erysipelothrix rhusiopathiae,* and it appears similar to erysipelas. It occurs most commonly on the hands and fingers of individuals handling fresh seafood and meat products. The lesion is a well-circumscribed violaceous plaque that is not as hot or as tender as that of erysipelas. The presence of fever is also atypical for erysipeloid. Most prevalent in summer, the infection is introduced through an abrasion on the hand.

Cellulitis is an acute spreading infection of the skin and subcutaneous tissue. Group A streptococci and *S. aureus* represent the most common etiologic agents. *Hemophilus influenzae* is also an important pathogen, especially in children. The borders of an area of cellulitis, in contrast to erysipelas, are not well demarcated and raised. When cellulitis is severe, frank necrosis can occur, in addition to vesiculation and pustulation. Predisposing factors include previous trauma, such as an abrasion or laceration, and the presence of preceding skin lesions. Individuals whose saphenous veins have been removed for coronary artery bypass surgery may suffer from recurrent cellulitis of the involved leg. Areas of tinea pedis are often the portal of entry for the infection. Patients often present with constitutional symptoms of malaise and fatigue, and are febrile. Regional lymphadenopathy is common. With the potential to spread via lymphatics and the blood stream, it is a serious infection. When lymphatic vessels are involved, lymphangitis follows. Clinically, a pink to red macular streak is seen along the course of inflamed vessels, with palpable tender lymphadenitis.

The potential for a vicious cycle is obvious. Inflammation from an initial episode of erysipelas, cellulitis, or lymphangitis will obstruct lymphatic drainage, which in turn will predispose the patient to further episodes of infection. With recurrent infections, permanent changes, such as chronic edema or elephantiasis nostras verrucosa can occur.

Culture of tissue fluid aspirated from the advancing edge of the lesion is rarely fruitful, yielding positive results in only 5% to 10% of procedures. It seems likely that immunocompetent cells in the skin reduce or eliminate bacteria from tissue, and that the intense inflammation is produced by soluble mediators of inflammation released by epidermal cells in response to the infection.

Treatment of both erysipelas and cellulitis requires systemic antibiotics active against gram-positive cocci. For mild cases of erysipelas, oral penicillin V or erythromycin (250–500 mg PO every 6 hours) may be adequate. When severe, high levels of parenteral penicillin G or a first-generation cephalosporin are indicated. When staphylococcal infection is suspected, a penicillinase-resistant penicillin such as oxacillin or dicloxacillin (0.5–1.0 g PO every 6 hours) can be used. Erythromycin is an alternative for penicillin-allergic patients. For a severe infection, intravenous administration of nafcillin (1.0–1.5 g PO every 4 hours) is appropriate. Vancomycin (1.0–1.5 g every day) is an alternative for penicillin-allergic patients. The decision to use intravenous rather than oral antibiotics is based on the clinical picture of each patient. When confronted with a facial cellulitis, especially in a child, the clinician must also consider the possibility of *H. influenzae* infection. Ampicillin can no longer be assumed to be effective against that organism, and resistance to chloramphenicol has been encountered as well. Second-generation cephalosporins, such as cefuroxime, provide adequate coverage.

Baltimore RS: Treatment of impetigo: a review. *Pediatr Infect Dis.* 1985;4(5):597–601.
  A nice, readable review of the topic with an informative historic perspective.
Becker LE, Tschen E: Common bacterial infections of the skin. Symposium on Office Dermatology. *Primary Care.* 1983;10(3):307–409.
  A thorough discussion of primary skin infections.
Gustafson TL, Bank JD, Hutcheson RH, et al.: Pseudomonas folliculitis: an outbreak and review. *Rev Infect Dis.* 1983;5(1):1–8.
  An epidemiologic investigation of an outbreak involving 60 members of a health spa.
Hirschmann JV: Topical antibiotics in dermatology. *Arch Dermatol.* 1988;124:1691–1700.
  An extensive critical review.
James WD, Leyden JJ: Treatment of gram-negative folliculitis with isotretinoin: positive clinical and microbiologic response. *J Am Acad Dermatol.* 1985;12:319–324.
  Impressive efficacy of the retinoid in this disease is shown. All 32 patients had complete clearing of the folliculitis with 26 out of 32 developing S. aureus nasal carriage by the end of therapy.
Kremer M, Zuckerman R, Avraham Z, et al.: Long-term antimicrobial therapy in the prevention of recurrent soft tissue infections. *J Infect.* 1991;22:37–40.
  Thirty-six patients with a history of more than one episode of cellulitis or erysipelas in the past year were randomly assigned to daily prophylaxis with erythromycin or no treatment for 18 months. Fifty percent of untreated patients relapsed while those treated had no new infectious episodes.
Leyden JJ, Stewart R, Kligman AM: Experimental infections with group A streptococci in humans. *J Invest Dermatol.* 1980;75:196–201.
  An important study demonstrating the need for skin damage if infection is to occur with the pathogen.
Leyden JJ: Pyoderma: pathophysiology and management. *Arch Dermatol.* 1988;124:753–755.
  An excellent summary of conditions that favor staphylococcal and streptococcal skin infections. This article also discusses skin care in epidermolysis bullosa patients, where secondary pyoderma is a frequent problem.
Maddox JS, Ware JC, Dillon HC: The natural history of streptococcal skin infection: prevention with topical antibiotics. *J Am Acad Dermatol.* 1985;13:207–212.
  A nice study showing a statistically significant difference in the incidence of pyoderma with the use of a topical antibiotic ointment (47%) vs. a placebo (15%).
Mertz PM, Marshall DA, Eaglstein WH, et al.: Topical mupirocin treatment of im-

petigo is equal to oral erythromycin therapy. *Arch Dermatol.* 1989;125:1069–1073.
Seventy-five patients with clinically and bacteriologically confirmed lesions of staph-
ylococcal and/or streptococcal impetigo were treated with mupirocin or oral eryth-
romycin for 8 days. There was no difference in clinical response between the two
groups. Forty-five percent of lesions were positive for both S. aureus *and* S. pyogenes,
29% for S. aureus *only, and 26% for* S. pyogenes.

Sachs MK: Cutaneous cellulitis. *Arch Dermatol.* 1991;127:493–496.
The author hypothesizes that the inflammation present in cellulitis is primarily a
result of the release of mediators from epidermal cells, and not a direct result of the
causative organisms. This theory is consistent with the paucity of organisms able
to be cultured from lesion—only 8.7% of 173 aspirates in the largest retrospective
study, and 3 (10%) of 30 in one prospective study.

35. SUPERFICIAL FUNGAL INFECTIONS
Lynn A. Baden

Fungi are dimorphic, eucaryotic organisms whose cytoplasms are enclosed by rigid
walls. Yeasts are unicellular fungi. Fungi are currently divided into four classes.
The first three, Phycomycetes, Ascomycetes, and Basidiomycetes, differ in their method
of sexual reproduction and are identified by the morphology of their sexual spores.
The fourth class, Fungi Imperfecti, includes *Candida, Microsporum, Trichophyton,*
and *Histoplasma.* These fungi were thought to reproduce only by asexual spores
(conidia); however under special laboratory conditions, sometimes a sexual state may
be found. Most superficial fungal infections are caused by organisms belonging to
the fourth class.

Direct microscopy, culture, and Wood's lamp examination are all used to evaluate
and diagnose fungal infections. Scrapings of scale collected from the active margin
of a skin lesion can be placed on a slide, and Shwartz-Lamkin stain or potassium
hydroxide solution applied. With gentle heating, the epithelial cells are slowly destroyed, but the chitinous fungal cell walls resist digestion. Specimens containing
fungi will reveal septate, branching hyphal elements, yeasts, and spores. Sabouraud's
agar, which contains an organic nitrogen source, glucose, and antibiotics, is used for
culture of scrapings or pieces of biopsies. Bacterial contamination and saprophytic
molds can be controlled with appropriate antibiotic additives. Commercial products
of these combinations are available. Some products include phenol red, which turns
from yellow to red when dermatophytes are present. Cultures must be kept for up
to 1 month. Some fungi fluoresce when illuminated with a Wood's lamp, which emits
light at wavelengths greater than 365 nm. Wood's lamp examination of the patient
is helpful in identifying superficial infections caused by these fungi, which include
Microsporum canis, M. audouini, and *Trichophyton schoenleinii.* Serology and skin
tests can sometimes be useful to identify systemic fungal infections.

Most superficial fungal infections, with exceptions noted below, are treatable with
the use of topical antifungal preparations, which are numerous and readily available
over the counter or by prescription. Imidazoles are the most popular antifungal agents
because they are effective and work for both *Candida* and dermatophyte infections.
Examples include clotrimazole, miconazole, econazole, and ketoconazole. Ciclopirox
olamine and haloprogin are effective against bacteria, yeasts, and dermatophytes.
Allylamines and naftitine are new additions to dermatophyte therapy.

Superficial fungi cause a wide variety of cutaneous infections. **Tinea versicolor**
is a noninflammatory, chronic, superficial infection caused by a fungus variably
known as *Pityrosporum orbiculare, P. ovale,* or *Malassezia furfur.* The clinical appearance is often characteristic. Typically, there are irregular, scaly macules or thin
plaques of various sizes on the upper trunk and proximal extremities. The macules
or plaques commonly yield surprisingly large amounts of scale when scraped. Macules

may be hypopigmented, hyperpigmented, or erythematous. Predisposing factors include heat, humidity, and immunosuppression. Patients with AIDS often have extensive and recalcitrant disease.

The diagnosis of tinea versicolor is made by microscopically examining a KOH preparation of scrapings from a macule and visualizing short, nonbranching hyphae and clusters of spores (which often resemble spaghetti and meatballs). Treatments include 2.5% selenium sulfide lotion, topical antifungal creams, keratolytics, and a short course of systemic ketoconazole. Griseofulvin is ineffective. Recurrences are common and may be prevented by periodic use of selenium sulfide, salicylic acid/sulfur, or pyrithione zinc soaps or shampoos. Pigmentary changes may persist for months.

Pityrosporum folliculitis is caused by the same organism. It presents with pruritic, 2- to 3-mm follicular papules and pustules usually occurring on the upper back and chest. Microscopic examination of scrapings occasionally reveals typical hyphae and spores, but a biopsy is often needed for diagnosis. Pathologic examination will reveal dilated follicles plugged with the organism. *Pityrosporum* folliculitis will respond to the same treatments used for tinea versicolor.

Tinea nigra is caused by *Cladosporium wernecki* (syn. *Exophiala werneckii*) and is characterized by dark macules with little scale resembling silver nitrate stains. Lesions occur almost exclusively on the wrists and palms. Treatment includes stripping or paring the lesions to normal skin followed by topical therapy with keratolytics.

Piedra is an asymptomatic fungal infection of the hair shaft. Black piedra, caused by *Piedraia hortae,* is seen most often in the tropics, with scalp hair examination revealing characteristic small dark nodules along the shaft both microscopically and grossly visible. White piedra (trichosporosis), caused by *Trichosporon beigelii,* is seen worldwide, and the hair (mostly facial and pubic) shows soft, mucilaginous nodules. Shaving is curative.

Tinea corporis is a term used for all dermatophyte infections of glabrous skin except for the palms, soles, and groin, generally manifested by solitary or multiple annular, sharply marginated plaques with elevated scaling, erythematous borders and central clearing. Common causative organisms are *T. rubrum, M. canis, T. tonsurans,* and *T. mentagrophytes*. Diagnosis is established by microscopic examination of a KOH preparation of scrapings from the active border where fungal elements are commonly found. Precise identification of causative organisms requires identification of characteristic features on culture. Tinea corporis usually responds to topical therapy with antifungal creams. Oral griseofulvin or ketoconazole may be used for extensive or recalcitrant infections.

There are several uncommon or unusual variants of tinea corporis. Tinea imbricata is caused by *T. concentricum*. This disease presents as numerous concentric, scaly rings, which may affect the entire body. It is seen in southeast Asia, the South Pacific, and parts of South America. Another variant of tinea corporis is Majocchi's granuloma, which is a granulomatous response to perifollicular infection; *T. rubrum* is most commonly implicated. It presents as an annular arrangement of irregularly sized follicular papules. Tinea incognito is a dermatophyte infection in which the clinical diagnosis is difficult to make because the inflammatory response has been modified by corticosteroid treatment. Tinea faciei, caused by *T. mentagrophytes* or *T. rubrum,* presents with red scaly plaques or papules, itching, and burning on the face. When accompanied by telangiectasia, atrophy, and photoexacerbation, it may mimic lupus erythematosus.

Tinea pedis is the most common dermatophyte infection in the United States and the United Kingdom. It is uncommon before puberty and occurs more often in males. Causative organisms include *T. rubrum* (60%), *T. mentagrophytes* (25%), and *E. floccosum* (10%). There are four patterns of involvement: (1) intertriginous fissuring and maceration; (2) chronic papulosquamous eruption (moccasin foot), often accompanied by multiple toenail involvement; (3) vesicules and bullae; and (4) acute ulceration. The latter two are often associated with a dyshidrotic-like id reaction of the hands. Pruritus is common in all patterns. Treatment with topical antifungal preparations is effective, but must often be continued intermittently for the rest of the patient's life.

Tinea cruris is caused most commonly by *T. rubrum, E. floccosum,* or *T. men-tagrophytes.* It occurs more commonly in men and is usually associated with tinea pedis. Both infections occur in epidemics, especially among soldiers or athletic teams. Tinea cruris is characterized by bilateral involvement of the genital-crural skin and medial upper thigh, sparing the scrotum, with well-marginated erythematous plaques and arciform raised edges. Scaling and central clearing are commonly seen. Pruritus or pain may accompany the rash. Treatment is similar to that for tinea corporis. Topical antifungal powders are useful to prevent recurrence.

Tinea manuum is most often caused by *T. rubrum* and usually exists with concomitant foot infections. The disease is unilateral in 50% of cases. Hyperkeratosis of the palms and fingers with accentuation of the flexural creases is typical. The infection may creep over to the dorsum of the hand.

Tinea unguium refers to infection of the nail plate by dermatophytes; **onychomycosis** includes nondermatophytes and yeasts. Both are often associated with tinea pedis and are also rarely seen before puberty. Diagnosis is made by obtaining nail clippings or subungual debris for cultures and microscopic examination.

There are four patterns of onychomycosis. Distal subungual involvement is the most common. Clinically, there is darkening and thickening of the nail plate and hyperkeratotic subungual debris. White superficial onychomycosis is caused by invasion of the superficial surface of the nail plate, leading to opaque, white, rough areas. It is most commonly caused by *T. mentagrophytes* and is easily diagnosed by microscopic examination of shavings of the surface of the nail. Proximal subungual involvement is uncommon. White areas and subungual debris begin at the proximal nail fold and extend distally. *Candida* onychomycosis involves the whole nail plate and is seen only in patients with chronic mucocutaneous candidiasis.

Systemic therapy is generally required for all types of onychomycosis. The treatment of choice for onychomycosis caused by dermatophytes is griseofulvin. Therapy must continue for months until a normal nail is formed. The relapse rate is high. Avulsion of the nail probably does not improve the poor long-term cure rate. Candidal infections may be treated with oral ketoconazole. Topical treatment of onychomycosis is rarely effective.

Tinea capitis is caused by *Trichophyton* or *Microsporum* species. The fungus penetrates the follicle to Adamson's ring (keratinization zone). Depending on the organism, arthrospores are produced just under the cuticle of the hair (ectothrix) or within the hair shaft (endothrix). Invading fungi produce enzymes that dissolve and weaken the hair.

Tinea capitis is seen most often in children. *T. tonsurans* is currently the most common cause in the United States. In two recently reported studies, 90% of infections were seen in black and Hispanic children. Infection appears to be caused by person-to-person contact, and asymptomatic carrier states have been documented.

There are four clinical forms of tinea capitis. Noninflammatory tinea capitis is the most common. This pattern resembles seborrheic dermatitis and is characterized by scaly, pruritic patches spread diffusely on the scalp. Involved areas contain numerous broken-off, dull gray hairs several millimeters in length and hair loss may be striking. Inflammatory tinea capitis varies from pustular folliculitis (agminate folliculitis) to kerion formation. A kerion is a large, tender, boggy mass with erythema, pustules, and crusting, and may result in scarring alopecia. It represents an intense host response to infection. Inflammatory tinea capitis may be accompanied by pruritus, fever, pain, and lymphadenopathy. "Black dot" tinea capitis is uncommon. This is a relatively noninflammatory infection in which the hair breaks at the surface of the scalp when the support of the follicle is lost, resulting in alopecia and a "black dot" appearance. Multiple areas are often affected. Tinea favus caused by *T. schoenleinii* is seen most frequently in the Middle East and southern Africa. It is characterized by yellow, cup-shaped crusts called scutulum. Each scutulum develops around a hair, which pierces it centrally. Patchy hair loss and scarring alopecia are seen. It is a chronic infection that may persist from childhood to adulthood.

The diagnosis of tinea capitis is established by microscopically demonstrating spores or hyphae in or on hairs removed from affected areas, or by culturing fungi from specimens obtained from affected areas. Methods for obtaining material for direct examination or culture include scraping or brushing affected areas or plucking several affected hairs. Wood's lamp examination is currently of limited value, since the majority of cases are caused by *T. tonsurans,* which does not fluoresce.

Treatment is with griseofulvin for 6 to 8 weeks. Absorption is enhanced when the drug is administered with food. Griseofulvin is well tolerated in children and has few side effects. Concomitant daily shampooing with 2.5% selenium sulfide shampoo shortens the time that viable fungi can be cultured from infected children.

Tinea barbae is an infection of the beard, caused most commonly by *T. mentagrophytes* or *T. verrucosum.* The clinical appearance may vary from an inflammatory, kerionlike picture to a superficial folliculitis or circinate-spreading plaques. Griseofulvin is curative.

Candida is a yeastlike fungus consisting of over 100 species. *C. albicans* and *C. tropicalis* account for 80% of pathogenic isolates. *Candida* forms true hyphae and pseudohyphae that arise from buds of elongate cells that remain attached to the parent. *Candida* species are asymptomatic colonists of the gut in 60% of individuals and of the mouth in 15% of individuals. Although not a usual member of the normal skin flora, it can often be recovered from periorificial areas. Most symptomatic candidal infections result from autoinoculation by commensal yeast. Predisposing factors include mechanical factors (trauma and moisture), nutrition (avitaminosis, iron deficiency), physiologic states (pregnancy, age extremes), underlying systemic disorders (Down's syndrome, AIDS, diabetes mellitus, uremia, malignancy, immune deficiency), and medications (antibiotic therapy, oral contraceptive pills). Cell-mediated immunity is important in host defense.

Diagnosis is made by direct microscopic examination of smears and biopsies revealing budding yeasts, hyphae, or pseudohyphae. Positive cultures can be considered significant only if the site from which they are taken is one that is not often colonized.

Candidal infections of the mucous membranes occur in several clinically distinct syndromes. **Oral candidiasis** (thrush) presents as sharply defined patches of creamy, curdlike, white pseudomembrane overlying an erythematous base. **Acute atrophic oral candidiasis** may follow thrush and is associated with antibiotic use. It presents as denuded atrophic inflamed patches. **Perlèche** is cracks and fissures of the mouth corners. It is usually multifactorial in etiology, but the presence of *Candida* may often be documented by microscopic examination of scrapings. Other types of oral candidiasis include **denture stomatitis, angular stomatitis,** and **median rhomboid glossitis. Candida esophagitis** may be seen in AIDS patients. **Vulvovaginitis** presents as a pruritic, sore, red, and inflamed perineum with a thick, creamy, white vaginal discharge. It is associated with pregnancy, diabetes mellitus, oral contraceptives, and antibiotics. **Candidal balanitis** is usually an asymptomatic infection of the glans of the uncircumcised penis; often the sexual partner has a candidal infection as well. Tiny papules may evolve into pustules. Treatment of mucosal lesions is with anticandidal agents such as nystatin or the imidazoles. Oral and esophageal disease is treated with nystatin (swish and swallow) 3 times a day. Clotrimazole troches are also effective. Vaginal infections are treated with the same agents prepared as creams or suppositories.

Intertriginous candidal infection is seen in normal skin folds, especially in obese people or diapered babies. Wetness with occlusion predisposes an individual to infection. A well-defined, intensely erythematous eroded plaque studded with subcorneal pustules is typically present. Classically, there are satellite papules, pustules, or erosions with a collarette of scale. **Erosio interdigitalis blastomycetica** is a candidal infection occurring between the third and fourth web space of fingers. Treatment consists of keeping the affected areas dry and using topical anticandidal creams.

Nodular or **granulomatous candidiasis** can occur as an atypical reaction to the *Candida* infection, manifesting as bluish-brown nodules or cutaneous hornlike lesions. **Candidal paronychia** presents as tender, red swellings around the nails, often accompanied by a bacterial superinfection. Wet hands predispose an individual to infection. One nail or all may be involved, with loss of cuticle and onycholysis. *Candida* species do not produce keratolytic enzymes; therefore, nail dystrophy is secondary to chronic paronychia causing matrix damage.

Congenital candidiasis, from intrauterine infection, is an uncommon disorder detectable usually within the first 12 hours of life. It is a widespread eczematous, exudative, or vesiculopustular disease. Resolution occurs within 4 to 7 days with topical therapy alone. Blood and cerebrospinal fluid are usually sterile; however, systemic disease is seen in compromised infants.

Disseminated candidiasis is seen most often in severely immunocompromised hosts or in patients with invasive catheters. The mortality rate is 50%. Organs and tissues involved often include the kidneys, heart, meninges, and joints. Only 50% of patients may have positive blood cultures. Skin lesions are seen in 10% of patients and typically are firm red papulopustules or nodules, which may become hemorrhagic and ulcerate. Treatment includes intravenous amphotericin or ketoconazole.

Chronic mucocutaneous candidiasis is a group of chronic, treatment-resistant, superficial candidal infections of the skin, nails, and oropharynx without visceral involvement. Although up to one-third of patients have no demonstrable immunologic defect, the disease is a manifestation of various underlying primary defects in immunity, most commonly leading to defects in T–cell–mediated immune responses. Cases may be sporadic or inherited and may be apparent in infancy or early childhood. Clinical features include persistent oral candidiasis, intertrigo, paronychia with severe nail plate invasion and dystrophy, and vulvovaginitis. Five clinical syndromes are noted: oral candidiasis, candidiasis with endocrinopathy, localized mucocutaneous candidiasis, diffuse candidiasis, and candidiasis with thymoma.

Ahmed AR: Immunology of human dermatophyte infections. *Arch Dermatol.* 1982;118:521–525.
An excellent review covering the immunologic basis of acute and chronic dermatophyte infections.

Elewski BE, Hazen PG: The superficial mycoses and the dermatophytes. *J Am Acad Dermatol.* 1989;21:655–673.
A review of superficial mycoses with emphasis on exact identification of fungi according to their macroscopic and microscopic features when grown on appropriate media.

Haneke E: Fungal infections of the nail. *Semin Dermatol.* 1991;10:41–53.
Detailed review of the onychomycoses and their differential diagnosis. Author concludes that treatment has remained difficult because predisposing factors are not usually amenable to therapy.

Jacobs PH: Treatment of fungal skin infections: state of the art. *J Am Acad Dermatol.* 1990;23:549–551.
An overview of the use of topical and oral agents is presented, and treatment of specific infections is detailed. Ketoconazole is particularly well reviewed.

Jorizzo JL: Chronic mucocutaneous candidosis: an update. *Arch Dermatol.* 1982;118:963–965.
Succinct review of this subject.

Kaplan MH, Sadick N, McNutt S, et al.: Dermatologic findings and manifestations of acquired immunodeficiency syndrome (AIDS). *J Am Acad Dermatol.* 1987;16:485–506.
Discussion of fungal infections, including those with atypical presentations and courses, seen in AIDS.

Lesher JL, Smith JG: Antifungal agents in dermatology. *J Am Acad Dermatol.* 1987;17:383–394.
A clear review of this subject.

Pariser DM: Superficial fungal infections. A practical guide for primary care physicians. *Postgrad Med.* 1990;87:101–103, 106–108.
Review of diagnosis and management of dermatophyte infections and cutaneous candidiasis.

Stein DH: Superficial fungal infections. *Pediatr Clin North Am.* 1983;30:545–561.
Well-written review of this subject in the pediatric population, but also helpful in adult dermatology.

36. SUBCUTANEOUS AND SYSTEMIC MYCOSES
Lynn A. Baden

Some fungi are not confined to keratinized tissue and may cause subcutaneous and systemic infections. Subcutaneous mycoses are usually caused by fungi that live in the soil or water. Infections are characterized by the development of lesions at the site of inoculation and subsequent deep localized chronic infection. Systemic mycoses can be divided into two groups: true pathogenic infections and opportunistic infections. Infection with true pathogenic fungi usually occurs in a normal host through a pulmonary source. The opportunistic fungi are commonly soil inhabitants but cause disease in an immunocompromised host. Skin manifestations usually represent disseminated diseases. Opportunistic infections are increasingly important because of the number of immunocompromised hosts, including people with AIDS, patients on chemotherapy for malignancy, and transplant patients on chronic immunosuppressive therapy. Biopsy specimens are often required for histology and culture, since the clinical features of lesions are not diagnostic.

Sporotrichosis, infection with *Sporothrix schenckii,* is a chronic lymphatic or subcutaneous granulomatous mycosis seen worldwide. Classically, the portal of entry occurs on the hand or arm through a small wound induced by a thorn or splinter. Initially a chancriform lesion develops. Over weeks to months an ascending lymphangitis occurs, characterized by thickening of lymphatics studded with enlarging subcutaneous nodules. Rarely, hematogenous spread occurs. The differential diagnosis of sporotrichosis with clinically evident lymphatic spread includes atypical mycobacterial infections, tularemia, tuberculosis, anthrax, and other mycotic infections. Diagnosis is best established by culturing the organism from suspected lesions. Serologic tests are also available and are generally sensitive and specific. Treatment of cutaneous infection is with oral iodides. Parenteral amphotericin B or oral ketoconazole may be effective for patients who cannot tolerate iodides.

Chromoblastomycosis is an uncommon disease seen mostly in the tropics and subtropics, caused by a variety of fungi. The clinical picture of warty and papillomatous excrescences led to the name "mossy foot." Typical lesions are slow-growing verrucous plaques with crops of satellites. The disease is normally painless, and there is no bony invasion. Early diagnosis leads to cure with local excision. More-extensive disease may be treated with flucytosine alone or in combination with amphotericin B.

Mycetoma, also known as Madura foot, is a chronic granulomatous foot infection caused by usually harmless, common fungi or actinomycetes, most often affecting farm laborers. Once inoculated, these wound pathogens can cause severe skin damage, progressing to involve the subcutaneous tissue and bone. The infection begins as a firm nondescript papule. After months to years, nodules stud the foot and marked fibrosis, draining sinuses, and abscesses are seen. Diagnostic features include extrusion of tiny granules containing crops of organisms from sinus openings. Treatment depends on the organism that is seen in the granules, but includes 6 to 12 months of ketoconazole, griseofulvin, sulfonamides, penicillin, or tetracycline.

Rhinosporidiosis is a chronic granulomatous disease typified by pedunculated polyps, sometimes quite large, hanging from the nose. The cauliflower-like lesions are studded with small white spots that contain the fungus. Disease is seen in India and Ceylon. The causative organism is a water inhabitant.

Lobomycosis (Lobo's disease) is a chronic localized disease seen in the Caribbean and South America. It is characterized by intracutaneous, keloidal-like lesions that may become verrucous, often on exposed skin. Excision is curative.

Systemic mycoses may be due to true pathogenic fungi. In **histoplasmosis** (*Histoplasma capsulatum*) infection, subclinical disease accounts for most cases. In endemic areas such as the Mississippi River and Ohio River valleys, up to 80% of the population has delayed type hypersensitivity to histoplasma antigens. There is a wide spectrum of disease, ranging from asymptomatic to acute and fulminant. Acute disseminated disease is uncommon and may be accompanied by indurated granulomas of the mucous membranes or skin. Except for rare cases of primary cutaneous inoculation, mucocutaneous histoplasmosis represents fulminant disseminated disease and is fatal without intravenous amphotericin B therapy. Biopsy and culture reveal small intracellular yeastlike organisms. Serology is valuable in diagnosis. Primary cutaneous lesions are rare and self-limited.

Coccidioidomycosis (San Joaquin Valley fever) occurs 100,000 times per year in the United States, most often in a subclinical or self-limited form. Cutaneous involvement follows disseminated disease from a primary pulmonary infection in a small number of cases. It is 5 times more common in blacks and Filipinos than in whites. When involved, the skin reveals verrucous granulomas that occur as solitary lesions or as disseminated miliary disease. Primary cutaneous disease is a medical rarity, presenting as a chancriform syndrome at the inoculation site and becoming sporotrichoid in appearance. Therapy for disseminated disease consists of intravenous amphotericin B. Diagnosis is aided by serologic studies.

North American blastomycosis is a chronic granulomatous and suppurative mycosis mainly affecting the lungs but which may disseminate to affect skin, bones, and the CNS. The Mississippi River valley has the largest number of cases. Most pulmonary infections are asymptomatic or acute and self-limited. Patients with disseminated disease may have one or more skin lesions presenting on the trunk that extend slowly and show central clearing, but have borders that are persistent, sharply elevated, and verrucous. Miliary abscesses containing the organism are found at the border. Mucosal lesions may be seen. Treatment consists of intravenous amphotericin B. Stilbamidine derivatives and miconazole are also useful. Primary skin lesions are rare and are chancriform in appearance; they tend toward spontaneous recovery.

Paracoccidioidomycosis (South American blastomycosis) is a chronic granulomatous fungal infection affecting the skin, mucous membranes, lymph nodes, and viscera. The disease is endemic in Central and South America. The primary lesion is usually in the mouth and presents as a firm ulcer with punctate hemorrhages. Indurated ulcerations of the oral pharynx or crusted granulomatous lesions on the mucocutaneous borders are seen in 65% of patients. Acneiform or granulomatous lesions are seen on the skin of 10% of patients. Regional lymph nodes, always severely affected, are painful, adherent to the skin, and suppurative. Ketoconazole is the drug of choice.

Opportunistic fungal infections have become common. **Cryptococcosis,** caused by *Cryptococcus neoformans,* is an acute, subacute, or chronic infection with marked predilection for the brain or meninges. The organism is found worldwide, classically in pigeon droppings. The respiratory tract is the primary portal of entry, and disease is usually subclinical or mild. Approximately 50% of cases occur in the immunosuppressed, including people with AIDS. Skin lesions, which are considered a bad prognostic sign, are most common on the face, scalp, and neck, occurring in 10% of patients with systemic involvement. These lesions begin as painless red papules or pustules and evolve into warty infiltrated plaques and nodules that may ulcerate and have rolled edges. The organism is readily cultured from cerebrospinal fluid or smears. Without treatment, disease can be expected to lead to coma and death. A combination of amphotericin B and flucytosine for systemic and meningeal disease is recommended. Serologic tests are useful, especially for disseminated disease. Primary cutaneous lesions rarely occur.

Aspergillosis is an uncommon opportunistic fungal infection caused by any of 600 species of *Aspergillus.* It is a common household mold, usually causing superficial infections such as external otitis or pulmonary aspergilloma. In those with reduced resistance, fatal disseminated disease may follow. In disseminated disease, erythematous to violaceous plaques are seen, which may be important sites to biopsy, obviating the need for more-invasive techniques. Primary cutaneous lesions are uncommon, but may be seen in the immunosuppressed. They are red papules, nodules, and plaques that may enlarge, ulcerate, and develop eschar. Lesions often begin in sites where intravenous catheters are taped to the skin of immunocompromised patients. Paranasal sinus and oropharyngeal involvement may be severe.

Mucormycosis is a lung and CNS infection most often associated with diabetic ketoacidosis, renal transplantation, or hematopoietic malignancy. Rhinocerebral subcutaneous mucormycosis is a paranasal sinus infection, presenting with orbital cellulitis and evolving into black necrotic lesions on the palate or nasal mucous membrane through which the fungus invades the sinuses or brain. Disseminated mucormycosis occurs from a pulmonary source and resembles aspergillosis. Burn wound infections are common with this fungus. Primary cutaneous infection is rare. Therapy consists of intravenous amphotericin B and correction of any underlying metabolic defect.

Nocardia asteroides is a microbiologic intermediate between true fungi and bacteria. It causes an acute or subacute respiratory disease. Skin lesions are limited to sinus tracts from abscesses. Sulfonamides are the treatment of choice.

Actinomycetes are bacteria that produce filamentous branching hyphae and therefore are considered in this discussion. There are three clinical presentations, including cervicofacial "lumpy jaw" infection, thoracic disease mimicking tuberculosis, and abdominal disease presenting with a mass. Primary cutaneous disease is very uncommon; however, any of the three syndromes may have draining sinuses from subcutaneous abscesses. Diagnosis is made by "sulfur" granules in tissue exudate. Treatment consists of debridement and high-dose penicillin.

Meyer RD: Cutaneous and mucosal manifestations of the deep mycotic infections. *Acta Dermatol Venereol (Stockh).* 1986;121:57–72.
An excellent review of this subject, written in a concise manner.

Penn RL, Lambert RS, George RB: Invasive fungal infections: the use of serologic tests in diagnosis and management. *Arch Intern Med.* 1983;143:1215–1220.
This review is a summary of available serologic tests for common invasive mycoses and discusses the tests' utility.

Saral R: Candida and aspergillus infections in immunocompromised patients: an overview. *Rev Infect Dis.* 1991;13:487–492.
These two common fungal pathogens are responsible for many disseminated infections and may be difficult to document. Treatment of clinically suspect cases and prophylaxis are discussed in detail.

Tomecki KJ, Steck WD, Hall GS, Dijkstra JWE: Subcutaneous mycoses. *J Am Acad Dermatol.* 1989;21:785–790.
Periodic synopsis of subcutaneous mycoses that covers recent references and key points. Disorders covered include sporotrichosis, chromoblastomycosis, mycetoma, cryptococcosis, histoplasmosis, and aspergillosis.

Wolfson JS, Sober AJ, Rubin RH: Dermatologic manifestations of infection in the compromised host. *Annu Rev Med.* 1983;34:205–217.
Review of the numerous cutaneous infections occurring in immunocompromised patients. Aggressive diagnostic evaluation is emphasized.

Yalisove BL, Berzin M, Williams CM: Multiple pruritic purple plaques. Cutaneous sporotrichosis. *Arch Dermatol.* 1991;127:721–722, 724–725.
Brief presentation of a classic case with good photographs and a cogent discussion.

37. WARTS
Edward V. Maytin

Warts, or verrucae ("little hills"), are benign epithelial tumors caused by human papillomaviruses (HPV). They are very common, generating an estimated 4 million yearly patient visits to office-based physicians for nongenital warts and another 1 million for anogenital warts. Certain patients with impaired cell-mediated immunity are particularly susceptible to frequent and recalcitrant HPV infections, such as patients with AIDS, lymphoma, or leukemia, those on immunosuppressive drugs after organ transplantation, or those with the rare familial disease epidermodysplasia verruciformis. In all patients, however, warts can be frustratingly difficult to treat. The need for therapy may be more important in the light of increasing evidence that infections by certain HPV strains can predispose patients to malignancy.

Most HPV infections affect only the skin, although involvement of other epithelial surfaces, such as laryngeal papillomatosis or warts in the urethra and bladder, can occur. The infection and resulting changes are confined to the epidermis. Different clinical appearances (common, plantar, flat, or genital warts) arise from varying degrees of epidermal proliferation and keratinization. While the virus is thought to be present throughout the epidermis, it is only actively expressed in the upper layers, where dense spherical nuclei (laden with intranuclear viral particles) are sometimes seen histologically. Usually the only cytologic evidence of HPV infection is the presence of koilocytes (vacuolated cells with irregular, popcorn-shaped nuclei and peri-nuclear halos), seen in the upper stratum spinosum and granulosum. The basal layer appears normal. If, on biopsy, atypia appears in the lower epidermis, the possibility of Bowen's disease (carcinoma in situ) or squamous cell carcinoma should be entertained.

Common warts (verrucae vulgaris) are flesh-colored, rough, hyperkeratotic pap-ules, found singly or grouped on any skin surface but most often on the hands. Trauma or infectious spread may explain the predilection for fingers and periungual skin. Autoinoculation may lead to warts on adjacent surfaces of fingers and toes ("kissing warts"). While the appearance of common warts is usually distinctive (rough and dome-shaped), they can present on a stalk (filiform) or as a cutaneous horn and may occasionally resemble seborrheic keratoses, acrochordons (skin tags), squamous cell carcinomas, or one of the rare hereditary disorders of cornification (e.g., acrokeratosis verruciformis).

Plantar warts are thick, hyperkeratotic lesions on the soles, especially on the heel, metatarsal head region, and plantar toe. Multiple plantar warts that coalesce into plaques are called mosaic warts. Unlike warts in most other sites, plantar warts can be very painful. The principal differential diagnosis are calluses, corns (clavi), and scarring from previous overtreatment. Unlike a callus or a corn, a plantar wart will exhibit punctate black dots ("seeds") after the keratin is shaved away; these dots represent thrombosed capillaries in elongated dermal papillae. Calluses and corns are generally painful on direct pressure, while warts are often more painful on lateral pressure.

Anogenital warts (condylomata acuminata, genital warts, venereal warts) are moist, cauliflower-like masses that involve the genitalia, anorectal region, and oc-casionally the urethra, bladder, and ureters. They can range from discrete, pinpoint to 3 mm, soft, nonscaly papules on the penis or vulva to incredibly large exophytic growths. Pinpoint lesions may be difficult to see unless they are hydrated with water or acetic acid and then inspected with $10 \times$ magnification. The smaller warts may be hyperpigmented and resemble seborrheic keratoses or melanocytic nevi (moles). They may also be confused with bowenoid papulosis, a recently described entity in which velvety, red or hyperpigmented, 2- to 3-mm papules on external genitalia show both histologic evidence of HPV infection and cellular atypia similar to that of car-cinoma in situ. Occasionally, enlarged sebaceous glands near the glans penis may resemble genital warts. A large, exophytic anogenital wart must be distinguished from condyloma lata (secondary syphilis) and from verrucous carcinoma (also called giant condylomata of Buschke and Löwenstein), which is a low-grade, locally invasive tumor usually seen on the glans penis and foreskin of uncircumcised males. Verrucous carcinomas have also been seen in the vulvar and anal mucosa of women, however.

Anogenital warts are uncommon in children. A few years ago, many believed that such warts constituted very strong evidence for sexual abuse (see the advisory issued by the American Academy of Dermatology Task Force on Pediatric Dermatology in 1984). This belief was strengthened by the finding of genital types of HPV (e.g., HPV 6, 11, 16, and 18) in children's condylomata. However, more recent evidence from DNA hybridization studies has shown that skin types (e.g., HPV 1–4) can also occur in these lesions, with little correlation to either social history or wart morphology. Judging from the fact that laryngeal papillomatosis (caused by HPV type 11 and transmitted at birth) sometimes may not appear clinically until 5 years of age, it remains possible that many condylomata in young children are the result of trans-mission at birth. Therefore, caution should be exercised in interpreting the finding of anogenital warts in a child, and the decision to institute social or criminal investigation should be made only on the basis of other clinical and social information available.

Flat warts (verrucae planae), seen mostly on the face and hands of children, are small, 2- to 5-mm, flat-topped, hyperpigmented papules. They often occur in linear streaks, perhaps as a result of scratching and autoinoculation of the virus. On the face they can mimic acne, melanocytic nevi, or seborrheic keratoses. Flat warts on the extremities may look like lichen planus but lack Wickham's striae and associated buccal involvement.

Since the mid-1970s, when advances in molecular biology allowed the first identification of **distinct papillomavirus types** by DNA hybridization techniques, the number of different HPV types has grown from a half-dozen to at least 56. (By definition, a new HPV type has less than 50% DNA sequence homology with existing HPV types.) Early expectations for a strict classification have not been met; any given virus type may be found in multiple locations or have varying gross morphology. In general, types 1 through 4, among the first discovered and most widespread HPV, predominate in nongenital cutaneous warts, while types 6, 11, 16, 18, 31, and 35 are seen more often in genital warts. The very high prevalence of HPV types 16, 18, and 31 in cancerous or precancerous lesions of the genitalia (e.g., 70% to 100% for HPV type 16 in high-grade cervical intraepithelial neoplasia, carcinoma in situ, and squamous cell carcinoma) suggests a strong association between HPV-induced genital warts and malignancy. The oncogenic potential of certain HPV types may also pertain to nongenital skin, as suggested by recent reports of periungual squamous cell carcinoma harboring HPV 16 and 35. Atypical changes on Pap smears, previously interpreted as evidence of cervical dysplasia or carcinoma in situ, may actually represent viral-induced changes from subclinical HPV infection (the shed cells may be the koilocytes described above). HPV genetic material has even been reported in histologically and clinically normal tissue, 2 to 5 cm distant from a genital carcinoma. Although not all of Koch's postulates for HPV as the oncogenic agent have been fulfilled, clearly the patient with genital warts should receive close scrutiny and follow-up (e.g., colposcopy in women with genital lesions) for possible development of malignancy.

Many nonspecific **therapies** for warts seem to work, but none consistently. In the few comparative studies available, similar results were obtained with different techniques. For example, either liquid nitrogen applied every 2 or 3 weeks for up to six treatments or salicylic acid–lactic acid (SAL) applied nightly for 12 weeks cured hand warts in 70% to 80% of patients. Likewise, either SAL or podophyllin applied nightly for 12 weeks was 80% to 85% effective for simple plantar warts, while 30% of hand wart patients were resistant to treatment. All these agents may be working by stimulating cell-mediated immunity, as evidenced by a similar histologic picture (mononuclear inflammatory cell infiltrate) in warts that spontaneously regress or in those involuting because of therapy.

It is crucial to remember that warts are, in general, benign growths and that overzealous therapy can cause permanent pain and scarring. Sometimes treatment of a few warts will induce generalized regression of other warts. Only in the case of genital warts with premalignant potential could treatment be considered mandatory, and even then, close regular follow-up may be an alternative before surgery or other definitive procedures are undertaken.

Common warts are frequently treated with keratolytics (generally SAL mixtures), repeated sessions of cryosurgery, electrodesiccation and curettage, or repeated applications of trichloroacetic acid. Plantar warts may be left untreated if not painful, or pared periodically, or removed by blunt dissection, or treated like common warts. The first choice for treating genital warts is usually podophyllin applied every 5 to 7 days or cryosurgery every 7 to 14 days. They may also be treated with electrosurgery or repeated applications of 5-fluorouracil cream or solution. The presence of external genital warts may necessitate further examination by proctoscopy or colposcopy (one-third of women with vulvar warts have internal involvement on colposcopy). Five percent acetic acid may be painted on mucosal surfaces to whiten affected areas thus making them more visible.

Recent advances have been made in the treatment of recalcitrant lesions. The carbon dioxide laser has been used to melt away the wart and surrounding infected but clinically normal skin or mucosa. It is best used for recalcitrant genital warts that are on mucosal surfaces since such warts heal rapidly without hypertrophic scarring. The carbon dioxide laser can also be used for difficult cutaneous warts, although it generally produces wounds requiring 4 to 8 weeks to heal and a permanent scar. Intralesional bleomycin is expensive and painful but sometimes produces spectacular results with relatively quick involution of the wart. Interferon injections may be administered systemically or intralesionally with involution of the warts, though the remission is generally temporary. An allergic reaction to DNCB (dinitrochlorobenzene) can also be used. The antigen (2% DNCB) is dripped onto normal skin, and the patient becomes sensitized within 12 to 14 days; then 0.1% DNCB ointment is applied to the wart. The resulting contact hypersensitivity reaction attracts inflammatory cells, which induce resolution of the wart. Severe allergic contact dermatitis can result from indiscriminate application of the ointment, and the long-term effects of this sort of immune modulation are unknown. Finally, hypnosis can sometimes induce wart regression and may be particularly helpful for children.

American Academy of Dermatology Task Force on Pediatric Dermatology: Special report: Genital warts and sexual abuse in children. *J Am Acad Dermatol.* 1984;11:529–530.
  A statement emphasizing that if warts are noted in the anal or genital areas of children less than 12 years of age, child abuse must be considered. Suggestions for further investigation and notification of the appropriate state agency are given.
Arndt KA: *Manual of Dermatologic Therapeutics.* 4th ed. Boston, MA: Little, Brown and Co.; 1988. Chapter 34 on the treatment of warts and chapter 7 on corns and calluses are succinct and practical.
Beutner KR: Human papillomavirus infection. *J Am Acad Dermatol.* 1989;20:114–123.
  A current synopsis of key advances and concepts in HPV biology, epidemiology, genital infection, transmission in children, diagnostic tests, and clinical treatment modalities. Recent references.
Bunney MH, Nolan MW, Williams DA: An assessment of methods of treating viral warts by comparative treatment trials based on a standard design. *Brit J Derm.* 1976;94:667–678.
  Best available study comparing standard protocols in treatment of common hand and plantar warts.
Chuang T-Y: Condylomata acuminata: an epidemiologic view. *J Am Acad Derm.* 1987;16:376–384.
  An overview of HPV types and clinical associations as of 1986.
Jones SK, Darville JM: Transmission of virus particles by cryotherapy and multi-use caustic pencils: a problem to dermatologists? *Brit J Dermatol.* 1989;121:481–486.
  Because many virus particles can apparently survive in the liquid nitrogen that is used to treat warts, it would seem prudent to discard cotton swabs and aliquots of liquid nitrogen after every patient. Alternatively, a cryotherapy gun can be used for spray delivery.
Kraus, SJ, Stone KM: Management of genital infection caused by human papillomavirus. *Reviews Infect Dis.* 1990;12 (suppl. 6):S620–S632.
  A nice quantitative review from the CDC in Atlanta regarding the relatively efficacy, cost, side effects, and rates of recurrence of cryotherapy, laser surgery, interferon, podophyllin, and 5-fluorouracil in the treatment of genital warts. Simple methods (podophyllin and liquid nitrogen cryotherapy) come out ahead.
Macnab JCM, Walkinshaw SA, Cordiner JW, et al.: Human papillomavirus in clinically and histologically normal tissue of patients with genital cancer. *New Engl J Med.* 1986;315:1052–1058.
  In this study of 30 patients, DNA sequences of HPV 16 were detected in 84% of tumors from women with genital cancers and in 73% of clinically and histologically normal neighboring tissues from the same patients but in only 11% of normal cervix

specimens. In addition to showing a strong association between the presence of HPV 16 genomes and genital tumors, these investigators identified HPV 16 DNA in apparently normal tissue as far as 5 cm from the tumor.

Ostrow RS, Shaver MK, Turnquist S, et al.: Human papillomavirus-16 DNA in a cutaneous invasive cancer. *Arch Dermatol.* 1989;125:666–669.

This case report demonstrates that certain HPV types associated with neoplasia of the genital region may also have oncogenic potential elsewhere on the skin.

Padel AF, Venning VA, Evans MF, et al.: Human papillomaviruses in anogenital warts in children: typing by in situ hybridisation. *Brit Med J.* 1990;300:1491–1494.

DNA probes to 11 different HPV types were used to characterize anogenital wart biopsies from 17 children, aged 1 to 9 years. While two-thirds (10 specimens) were positive for genital HPV types 6 or 11, the other one-third (6 specimens) contained skin HPV types 2 or 3. There was no correlation between the morphologic appearance of the warts and HPV type. In only 5 children was there evidence of sexual abuse. The authors suggest that nonvenereal transmission of anogenital warts in children is more common than previously thought, and that neither the presence of such warts, nor their HPV type, can be used as proof for or against sexual transmission.

Ruedlinger R, Grob R, Yu YX, et al.: Human papillomavirus-35-positive bowenoid papulosis of the anogenital area and concurrent human papillomavirus-35-positive verruca with bowenoid dysplasia of the periungual area. *Arch Dermatol.* 1989;125:655–659.

Expands on the theme of Ostrow et al.

Schneider A, Grubert T: Diagnosis of HPV infection by recombinant DNA technology. *Clin Obstet Gynecol.* 1989;32:127–140.

A review of currently available DNA hybridization techniques to identify HPV genomes.

Syrjanen K, Vayrynen M, Saarikoski S, et al.: Natural history of cervical human papillomavirus (HPV) infections based on prospective follow-up. *Brit J Obstet Gynaecol.* 1985;92:1086–1092.

A prospective study of 418 women over a 2-year period showed that lesions infected with HPV 16 and 18 were more rapidly progressive, more likely to recur after treatment, and more likely to progress to high-grade neoplasia than were lesions infected with HPV 6 and 11.

Turner MLC: Human papillomavirus infection of the genital tract *Progr Dermatol.* 1989;23(2):1–12.

An excellent short review with 165 recent references and concise summaries on wart biology, relationships to genital cancer, clinical diagnosis, and treatment.

38. GENITAL ULCERS
Joseph C. Kvedar

The patient presenting with genital ulcerations poses a unique diagnostic and therapeutic challenge. Textbooks of dermatologic and infectious diseases outline the various entities and stress clinical features that differentiate them. In reality, it has been demonstrated that the accuracy with which even experienced clinicians make the correct diagnosis without laboratory aids is about 60%. Moreover, it is not uncommon to have multiple pathogens in the same lesion. Therefore, accurate laboratory tests are necessary to facilitate correct treatment. Other factors that complicate this already difficult area are the public health implications of improper treatment and the unreliability of some patients.

The following discussion reviews the sexually transmitted diseases that can result in genital ulcers. Diseases that can cause genital ulcers but are not within the scope of this discussion include Behçet's disease, deep fungal infections, carcinoma, blistering diseases, fixed drug eruptions, lichen planus, and erosive balanitis.

The incidence of **syphilis** is now increasing after a steady post–World War II decline. Rates of primary and secondary syphilis increased 34% from 1981 to 1989. The incidence varies according to the population studied. In urban populations the incidence is estimated to be 25 to 50 per 100,000. Syphilis is a common cause of genital ulcers. Since it occurs in sexually active populations, it may be associated with HIV infection, which alters the clinical manifestations and response to treatment.

After an average incubation period of 3 weeks (the range is 10 days to 3 months), a papule forms at the site of inoculation. The papule rapidly breaks down to form a slowly growing ulcer. The ulcer enlarges to a maximum diameter of 1 to 2 cm and involutes spontaneously in 3 to 9 weeks. Clinical characteristics include the painless nature of the ulcer as well as the round, rolled, indurated border and clean, granulating base. While a single ulcer is most common, multiple lesions have been observed. Bilateral painless adenopathy is most common, but unilateral or painful adenopathy can be seen.

The causative organism is a spirochete, *Treponema pallidum,* which cannot be readily cultured but is easily viewed by dark-field examination of serum from the ulcer base. The ulcer is squeezed until a drop of serum can be touched to a cover slip, inverted onto a slide, and viewed immediately under the dark-field microscope. The accuracy of the test can be increased if the ulcer bed is cleaned with sterile saline before the serum is expressed.

Since serologic tests for syphilis begin to show reactivity 14 to 21 days after inoculation, they are unreliable in the diagnosis of primary syphilis. If the initial serology of a patient with a suspected chancre is negative, the test should be repeated weekly for 4 weeks and then monthly for 2 months. While histopathology is seldom necessary for diagnosis, primary syphilis can be distinguished from other ulcerative lesions by the presence of a marked plasma cell infiltrate and endothelial cell proliferation. If the tissue specimen is prepared with Warthin-Starry stain or modified Steiner stain, numerous organisms are readily identified.

A genital ulcer is often the first evidence of syphilis but does not occur in all patients. Secondary syphilis, a manifestation of disseminated disease, develops in 25% of patients who have had untreated chancres. It sometimes appears when the chancre is still present or in patients who have no history of suspicious ulcers, but usually follows a chancre in 2 to 6 months. In secondary syphilis, the skin and mucous membranes are involved with a generalized eruption, with morphologies varying from maculopapular, papulosquamous, verrucous, follicular, and pustular to nodular varieties. Constitutional signs and symptoms may accompany the rash. Central nervous system involvement may be documented in up to 5% of patients by CSF examination. Latent syphilis may also occur, with or without a history of chancres or secondary syphilis. Twenty-five percent of these patients develop nodular or noduloulcerative lesions or life-threatening neurosyphilis or cardiovascular syphilis.

Treatment is with benzathine penicillin G, 2.4 million units IM, or tetracycline, 500 mg qid for 2 weeks.

While **chancroid** was once an uncommon disease in the United States, the incidence of this disease increased in the 1980s, particularly in large coastal cities.

Following an incubation period of 12 to 72 hours, an ulcer or ulcers form at the site of inoculation. Typically, there are multiple, round to oval, deep ulcers with irregular, nonindurated and undermined borders. The edges of the ulcers tend to have a ragged appearance, and the bases are purulent. The most distinguishing clinical characteristic of this disease is the exquisite tenderness of the ulcers. Without treatment, lesions remain for several months. The infection remains localized. Approximately half of the patients will develop unilateral inguinal adenitis and occasional bubo formation. There may be sinus tract formation and drainage.

Chancroid is easily confused clinically with herpes genitalis, which also produces multiple painful ulcerations. A variant of chancroid resembling granuloma inguinale has also been described.

The causative organism is *Hemophilus ducreyi,* a gram-negative pleomorphic coccobacillus. It is easily identified on a Gram stain by its tendency to group with the appearance of "railroad tracks" or "schools of fish." The organism is difficult to culture. The most successful culture medium is enriched chocolate agar with added vancomycin. The organism has also been successfully cultured in defibrinated blood.

The diagnosis is usually made on clinical grounds and by response to therapy. However, laboratory confirmation of clinical impressions should be pursued. A Gram-stain demonstration of the gram-negative coccobacilli in characteristic array is diagnostic. The specimen should be taken from the undermined edge of an ulcer and rolled rather than smeared onto the slide. If culture by the microbiology laboratory is unavailable, a tube of the patient's clotted blood can be used as an inoculation medium, stored at 37°C, and the serum Gram-stained at 24 to 48 hours.

The histopathology of chancroid is distinctive, showing a superficial zone of necrotic debris, a middle layer of proliferating blood vessels, and a deep zone with an intense bandlike array of plasma cells and lymphocytes.

Treatment is with erythromycin (500 mg PO qid for 7 days), sulfamethoxazole (800 mg bid for at least 7 days), ceftriaxone (250 mg IM) or amoxicillin (500 mg) plus clavulanic acid (125 mg tid for 7 days).

Herpes genitalis is produced by the herpes simplex virus (HSV) and presents as a primary lesion of grouped vesicles on an erythematous base. These lesions commonly break down to form painful erosions.

It is useful to distinguish a primary, initial clinical episode from recurrent infections in an immune host. The primary infection is variable in presentation. It can range from an inapparent episode to a 2- to 3-week systemic illness characterized by fever, malaise, adenopathy, and painful cutaneous lesions. Recurrent disease is more predictable and tends to present as grouped vesicles or erosions that are either in the same location as the primary infection or in the distribution of cutaneous nerve innervation. The erosions of HSV infection are shallow, multiple, often painful, and have ragged, nonindurated borders and clean bases. There is sometimes a scalloping of the ulcer borders. The duration of untreated recurrent lesions is 8 to 12 days in the normal immune host. In the immunocompromised patient, the clinical presentation and duration are variable. HSV infection should always be considered in the differential diagnosis of cutaneous ulceration in the immunocompromised patient.

The diagnosis can be confirmed by an examination of scrapings from the base of an ulcer with Wright or Giemsa stain (Tzanck smear). The presence of multinucleated giant cells is confirmatory. Identification of viral antigens in scrapings with fluorescein-conjugated monoclonal antibodies is increasingly available and improves the accuracy of the diagnosis. Isolation of the virus in tissue culture is now routinely available in most virology laboratories. A skin biopsy is not usually performed for the diagnosis of HSV infections.

Oral administration of acyclovir is useful for primary genital herpes. It shortens the course of the disease and decreases symptoms. Its efficacy in recurrent disease is debatable. The standard dosage is 200 mg 5 times a day for 10 days. Patients with frequently recurring genital herpes have a decrease in the number of recurrences while taking oral acyclovir in a dosage of 200 mg tid.

While common in the tropics and in Africa, **granuloma inguinale,** a chronic disease caused by *Calymmatobacterium granulomatis* is quite unusual in the United States. After an incubation period of 3 to 6 weeks, a soft, nontender, eroded papule appears and rapidly breaks down to form an ulcer. The classic lesion is a soft, painless, irregularly shaped erosion with a beefy red, granular base and rolled, elevated border. The unusual features of this disease are its chronicity, the lack of associated adenopathy, and the presence of characteristic Donovan bodies on tissue smears. If untreated, the ulcer will last indefinitely, with slow expansion. The expansion can occur along skin folds, resulting in bizarre furrows, and can track subcutaneously, producing pseudo-bubos. True adenopathy is not usually present.

By crushing a snip of tissue between two microscope slides and staining it with Giemsa stain, the clinician can confirm the diagnosis. The organism appears as numerous rod-shaped or safety pin–shaped cytoplasmic inclusions in mononuclear cells (Donovan bodies). This finding can also be seen on biopsy, if the tissue is processed and stained with Giemsa stain. Treatment is with tetracycline, 500 mg qid for 3 weeks, or trimethoprim-sulfamethoxazole, 160–800 mg bid for 2 to 5 weeks.

While **lymphogranuloma venereum** (LGV) is commonly included in any discussion of genital ulcers, it is not primarily a disease of ulcerations. The infection is with *Chlamydia trachomatis* immunotypes L_1, L_2, and L_3. After a variable incubation period of days to weeks, an evanescent, painless papule or ulcer forms on the genitalia at the site of inoculation. This lesion usually resolves spontaneously without being noticed. Two to four weeks later, unilateral or bilateral adenitis with suppuration and bubo formation occurs. If untreated, LGV may lead to scarring, lymphedema, and urethral strictures.

The diagnosis is suspected when there is painful, suppurative inguinal adenitis and no obvious primary ulcer. It is confirmed by the demonstration of a rise in complement-fixation titer to the organism. Treatment is with tetracycline, 500 mg qid for 3 weeks, and surgical drainage as needed.

Boyd AS: Chemical efficacy of antimicrobial therapy in *Hemophilus ducreyi* infections. *Arch Dermatol.* 1989;125:1399–1405.

Evaluations of multiple antibiotics and varying dosing schedules have been undertaken to circumvent the extensive resistance to previously effective antimicrobials. This article reviews the incidence, clinical features, diagnosis, and therapy of chancroid. Erythromycin PO or ceftriaxone IM are the current drugs of choice.

Gregory N: Clinical problems of syphilis in the presence of HIV. *Clin Dermatol.* 1991;9:71–74.

The manifestations of syphilis in patients with HIV disease are detailed. Since presentations of the infection may be atypical or even bizarre, the diagnosis may be difficult to make.

Rolfs RT, Cates W Jr.: The perpetual lessons of syphilis. *Arch Dermatol.* 1989;125:107–109.

This editorial comments on recent changes in syphilis and on two articles published in the same issue of the Archives, *one reporting four cases of a vesicular variant of the Jarish-Herxheimer reaction, and the other reporting the failure of erythromycin to cure secondary syphilis in patients with the human immunodeficiency virus. Noted in this paper are (1) a change in the dominant mode of transmission from homosexual to heterosexual; (2) the rise of crack houses and other drug settings as foci of syphilis transmission; and (3) the observation that syphilis is increasing dramatically in the same inner city populations already at risk for HIV infection.*

Rolfs RT, Nakashima AK: Epidemiology of primary and secondary syphilis in the United States, 1981 through 1989. *J Am Med Assoc.* 1990;264:1432–1437.

Rates of primary and secondary syphilis increased 34% from 1981 to 1989, and rates increased from 13.7 to 18.4 cases per 100,000 population. There were dramatic changes in the incidence in certain subpopulations. The incidence among white men decreased by 69%, while that among blacks more than doubled.

Ronald AR, Plummer FA: Chancroid and granuloma inguinale. *Clin Lab Med.* 1989;9:535–543.

In Africa chancroid has emerged as a major risk factor for the acquisition of HIV-I infection. The gram-negative rod that causes granuloma inguinale remains poorly characterized. The presence of Donovan bodies is a specific and sensitive finding for granuloma inguinale. This article reviews both sexually transmitted diseases in depth.

Salzman RS, Kraus SJ, Miller RG, et al.: Chancroidal ulcers that are not chancroid. Cause and epidemiology. *Arch Dermatol.* 1984;120:636–639.

Herpes simplex virus was isolated from 16 to 33 patients in whom chancroid had been diagnosed clinically. The availability of herpes simplex virus cultures and a selective H. ducreyi culture medium will assist in the correct diagnosis of genital ulcers.

Scieux C, Barnes R, Branchi A, et al.: Lymphogranuloma venereum: 27 cases in Paris. *J Infect Dis.* 1989;160:662–668.

Twenty-seven men with laboratory-confirmed LGV were identified among 211 patients tested for LGV or chancroid during a 6-year period. Presenting findings were inguinal adenopathy in 25 and proctitis in 2. C. trachomatis of the LGV subtype was isolated in 9 patients.

Spence MR: The treatment of gonorrhea, syphilis, chancroid, lymphogranuloma venereum, and granuloma inguinale. *Clin Obstet Gynecol.* 1988;31:453–465.
A review of preventative methods and treatment for the classic venereal diseases.

39. BITES AND INFESTATIONS
Anita M. Grassi

Arthropod bites and infestations are a common presenting complaint to the primary care physician or dermatologist. Five out of the nine classes of arthropods are capable of producing cutaneous disease in humans, with clinical manifestations ranging from self-limited, pruritic dermatoses to life-threatening disease. Some of the more commonly encountered problems are discussed below.

Approximately 50 species of **mites** (class Arachnida, order Acari) may cause cutaneous lesions in humans. They have a variety of feeding habits whereby they infest food, grain, birds, and rodents, as well as humans. They may produce skin lesions in humans either by direct biting or by causing a hypersensitivity reaction to secretions produced during feeding.

Scabies is the most common human mite infestation. It is caused by the mite *Sarcoptes scabiei* var. *hominis* and produces intense, generalized pruritus. There is also an animal variant of the mite that can create similar skin lesions in humans and may infest dogs and cats, acting as a reservoir for infection. The adult mite, like all insects of the Arachnida class, has four pairs of legs. It has an oval, flat body and measures about 0.3 mm in length. The adult female mite digs burrows into the stratum corneum, depositing fecal pellets (scybala) and ova. The eggs hatch, and larvae mature in about 2 weeks, repeating their 30-day life cycle. After initial infestation, it may take 3 to 5 weeks before enough mites are present to create intense, generalized pruritus.

Clinically the lesions of scabies include pinpoint, erythematous vesicles and papules with secondary excoriations often located on the interdigital webs, wrists, axillae, buttocks, and groin. The most characteristic finding is a linear, pink burrow with tentlike scale up to 15 mm in length. A minute black speck (the mite) may be present at one end of the burrow. Nodules may be present on the scrotum and penis. Patients usually complain of mild, localized pruritus, which then progresses to intense, generalized pruritus with nocturnal itching. The cutaneous lesions are probably a result of a hypersensitivity reaction to the mites. Some patients develop elevated immunoglobulin E titers and peripheral eosinophilia, which resolve after therapy.

Diagnosis should be made on the clinical presentation, in particular the presence of burrows, and by the demonstration of mites, scybala, ova or egg casings on microscopic examination. Burrows may be shaved superficially or scraped with a No. 15 scalpel blade, and the material obtained placed on a glass slide with mineral oil and topped with a coverslip. At any one time, only about 30 to 50 mites are present on a single infested individual. However, in Norwegian scabies, a particularly severe form seen in immunocompromised, or institutionalized, patients, thousands of adult mites can be present.

The most commonly used treatment for adults is a single, overnight application of 1% lindane lotion (Kwell). No more than 1 oz of Kwell should be applied to the entire body below the neck, and it should be washed off in 8 to 12 hours. Caution should be exercised with infants and pregnant women. Neurotoxicity including seizures has been reported in premature infants after topical application and in older children who mistakenly ingested the drug. Kwell may be passed through breast milk by nursing mothers. Six percent precipitated sulfur in petrolatum is a messy but effective treatment and can be an alternative to lindane for infants and pregnant women. Precipitated sulfur is applied to the entire body below the neck daily for 3 days, the patient bathing 24 hours after each application. Crotamiton (Eurax lotion) is less effective, and its toxicity is unknown. It is applied to the whole body below the neck twice, 24 hours apart, and left on for the entire 48-hour period and then washed off thoroughly. Permethrin 5% cream (Elimite) has been shown to be safe and effective against scabies and is currently gaining popularity as a useful agent in lindane treatment failures and as a first-line treatment in children.

The pruritus from scabies usually improves significantly 24 hours following therapy, but it may persist for days to weeks. As scabies is spread by close physical contact, sexual partners and family members should also be treated. Clothing, sheets, and towels should be washed in an automatic washing machine. Because the mite does not survive more than 2 days away from a moist environment, transmission via clothing is unlikely.

The larvae of mites of the genus *Trombidioidae,* popularly called chiggers or harvest bugs/mites, are found throughout the southeastern United States. Especially active in grassy areas near trees only in warm months, these mites can cause severe pruritic erythematous eruptions, which generally resolve without treatment in 3 days to a week. The females are attracted to warm, moist areas of the body such as the skin beneath clothing bands, where they burrow beneath the skin surface. Secondary infections can result from excoriation. Wearing tight clothing with shirts tucked into pants and pants tucked into socks may prevent these insects from entering the skin.

Three varieties of **lice** infest humans: *Pediculus humanus* var. *corporis* (body lice), *Pediculus humanus* var. *capitis* (head lice), and *Phthirus pubis* (pubic lice). They are ectoparasites that feed on blood and cannot survive more than 48 hours away from their human hosts. The ova or nits, however, which are cemented to the base of the hair shafts, may remain viable up to 1 month away from the human body. Skin lesions are induced by a hypersensitivity reaction to the lice saliva and feces. These lice are less than 2 mm in size and have three pairs of legs. Pubic lice in particular have prominent clawlike appendages and are often called crabs.

Pediculosis capitis is most commonly seen in children and has an incidence of up to 30% in some populations. Girls are affected more often than boys, probably because of their longer hair. Head lice are transmitted by close physical contact as well as via shared personal items such as combs, pillows, and hats. Clinically, only a few lice may be visible, but many nits can be found firmly adherent to hair shafts. Secondary infection with crusts, pustules, and cervical adenopathy can be seen. Wood's lamp examination will demonstrate the fluorescent, live nits.

Pediculosis pubis is a sexually transmitted disease of unknown incidence. It is associated with a second sexually transmitted disease in 30% of the patients infested. Pubic lice may also be transmitted by clothing and bedding. Crab lice prefer the coarse hair of the anogenital region but can spread to the thighs, axillae, and even beard hair. The eyelashes may become involved, especially in children, usually from contact with an infested parent but occasionally as a manifestation of child abuse. The most prominent clinical symptom is pruritus. Inguinal lymphadenopathy and blue-gray macules, called maculae caeruleae, may likewise be seen.

Pediculosis corporis is a much less common infestation seen mostly in people with poor personal hygiene. Body lice hide in the seams of clothing. The skin manifestations consist of pruritic, red macules that can become secondarily infected.

Effective treatment for all three forms of pediculosis includes 1% lindane (Kwell), 1% permethrin (Nix), and pyrethrins (Rid). The shampoo form of each medication should be applied for 5 minutes and then washed off. A single 8- to 12-hour application of 0.5% malathion lotion (Prioderm) may be useful for treatment of lindane-resistant head lice. Body and pubic lice may be treated either as described above for head lice or with an 8- to 12-hour application of the lotion form of lindane or pyrethrins. The new synthetic pyrethrin, permethrin 1% lotion, has also been shown to be effective against lice and may be less toxic than lindane. All preparations are ovicidal, but dead nits will remain cemented to the hair shafts until combed out. School policies generally require all nits to be removed from the scalp before a student with pediculosis capitis may return to school. Following therapy, all clothing, bedding, and towels should be washed in hot water.

Ticks can produce localized cutaneous lesions and can also serve as vectors for life-threatening systemic diseases. Like lice, they are ectoparasites that feed on blood from human hosts. They also infest birds, reptiles, and wild and domestic animals, through which humans can become unwitting victims. Two families of ticks exist: soft ticks and hard ticks. Only hard ticks (*Ixodidae*) cause serious human illness. Both varieties may reach 1 cm in length. They have a barbed feeding apparatus (hypostome) through which they suck blood. Ticks are frequently nocturnal and are most active during the spring and summer months. Soft ticks release themselves from their host after 2 hours, but hard ticks may feed slowly for several days. The initial bite may be painless, but the resultant lesion can consist of an erythematous papule or indurated nodule with surrounding edema. Soft ticks can induce ecchymosis due to an anticoagulant in their saliva. Tick bites may also produce persistent local granulomas and temporary perilesional alopecia of the scalp.

Lyme disease is an inflammatory illness produced by a spirochete, *Borrelia burgdorferi*. The deer tick, *Ixodes dammini*, is the vector in the eastern United States, with endemic areas including the coastal Northeast from Massachusetts to Delaware, Minnesota, and Wisconsin. *Ixodes pacificus* is the principal vector in the western United States, where cases have been reported in California, Oregon, Utah, Nevada, and Idaho. The spirochete is transmitted by a tick bite on exposed skin of hikers or campers in wooded or coastal areas.

One of the characteristic skin findings in Lyme disease is the skin lesion, erythema chronicum migrans. Erythema chronicum migrans begins as an erythematous papule at the site of the tick bite and expands in 1 to 4 weeks to form a red, macular ring with central clearing. This ring blanches under pressure and usually lacks any epidermal changes such as scaling or vesicles. It may continue to expand slowly to the size of 50 cm. Multiple secondary lesions of similar morphology will develop within several days of the first lesion. These may occur anywhere but usually not on the palms and soles. Other skin findings associated with Lyme disease include a malar rash and conjunctivitis.

Constitutional symptoms may accompany the skin rash, including fever, headache, fatigue, malaise, myalgias, and arthralgias. Signs and symptoms suggestive of hepatitis can occur, such as anorexia, vomiting, weight loss, and hepatosplenomegaly. Common abnormalities revealed by laboratory studies include elevated erythrocyte sedimentation rate (53%), SGOT (19%), and serum IgM (33%). Lyme disease can have neurologic and cardiac complications including meningitis, encephalitis, and myocarditis. Arthritis is a late manifestation.

Treatment regimens for Lyme disease are subject to ongoing evaluation. Recommended treatment is tetracycline, 250 mg 4 times daily for 10 days, up to 20 days if symptoms persist, or doxycycline, 100 mg 2 times daily for 10 to 20 days. Alternatives are penicillin VK, 250 to 500 mg 4 times daily for adults (50 mg/kg/d divided into 4 doses for children) or erythromycin, 250 mg 4 times daily for adults (30 mg/kg/day for children).

Acrodermatitis chronica atrophicans is a rare skin disorder that begins as localized areas of erythema and edema on the extremities and progresses to atrophic plaques. It is associated with the bite of a wood tick in Europe, and recently a spirochete similar to the etiologic agent of Lyme disease has been isolated from these lesions.

Rocky Mountain spotted fever is the most frequent rickettsial infection in the United States and is transmitted via tick bites. It is a potentially fatal disease with high mortality rates if untreated. The causative agent, *Rickettsia rickettsii*, has two principal vectors: the wood tick, *Dermacentor andersoni*, in the western United States and the dog tick, *Dermacentor variabilis*, in the eastern United States. Peak incidence occurs in late spring and early summer, when the ticks are most active.

Clinically, about 7 days after the tick bite, the patient will experience fever, chills, myalgias, arthralgias, and headache. The rash often erupts on the fourth day, usually peripherally on wrists and ankles, progressing more centrally to the trunk and face. It may involve the palms and soles. It typically begins as discrete, pink, blanchable macules that become more papular and petechial in 2 to 4 days. Pressure such as that from a blood pressure cuff can create further petechiae. Small necrotic lesions may develop on fingers, toes, earlobes, nose, vulva, and scrotum. Ten percent of cases may have no cutaneous findings. Splenomegaly can be present in 50% of cases. Laboratory test results are not rewarding. The WBC is usually within normal limits.

Thrombocytopenia and clotting factor abnormalities may be present in severe cases, probably from disseminated intravascular coagulation. The BUN may be elevated because of prerenal azotemia. Serum albumin can be low. Rickettsial antibody titers may be performed on acute and convalescent sera to confirm the diagnosis.

A diffuse vasculitis with thrombosis and microinfarction of small vessels is the underlying pathologic finding in rickettsial disease. If this vasculitis affects larger vessels, then infarction of tissue is more extensive, causing myocarditis, liver damage, interstitial nephritis, neurologic damage, even shock and death in fulminant cases. Treatment with tetracycline and chloramphenicol should be instituted promptly in patients from endemic areas with a consistent clinical picture.

Spiders belong to the class Arachnida, order aranae. Like all arthropods, they are bilaterally symmetric invertebrates with an exoskeleton, true body segmentation, and jointed appendages. They have four pairs of legs. Their bodies are divided into two regions: an anterior cephalothorax and a posterior abdomen. All spiders are carnivorous, usually preying on insects. Most are venomous and bite, although they are shy and avoid human contact. Only about 50 of the 100,000 known species of spiders bite humans. Of these species, the black widow and brown recluse spiders are the only truly dangerous species native to the United States.

The female **black widow spider,** *Latrodectus mactans,* is typically black with a characteristic red, hourglass-shaped marking on the underside of the abdomen. Female spiders are quite large, growing up to 1 cm in length. They are found throughout the continental United States. They live in webs in secluded locations such as vacant rodent burrows, under rocks and logs, and in barns and outhouses.

The bite of the black widow spider may be painless or may produce sharp stinging. The local reaction consists only of mild erythema and edema with two small red fang marks. The spider's venom, however, acts as a neurotoxin that may cause depletion of acetylcholine and catecholamines at motor nerve endings, leading to neuromuscular symptoms. Within 15 minutes to an hour after the initial bite, muscle cramps may begin at the area of the bite and radiate to other parts of the body. The abdomen in particular may become extremely painful and rigid, resembling an acute surgical abdomen. The pain progresses over 2 to 3 hours and then resolves in 2 to 3 days. Other signs and symptoms include increased deep tendon reflexes, muscle spasms, fasciculations, nausea, vomiting, diaphoresis, salivation, respiratory distress, and urinary retention. Shock and death may occur in 5% of victims, especially children and the elderly.

Treatment of healthy individuals between the ages of 16 and 60 probably can consist of muscle relaxants and ice compresses applied to the inoculation site to prevent the spread of the toxin. Severe cases, especially in patients with dyspnea or hypertensive heart disease, as well as children, the elderly, and pregnant women should be treated with *Latrodectus mactans* antivenom. One ampule or 2.5 ml given either intravenously or intramuscularly to individuals not sensitive to horse serum will relieve the symptoms within 1 to 2 hours.

The bites of *Loxosceles reclusa,* or the **brown recluse spider,** are the most commonly reported spider bites in the United States, and probably the most dangerous as well. This spider can be larger than 2.5 cm in length and ranges in color from tan to brown with a dark brown, violin-shaped marking on its back. *Loxosceles reclusa,* as its name suggests, is naturally shy and nocturnal, and usually lives in hidden outdoor locations (e.g., under rocks and in caves). However, it will live in secluded indoor places such as attics and closets, and bite humans when provoked. *Loxosceles reclusa* can be found throughout the United States but prefers the warmer weather of the South.

The initial brown recluse spider bite may sting, but it is generally not painful and often remains asymptomatic for 8 hours. If the bite is severe enough to produce necrosis, local hemolysis and arterial constriction will cause a blue-gray macular ring to appear at the site within a few hours to a few days. Furthermore, vesicles, bullae, or pustules may arise at the site with surrounding erythema and edema. The necrosis can progress with eschar formation and ulceration, taking months to heal. In some individuals, the reaction may become more systemic, leading to the signs and symptoms of viscerocutaneous loxoscelism. Within 3 days these patients may develop fever, headache, myalgias, nausea, vomiting, urticaria, and seizures. They may progress to renal failure, disseminated intravascular coagulation, shock, and death.

Treatment remains controversial. Patients having minor bites with less than 2 cm of necrosis may be treated with analgesics, antihistamines, and dressings. Patients having larger lesions with necrosis greater than 2 cm should receive systemic steroids for the first 5 days. Excision of large necrotic areas was once advocated, but this treatment does not seem uniformly effective, probably because the toxin spreads rapidly in tissue, making it difficult to estimate surgical margins. Dapsone has been reported to help heal necrotic ulcerations. Severe systemic loxoscelism may be treated promptly with prednisone, 1 mg/kg, to prevent hematologic abnormalities.

Flies, mosquitoes, and **fleas** will "bite" their victims by inserting sharp mouthparts and injecting saliva. All of these insects can be vectors for infectious diseases—especially mosquitoes, which may transmit malaria, dengue fever, and encephalitis. The extent of the cutaneous reaction produced depends on the victim's sensitivity. Sensitive individuals will immediately develop localized urticarial plaques, but patients without prior exposure or those with a history of multiple bites may have no local reaction. Bites by these insects may be prevented by the use of a repellent containing diethyltoluamide (DEET). The repellent should be applied to all exposed body surfaces. Actual bites can be treated with oral antihistamines, topical corticosteroids, and cool compresses.

Mosquitoes are attracted to warm, scented skin, brightly colored clothing, and children more than adults. They inject secretions that cause pruritus, erythema, and edema. Children are particularly vulnerable and may develop urticarial papules that are intensely pruritic; excoriations and scars can result.

Black flies can inject an anesthetic substance into the skin, creating delayed pain and pruritus. Fly bites are often seasonal, occurring in late spring and early summer.

Fleas usually live on animals, rugs, and furniture, and will jump onto humans. They often produce clusters of erythematous papules with a central punctum, typically on the lower extremities.

Bedbugs of the order Hemiptera are blood-sucking insects that feed at night. The females infest dwellings by laying their eggs in the cracks of walls and furniture. Clinically, bedbug bites present as linear pruritic papules in groups of twos and threes on the face and extremities. The bites are usually painless initially, so they may not awaken a victim.

Stinging insects such as **wasps, hornets, yellow jackets,** and **bees** inject venom that produces both localized toxic reactions and generalized allergic reactions including anaphylaxis. The initial sting causes a sharp, painful sensation, and results in an erythematous papule or wheal. For allergic individuals, the reaction is more pronounced, with a localized, indurated urticarial plaque that may persist for several days. Generalized allergic reactions to insect stings in the United States occur with a prevalence rate up to 0.8%, and account for about 40 deaths annually. The symptoms of generalized allergic reactions typically begin within 1 hour after the sting and include pruritus, urticaria, nausea, abdominal pain, wheezing, and dyspnea from upper airway edema.

Insect repellents are not effective against stinging insects. Patients who have experienced extensive localized reactions or generalized allergic symptoms should have skin testing and desensitization performed with species-specific venom extracts. Localized lesions can be treated with antihistamines and cool compresses. Generalized reactions may require a 0.3-ml subcutaneous injection of epinephrine in a 1:1000 dilution, or a 50-mg intramuscular injection of Benadryl, or the currently recommended regimen.

The **gypsy moth caterpillar,** from the order Lepidoptera, has been reported to produce a pruritic eruption and rhinitis. The rash consists of erythematous, edematous papules and linear streaks on both exposed and unexposed skin, including the neck, extremities, and abdomen. This dermatitis probably represents a hypersensitivity to contact with the hairs of the caterpillar.

Berger BW: Treating erythema chronicum migrans of Lyme disease. *J Am Acad Dermatol.* 1986;15:459–463.
Evaluation of antibiotic therapy for 117 patients with Lyme disease.

King LE: Spider bites. *Arch Dermatol.* 1987;123:41–43.
Editorial with concise discussion of important clinical points in the management of spider bites.

Krinsky WL: Dermatoses associated with the bites of mites and ticks (*Arthropoda acari*). *Int J Dermatol.* 1983;22:75–91.
Thorough review of the topic with detailed classification of the sources and distributions of these insects.

Meinking TL, Taplin D, Kalter DC, et al.: Comparative efficacy of treatments for pediculosis capitis infestations. *Arch Dermatol.* 1986;122:267–271.
A good discussion of the available treatments for head lice.

Shama SK, Etkind PH, Odell TM, et al.: Gypsy-moth-caterpillar dermatitis. *New Engl J Med.* 1982;21:1300–1301.
A report of the characteristic eruption caused by this caterpillar.

Steere AC: Lyme disease. *N Engl J Med.* 1989;321:586–596.
Review of the epidemiology, clinical course, laboratory manifestations, and treatment of Lyme disease.

Steere AC, Bartenhagen NH, Craft JE, et al.: The early clinical manifestations of Lyme disease. *Ann Intern Med.* 1983;99:76–82.
One of the most frequently quoted articles on the clinical signs and symptoms of Lyme disease.

Szer IS, Taylor E, Steere AC: The longterm course of Lyme arthritis in children. *N Engl J Med.* 1991;325:159–163.
The course of initially untreated Lyme disease in children may include acute infection followed by attacks of arthritis and then by keratitis, subtle joint pain, or chronic encephalopathy.

Wong RC, Hughes SE, Voorhees JJ: Spider bites. *Arch Dermatol.* 1987;123:98–104.
An excellent, comprehensive review of the biology of spiders as well as the diagnosis and treatment of their bites.

VII. ALTERED PIGMENTATION

40. LIGHT MACULES
David A. Laub

Clinicians frequently encounter patients with complaints of pigmentary loss. The conditions associated with diffuse pigmentary loss are addressed in Chapter 42, while conditions with light macules will be discussed here. Isolated light macules are most commonly brought to a patient's attention following an extended exposure to the sun. In response to the sun, normal skin will tan, but hypopigmented macules will either remain light or develop a sunburn erythema, resulting in increased contrast and thus easier visualization.

The first step in the management of these patients is to make an accurate **diagnosis.** This is established by an assessment of the lesions' onset, shape configuration, morphology, distribution, degree of pigmentary dilution, and associated abnormalities.

Conditions present at birth include the inheritable diseases tuberous sclerosis, piebaldism, and incontinentia pigmenti achromians. Acquired conditions secondary to inflammation or infection include postinflammatory hypopigmentation, leprosy, and tinea versicolor.

The shape, configuration, and morphologic features of the lesions provide additional clues to the correct diagnosis. The presence of ash leaf–shaped macules suggests a diagnosis of tuberous sclerosis, and quasidermatomal patterns are seen in nevus depigmentosus. The hypopigmentation of nevus depigmentosus often has a whorl-like pattern, as does incontinentia pigmenti achromians. The macules of halo nevi are usually round, while those of vitiligo frequently have scalloped margins. The borders of individual lesions may be sharp and discrete, as in vitiligo, piebaldism, and nevus depigmentosus, or ill-defined, as in pityriasis alba, leprosy, and postinflammatory hypopigmentation. Several conditions have characteristic areas of involvement. A central white forelock associated with amelanotic macules on the abdomen suggests piebaldism. The macules of tuberous sclerosis are most common on the lower back, tinea versicolor usually involves the upper back and chest, and vitiligo is usually seen in the periorificial and extensor extremity areas.

The degree of pigmentary loss may be partial (hypomelanotic or hypopigmented) or complete (amelanotic or depigmented). Hypomelanotic lesions generally are pale white, the color of macules in incontinentia pigmenti achromians, tinea versicolor, pityriasis alba, tuberous sclerosis, and leprosy. Amelanotic macules, which are chalk white, are seen in vitiligo, piebaldism, chemical leukoderma, and discoid lupus erythematosus.

Detecting abnormalities beyond the disturbances of pigmentation can be very helpful in confirming a diagnosis. Hypopigmented macules of leprosy may be anesthetic. Thorough examination of the cutaneous surface may reveal more active inflammatory lesions of tinea versicolor, discoid lupus erythematosus, and atopic dermatitis. An early halo nevus may have an intact pigmented or hypopigmented nevus in the center of a hypopigmented macule. Even extracutaneous findings should be sought. Seizures, mental retardation, and CNS tubers are seen in tuberous sclerosis, while strabismus and hypertelorism are found in incontinentia pigmenti achromians.

In addition to the clinical clues, a Wood's lamp examination, a potassium hydroxide preparation, or a skin biopsy may be necessary to make a diagnosis. Wood's lamp, which emits light in the ultraviolet-A range, fluoresces epidermal proteins. Melanin-containing skin absorbs the UVA light while nonpigmented skin (e.g., vitiligo) strongly fluoresces. The lamp is especially helpful when examining infants for white macules in tuberous sclerosis and to determine the extent of hypopigmented conditions. A potassium hydroxide preparation of superficial scale will readily confirm the diagnosis of tinea versicolor. A specimen obtained by punch biopsy may be examined microscopically to detect an inflammatory infiltrate in vitiligo or leprosy, or may be processed for electron microscopic analysis to detect the small melanosomes found in tuberous sclerosis.

Piebaldism is an inheritable, autosomal dominant condition characterized by a white forelock and stable white macules with hyperpigmented areas in the center.

The chalk white macules are usually on the trunk, face, forearms, and midleg areas; the hands and feet are spared. A skin biopsy reveals no melanocytes in the nonpigmented skin. Some patients with piebaldism have deafness (Waardenburg's syndrome) or heterochromic irides, and variants with other systemic findings have been described. Repigmentation of piebald white macules is difficult. The lack of melanocytes in hair follicles adjacent to affected skin leads to poor results with psoralen and UVA (PUVA) therapy. Full-thickness autografts of normal skin onto amelanotic areas have been reported to produce repigmentation.

Tuberous sclerosis is an autosomal dominant condition characterized by adenoma sebaceum, seizures, and mental retardation. Hypomelanotic, pale white macules are the earliest sign of tuberous sclerosis and appear in approximately 85% of all patients. The macules are stable, may appear in polygonal, ash leaf, confetti, or dermatomal patterns, and are seen predominantly on the trunk, arms, legs, and face. Electron microscopy reveals melanocytes with abnormally small melanosomes.

Tuberous sclerosis should be suspected in any child with white spots and seizures. A work-up for tuberous sclerosis includes a thorough skin examination with Wood's lamp, a cranial nuclear magnetic resonance (NMR) or CT scan, a renal ultrasound, an eye examination, and examination of family members. Genetic counseling is very important and sometimes difficult since the spontaneous mutation rate is as high as 75%.

Incontinentia pigmenti achromians is a rare, autosomal dominant hypomelanotic condition associated with neuromuscular abnormalities. The pale white macules are usually bilateral, with a whorled or streaklike shape, and are commonly distributed on the trunk, extremities, and face. Skin changes are usually present at birth; however, they have been reported to first appear as late as age 12. Spontaneous repigmentation is seen, especially with lesions of late onset. Associated abnormalities include seizures, mental retardation, hypertelorism, scoliosis, strabismus, and myopia.

This condition should be suspected in any child with a bizarre, whorled-like hypopigmented area. Diagnosis is based on finding associated abnormalities and establishing a familial inheritance. A skin biopsy with vacuolated keratinocytes and decreased melanocytes can provide confirmatory information. Genetic counseling is important.

Nevus depigmentosus is a rare, nonfamilial condition that presents at birth with quasidermatomal pale white macules. The macules are stable and rarely associated with neuromuscular abnormalities. No treatment is known.

Vitiligo is an acquired, idiopathic, progressive whitening of the skin and hair characterized by the total absence of melanocytes in the skin. An autosomal dominant condition, vitiligo has an incidence of 1%. It usually appears in the late teens and early 20s with discrete, well-circumscribed chalk white macules on the extensor surfaces and in periorificial areas. Spontaneous repigmentation, while seen, is not clinically significant.

The etiology of vitiligo is unknown. Most researchers believe it is an autoimmune disease. This opinion is supported by vitiligo's association with antithyroid and antimelanocyte antibodies, and by the prevalence of thyroid disease, diabetes mellitus, pernicious anemia, Addison's disease, and iritis among vitiligo patients. A work-up in these patients includes an eye examination, thyroid function tests, a complete blood count, and a fasting blood sugar test. An AM cortisol level is optional. Treatment should include avoidance of sun exposure and use of sunscreens and camouflage preparations (Vita Dye, Dermablend). Topical steroids can be useful for inducing repigmentation in localized variants, while PUVA may be required for therapy for generalized involvement. Pigment transplantation through autografts has been used for stable localized variants, while topical monobenzylether of hydroquinone is available for patients who are willing to undergo depigmentation of remaining pigment in order to obtain a uniform skin color.

Tinea versicolor is a chronic skin condition characterized by discrete round to oval macules or thin plaques with fine scaly margins. Lesions are white, red, or brown and usually on the upper trunk. The lesions are attributed to the fungus *Pityrosporum orbiculare,* which is demonstrated on a potassium hydroxide preparation of superficial scale as hyphae and yeast forms. Topical treatments include

2.5% selenium sulfide suspension, zinc pyrithione, and imidazole and other antifungal creams. Oral ketoconazole administered as one 400-mg dose, or in a dosage of 200 mg/d for 1 week, will consistently clear widespread tinea vesicolor.

Pityriasis alba is a common, acquired hypomelanosis characterized by poorly circumscribed, fine scaly macules on the face of dark-skinned children. The lesions are occasionally pruritic and may be seen also on the neck, trunk, extremities, and scrotum. A skin biopsy shows a nonspecific eczematous dermatitis. Although treatment is not very effective (topical corticosteroids may be used with partial success), spontaneous resolution slowly occurs.

Finally, though the most common conditions associated with white spots have been mentioned, it is important to note the less common diseases associated with light macules. These diseases include leprosy, secondary syphilis, pinta, yaws, idiopathic guttate hypomelanosis, and chemical leukoderma.

Falabella R: Treatment of localized vitiligo by autologous minigrafting. *Arch Dermatol.* 1988;124:1649–1655.
Thirteen of twenty-two patients attained a 90% to 100% repigmentation after minigrafting, two others had partial improvement, and five had a positive test area. This technique may be a reasonable alternative for treating localized vitiligo when medical therapy has failed.
Gilhar A, Pillar T, Eidelman S, et al.: Vitiligo and idiopathic guttate hypomelanosis. Repigmentation of skin following engraftment onto nude mice. *Arch Dermatol.* 1989;125:1363–1366.
Split-thickness grafts from patients with vitiligo, idiopathic guttate hypomelanosis and tyrosinase-negative albinism were grafted onto nude mice and studied by histology and dopa staining. The results suggested that systemic factors play a role in the pathogenesis of vitiligo and acquired hypomelanosis guttata.
Honigsmann H: Phototherapy and photochemotherapy, *Semin Dermatol.* 1990;9: 84–90.
The treatment of vitiligo with PUVA is detailed; treatment results and acute and chronic side effects, especially skin carcinogenesis, are emphasized.
Ortonne JP: Piebaldism, Waardenburg's syndrome, and related disorders. "Neural crest depigmentation syndromes." *Dermatol Clin.* 1988;6:205–216.
The striking parallel in the pigmentary abnormalities in these syndromes suggests that they all result from defective development of the neural crest.
Urano-Suehisa S, Tagami H: Functional and morphological analysis of the horny layer of pityriasis alba. *Acta Derm Venerol.* 1985;65:164–167.
This study of the skin surface in five patients demonstrated abnormalities of the horny layer similar to that of a dermatitic change. These findings suggest that the hypopigmentation may be due to postinflammatory mechanisms.

41. DARK MACULES
Paul B. Googe

The evaluation and diagnosis of dark macules require attention to the details of size, shape, color, number, distribution, and duration of the lesions present. Historical information may also be necessary to implicate etiologic agents or to define conditions of prognostic significance. A complete skin examination including the oral cavity and genitalia is necessary to establish the number and distribution of lesions.

The color of the macule is a master clue to its identification. The color of the lesion should be compared to the patient's normal constitutive skin color as may be found on the volar forearm or other non–sun-exposed, nonlesional area. In this comparison, true increases or decreases in pigmentation may be detected, and the basis for the coloration of the lesion (i.e., melanin, heme, hemosiderin, or other pigment) may become apparent. Melanin in the epidermis tends to be brown. Blue lesions are dermal processes in which the pigment may be melanin, blood, foreign material, or metabolites of endogenous or exogenous chemicals. The response of the lesion to physical manipulation is another diagnostic clue. For example, vascular lesions such as venous lakes and telangiectases will blanch with pressure, while melanocytic lesions will not. Important information can also be obtained from sidelighting the lesion—i.e., whether the lesion is flat or elevated. Wood's lamp can reveal the location of pigments within the skin of a light-skinned individual: an area of increased melanin in the epidermis will appear relatively darker than the surrounding skin, while an area of increased dermal pigmentation will not be enhanced. The location of pigment in the skin is important since only epidermal pigment may be expected to respond to topical hypopigmenting (bleaching) agents, cryotherapy, or standard laser treatment. Dermal pigmentation does not respond to currently available therapeutic methods other than excision and ablation, either of which may leave scarring or hyperpigmentation more noticeable than the original lesion. Use of the Q-switched ruby laser or Q-switched neodymium: YAG laser is promising, and this laser will likely become a useful clinical tool. The treatment of pigmented lesions must therefore be individualized according to the process causing them. Accurate diagnosis is essential.

Benign lesions considered to be of melanocytic origin are stable in regard to size and color. A pigmented macule that changes in any way over time and is considered melanocytic or is of uncertain etiology should be biopsied. Excision allows histopathologic examination to confirm the diagnosis and exclude a malignancy masquerading as a benign lesion. Lesions treated by destructive methods such as cryosurgery or laser may escape proper identification, only to recur or metastasize and declare their true nature.

Freckles (ephelides) are acquired macules several millimeters in size that appear in sun-exposed areas of individuals with fair hair and fair complexions. Freckles may be various shades of brown (but not black), have irregular outlines, and are well demarcated from surrounding skin. They are usually numerous and their onset may be directly related to memorable instances of intense sun exposure producing sunburn. Freckles may appear darker in summer than in winter. The lesions are due to focal increases in epidermal melanin content and, therefore, stand out dramatically when examined with Wood's lamp. They are stable lesions with no known premalignant potential. Freckles are markers, however, for individuals at risk for actinic damage and subsequent UV-induced neoplasms, basal cell carcinoma, squamous cell carcinoma, and melanoma. Sunscreens, protective clothing, and avoidance of midday sun exposure will help prevent the development of more freckles. Hypopigmenting agents such as 2% hydroquinone cream may be slightly effective. In addition, some freckles may fade after application of liquid nitrogen for 10 to 15 seconds. Laser therapy for freckles warrants further study with scrutiny of risks versus benefits.

Similar lesions may occur in other, less typical locations. The **lower lip macule** is a dark brown to blackish brown lesion, 2 to 6 mm in diameter, occurring on the sun-exposed portion of the lip and often considered a large freckle of the lip. It requires no therapy. If desired, excision in toto with primary repair usually heals with little scarring; cryotherapy or laser surgery may also be effective. Pigmented macules also occur in **surgical scars**, presenting as flat, tan discolorations in round or streaklike patterns. These macules may raise concerns of tumor recurrence in scars produced by excision of melanomas; however, they usually evolve slowly and have no known malignant potential. A biopsy can settle any uncertainty.

Lentigines are flat, small, 2- to 5-mm macules that vary in color from tan to dark brown. They are due to increased numbers of melanocytes as well as to increased melanin. They may occur after sun exposure, particularly sunburn, or they may be found in sun-protected skin. In contrast to freckles, lentigines may be very dark brown or even black in color. Some authors consider them a possible precursor to benign nevi, although certainly this fate is not universal. Junctional nevi may be similar in appearance to lentigines and may be distinguished only if they become elevated or by a biopsy that demonstrates nests of melanocytes at the dermal-epidermal junction. Lentigines and junctional nevi, lesions of increased numbers of melanocytes could theoretically be precursors to melanoma; however, the occurrence is exceedingly rare.

Solar lentigines are also known as liver spots, old-age spots, and senile lentigines. They are several millimeters to a centimeter in size and may be various shades of brown and dark yellow. They are present in sun-damaged skin of older adults and are sometimes difficult to distinguish from pigmented actinic keratoses. Unlike freckles, solar lentigines may occur in individuals with dark hair and dark complexions, and they do not vary in color with the seasons. The pigmentation is due to increased melanin in the epidermis and dermis. The lesions are not premalignant, but do indicate actinic damage and may coexist with other premalignant and malignant skin tumors. These lesions may also be induced by UV light radiation received for cosmetic reasons in tanning salons or as phototherapy for various skin diseases (especially psoriasis treated with chronic PUVA therapy). Light cryotherapy is an effective method for lightening the lesion, although often the result is temporary.

Lentigo maligna appears as a pigmented lesion on sun-exposed areas of individuals who usually have evidence of actinic damage. The face, back, and dorsal hands and forearms are typical locations. The macule may have subtle variation in hues of brown, and the borders are irregular, indistinct, and ill-defined, It may be many millimeters to several centimeters in diameter. Deepening of color around follicles, notching of the border, enlargement, and variegation in color are clues to the sinister nature of what may otherwise appear to be a giant freckle. The occurrence of a papule, ulcer, or nodule or marked change in color or size are signs of aggressive behavior that suggest lentigo maligna melanoma (invasive melanoma) and should prompt pathologic evaluation, preferably of the entire lesion by excision in toto.

Café-au-lait macules are hyperpigmented areas that are not related to UV radiation exposure, and they occur on any cutaneous surface. Characteristically homogeneous in color, typically light brown, they vary in size (from 1 millimeter to many centimeters) and number, and may be present at birth or acquired in early childhood. They have a sharp demarcation from surrounding skin and usually a smooth contour. While the macule may increase in size as a child grows, they remain flat and are stable in size in adulthood. The hyperpigmentation is due to increased melanin within epidermal keratinocytes and therefore is enhanced by Wood's lamp. Café-au-lait macules occur as solitary lesions in 10% to 15% of the general population. However, the presence of six or more café-au-lait macules greater than 1.5 cm in diameter is usually a sign of neurofibromatosis. Axillary freckling, numerous tiny café-au-lait macules, is a sign of neurofibromatosis as well. Café-au-lait–like macules have been described in a variety of other syndromes, including tuberous sclerosis, Bloom's syndrome, and Cowden's disease. No useful treatments have been described.

The dark macules of **Albright's syndrome** are usually large and few in number. They tend to be unilateral and may be arranged in a linear or segmental pattern. The hairs within the macules are often darker as well. While a single lesion may be indistinguishable from a café-au-lait macule, the macules of Albright's syndrome tend to have very irregular contours, likened to the coast of Maine. Other manifestations of the syndrome are fibrous dysplasia of bone and endocrine dysfunction. The bony lesions tend to be on the same side of the body as the macules. Axillary freckling has not been described in Albright's syndrome.

Blue nevi appear as blue or blue-black, round or oval lesions. These benign nevi may occur anyplace, but are common on the extensor surfaces of the extremities, buttocks, and face. They are 1 to 6 mm in diameter, well-circumscribed, and evenly colored. They are more common in women and individuals with dark complexions. Blue nevi are often flat, but may become papules or even exophytic nodules. Malignant transformation is exceedingly rare. If the diagnosis is uncertain or the lesion changing, an excisional biopsy should be performed to exclude the possibility of a primary melanoma.

The **mongolian spot** occurs in infants as a pale slate-gray, blue-gray, or blue macule over the midline lumbosacral area. These lesions are present at, or appear soon after, birth and are more common in dark-skinned races. Mongolian spots are sometimes multiple and scattered over the posterior trunk. The lesion is of cosmetic consequence only and usually fades by adulthood.

The **nevus of Ota** and the **nevus of Ito** are similar in appearance to the mongolian spot but different in location. The nevus of Ota occurs over the temple and cheek, typically in dark-skinned people, particularly Orientals. It is usually unilateral and may be associated with nevomelanocytic pigmentation of the ipsilateral retina, pharynx, and middle ear. The nevus of Ito occurs over the shoulder girdle. Both nevi may be seen at birth or not until the early 30s and do not fade with age. They are benign; however, melanoma has been rarely reported in association with them. No good treatment has been described at present, although the effectiveness of the Q-switched ruby laser is being studied.

A blue or violet macule with an irregular border may be the earliest manifestation of **Kaposi's sarcoma** (KS). Often beginning as a discoloration similar to a bruise, KS may appear on any cutaneous or mucosal surface. Solitary or multiple, the lesions evolve into bluish nodules. They may or may not blanch with pressure. KS is now most commonly seen as a manifestation of AIDS; however, it was originally described as a disease of the lower extremities in elderly patients, particularly men, and is still not infrequently seen in that population. Pertinent risk factors elaborated in the patient's history may support a high index of suspicion, which may be verified by a biopsy. Excision, radiotherapy, intralesional chemotherapy, and laser ablation may be effective treatments depending on the site and size of the lesions and the general state of the patient's health.

A purple macule or soft papule that compresses and blanches defines a **venous lake.** Common in elderly individuals, they occur as single, or sometimes grouped, multiple lesions on the head, neck, and upper trunk. The lip and ear are frequent sites. These lesions are often mistaken for melanomas, which are not, of course, compressible. Treatment is optional, but may be accomplished by excision, electrosurgery, or laser surgery.

Nevus flammeus is the name given to a group of congenital malformations of cutaneous capillaries with variable clinical significance. The most common type, also known as a salmon patch, is a sharply defined, pink macule over the nape of the neck or face. Up to 75% of newborns may have these lesions on the nuchal area. The majority of the facial lesions fade with time, although 20% of adults may have persistent nuchal lesions. Port-wine stains are lesions of a similar nature but with a more exaggerated appearance. They tend to be a deeper color and larger size. A minority of port-wine stains have underlying bony or soft tissue hypertrophy or may be associated with other congenital anomalies or syndromes. Sturge-Weber disease is an example of a congenital disorder with a port-wine stain associated with vascular malformations of the cortical leptomeninges, seizures, intracranial calcifications, and mental retardation. A port-wine stain present on the eyelids or temple may extend into the orbit, producing glaucoma and blindness. Visible light lasers (argon, dye, heavy metal lasers) are the modalities of choice for treatment, although lesions respond variably according to their color, thickness, size, and site.

Telangiectasias, although usually linear, may appear as red or blue macules several millimeters in diameter. Close inspection will reveal a vascular appearance with either spiderlike or matlike arrangements of tiny vessels that empty with pressure. Compression with a transparent object such as a glass slide, lens, or piece of plastic will allow direct observation of the lesion. Multiple telangiectases, sometimes unilateral, may occur as a benign, essential condition. Their incidence is also increased in patients with a history of excessive sun exposure or familial predisposition. Leg lesions are particularly common, especially in the setting of venous incompetency. Although the lesions are generally idiopathic, an evaluation is appropriate if the lesions are particularly numerous or associated with gastrointestinal or respiratory hemorrhage. Conditions associated with multiple telangiectases include liver disease, ataxia-telangiectasia, and hereditary hemorrhagic telangiectasia (Osler-Weber-Rendu syndrome). Treatment can be accomplished with electrocoagulation or a visible light laser. Leg telangiectasias are best treated with sclerotherapy.

Melasma, or chloasma, is an increase in epidermal or dermal pigmentation (or both) that usually occurs in premenopausal women. It typically appears as an irregular, splotchy, gray-brown darkening of the skin over the cheeks, temples, forehead, upper lip, and chin. The hyperpigmentation is usually symmetric, but it is sometimes irregularly distributed. A Wood's lamp examination will demonstrate areas of increased pigmentation compared to normal skin. Melasma is frequently seen in women who have overindulged in sun exposure. The alteration may occur during pregnancy (mask of pregnancy) or result from the use of oral contraceptives. Occasional cases may occur in men or postmenopausal women. The tendency to develop melasma may be familial. Melasma with predominant epidermal hyperpigmentation may respond to hypopigmenting agents containing hydroquinone or to the combination of 0.1% tretinoin cream and hydroquinone with or without concomitant use of a topical steroid. Melasma is definitely worsened by even brief exposure to sunlight, and effective treatment must include the continuous use of potent sun-blocking agents. Melasma in premenopausal women may improve after menopause without therapy.

Exogenous ochronosis is an uncommon complication of topical hydroquinone therapy that has primarily been reported in patients using hydroquinone-containing hypopigmenting agents for melasma. The melasma may initially improve; however, with continued therapy, blue-brown or brown hyperpigmentation appears in the treated area. A skin biopsy confirms the presence of pigmented material in the dermis similar to that found in ochronosis. The cessastion of hydroquinone therapy usually results in clinical improvement of the hyperpigmentation.

Postinflammatory hyperpigmentation is a brown or purple-brown discoloration from the accumulation of heme, iron, and melanin pigments in the dermis with or without increased melanin in the epidermis. It occurs after trauma or thermal injury, or after inflammatory dermatoses such as atopic dermatitis, stasis dermatitis, acne, psoriasis, lupus erythematosus, and lichen planus. The discoloration intensifies and persists after primary lesions have resolved. It is particularly likely to occur in dark-skinned individuals. A unique condition is that of the **fixed drug reaction.** A well-circumscribed, coin-shaped patch first appears with an orange-red discoloration, and may scale or blister. Within days the color becomes violaceous and then a persistent dark brown. The oral mucosa or genitalia may be involved. Sometimes multiple lesions appear, but usually there are only a few. The reaction follows ingestion of a specific agent within days. The lesions recur at the same site or sites with easy subsequent exposure. Phenolphthalein (commonly found in laxatives), tetracycline, and barbiturates are among the many drugs that cause such an eruption. Thus the identification of the cause of postinflammatory pigmentation relies on a history of a preexisting condition and on an examination of coexisting lesions. A biopsy usually documents a postinflammatory state but is often unable to identify the preexisting condition. Treatments are generally unsatisfactory. It is necessary to determine the preexisting condition so that it and the resulting pigmentary change can be prevented.

Exogenous material may **stain** the skin or be injected into the skin or be implanted during trauma to produce a dark macule or **tattoo.** Staining is generally easily identified by history. Vegetable or industrial dyes are common agents. Topical exposure to tars or anthralin may also discolor the skin. Stains generally resolve within a month. Tattoos are produced inadvertently by materials such as carbon, asphalt, gunpowder, ink, paint, and glass or produced intentionally for decorative purposes by metallic or vegetable dyes. Styptics such as Monsel's solution and silver nitrate may also leave tattoos. Amalgam used in dental procedures can produce tattoos in the oral cavity. Historical information is sometimes misleading. For example, a blue nevus may be erroneously attributed to a pencil stab, or lead pencil tattoo. Tattoos are stable, and any change in the color, shape, or size should prompt a biopsy to exclude malignancy, secondary infection, or a granulomatous response. Tattoos may be removed by excision, dermabrasion, salabrasion, or laser ablation, with the results depending on the depth, site, and size of the tattoo, and the skill of the therapist. The Q-switched ruby laser is currently the treatment of choice for many tattoos, particularly those with blue-black colors, because of the lack of significant scarring and nearly complete resolution of the discoloration.

Systemic medications may produce localized dark discoloration of the skin. Blue-gray macules over the shins, nail beds, face, and hard palate may appear after many months of therapy with the antimalarial medications quinine, chloroquine, and hydroxychloroquine. Similar discoloration has been rarely reported after prolonged use of quinidine, which is chemically related to the antimalarials. Although quinacrine may produce macular blue-gray discoloration of the palate, it more commonly causes generalized yellowing of the skin. These pigmentary changes usually diminish after cessation of the drug.

Therapy with minocycline over many months or years may cause macular blue-gray pigmentation similar in distribution to that caused by the antimalarials over the shins, nail beds, face, and hard palate. It may also appear at the sites of acne scars or at the sites of active inflammation. Generalized muddy-colored skin has also been described. Prolonged minocycline therapy may also cause black discoloration of bone, teeth, the thyroid gland, and breast milk. Chlorpromazine can produce cutaneous hyperpigmentation similar to that caused by minocycline. The pigmentation resolves very slowly after discontinuation of the causative agent.

Other drugs known to produce macular hyperpigmentation include amiodarone—which, in addition to causing a photosensitivity reaction, may produce slate gray discoloration of the face and other sun-exposed skin surfaces. This complication usually occurs after 1 to 2 years of therapy and is related to the cumulative dose. The discoloration persists for many months after discontinuation of the drug. Azidothymidine (zidovudine, AZT, Retrovir) has been reported to cause generalized cutaneous hyperpigmentation, longitudinal brown streaks of the nail beds, diffuse blue discoloration of the nail beds, and circumscribed brown spots on the palms and soles. These alterations have appeared after several weeks to months of therapy. Bleomycin may cause localized linear hyperpigmentation or hyperpigmentation over pressure points. Oral mucosal pigmentation has been reported following administration of doxorubicin, busulfan, cyclophosphamide, and fluorouracil. These medications may also produce a generalized cutaneous hyperpigmentation. Long-term exposure to gold, silver, bismuth, and mercury also causes discoloration of the skin.

Systemic disorders may have associated cutaneous areas of hyperpigmentation. Addison's disease, Fanconi's syndrome, Gaucher's disease, hemochromatosis, incontinentia pigmenti, Peutz-Jeghers syndrome, and ochronosis are disorders that characteristically present with cutaneous and oral hyperpigmentation. **Local processes** such as erythema dyschromicum perstans, erythema ab igne, poikiloderma of Civatte, and Riehl's melanosis are also diagnosed because of typical macular hyperpigmentation. These disorders are well described in dermatology texts.

Basler RSW: Minocycline-related hyperpigmentation. *Arch Dermatol.* 1985;121:606–608.
> *An editorial review of the appearance and pathophysiology of skin hyperpigmentation due to minocycline therapy.*

Bendick C, Rasokat H, Steigleder FK: Azidothymidine-induced hyperpigmentation of the skin and nails. *Arch Dermatol.* 1989;125:1285–1286.
> *Two case reports and a synopsis of cutaneous pigmentation caused by azidothymidine (AZT).*

Engasser PG, Maibach HI: Cosmetics and dermatology: Bleaching creams. *J Am Acad Dermatol.* 1981;5:143–147.
> *A concise review of the use of hydroquinone preparations as bleaching agents.*

Ferguson J, Frain-Bell W: Pigmentary disorders and systemic drug therapy. *Clin Dermatol.* 1989;7:44–54.
> *A review of medications causing cutaneous pigmentation.*

Hood AF: Cutaneous side effects of cancer chemotherapy. *Med Clin North Am.* 1986;70:187–209.
> *A review of skin complications and manifestations of chemotherapy drugs and immunosuppression.*

Lawrence N, Bligard CA, Reed R, et al.: Exogenous ochronosis in the United States. *J Am Acad Dermatol.* 1988;5:1207–1211.
> *Case reports and a literature review with discussion of the pathogenesis of exogenous ochronosis.*

Maize JC, Ackerman AB: *Pigmented Lesions of the Skin.* Philadelphia, PA: Lea & Febiger; 1987.
> *A thorough clinicopathologic atlas of cutaneous pigmented lesions.*

Pathak MA, Fitzpatrick TB, Parrish JA: Treatment of melasma with hydroquinone. *J Invest Dermatol.* 1981;76:324.
A blind study comparing various combinations of hydroquinone, retinoic acid, corticosteroids, and sunscreens in the treatment of melasma.

Rappersberger K, Hönigsmann H, Ortel B, et al.: Photosensitivity and hyperpigmentation in amiodarone-treated patients: Incidence, time course and recovery. *J Invest Dermatol.* 1989;93:201–209.
One medical center's experience with amiodarone-induced skin disease.

Taylor CR, Gange RW, Dover JS, et al.: Treatment of tattoos by Q-switched ruby laser. A dose-response study. *Arch Dermatol.* 1990;126:893–899.
Fifty-seven tattoos were treated with the Q-switched ruby laser. Substantial lightening or total clearing was achieved in 78% of amateur tattoos and 23% of professional tattoos. Optimal treatment protocol and side effects are discussed.

Wintroub BU, Stern R: Cutaneous drug reactions: Pathogenesis and clinical classification. *J Am Acad Dermatol.* 1985;13:167–179.
A comprehensive review of cutaneous complications of drug therapy, including pigmentary alterations.

42. DIFFUSE HYPOPIGMENTATION
David A. Laub

While conditions featuring diffuse hypopigmentation are rare, they illustrate the importance of an intact pigment shield. Patients lacking such a shield are extremely sensitive to the harmful effects of solar radiation, which include UV light–induced damage to DNA, promotion of skin cancer formation, and aging of exposed skin. Most conditions with diffuse hypopigmentation, such as albinism and phenylketonuria (PKU), are congenital and are associated with various neuromuscular abnormalities. In contrast, vitiligo, a suspected autoimmune disease, can produce a generalized amelanotic state typically after the adolescent stage of life.

An accurate **diagnosis** is important for proper management of patients with diffuse hypopigmentation. Attention to inheritance pattern, extent of pigmentary dilution, and extracutaneous findings is required. Albinism and PKU are autosomal recessive disorders, while oculocutaneous albinoidism and vitiligo are autosomal dominant. Pigmentary dilution of skin, hair, and eyes is seen in albinism, PKU, and oculocutaneous albinoidism, but eye pigmentation is usually normal in vitiligo. Nystagmus, photophobia, and decreased visual acuity are characteristic of albinism. Abnormalities of phenylalanine metabolism and mental retardation are seen in PKU. Vitiligo is often associated with thyroid abnormalities, diabetes, Addison's disease, and pernicious anemia.

The group of disorders called **oculocutaneous albinism (OCA)** are characterized by varying degrees of skin, hair, and eye pigmentary dilution. Nystagmus, photophobia, and reduced visual acuity are often associated. Ten types of OCA have been identified, one of which is inherited as an autosomal dominant trait and the rest as autosomal recessive traits. Types with findings limited to the skin, hair, and eyes include autosomal dominant OCA, tyrosinase-negative OCA, tyrosinase-positive OCA, yellow-mutant OCA, platinum OCA, brown OCA, and rufous OCA. Tyrosinase is an enzyme found in melanocytes necessary for pigment (melanin) production. The tyrosinase-negative form of albinism, which presents with no visible pigment, results from the total absence of tyrosinase. The other forms have identifiable tyrosinase enzyme and trace amounts of pigment, and the cause of their decreased pigment is unknown. Tyrosinase-positive OCA is the most common type of albinism.

Three types of OCA are associated with significant systemic abnormalities. In **Hermansky-Pudlak syndrome,** patients have albinism associated with a bleeding diathesis and interstitial lung fibrosis. The syndrome is believed to be due to an enzyme defect resulting in the accumulation of ceroid material in the reticuloendothelial system of the lungs and visceral organs. In **Chediak-Higashi syndrome,** patients suffer from bacterial infections, neuropathy, and lymphoreticular malignancy. Their neutrophils, which are deficient in lysosomal enzymes, are characterized by giant lysosomal granules detected on peripheral blood smear examination. In **Cross-McKusick-Breen syndrome,** patients have mental retardation, short stature, athetoid movements, and gingival fibromatosis accompanying their pigmentary findings. When confronted with a patient with albinism, it is important to do a complete history and physical to rule out the syndromes associated with systemic abnormalities, paying close attention to the neurologic, ophthalmologic, and hematologic systems.

Treatment recommendations stress avoidance of mid-day sun and use of UVA-UVB sunscreens with a minimum effectiveness of SPF 15. Sunglasses will reduce photophobia, and corrective glasses may improve visual acuity. Neither oral beta-carotene nor PUVA has been shown to offer solar protection. However, beta-carotene is sometimes employed to provide skin color and improve cosmesis. Many albino children suffer from distant vision impairment, making proper seating selection in school classrooms important. Finally, genetic counseling is very important in the prevention of further occurrences among families.

Oculocutaneous albinoidism is a congenital hypomelanosis of the skin, hair, and eyes inherited in an autosomal dominant pattern. The irides are blue, while nystagmus and visual acuity defects are absent. The patients are otherwise healthy.

PKU is an autosomal recessive disorder with a deficiency in hepatic phenylalanine hydroxylase enzyme. Affected patients are characterized by blond hair, blue eyes, and fair skin color. If PKU is not detected early, mental and growth retardation may develop along with many other neuromuscular abnormalities. Neonatal urinary screening for phenylalanine metabolites is now routinely performed. Once the disorder is detected, phenylalanine dietary restriction is effective in preventing further structural abnormalities and mental retardation.

Vitiligo is an acquired idiopathic progressive depigmentation of the skin and hair. An autosomal dominant condition with an incidence of 1%, vitiligo usually presents with localized chalk white macules in periorificial areas and on extensor surfaces, as discussed in the chapter on light macules (Ch. 40). It occasionally presents as a generalized process involving both skin and hair. Patients with generalized vitiligo have a very high incidence of various autoimmune diseases including thyroid disease, diabetes mellitus, pernicious anemia, and Addison's disease. Repigmentation of the skin in generalized vitiligo is very difficult. Patients with very little normally pigmented skin may choose to depigment the normal skin to achieve a cosmetically acceptable uniform color. The monobenzyl ether derivative of hydroquinone induces irreversible pigmentation with topical use. As with all diseases of diffuse hypopigmentation, solar protection is of paramount importance to prevent skin cancer and premature aging of the skin.

Depinho RA, Kaplan KL: The Hermansky-Pudlak Syndrome. *Medicine.* 1985;64:192–202.
A complete review of this important type of albinism with emphasis placed on pathophysioloy and management of this condition.
Kronberg JG, Castle D, Zwane EM, et al.: Albinism and skin cancer in Southern Africa. *Clin Genet.* 1989;36:43–52.
Skin cancer presence was investigated in 111 black albinos in South Africa. The rate was 23.4% and the risk increased with age.
Schachne JP, Glaser N, Lee SH, et al.: Hermansky-Pudlak syndrome: case report and clinicopathologic review. *J Am Acad Dermatol.* 1990;221:926–932.
Hermansky-Pudlak syndrome is an autosomal recessive disorder consisting of albinism, a bleeding diathesis, and ceroid deposition in the reticuloendothelial syndrome. In the patients studied, ceroid was demonstrated within dermal macrophages, and electron microscopy studies suggested that melanosomes may be a substrate for the formation of ceroid in skin.
Witkop CJ, Quevado WC, Fitzpatrick TB: Albinism and other disorders of pigment

metabolism. In: Stanbury JB, ed. *Metabolic Basis of Inherited Disease*. 5th ed. New York, NY: McGraw-Hill; 1983:301–346.
A comprehensive review of albinism.

43. MUCOSAL PIGMENTATION
Scott B. Phillips

Mucosal surfaces that are easily examined by the clinician include the mouth, conjunctivae, vagina, and distal rectum. These mucosal membranes are generally moist and pink; however, pigmentation may be present as a normal variant, especially in blacks and Asians. Normal coloration can vary from pale pink to deep bluish purple to brown or brownish black, and it may be present unilaterally or bilaterally in patchy or diffuse, uniform or mottled patterns. Pigmentation may also represent local or systemic disease, or result from deposition or contact with exogenous pigmented substances. Identification of mucosal pigmented lesions is therefore essential since the pigmentation may represent benign, potentially harmful, or malignant conditions, or may indicate disease elsewhere.

Nevi are commonly found on mucosal surfaces. Most oral nevi are raised, though they can be flat, sessile, or polypoid. The surface may be smooth or verrucous. Nevi are frequently unpigmented and usually small, between 1 and 6 mm in diameter. Forty percent occur on the palate. Oral nevi may be intramucosal, junctional, or compound, depending on the histologic level of involvement by nevus cells. Blue nevi and combined nevi (intramucosal nevi associated with blue nevi) also occur, as well as melanoma. When diagnosed in the mouth, **malignant melanoma** exhibits clinical features not usually associated with benign pigmented lesions, such as large size, irregular shape, tendency to ulcerate or bleed, peripheral erythema, and spreading melanosis, and it has a poor prognosis. Theoretically, however, it begins with a small pigmented macule or papule. Because the malignant potential of oral nevi is unclear and because preexisting macular pigmentation is present in about one-third of all patients with melanoma of the mucosa, it is advisable to identify all oral pigmented lesions carefully. Evaluation may require a biopsy or excision and microscopic examination.

Other **local processes** may present with pigmented lesions in the oral mucosa. Ecchymoses, hematomas, hemangiomas, and dilated veins (venous lakes) may appear as bluish macules or nodules. Brown or brownish black macules may represent postinflammatory pigmentation, which occurs after mucosal trauma from friction, heat, irritants, and infection. Tobacco smoking is particularly incriminated in this process. Smoker's melanosis develops within the first year of smoking, and does not usually disappear until several years after cessation. Riehl's melanosis is characterized by reticular pigment, black to brown-violet in color, usually in sun-exposed areas and rarely in the oral mucosa. It occurs as a result of pigmentary incontinence caused by chemical and physical irritations of the skin and mucous membranes. Melanotic macules or lower labial macules are dark brown to brownish black macules, 2 to 10 mm in diameter, found on the vermilion border of the lower lip. They usually appear after intense sun exposure and have no malignant potential.

Local conditions causing **hyperplasia** of the mucosa may give rise to diffuse or patchy oral pigmentation. In acanthosis nigricans, the tongue and lips are often involved, with pigmented patches that appear velvety and sometimes verrucous on close inspection. Black hairy tongue is a benign hyperplasia of the filiform papillae of the midline anterior two-thirds of the tongue. A matted, jet black to yellowish white hairy mass is produced by retention of long conical masses of ortho- and para-keratinized cells. It is seen in association with smoking, use of oral antibiotics, and prolonged use of oxidizing agents. Therapy for either condition includes treatment of predisposing factors and careful attention to oral hygiene, including scrubbing the tongue with a toothbrush. Hairy leukoplakia, poorly demarcated white to dark brown verrucous plaques on the sides of the tongue, is a manifestation of AIDS and is caused by a mixed viral infection. Human papillomavirus, Epstein-Barr virus, and herpes simplex have been incriminated. Topical fluorouracil, tretinoin, and acyclovir have been used for treatment.

Pigmentation of the oral mucosa may be the first evidence of **systemic disease.** In Addison's disease, which is due to a chronic insufficiency of adrenocortical hormones, blue-black to dark brown streaks, irregular patches, and small macules are usually seen on the buccal mucosa bilaterally and the tongue. Although not pathognomonic, oral pigmentation of this sort in conjunction with malaise and low blood pressure may be the earliest sign of the disorder. The pigmentation is a result of increased melanin deposition and often persists despite successful therapy for other manifestations of the disease. In hemochromatosis, 15% to 20% of patients have mucosal pigmentation resembling that of Addison's disease. A diffuse bluish gray color from the iron deposition may also be seen. Patients with polycythemia often develop a generalized purple erythema and hypertrophy of the mucosa of the gingivae, buccal mucosa, palate, and tongue. In jaundiced patients, persistent hyperbilirubinemia of greater than 1.5 mg/100 ml results in the yellowish green staining of the skin and mucous membranes from deposition of bile pigments. The discoloration may be easy to see in the sclera, buccal mucosa, and soft palate. Cyanosis due to cardiopulmonary decompensation or sickle cell anemia may cause mucous membranes to appear deep blue or purple. Vitamin B_{12} deficiency also causes a diffuse bluish purple (magenta) discoloration of the buccal mucosa, tongue, and vermilion border of the lips; this condition can be treated with riboflavin administration. Occult malignancy is a rare cause of oral hyperpigmentation. Some tumors produce specific circulating peptides that stimulate melanocytes in the oral and laryngeal mucosa.

Oral pigmentation can be a manifestation of several **genetic disorders.** Albright's disease (polyostotic fibrous dysplasia) is characterized by fibrous dysplasia of bone; irregular, well-demarcated brown macules on the skin and mucous membranes; and sexual precocity in the female. Lips are a common area of involvement. Peutz-Jeghers syndrome is characterized by mucocutaneous melanosis and gastrointestinal polyposis. Brown to black macules from a few tenths to several millimeters in size occur around the mouth, lips, and buccal mucosa. The hyperpigmentation that is seen in incontinentia pigmenti can involve mucosal surfaces. In von Recklinghausen's neurofibromatosis, the characteristic light to dark brown pigmented macules (called café au lait spots) are rarely seen on mucosal surfaces. Alkaptonuria is an inherited deficiency of homogentisic acid oxidase that results in the accumulation and deposition of homogentisic acid and its polymers in various tissues. Clinically, the disorder is characterized by dark urine, arthropathy, and diffuse bluish-black pigmentation of connective tissue that can easily be appreciated in sites such as the ears, nose, extensor tendons of the hands, nails, intertriginous areas and oral mucosa. The pigment deposition is called ochronosis.

Exogenous pigments may be deposited in the oral mucosa. Amalgam particles introduced into the oral mucosa during dental procedures can produce an asymptomatic bluish black tattoo. Histologically, the amalgam is identified in the tissues as discrete, fine dark granules, or as irregular, solid fragments arranged predominantly along collagen bundles and around blood vessels. Other foreign material such as pencil lead, ink, and carbon may also tattoo the mucosa. External agents can also stain the oral mucosa as well as the teeth. Tobacco stains, a process different from smoker's melanosis, impart a yellowish brown color. Artificial coloring agents and food such as grapes and berries may cause temporary staining. Betel or areca nut chewing is a common cause of brownish discoloration in some parts of the world. Similar in appearance to a stain, berloque dermatitis is an irregularly patterned hyperpigmentation usually located on the front and sides of the neck because of photosensitization by 5-methoxypsoralen and other furocoumarins in perfumes, but it can also rarely affect the oral mucosa.

Systemic medications may deposit at the gingival margin and other mucosal surfaces, especially if the gingivae are already mildly inflamed with local vasodilation and stasis. Chronic administration of gold for rheumatoid arthritis and other conditions causes a blue-gray pigmentation, identified histologically as granules, located around blood vessels and in dermal macrophages. Antimalarials such as chloroquine, quinacrine, and quinine cause greenish yellow or yellowish brown pigmentation of the palate. The antibiotics minocycline (100 to 200 mg/d for 1 to 3 years) and tetracycline (also substantial, prolonged use) may give a blue-gray pigmentation, particularly of the gingivae. Administration of doxorubicin has been reported to result in the development of hyperpigmentation of the tongue and buccal mucosa, which improves when the drug is withdrawn. Phenolphthalein, common in over-the-counter laxative medications, can cause a fixed drug eruption in which the inflammatory component is fleeting and subsequent macular hyperpigmentation is persistent. Chlorpromazine may produce patchy, melanin hyperpigmentation. Carotenemia, caused by an excessive intake of beta-carotene either as a natural substance in fruits and vegetables or as a synthetic pharmacologic agent, produces yellow discoloration most markedly on the palate and palms. Heavy metals such as bismuth, mercury, silver nitrate, and arsenic are not commonly used as medications today, although occupational exposure may still give rise to gingival hyperpigmentation. Other substances, such as lead, zinc, cadmium, copper, tin, and manganese, can result in a blue line, on the gingival margin, called a Burtonian line. Exposure to these metals is usually from occupational sources or accidental ingestion.

Pigmented lesions of the **conjunctivae** have a similar list of causes and associations. Racial variations in pigment deposition are common. Nevi may occur, and melanomas are not rare. Ephelides (freckles) and lentigenes may be found. In a nevus of Ota, the skin and adjacent conjunctiva have a bluish gray pigmentation, and the patient has an increased risk of glaucoma. Melanoma has also been reported to arise in these lesions. Discoloration of the conjunctivae may also result from deposition of exogenous pigments. A melanin-related pigment in conjunctival crypts and cysts along the microvilli has been reported after local instillation of epinephrine. Tetracycline or minocycline form extracellular chelation complexes with calcium, which accumulate as dark brown to black concretions in the palpebral conjunctival cysts. These deposits display a characteristic yellow fluorescence under ultraviolet light. Polychlorinated biphenyl exposure with blood levels above 41 ppb has resulted in pigmentation of the conjunctivae. Eye cosmetics containing carbon-black may also be associated with conjunctival pigmentation.

The **genital mucosa** is another easily examined mucosal surface in which pigmented lesions may be found. The differential diagnosis is similar to that discussed for the oral and conjunctival mucous membranes. Nevi and their variants are of primary concern. Malignant melanoma can occur and has a dismal prognosis even with radical therapy. Therefore, all pigmented lesions should be identified, fully evaluated, excised, or carefully charted and followed. In addition, the NAME and LAMB syndromes, are important, recently described disorders that include (a) cardiac, cutaneous, and eyelid myxomas; (b) cutaneous (including lips), conjunctival, and genital mucosal pigmented lesions: ephelides, nevocellular nevi, lentigenes, blue nevi; and (c) endocrine overactivity. The morbidity and mortality caused by the cardiac myxomas can be avoided if affected individuals are appropriately identified and treated; therefore, the prompt recognition of other features of these syndromes is important. Bowenoid papulosis, a human papillomavirus infection associated with the histologic picture of squamous cell carcinoma in situ, presents with thin hyperpigmented, slightly verrucous plaques. Patients with this disorder need to have all warty lesions on the genital mucosa identified by colposcopy and eradicated. Careful long-term follow-up is necessary to prevent the development of invasive squamous cell carcinoma. Finally, lichen simplex chronicus is a common, annoying condition of the genitalia that presents with large, pruritic, poorly demarcated, hyperpigmented, scaly, lichenified plaques. What initiates the process is unknown, but when fully developed, it represents chronic inflammation due to scratching or rubbing.

Axell T, Hedin CA: Epidemiologic study of excessive oral melanin pigmentation with special reference to the influence of tobacco habits. *Scand J Dental Res.* 1982;90:434–442.
The prevalence and location of oral melanin pigmentation were studied in a population of 30,118 adults in Sweden and found to increase prominently during the

first year of smoking but also to decrease to the level found among nonsmokers about 3 years after cessation of smoking.

Buchner A, Hansen LS: Melanotic macule of the oral mucosa. A clinicopathologic study of 105 cases. *Oral Surg, Oral Med, Oral Pathol.* 1979;48:244–249.

Most melanotic macules in the oral cavity are single and found on the vermilion border or on the gingivae. Histologic examination reveals only increased pigmentation either in the basal cell layer or in macrophages in the lamina propria.

Buchner A, Hansen LS: Amalgam pigmentation (amalgam tattoo) of the oral mucosa. A clinicopathologic study of 268 cases. *Oral Surg, Oral Med, Oral Pathol.* 1980;49:139–147.

Amalgam tattoos are found most commonly on the gingivae and alveolar mucosa, followed by the buccal mucosa. A chronic inflammatory reaction may accompany the pigment.

Buchner A, Hansen LS: Pigmented nevi of the oral mucosa: A clinicopathologic study of 36 new cases and review of 155 cases from the literature. Part I: A clinicopathologic study of 36 new cases. Part II: Analysis of 191 cases. *Oral Surg, Oral Med, Oral Pathol.* 1987;63:566–572 (Part I), 676–682 (Part II).

Review and analysis of data of 191 cases of oral pigmented nevi with discussion of frequency and location of oral pigmented lesions.

Dummett CO: Systemic significance of oral pigmentation and discoloration. *Postgrad Med.* 1971;49:78–82.

An easy-to-read discussion of oral pigmentation and its significance is accompanied by excellent photographs.

Langford A, Pohle HD, Gelderblom H, et al.: Oral hyperpigmentation in HIV-infected patients. *Oral Surg, Oral Med, Oral Pathol.* 1989;67:301–307.

Six cases of oral hyperpigmentation in HIV-infected patients are reported. The clinical and histologic findings as well as the differential diagnosis are discussed.

McCarthy PL, Shklar G: *Diseases of the Oral Mucosa.* Philadelphia, PA: Lea & Febiger; 1980.

A complete text of the subject with excellent discussions of local and systemic etiologies of normal and pathologic mucosal pigmentation.

Moss AP, Sugar A, Hargett NA, et al.: The ocular manifestations and functional effects of occupational argyrosis. *Arch Ophthalmol.* 1979;97:906–908.

Workers involved in the manufacture of silver nitrate and silver oxide were examined. A direct relationship was observed between the prevalence of conjunctival and corneal pigmentation and the duration of employment.

Rhodes AR, Silverman R, Harrist TJ, et al.: Mucocutaneous lentiginosis, cardiocutaneous myxomas, and multiple blue nevi: The LAMB Syndrome. *J Am Acad Dermatol.* 1984;10:72–82.

Report of a case and review of the literature.

ten Bruggenkate CM, Lopes-Cardozo E, Maaskant P, et al.: Lead poisoning with pigmentation of the oral mucosa. Review of the literature and report of a case. *Oral Surg, Oral Med, Oral Pathol.* 1975;39:747–753.

Some general aspects of the pathogenesis and the clinical and oral symptoms of chronic lead intoxication are presented.

VIII. TUMORS

Suzanne M. Olbricht

More than 500,000 new cases of skin cancer are diagnosed in the United States per year, an increase of 15% to 20% over the previous decade. Basal cell carcinoma (BCC) is the most common type, constituting 65% to 80% of these cases. Squamous cell carcinoma (SCC) accounts for 10% to 25%, and melanoma, which is discussed in chapter 45, accounts for most of the remainder. Some rare types of skin cancer that may be primary in the skin include sebaceous gland carcinoma, eccrine gland carcinoma, Merkel cell tumor, Kaposi's sarcoma, angiosarcoma, dermatofibroma sarcoma protuberans, and leiomyosarcoma. The incidence of the three most common skin cancers varies by region; all occur more commonly in the southern United States, where, in addition, SCC accounts for a larger percentage of skin cancers.

Some aspects of the **biologic behavior** of skin cancers are known. The BCC is thought to arise from a pluripotential cell residing in the basal layer of the epidermis or appendageal epithelium. The SCC probably arises from atypical epidermal keratinocytes. Although these tumors have been reported on any cutaneous or mucosal surface, 85% are found in the head and neck areas. A BCC may arise from normal skin; however, an SCC generally appears on sun-damaged skin or in actinic keratoses. A BCC is usually a stable, slowly growing lesion present for months to years. Rapid and destructive growth occurs infrequently. Massive silent penetration along deep tissue planes or along nerves is rare, and metastasis is quite rare. An SCC may have a similar biologic behavior; however, typically it appears as a rapidly growing lesion, and deep invasion, with extension along nerves, occurs more frequently. The rate of metastasis of SCC is debated. Dermatologic studies suggest that less than 0.1% of SCCs arising in sun-damaged skin metastasize, while other studies suggest a metastatic rate of 2% to 3%. The rate of metastasis approaches 10% to 15% for SCC of the ear, forehead, temple, dorsa of the hands, and the lip.

Although the **pathogenesis** remains undefined, chronic cumulative sun exposure as estimated by the age of the patient, vocational and recreational exposure history, and complexion (fair, poor tanning ability) is a prominent factor for the development of both BCC and SCC. The presence of sun-damaged skin manifested by actinic keratoses, elastosis, localized pigmentary disorders, senile lentigines, freckles, spider angiomas, telangiectasia, dry skin, wrinkled skin, and arcus senilis defines a population at great risk for skin cancer. The risk of a second cutaneous carcinoma is reported to be 20% within 18 months and 36% within 5 years. Ultraviolet B (UVB) light has been most strongly implicated, but UVA probably also plays a role, particularly in the development of SCC. Other conditions predisposing individuals to the development of both tumors include therapeutic, diagnostic, or accidental exposure to radiation with a latent period of 15 to 25 years; long-term PUVA therapy (psoralens and UVA radiation); chronic arsenical intoxication from medicaments or well water; renal transplantation; and immunosuppression. Skin cancer in renal transplant patients may be associated with some mismatches of HLA subtypes. The risk of SCC in immunosuppressed patients is 18 times that of the general population, and the risk for BCC is 3 times. This increased risk also correlates with sun exposure and evidence of photodamage. Other predisposing lesions include old burn scars, tattoos, vaccination scars, chronic ulcers, sinus tracts, epidermal nevi, nevus sebaceous of Jadassohn, and areas of trauma. Infection with particularly specific subtypes of human papillomavirus has been incriminated in the development of SCC as well as exposure to tars and polycyclic aromatic hydrocarbons.

Several **genetic disorders** are associated with an increased incidence of skin cancer. Xeroderma pigmentosum is a group of autosomally recessive disorders with biochemical defects in the excision and repair of UV light–induced pyrimidine dimers in DNA or in the synthesis of DNA after UV radiation. These patients have acute photosensitivity, photophobia, conjunctivitis, and multiple cutaneous neoplasms (BCC, SCC, and melanoma) usually before the age of 10, often with horrifying results. The basal cell nevus syndrome is inherited in an autosomal dominant fashion, although expression in affected family members may be dissimilar. The cutaneous manifestations include multiple BCC (often hundreds), palmar pits, milia, epidermal inclusion cysts, and extreme sensitivity to radiation with a short latency period of 4 to 5 years to the onset of numerous tumors. Jaw cysts, bony abnormalities (hypertelorism, calcification of the falx cerebri, spina bifida, and bifid ribs), ovarian fibromas, cardiac fibromas, mesenteric cysts, gastric polyps, and rare neuromuscular tumors also occur. Patients with the Bazex syndrome have multiple BCC developing between the ages of 15 and 25 years, follicular atrophoderma on the dorsum of the hands and elbows, and localized areas of anhidrosis. Epidermodysplasia verruciformis is a rare autosomal recessive disorder in which several subtypes of human papillomavirus induce widespread, polymorphic, and verrucous lesions beginning in childhood. The SCC develop within the warty plaques, and metastasis and death have been reported. The genetic defect is probably in cell-mediated immunity.

The diagnosis of a skin cancer depends on **physical examination** and histologic confirmation. The most common appearance of a BCC is a slightly translucent, waxy, or pearly papule or nodule with surrounding and overlying telangiectasia and an easily defined border. Secondary changes may include ulceration, crusting, scaling, pigmentation, erythema, cystic collection, and scarring. Sometimes ulceration is so prominent that the tumor mass is inapparent grossly. A superficial BCC, typically on the back, is an erythematous, telangiectatic, well-demarcated macule with fine scale. A primary sclerosing BCC (also called a morpheaform or an infiltrating BCC) is relatively rare and appears as an ill-defined flat or depressed, yellowish indurated plaque, sometimes with overlying telangiectasia. An SCC may appear similar, but is often distinguishable as a poorly defined, firm dome-shaped nodule, flesh-colored to red, with a hyperkeratotic crust. It may also ulcerate as it grows, or produce large amounts of compacted parakeratosis, mimicking a wart or producing a cutaneous horn. An SCC of the lower lip appears as a nonhealing erosion, a white plaque, or a rapidly growing inflammatory nodule.

The **differential diagnosis** of suspicious lesions includes a host of benign tumors (usually nevocellular or appendageal in origin), actinic keratoses, malignant melanoma, and, rarely, an inflammatory condition (acneiform papule) or traumatic event (excoriation, shaving cut). The most important diagnosis to make accurately is that of malignant melanoma. While a pigmented BCC may obviously suggest melanoma, an amelanotic melanoma may be difficult to diagnose clinically.

Documentation of the presence of a BCC or an SCC is by **pathologic examination.** The lesion may be sampled by curettage, shave biopsy, punch biopsy (a 3- or 4-mm disposable Keyes punch is sufficient), incisional biopsy, or excision in toto. Curettage yields fragments of disoriented tissue that are adequate only for confirming BCC and will not afford definitive diagnosis of an SCC nor exclude other tumors or disease processes. Shave biopsy is easy to perform and the site heals well. If a melanoma is being considered in the differential diagnosis, only a punch biopsy of at least 4 mm in diameter or an incisional or excisional biopsy will obtain a specimen appropriate for evaluation. Pathologic changes that indicate the presence of a BCC include cytologically atypical cells with darkly staining, large, oval, elongated nuclei and little cytoplasm collected in masses of various sizes with palisading of cells at the periphery of the masses and retraction artefact about the masses. Stromal changes include mucin deposition and fibrosis of varying degree. The tumor may differentiate toward hair structures, sebaceous glands, apocrine glands, or eccrine glands. In SCC there is atypia of keratinocytes throughout the full thickness of the epidermis, in contrast to actinic keratosis in which the atypical keratinocytes are found only in the lower third of the epidermis. Invasive SCC is diagnosed when the atypical cells invade the dermis in tumor masses, typically containing keratin pearls.

Several distinct clinical and pathologic entities are often considered as **variants of SCC.** An SCC in situ, defined histologically by full-thickness epidermal atypia without invasion into the dermis, appears as a poorly demarcated inflammatory scaling papule or plaque in the midst of marked actinic damage. Bowen's disease is histologically similar; however, clinically it is manifested as a well-demarcated macule or as a slightly indurated plaque with sharp but irregular outline, often with gray-brown hyperpigmentation and a fine superficial scaling. By definition, it does not arise in skin with actinic damage. The significance of distinguishing these two lesions is debated; some reports in the literature indicate that patients with Bowen's disease have an increased incidence of internal malignancy, but most conclude the apparent association is the result of studying an older group of patients in which internal malignancies are commonly found. Both SCC in situ and Bowen's disease may progress to invasive SCC. Bowenoid papulosis is the name used for single or multiple verrucous papules on the genitalia that are resistant to therapy and have atypia reminiscent of Bowen's disease on histologic examination. These lesions are probably induced by human papillomavirus and may have significant malignant potential. Erythroplasia of Queyrat is a term used to identify an asymptomatic, sharply demarcated, bright red, shiny, slightly indurated plaque on the glans penis with the histologic picture of SCC in situ. It develops almost exclusively in uncircumcised men, and progression into invasive SCC and metastasis has been reported. Carcinoma cuniculatum, or verrucous carcinoma, is a warty, slowly growing plaque, generally developing on the feet. A deep biopsy is necessary to identify the characteristic broad, invading tumor masses at the base of the lesion, often found without significant cytologic atypia. Keratoacanthoma is a common lesion that has been described as self-resolving SCC. Clinically, it is a well-demarcated nodule with rolled, firm borders and a central cup filled with keratinaceous debris. It typically grows large quite rapidly and then stabilizes over a few months. A classic keratoacanthoma then regresses, usually with scarring. Multiple keratoacanthomas have been related to internal malignancies and sebaceous adenomas in a hereditary syndrome, the Muir-Torre syndrome. Histologically, the lesion has cup-shaped acanthosis; glassy, mildly atypical keratinocytes pushing into the dermis; a pronounced inflammatory infiltrate; horn pearls; intraepithelial abscesses; and elimination of elastic tissue in epithelial tongues. It is difficult to impossible to definitively differentiate pathologically between keratoacanthoma and SCC, so that generally these lesions are treated similarly to SCC.

Treatment of BCC and SCC is primarily surgical or destructive, and in most cases curative. Most studies have found that a minimum margin of 2 to 4 mm of normal skin surrounding the tumor must be included in the treatment to eradicate a BCC or an SCC totally in more than 95% of the cases. Sclerosing BCC presents a special problem with subclinical extension averaging 7 mm and ranging from 4 to 10 mm. Optimal therapy for a primary lesion may depend on multiple factors, including size and location of the tumor, possible invasion of vital structures, age and general health of the patient, and the patient's cosmetic concerns. Modalities commonly employed include surgical excision, cryotherapy, electrodesiccation and curettage, radiation, laser surgery, topical application of fluorouracil, and Mohs micrographic surgery. Surgical excision is often the treatment of choice. The recurrence rate after primary excision is 5% to 6%. Cryotherapy, and electrodesiccation and curettage, have similar cure rates when performed according to a specific protocol. Superficial radiotherapy may be delivered to a field encompassing the tumor and its margins, usually in one to five visits, resulting in acute radiation dermatitis and healing in 4 to 6 weeks. Because of the high risk of a radiation-induced secondary cutaneous carcinoma and the production of a scar that worsens in appearance over time, this method of treatment is inadvisable for patients less than 70 years old. In addition, there is some evidence that BCC recurrent after radiotherapy is wider, deeper, and more difficult to eradicate than BCC recurrent after other treatments. Laser technology for treating skin cancers, including photodynamic therapy, is relatively new and has no advantage at the current time in either reducing the recurrence rate or improving the cosmetic results. Topical 5-fluorouracil is most helpful in very superficial lesions. It is applied twice a day for 4 to 6 weeks, depending on the site. Cure rates are enhanced by curettage immediately before beginning therapy. Mohs micrographic surgery, in which the tumor is removed in stages and margins evaluated by horizontally cut frozen sections, has the highest cure rates and does not require removal of an additional 2 to 4 mm of normal skin. It is the treatment of choice for recurrent tumors, primary lesions known to have high recurrence rates (large tumors, tumors on the ear, lip, nasolabial triangle), sclerosing BCC, and primary lesions where maximal preservation of normal skin is required because of tumor location. Medical therapies using synthetic retinoids and interferon are in experimental stages.

Persistent long-term **follow-up** care of patients who have had skin cancer is essential. Visible recurrence at the site of the treated lesion may not be apparent for 3 or more years. In addition, patients are highly likely to develop a second primary. The patient's entire cutaneous surface should therefore be examined every 6 to 12 months with particular attention to sun-exposed surfaces, sites previously treated by radiotherapy, and areas difficult for the patient to examine. Most important, patients need instruction concerning risky behavior relating to sun exposure, since cumulative sun exposure is the most common and preventable inciting factor. Infants less than 6 months of age should not be exposed to direct sunlight. All other individuals, except dark-skinned blacks, should wear a sunscreen with a sun protection factor of 15 or greater, large-brimmed hats, and adequate clothing at all times and should avoid noonday sun.

Bart RS, Kopf AW: Techniques of biopsy of cutaneous neoplasms. *J Dermatol Surg Oncol.* 1979;5:979–987.
Diagrams and text illustrate the methods of biopsy that best achieve accurate histologic diagnosis.

Dinehart SM, Pollack SV: Metastases from squamous cell carcinoma of the skin and lip. *J Am Acad Dermatol.* 1989;21:241–248.
In this series of relatively large and complicated SCC treated by Mohs surgery, metastasis occurred in 10% to 15% of lesions located on the ear, forehead, temple, lip, and dorsa of the hands.

Koff AW, Bart RS, Andrade R: *Atlas of Tumors of the Skin.* Philadelphia, PA: W.B. Saunders Co.; 1978.
Excellent photographs illustrate the full range of presentation of SCC and BCC.

Miller SJ: Biology of basal cell carcinoma. *J Am Acad Dermatol.* 1991;24:1–13, 161–175.
This two-part review discusses features that relate to invasive potential, host immunologic responses, and theories of pathogenesis.

Robinson JK: Risk of developing another basal cell carcinoma. A 5-year prospective study. *Cancer.* 1987;60:118–120.
In a series of patients who were treated surgically for one BCC, 36% developed a second BCC within 5 years. The majority of these new skin cancers were unsuspected by the patient.

Robinson JK: What are adequate treatment and follow-up care for nonmelanoma cutaneous cancer? *Arch Dermatol.* 1987;123:331–333.
In this editorial, it is suggested that the physician inspect each patient after treatment of a BCC at 6-month intervals for the first 2 years and then yearly for 5 years to detect recurrences of previously treated BCC and new primary BCC while they are small enough to remove without significant cosmetic loss.

Schwartz RA: *Skin Cancer: Recognition and Management.* New York, NY: Springer-Verlag; 1988.
This encyclopedic textbook is well referenced.

Stern RS, Weinstein MC, Baker SG: Risk reduction for nonmelanoma skin cancer with childhood sunscreen use. *Arch Dermatol.* 1986;122:537–545.
Using a mathematical model based on epidemiologic data, the authors assert that regular use of a sunscreen with a sun protection factor of 15 during the first 18 years of life would reduce lifetime incidence of skin cancer by 78%.

Wolf DJ, Zitelli JA: Surgical margins for basal cell carcinoma. *Arch Dermatol.* 1987;123:340–344.
In 117 cases of previously untreated, well-demarcated BCC less than 2 cm in diameter, a minimum margin of 4 mm was necessary to totally eradicate the tumor in 95% of cases.

45. MELANOMA
Martin A. Weinstock

The incidence and mortality of melanoma are increasing dramatically in white populations throughout the world. The current estimate of lifetime risk of melanoma among whites in the United States is 1%. Among dermatologic conditions, malignant melanoma is the leading cause of death. Melanoma diagnosed early in its evolution is nearly 100% curable; melanoma not diagnosed until it has spread beyond the site of the primary lesion is usually fatal.

Numerous guides to the **recognition of melanoma** have been published. Melanoma lesions are typically elevated above the skin surface, haphazard in color pattern (often including shades of brown, black, blue, red, and gray), irregular in shape, and changing in appearance over a period of months to years. An early lesion may appear simply as a brown "mole" that has a notched border, whereas a later lesion may be nodular and have persistent ulceration, satellite lesions, white scarlike areas of tumor regression, and regional adenopathy of metastatic disease. There are other presentations of melanoma: amelanotic melanoma is pink or red with no visible pigmentation; melanoma in situ may be completely flat; nodular melanoma may have a uniform brown, black, or blue color; and a flat white spot on the skin may be the only remaining evidence of the regressed primary melanoma that gave rise to metastatic disease. Finally, melanoma may present as metastatic disease with no evidence of a primary lesion.

Melanomas typically spread along the epidermis prior to developing an invasive nodule that penetrates deeper into the dermis and subcutaneous tissue. The horizontal array of tumor cells relatively close to the skin surface is described as the "radial growth phase." It forms the basis of the histologic categorization of melanomas as superficial spreading (which is the most common type), lentigo maligna (which typically occurs on the sun-damaged skin of elderly individuals), acral lentiginous (which occurs on palms and soles), or nodular (which has no remaining radial growth phase).

The past decade has seen tremendous advances in our understanding of the **risk factors** for melanoma. Foremost among these risk factors are melanoma precursors, i.e., changing nevi, dysplastic nevi, lentigo maligna, congenital nevi, and other melanocytic dysplasias. These precursors are discussed in detail in Chap. 46.

Melanoma is rare in children; incidence in whites under the age of 10 is approximately 1:1,000,000 per year. The incidence increases exponentially with age. Black and Oriental individuals have approximately one-twelfth the risk of a white individual because they are essentially free of the superficial spreading and lentigo maligna types of melanomas. Their melanomas are typically located on hands, feet, mucous membranes, and the eye. Their risk factors are poorly understood.

Among whites, a personal history of melanoma is associated with an approximately eightfold increased risk of melanoma, and a family history of melanoma is also associated with a substantially increased risk. Indicators of sun sensitivity such as the following have been associated with a two- to fourfold increased risk: poor tanning ability, susceptibility to sunburn, freckles, fair skin, red or blonde hair, and blue or hazel eyes. Signs of sun-induced damage such as fine wrinkling or actinic keratoses, basal cell carcinomas, and cutaneous squamous cell carcinomas each indicate a three- to fivefold increased risk. There is a small increase in risk among indoor workers and people of higher socioeconomic status. Finally, individuals who have had a lymphoma, leukemia, or renal transplant appear to be at increased risk, presumably due to their immunosuppressed state.

Several lines of evidence indicate that sun exposure is an important cause of melanoma. Residents of sunnier climates have a higher incidence of melanoma; melanomas occur more frequently (per unit of skin surface) on sun-exposed areas; trends over time in anatomic location of melanomas correspond to changes in sun exposure due to changing styles of dress, particularly swimsuits; and migrants to sunnier climates at an early age have a markedly higher risk of melanoma than those who migrate at a later age. There is some recent evidence that these findings may be explainable, at least in part, by the role of sun exposure during childhood in producing nevi.

The following parameters are used for assessment of the patient's prognosis:

Clinical stage: stage I—no palpable lymph nodes containing metastatic disease, and no evidence of distant cutaneous, nodal, or visceral metastases; stage II—palpable regional adenopathy due to metastatic deposits, but no distant cutaneous, nodal, or visceral metastases; stage III—distant metastases.

Thickness (Breslow): distance from the granular layer of the epidermis to the deepest tumor cell in primary lesion.

Level (Clark): level I—malignant cells in the epidermis only (i.e., melanoma in situ; level II—malignant cells in the papillary dermis; level III—malignant cells fill the papillary dermis and extend to the reticular dermis but do not invade it; level IV—malignant cells invade the reticular dermis; level V—malignant cells invade the subcutaneous fat.

For patients with clinical stage I disease, the prognosis is primarily determined by tumor thickness. Patients with tumors less than 0.75 mm thick have a 95% 10-year survival rate; patients with tumors 0.76 to 1.5 mm thick have an 85% 10-year survival rate. Those patients with thicker tumors have a correspondingly poorer prognosis: patients with tumors greater than 4.0 mm thick have a 25% to 40% 10-year survival rate. Other factors that worsen the prognosis include a deeper Clark level, the presence of ulceration or microscopic satellites, and a high mitotic rate among the malignant cells. If an elective regional lymph node dissection is performed in clinical stage I disease, the number and proportion of nodes found to contain microscopic tumor predictably affect the prognosis. However, even patients with metastatic melanoma in the nodes (they are classified as clinical stage I, pathologic stage II) have a better prognosis than clinical stage II patients.

The period between treatment of the primary disease and detection of the first metastasis is of variable duration, and appears to be longer for thinner lesions. For melanomas less than 0.75 mm thick, the chance of diagnosing metastatic disease is said to increase steadily until the sixth year after excision of the primary lesion. Although disease-free intervals of up to 26 years have been reported, it is unusual to have a first recurrence more than 10 years after excision of the primary lesion.

Clinical stage II disease is associated with a 20% to 35% long-term survival rate. Forty percent of these patients survive 10 years if only one node is found to be involved, whereas only one in eight is a 10-year survivor if multiple nodes contain metastatic tumor.

The most common sites of clinically detected distant metastasis are the skin, subcutaneous tissue, distant lymph nodes, lung, liver, brain, and bone. Patients with stage III melanoma have a dismal prognosis: most succumb within 1 year. A single metastatic site and the absence of visceral involvement are both associated with a somewhat improved survival rate. Complete spontaneous regression of metastatic disease is documented.

When melanoma is suspected, the **evaluation** begins with a biopsy, which is necessary for diagnosis. An excisional biopsy is generally recommended in order to insure optimal histopathologic analysis. The possibility of metastasis is routinely investigated with history, physical examination, and chest x ray.

The purposes of **follow-up** visits include early detection of residual or recurrent disease, early detection of a second primary melanoma, surveillance for precursor lesions, and instruction regarding both sun protection and screening of family members. The entire cutaneous surface should be carefully reviewed at each visit. For a patient with a thin melanoma, the risk of a second primary melanoma is greater than the risk of recurrence or metastasis. The optimal frequency of follow-up examinations is unclear, but at least annual follow-up for life is typically recommended in addition to more-frequent evaluations when the risk of recurrence is highest.

The **treatment** of primary cutaneous malignant melanoma is complete surgical excision of the lesion along with a margin of clinically uninvolved skin. The width of the margin of normal skin that must be excised is the subject of ongoing clinical trials; a reasonable recommendation at present is to excise a 1- to 1.5-cm margin for lesions less than 0.75 mm thick, and a 2- to 3-cm margin for thicker lesions. Smaller margins may be acceptable if functionally important structures would otherwise be sacrificed.

Hyperthermic regional perfusion is sometimes performed for clinical stage II and thick (>0.75 or 1.5 mm) stage I tumors located on limbs. The usual chemotherapeutic agent is melphalan.

Elective dissection of regional lymph nodes is sometimes recommended in clinical stage I disease. This procedure will not influence survival for most patients. However, it is the subject of ongoing clinical trials and may be beneficial for some patients with lesions 1.5 to 4.0 mm thick. If elective node dissection is performed for a melanoma on the trunk, cutaneous lymphoscintigraphy may be used to define the pattern of lymphatic drainage.

Treatment of metastatic disease is unsatisfactory. Excision of isolated metastases is associated with long-term survival in some cases. Dicarbazine is the most effective chemotherapeutic agent available for systemic treatment at this time, and it is associated with a dismal 20% response rate. Combination chemotherapy offers little advantage over dicarbazine alone. Radiation may be used for palliation, particularly for metastases to the brain. There are several agents under investigation, most notably interleukin-2, interferons, monoclonal antibodies, and dopa analogues. Their potential remains to be elucidated.

Balch CM, Milton GW: *Cutaneous Melanoma: Clinical Management and Treatment Results Worldwide.* Philadelphia, PA: J.B. Lippincott; 1985.
   This is an excellent book-length review of melanoma. It focuses on prognosis and treatment.
Friedman RJ, Rigel DS, Kopf AW; Early detection of malignant melanoma: the role of physician examination and self-examination of the skin. *CA.* 1985;35:130–151.
   An introduction to the recognition of melanoma, which includes color photographs.
Gupta BK, Piedmonte MR, Karakousis CP: Attributes and survival patterns of multiple primary cutaneous malignant melanoma. *Cancer.* 1991;67:1984–1989.
   Of 1495 patients with melanoma, 1.73% had multiple primary melanomas, with a median interval between occurrence of the melanomas of 1.93 years.
Koh HK: Cutaneous melanoma. *N Engl J Med.* 1991;325:171–182.
   Detailed review of melanoma and precursors, with extensive references.
Mihm MC Jr, Fitzpatrick TB, Lane-Brown MM, et al.: Early detection of primary cutaneous melanoma: a color atlas. *N Engl J Med.* 1973;289:989–996.
   An introduction to the recognition of melanoma, which includes color photographs.
Rhodes AR, Weinstock MA, Fitzpatrick TB, et al.: Risk factors for cutaneous melanoma: a practical method of recognizing high risk individuals. *JAMA.* 1987;258:3146–3154.
   This review summarizes our knowledge to date of the major risk factors for melanoma and discusses their relative importance. It also serves as a guide to the literature on the etiology of melanoma.
Veronesi U, Cascinelli N, Adamus J, et al.: Thin stage I primary cutaneous malignant melanoma: comparison of excision with margins of 1 or 3 cm. *N Engl J Med.* 1988;318:1159–1162.
   Preliminary results of a controlled trial suggest that 1-cm margins are adequate for melanomas less than 2 mm in Breslow thickness.
Weinstock MA: Treatment of thin melanomas. *N Engl J Med.* 1988;319:1669.
   In this editorial accompanying the Veronesi et al. article, the author notes that patients were not followed long enough for a definitive conclusion to be drawn.

46. NEVI AND MELANOMA PRECURSORS
Martin A. Weinstock

Detection of melanoma precursors has become an important strategy for the prevention of malignant melanoma. Four types of pigmented lesions have been associated with melanoma risk: common acquired nevi, dysplastic nevi, congenital nevi, and lentigo maligna.

Nevomelanocytic nevi (moles) that are not present at birth and are not dysplastic (see below) are classified as **common acquired nevi.** They are typically smaller than 5 mm in diameter, have well-defined smooth borders, and have no irregularity of color, shape, or contour. The pigmentation, when present, is typically speckled or uniform, and may be tan or brown. In general, there is little or no change in common acquired nevi from year to year. Pronounced changes may occur during early childhood, puberty, or pregnancy; however, even during these periods, the expected changes are increased size or uniform darkening and do not include the development of irregularities of color, shape, or contour.

Dysplastic nevi are recognized by their clinical features. They are usually large (greater than 5 mm) and classically have an asymmetric distribution of pigment. The center of the nevus may be obviously raised or relatively flat, yet the edges often exhibit a splaying of pigment onto the surrounding skin, without any clear border. The contour or shape may be irregular. Although the color often varies from one area of the nevus to another, this variation is restricted to tones of tan and brown, sometimes mixed with erythema. Colors such as white, blue, or jet black in a lesion that otherwise appears to be a dysplastic nevus suggest the presence of a malignant melanoma.

Some dermatologists believe that histologic confirmation is required for diagnosis of a dysplastic nevus. The key histologic features include cytologic atypia of the epidermal melanocytes, proliferation of melanocytes in the epidermis, extension of this epidermal proliferation beyond the dermal nevus cells, fibrosis of the superficial dermis in a characteristic pattern, lymphocytic infiltration in the dermis, and bridging of the epidermal nests of nevus cells. Consensus regarding the relative importance of these criteria for the diagnosis of a dysplastic nevus has not yet been achieved.

Most adults have common acquired nevi. Individuals who have a great many nevi are at higher risk for melanoma than those with few nevi, and are also more likely to have dysplastic nevi. People who have dysplastic nevi and a history of at least two relatives with melanoma have more than a 100-fold risk of melanoma; their chance of developing a melanoma exceeds 50% by age 60. Other individuals with dysplastic nevi have a 7- to 40-fold increase in melanoma risk.

Congenital nevi are simply defined as nevomelanocytic nevi that were present at birth. Classically they are larger than common acquired nevi and are hypertrichotic, although neither of these criteria is a reliable sign. The differentiation from common acquired nevi is particularly difficult because patients will often state they were born with a nevus if the nevus became evident in early childhood. A history taken directly from the parents may be helpful.

Nevi are present in 1% of children at birth. The lifetime risk of melanoma in patients with congenital nevi has been estimated to be increased 20-fold over that of the general population, although this is controversial. The subgroup with giant nevi appear to be at even higher risk, and the melanomas that develop in the giant congenital nevi may arise early in childhood and may be difficult to detect by clinical examination at a curable stage. Fortunately, less than 1% of children with congenital nevi have giant congenital nevi.

Lentigo maligna is a brown macule that is usually irregular in shape and pigmentation, typically presenting on the sun-exposed skin of an elderly patient. Histologic examination reveals an epidermal melanocytic hyperplasia with no nevus cells but with pronounced atypism of the melanocytes. These lesions typically grow slowly for many years. If left untreated, a small but significant proportion of them will give rise to lentigo maligna melanoma.

The **treatment** of melanoma precursors is controversial, and must be individualized. Excision of common acquired nevi is not indicated for the prevention of melanoma. Dysplastic nevi are both precursors of melanoma and indicators of melanoma risk. If a dysplastic nevus has undergone dramatic change, or if its clinical features suggest the possibility of melanoma, then an excisional biopsy is generally performed to rule out melanoma and to eliminate further concern about malignant change in the lesion. It is not clear whether excision of dysplastic nevi that have a less worrisome appearance has a significant impact on melanoma risk. Most dysplastic nevi do not give rise to melanoma; and melanoma may arise in individuals with no dysplastic nevi, or in those who have had all of their dysplastic nevi removed, or in sites not previously involved with dysplastic nevi. Regardless of whether excisions have been performed, individuals at high risk for melanoma because of their nevi should periodically perform self-examination and be regularly examined by a physician skilled in the diagnosis of melanoma. Patient education materials with pictures may be obtained from the American Academy of Dermatology, Evanston, Illinois, American Cancer Society, New York, New York, National Cancer Institute, Bethesda, Maryland, and the Skin Cancer Foundation, New York, New York.

The risk associated with congenital nevi and lentigo maligna appears to be due primarily to the risk of melanoma arising within the clinical lesion. Hence surgical excision is the definitive therapy for both. However, since the probability of melanoma arising in any individual congenital nevus or lentigo maligna is small, this risk must be compared to the consequences of surgery in each case. For example, congenital nevi in children, with the exception of the giant variety, rarely give rise to melanoma before puberty, so surgery is generally deferred until the child is old enough to cooperate with excision under local anesthesia. When a lentigo maligna is large or involves critical areas, or when the patient has other significant medical problems, excision may involve considerable morbidity, and alternative management may be considered. The alternative to surgery is long-term periodic follow-up, whether or not a partial excision or other therapy is performed, so that any melanoma that does develop will be caught at an early stage when the probability of cure is high.

Armstrong BK, English DR: The epidemiology of acquired melanocytic nevi and their relationship to malignant melanoma. *Pigment Cell.* 1988;9:27–47.
A review of the association of nevi with melanoma in epidemiologic investigations.
Elder DE: The blind men and the elephant: different views of small congenital nevi. *Arch Dermatol.* 1985;121:1263–1265.
Discussion of the prognosis of congenital nevi.
Green MH, Clark WH, Tucker MA, et al.: Acquired precursors of malignant melanoma: the familial dysplastic nevus syndrome. *N Engl J Med.* 1985;312:91–97.
This article discusses the management of dysplastic nevi and includes color photographs.
Green MH, Clark WH, Tucker MA, et al.: The prospective diagnosis of malignant melanoma in a population at high risk: hereditary melanoma and the dysplastic nevus syndrome. *Ann Intern Med.* 1985;102:458–465.
Report of the prognosis and management of dysplastic nevi in the setting of familial melanoma.
Halpern AC, Guerry D IV, Elder DE, et al.:Dysplastic nevi as risk markers of sporadic (nonfamilial) melanoma. A case-control study. *Arch Dermatol.* 1991;127:995–999.
The prevalence of dysplastic nevi in 105 cases of melanoma without familial melanoma was 39%, compared to 15% in 181 controls, supporting the concept that dysplastic nevi are markers of increased risk for nonfamilial melanoma.
Rhodes AR, Melski JW: Small congenital nevocellular nevi and the risk of cutaneous melanoma. *J Pediatr.* 1982;100:219–224.
Discussion of the prognosis of congenital nevi.
Rhodes AR, Weinstock MA, Fitzpatrick TB, et al.: Risk factors for cutaneous melanoma: a practical method of recognizing predisposed individuals. *JAMA.* 1987;258:3146–3154.
A review of the relation between melanoma precursors and melanoma. Color photographs are included.

Slue W, Kopf AW, Rivers JK: Total-body photographs of dysplastic nevi. *Arch Dermatol.* 1988;124:1239–1243.
  This article describes one system for following dysplastic nevus patients photographically.
Weinstock MA, Sober AJ: Risk of progression of lentigo maligna to lentigo maligna melanoma. *Br J Dermatol.* 1987;16:303–310.
  Discussion of the prognosis of lentigo maligna.

47. KELOIDS AND SCARS

Andree A. Haas

Keloids and hypertrophic scars are results of abnormal wound healing. Keloids present as large, firm, pruritic masses of scar tissue that originate in a site of injury and grow or persist. In contrast, hypertrophic scars, which initially may appear similar, tend to flatten over time. Keloids are also differentiated from hypertrophic scars by extension beyond the dimensions of the original injury, forming a clawlike appearance. The size and configuration of the keloid may or may not be related to the trauma, while a hypertrophic scar is generally a thickening corresponding to the shape and extent of the original injury.

Strict definitions of keloids and hypertrophic scars, differentiating the two lesions, are not generally used by patients, clinicians, or researchers. In young people, surgical procedures in some sites, e.g., the neck, are almost universally followed by hypertrophic scarring for periods of 6 months to 3 years, and thus it might operationally be described as a normal stage of wound healing. Both keloids and hypertrophic scars may range in size from small papules to large linear plaques, and some keloids develop into very large tumors. The color can vary from light pink to red to darkly pigmented, and the epidermis is often thin and shiny. Keloids and hypertrophic scars may occur anywhere. The most frequent locations are the shoulder, anterior chest, and upper arms. They may be found less frequently on the lower extremities, face, and neck and are only rarely found on the eyelids, genitalia, palms, soles, cornea, and mucous membranes. Both develop rapidly over weeks to months after trauma or some other event. Hypertrophic scars stabilize, then improve within several years; however, keloids may continue to enlarge, may remain stable, or may undergo suppurative necrosis. Keloids tend to involute in the sixth and seventh decades of life.

Keloids occur equally in males and females. Most reported cases have occurred in patients between the ages of 10 and 30 years of age. The prevalence of keloids in the total population is not known. Keloids are more common in individuals with darker pigmentation. In some African populations, the incidence is as high as 6%. Keloids have not been reported in Negroid albinos, and Europeans living in the tropics have a greater keloidal diathesis than those living in more temperate zones.

The **etiology** of keloids is uncertain. A familial susceptibility to keloid formation has been reported; inheritance is thought to be an autosomal gene of incomplete dominance and variable expressivity. Most keloids appear within a year after local trauma including surgery, laceration, tattoos, burns, injection, bites, and vaccination. Keloids have also formed in skin injured by dissecting cellulitis of the scalp, acne vulgaris, acne conglobata, hidradenitis suppurativa, pilonidal cysts, foreign body reaction, and local infections with herpes, smallpox, or the vaccinia virus. Postsurgical keloid formation may be seen in association with a wound infection or other interference with the dynamics of wound healing, such as the presence of excessive tension on the wound edges from poor orientation to the lines of relaxed skin tension or movement, but also occurs in scars resulting from uncomplicated surgery performed with good technique. Keloid formation has been reported in Ehlers-Danlos syndrome, Rubenstein-Taybi syndrome, and pachydermoperiostosis.

Numerous studies have compared the biochemical and physical processes measurable in normal skin, normal scars, and keloids. The results are not uniform and are even sometimes confusing, since a clear differentiation between hypertrophic scars and keloids is not often made. Regardless, some aspects of keloid formation are known. Normal wound healing and keloids both show an early inflammatory stage that is followed by fibroplasia with increased vascularity and a perivascular mononuclear infiltrate, which consists of mast cells, plasma cells, and lymphocytes. Fibroplasia slows down after the third week of wound healing in normal scars, but continues in keloids, where a thickened nodular mass of collagen and proteoglycan is formed from swirl-like fibroblast (or myofibroblast) clusters. In normal wound maturation, the number of fibroblasts decreases by the fifth week, and the collagen fibers become more organized and parallel to the epithelial surface. In contrast, the collagen bundles and fibers in keloids remain disorganized.

Fibroblasts isolated from keloids and hypertrophic scars show hyperplasia and increased metabolic activity, but growth characteristics are similar to those of normal dermal fibroblasts. Most of the extracellular material found in keloids is either proteoglycan or water. The proteoglycan is composed mostly of chrondoitin-4-sulfate (4.5% in normal skin vs. 26% in keloids and hypertrophic scars).

Collagen synthesis is increased in keloids, but collagen concentration is not increased. Proline hydroxylase is required for collagen synthesis, and this activity is increased in keloidal tissue when compared with hypertrophic scars. The type of collagen synthesized differs from that which is found in the normal dermis. In adult human skin, 85% of dermal collagen is type I, whereas only 15% is type III. In early scar formation, type III is synthesized. During maturation of the scar, type III collagen is replaced by type I collagen until the normal adult ratio is reestablished. In hypertrophic scars, replacement of type III collagen with type I collagen is delayed or absent.

Collagenase activity in keloids has been found to be normal or increased. The accumulation of fibrous tissue could result from altered digestion. Collagenase is inhibited by alpha-2-macroglobulin and alpha-1-antitrypsin. Immunofluorescence studies have shown accumulation of these substances in keloidal tissue. Some researchers have also suggested that the increased concentration of chrondoitin-4-sulfate may prevent collagenase digestion.

An immunologic derangement may also be responsible, in part, for keloid formation. Tissue immunoglobulin is present in greater quantities in keloids than in normal skin or scar tissue, and is also found elevated in hypertrophic burn scars. Antibody-antigen interaction could stimulate a chronic inflammatory response that enhances fibroblast proliferation and collagen deposition.

Other studies have shown elevated testosterone binding in keloids, suggesting that a localized hyperandrogen metabolism may contribute to the formation of keloids. Estrogens have also been implicated in the pathogenesis of keloids because of the observation of exacerbations during pregnancy and resolution during menopause.

The **treatment** of a true keloid can be a long-term and difficult management problem. Regardless of the technique used, an observation and treatment period of at least 2 years is necessary to effectively limit the chance and degree of recurrence. No single modality alone is likely to be effective in managing most keloids. Surgical excision of keloids alone has been associated with a high recurrence rate. It is important that the actual excision be performed atraumatically. The wound closure should include eversion of the wound edges by use of a vertical mattress suture and use of inert, nonabsorbable material. Postsurgical therapy must include an adjunctive therapy such as compression, intralesional steroids, or radiotherapy.

Intralesional corticosteroid therapy has been used as a sole treatment modality or in conjunction with surgery or other techniques. Corticosteroids are felt to act both by decreasing collagen synthesis and by increasing collagen degradation through reducing the levels of collagenase inhibitors such as alpha-2-macroglobulin and alpha-1-antitrypsin. When used in conjunction with surgery, presurgical intralesional injection of triamcinolone diacetate 40 mg/cc at least 1 month prior to the procedure is advocated, along with injection at the wound edges at the time of surgery. The patient should then be followed and injected monthly for more than 6 months. Care must be taken to inject the steroid directly into the firm scar tissue. If the steroid is injected into soft subcutaneous tissue below the keloid, atrophy and hypopigmentation of normal tissues will result.

Pressure is another adjunctive modality that is particularly useful after surgery for earlobe keloids. It has been found that pressure can restore the patency of the microvasculature lumina that are partially occluded in hypertrophic scars. It is interesting to speculate that hypoxia secondary to occluded microvasculature lumen may account for the formation of hypertrophic scars. Other speculations for the effectiveness of pressure in treatment of keloids include the possibility that the more linearly organized fibroblasts may deposit collagen in a more organized manner or that focal degeneration of selected cells occurs secondary to anoxia brought about by total microvascular occlusion. Effective pressure devices and garments include surgical compression earrings, polyurethane sponges, nylon compression suits, corsets, foam splints, Jobst compression garments, and polymethylmethacrylate molded splints, and are used continuously for at least 2 years following surgical excision.

In the past, radiotherapy has been used with total doses ranging from 1500 to 2000 rads. The best results have been obtained when radiotherapy was used early in the postoperative period. Radiotherapy probably exerts some inhibitory effect on both fibroplasia and endothelial vascular budding. However, because of the complications of cutaneous or thyroid cancer seen up to 20 years after exposure, this modality is not currently used frequently. It probably, however, should be considered more often for particularly troublesome keloids.

Cryotherapy has also been used, but it is not generally recommended for darkly pigmented skin, because of the complication of hypopigmentation. Cryotherapy has been used with a linear probe to treat keloids following thyroidectomy, cholecystectomy, or suprapubic incisions. The results may be improved with the adjuvant use of intralesional corticosteroids.

The carbon dioxide laser has been used in treating keloids. It is primarily effective as a debulking tool. Regrowth of the keloid is almost universal if the patient is followed for more than 2 years. Postoperative management with pressure devices and intralesional corticosteroids may delay and minimize recurrence. The argon laser has also been used, but the results have been disappointing. The neodymium:YAG laser selectively suppresses collagen production in keloid fibroblast cultures. Very few patients have been treated with this modality, and none have been reported with adequate long-term follow-up.

Other novel approaches have been tried. Several pharmacologic agents may prove efficacious in treatment. These include colchicine, which retards fibroblast collagen secretion, enhances collagenase activity, and thus inhibits wound contraction. Beta-aminopropionitile irreversibly inhibits lysyl oxidase and prevents subsequent collagen cross-linking. High doses of D-penicillamine produce a similar effect by chelating copper. Systemic use of these agents may retard excess collagen deposition, but they may also have unwanted effects on systemic collagen metabolism. Antineoplastic agents, such as nitrogen mustard, thiotepa, and methotrexate, have also been used, and many patients have experienced improvement. One study reported that topical retinoic acid improved the itch, size, and coloration of keloids and hypertrophic scars. It was hypothesized that retinoic acid inhibited the DNA synthesis in fibroblasts. Other studies noted improvement with asiatic acid (Madecassol), which is thought to interfere with the metabolism of fibroblasts; tetrahydroquinone; intralesional interferon; and zinc oxide, which may inhibit lysyl oxidase and/or stimulate collagenase. One of the newest forms of treatment is a silicone gel sheeting that is used as a dressing, applied without compression to a thickened scar. The sheeting may induce appropriate orientation of collagen bundles, assisting degradation and remodeling.

Abergel RP, Pizzuro D, Meeker CA, et al.: Biochemical composition of the connective tissue in keloids and analysis of collagen metabolism in keloid fibroblast cultures. *J Invest Dermatol.* 1985;84:384–390.
Excellent study of the connective tissue composition of keloids.
Brown LA, Pierce HE: Keloids: scar revision. *J Dermatol Surg Oncol.* 1986;12:51–56.

Review of a number of conventional and new therapeutic approaches in the management of keloids and scars.

Datubo-Brown DD: Keloids: a review of the literature. *Br J Plast Surg.* 1990;43:70–77.

Well-referenced current article reviewing treatment in an up-to-date fashion.

de Castro JLC, dos Santos AP, Cardoso JPM, et al.: Cryosurgical treatment of a large keloid. *J Dermatol Surg Oncol.* 1986;12:740–742.

Successful treatment of a keloid with cryotherapy.

Kanzler MH: Basic mechanisms in the healing cutaneous wound. *J Dermatol Surg Oncol.* 1986;12:1156–1164.

Excellent summary of wound healing.

Mercer NS: Silicone gel in the treatment of keloid scars. *Br J Plast Surg.* 1989;42:83–87.

Silicone gel sheeting was applied to 22 scars in 18 patients with improvement in texture, color, and volume at 6 months.

Murray JC, Pollack SV, Pinnell SR, et al.: Keloids: a review. *J Am Acad Dermatol.* 1981;4:461–470.

An excellent overall summary of keloids.

Peacock EE: Pharmacologic control of surface scarring in human beings. *Ann Surg.* 1981;193:592–597.

Control of surface scarring by the use of colchicine, penicillamine, and beta-aminopropionitrile.

Sallstrom KO, Larson O, Heden P, et al.: Treatment of keloids with surgical excision and postoperative x-ray radiation. *Scand J Plast Reconstr Surg.* 1989;23:211–215.

One hundred twenty-four patients had keloids treated with surgical excision followed by postoperative x-ray radiation begun within 24 hours after surgery. In 92% of patients, there was improvement noted at follow-up in 6 months and 24 months.

Soderberg T, Hallmans G, Bartholdson L: Treatment of keloids and hypertrophic scars with adhesive zinc tape. *Scand J Plast Reconstr Surg.* 1982;16:261–266.

Treatment of 41 patients with occlusive zinc tape for 6 months.

Uitto J, Murray LW, Blumberg B. Shamban A: UCLA conference: Biochemistry of collagen in diseases. *Ann Intern Med.* 1986;105:740–756.

Review of the latest discoveries in the biochemistry of collagen, highlighting some disease entities in which definitive information in molecular alterations in collagen is available.

48. BENIGN TUMORS

Jerome D. Fallon and Michael E. Bigby

Benign tumors may arise from virtually every tissue present in the skin. Benign-appearing tumors may actually be malignant or may be indicators of systemic illnesses. The ability to accurately diagnose and manage benign tumors is, therefore, important. This chapter will include a brief discussion of frequently occurring and medically significant tumors.

Epidermal nevi are thin plaques that have a characteristic verrucous surface. The color ranges from normal skin color to dark brown or black. They are often arranged in linear configurations that follow Blashko's lines. Epidermal nevi are present at birth or arise in early infancy. Extensive epidermal nevi may rarely be associated with congenital nervous system and skeletal system defects. The differential diagnosis of epidermal nevi includes nevus sebaceous, seborrheic keratoses, warts, and the shagreen patch of tuberous sclerosis. Diagnosis can be established with a biopsy that reveals acanthosis, hyperkeratosis, papillomatosis, and elongation of the rete ridges.

While epidermal nevi can be treated by many modalities, including surgical excision, carbon dioxide laser, dermabrasion, and cryotherapy, recurrences of the epidermal nevus at the site are common. The patient's desire for treatment often diminishes when the benign and stable nature of these tumors is explained.

Seborrheic keratoses appear in adults as acquired plaques, tumors, or papules that have a verrucous surface. They range in color from yellow to dark brown or black. They occur most commonly on the trunk but may appear anywhere. The superficial nature of these keratoses gives them their distinctive "stuck on" appearance. These tumors may be mistaken for malignant melanomas, basal cell carcinomas, nevi, or warts. Actinic keratoses and early squamous cell carcinomas may also appear similar but usually have a thin red plaque with an irregular surface and sandpaper-like scale. Any question about diagnosis should be resolved by a biopsy to avoid unnecessary surgery. Specimens obtained by punch biopsy, shave biopsy, or curretage are usually adequate for histopathologic examination. Liquid nitrogen cryotherapy or curretage is effective therapy.

The onset of numerous generalized seborrheic keratoses has been described in several patients as a sign of an underlying malignancy (the sign of Leser and Trélat). There is some evidence that this sign may be due to production of epidermal growth factors by the tumor. This phenomenon has been described with a variety of internal malignancies including lung, breast, and colon tumors.

Keratoacanthoma is a tumor composed of hyperplastic epithelium, manifested by a rapidly growing dome- or bud-shaped nodule, most often found on sun-exposed skin of elderly patients. The mature lesion displays a central plug of keratin surrounded by a scaly, erythematous, rolled border. The tumor is most commonly solitary. Rare cases of multiple or recurring, giant, superficial, or subungual keratoacanthomas have been reported. The typical behavior of these tumors is marked by rapid growth over 2 to 4 weeks, usually followed by spontaneous regression in 2 months to 1 year.

It is frequently difficult to differentiate keratoacanthoma from squamous cell carcinoma, both clinically and histopathologically. The pathologic distinction is made principally on the basis of the architecture of the lesion (i.e., a cup shaped tumor that is surrounded by a collar of hyperplastic epithelium and evidences no invasion of malignant cells through the basement membrane). Other findings usually present include elimination of elastic fibers, lack of extension below eccrine glands, large, atypical epithelial cells with glassy cytoplasm, and intraepithelial microabscesses. A biopsy of the lesion should therefore be fusiform (wedge) and include sides, center, and enough depth to include subcutaneous fat below the tumor. Alternatively, an excisional biopsy with narrow margins can also be performed.

Once a firm diagnosis of keratoacanthoma has been made on the basis of clinical features and pathologic examination, many methods for managing the tumor have been successfully employed, including excision, curretage and electrodesiccation, radiation therapy, cryotherapy, and topical and intalesional fluorouracil. Rare, carefully selected lesions may be left untreated but should be closely followed to insure that they regress completely. Those lesions that cannot be distinguished from squamous cell carcinoma, and lesions whose behavior is not typical for keratoacanthomas should be treated like squamous cell carcinomas (i.e., with total excision or radiation therapy).

Cutaneous horns appear as hard, conical, hornlike projections. They have a predilection for sun-exposed skin in the elderly. The cutaneous horn is a clinical description of the tumor and is not a diagnosis. Cutaneous horns may be due to hypertrophic actinic keratoses, squamous cell carcinomas, seborrheic keratoses, or warts. Diagnosis can be made by a biopsy, which must include the base of the lesion, preferably to a depth that extends well into the dermis. Therapy is determined by the underlying etiology of the horn.

Epidermal cysts and **milia** are slowly growing, soft, round papules or nodules within normal surrounding skin. They represent entrapment of epidermal cells within the epidermis. They are distributed primarily on the face, neck, and back, and they exhibit no age or sex predilection. Milia are miniature epidermal cysts lying in the superficial epidermis. They are often multiple and may follow acute or chronic UV exposure or may develop during the healing of surgical wounds or bullous lesions.

Epidermal cysts are commonly and erroneously called sebaceous cysts. Large epidermal cysts may rupture into the surrounding tissue, forming large, tender, warm, erythematous nodules. The inflammation is most likely due to a brisk inflammatory response to the keratinaceous material found in the cyst, and only rarely involves pathogenic bacteria. These inflamed lesions respond well to incision and drainage; antibiotic therapy is only rarely required if pathogenic bacteria are present. Surgical excision in toto may be undertaken when all evidence of inflammation has resolved. Epidermal cysts and milia may be removed for cosmetic reasons or to prevent recurrence or rupture.

Appendageal tumors arise from adnexal tissue and are many in number and myriad in morphology. They can originate from any appendageal structure, including hair follicles, sebaceous glands, and apocrine and eccrine sweat glands. Many of the tumors in this group are rare.

Some appendageal tumors occur as part of inherited or acquired syndromes associated with cancer. **Cowden's disease** is an autosomal dominant disorder characterized by the presence of multiple trichilemmomas on the face, by a high prevalence of breast carcinoma in females, and by thyroid and gastrointestinal cancer in males and females. Trichilemmomas are flesh-colored papules that have no distinctive clinical features that allow for recognition. The diagnosis is therefore made by pathologic examination. Other cutaneous features of Cowden's disease are oral mucosal papules that have a cobblestone-like appearance, multiple other benign epithelial and appendageal tumors, such as flat warts, and tumors of follicular infundibulum, in a generalized distribution. Bilateral prophylactic mastectomies should be carefully considered for women with a definitive personal and family history of Cowden's disease.

The **Muir-Torre syndrome** describes a disease in which sebaceous adenomas occur in association with multiple visceral carcinomas. Patients with other sebaceous gland tumors and multiple keratoacanthomas have also been described. Associated visceral carcinomas include those of the colon, stomach, duodenum, kidney, ureter, uterus, and respiratory tract.

Trichilemmal (pilar) cysts represent the second most common type of intracutaneous cyst. Clinically, trichilemmal and epidermal cysts are indistinguishable, although trichilemmal cysts occur most commonly in the scalp. Affected individuals often have a family history of multiple cysts. Histologically, trichilemmal cysts are recognized by their lack of a granular layer, reflecting their follicular origin. If treatment is desired, they may be excised in toto.

Trichoepithelioma is a tumor of pilar origin and presents as a flesh-colored papule on the face. Solitary lesions appear in adults and must be distinguished from basal cell carcinomas, fibrous papules, nevi, and sebaceous hyperplasia. Multiple trichoepitheliomas occur as an inherited autosomal dominant trait and appear often in children as multiple nasolabial tumors that may clinically resemble adenoma sebaceum and neurofibromatosis. Multiple trichoepitheliomas show a high frequency of recurrence when treated.

Nevus sebaceous presents as a hairless, yellow, verrucous plaque on the scalp of infants. The predominant histopathologic feature is atypical sebaceous hyperplasia, often associated with epidermal and apocrine hyperplasia. Other benign and malignant tumors may arise within a nevus sebaceous, and the tumor is associated with the later development of basal cell carcinoma in 25% of cases. Complete surgical excision, if possible, is advised by most authors.

Discrete papules of **sebaceous hyperplasia** appear on the face of older patients as solitary or multiple yellow to flesh-colored tumors 2 to 5 mm in diameter with a lobulated appearance and a central depression. Because of the appearance and distribution, these papules must be distinguished from basal cell carcinomas. Sebaceous hyperplasia may be excised in toto with minimal margins of normal appearing skin. Histopathologic examination reveals only hyperplastic sebaceous glands. These lesions are not thought to predispose to cutaneous malignancy.

Tumors arising from structures in the **dermis** are also numerous and common. Any cell type may predominate. The tumors may be solitary or they may be multiple and a manifestation of a congenital disorder.

Acrochordae, or skin tags, are very common, soft, flesh-colored polyps composed of loose dermal stroma covered by rugose epidermis. They occur most commonly on the neck, in the axillae, and in the groin. They may be confused with neurofibromas or dermal nevi. Questionable lesions should be considered for histologic evaluation. Management is by shave or scissor excision or electrosurgery. A purported association of acrochordae with colonic polyps has been claimed by several investigators, but the current weight of evidence suggests that this association is not justifiable.

Dermatofibromas are very common, solitary or multiple, discrete, round, firm, brown or purple papules or nodules distributed primarily on the extremities. They may be dome shaped or flat topped, and vary in size from 3 to less than 10 mm in diameter. They may lie above, level with, or below the epidermis and generally exhibit dimpling on lateral pressure. Histopathologically, lesions are fibrohistiocytic tumors associated with a hyperplastic epidermis. Treatment is excision in toto, but is rarely necessary because of their slow growth and benign behavior. Dermatofibromas must be distinguished from dermatofibrosarcoma protuberans, which are usually larger, solitary, rapidly growing, and occur most commonly on the upper trunk and shoulders. Dermatofibrosarcoma protuberans is malignant and recurs locally unless widely excised. Margin of normal skin recommended to be removed is 5 cm, and underlying fascia and thin layer of muscle must be included. Mohs surgery has also been used successfully as primary therapy.

Lipomas are very common tumors of cytologically normal subcutaneous adipose tissue surrounded by a fibrous capsule. They are round, soft tumors appearing on the trunk, neck, and arms. Subgaleal lipomas are not uncommon on the forehead or in the scalp. Given these tumors' subcutaneous location, the skin overlying lipomas looks normal and slides freely over the top of the tumor. This feature helps distinguish them from intraepidermal cysts, which are mobile but connected intimately with the epidermis. Treatment of lipomas is not necessary, but may be accomplished for cosmetic reasons by surgical excision or liposuction.

Neurofibromas are benign neoplasms of the nerve sheath. The tumors present as soft, flesh-colored papules and nodules. They typically herniate downward through an underlying cutaneous defect on vertical pressure, a phenomenon termed buttonholing. Solitary neurofibromas may be seen in normal individuals. In neurofibromatosis, multiple neurofibromas occur, and individual lesions may be large and disfiguring. The tumors may occur not only on the skin but in virtually any enervated tissue. Two pigmentary abnormalities frequently seen in neurofibromatosis are multiple café-au-lait macules and axillary freckling. While isolated café-au-lait spots occur in 10% of the normal population, multiple lesions are highly suggestive of neurofibromatosis. Axillary freckling is seen in virtually no other illnesses. The minimal necessary evaluation, if neurofibromatosis is suspected, includes a family history, and thorough examination of skin, eye (looking for Lesch nodules, which are hamartomas on the iris), and ear (looking for subtle signs of sensory neural hearing loss). Several distinct types of inheritable neurofibromatosis have been described, the most common of which are the classic von Recklinghausen's disease (type 1) and a syndrome in which acoustic neuromas or other hamartomas of the cranial nerves predominate (type 2). The genetic mutation in type 1 disease has been mapped to a distinct locus on chromosome 17, and exciting studies are underway to delineate the pathogenesis of its manifestations. Once a diagnosis of neurofibromatosis is made, genetic counseling and careful medical follow-up are essential.

Adenoma sebaceum is a misnomer, since these tumors are angiofibromas and not of adenomatous or sebaceous origin. Adenoma sebaceum is one of the triad of findings in **tuberous sclerosis**, the other two being mental retardation and seizures. Clinically, adenoma sebaceum appears as grouped erythematous or flesh-colored papules that are characteristically clustered around the nose and are also commonly found in the periungual regions of the fingers and toes. Other cutaneous manifestations of tuberous sclerosis include digital fibromas; the shagreen patch, which is a dermal proliferation of connective tissue found usually on the lower back; and multiple hypopigmented macules, often in the elongate and oval shape of an ash leaf. The ash-leaf spots are best seen on Wood's lamp examination.

Tuberous sclerosis is an autosomal dominant disorder often associated wtih CNS, renal, and cardiac tumors. Medical care of a patient with tuberous sclerosis should include a careful family history, physical and ophthalmic examinations, careful follow-up, and genetic counseling. A CT scan may allow early detection of calcified brain tumors in patients at risk for having tuberous sclerosis even prior to the appearance of characteristic skin lesions, suggestive symptoms, or x ray abnormalities.

Strawberry hemangioma is the most common tumor found in infants. Histopathologically, it is defined as a capillary hemangioma composed of excessive numbers of large capillaries arranged in lobules. A strawberry hemangioma is characteristically a red or purple nodule presenting usually on the head and neck shortly after birth. It is usually solitary, although multiple tumors are not rare. Even at a very young age, it is easily distinguished from a portwine stain, which is a variably sized, pink macule that does not develop angiomatous proliferations until adulthood. A strawberry hemangioma initially grows rapidly, but up to 85% of lesions involute spontaneously, beginning in the preschool years, and leaving a hypotrophic scar by 6 to 12 years of age. The tumor can interfere with a vital structure, bleed, ulcerate or become infected. Very large lesions may cause high output cardiac failure or platelet sequestration (Kasabach-Merritt syndrome). Many modalities have been used to treat strawberry hemangiomas. Systemic or intralesional corticosteroids may cause the lesions to shrink. Ablation by cryotherapy, electrodesiccation, or carbon dioxide or argon laser has been successful. Selective vessel embolization followed by excision has also been employed. Recently, excellent results with minimal complications have been reported in several series from different centers of children treated in infancy with the flash-lamp pulsed dye laser. These reports suggest that this laser is the treatment of choice for strawberry hemangiomas if treatment is initiated early, before the lesion is fully evolved, although early elective treatment is controversial. Some authors argue that since 85% of lesions spontaneously involute and leave minimal cosmetic defect, uncomplicated lesions should not be treated. In contrast, other authors argue that selective destruction of early lesions (i.e., before vascular proliferation and rapid growth occurs) with the flash-lamp pulsed dye laser will prevent tumor expansion and result in a significant reduction in complications as well as size of the final cosmetic defect. Controlled studies to resolve this controversy are probably not possible.

Cavernous hemangiomas, like strawberry hemangiomas, most often occur in young children and have a predilection for the head and neck. Their color varies from blue or purple for deep lesions to red for superficial lesions. Cavernous hemangiomas are composed of dilated venules and veins rather than capillaries. Cavernous lesions are also distinguished by their slow growth and lack of involution. Treatment for cosmesis and for complications is often necessary. Therapeutic modalities are the same as those used for strawberry hemangiomas. Reported results are, however, less gratifying and complete, and complications and scarring are more common.

Pyogenic granuloma is a misnamed capillary proliferation that is neither infectious nor granulomatous. The lesions are polypoid tumors usually occurring on the extremities, frequently following trauma. Pathologically, the tumors are composed of proliferating capillary tufts embedded in an edematous fibrous stroma. The tumors may grow rapidly but may also spontaneously necrose or ulcerate. The differential diagnosis includes cavernous or capillary hemangiomas, nodular melanoma, granulation tissue, and Kaposi's sarcoma. Treatment may be accomplished by surgical excision or by ablation with cryotherapy, electrodesiccation, or laser surgery (argon, CO_2, and dye lasers have all been reported to be successful). Recurrences are uncommon but may be multiple and difficult to treat.

Angiokeratomas appear as 1- to 3-mm red, hyperkeratotic papules, commonly found on the scrotum of adult men. They are usually asymptomatic, but can bleed with minimal trauma. Generalized angiokeratomas may be a manifestation of Fabry's disease, an X-linked, recessive lipid-storage disease due to a deficiency of alpha-galactosidase. In this disease, angiokeratomas are commonly found on the back, buttocks, and genitalia (angiokeratoma corpus diffusum), and are associated with episodes of pain in the hands and feet, and renal failure.

Ashinoff R, Geronemus RG: Capillary hemangiomas and treatment with the flash lamp-pumped pulsed dye laser. *Arch Dermatol.* 1991;127:202–205.
After an average of three treatments, lesions in 10 patients exhibited mean regression of 70%. Pulsed dye laser therapy should be considered as an option in the treatment of capillary hemangiomas, preferably prior to their full evolution.

Baldwin HE, Berck CM, Lynfield YL: Subcutaneous nodules of the scalp: preoperative management. *J Am Acad Dermatol.* 1991;25:819–830.
Although the vast majority of scalp nodules are benign and may be diagnosed as epidermal inclusion cysts or lipomas, the differential diagnosis includes dermoid cysts, metastases, and extensions of intracranial tumors or cysts. Important features and a schema for workup are presented in detail.

Burkhart CG, El Shaar A: Computerized axial tomography in the early diagnosis of tuberous sclerosis. *J Am Acad Dermatol.* 1981;4:59–63.
A CT scan used in young patients may prove positive prior to other diagnostic clinical findings.

Crowe FW, Schull WJ, Neel JV: *A Clinical, Pathological, and Genetic Study of Multiple Neurofibromatoses.* Springfield, IL: Charles C. Thomas; 1986:1–181.
An often-cited and authoritative text on neurofibromatosis. This text established the standard of enumerating café-au-lait macules and describes the "buttonholing" of neurofibromas.

Mallory SB, Stough DB: Genodermatoses with malignant potential. *Dermatol Clin.* 1987;5:221–230.
Cowden's syndrome is reviewed.

Mulliken JB, Young AE: *Vascular Birthmarks: Hemangiomas and Malformations.* Philadelphia, PA: W.B. Saunders; 1988:1–462.
Comprehensive text emphasizing classification and treatment. Includes excellent illustrations and entertaining historical background.

Riccardi VM: Neurofibromatosis: past, present, and future. *N Engl J Med.* 1991;324:1283–1285.
An editorial reviewing current knowledge of the genetics of neurofibromatosis and the exciting hypotheses concerning pathogenesis.

Riccardi VM, Eichner JE: *Neurofibromatosis. Phenotype, Natural History, Pathogenesis.* Baltimore, MD: Johns Hopkins University Press; 1986:3–301.
A comprehensive review by a recognized authority on the subject, including a new classification scheme.

Robinson JK: Dermatofibrosarcoma protuberans resected by Mohs' surgery. *J Am Acad Dermatol.* 1985;12:1093–1098.
Report of four cases treated by Mohs' surgery and followed for five years without evidence of recurrence.

IX. ADVERSE REACTIONS TO ENVIRONMENTAL FACTORS

49. PHOTOSENSITIVITY
Richard J. Sharpe and Jeffrey S. Dover

Exposure to light causes a wide variety of photosensitive disorders by many different mechanisms. Some dermatoses are photoaggravated dermatoses (i.e., light aggravates but does not cause the disorder), while others are primary photosensitivity disorders that would not develop without sun exposure. For example, cutaneous herpes simplex infection occurs without light but an acute herpetic blister can be triggered by sunlight. Polymorphous light eruption, however, does not occur without sun exposure.

Light energy (electromagnetic radiation) commonly encountered at the earth's surface represents a continuum from radio waves to UV waves. Radio waves, at the intensities normally encountered, have no known significant biologic effect. The other wavelengths, however, have numerous photobiologic effects. The action spectrum of a photosensitivity disorder is defined as the wavelength range that produces the reaction. Infrared radiation (wavelengths 800 to 1,000,000 nm) is felt as heat and can cause thermal burns. Visible light (wavelengths 400 to 700 nm) is rarely implicated in photosensitivity. The UV spectrum is arbitrarily divided into UVA, UVB, and UVC wavelength ranges. The UVA (wavelengths 320 to 400 nm) and UVB (wavelengths 290 to 320 nm) bands are the primary inducers of most photosensitivity reactions, the action spectra of which are sometimes specific for the disorder or sometimes specific only for a certain individual. The UVB band is almost completely absorbed by ordinary window glass, but the UVA is not. The UVC band is the region of the shortest wavelength in the UV spectrum (wavelengths 200 to 290 nm) and is essentially completely absorbed by the ozone layer, so that little or no UVC radiation reaches the earth's surface. This may change if the human race continues to cause depletion of the ozone layer.

Effective evaluation of the photosensitive patient includes a history and physical examination. The history should supply such information as the age at which the photosensitive reaction first occurred, the temporal relationship between sun exposure and the eruption, the duration of the eruption, the nature of associated symptoms, the relationship to potential photosensitizers including medications the patient has recently taken, and a family history. Conditions that can mimic photodermatoses by occurring on primarily sun-exposed surfaces—such as arthropod bites, primary irritant dermatitis (such as that caused by solvents), and allergic contact dermatitis—can usually be eliminated with a thorough history. In performing the physical examination, the observer must pay particular attention to the distribution of the eruption, in addition to its morphology. Regions of the body that receive relatively less ambient light are typically less involved in a photodistributed reaction. Classic photodermatoses involve the forehead, malar region, nose, rims of the ears, sides and back of the neck, V of the chest, and extensor surfaces of the distal extremities. Areas of partial sparing are also very important diagnostically. They usually include the area below the alae nasae, the submental region, Wilkinson's triangle (the shaded triangle behind each ear), the recessed area of the eyelids, the back of the neck, the nasolabial line, the web spaces of the fingers, and skin that is covered by fixed jewelry such as a watch band. Sunbathing habits and other clues, such as whether an individual drives a car with one arm on the window ledge of a rolled-down window, should be used in determining whether lesions are photodistributed.

Evaluation or treatment of the photosensitive patient may be aided by phototesting. The patient is exposed to various doses of light at wavelengths including the visible, UVA, UVB, and UVC bands at different sites on the skin. Test sites are evaluated at 5 and 30 minutes and at 24 and 48 hours for erythema, edema, papules, and vesicles. The range of wavelengths (action spectrum) and dose of light that produce the biologic response (erythema, edema, papules or vesicles) can therefore be determined. If a photoallergic or phototoxic process is suspected, the testing procedures are modified to include systemic administration of a drug or topical application of a photoallergen or photosensitizer.

Sunburn (UV erythema), primarily due to UVB, which reaches the earth's surface in abundance, is one of the most common reactions to light. Such erythema becomes visible 2 to 6 hours following exposure and reaches a maximum at 24 to 72 hours. The erythema then typically fades over 3 to 5 days and is followed by increased skin pigmentation (tanning) in most individuals. After intense exposure, the erythema may be associated with blistering, similar to that of a second-degree thermal burn. Large amounts of UVA also reach the earth's surface, but it has little or no role in this process because the dose required to produce erythema in human skin is 100 to 1000 times greater than that contained in natural sunlight. However, high-intensity artificial UVA sources encountered in tanning booths can induce erythema and melanogenesis. Erythema can occasionally be caused by UVC, generally in laboratory workers exposed to germicidal lighting.

The pain associated with a severe sunburn can be blunted with nonsteroidal anti-inflammatory drugs such as aspirin and indomethacin. Nonblistering sunburn reactions can also be treated topically with bland emollients such as hydrated petrolatum or potent topical steroids that induce vasoconstriction and sometimes reduce patient discomfort. Blistering sunburn reactions should be treated as second-degree thermal burns with topical silver sulfadiazine cream or topical antibiotic ointments. Sunburn is more easily prevented than treated. Recommendations include wearing protective hats and clothing, avoiding outdoor activities between 10:00 a.m. and 2:00 p.m., and using sunscreens with a sun protection factor (SPF) of at least 15 liberally. The SPF measures the ability of the sunscreen to filter out erythemogenic solar irradiation and is defined as the minimal dose of light required to produce erythema in protected skin divided by the minimal erythema dose in unprotected skin.

Sunlight-induced carcinogenesis is currently thought to be due primarily to UVB exposure with some probable, as yet undefined, participation by UVA. Cutaneous basal cell and squamous cell carcinomas as well as melanomas are correlated with sun exposure. Nonmelanoma skin cancers appear to arise secondary to chronic, cumulative sun exposure, while repeated intense exposures are implicated as a primary risk factor for melanoma. The mechanism of UV carcinogenesis is complex but probably involves direct mutagenic effects, mutagenesis in conjunction with co-carcinogens or viruses (e.g., certain human papillomavirus subtypes), and induction of immune tolerance to tumor-associated antigens. Fair-skinned individuals and immunologically suppressed individuals are particularly susceptible. The best "treatment" is routine daily prevention of excessive exposure to sunlight.

Polymorphous light eruption (PMLE) is a pruritic eruption that usually develops 1 to 72 hours following sun exposure and lasts days to weeks. As its name implies, PMLE can have various morphologies. The most common cutaneous lesions of PMLE are papules; but macular erythema, plaques, vesicles and eczematous plaques also occur. Despite this wide variation in type of lesion, the morphology is usually constant in a given individual. Lesions are primarily but not exclusively confined to sun-exposed body areas. Thirty percent to fifty percent of patients with PMLE develop their most severe eruptions after the first several sun exposures of the spring or summer. Subsequent sun exposures, however, lead to progressively less reaction in this subset of patients, so that by the middle of the summer many of these individuals develop no eruption whatsoever. This type of photosensitivity affects up to 10% of the population, is more common in females, and usually has its onset before age 30. The diagnosis is most often made on clinical grounds. Phototesting is helpful only rarely, since PMLE may be caused by light in the visible, UVA, or UVB wavelength ranges. If performed, appropriate phototesting involves all of these ranges of light at multiple doses in different sites. A biopsy of involved skin, whether the eruption is induced naturally or by phototesting, may substantiate the diagnosis. An antinuclear antibody titer is often obtained to help exclude the possibility of photosensitivity associated with systemic lupus erythematosus.

Protective clothing in combination with broad-spectrum sunscreens and avoidance of solar radiation is the treatment of choice for PMLE. Short courses of high-potency topical corticosteroids may be helpful in relieving symptoms associated with established eruptions. Systemic corticosteroids can be useful in preventing and treating PMLE, but potential toxicities limit their long-term and frequent use. Similarly, antimalarials are useful agents for prevention and possible treatment of the PMLE response but have potentially serious toxicities. One strategy that may minimize risk and optimize the benefit of both systemic corticosteroids and antimalarials is to use them as prophylaxis prior to spring or a holiday involving known exposure to sunlight. Another treatment approach depends on the known ability of many PMLE patients to become less photosensitive over a course of increasing dose and frequency of sunlight exposure. By exposing patients to gradually increasing doses of UVB or PUVA (psoralen plus UVA) beginning 4 to 8 weeks prior to the onset of spring, tolerance to natural sunlight is possible in many patients.

Drug-induced photosensitivity may result from phototoxicity or photoallergy. In phototoxicity, both light and a topically or systemically administered drug must be present locally to cause tissue damage. Phototoxic eruptions usually occur only on sun-exposed sites. They have varied clinical features but frequently resemble a sunburn that has become eczematous. A wide variety of compounds have been implicated in phototoxic eruptions—including dyes, coal tar derivatives, furocoumarins such as psoralens (in limes, fragrances, and moldy celery), and drugs such as the tetracyclines, phenothiazines, sulfonamides, thiazides and amiodarone. The best therapy for drug-induced phototoxicity is discontinuation of the offending compound. However, if a drug necessary for the patient's well-being is implicated and if the photosensitivity is mild, avoidance of sun exposure and the use of sunscreens may be adequate. If sunscreens are to be used effectively, determination of the action spectrum of the photosensitivity reaction may be useful. Usually the action spectrum of the reaction is in the UVA range, and a sunscreen that absorbs the UVA range as well as the UVB should be chosen. If the reaction has an action spectrum that includes visible light, then an opaque screen should be used in conjunction with protective clothing. Readily available opaque screens usually contain zinc oxide, titanium dioxide, or coloring pigments (e.g., Clinique Continuous Coverage).

Photoallergy is much less common than phototoxicity. The mechanism in photoallergy is similar to T-cell–mediated contact dermatitis. The "antigen" is probably a drug-protein conjugate whose formation is enhanced by light, or a drug-protein conjugate that is altered by light to become antigenic. Phenothiazines, quinidine, halogenated salicylanilides (in deodorant soaps), para-aminobenzoic acid (in sunscreens), and musk ambrette (in after-shave lotion) have been implicated in photoallergic reactions. Optimal therapy for this type of disorder is discontinuation of the offending agent; however, response may be slow because even minute quantities of residual drug-protein conjugate can be responsible for continued photoallergy.

Solar urticaria develops within seconds to minutes following sun exposure and subsequently resolves over minutes to hours. The mechanism of this response may involve direct stimulation of vasoactive mediator release or an indirect effect involving immunoglobulin E. Clinically, pruritic, edematous, erythematous plaques (urticarial plaques) occur and often times coalesce and assume bizarre forms. Rarely, solar urticaria may be associated with systemic anaphylaxis. Urticarial plaques are almost never present at the time of examination. Diagnosis, therefore, is based on the extremely short lag time between exposure and the onset of the eruption. It can be confirmed with phototesting. The action spectrum of solar urticaria may involve the visible, UVA, UVB, or UVC wavelengths.

Protective clothing, sunscreens, corticosteroids, and nonsteroidal anti-inflammatory drugs are of little utility in treating solar urticaria. Antimalarials and beta-carotene provide variable and unpredictable results. Antihistamines appear to delay the onset and limit the severity of the urticarial reaction in a subset of individuals. Desensitization is the treatment of choice. After determining the action spectrum, the clinician then exposes the patient to increasing doses of light at that wavelength over several weeks.

Chronic actinic dermatitis (CAD), also known as photosensitivity dermatitis or as actinic reticuloid, is a chronic form of photosensitivity with no known spontaneous remissions. Elderly males are most commonly affected, developing a slowly progressive dermatitis in sun-exposed sites that often eventually involves unexposed areas. The spectrum of disease ranges from mild UVB sensitivity to severe photosensitivity involving UVB, UVA, and visible light, and may prevent patients from venturing out of doors during daylight hours. Patients with chronic actinic dermatitis often have positive patch and photopatch tests to many allergens.

In the actinic reticuloid variant, atypical lymphoid and histiocytic cells may be seen on a biopsy. The degree of atypia may be so great that the condition is misdiagnosed as lymphoma. The pathogenesis of this disease may be understood soon on a cellular level. Researchers currently hypothesize that a clone or clones of lymphocytes appear that are particularly responsive to epidermal cytokines, such as epidermal thymocyte activating factor (ETAF, IL-1). Sunlight is known to enhance the release of these cytokines, which may then activate the atypical lymphocytes and cause them to migrate to the epidermis. Alternatively, sunlight may enhance expressions of adhesion receptors, such as ICAM or ELAM, in the skin of these individuals, and this may be the basis of the migration into the skin of activated lymphocytes expressing complementary adhesion receptors.

Complete sun avoidance, protective garb, and sunscreens are essentials of treatment. Induction of tolerance with PUVA therapy and immunosuppression with azathioprine are also effective.

The **porphyrias** are a group of diseases in which porphyrin-heme biosynthesis is altered in such a way that porphyrins accumulate at the site of the biochemical defect, generally in erythropoietic tissues or in the liver and skin. Porphyrins deposited in the skin cause tissue injury when activated by 400-nm light (UVA range) through interaction with water and lipids in the presence of oxygen to form peroxides that damage cell membranes.

Cutaneous manifestations may occur in all porphyrias except acute intermittent porphyria. Porphyria cutaneous tarda (PCT), the most common of the disorders, is caused by a deficiency of uroporphyrin decarboxylase, clinically significant when a patient is chronically exposed to ethanol, exogenous estrogens, iron, hexachlorobenzene, polychlorinated biphenyls, chlorinated phenols, and tetracholorodibenzo-paradoxin. Human immunodeficiency virus infection may be associated with the development of PCT. Early clinical manifestations in PCT include hypertrichosis, increased skin fragility with bullae formation, and hyperpigmentation of sun-exposed sites, usually the face and the dorsa of the hands. Late in PCT, sclerodermoid changes, scarring, and milia formation become prominent. Iron overload is the prominent systemic feature. Diabetes mellitus occasionally occurs, and in rare instances hepatomas develop. Patients with variegate porphyria (VP) have identical cutaneous findings but also develop acute abdominal pain and neuropsychiatric crises that can be avoided if the disease is accurately identified.

Patients with PCT and VP are often unaware that sunlight plays a role in producing their lesions since there is no acute photosensitivity reaction; they may, however, note that their skin condition worsens in the spring and summer. In contrast, acute severe photosensitivity with pain and blistering, resolving over years with mutilating scars, occurs in erythropoietic porphyria. Acute but less severe photosensitivity is also seen in erythropoietic protoporphyria. Acute intermittent porphyria is caused by porphyrin metabolites that are not photosensitizing; it has no cutaneous manifestations. The term *pseudoporphyria* is used to describe a skin disease with increased skin fragility and blistering that resolves with scarring and milia and histologically resembles PCT. The condition may or may not be associated with abnormal porphyrin metabolism and generally occurs in patients who are undergoing hemodialysis or who are on medications such as nalidixic acid, furosemide, or tetracycline. Accurate diagnosis and classification of the porphyrias involve testing the blood, urine, and feces for various intermediates and enzymes present in the heme biosynthetic pathway.

The best treatment for PCT is strict avoidance of exacerbating agents, including sunlight and alcohol. Second-line therapies are phlebotomy, low-dose chloroquine, or both. Other agents such as iron chelators and oral cholestyramine may be somewhat effective.

Xeroderma pigmentosa is a group of autosomal recessive disorders associated with excessive sunburn reactions to minimal light, with early onset of freckling, and with severe actinic damage. The major defect in XP is inability to correctly repair UVB-induced defects in DNA. Affected individuals commonly develop myriad skin cancers, usually basal cell carcinomas and squamous cell carcinomas, but also melanomas. The defective DNA repair mechanism in these patients has been implicated as causing or contributing to other manifestations: deafness, progressive mental deterioration, photophobia, conjunctivitis, and UV keratitis. Death usually occurs in the second or third decade. The cornerstone of managing XP involves early diagnosis and protection from UV irradiation. Potent sunscreens (SPF 30 or greater) combined with restricted sun exposure and protective garb can reduce actinic damage to the skin. The eyes of XP patients should be constantly protected with wraparound UV-absorbing glasses. In addition, cutaneous neoplasms should be detected and treated as early as possible.

A large number of rare or incompletely described processes are also associated with photosensitivity. **Hydroa vacciniforme** is an extremely rare photodermatosis that first presents in late infancy or early childhood. The action spectrum is in the UVA range; natural or artificial UVA exposure results in vesicles that heal with chickenpox-like scarring. **Bloom's syndrome** is an autosomally recessive disease associated with a high frequency of chromosomal rearrangements and breaks. Patients with this disorder are prone to a host of internal malignancies. The increased risk of photocarcinogenesis seen in Bloom's syndrome is probably related to defective DNA repair mechanisms. **Rothmund-Thomson syndrome** is a rare, hereditary oculocutaneous photosensitivity disorder with an increased risk of cancer and cutaneous poikiloderma. **Pellagra** is a photodermatitis caused by niacin deficiency. Intake of isoniazid, a niacin analogue, can also cause a similar photodermatitis. **Hartnup's disease** is a photosensitivity disorder characterized by a defect in the transport of neutral charge alpha-amino acids. The mechanism behind this pellagra-like photodermatitis may be reduced synthesis of niacin.

Many cutaneous and systemic disorders, including systemic lupus erythematosus, pemphigus, erythema multiforme, and herpes simplex infection, are photoaggravated. In addition, acne, atopic dermatitis, lichen planus, and psoriasis are exacerbated by sun exposure in some patients. In **systemic lupus erythematosus,** photosensitivity may be the presenting complaint and is found in about 30% of cases. Discoid lupus erythematosus is occasionally exacerbated by sun exposure, and lesions commonly occur in light-exposed skin. The mechanism by which light exacerbates lupus erythematosus is not fully known. UV-irradiated DNA is a good immunogen, while nonirradiated DNA is not. Thus, alterations of DNA by UV light might influence the autoimmune features of lupus erythematosus. An alternative hypothesis is that keratinocyte cytokine production is altered in such a way as to boost the autoimmune response. Most sun-induced exacerbations of systemic lupus erythematosus are limited to cutaneous disease; however, in a small subset of patients, intense sun exposure may cause the systemic disease to flare. The action spectrum of disease exacerbation is in the UVB band; therefore, UVB sunscreens in conjunction with prudent sun avoidance are useful adjuncts to therapy.

Bickers DR: Sun-induced disorders. *Emerg Med Clin N Am.* 1985;3:659–676.
  A practical, clinically oriented review of common photosensitivity disorders.
Cohen PR, Suarez SM, DeLeo VA: Porphyria cutanea tarda in human immunodeficiency virus-infected patients. *JAMA.* 1990;264:1315–1316.
  HIV infection appears to predispose to the development of PCT either by affecting porphyrin metabolism directly or by causing a hepatopathy.
Cripps DJ: Natural and artificial photoprotection. *J Invest Dermatol.* 1981;76:154–157.
  Basics of sun protection clearly and concisely reviewed.
Epstein JH: Polymorphous light eruption. *J Am Acad Dermatol.* 1980;3:329–343.
  A comprehensive review of polymorphous light eruption, phototoxicity and phototesting.
Epstein JH: Phototoxicity and photoallergy in man. *J Am Acad Dermatol.* 1983;8:141–147.
  Both basic and practical aspects of these entities are discussed in the review.
Epstein JH, Wintroub BU: Photosensitivity due to drugs. *Drugs.* 1985;30:42–57.
  An excellent review of phototoxic and photoallergic reactions induced by drugs, including a discussion of clinical presentations and mechanisms.
Frain-Bell W: *Cutaneous photobiology.* Oxford: Oxford University Press; 1985.

A comprehensive presentation of photosensitivity with an emphasis on clinical aspects. Included is an excellent section on phototesting.

Harber LC, Bickers DR: *Photosensitivity Disorders: Principles of Diagnosis and Treatment.* Toronto; B.C. Decker; 1989.

An easy-to-read, comprehensive presentation of photosensitivity.

Lehmann AR, Norris PG: DNA repair deficient photodermatoses. *Semin Dermatol.* 1990;9:55–62.

This review discusses xeroderma pigmentosum, Cockayne's syndrome, trichothiodystrophy, and Bloom's syndrome, emphasizing molecular pathophysiology and associated immunologic factors.

Marx JL, Eisenstat BA, Gladstein AH: Quinidine photosensitivity. *Arch Dermatol.* 1983;119:39–43.

The characteristics of quinidine-induced photosensitivity are described.

50. REACTIONS TO HEAT AND COLD
Edward V. Maytin

Skin interacts with the environment through exchange of radiant energy in a variety of forms. "Heat" and "cold" are often regarded as states of high or low kinetic energy in molecules, transmitted by mechanisms of conduction, convection, or infrared radiation. However, to understand the cutaneous interactions, we may also need to consider thermal interactions in the context of the broad electromagnetic spectrum. This spectrum is defined in terms of wavelengths: gamma rays and x rays (0.01–1.0 nm), UV radiation (UVC 200–290 nm, UVB 290–320 mm, UVA 320–400 nm), visible light (400–700 nm) and infrared (700–1,000,000 nm). While these different wavelengths do vary in their effects on the skin, a remarkable similarity exists in the types of cutaneous reaction patterns seen with many of the different wavelength categories. For example, chronic heat exposure, sun damage, and x-ray exposure share a common clinical appearance characterized by pigmentary changes, telangiectasia, and atrophy. Histologic similarities between exposure to UV light or to infrared radiation (heat) include proliferation of elastic fibers, increased cellularity of the dermis, and tortuous blood vessels.

Concerning pathophysiologic mechanisms, the dogma that UV radiation causes damage through photochemical reactions (e.g., breakage of DNA), while infrared wavelengths act through separate thermal mechanisms, may have to be reassessed. For example, some experimental studies suggest that heat enhances the effects of sun-induced erythema in mice. Heat in the range of 41°C to 43°C inhibits DNA repair and acts synergistically with UV radiation to denature DNA in squamous cells. Infrared radiation alone can evoke elastic fiber hyperplasia in the dermis, and may therefore be a strong contributor to chronic sun damage. Finally, thermal, UV, and x-ray exposure each tend to increase the incidence of skin cancer at the exposed site.

The two broad categories of reactions to heat and reactions to cold can be further subdivided into normal reactions that occur in all individuals who receive adequate exposure (e.g., burns, or erythema ab igne), and abnormal reactions, defined as syndromes that are only seen in certain patients (e.g., Raynaud's phenomenon).

Acute heat injury (thermal burns) results from exposure to extreme heat. "Extreme" is defined by factors such as the type of heat source, temperature of exposure, and duration of exposure. The minimal temperature at which a burn can occur is 44°C. With increasing temperatures, shorter times are required, so that epidermal necrosis will occur in 45 minutes at 47°C or in 1 second at 70°C. Superficial burns cause erythema, partial-thickness burns cause bullae and eschars, and full-thickness burns form an eschar, which then sloughs. Pain is prominent in superficial and partial thickness burns.

Burns are classified by the depth of necrosis: superficial (epidermis alone), partial thickness (down to mid-dermis), or full thickness (dermis down to fat). The pathogenesis of heat injury involves denaturation and coagulation of cellular proteins, with enzyme inactivation. Edema results from increased capillary permeability and the release of vasoactive mediators. Severe systemic alterations occur as well. Susceptibility to infection may result, in part, from impaired neutrophil and T-cell function and from loss of the integument. Fever results from the release of interleukin-1 and other cytokines from keratinocytes and other cells. Cellular responses in the burn area may include induction of heat shock proteins.

Pain, infections, metabolic derangements, scarring, and death constitute the major complications of burns. Skin cancers, usually squamous cell carcinomas, may arise within burn scars. First aid measures include flooding with cool water, tetanus prophylaxis, and anticipation of shock, with immediate intravenous fluid replacement. Any burns involving the face, hands, and genitalia, as well as those involving more than 10% to 15% of the body surface, should be referred to a specialized burn center. Such specialized attention can reduce the risk of infection and contraction deformities.

Erythema ab igne, a netlike pattern of telangiectasia and reddish brown pigmentation on the legs of patients who sat in front of open fires or coal stoves, was seen in Great Britain and Europe in the past. It became less common with the advent of central heating, but there has been a recent resurgence of erythema ab igne in America with the increased popularity of space heaters, woodburning stoves, and fireplaces. Erythema ab igne can also be seen with chronic use of heating pads and water bottles, and on the skin of glassblowers, bakers, and kitchen workers.

Clinical features include mild and transient reticular erythema that may progress to hyperpigmentation, atrophy, and telangiectasia (poikiloderma). The pathological changes are similar to those of solar damage, and include proliferating elastic fibers, increased cellularity of the telangiectatic vessels, and marked cellular atypia of the epidermis. However, compared to ultraviolet damage, erythema ab igne shows more dermal deposition of melanin and less degeneration of elastic fibers.

Complications include skin cancers, which can arise in areas of erythema ab igne or in areas of chronic heat exposure. Many examples of these heat-damage–related neoplasms have been described throughout the world, with exotic names such as the Kangri cancer of India (from pots of coal being held next to the skin), the Kange cancer of China (from sleeping on hot bricks), the Kairo cancer of Japan (from benzene-burning flasks next to the skin), and the Turf or Peat Fire cancer on the legs of rural Irish women. Thermally induced cancers are usually squamous cell carcinomas, and occur after a long latency period of 30 years or more. They may be aggressive, with metastases occurring in over 30%.

Abnormal reactions to heat include cholinergic urticaria and erythermalgia. **Cholinergic urticaria** is common, especially in young adults, and is one of many forms of physical urticarias. Triggered not only by heat but also by exercise or emotion, a warm sensation is followed by the appearance of itchy 1- to 3-mm urticarial papules with a surrounding flare, typically over the chest and back. Symptoms of angioedema, with wheezing, nausea, and other systemic symptoms, may occur. The urticaria may be reproduced by a hot bath or by vigorous exercise. Pathologically, there is intradermal edema. Treatment consists of avoidance of trigger factors, and use of an H_1 antihistamine such as hydroxyzine. Very sensitive individuals should carry an injectable epinephrine kit, avoid aspirin (it may aggravate the urticaria), and should never exercise alone.

In another form of urticaria, called localized heat urticaria, direct application of heat will cause wheals at the site. This entity is very rare. Treatment is similar to that for cholinergic urticaria.

In **erythermalgia** (also called erythromelalgia), attacks of burning pain occur in the feet or hands. Attacks of prickling, burning, or erythema and cyanotic discoloration of the feet and hands are provoked by standing, exercise, or exposure to heat. Elevating or cooling the affected limbs relieves the symptoms. Patients seek relief by walking on snow or cold floors or by sleeping outside the bedcovers. The primary (idiopathic) form seems to predominate in young adult males, while the secondary form occurs in patients over 40 years of age and is associated with hematologic disease such as polycythemia rubra vera, chronic myeloproliferative disorders, and primary thrombocythemia.

Pathologically, arterioles show inflammation and proliferation of the fibromuscular intima, with thrombi in the vessels. Raising the temperature or lowering the limb may increase the swelling and occlusion of these vessels, resulting in sludging of blood and platelet aggregation.

The presence of polycythemia vera, thrombocythemia, or other hematologic proliferative disorders should be ruled out. Aspirin, 650 mg/d, is the only therapy that has given consistently good results. Heat should be avoided.

Cutaneous **reactions to cold,** whether at freezing temperatures (frostbite) or nonfreezing temperatures (trench foot), show a common sequence of events. These mechanisms are different from those seen with extreme heat. At a cellular level, freezing creates damage through the formation of ice crystals. A slow freeze results in extracellular crystals, which raise the osmolarity and dehydrate cells. Rapid freezing creates tiny intracellular ice crystals, which are highly destructive through disruptive effects on cell membranes, enzymes, and structural molecules. The rate of rewarming is also important. Slow rewarming causes formation of larger, more damaging intracellular ice crystals. Therefore, rapid rewarming is desirable. Also, repeated freeze/thaw cycles cause greater damage, a principle used to advantage in cryotherapy for tumors and other skin lesions.

Different types of cells vary in their sensitivity to cold injury, with melanocytes being very sensitive (damage seen at $-4°C$ to $-7°C$). Almost all tissues exposed to a temperature of $-20°C$ or below for 1 minute will undergo necrosis. However, certain malignant tumors in mouse skin require at least $-60°C$. Current recommendations in cryotherapy suggest obtaining a tissue temperature of $-20°C$ for inflammatory lesions and benign tumors, and $-50°C$ or colder for squamous cell carcinomas.

Pathophysiologic events during cold injury center around blood vessels. Three stages of cooling are seen. The first is a massive vasoconstriction, which causes a rapid fall in skin temperature. The second is a paradoxical cyclic vasodilation, called the "hunting phenomenon of Lewis," that seems to exist as a protective mechanism against skin necrosis. Lewis demonstrated that the temperature of a finger immersed in water at 0°C will initially drop to 2°C to 4°C, but will then rise to about 7°C with reflex vasodilation and then cycle around a set point. If cold exposure continues, the third stage (actual freezing) sets in. Events include (1) arterial vasoconstriction, (2) excessive vein and capillary vasodilatation, (3) endothelial leakage, (4) stasis of red blood cells, (5) arterial-venous shunting, (6) segmental vascular necrosis, and (7) massive thrombosis.

Frostbite represents actual freezing of tissue. Risk factors include alcohol intoxication, peripheral vascular disease, tight constrictive clothing, previous frostbite, and cigarette smoking. The affected part, usually a finger, toe, ear, or cheek, becomes white or blue-white. The skin may actually feel hard and solid. After rewarming, large blisters form in 1 to 2 days, leading to formation of a hard, black eschar within 1 to 2 weeks. Within weeks, a line of demarcation occurs, with sloughing of tissue distal to this line.

Pathologically, necrosis of the dermis and epidermis occurs. Complications include hypersensitivity to cold, hyperhydrosis (sweating), damage of the epiphysial plate in children, and frostbite arthritis.

Rapid rewarming should be performed in a water bath at 40°C to 42°C until the most distal part becomes flushed. Generous analgesia, elevation of the affected part, and bed rest are required. Twenty-minute twice-daily soaks in a warm whirlpool bath will gently debride the eschar and encourage joint mobility and circulation. Debridement of necrotic eschar should be delayed until the extent of permanent damage has been defined. Tetanus toxoid should be given.

Nonfreezing cold injury (trench foot, immersion foot) comprises a variety of related syndromes, seen historically in soldiers exposed to cold and wet conditions. These include trench foot, immersion foot, tropical immersion foot, and a new entity called "pulling boat hands," described among Outward Bound students living in an open boat on the North Atlantic. In all these entities, cold and wet conditions, along with venous stagnation from immobility and constrictive footwear, seem to be important in the pathogenesis. Trench foot (World War I), immersion foot, and tropical immersion foot (shipwrecked sailors in World War II) are clinically similar except that tropical immersion foot appears to be a milder form in which the role of cold is unclear. Clinical features include initial erythema, edema, and tenderness, followed within 24 hours by paresthesia, increased edema, numbness, and blistering. Progression to gangrene occurs if any of these conditions is left untreated. Pathologically there is swelling of endothelial cells, thrombosis of intradermal vessels, dermal edema, and subepidermal blistering. Complications include sensitivity to cold and hyperhydrosis that may persist for years. Maintaining dry, warm conditions is paramount to prevention. Rest, analgesics, and antibiotics are employed for therapy.

There are several **abnormal reactions to cold. Chilblains,** also called pernio, is a painful condition of localized inflammatory lesions of the hands and feet, seen most commonly in the cold, damp environments of Britain and Europe. It was very common in the last century, but has become less common since the onset of central heating. Clinical features include the acute onset of multiple, erythematous, purplish papules and nodules accompanied by symptoms of itching, burning, or pain. Lesions occur on the fingers and toes, heels, thighs, nose, and ears. In horse riders, lesions may occur on the outer thighs. Each lesion is an acute, itchy swelling of dermis and subcutaneous tissue that arises over a few hours or days and slowly subsides. Severe cases may blister and ulcerate. Lesions of chilblains have been described in lupus erythematosus. Most cases are self-limited, although lesions may persist for months. Pathological patterns are similar to those of other conditions due to nonfreezing cold injury: thickening of blood vessel walls with intimal proliferation, superficial and deep perivascular lymphocytic infiltrates, edema of the papillary dermis, and overlying epidermal changes. Prophylaxis with adequate clothing and home heating is most important. A short course of UV light at the beginning of winter may prevent chilblains. Symptomatic treatment of established chilblains with rest, warmth, antipruritics, and analgesics is used. Nifedipine, 20 mg tid, has been effective in some patients.

Acrocyanosis and **erythrocyanosis** are characterized by dusky, mottled discoloration of the skin, exacerbated during the winter months and by cold exposure. Clinically these persistent conditions differ from Raynaud's phenomenon, which is episodic. In acrocyanosis, persistent discoloration of the hands and feet is found; they may be bright red when very cold, but usually are more dusky, cyanotic, and mottled. In erythrocyanosis, the distribution of the discoloration occurs over areas that have thick layers of subcutaneous fat, such as on the buttocks of prepubertal boys or on the lower legs of adolescent girls or on the forearms of infants. In both conditions, evidence for arterial disease is usually lacking. The pathology is similar to that of chilblains. Both conditions are thought to result from abnormal shunting of blood within the cutaneous vascular plexus. Treatments are similar to those used for chilblains.

Livedo reticularis is not a diagnosis but a reaction pattern that may be primary (idiopathic) or secondary to a number of systemic diseases. Clinical features include a mottled, blue or erythematous discoloration of the skin that occurs in a netlike pattern and becomes more pronounced on exposure to cold. Numbness and tingling may be associated. Ulceration may occur. Livedo reticularis must be distinguished from cutis marmorata, a normal, transient physiologic reaction to cold exposure, seen in 50% of normal children and in many adults.

The netlike pattern may be due to the arrangement of the superficial venous plexus within the skin. When cold or other factors, such as arterial obstruction and increased blood viscosity, cause low flow rates and deoxygenation within these veins, the cyanotic reticulated pattern becomes more pronounced. A skin biopsy may show necrosis of small blood vessels and hyaline thrombi. The main significance of livedo reticularis is its role as a marker for possible underlying systemic disease. Secondary livedo reticularis is often asymmetric and patchy. Conditions such as cholesterol emboli, thrombocythemia, cryoglobulinemia, and systemic collagen vascular diseases including polyarteritis nodosa, rheumatoid arthritis, and lupus, as well as syphilis and tuberculosis, must all be investigated.

In **Raynaud's phenomenon,** episodic, reversible color changes in the extremities occur because of vascular spasm. The idiopathic form is called Raynaud's disease; when secondary to other underlying diseases, the condition is called Raynaud's phenomenon. Attacks are precipitated by cold or emotional stress. A biphasic or triphasic color change occurs, with succession of pallor, cyanosis, and erythema (white, blue, and red), which presumably represents vasospasm, venostasis, and reactive hyperemia in the blood vessels of the digit. Raynaud's disease is most common in women under the age of 40, affecting the hands and rarely the feet. It runs a variable course, with a good prognosis in 80% of cases but progressive disability in the remainder. In Raynaud's phenomenon, the prognosis depends on the nature of the underlying disease. No histologic abnormality is detectable early on. Later, thrombosis within vessels may be found.

It is extremely important to rule out an underlying cause for Raynaud's phenomenon, such as arteriosclerosis, Buerger's disease (thromboangiitis obliterans), or one of the collagen vascular diseases such as scleroderma, lupus, dermatomyositis, or cryoglobulinemia. Patients should be advised to quit smoking, avoid sudden changes of temperature, and use warm (e.g., electrically heated) gloves and socks. Among therapies, the best appear to be diltiazem or nifedipine, with benefits in about 60% of patients.

Cryoglobulins are serum immunoglobulins that undergo reversible precipitation at low temperatures, and cause symptoms related to vascular sludging. Various cutaneous symptoms, such as vascular purpura, distal necrosis, livedo reticularis, leg ulcers, and Raynaud's phenomenon, may be seen. However, cold sensitivity is not a consistent feature and occurs in less than half of the cases. Typical findings are crops of purpuric lesions that are precipitated by standing, or in 30% of patients, by cold. Diagnosis is made by the detection of cryoglobulins in the blood.

Other cold precipitable proteins include cold agglutinins, which are antibodies that bind to red blood cell antigens at cold temperatures, causing the cells to agglutinate, and the cold hemolysins, seen mainly in the past with tertiary or congenital syphilis.

Cold panniculitis produces tender erythematous nodules and induration that appear beneath the chins of young children exposed to cold. This picture may also occur in adults with very extensive cold exposure. Lesions appear between 1 and 3 days after cold exposure, and subside within 2 weeks. An ice cube applied to the child's skin for 10 minutes will re-create the erythematous plaque 12 to 18 hours after exposure. Children who suck on popsicles can develop indurated nodules in the buccal area, so-called popsicle panniculitis. Pathologically, one sees a perivascular lymphohistiocytic infiltrate at the dermal-subcutaneous junction within 24 hours, and a well-developed panniculitis at 48 to 72 hours.

In **sclerema neonatorum** and **subcutaneous fat necrosis of the newborn,** a relationship to cold exposure has not been firmly established. However, similar clinical findings have been described in infants in Britain admitted to the hospital with primary hypothermic injury, usually due to poorly heated homes.

In sclerema neonatorum, fortunately a rare disorder, hardening of the skin and subcutaneous tissues spreads rapidly from the buttocks and trunk to include the entire body of the infant. It usually occurs in the setting of a major illness, for example, sepsis or a congenital anomaly. Infants may be cyanotic at birth and have difficulty in maintaining body temperature. Mortality is high. Pathologically, fat necrosis is absent. Fat cells contain needlelike clefts. Some suggest that the disorder is caused by an exaggeration of the normal saturated-unsaturated fatty acid ratio seen in the brown fat of infants.

Subcutaneous fat necrosis is a more benign condition seen in newborns, and is characterized by discrete plaques and nodules appearing within a few days after birth. It is generally self-limited.

Copeman PWM: Livedo reticularis: signs in the skin of disturbance of blood viscosity and of blood flow. *Br J Dermatol.* 1975;93:519–529.
A beautiful review, with discussion of pathophysiology as well as clinical features.
Dana AS, Rex IH, Samitz MH: The hunting reaction. *Arch Dermatol.* 1969;99:441–450.

A landmark paper, describing a physiologic compensatory, vasodilatory reaction to cold that occurs in the microvasculature of the distal extremities at temperatures near freezing.

Demling RH: Burns. *N Eng J Med.* 1985;313:1389–1398.

An authoritative review of the pathophysiology and therapeutic management of burns.

Dover JS, Phillips TJ, Arndt KA: Cutaneous effects and therapeutic uses of heat with emphasis on infrared radiation. *J Amer Acad Dermatol.* 1989;278–286.

A review of the currently limited literature available about acute, chronic, and carcinogenic effects of infrared radiation.

Dowd PM: The treatment of Raynaud's phenomenon. *Br J Dermatol.* 1986;114:527–533.

Reviews the pros and cons of each of a plethora of remedies for this frustrating affliction. Nifedipine may be most effective.

Eun HC, Kim JA, Lee YS: Squamous cell carcinoma in a frost-bite scar. *Clin Exper Dermatol.* 1986;11:517–520.

One of many examples of epithelial tumors arising within scars. Similar cancers have been reported in scars from thermal burns or x-irradiation.

Fitzgerald O, Hess EV, O'Connor GT, Spencer-Green G: Prospective study of the evolution of Raynaud's phenomenon. *Am J Med.* 1988;84:718–726.

Among a cohort of 58 patients with Raynaud's phenomenon, initially without any known associated illness, 11 patients (19%) eventually developed either systemic sclerosis or CREST syndrome. This underscores the need for a high index of suspicion for underlying diseases in patients with episodic vascular spasm of the distal extremities.

Gage AA: What temperature is lethal for cells? *J Dermatol Surg Oncol.* 1979;5:459–464.

Discussion of the temperature requirements for cold injury.

Kligman LH, Kligman AM: Reflections on heat. *Br J Dermatol.* 1984;110:369–375.

A thoughtful discussion of the similarities between the cutaneous effects of infrared (heat) versus those of UV radiation, suggesting that we keep an open mind about the possible mechanisms of damage.

Maytin EV, Wimberly JM, Anderson RR: Thermotolerance and the heat shock response in normal human keratinocytes in culture. *J Invest Dermatol.* 1990;95:635–642.

Normal protective mechanisms exist in skin cells exposed to heat. These include production of heat shock proteins, and acquisition of resistance against further heat injury (thermotolerance).

Michiels JJ, et al.: Erythromelalgia caused by platelet-mediated arteriolar inflammation and thrombosis in thrombocythemia. *Ann Int Med.* 1985;102:466–471.

Erythromelalgia (erythermalgia) was the presenting symptom in 26 of 40 patients with thrombocythemia, suggesting that microvascular occlusive changes play a role in the pathogenesis of erythromelalgia.

Page EH, Shear NH: Temperature-dependent skin disorders. *J Am Acad Dermatol.* 1988;18:1003–1019.

A broad review of cutaneous disorders either caused or exacerbated by thermal excesses (heat or cold).

Toback AC, Korson R, Krusinski PA: Pulling boat hands: a unique dermatosis from coastal New England. *J Am Acad Dermatol.* 1985;12:649–655.

Painful plaques, similar to those of nonfreezing cold injury (trench foot) except for the additional feature of vesicles, was described in participants of an Outward Bound program who spent many days in a boat exposed to cold air, wind, and ocean spume. Trauma as well as cold injury is implicated.

Treatment of Frostbite. *Med Lett Drugs Ther.* 1980;22:112–114.

Often-quoted recommendations for treatment of this common problem.

51. RADIATION AND THE SKIN
R. Rox Anderson

For the first half of this century an x-ray machine was essential equipment for the modern office practice of dermatology. This is no longer the case. Alarming and late sequelae, such as iatrogenic radiation-induced ulcers and carcinomas, became apparent over decades. These effects are rather easily controlled by proper dosimetry and application, but led to a proper reluctance to employ radiotherapy. This reluctance intensified with the dawn of nuclear weapons. More importantly, the advent of antibacterial, antifungal, corticosteroid, chemotherapeutic, and improved surgical treatments has drastically reduced the need for dermatologic radiotherapy. Today, radiotherapy is essentially confined to the treatment of neoplasms. Under specific conditions, radiotherapy may be the treatment of choice.

X rays and gamma rays make up the shortest-wavelength portion of the spectrum of electromagnetic radiation, which also includes UV, visible light, infrared, microwave, and radio waves. As noted by Planck and Einstein, shorter-wavelength radiation carries greater energy. Unlike longer-wavelength spectral regions, the energy carried by x rays is sufficient to strip electrons from their atomic or molecular orbitals. Therefore, x-ray radiation is ionizing, a fact that accounts for essentially all of its biologic effects.

The production of x rays occurs when electrons strike a metal target, converting their kinetic energy into photon radiation. Correspondingly, the higher the voltage used to accelerate the electrons, the higher the average energy (and the greater the penetration) of the x rays produced. Thus, the voltage, expressed in kilovolts, is set for the maximum desired tissue penetration. X-ray tubes produce a broad spectrum of x-ray energies. In addition to the x-ray tube voltage, the x-ray tube window material and any filters interposed between the source and tissue modify the spectrum reaching the patient. Aluminum filters, typically from 0.1 to 1 mm thick, are frequently interposed to absorb low-energy rays up to specific energies, such that a narrower band of higher-energy rays reaches the patient. This allows a more uniform penetration depth, such that superficial tissue is not overexposed while underlying tissue is treated to some well-defined depth.

The penetration of x-ray radiation varies widely, such that shorter-wavelength, higher-energy x rays penetrate tissue more deeply. Fundamentally, therefore, x-ray energies should always be carefully chosen to match tissue penetration with that of the tumor or pathologic process. Table 51.1 lists x-ray energies, tissue penetration, and nomenclature for different portions of the x-ray spectrum. Grenz rays (after the German *Grenze,* meaning "border") penetrate very superficially and were one of the mainstays of dermatologic therapy for superficial inflammatory and infectious conditions. Soft versus hard x rays refer roughly to millimeter versus centimeter tissue penetration, respectively.

The x-ray tube current, exposure time, and target-to-skin distance determine the

Table 51-1 The x-ray spectrum

Therapy	Energy (kilovolts)	$D_{1/2}$ in tissue* (mm)
megavoltage	>1000	200
supervoltage	400–800	100
orthovoltage	200–400	50–80
intermediate	110–130	30
superficial	60–100	7–10
soft x ray	20–100	1–10
grenz	5–20	0.2–0.8

*$D_{1/2}$ is the depth of penetration at which 50% of the energy has been absorbed.

dose delivered to skin. Various masks and treatment cones exist to define the treated area while shielding against scattered and stray radiation. Masks made of metal or lead-impregnated rubber can also be applied to perilesional skin to limit exposure to surrounding uninvolved tissue. Modern x-ray machines have been standardized to reduce confusion regarding voltage, current, filters, and dosimetry.

High-energy particle radiation, such as electrons (beta particles), neutrons, and helium nuclei (alpha particles), is also ionizing. These forms of ionizing radiation produce a greater number of ionizations per unit path length than x-ray radiation. In particular, electron beam radiation in the 1- to 10-MeV range is used for treatment of cutaneous T-cell lymphomas. Because of scattering and progressive loss of particle velocity, electron beam therapy produces greater ionization well below the surface of the skin, resulting in a "skin-sparing" effect.

The standard **unit** of ionizing radiation is the roentgen (R), which describes the number of ionizations per unit volume in air. The dose of radiation describes the energy absorbed per unit mass of material, and is measured in rads or grays (1 Gy = 100 rad). The rem (radiation equivalent in man) and sievery (Sv) are biologically effective dose units (1 Sv = 100 rem), weighted to reflect biologic sensitivity of given tissues to specific types of ionizing radiation.

Ionizing radiation interacts with tissue primarily by producing free radicals, i.e., chemical species with an unpaired electron resulting from ionization. These include hydrated electrons, and hydroxyl and superoxide anion radicals, which lead to oxidative damage and structural changes in essentially all classes of macromolecules. Therefore, ionizing radiation produces responses related to acute toxicity, structural damage, and genetic alteration. The lifetime of most reactive radicals is only about 10^{-5} seconds, which accounts for the localization of biological effect to sites of x-ray absorption. Free radical scavengers can act as radioprotectants.

Acute effects on cells include delayed growth and cell death. In general, cell sensitivity to ionizing radiation increases with the rate of proliferation and metabolic activity. This fact accounts for the ability to eradicate tumors while largely preserving surrounding normal tissues. There are notable exceptions, however, such as the radiosensitivity of resting lymphocytes. Sensitivity is also highly cell-cycle dependent. The greatest sensitivity occurs in the premitotic phase, and the greatest resistance during the period of active DNA synthesis. In general, well-oxygenated cells are more sensitive than hypoxic cells, in part because oxygen radicals participate in producing damage. Compounds with high electron affinity other than oxygen, e.g., metronidazole, have been used as radiosensitizers, but are not in widespread use. Hyperthermia is synergistic with ionizing radiation injury, especially in hypoxic tissues, and is often used adjunctively with ionizing radiation.

Mutagenesis occurs by direct damage to DNA, which may eventuate in carcinogenesis. Paradoxically, high radiation doses tend to avoid carcinogenesis, since lethality supervenes. Tumors appearing after high doses of radiation are often in the periphery of the exposure field, where intermediate (2000–3000 rad) doses exist. The repair of specific DNA damage is an important factor in cell sensitivity and mutagenesis; some disorders, such as ataxia telangiectasia and Gardner's syndrome, are associated with abnormal repair of DNA damaged by ionizing radiation. There is some evidence that fibroblasts from patients with basal cell nevus syndrome exhibit abnormal sensitivity to ionizing radiation.

The fractionation of exposures is an important tool that allows normal tissue repair to decrease the incidence of unwanted acute radiation effects, while providing tumoricidal effects that depend primarily on the cumulative dose. Tumor cells in a resistant portion of the cell cycle are also more apt to be eliminated by fractionated exposures.

Cutaneous reactions are conveniently divided into groups based on the sequence of appearance. **Roentgen erythema** is delayed erythema with varying amounts of edema, beginning half a day to 2 days after doses of 350–450 rad (3.5–4.5 Gy). For grenz rays, the erythema dose is considerably higher. Roentgen erythema is mediated by histamine, serotonin, and prostaglandins, and appears to be an early response to both epidermal and direct dermal vascular injury. Histologically, there is vasodilation and edema, with a mild mononuclear perivascular infiltrate. Abnormal mitoses and scattered pyknotic epidermal cells are seen. Roentgen erythema may subside or may blend with acute radiation dermatitis.

Acute radiation dermatitis is a more prolonged, dose-dependent reaction to injury of cutaneous germinative epithelia, which may begin within 1 to 2 weeks after exposures in excess of about 100 rad. Erythema is followed by moist desquamation and erosions, as a result of epidermal basal cell reproductive failure. Epilation occurs because of similar changes in follicular epithelium and hair bulbs. Vascular injury and thrombosis occur because of endothelial cell injury. Histologically, there is liquefactive necrosis of basal cells, blister formation, edema, a mononuclear infiltrate, endothelial cell swelling, and thrombosis. Typically, acute radiation dermatitis resolves by 4 weeks after exposure, but may persist into chronic radiation dermatitis, especially at high doses. A rebound phase of epidermal hyperplasia occurs, followed by return to a variably atrophic but intact epidermis and dermis. At doses used for skin tumor treatment, acute radiation dermatitis should be anticipated, and treated as a second-degree burn, with local or systemic antibiotics, analgesia, wet compresses, and dressings. Sun exposure and trauma exacerbate radiation dermatitis and should be avoided. Corticosteroids do not appear to be helpful.

Pigmentation is stimulated at low doses, which produce an increase in both the number and the activity of epidermal melanocytes. At typical tumor-treatment doses, mottled or confluent hypopigmentation with islands of macular hyperpigmentation may result. Poliosis (gray regrowing hairs) is frequent.

Alopecia may be transient or permanent, depending on the dose (in the range of approximately 200–800 rad). Anagen follicles are about 3 times more sensitive than telogen follicles. Destruction of anagen hair follicles may, therefore, lead to permanent thinning of hair. A phase of epilation coincides chronologically with acute radiation dermatitis and is followed by complete or partial regrowth of normal, dystrophic, or gray hairs, depending on both the doses and the depth of penetration used.

Chronic radiation dermatitis can be progressive, beginning months to years after exposures that may or may not have induced acute changes. Chronic radiation dermatitis appears to be primarily due to permanent alterations in the dermis. Atrophy, telangiectasia, fibrosis, hyperpigmentation, hypopigmentation, and absence of adnexae are present to varying degrees. This constellation of signs is known as poikiloderma. Pathologically, there is dermal hypocellularity with enlarged, sometimes bizarre fibroblasts and thickened vascular walls. These chronic histologic alterations are frequently present even in clinically normal exposed skin. The epidermis may be mildly to severely atrophic, frequently with keratoses and hypopigmentation. Atypical epidermal mitoses and patchy parakeratosis may be seen chronically.

Poorly healing ulcers can occur in irradiated skin years after x-ray exposure, either spontaneously or after simple trauma, infection, or pressure. Ulcers may also occur subacutely after doses of about 5000 rad at 90 kV or more, but essentially never occur after grenz ray therapy. The severity of acute reactions does not correlate well with chronic sequelae, including ulceration and radiation-induced carcinomas. It is therefore important to periodically follow patients after radiation therapy, regardless of acute reaction or apparent early treatment success. The ulcers may periodically heal and then recur. Treatment for radiation-induced ulcers includes aggressive local care by antibiotics, debridement, and appropriate dressings. Wound healing is permanently altered by radiation, however; and when possible, surgical excision, with repair by graft or flap techniques, often gives the best result.

Skin carcinomas induced by ionizing radiation may occur any time after exposure, but typically they appear after years or decades, in approximately 5% to 10% of patients. Carcinomas occurring in ulcers are not infrequent, and a biopsy is necessary in essentially all nonhealing radiation-induced ulcers. Squamous cell and basal cell carcinomas are most frequent. Mesenchymal spindle cell carcinoma, sebaceous adenocarcinoma, appendageal carcinomas, melanoma, and other skin tumors may also appear. Ionizing radiation-induced squamous cell carcinomas are more frequently aggressive and metastatic than their UV-induced counterparts. There is no firm dose-response data for radiation-induced tumors in human skin, but some retrospective studies suggest that doses of 2000–3000 rad account for most radiation-induced squamous carcinomas, with decreased tumorigenesis both below and above this dose.

Poor shielding at the time of radiotherapy used on the head and neck can result in **other carcinomas,** such as thyroid, brain, bone, or parotid tumors. A recent study conducted in over 10,000 patients irradiated as children for treatment of tinea capitis showed a dose-dependent incidence of neural tumors up to 20 times that of age-matched or sibling controls.

Infertility in males occurs at low doses, starting at approximately 250 rad. Transient aspermia may occur after as little as 25 rad, a dose which is within an order of magnitude of some CT scanners. There is little reliable data regarding the expression of germ-line mutations in offspring of x-irradiated humans. **Cataracts** can occur if the eyes are not properly shielded.

Grenz ray therapy was widely used for eczema, psoriasis, lichen planus, tinea capitis, and acne. Although transiently effective for all of these disorders, grenz ray therapy for inflammatory skin disease has been, rightly, nearly abandoned. Superficial mycosis fungoides, Sézary syndrome, Kaposi's sarcoma, and superficial basal cell carcinomas also respond to grenz ray therapy, but soft x rays with greater penetration are currently preferred over grenz rays for radiotherapy for these tumors.

X-ray therapy is widely but judiciously used for skin tumors that (1) are inoperable, (2) would yield poor surgical results due to local destruction, (3) are exquisitely radiosensitive, or (4) are present in elderly patients who may at times choose the risk of long-term sequelae over the risks of specialized surgery or other therapy. In some hospitals, up to 20% of patients with **basal** or **squamous cell tumors** of the head and neck are treated with radiation therapy. This is undoubtedly the most frequent use of radiotherapy in dermatology. Preservation of periorbital and other facial structures can be excellent and there is less tendency for chronic dermatitis on the face compared with the extremities. Basal and squamous cell carcinomas and keratoacanthomas are typically treated with up to 6000 rad in fractionated doses, aiming to deliver approximately 2500 rad at the base of the tumor. The efficacy in most series exceeds 90%, and various fractionations, kilovoltages, and treatment schedules are in use. Less commonly, Bowen's disease and erythroplasia of Queyrat (squamous cell carcinomas in situ) and lentigo maligna are treated with radiotherapy.

Kaposi's sarcoma is a radiosensitive tumor that typically regresses after a total dose of 200–1000 rad. The present AIDS epidemic has led to many cases of this previously uncommon tumor. The local effectiveness of radiotherapy with little or no immunosuppression is often preferable to chemotherapy in these patients. The long-term sequelae of radiotherapy are, at present, of secondary importance.

Radiotherapy is relatively contraindicated in (1) lesions on the trunk and extremities, (2) lesions grater than about 8 cm, (3) young patients, (4) cutaneous tumors with bony invasion, (5) radiation-induced tumors, or (6) tumors occurring in ulcers or burn scars.

Bernhardt M (ed.): Roentgen-rays in the treatment of skin diseases and for the removal of hair. *Arch Dermatol.* 1983;119:162-177.
A reprint of a classic article published in the July 1900 issue of Cutan Genitourin Dis.

Freeman RG, Knox JM, Heaton CL: The treatment of skin cancer. A statistical study of 1,341 skin tumors comparing results obtained with irradiation, surgery, and curettage followed with electrodesiccation. *Cancer.* 1964; 17:535–538.
Radiotherapy is comparable in efficacy (90% to 95%) to standard surgical modalities for treating basal and squamous cell carcinomas. (The efficacy of Moh's surgery is, however, higher.)

Furst CJ, Lundell M, Holm LE: Tumors after radiotherapy for skin hemangioma in childhood. A case-control study. *Acta Oncol.* 1990;29(5):557–562.
A positive relationship was found between childhood radiotherapy and cancers of the thyroid, bone, and soft tissues.

Malkinson FD, Keane JT: Radiobiology of the skin. In: Goldsmith LA, ed. *Biochemistry and Physiology of the Skin.* Vol. 2. Oxford: Oxford Univ. Press; 1983:769–782.

Informative review of both basic radiobiology and cutaneous reactions to ionizing radiation.

Murphy WJ: *Radiation Therapy.* Philadelphia, PA: W.B. Saunders Co.; 1967.
A good general reference for both modern and past uses of radiation in dermatology.

Ron E, Modan B, Preston D, et al.: Radiation-induced skin carcinomas of the head and neck. *Rad Res.* 1991 Mar;125(3):318–325.
Radiation exposures to the scalp during childhood for tinea capitis were associated with a fourfold increase in nonmelanoma skin cancers.

Ron E, Modan B, Boice JD Jr., et al.: Tumors of the brain and nervous system after radiotherapy in childhood. *N Engl J Med.* 1988;319:1033–1039.
A study of the incidence of benign and malignant brain neoplasms in 10, 834 Israelis who were irradiated for tinea capitis as children. There was, in comparison with unirradiated age-matched and sibling controls, a relative risk of 6.9 overall, which increased to 20 for those exposed to estimated brain doses of 2.5 Gy (250 rad) or greater.

Rowell NR: A follow up study of superficial radiotherapy for benign dermatoses: recommendations for the use of x-rays in dermatology. *Br J Dermatol.* 1973;88:583–590.
In 100 cases of patients exposed to over 20 Gy (2000 rad), 5% developed skin tumors. Interestingly, some patients who received over 30 Gy (3000 rad) had clinically normal skin. The study illustrates both the interesting dose-response relationship for x-ray carcinogenesis and the lack of correlation between acute radiodermatitis, and carcinogenesis.

Shore RE: Follow up study of patients treated by x-ray epilation for tinea capitis. Resurvey of post-treatment illness and mortality experience. *Arch Environ Health.* 1976;31:21–28.
Radiation-induced squamous cell carcinomas are aggressive tumors with increased metastatic potential.

52. SKIN PROBLEMS IN THE WORKPLACE
Christopher R. Shea

Because of the special position of the skin as the definitive interface with the outside world, it is uniquely at risk from environmental insults. Indeed, disorders of the skin make up approximately half of the reported cases of occupational illness in the United States. The economic costs, both direct and indirect, of occupational dermatoses therefore run into hundreds of millions of dollars per year.

Skin problems that occur in the workplace are difficult to summarize in a few pages, as they embrace virtually the entire spectrum of cutaneous reaction patterns, from simple irritation to malignant neoplasia, resulting from exposure to exogenous agents, whether physical, chemical, or biologic. Not only do these agents cause dermatoses de novo, they can exacerbate or otherwise alter the presentation, course, or prognosis of almost any preexisting dermatosis. The possible relationship of occupation to skin disease should, therefore, be viewed not as the purview of the subspecialist but as a matter for all students of skin disease to keep in mind when evaluating any patient's skin problem. In complex cases, especially where issues of workers' compensation and litigation arise, the determination of a possible occupational role in pathogenesis can require considerable time and thought. In no other area of dermatology is a thorough history more important. A visit to the patient's workplace may also be required in order to assess possible exposure to hazards, adequacy of ventilation, temperature conditions, and washing facilities.

Chemical agents, organic and inorganic, are responsible for the majority of occupational dermatoses. Acute and chronic contact dermatitis represents approximately 90% of occupational dermatoses; most of these reactions, in turn, are mediated by irritant rather than allergic mechanisms. Irritant reactions, in contrast to allergic reactions, can occur upon first exposure to an agent, are typically dose-related, can be induced in almost anybody with sufficient exposure, and are more likely to respond to the use of protective barrier creams and simple emollients. Irritants can be as seemingly innocuous as soap and water when repeated handwashing is required, or as obviously hazardous as strong alkalies or acids.

Occupation-related allergic contact dermatitis is also common, and can be a particularly trying problem in the event of a reaction that is persistent or a cross-reaction to agents that are present outside the workplace. A single agent can be both irritant and allergenic, depending on the patient and on the conditions of exposure. Examples of important causes of contact dermatitis in the workplace include cement (chromate) and formaldehyde products for construction workers, poison ivy or other Rhus plants for forestry workers, feed additives (ethoxyquin, cobalt, antibiotics) and pesticides for farmers, rubber in gloves and hair dyes for beauticians, nickel in paper clips for office workers, and flour (potassium persulfate) for bakers. The chapters on contact dermatitis and hand dermatitis also contain more information on these important topics.

Folliculitis and acne can result from exposure to petroleum derivatives and coal-tar derivatives. Thus, metal workers using cutting oils, automobile mechanics exposed to grease and lubricants, and roofers and road workers exposed to tars are examples of workers at high risk. The presence of preexisting acne, occlusive clothing or friction, and comedogenic cosmetics can act in concert with these chemicals to produce lesions. The clinical picture may resemble acne vulgaris (i.e., predominance in areas containing many sebaceous glands) or folliculitis. Chloracne is a particularly severe form of acne produced by exposure to halogenated aromatic compounds (e.g., dioxin, a contaminant present in Agent Orange). Occupational exposure to chloracnegens is possible for chemical manufacturers, those working with herbicides, and laboratory workers, while industrial and transportation accidents, food contamination, and environmental pollution are routes by which the general public may be exposed. Chloracne has a characteristic clinical presentation. The primary lesions are relatively noninflamed comedones and straw-colored cysts that may number in the hundreds. The distribution of lesions is also typical, with sparing of the nose and prominent involvement of retroauricular, malar, and temporal areas. In severe cases, there may be extension to the back, buttocks, and groin. The presence of typical chloracne should prompt an assessment to exclude possible systemic toxicity, specifically porphyria and liver disease.

Pigmentary changes are another important group of chemically induced findings. Either hyper- or hypopigmentation may occur as a nonspecific sequela to inflammation, e.g., from irritant or allergic contact dermatitis or thermal injury. Such changes are both more common in, and more distressing to, patients with a constitutively dark complexion. Chemically induced leukoderma, in contrast, is the result of a specific toxic insult to melanocytes and can be produced by a variety of derivatives of quinone, phenol, and catechol. The mechanism of this injury is probably related to the structural similarity of these compounds to the intermediate metabolites involved in melanin biosynthesis, so that they act as false substrates within melanocytes. Chemical leukoderma may occur in the workplace as a result of exposure to the monobenzylether of hydroquinone, formerly used as an antioxidant in rubber gloves, and to cresol, still present in some disinfectant solutions. The primary lesion is an amelanotic macule, confined originally to the site of contact with the chemical. With prolonged exposure, however, distant skin may become affected, presumably on an autoimmune basis, and a clinical picture indistinguishable from idiopathic vitiligo may result. Hypermelanosis, in contrast, can result from exposure to photosensitizing chemicals plus ultraviolet radiation (UVR). Occupational groups at risk include individuals working with coal-tar derivatives, who can develop both an immediate, smarting, phototoxic reaction and a delayed pigmentary response on exposed skin. Similarly, workers handling psoralen-producing plants (e.g., lime, celery, parsley) can develop phytophotodermatitis following UVR exposure.

Finally, some other distinctive responses to occupational chemicals deserve mention. Berylliosis, either in systemic or primary cutaneous form, is typically seen in lamp manufacturers and is manifested by allergic granulomatosis. The PVC syndrome, a response to polyvinyl chloride, is seen in chemical workers and others, consisting of the triad of acro-osteolysis, sclerodactyly, and Raynaud's phenomenon of the fingers. Skin cancer may be induced by coal-tar derivatives (e.g., in pitch workers, roofers) and arsenic (e.g., in agricultural workers). The development of mycosis fungoides is possibly related to chronic contact dermatitis in the manufacturing and construction industries. Perforation of the nasal septum may occur with aerosol exposure to chromium, cobalt, and mercury, seen in various industrial occupations. Lichen planus may be induced by chemicals used for color film developing.

Numerous **physical agents** at the workplace may cause or exacerbate skin disease. Excessive ambient heat can lead to miliaria, erythema ab igne, and intertrigo. Furthermore, sweating increases the hazard of chemical exposures by increasing percutaneous absorption of certain particulates or solutions. Extreme thermal exposure can lead to heat prostration or, if localized, to burns. Workers at special risk include bakers, foundry workers, and those working outdoors under extreme conditions. The opposite problem, hypothermia leading to frostbite, is most often seen in outdoor workers. Prolonged exposure to moisture can lead to maceration, as in immersion foot seen in combat soldiers. In this condition, superinfection by *Corynebacterium* species may further damage the macerated stratum corneum, leading to pitted keratolysis of the soles. The potential hazards of electrical shocks need no elaboration. Exposure to high-frequency vibrating tools, such as chain saws and pneumatic drills, can produce Raynaud's phenomenon (so-called white hand), with vasospasm, objective sensory and motor neurologic deficits, and the potential for progression to gangrene. Less extreme but repetitive mechanical trauma produces characteristic occupational stigmata such as calluses, knuckle pads, and dystrophic fingernails. Minor trauma in susceptible persons may also produce lesions of psoriasis, lichen planus, and vitiligo by the isomorphic (Koebner) reaction.

Occupational exposure to electromagnetic radiation is a major cause of skin disease; UVR causes acute erythema (sunburn) and chronic changes such as photoaging and cancer. Workers traditionally at risk for such effects include arc welders, farmers, outdoor laborers, and sailors. These effects may be seen in the future in indoor workers with the increasing use of artificial UVR sources in the printing and plastics industries. The role of occupational exposure in producing chronic solar damage can be difficult to assess since the disease may follow the exposure by many years and there is frequently a strong history of recreational exposure to sunlight as well. Phototoxicity may also occur from the combination of occupational light exposure and non-occupational chemicals (e.g., thiazide diuretics, tetracyclines, nonsteroidal anti-inflammatory drugs). Occupational exposure to ionizing radiation occurs chiefly among medical, dental, and laboratory workers, and can produce characteristic radiodermatitis and aggressive squamous cell cancers. Any potential hazards posed by exposure to microwave radiation and to video display terminals are not well defined at present.

Fiberglass dermatitis represents a unique type of physical irritation. Spicules of spun fiberglass enter the epidermis and produce intense localized pruritus, often without an objective primary lesion, rarely with small urticarial papules. Typically, those working with fiberglass develop some tolerance over the course of repeated exposures. Proper cleansing of skin and clothing is important lest a family epidemic occur through contamination. The presence of fiberglass can be demonstrated by rinsing the affected areas and then touching them with cellophane tape; the tape is then mounted on a glass slide for microscopic examination and evaluated with the use of a polarizing lens.

The vast taxonomic array of organisms able to injure skin, and the countless connections between them and the paths of human endeavor, are seemingly endless. Some of the **cutaneous infections** and **infestations,** many of them zoonoses, have a particular relevance in the evaluation of eruptions acquired in the workplace.

Of bacterial infections, anthrax, caused by *Bacillus anthracis,* is a striking and fortunately rare example. Inoculation with infected animal tissue causes the typical primary malignant pustule, which evolves into a gelatinous plaque, subsequently breaking down into a hemorrhagic, necrotic ulcer with associated tender regional lymphadenopathy. Systemic dissemination can be prevented by timely incision and drainage plus antibiotic therapy. Wool, bone, and ivory are typical fomites for anthrax spores, and hence, it is seen in workers such as shepherds, wool-sorters, carvers, and buttonmakers. Erysipeloid, caused by *Erysipelothrix rhusiopathiae* (also known as *E. insidiosa*), is acquired by fish handlers, butchers, and veterinarians via skin contact with infected shellfish or swine, and has a typical appearance of circumscribed erythema and edema, often forming geographic patterns with central clearing. *Mycobacterium marinum* is the cause of fish-tank granuloma or swimming-pool granuloma. A primary lesion at the inoculation site often is followed by the sporotrichoid spread of metastatic infectious foci via the regional lymphatics. Primary inoculation tuberculosis is rarely seen in anatomists; *M. tuberculosis* var. *bovis* is usually the causative agent in farmers and butchers. Numerous other infections, including brucellosis, glanders, tularemia, and leptospirosis, can be acquired occupationally by the cutaneous route, but systemic rather than cutaneous signs and symptoms generally dominate the resulting clinical syndromes.

Infections with yeasts and fungi are also sometimes occupationally related. People doing wet work (e.g., bartenders, food handlers, dishwashers) can develop chronic candidal paronychias. Dermatophyte infections acquired by ranchers or other animal handlers from their beasts can involve less common organisms (e.g., *Trichophyton verrucosum*) and may be highly inflammatory. Sporotrichosis, caused by *Sporothrix schenckii,* is an occupational illness of miners, foresters, and gardeners, and usually causes a classic pattern, with a chain of lymphatic satellite granulomas proximal to the inoculation site. If the diagnosis is suspected, special culture medium should be used for diagnostic studies of tissue specimens.

Occupational viral dermatoses include molluscum contagiosum in caretakers of children, warts in physicians and podiatrists, herpetic whitlows in health care workers (especially dentists), milkers' nodule, and orf. The latter two diseases are caused by poxviruses acquired from cattle and sheep, respectively. They typically present as erythematous papules on the dorsum of a finger, undergoing evolution over the course of several weeks to form targetlike vesicular lesions and then crusted and verrucous nodules, finally resolving spontaneously. Deep mycotic infections may occur occupationally in agricultural and laboratory workers.

Arthropods can cause disease and disability by direct local actions, through the systemic effects of an injected toxin or antigen, or by acting as vectors for infection by microbes. Superinfection at bite sites is another potential cause of disease. Exposure to arthropods is common in outdoor workers of all kinds, but is not limited to them. Mites associated with foodstuffs and other agricultural products frequently cause eruptions, "grain itch," in those involved in harvesting, transporting, and processing grain, cheese, and fruits. Animal handlers acquire mites infesting domestic and wild animals, and health care workers are exposed to scabies infections.

Adams RM: *Occupational Skin Disease,* 2d ed. Philadelphia, PA: Saunders, 1990.
   The best and most complete general reference on this topic; to be consulted first.
Berkley SF, Hightower AW, Beier RC, et al.: Dermatitis in grocery workers associated with high natural concentrations of furanocoumarins in celery. *Ann Intern Med.* 1986;105:351–355.
   Great example of sleuthing by the Centers for Disease Control, leading to identification of phytophotodermatitis in celery handlers.
Emmett EA: Dermatologic screening. *J Occup Med.* 1986;28:1045–1050.
   This review discusses the value of screening programs in order to reduce risks in particular workers and to facilitate early detection and treatment.
Keil JE, Shmunes E: The epidemiology of work-related skin disease in South Carolina. *Arch Dermatol.* 1983;119:650–654.
   The hands were involved in 88% of cases reported. Over 90% of cases represented contact dermatitis, especially from oils, solvents, and other chemicals.
Knox JM, Knox JM, Dinehart SM, et al.: Acquired perforating disease in oil field workers. *J Am Acad Dermatol.* 1986;14:605–611.

Eight cases with transepidermal elimination of calcium were studied. The lesions were secondary to caustic drilling fluid, and could be reproduced in an animal model.

Maibach H: *Occupational and Industrial Dermatology.* 2d ed. Chicago, IL: Yearbook Medical Publishers; 1987.
Useful general reference with good bibliographies, covering basic aspects as well as specific occupational problems.

Marks JG, Trautlein JJ, Zwillich CW, et al.: Contact urticaria and airway obstruction from carbonless copy paper. *JAMA.* 1984;252:1038–1040.
Well-documented case report with positive challenge tests and evidence for PGF$_{2\alpha}$ and thromboxane B$_2$ as mediators of urticaria and objective changes on pulmonary function tests.

Mathias CG: Periodic synopsis: Occupational dermatoses. *J Am Acad Dermatol.* 1988;19:1107–1114.
Bibliography and review of pertinent points from literature.

Peahy RD: Skin hazards in farming. *Br J. Dermatol.* 1981;105 (Suppl. 21):45–50.
Brief review of plant dermatitis, bacterial, viral, and fungal infections, parasitic infestations, and contact dermatitis from pesticides, herbicides, feed additives, all commonly associated with farming.

Shelley WB, Shelley ED, Welbourn WC: Polypodium fern wreaths (Hagnaya): a new source of occupational mite dermatitis. *JAMA.* 1985;253:3137–3138.
Interesting case report that includes a helpful table of the varieties of mites involved in occupational dermatitis.

Shmunes E, Keil JE: Occupational dermatoses in South Carolina: a descriptive analysis of cost variables. *J Am Acad Dermatol.* 1983;9:861–866.
Atopic patients have a 13.5 times greater relative risk of developing occupational skin disease than do nonatopics.

Stevenson CJ: Occupational vitiligo: clinical and epidemiological aspects. *Br J Dermatol.* 1981;105 (Suppl. 21):51–56.
P-tert butyl catechol, p-tert butyl phenol, p-tert amylphenol, and monomethylether of hydroquinone are all well-documented causes of occupational leukoderma. Spontaneous repigmentation is rarely if ever cosmetically significant.

53. PHOTOAGING
Serge A. Coopman

Exposure to sunlight has increased considerably over the past decades because of changing lifestyles. Tanned skin has often been considered a symbol of health and beauty. The appearance of youth is also desired. Unfortunately, aging of the skin is appreciated by a variety of distinctive gross and microscopic skin changes that are most prominent on the face, exposed part of the neck, bald head, dorsal surface of the hands, forearms, and exposed lower legs. These changes develop in response to repeated sun exposure rather than as a result of the passage of time alone, and are most appropriately termed photoaging or dermatoheliosis. Photodamage results from sun exposure in a cumulative fashion. Factors that influence the severity of photodamage are both intrinsic (e.g., the degree of skin pigmentation and thickness of the stratum corneum) and extrinsic (e.g., indoor v. outdoor work, recreational activities, exposure to artificial UV sources, geographic, seasonal, and environmental factors). A fair person who tans poorly and lives in the southern United States will develop more photoaging than a person who tans well and lives farther north.

Because of the major medical, aesthetic, and psychosocial consequences of photoaging, interest in cutaneous aging and the underlying biological processes has increased greatly in recent years. The precise determination of the UV action spectrum responsible for this phenomenon is difficult because of the long latency period between sun exposure and clinical manifestations and because of the lack of suitable animal models. On the basis of epidemiologic data and a limited number of experimental findings, however, it is currently assumed that both the UVB (290–320 nm) and the UVA (320–400 nm) components of UV light contribute to this process. The potential hazards of UVA, both direct and through augmentation of UVB-associated side effects, have only been appreciated more recently.

Although the manifestations of actinic damage are often misinterpreted as signs of chronological aging, photoaging is characterized by unique **clinical features.** Morphologic changes in old, sun-protected skin are relatively subtle and consist primarily of fine wrinkles, laxity, and a variety of benign neoplasms. In addition, the skin shows increased fragility and poor wound healing. Photoaging refers to the following clinical skin changes superimposed on the alterations of intrinsic aging: coarsening, deep wrinkling, roughness or dryness, loss of elasticity, irregular hyper- and hypopigmentation, telangiectasia, purpura, atrophy, fibrotic changes and stellate pseudoscars, and ultimately the development of premalignant and malignant lesions. Sun-induced wrinkling on the back of the neck presents with a typical rhomboidal pattern and is called cutis rhomboidalis nuchae. Senile comedones and cysts may form around the eyes (Favre-Racouchot). Arcus senilis and cataracts are also manifestations of excessive cumulative sun exposure.

The **histologic characteristics** of photoaged skin also differ from those of chronologically aged skin. A biopsy specimen of aged, sun-protected skin reveals a hypocellularity in the dermis with only slight alterations in the structure and quantity of elastic fibers and collagen. There is epidermal thinning and flattening of the dermoepidermal junction. The microcirculation is decreased, but the appearance of the blood vessels is not greatly altered. In contrast, photoaged skin shows an abundance of thickened, tangled, and ultimately granular amorphous elastic fibers that replace most of the collagen in the upper dermis. The glycosaminoglycans composing the ground substance are greatly increased. Fibroblasts are numerous and hyperplastic. There is a considerable depletion of the microcirculation, and the remaining blood vessels are tortuous and dilated. The photoaged epidermis is characterized by alternating areas of severe atrophy and hyperplasia, and there are variable degrees of cellular atypia, loss of polarity, and other preneoplastic alterations. Retention of melanin clumps can be observed in basal keratinocytes.

Much attention has recently been given to possible **therapies** for photoaging. Several authors claim that photoaging is to some degree a reversible process when the damage/repair balance is allowed to shift towards dermal repair mechanisms. The application of topical tretinoin (Retin-A) in varying strengths is reported to partially reverse the structural alternations of photodamaged skin; however, the results obtained in nonblind open-label studies and short-term double-blind studies still need confirmation by data gathered in formally controlled long-term studies. Tretinoin may be applied as a cream (0.025%, 0.05%, 0.1%), solution (0.05%), or gel (0.025%, 0.01%). Most patients experience an irritant dermatitis when treatment is initiated, especially with higher concentrations or with the solution- or gel-based topicals. Intermittent nighttime applications of a very small amount of 0.025% tretinoin cream and the use of moisturizers in the initial treatment phase can allow gradually increasing tolerance of the product. Initial changes include a pink, rosy glow of the treated skin and a subjective sense of tightening of the skin. According to several investigators, significant improvements in wrinkling can be noted after 6 to 10 months of treatment. Fine wrinkles may benefit most from treatment, and the number of lentigines is also reported to decrease substantially. The continuous and concomitant use of sunscreens is essential. Histologic and ultrastructural changes seen in tretinoin-treated skin include compaction of the stratum corneum, increased granular layer and epidermal thickness, increased number of mitoses in keratinocytes, elimination of epidermal atypia, and, according to some authors, the formation of collagen with normal-appearing structure and orientation in the papillary dermis as well as increased numbers of anchoring fibrils at the dermoepidermal junction.

Facial wrinkling can also be treated surgically with rhytidectomy (face lift) and soft tissue implants. Bovine type I collagen (Zyderm I and II) can be used for correction of superficial wrinkles, and a cross-linked bovine collagen product (Zyplast) is designed to raise deeper depressed areas. Autologous fat obtained from liposuction may also be used for soft tissue augmentation. Telangiectasia can be treated with electrocoagulation, argon laser, or pulsed dye laser. Chemical peels and dermabrasion correct wrinkling and diminish the size and number of benign or premalignant growths.

Prevention is the cornerstone of the management of photoaging, and there are several strategies for insuring proper sun protection. Because photodamage is the result of cumulative exposure to UVA and UVB, there is no "safe" tan.

Sun exposure should be avoided between the peak hours of 11:00 a.m. and 3:00 p.m. Initial exposures should be limited to 15 to 20 minutes in the morning or late afternoon. Window glass blocks virtually all UVB but offers only limited photoprotection against UVA.

Sunscreens with a sun protection factor (SPF) of at least 15 (see below) should be used on a *daily* basis, and they should be reapplied after sweating or bathing. Contrary to popular belief, the intensity of solar radiation is reduced by only half or less on a moderately cloudy day.

Adequate clothing should be worn at all times, including a wide-brimmed hat. Wet or loosely woven clothes can allow significant UV radiation to pass through to the skin.

Because photodamage is cumulative and significant sun exposure occurs during the early years of life, these measures should begin in childhood. Sunscreens may be used as early as 6 months. Prior to that time, the infant should not be exposed to direct sunlight.

The SPF is the principal measure of a sunscreen's effectiveness: SPF is defined as the ratio of the amount of UVB energy required to produce a minimal erythema reaction after application of the sunscreen to the amount of energy required to produce the same erythema without any sunscreen application. In actual use, the SPF achieved in natural sunlight tends to be somewhat lower than the SPF derived from tests with laboratory light sources. Under most conditions, a sunscreen with an SPF of 15 or greater is recommended.

Sunscreens contain active ingredients that prevent photodamage by either chemical or physical means. Chemical sunscreens contain one or more UV-absorbing chemicals in cosmetically acceptable lotions or cream bases. The most widely used chemical sunscreens contain para-aminobenzoic acid (PABA) and its esters, benzophenones, or cinnamates. PABA and PABA esters absorb predominantly in the UVB range, and they may cause irritant and contact allergic reactions with cross-reactions to a broad variety of so-called aromatic para-compounds. Benzophenones and cinnamates absorb UVB and shorter wavelengths of UVA. Cinnamates may also cause allergic contact dermatitis, and they are generally more easily removed by water or sweat. In general, most of the current chemical sunscreens offer protection against UVB but are less effective against UVA. Because of the new appreciation for the deleterious effects of UVA, there has recently been an increased interest in developing and assessing sunscreens that provide adequate protection against this type of UV radiation. Recently, a new sunscreen, butylmethoxydibenzoylmethane (Parsol 1789), has become available. This compound appears to be an effective UV screen throughout the UVA region but has poor UVB absorption and may therefore be complementary to the classic UVB screens. Physical sunscreens are usually opaque formulations that reflect and scatter UV radiation. Examples include titanium dioxide, talc, kaolin, zinc oxide, and iron oxide. They provide a broad spectrum of photoprotection; however, since they are visible, they are often cosmetically less acceptable, and because of their occlusive effects, they may also provoke folliculitis. Zinc oxide was recently shown to be a less effective sunscreen than opaque sunscreens that contain a visible light absorber, such as iron oxide.

Sunscreens containing photosensitizing substances are widely used in certain European countries. These are marketed as "agents that allow rapid, safe, and controlled tanning." The use of these products is not recommended, since the long-term safety of these substances has not been established and because the presentation of sunscreens as tanning promoters is confusing at a time when accurate public education is a priority.

Ellis CN, Weiss JS, Hamilton TA, et al.: Sustained improvement with prolonged topical tretinoin (retinoic acid) for photoaged skin. *J Am Acad Dermatol.* 1990;23:629–637.
This article presents the clinical and histologic results of an open-label, nonblind, 22-month trial of topical tretinoin in the treatment of photoaging. Of the original group of 30 patients who participated in a 4-month double-blind study, 16 continued treatment for 22 months.
Gilchrest BA: Skin aging and photoaging: an overview. *J Am Acad Dermatol.* 1989;21:610–613.
A concise overview of age-associated skin changes at the cellular and histologic level and their clinical correlates.
Kaye ET, Levin JA, Blank IH, et al. Efficiency of opaque photoprotective agents in the visible light range. *Arch Dermatol.* 1991;127(3):351–355.
Transmittance using zinc oxide paste was high despite high layer thickness. Opaque sunscreens containing visible light absorbers were more effective.
Menter JM: Recent developments in UVA photoprotection. *Int J Dermatol.* 1990;29:389–394.
This article highlights some recent developments in the area of UVA photoprotection. Several methods for evaluating the effectiveness of UVA-absorbing sunscreens are critically discussed.
Taylor CR, Stern RS, Leyden JJ, Gilchrest BA: Photoaging, photodamage, and photoprotection. *J Am Acad Dermatol.* 1990;22:1–15.
A recent and well-written review that attempts to situate the problem of photoaging in a broader psychosocial frame of reference.

54. HAND DERMATITIS
Susan D. DeCoste

Hand dermatitis is an eczematous eruption localized to the hands, with little dermatitis elsewhere. Afflicting about 4% to 8% of the population, it is a common problem that challenges clinicians both diagnostically and therapeutically. Hand dermatitis may be multifactorial in etiology; an underlying endogenous cause of dermatitis is often exacerbated by exogenous contactants.

Contact dermatitis is the most common type of exogenous hand dermatitis. Contactants can produce irritant or allergic eczematous reactions and, less commonly, urticarial contact or systemic contact reactions.

Irritant dermatitis accounts for about 70% of contact hand dermatitis. Irritants directly damage the skin and produce dermatitis without antecedent sensitization. Detergents, soaps, and solvents are important causes of irritant hand dermatitis. Severe reactions can be produced by strong acids and alkalies. Topical medications are frequently incriminated, especially those containing propylene glycol and other potentially irritating ingredients. *Housewife's eczema* is the term given to irritant dermatitis affecting those who do wet work. Housewives are affected, as are medical personnel and kitchen workers. Fruit and vegetable juices may contribute in those who handle foods. Friction, occlusion, lacerations, cold dry air, and an atopic background are factors that contribute to irritant dermatitis.

Irritant hand dermatitis may clinically range from slight erythema to large bullae with necrosis. It is usually characterized by scaling, erythema, and dryness with fissuring and thickening of the dorsal and lateral surface of the hands and fingers; palmar skin is rarely involved. The reaction may be localized to the skin under a ring, as soaps and detergents are often trapped in such an area.

Contact allergic hand dermatitis is seen in 25% to 30% of cases. It is of major importance because it leads to the need for job change if allergen avoidance is not otherwise possible. The mechanism of sensitization is a delayed-type hypersensitivity reaction. Preexisting irritant dermatitis can predispose the individual to the development of allergy due to increased antigen absorption through dermatitic skin. Clinically, allergic contact hand dermatitis begins as an acute eczematous process. It usually evolves into chronically thickened and lichenified skin indistinguishable from that caused by irritant dermatitis.

Significant etiologic agents in allergic hand dermatitis include nickel, chromate, rubber compounds, paraphenylenediamine, and parabens. Nickel allergy is present in about 5% of the population, more commonly in women. Nickel is present in costume jewelry, coins, handles, pens, surgical instruments, and kitchen utensils, all of which can play a role in hand dermatitis. Chromate-sensitized individuals can develop hand dermatitis from industrial exposure, especially to cement, leather goods, certain paints, and photography dyes. Chemicals added to natural rubber, such as mercaptobenzothiazole and thiuram, are causes of rubber sensitization, producing hand dermatitis through contact with rubber gloves and rubber tubing. Paraphenylenediamine is present in azo dyes and frequently causes problems for hairdressers. Paraben-sensitive patients experience flares from the use of many topical medications, cosmetics, and foods.

Contact urticarial dermatitis refers to a localized wheal-and-flare response elicited within minutes to about an hour after contact with intact skin. The prevalence of contact urticaria involving the hands is unknown. Contact urticarial hand dermatitis is most significant in food handlers, especially those working with seafood.

Systemic contact-type dermatitis involving the hands can occur with ingestion of certain allergens. Ingestion of nickel or chromate in some patients with contact hypersensitivity to those agents can cause a flare of hand dermatitis or produce pompholyx (dyshidrotic eczema) of the hands. The hand dermatitis caused by nickel ingestion may be improved with a nickel-free diet or chelation of nickel with disulfuram.

Photocontact hand dermatitis is most often a phototoxic reaction. This nonimmunologic reaction occurs with certain photosensitive agents such as celery, parsley, parsnips, and limes in the presence of sunlight, and requires no previous exposure to the agent.

Atopic dermatitis is the major endogenous cause of hand dermatitis. Affected individuals generally have a history of atopic eczema in infancy or childhood, asthma or allergic rhinitis, or a positive family history of atopy. Flexural areas are often involved with lichenification, but hand dermatitis may be the sole manifestation. Most commonly, contact with an irritant exacerbates an atopic diathesis. About 70% of people with an atopic background who do wet work will develop hand dermatitis.

Psoriasis is a common endogenous cause of hand dermatitis. The lesions may be localized to the hands, and often involve mostly the palms, unlike the lesions of contact hand dermatitis. There is often a positive family history of psoriasis, and examination of the scalp, nails, intergluteal and extensor areas will commonly reveal typical lesions of psoriasis.

Pustular dermatoses of the hands are often variants of psoriasis. Pustular palmoplantar psoriasis is a chronic recurrent condition with crops of sterile pustules on the palms and soles. There may be a family history of psoriasis, but psoriasis may not be present elsewhere on the body. The lesions display eczematous hyperkeratotic features in late stages when they dry. Acrodermatitis continua of Hallopeau is a rare sterile pustular eruption involving distal fingers and toes with nail destruction and is probably a variant of psoriasis.

Dyshidrotic eczema, or pompholyx, is an entity involving the hands and the feet with very pruritic, deep-seated vesicles. The sides of the digits are usually affected. The etiology is most often unknown. The course is recurrent, with episodes having sudden onset and lasting about 3 weeks. Exogenous factors such as ingested allergens can produce similar eruptions. Active dermatophyte infection elsewhere can produce a hypersensitivity id reaction with pompholyx-like lesions on the palms.

Nummular eczema is a condition characterized by coin-shaped eczematous plaques, usually on the dorsal surface of the hands. Lesions may be present elsewhere, including the extremities. The etiology is probably multifactorial, with an association with dry skin, especially in the elderly, and exacerbation by irritants.

Other endogenous causes of hand dermatitis are uncommon. Hyperkeratotic palmar dermatitis is an eczematous condition characterized by scaly fissured plaques on the palms, with no evidence of psoriasis, atopy, or contact dermatitis.

Establishing the **diagnosis** of hand dermatitis begins with a thorough history and physical examination. A personal or family history of psoriasis or atopy is significant. A detailed history of exposure at work, at home, with hobbies, and to topical medicaments should be obtained. The effect of vacations on the dermatitis may also give useful information regarding occupational exposure. On physical examination, palmar involvement is suggestive of endogenous causes. When nail folds are involved with dermatitis, nail changes such as pitting and dystrophy may develop; however, if there is no periungual involvement, an endogenous cause such as psoriasis is suggested. Examination of the entire skin is important, particularly the feet.

Patch testing is needed when allergic contact dermatitis is suspected or in recalcitrant cases of unclear etiology (see Chap. 60). The patient should be tested with the standard patch test series, as well as with potential allergens at work and at home. Positive patch tests indicate allergens that can then be documented to contribute to the initiation or exacerbation of the hand dermatitis. In cases of suspected contact urticaria, the suspected allergen is applied to intact skin and examined for a wheal in 20 to 30 minutes. If this test is negative, it should be repeated on mildly dermatitic skin.

The **differential diagnosis** of hand dermatitis includes infectious and neoplastic disorders and various other dermatoses that can present on the hands. Tinea manum is seen with palmar fissuring and scaling or with vesicles, often on only one hand. Onychomycosis and tinea pedis are usually present. Primary or recurrent herpes simplex can produce localized vesicles on the hand, often localized to one digit. Bowen's disease may present as a well-demarcated erythematous plaque on the palm or dorsal surface of the hand. Keratodermas of the palms and soles, with localized thickening of the stratum corneum, can mimic hand dermatitis. Lichen planus can be extensive on the hands, including the palms. Erythema multiforme and secondary syphilis can present with localized palmar lesions. Bullous dermatoses such as porphyria cutanea tarda and epidermolysis bullosa acquisita are often localized to the dorsal surface of the hands. Dermatitis herpetiformis may also uncommonly present on the hands.

The **management** of hand dermatitis entails certain principles that apply regardless of etiology. Avoidance of irritants is crucial in all cases, as irritants can cause a flare in any type of hand dermatitis. Wet work should be avoided, and hand washing should be minimized and should always be followed by application of an emollient. Vinyl gloves provide the most effective protection for hands because they are hypoallergenic and impermeable to many potential allergens. It is helpful to have patients wear white cotton gloves inside of vinyl gloves to ensure that the hands remain dry. Skin lubrication is also important. Bland emollients, such as white petrolatum, should be frequently applied during the day to all scaly, fissuring dermatoses. Their effectiveness is enhanced if applied while the skin is wet.

Topical corticosteroids are the mainstay of treatment to suppress inflammation. In mild cases, a mid-potency agent can be effective and should be used in conjunction with separate applications of lubricants. In moderate or severe cases, a high-potency agent should be used twice daily. Ointment vehicles are preferable because of their increased penetration and lubricating effects. Palmar dermatitis is generally more recalcitrant, and occlusion with a mid- to high-potency agent overnight may be necessary. Patients with moderate to severe dermatitis should be reevaluated in 1 to 2 weeks and weaned gradually off high-potency medications. The potential for overuse producing the unwanted side effect of skin atrophy should be explained to patients.

In acute exudative or vesicular dermatitis, aluminum acetate soaks for 15 minutes 3 or 4 times daily are beneficial. Corticosteroid creams can be used initially, then ointments. In acute, severe cases with marked blistering, early treatment with systemic corticosteroids may be warranted if there are no contraindications. The course, starting with about 1 mg of prednisone per kilogram body weight, should be tapered over approximately 2 weeks. This therapy is not indicated for chronic dermatitis.

Bacterial superinfection may be present in acute and chronic cases of hand dermatitis. Systemic antibiotics may be used for 7 to 10 days in suspected cases of infection, especially when there is crust and exudate. Candidal superinfection can also occur, especially in those patients doing wet work. Erosio interdigitalis blastomycetica is an interdigital candidal infection of the hands, often presenting with maceration in the space between the third and fourth fingers. Topical antiyeast medications and reduction of wet work should lead to resolution.

Adjunctive therapy is needed with topical corticosteroids in some cases. Tar preparations may be helpful, especially in chronic cases, and may be used in the form of tar soaks or tar gels. Oral antihistamines are beneficial when pruritus is significant. Flexible collodion or Epilyt may be used on fissured areas.

Recalcitrant hand dermatitis may respond to some other treatments. Intralesional corticosteroids can be used when there is localized resistant plaque-type psoriasis. Triamcinolone diacetate, 2–10 mg/ml, can be injected at 6- to 8-week intervals. Photochemotherapy has been shown to be beneficial in some cases of recalcitrant endogenous hand dermatitis. Oral 8-methoxypsoralen with UVA (PUVA) may clear plaque-type psoriasis of the hands, chronic pustular palmar eruptions, endogenous eczema, and pompholyx. Long-term maintenance therapy may be needed. The combination of PUVA with retinoids such as etretinate in pustular hand dermatitis is also reported to be effective. Because of the significant short-term side effects of the retinoids as well as their teratogenicity, these agents should be administered only for severe resistant cases.

Epstein E: Hand dermatitis: Practical management and current concepts. *J Am Acad Dermatol.* 1984;10:395–424.
Excellent comprehensive review of hand dermatitis, including etiology and treatment.

Fisher AA: Hand dermatitis due to contactants. In: *Contact Dermatitis.* 3rd ed. Philadelphia, PA: Lea & Febiger:1986.
Practical aspects of irritant and allergic hand dermatitis.

Hersle K, Mobacken H: Hyperkerototic dermatitis of the palms. *Br J Dermatol.* 1982;107:195–202.
Characterization of this distinct entity in 32 patients.

Holness DL, Nethercott JR: Dermatitis in hairdressers. *Dermatol Clin.* 1990 Jan;8(1):119–126.
Hand dermatitis in hairdressers is commonly secondary to irritant contact dermatitis due to shampooing or allergic contact dermatitis due to dyes and waving components.

Jordan WP: Allergic contact dermatitis in hand eczema. *Arch Dermatol.* 1974;110:567–569.
Evaluation of 220 patients with hand eczema revealed allergic contact dermatitis in 17% in whom the eruption cleared with allergen avoidance.

Lantinga H, Nater JP, Coenraads PJ: Prevalence, incidence and course of eczema on the hands and forearms in a sample of the general population. *Contact Dermatitis.* 1984;10:135–139.
Epidemiologic study of contact hand dermatitis.

Morison, WL, Parrish, JA, Fitzpatrick TB: Oral methoxypsoralen photochemotherapy of recalcitrant dermatoses of the palms and soles. *Br J Dermatol.* 1978;99:297–302.
Successful treatment of psoriasis and endogenous eczema of the hands with PUVA.

von Krogh G, Maibach HI: The contact urticaria syndrome—an updated review. *J Am Acad Dermatol.* 1981;5:328–342.
Summary of the pathogenesis and diagnostic evaluation of contact urticaria.

55. DIAPER DERMATITIS
Clarence E. Boudreaux

Diaper dermatitis is not a specific diagnosis but a localized response to a combination of factors unique to the diaper area. The exact incidence of diaper dermatitis is unknown; however, between 10% and 20% of all skin consultations for children up to 5 years old are accountable to diaper rash.

Chafing is the most common type of diaper dermatitis. In chafing, the convex surfaces of the diaper area are involved and skin folds are spared. The eruption quickly waxes and wanes and occurs on areas where friction is greatest: over the buttocks, mons pubis, lower abdomen, and inner surface of the thighs. The skin is shiny and erythematous, with occasional development of papules. Friction in a chronically wet environment is the major cause; ammonia and microorganisms play no demonstrable role.

Candidal diaper dermatitis presents with confluent erythema involving the intertriginous folds. The border of the erythema is sharply demarcated, and beyond it there are satellite papules, pustules, and small erosions. Satellite lesions will give the highest yield for KOH and cultures. Pseudohyphae, hyphae, and budding yeasts are characteristically found in the bullae and pustules. The central area of erythema will often give false-negative KOH and culture results due to the localized suppression of the organism by the host's inflammatory response.

Occasionally an infant with candidiasis will develop a disseminated eruption of papules and plaques on the trunk, extremities, and neck. This id or autosensitivity reaction is poorly understood but is believed to result from antigenic dissemination. *Candida* is rarely found in the diaper area of normal infants.

Infants with candidal diaper dermatitis will have *Candida* recoverable from the gastrointestinal tract in 93% of cases. Whether treatment of these patients with oral nystatin may help clear the diaper dermatitis more quickly and decrease the incidence of recurrence is controversial. Other sources may be responsible for repeated introduction of *C. albicans,* including maternal vaginal candidiasis, candidal infection of the nipple, pacifiers, and bottle nipples. These sources should be sought and removed. Recurrences are frequent. Repeated candidal diaper dermatitis without other signs or symptoms suggesting immunologic incompetency does not warrant an evaluation for an immunodeficiency disorder.

The clinical features of the diaper rash of **atopic dermatitis** are variable. Some cases are similar to chafing dermatitis. In other cases a more characteristic eczematous dermatitis (an erythematous papular eruption with scaling, small vesicles, exudates, and honey-colored crusts) is present. Diaper-area atopic dermatitis is chronic and more difficult to treat. Other evidence for atopic dermatitis can usually be found on the cheeks, neck, extremities, or antecubital fossae. A family history of asthma, seasonal rhinitis, or atopic dermatitis helps to establish the diagnosis.

Atopic dermatitis of the diaper area has an extremely high rate of secondary infection with *Staphylococcus aureus.* Cultures have shown that in up to 100% of atopic infants, *S. aureus* colonizes the affected areas. Although this organism may account for 80% of the bacterial flora in the affected areas, typical signs of pyoderma (crusting, weeping, exudate, and fever) are not usually present. Nonetheless, antibacterials may be helpful for treating recalcitrant atopic diaper dermatitis.

In **seborrheic dermatitis** the folds are involved and affected areas are sharply demarcated. Erythema and scaling occur most predominantly in the groin and gluteal cleft. Similar lesions with greasy scale and yellowish color may be found on the scalp ("cradle cap"), in the folds of the neck or arms, and in the axillae.

C. albicans is thought by some authors to be involved in the pathogenesis of diaper-area seborrheic dermatitis. In one study, 80% of cultures from infants with seborrheic dermatitis were positive for *Candida; C. albicans* was therefore considered a major factor in continuance of the rash. These authors contend that therapy for diaper-area seborrheic dermatitis should include an anticandidal agent.

Several factors are involved in the development of **irritant diaper dermatitis.**

These factors include characteristics of the host, colonization and invasion by microorganisms, contact with irritants, occlusion, friction, and wetness. Some infants have skin types that are more easily irritated by environmental factors or penetrable by microorganisms. This predisposition is especially evident in patients with atopic dermatitis. Infants may also have inherited diatheses for psoriasis or seborrheic dermatitis.

Classic **impetigo** may occur in the diaper area, presenting as weeping erosions that often have honey-colored crusts. A bullous form of impetigo may occur also, due to a localized infection with *S. aureus* phage type II, which produces exfoliative toxin. This toxin causes separation of the upper epidermis and formation of flaccid bullae filled with straw-colored fluid. Diagnosis can be established by culture and Gram stain.

In 1921, Cooke first implicated ammonia in the pathogenesis of diaper dermatitis and isolated *Bacillus ammoniagines* as the microorganism responsible for the degradation of urea to ammonia. For decades this theory for ammoniacal diaper dermatitis has been accepted by pediatric authorities and textbooks. However, recent investigations have shown no difference in ammonia content or ammonia-producing organisms in infants with or without diaper rash. Furthermore, application of ammonia under occlusion at concentrations 19 times greater than that found in diapers of infants with diaper rash failed to produce erythema on the skin of normal infants after 24 hours. Present data suggest that ammonia is not involved in the pathogenesis of diaper dermatitis. Once erosions have developed from wetness, heat, and friction, however, ammonia may contribute to the irritation of the damaged skin.

Occlusion of skin by diapers traps water against the skin. This trapping causes hydration of the stratum corneum and increases the penetration of irritants and may increase susceptibility to the forces of friction and invasion by bacteria and yeast. Diapers that keep the diaper area drier are associated with a lower incidence of diaper rash.

Treatment of diaper dermatitis includes general measures that are applicable in nearly all cases. Diapers should be changed promptly after voiding or soiling or at least every 4 hours. Parents should be encouraged to use disposable or superabsorbent diapers at least temporarily. Rubber and plastic pants should be avoided. Occasional diaper-free periods are helpful. Soaps, detergents, and commercial diaper wipes should be avoided. Plain water and a soft cloth or paper towels should be used to clean the diaper area. If diaper dermatitis has been present for more than 3 to 4 days, infection by *C. albicans* should be suspected. Fluorinated steroids should not be used in the diaper area.

Specific treatments are dictated by the type of dermatitis encountered. Candidal diaper dermatitis can be treated with a wide variety of anticandidal creams. If candidal diaper dermatitis is frequently recurrent or recalcitrant, a course of nystatin oral suspension may be considered. A 1% hydrocortisone cream is frequently adequate for decreasing the inflammation of seborrheic dermatitis or atopic dermatitis. Infants with atopic diaper dermatitis should also be examined for the presence of *S. aureus*. In nonexudative dermatitis associated with *S. aureus,* topical antibacterial agents applied 3 to 4 times a day may be effective. If exudation is present, systemic dicloxacillin may be needed. Erythromycin, 40 mg/kg/d in four divided doses, may be used as an alternative to dicloxacillin.

If a rash in the diaper area does not respond to general and specific treatment measures, other diagnoses need to be considered. **Letterer-Siwe disease** is a malignant proliferation of histiocytic cells and is a form of **histiocytosis X.** Clinically it presents with scaling and erosions of the scalp, behind the ears, in the axillae, and the diaper area. It may be mistaken for seborrheic dermatitis. A tendency for the rash to become purpuric is a helpful clinical feature.

Granuloma gluteale infantum presents with red-purple granulomatous nodules that resemble those of Kaposi's sarcoma. The nodules appear to be a response to inflammation, maceration, and secondary candidal infection that has been inappropriately treated with topical fluorinated steroids.

Acrodermatitis enteropathica is a sign of zinc deficiency. Manifestations may occur at the time of weaning from breast feeding and consist of acral and periorificial blisters, erosions, and pustules; eczematous dermatitis; glossitis; diarrhea; alopecia; and frequent infections with *C. albicans*. It responds to zinc replacement.

Psoriasis of the diaper area has well-demarcated ruby red plaques, often with a heavy scale. Involvement of the scalp and trunk with typical psoriasiform lesions and a positive family history of psoriasis are helpful in confirming the diagnosis. Bullous lesions in the diaper area may represent bullous impetigo, congenital syphilis, herpes simplex, epidermolysis bullosa, contact dermatitis, or staphylococcal scalded skin syndrome.

Campbell RL, Bartlett AV, Sarbaugh FC, et al.: Effects of diaper types on diaper dermatitis associated with diarrhea and antibiotic use in children in day-care centers. *Pediatr Dermatol.* 1988;5:83–87.
The severity of diaper dermatitis was less in children wearing absorbent gelling material disposable diapers than those wearing conventional disposable diapers.

Honig PJ: Diaper dermatitis. Factors to consider in diagnosis and treatment. *Postgrad Med.* 1983;74:79–84.
A critical review of diaper dermatitis and therapeutic factors.

Honig PJ, Gribetz B, Leyden JJ, McGinley KJ, Burke LA: Amoxicillin and diaper dermatitis. *J Am Acad Dermatol.* 1988;19:275–279.
Antibiotic therapy was associated with a twofold increase in the recovery of C. albicans *from the rectum and skin, and infants who developed diaper dermatitis had increase in* C. albicans *from those sites. The use of amoxicillin increased the risks of developing diaper rash.*

Lane AT, Rehder PA, Helm K: Evaluations of diapers containing absorbent gelling material with conventional disposable diapers in newborn infants. *Am J Dis Child.* 1990 Mar;144(3):315–318.
Infants in diapers containing absorbent gelling materials had less diaper dermatitis than those in conventional disposable diapers.

Leyden JJ, Katz S, Stewart R, et al.: Urinary ammonia and ammonia-producing microorganisms in infants with and without diaper dermatitis. *Arch Dermatol.* 1977;113:1678–1680.
This study of 26 infants with "ammoniacal dermatitis" and 82 controls did not support the notion that ammonia is a primary factor in the common diaper rash.

Rebora A, Leyden JJ: Napkin (diaper) dermatitis and gastrointestinal carriage of Candida albicans. *Br J Dermatol.* 1981;105:551–555.
The authors define four clinically distinct types of diaper dermatitis based on the presence or absence of C. albicans *on the skin and in the gastrointestinal tract.*

Weston WL, Lane AT, Weston JA: Diaper dermatitis: current concepts. *Pediatrics.* 1980;66:532–536.
A review of the topic which notes that diaper dermatitis results from prolonged skin contact with wetness and bacteria and that ammonia plays no apparent role in the causation of this rash. The authors caution that potent topical corticosteroids, boric acid, and mercury-containing preparations should be avoided in the diaper area because of their toxicity.

X. ALLERGY AND IMMUNOLOGY

Mark S. Bernhardt

Vasculitis refers to a group of syndromes that involve inflammation and necrosis of blood vessels and are defined by distinctive clinical, pathologic, and laboratory findings. Organization by the predominant vessel type involved provides a framework that is both didactically and diagnostically useful. Cutaneous lesions usually allow one to predict the caliber of affected vessels. The "cayenne pepper spots" of capillaritis, the palpable purpura of venulitis, and the painful nodules of arteritis are the best-known examples. Within this broad classification, further differentiation is made by lesional morphology, associated internal organ involvement, predilection for anatomic region, and histologic features.

The various forms of capillaritis share a similar histologic picture, characterized by endothelial swelling, perivascular lymphocytic infiltration, extravasation of red blood cells, and hemosiderin deposits. With the exception of meprobamate-induced capillaritis, the etiology of these conditions is unknown. There are no associated systemic abnormalities. Adults are predominantly affected by all forms of capillaritis. Familial incidence is rare. The capillaritides are clinical syndromes distinguished by subtle morphologic differences.

The prototype of capillaritis is **progressive pigmented purpuric dermatosis** (Schamburg's disease). Lesions tend to involve the lower extremities and consist of asymptomatic, ill-defined, irregular, tan to orange macules speckled with discrete cayenne pepper spots. Purpuric lichenoid dermatosis of Gougerot-Blum and purpura annularis telangiectodes (Majocchi's disease) are clinical variants in which violaceous papules in the former, and an annular configuration in the latter, permit clinical subtyping. All forms of capillaritis tend to be chronic and resistant to therapy. Topical steroids or UVB phototherapy is occasionally helpful.

Lichen aureus has been classified as a capillaritis, but recent reports suggest that rather than being a form of vessel inflammation, it is due to a "hemosiderin tattoo" from incompetence of perforating veins or other anatomic abnormality. Lesions are single or few in number, unilateral, of sudden onset, and often pruritic. They have a distinctive golden hue and histologically show an intense, bandlike, lymphocytic infiltrate with erythrocyte extravasation.

Most cases of cutaneous vasculitis represent a hypersensitivity reaction involving the venules, known as **cutaneous necrotizing venulitis,** hypersensitivity vasculitis, or leukocytoclastic vasculitis. The latter is most appropriately a histologic rather than clinical term, referring to the changes of segmental endothelial cell swelling of the venule, fibrinoid necrosis, and neutrophilic perivascular infiltration with karyorrhexis (leukocytoclasia). Though demonstrable in only rare instances, necrotizing venulitis is considered to be an immune complex–mediated disease in which circulating immune complexes formed in mild antigen excess deposit in postcapillary venules and activate the complement cascade, thus attracting neutrophils with damage to the vessels secondary to neutrophilic enzymes.

The classic clinical manifestation of necrotizing venulitis is palpable purpura. Most common on the legs, other dependent parts, and areas subjected to external pressure, these lesions begin as erythematous macules that become slightly elevated and will not blanch with pressure. Necrotizing venulitis may also present with urticaria-like lesions, nodules, pustules, vesicles, ulcers, gangrene, and a netlike mottling of the skin (livedo reticularis).

Although the distinctions between the forms of capillaritis may appear trivial, the proper categorization of a patient with necrotizing venulitis makes a significant difference with regard to proper management and prognosis. An orderly approach first excludes a provocative factor or associated disorder. Infectious agents known to cause vasculitis include hepatitis B virus, group A beta-hemolytic streptococcus, *Staphylococcus aureus,* and *Mycobacterium leprae.* Numerous drugs have been implicated in necrotizing venulitis, most commonly sulfonamides, thiazides, penicillin and its derivatives, and serum products. The collagen-vascular diseases of rheumatoid arthritis, lupus erythematosus, and Sjögren's syndromes are frequently associated with necrotizing venulitis. In most of these patients the underlying disease is quite active with high titers of associated antibody abnormalities, although systemic lupus erythematosus may present with an urticarial vasculitis and few other manifestations. Hypergammaglobulinemia and cryoglobulinemia, either primary or secondary to another chronic disease such as a lymphoproliferative state or collagen-vascular disorder, may also present as necrotizing venulitis. Since the clinical manifestation offers little if any clue to the presence of an underlying disease, appropriate investigations must be performed before any case of necrotizing venulitis is considered idiopathic. Even then, further differentiation is clinically useful.

Henoch-Schönlein purpura is the most commonly recognized syndrome of idiopathic necrotizing venulitis. A typical case is a child with a history of recent upper respiratory tract symptoms followed by the acute onset of arthralgia, abdominal pain, and skin lesions. Papular, purpuric, and urticarial lesions are seen. A distinctive pattern of reticulate purpuric plaques and ulceration has also been described. Renal vasculitis with proteinuria or frank nephritis may be transitory or progressive. Perivascular deposition of immunoglobulin A on indirect immunofluorescence testing of a skin biopsy is highly suggestive of Henoch-Schönlein purpura, in contrast to the less discriminatory findings of IgG, IgM, fibrin, and complement factor 3 found in other varieties of necrotizing venulitis. Indeed, whether a diagnosis of Henoch-Schönlein purpura should be made in the absence of IgA deposition is debatable, depending on whether one views it as a primary clinical syndrome or as an immunologically distinct disease. This disorder is usually self-limited in children; adults tend to follow the chronic course typical of idiopathic necrotizing venulitis.

Erythema elevatum diutinum is a progressive, symmetric papulonodular eruption favoring the extensor extremities and the buttocks. Arthralgia of the underlying joints is not uncommon. Lesions vary in color from yellow to reddish purple and may assume polycyclic and annular configurations. Differentiation from granuloma annulare and xanthomatosis can be difficult on morphologic grounds alone, but histologic examination of early lesions reveals typical leukocytoclastic vasculitis, while more chronic lesions often have extracellular cholesterol deposits (extracellular cholesterosis).

Nodular vasculitis (erythema induratum) consists of painful, erythematous nodules on the legs; these nodules may ulcerate and heal with atrophic scarring. Nodular vasculitis clinically enters into the differential diagnosis of inflammatory diseases of the subcutaneous fat (panniculitis). Women are far more frequently affected; systemic symptoms are absent.

Livedo vasculitis has traditionally been considered a necrotizing venulitis, although a skin biopsy shows not a necrotizing vasculitis but the occlusion of vessels by fibrin thrombi with secondary necrosis. Clinically, livedo vasculitis is characterized by persistent livedo reticularis of the legs, episodic ulceration, and healing with sclerotic hypopigmented areas surrounded by pinpoint telangiectasia (atrophie blanche).

Urticarial vasculitis is a useful concept in morphologic distinction to typical chronic urticaria. Patients tend to complain of a burning sensation rather than pruritus, and lesions last longer than 24 hours, resolving with residual ecchymoses or discoloration. Constitutional symptoms such as fever, malaise, arthralgia, and myalgia occur. The incidence of vasculitis found on histologic examination of clinically typical urticaria remains unknown. Even when no evidence of associated disorders is apparent at the time of presentation, one must remain vigilant, as overt systemic lupus erythematosus or other collagen-vascular disease may develop.

Treatment of necrotizing venulitis depends on whether a provocative agent can be withdrawn or specifically treated, or whether an underlying condition exists that would dictate therapy. Idiopathic necrotizing venulitis is usually treated with systemic corticosteroids, although controlled studies demonstrating their effectiveness are lacking. Other modalities that may be useful include sulfones, nonsteroidal anti-inflammatory agents, colchicine, and immunosuppressive agents. Sulfones are highly effective in suppressing erythema elevatum diutinum; cessation of therapy is associated with prompt exacerbation. Pentoxifylline (Trental) appears beneficial in the treatment of livedo vasculitis. Urticarial vasculitis is typically unresponsive to antihistamines, requiring systemic corticosteroids. Finally high-dose intravenous pulse corticosteroid therapy may be worthwhile in refractory cases of severe necrotizing venulitis.

When **cutaneous arteritis** presents as tender, nodose swellings that follow the course of an affected vessel, clinical recognition is easy. Less distinctive manifestations include localized erythema, edema, ulceration, and gangrene. Histology will demonstrate necrotizing vasculitis, but proper site selection and depth of biopsy are paramount since large vessels are involved segmentally. An incisional wedge biopsy, as opposed to a punch biopsy, is preferable. Angiography is useful for diagnosis as well as for location of the best site for biopsy. The site of involvement is a key factor in classifying the arteritides, including organ systems (pulmonary vs. renal), sites within an organ (upper vs. lower respiratory tract), or even distinct arterial branches (temporal artery vs. aorta).

Polyarteritis nodosa is a multisystem small- and medium-vessel arteritis with a predilection for the skin, kidneys, gastrointestinal tract, and nerves. Several precipitating factors are known, including streptococcal infections, hepatitis B virus infection, Kawasaki's disease, collagen-vascular diseases, hairy cell leukemia, and intravenous amphetamine abuse. Patients usually present with fever and other constitutional symptoms, leukocytosis, and an elevated erythrocyte sedimentation rate. Specific symptoms, signs, and laboratory test results reflect particular organ involvement. Typical cutaneous lesions of polyarteritis nodosa are painful, deep nodules along the course of superficial arteries of the lower extremities. Aneurysms, thromboses, gangrene, and livedo reticularis occur secondary to the arteritis. When the skin alone is affected (cutaneous polyarteritis nodosa), the course tends to be mild. Renal arteritis is the most frequent site of internal involvement, frequently results in hypertension, and is associated with a poor prognosis. Intestinal and pancreatic arteritis may produce abdominal pain and the more catastrophic events of peritonitis, bowel perforation, or hemorrhage. There are myriad neurologic manifestations, most commonly mononeuritis multiplex. Antineutrophil cytoplasmic autoantibodies specific for myeloperoxidase are found in patients with systemic necrotizing vasculitis of the polyarteritis type. Pulmonary artery involvement is not seen in polyarteritis nodosa. Combined corticosteroid and immunosuppressive (azathioprine or cyclophosphamide) therapy is preferable to single-agent treatment.

Giant cell arteritis is a medium- and large-vessel arteritis. The histologic features are a necrotizing vasculitis with mixed histiocytic and giant cell infiltrate (granulomatous vasculitis). The two syndromes of giant cell arteritis are **temporal arteritis** (involvement of vessels of the head and neck) and **Takayasu's arteritis** (involvement of the aortic arch and its branches). Both syndromes more frequently affect females. Temporal arteritis is a disease of the elderly, while Takayasu's arteritis is most common in young Oriental and Hispanic women. Cutaneous lesions are rarely described in Takayasu's arteritis. Although not prominent in temporal arteritis, they may at times be diagnostically helpful. A beefy red glossitis is the most typical cutaneous lesion. Ulceration and alopecia of the skin overlying the affected vessel may also be noted. Systemic corticosteroids are the treatment of choice for temporal arteritis. Takayasu's arteritis is usually unresponsive to therapy.

Allergic granulomatosis of Churg-Strauss is a rare syndrome characterized by asthma, eosinophilia, and a granulomatous vasculitis affecting blood vessels of all sizes. The vasculitic manifestations of allergic granulomatosis resemble those of polyarteritis nodosa, although there tends to be less renal involvement. More commonly, there are serious cardiopulmonary complications. Skin manifestations occur more often in allergic granulomatosis than in polyarteritis nodosa, but with similar morphology. Allergic granulomatosis also has characteristic subcutaneous granulomatous nodules of the scalp and extremities. Corticosteroids are the treatment of choice.

Wegener's granulomatosis is a granulomatous vasculitis that preferentially involves the skin, upper respiratory tract, and kidneys. Vessels of all sizes are affected. Although the cutaneous lesions of Wegener's granulomatosis are protean and clinically nonspecific, they are often the first manifestation of disease. Ulcers, papules, and plaques are commonly present on the lower extremities, but vesicles, petechiae, and subcutaneous nodules may also be seen. Paranasal sinusitis is the usual respiratory presentation. "Saddle nose" results from destruction of the septal cartilage. Glomerulonephritis is almost invariable. Antineutrophil cytoplasmic autoantibodies are detected in the majority of patients, but their role in pathogenesis remains to be determined. The differential diagnosis of Wegener's granulomatosis includes other vasculitic and granulomatous diseases, especially allergic granulomatosis, sarcoidosis, and lymphomatoid granulomatosis. Cyclophosphamide is the most effective therapy.

The clinical spectrum of **lymphomatoid granulomatosis** closely resembles that of Wegener's granulomatosis, with the former more commonly affecting the lower rather than the upper respiratory tract. Histologically, lymphomatoid granulomatosis demonstrates a granulomatous vasculitis with atypical lymphocytes (lymphomatoid vasculitis). Other processes with lymphomatoid vasculitis are angioimmunoblastic lymphadenopathy with dysproteinemia and lymphomatoid papulosis. **Angioimmunoblastic lymphadenopathy with dysproteinemia** (AILD) is characterized by lymphadenopathy, hepatosplenomegaly, anemia, hypergammaglobulinemia, and constitutional symptoms. A maculopapular erythematous eruption resembling an exanthem is common, but clinically nonspecific. **Lymphomatoid papulosis** affects only the skin with recurrent crops of erythematous lesions evolving as papules or nodules that crust or ulcerate and then heal with scarring. Approximately 10% of patients with lymphomatoid vasculitis eventually develop a full-fledged fatal lymphoma. In lymphomatoid granulomatosis, early therapy with corticosteroids and cyclophosphamide can induce remissions and apparently reduce the risk of malignant transformation. Effective treatment of AILD and lymphomatoid papulosis has not yet been found.

Baum EW, Sams WM Jr., Payne RR: Giant cell arteritis: Systemic disease with rare cutaneous manifestations. *J Am Acad Dermatol.* 1982;6:1081–1088.
Giant cell arteritis may present with scalp necrosis or gangrene of the tongue.

Crotty CP, DeRemee RA, Winkelmann RK: Cutaneous clinicopathologic correlation of allergic granulomatosis. *J Am Acad Dermatol.* 1981;5:571–581.
Authors present clinical and pathologic data suggesting that the disease represents a unique host response to multiple antigens.

Ewert BH, Jennette JC, Falk RJ: The pathogenic role of antineutrophil cytoplasmic autoantibodies. *Am J Kidney Dis.* 1991;18(2):188–195.
Antineutrophil cytoplasmic autoantibodies may play a pathogenic role in polyarteritis nodosa and Wegener's granulomatosus by activating neutrophils and monocytes.

Fauci AS, Hagnes BF, Katz P, et al.: Wegener's granulomatosis: Prospective clinical and therapeutic experience with 85 patients for 21 years. *Ann Intern Med.* 1983;98:76–85.
Long-term remissions were induced and maintained in the vast majority of patients by a combination of daily cyclophosphamide and alternate-day prednisone therapy.

Katz SI, Gallin JI, Hertz KC, et al.: Erythema elevatum diutinum—skin and systemic manifestations, immunologic studies, and successful treatment with dapsone. *Medicine (Baltimore).* 1977;56:443–455.
Review of five cases with excellent clinical and histological photographs. No single immunologic dysfunction was found, although all five had some impairment. Each of four patients treated with dapsone responded dramatically.

Patton WF, Lynch PJ II: Lymphomatoid granulomatosis: clinicopathologic study of four cases and literature review. *Medicine (Baltimore).* 1982;61:1–12.
Description of patients and review of the literature indicate the frequency of diagnostic delay, high mortality, and poor responsiveness to therapy in this disorder.

Piette WW, Stone MS: A cutaneous sign of IgA-associated small dermal vessel leukocytoclastic vasculitis in adults (Henoch-Schönlein purpura). *Arch Dermatol.* 1989;125:53–56.
Large purpuric plaques with retiform margins may be a specific presenting sign of IgA-associated necrotizing venulitis.

Sams WM Jr.: Necrotizing vasculitis. *J Am Acad Dermatol.* 1980;3:1–13.

Excellent review of currently understood pathogenesis, associated disorders, clinical manifestations, and therapy.

Sams WM Jr.: Livedo vasculitis: therapy with pentoxifylline. *Arch Dermatol.* 1988;124:684–687.

While receiving pentoxifylline, three of eight patients achieved complete healing and four noted much improvement.

Sanchez NP, Winkelmann RK, Schroeter AL, et al.: The clinical and histopathologic spectrums of urticarial vasculitis: study of 40 cases. *J Am Acad Dermatol.* 1982;7:599–605.

Authors divide patients with chronic urticaria and histologic features of necrotizing venulitis into two major groups: (1) hypocomplementemic (frequent renal disease, arthritis, and systemic disease) and (2) normocomplementemic (less severe clinical course).

Shelley WB, Swaminathan R, Shelley ED: Lichen aureus: hemosiderin tattoo associated with perforator vein incompetence. *J Am Acad Dermatol.* 1984;11:260–264.

Authors propose that lichen aureus is an "auto-tattoo" of insoluble hemosiderin granules.

Tervaert JW, Goldschmeding R, Elema JD, et al. Association of autoantibodies to myeloperoxidase with different forms of vasculitis. *Arthritis Rheum.* 1990;33(8):1264–1272.

Antineutrophil cytoplasmic autoantibodies (ANCA) recognize myeloperoxidase and a 29-Kd serine protease. The sensitivity and specificity of ANCA for these two disorders are 92% and 99%, respectively.

Verztman L: Polyarteritis nodosa. *Clin Rheum Dis.* 1980;6:297–317.

Excellent review with extensive reference list.

57. URTICARIA
Serge A. Coopman

Urticaria is a vascular reaction pattern characterized by transient localized swellings (wheals or hives) of the skin or mucous membranes. These swellings result from an increased permeability of blood vessel walls and a subsequent transudation of protein-rich fluid into the interstitium of the dermis. Because this fluid is gradually resorbed, individual lesions have a characteristic short life span and leave no trace. In angioedema, the process extends into the deeper dermis and the subcutis or the submucosal layers. Urticaria and angioedema may occur together or separately.

Wheal formation can be elicited by the action of several vasoactive mediators. Histamine seems to be an important mediator in most forms of urticaria. Injection of histamine into the skin produces the typical triple response of Lewis that consists of (1) an immediate red flush due to local vasodilation, (2) a more widespread erythematous flare due to reflex dilation of arterioles, and (3) wheal formation caused by increased capillary permeability. Histamine is stored in preformed granules of mast cells and basophils and can be released by a variety of immunologic and nonimmunologic triggers. In immune-mediated urticaria, an immunoglobulin E–dependent, type I hypersensitivity reaction occurs in which cell membrane–bound IgE interacts with antigens, resulting in mast cell degranulation. Histamine can also be released directly through the action of endogenous mediators (e.g., activated complement fragments) or pharmacologic agents. Well-known pharmacologic mast cell–releasing agents include opiates, curare, polymyxin-B, and radiocontrast media. Finally, there is some evidence that derivatives of arachidonic acid (especially the leukotrienes and prostaglandins) may play a role in the production or maintenance of urticaria.

Urticaria is a common **clinical problem,** affecting 20% of the population sometime during their lives. The characteristic wheals are evanescent, erythematous or white, sharply defined, nonpitting edematous papules or plaques that appear in crops. Lesions with pronounced edema often display a blanched center. Hives can vary considerably in size, from pinpoint to giant lesions that cover a substantial part of the body. They can enlarge by peripheral extension and become confluent, which results in striking polycyclic and geographic configurations (urticaria geographica). Individual lesions rarely persist longer than 12 to 24 hours, and they are usually seen in various stages of evolution and resolution. This is an important feature that distinguishes hives from other primary skin lesions. Intense pruritus is the cardinal symptom of urticaria, while a painful or burning sensation is more common in urticarial vasculitis or angioedema (see below).

For clinical convenience, urticaria is categorized as either acute or chronic. Acute urticaria is a self-limited disorder that evolves over a period of days or weeks, while chronic urticaria is arbitrarily defined as hives lasting longer than 6 weeks.

Acute urticaria may be limited to a single attack or consist of several brief recurrent episodes. Most cases of acute urticaria are caused by IgE-mediated mast cell degranulation triggered by foods, drugs, infections, or insect bites. The most common foods that cause recurrent attacks of urticaria are nuts, eggs, strawberries, tomatoes, chocolate, beans, fish, pork, yeast, citrus fruits, and seasonings. Hives usually appear within minutes to hours after ingestion of the food. Drugs that commonly provoke urticaria include aspirin and other nonsteroidal anti-inflammatory drugs, antibiotics (especially the penicillins and sulfonamides), and opiates. Urticaria is also commonly seen after the administration of blood, serum, or immunoglobulins. The presence of urticaria, fever, arthralgias, and lymphadenopathy in a patient receiving serum or immunoglobulins is strongly suggestive of serum sickness. Infections commonly implicated in urticaria include gastrointestinal infections with helminthic parasites, hepatitis B virus infections, dermatophytic infections of the skin, vaginal yeast infections, urinary tract infections, sinusitis, periapical dental abscesses, and tonsillitis.

Chronic urticaria represents a more challenging clinical problem, since an etiologic agent is often difficult to establish. Seventy to eighty percent of patients who have urticaria beyond 6 weeks will be classified as cases of chronic, idiopathic urticaria. Genetic factors (e.g., atopic diathesis) may determine an individual's reactivity to certain environmental allergens. Patients with atopy commonly have immediate type hypersensitivity to many environmental allergens, as demonstrated by scratch testing or a radioallergosorbent test. Many of these allergens (e.g., mold spores, animal danders, or pollen) are a relatively frequent cause of hives in people with atopy. A seasonal pattern and the concurrence of atopic dermatitis, asthma, or allergic rhinitis may suggest the diagnosis of atopy in some urticaria cases. Although foods are common causes of acute urticaria, they rarely cause chronic urticaria, with the well-known exception of sensitivity to food dyes such as tartrazine (FDA yellow dye #5), natural salicylates, and preservatives such as benzoic acid derivatives.

Some cases of chronic urticaria are caused by drugs. A regularly overlooked but frequent cause or perpetuating factor of chronic urticaria is aspirin. Aspirin intolerance may be found in as many as a third of the patients with chronic urticaria. People with aspirin intolerance may cross-react to other nonsteroidal anti-inflammatory drugs, and about one-fifth are expected to react to azo dyes, such as tartrazine and benzoates.

Low-grade chronic infections are also causes of chronic urticaria, but they are often symptomless and difficult to detect. However, it is debatable whether a rigorous search for occult infections should be conducted in urticaria patients, since the yield of such investigations is usually low and associations are probably often coincidental. Chronic urticaria can be the presenting sign of an underlying systemic disease, such as autoimmune thyroid disease, necrotizing vasculitis, collagen-vascular disease, and malignancy.

In some cases, hives are produced in response to a specific external physical trigger. The **physical urticarias** may be caused by both immunological mechanisms and direct stimulation of mast cell membrane receptors. **Dermatographism** (literally, the ability to write on skin) is the most common type of physical urticaria. Dermatographism (dermatographic urticaria) essentially represents an exaggeration of the physiologic triple response of Lewis and consists of itchy wheals developing within minutes at sites of friction or appearing as linear lesions from scratching. It is prevalent in many normal subjects as an idiopathic phenomenon. It can also appear after an illness, drug therapy, or pregnancy, and last for several months or years.

Cholinergic urticaria usually occurs in young adulthood and is triggered by an increase of global body temperature through heat, exercise, or emotion. In this condition, the hives are distinctive, small (2 to 4 mm), punctate, erythematous papules surrounded by a red flare. They typically appear on the neck and upper trunk, but they can spread distally to involve the whole body. The lesions usually last for 30 to 60 minutes and are often accompanied by itching, stinging, or burning. Other symptoms—such as wheezing, abdominal cramps, vomiting, diarrhea, hypotension, or angioedema—may occur. Unlike classic cholinergic urticaria, the localized form of heat urticaria is very rare. Exercise-induced anaphylaxis is a recently described, distinctive clinical entity characterized by urticarial lesions, upper airway obstruction, and hypotension only occurring after physical exercise. There is a high incidence of atopy in this syndrome, and the development of symptoms may be dependent on the prior ingestion of certain foods in some patients.

Solar urticaria is a form of urticaria in which pruritus and hives occur within minutes after exposure to either natural or artificial sources of light. The action spectrum seems to be complex and individually variable.

In **cold urticaria,** hives develop after exposure to cold air, water, or objects. Signs and symptoms may initially worsen upon rewarming but usually disappear within an hour. Cold urticaria occurs in a rare familial form, transmitted as an autosomal dominant trait, or can be acquired. In the familial variant, the urticarial lesions may be accompanied by fever, arthralgias, and leukocytosis. Acquired cold urticaria usually starts in young adulthood, often after an infection or drug therapy, and can last for years. The exact mechanism of wheal production is unknown. Cryoproteins are found in approximately one-third of the cases. Patients with total body exposure, such as when swimming in cold water, can experience severe reactions, with generalized hives, hypotension, fainting, shock, and even death.

Pressure urticaria is an uncommon form of urticaria characterized by a deep, often painful, swelling that occurs 4 to 6 hours after exposure to constant pressure and lasts hours to days. The disease usually runs a prolonged course. Spontaneous attacks can be elicited by tight clothing or belts, sitting, running, or manual labor. These episodes may be accompanied by flulike symptoms. A lack of response to antihistamines suggests that other mechanisms than the classic type I reaction are involved.

Contact urticaria is characterized by the occurrence of a wheal-and-flare response following direct contact of a chemical compound with the skin. It usually appears within 20 to 30 minutes. Contact urticaria can be elicited by immunologic (probably type I IgE-dependent) reactions toward a variety of antigens in foods (particularly meat and fish), drugs, textiles, and cosmetics, but can also be triggered by nonimmunologic mechanisms. Well-known causes of nonimmunologic contact urticaria include nettles, jellyfish, and chemicals such as dimethylsulfoxide. These reactions affect nearly all individuals exposed, without the need for specific sensitization. In some patients, an immediate urticarial response may be followed by an eczematous reaction of the delayed type. Finally, there are also a number of rare forms of urticaria/angioedema, such as **aquatic urticaria,** which occurs after contact with water, and **vibratory urticaria/angioedema.**

Thicker plaques that represent edema of the dermis and the subcutis are referred to as **angioedema.** These areas of deep swelling commonly involve the face and are usually not pruritic but are accompanied by a sense of pain or burning. They may last for 48 to 72 hours. There are both hereditary and acquired forms of angioedema, and only in the latter can urticaria and angioedema coexist. The hereditary forms, which are transmitted in an autosomal dominant manner, are caused by an absence or, more rarely, a functional deficiency of C1 inhibitor. Hereditary angioedema appears to involve both the complement- and the kinin-forming pathways. Affected persons have recurrent episodes of cutaneous angioedema, often with laryngeal and gastrointestinal involvement. Hoarseness, respiratory distress, and sore throat may be present. Acquired forms of angioedema can be triggered by a variety of factors, such as food, drugs (especially radiocontrast media), and insect stings. There is also an acquired form of C1 inhibitor deficiency that can be caused by a variety of lymphoproliferative and autoimmune diseases. Many cases of recurrent angioedema are idiopathic, however, occurring most frequently in middle-aged women.

Another distinctive entity, **urticarial vasculitis,** is clinically characterized by painful or burning urticarial plaques that persist longer than classic urticaria. The lesions may resolve with residual hyperpigmentation or purpura, and systemic manifestations of vasculitis may be present. This disease is thought to be caused by immune complex deposition, and, histologically, features of leukocytoclastic vasculitis are seen.

In the **diagnosis** of acute urticaria, a detailed history should be obtained with emphasis on foods, drugs (including agents that are often not considered, such as laxatives, mouthwashes, vitamins, and herbs), and exposure to pollen and chemicals. Gradual resolution of the urticaria is anticipated when the offending agents are identified and discontinued. A thorough physical examination focusing on the types and distribution of the lesions and testing for dermatographism may reveal a particular subtype of urticaria. Other causes of urticarial lesions should be considered in the differential diagnosis, such as papular urticaria (especially in small children), early bullous pemphigoid, urticaria pigmentosa, and erythema multiforme. Additional laboratory tests can be selected according to the findings in the history and physical examination. An extensive routine evaluation is usually not indicated or helpful in acute urticaria.

The evaluation of patients with chronic urticaria may be extensive and is often unrewarding. A detailed history and physical examination are essential. Physical urticaria can and should be ruled out by history and, if indicated, by some simple additional tests. In dermatographism, the clinician can elicit an exaggerated triple response of Lewis within a few minutes by firm stroking of the patient's skin with a tongue blade. Likewise, the clinician can elicit cholinergic urticaria by having the patient exercise or by immersing the patient in a warm bath. Caution should be exerted in cases in which exercise-induced anaphylaxis may occur. For pressure urticaria, a variety of testing devices using weights can be used. The area of pressure should be observed 4 to 8 hours later. To diagnose cold urticaria, the clinician can touch the patient's skin with an ice cube for 4 minutes and observe the area 10 minutes later, or immerse one of the patient's hands in cold water. If the history is suggestive of solar urticaria, phototesting may be performed. Contact urticaria can usually be diagnosed by an open patch test with readings after 30 minutes. Patch testing is first performed on nondiseased skin and, if negative, repeated on slightly or previously affected skin.

In the initial laboratory evaluation of chronic urticaria, a complete blood count, erythrocyte sedimentation rate, and urinalysis should be obtained. In selected cases, other useful diagnostic tests may include liver function tests, T4, thyroid microsomal antibodies, circulating immune complexes, complement levels, antinuclear antibodies, cryoglobulins, and hepatitis B surface antigen. In urticarial vasculitis, an elevated erythrocyte sedimentation rate, circulating immune complexes, and decreased complement may be found. A skin biopsy should be taken in cases suggestive of this entity. Radiographs of the chest, sinuses, and teeth can be indicated in some cases of urticaria. When a gastrointestinal infection is suspected, such as by history or on the basis of a prominent eosinophilia, a stool examination for parasites and ova can be performed. In possible cases of familial or acquired C1 inhibitor deficiency, a quantification and functional assay of C1 inhibitor is indicated. IgE-mediated reactions to specific foods, pollen, molds, and penicillin may be predicted by skin prick tests, but false-positive and false-negative reactions are common. These tests should not be performed in patients with dermatographism. The presence of specific IgE antibodies may be assessed with a radioallergosorbent test.

The best **treatment** of urticaria is the identification and elimination of the cause. The therapeutic approach in acute urticaria is conservative, since many cases end spontaneously and do not recur. If a specific causative antigen can be identified, suspected foods and drugs should be avoided and infections treated. Antihistamines can be given for symptomatic relief (see below).

The course of chronic urticaria is unpredictable. Fifty percent of patients with chronic urticaria without angioedema are symptom-free after 1 year, but 20% continue to experience lesions for more than 20 years. However, up to 75% of patients with chronic urticaria and angioedema still have attacks after 5 years. Since the yield of most work-ups for chronic urticaria is low, the physician must also provide reassurance and support.

In the physical urticarias, avoidance of the offending trigger is essential. In some cases (e.g., solar, cholinergic, or localized cold urticaria), it is possible to induce tolerance by graduated exposure to the inducing stimulus. Patients with cold urticaria should be warned that swimming is dangerous. In selected cases of chronic urticaria, dechallenge strategies can be tried under the form of a restricted diet or a change of environment. The disappearance of the hives and their recurrence upon rechallenge can identify potential triggers in food. There are several types and degrees of elimination diets, varying from the systematic avoidance of additives and salicylates to a very restrictive "lamb and rice" regimen. Patients with mold hypersensitivity, detected by a prick test, may benefit from a yeast-free diet (mainly avoiding fermented products) combined with a yeast elimination protocol with oral nystatin and a vaginal imidazole cream for 1 or 2 weeks. In cases in which a penicillin allergy is well documented, a diet free of dairy products that possibly contain penicillin contaminants (e.g., butter, cheese, ice cream, and creamed foods) can be tried. In some forms of chronic urticaria in which a focus of infection is suspected, a trial of a systemic antibiotic or anthelminthic may be indicated.

Antihistamines are the drugs of choice for the symptomatic treatment of urticaria. Antihistamines are chemical agents that prevent or block the action of histamine at its receptor sites. Although cutaneous blood vessels possess both H_1 and H_2 receptors, classic H_1 blockers are much more effective therapy for urticaria. Most antihistamines are well absorbed from the gastrointestinal tract and exert their action within 30 to 60 minutes. Their metabolism occurs mainly in the liver, and they are excreted by the kidneys. Many antihistamines stimulate their own metabolism by enzyme induction. The principal chemical classes of H_1 antihistamines are piperazines, e.g., hydroxyzine (Atarax); piperidines, e.g., cyproheptadine (Periactin); phenothiazines, e.g., promethazine (Phenergan); ethanolamines, e.g., diphenhydramine (Benadryl); ethylenediamines, e.g., pyrilamine maleate (Triaminic); and alkylamines, e.g., dexchlorpheniramine maleate (Polaramine). A list of antihistamines with their dosage is given in the chapter on pruritus. Common side effects of antihistamines include sedation and anticholinergic symptoms such as dry mouth, constipation, and blurred vision. Patients should be warned that antihistamines can potentiate the effects of alcohol and other CNS depressants. Topical antihistamine preparations have a considerable potential of inducing allergic contact dermatitis and should not be used. Some general and empirical guidelines can be given for the use of antihistamines. The drugs should be initiated at a low dose and increased on the basis of clinical response and individual tolerance. It is evident that uncolored antihistamine pills should be used in patients with dye sensitivity. A conventional antihistamine to start with is hydroxyzine (Atarax, Vistaril), 25 mg tid. If a particular agent is not sufficiently effective, a drug from a different chemical class can be substituted or added. For example, a combination of cyproheptadine and hydroxyzine may be more efficient than hydroxyzine alone. The combination of H_2 antagonists (cimetidine, 300 mg PO qid, or ranitidine, 150 mg bid) and H_1 antihistamines does not seem to have an additional beneficial effect in the majority of patients with urticaria. The combination may be more effective, however, in some cases of dermatographism or in selected cases refractory to conventional treatment. H_2 receptor blockade alone has virtually no effect on urticaria.

The development of new antihistamines with less penetration through the blood-brain barrier or with relatively low affinity for brain H_1 receptors has resulted in effective drugs that produce less sedation. Low-sedating H_1 antihistamines currently available in the United States include terfenadine (Seldane), 60 mg PO bid, and astemizole (Hismanal), 10 mg PO once daily. Astemizole should be taken on an empty stomach and has a delayed onset of action. Loratidine and cetirizine are two other drugs of this type that have been registered in other countries. Doxepin, a tricyclic antidepressant with strong H_1 and H_2 antagonist effects, may be a valuable alternative in the treatment of chronic urticaria. It is usually given in dosages of 10 to 25 mg tid. Side effects include sedation, constipation, and dry mouth.

In several subtypes of urticaria, a more specific approach is recommended. In cold urticaria, cyproheptadine (Periactin), an antihistamine with strong antiserotonin activity, may be more effective than classic antihistamines, and can be given in a dosage of 4 mg PO tid. Antihistamines have little effect on pressure urticaria. The only effective option in this condition is systemic corticosteroids, but their use should be limited to disabling disease. Potentially effective treatments of urticarial vasculitis include systemic corticosteroids, colchicine, and dapsone. Although the use of systemic corticosteroids is usually not justified in the management of chronic urticaria, a course of oral prednisone (started at approximately 1 mg/kg/d and tapered to a minimum alternate-day regimen) is often effective and may occasionally even stop the disease process. This approach should be restricted to very problematic cases. When a rapid effect is desirable, such as in severe angioedema or urticaria with laryngeal edema or hypotension, epinephrine (for adults: 0.005 mg/kg subcutaneously and repeated every 20 to 30 minutes as needed, up to three doses) should be given. Susceptible patients may carry this drug in autoinjector form. In patients with C1 inhibitor deficiency, replacement with fresh frozen plasma or purified C1 inhibitor is necessary during acute attacks. The prophylactic administration of anabolic steroids—e.g., danazol (Danocrine), started at 200 mg 2 or 3 times daily and gradually reduced—may be useful in the prevention of recurrences by increasing protease inhibitor levels.

Champion RH, Roberts SOB, Carpenter RG, Roger JH: Urticaria and angioedema: a review of 554 patients. *Br J Dermatol.* 1963;81:588–597.
  A retrospective analysis of the clinical findings in a mixed outpatient and inpatient population with urticaria or angioedema.
Flowers FP, Araujo OE, Nieves CH: Antihistamines. *Int J Dermatol.* 1986;25:224–231.
  A comprehensive overview of the different types of antihistamines and their trade names, dosage forms, and daily doses.
Guin JD: The evaluation of patients with urticaria. *Dermatologic Clinics.* 1985;3:29–49.
  Practical approach to evaluating patients with urticaria.
Lennart J (ed.): Urticaria. *Seminars in Dermatology.* 1987;6:271–356.
  Volume devoted to detailed review of all forms of urticaria.
Monroe EN: Urticarial vasculitis: An updated review. *J Am Acad Dermatol.* 1981;5:88–95.
  This article analyzes the clinical, laboratory, and immunopathological features of urticarial vasculitis.
Monroe EN: Chronic urticaria: Review of nonsedating H_1 antihistamines in treatment. *J Am Acad Dermatol.* 1988;19:842–849.
  This review focuses on the nonsedating antihistamines terfenadine, astemizole, loratadine, and cetirizine and evaluates their clinical efficacy, safety, and convenience in the treatment of chronic urticaria.
Noid HE, Schulze TW, Winkelmann RK: Diet plan for patients with salicylate-induced urticaria. *Arch Dermatol.* 1974;109:866–869.
  This article proposes concrete guidelines for the management of this relatively common clinical problem.
Winton GB, Lewis CW: Contact urticaria. *Int J Dermatol.* 1982;10:573–578.
  A review of the types of, and diagnostic approach to, contact urticaria.

58. MASTOCYTOSIS
Richard F. Horan

Mastocytosis refers to a variety of clinical conditions that are histologically characterized by mast cell hyperplasia. The clinical manifestations of these diseases are principally attributable to the actions of mast-cell-derived mediators. These mediators may be divided into granule-associated, preformed mediators (e.g., histamine, eosinophil chemotactic factors of anaphylaxis, high molecular weight neutrophil chemotactic factor, enzymes, structurally important proteoglycans, and other proinflammatory substances); newly generated mediators (including prostaglandin D_2; the sulfidopeptide leukotrienes LTC_4, LTD_4, and LTE_4; leukotriene B_4; platelet activating factor); and cytokines (including IL-3, IL-4, IL-5, IL-6, and GM-CSF). Mast-cell-derived mediators may act on a "systemic" level, causing flushing, hypotension, headache, or neuropsychiatric dysfunction, and on a "microenvironmental" level, causing localized pruritus, development of fibrosis in bone marrow or liver, or edema of the bowel wall upon ingestion of alcohol. Only secondarily are the manifestations of mastocytosis the result of the space-occupying nature of the mast cell infiltrates. Cutaneous involvement is part of the presentation of most patients with clinically evident mastocytosis, and may be what causes them to seek medical attention.

Urticaria pigmentosa (UP) is the most common form of cutaneous mastocytosis. In this condition, multiple reddish brown lesions (dozens, occasionally hundreds) are present, distributed symmetrically and diffusely. Individual lesions may be macular, papular, or nodular. Small lesions of UP tend to be oval or round. Occasionally, extensive involvement may present with confluent plaques in addition to more-typical smaller lesions. Rubbing lesions of UP will result in urtication (positive Darier's sign). Occasionally, they will also urticate spontaneously. Pruritus, usually mild, is a common complaint. Blistering is rare in children and adults but often occurs in infants. Bullous lesions also tend to occur more often in dependent areas.

Urticaria pigmentosa generally begins in infancy or childhood, although the condition may develop in adulthood. It occurs sporadically; only a few familial cases have been reported. No clear-cut sex predominance has been established. The eruption tends to resolve spontaneously in the vast majority of patients with onset in infancy or childhood. Even in patients who develop their eruption during adulthood there is a tendency toward resolution or, at least, considerable fading in color and flattening of papular or nodular lesions. The later in life the onset, the greater the likelihood of development of overt systemic mast cell disease. In the past it was felt that the majority of patients with adult-onset UP did not develop a systemic process. However, any such assessment is dependent on the rigor and technical ability with which involvement of other organs in the asymptomatic or minimally symptomatic individual is investigated. Currently it is thought that the majority of adult patients with UP have a generalized abnormality in regulation of mast cell proliferation.

The diagnosis of UP poses little difficulty to the experienced clinician. The differential diagnosis includes papular urticaria, secondary syphilis, older lesions of eruptive xanthomata, and multiple leiomyomata. Macular lesions may sometimes resemble freckles. Juvenile xanthogranuloma may also be in the differential diagnosis for infants and children. However, the typical red-brown hue, the symmetric and generalized nature of the eruption, and, most important, the presence of Darier's sign make the diagnosis of UP forthright in most instances. In infants, the presence of bullous lesions as a component of the eruption also favors the diagnosis of UP, although the appearance of bullae may antedate the more classic manifestations of UP, in which case the differential diagnosis of bullous diseases occurring in infancy must be entertained.

The diagnosis is established by a biopsy of lesional skin. Formalin-fixed, paraffin-embedded sections stained with Giemsa or toluidine blue will demonstrate significantly increased numbers of dermal mast cells. In macular or thin papular lesions, the mast cells are principally perivascular in location. With thicker lesions, mast cell hyperplasia increases in quantity and becomes more diffuse. The mast cells may form a true tumor and fill the dermis or, rarely, even involve subcutaneous fat. The cells appear cytologically benign and mitoses are exceedingly rare. Mast cell infiltrates in patients with UP and with systemic mast cell disease are currently being studied extensively with ultrastructural, immunohistochemical, and immunoelectron microscopic techniques to evaluate mast cell phenotypic and functional diversity and shed light on the factors that regulate mast cell differentiation in humans.

Solitary mastocytoma is an infrequent form of cutaneous mastocytosis. It accounts for at most 5% of patients with cutaneous mast cell disease. The presentation is generally at birth or within the first few weeks of life. Solitary mastocytoma presents as an isolated brown nodule, although macular and papular variants have been reported. Darier's sign is positive, and blistering may occur following stroking. The principal alternative diagnosis is a nevomelanocytic tumor, but the occurrence of urtication or bulla formation with pressure favors the diagnosis of mastocytoma. The diagnosis is readily established by a biopsy. Association with the development of systemic mast cell disease is said to be extremely infrequent.

Telangiectasia macularis eruptiva perstans (TMEP) is categorized as a distinct entity, although some lesions of UP may gradually develop a telangiectatic background. Localized variants have been reported, but the eruption is typically diffuse, with multiple red or brownish red macules consisting of fine telangiectasias. Pruritus is generally absent. Darier's sign may not be positive. The incidence of TMEP, its natural history, and its association with visceral disease have not been well established, although patients have been described in whom TMEP represents the cutaneous component of systemic mast cell disease. Other telangiectatic disorders, including CREST syndrome and Osler-Weber-Rendu syndrome, may be considered in the differential diagnosis. When the diagnosis of TMEP is under consideration, biopsy specimens should be carefully reviewed, since the degree of mast cell hyperplasia is less impressive in this condition than in other cutaneous mastocytosis variants.

Cutaneous mastocytosis may present with **diffuse erythroderma,** a generalized infiltration of the skin characterized by soft or doughy thickening, either reddish brown or yellowish in hue, and occasionally associated with the development of frank tumors or nodules. This form of the disease has been described in both infants and adults, and can be associated with systemic involvement. Because it is very rare, no well-documented studies of more than one patient have been undertaken. The differential diagnosis includes cutaneous T-cell lymphoma and lepromatous leprosy. A biopsy provides a definitive diagnosis.

Systemic mastocytosis can present with or without skin involvement. Most patients with systemic mast cell disease have some form of clinically evident cutaneous manifestation, generally UP or a plaque-like variant. In some patients, only a few small lesions of UP may be present, necessitating a careful examination of the skin. Systemic mastocytosis is also occasionally associated with TMEP or with the diffuse infiltrative form of cutaneous involvement. Symptoms in patients with systemic mastocytosis are variable and intermittent. The presentation may include flushing, pruritus, headache, rhinitis, episodic crampy abdominal pain (particularly after ingestion of alcohol), dyspeptic abdominal pain, nausea, vomiting, bloating, diarrhea (rarely accompanied by malabsorption), wheezing (in rare instances), bone pain, neuropsychiatric dysfunction (cognitive disorganization, irritability, and depression), intolerance of aspirin and nonsteroidal anti-inflammatory drugs, and vascular collapse. Physical findings may include hepatomegaly, splenomegaly, and adenopathy. Hepatic involvement has been infrequently associated with the development of frank portal hypertension. Laboratory studies occasionally reveal a mild anemia secondary to chronic disease, malabsorption, or iron deficiency due to gastrointestinal blood loss. In approximately 25% of patients, modest to marked eosinophilia may be noted. The white blood cell count is usually otherwise unremarkable, except in cases associated with hematologic dyscrasias. The platelet count is normal unless splenomegaly is significant. The erythrocyte sedimentation rate is generally normal. Blood chemistries may reveal mild elevations of AST and ALT, and moderate elevation of alkaline phosphatase. The presence of oligoclonal immunoglobulin spikes have been demonstrated in some patients by immunoelectrophoresis.

Demonstration of elevated excretion of histamine on 24-hour urine collection is the most useful and readily available means of documenting a biochemical correlate of increased mast cell numbers or activation. However, urinary histamine assays as performed by commercial laboratories are relatively insensitive, and, in addition, urinary histamine excretion may be at least in part dependent on disease activity, so that a normal result does not preclude the diagnosis of mastocytosis. Repeated collections on several occasions can sometimes be helpful, but may still yield normal results even in the setting of a symptomatic patient with known systemic mast cell disease. Sensitivity may be increased by more-sophisticated assays for histamine generally available only in a research setting, and increased still further by measurement of 24-hour urinary excretion of the histamine metabolites N-methylhistamine and N-methylimidazoleacetic acid performed by isotope dilution mass fragmentographic or gas chromatographic methods. Excretion of elevated quantities of histamine or its metabolites on 24-hour urinary collection is not diagnostic of mastocytosis; it can also be seen in a variety of settings including anaphylaxis, physical urticarias, myelodysplastic syndromes associated with basophilia, urinary tract infection, carcinoid syndrome, and ingestion of foods rich in histamine. Plasma histamine levels are similarly nonspecific, although repeated serial elevations make the diagnosis of mastocytosis likely. Elevation of serum levels of tryptase, presumably due to release of this enzyme in the process of mast cell degranulation, may be seen with exacerbation of the illness, but is also nonspecific and may occur in other conditions involving mast cell activation.

Radiographic studies of the gastrointestinal tract in patients with systemic mastocytosis may demonstrate nodular mucosal thickenings suggestive of mast cell hyperplasia. Gastritis, duodenitis, and peptic ulcer disease are not uncommon. Radiographic bone surveys and bone scans may reveal sclerotic, osteopenic, or mixed areas, either localized or diffuse. Bone marrow biopsies and, sometimes, aspirates may reveal evidence of mast cell hyperplasia. The processing of bone marrow biopsy specimens in a routine fashion may be associated with the loss of identifiable mast cells on an artefactual basis, but this can be avoided by the use of glycol methacrylate for plastic embedding. Other sites in which histologic confirmation of mast cell hyperplasia may be sought include the small bowel, the colon, and the liver. Assessment of the status of the bone marrow is particularly useful, however, in allowing simultaneous evaluation of the possibility of associated hematologic dyscrasia.

Establishing a diagnosis of systemic mast cell disease in the setting of a patient with symptoms suggestive of this diagnosis and classical skin lesions poses little difficulty. In the absence of clinically consistent skin lesions, establishing the diagnosis is more difficult. The clinical picture of unexplained flushing and episodic abdominal pain may be one such circumstance. Biochemical evidence of mast cell participation in the pathophysiology should be sought. A histologic diagnosis of mast cell hyperplasia is the gold standard, however, and is essential for a definite diagnosis of mastocytosis. Random biopsy of nonlesional skin is seldom a useful diagnostic procedure. Recent careful studies have shown that while increased numbers of mast cells are found in the skin of patients with unexplained flushing and unexplained anaphylaxis, the degree of elevation is not as striking as in nonlesional skin of patients with documented mastocytosis and is much less than in lesional skin. In the absence of convincing evidence of mast cell hyperplasia in the skin, such evidence should be sought in other tissues.

Most patients with systemic mast cell disease experience a chronic, indolent course characterized by episodic exacerbation of their symptoms. In perhaps 20% of cases, the presence of a systemic-mastocytosis-like illness has been associated with hematologic dyscrasias, including dysmyelopoietic bone marrow and occasionally development of chronic myelocytic leukemia. A few patients with systemic-mastocytosis-like symptoms associated with lymphadenopathy and a lymphoma-like illness have also been reported. The occurrence of true mast cell leukemia or of mast cell sarcoma is exceedingly rare. The absence of skin lesions is a poor prognostic factor in systemic mastocytosis. The presence of small groups of patients with natural histories distinct from that of the majority of patients with systemic mastocytosis implies that a better term for all these conditions may be *mastocytosis syndromes*. The factors eventuating in mast cell hyperplasia in a given patient are not understood and may vary from one patient to another.

The differential diagnosis of systemic mastocytosis without skin lesions includes idiopathic anaphylaxis, carcinoid syndrome, and unexplained flushing. The frequent occurrence of upper respiratory obstruction in idiopathic anaphylaxis helps to differentiate this condition from mastocytosis. Unlike carcinoid syndrome, mastocytosis is seldom associated with bronchospasm and is not associated with cardiac valvular disease or hepatic metastasis. The flushing in carcinoid syndrome may be more cyanotic, and that in mastocytosis more erythematous, but as a rule it is unwise to rely on this distinction as applied to the individual patient. Urinary histamine levels may occasionally be elevated in patients with carcinoid syndrome, but patients with mastocytosis do not demonstrate increased excretion of 5-hydroxyindoleacetic acid.

Treatment of the patient with mastocytosis is directed at alleviation of symptoms since a more pathophysiologic approach to the mast cell hyperplasia is not available at present. Solitary mastocytoma generally resolves spontaneously during childhood. Treatment is usually unnecessary, but can be accomplished by surgical excision. UP is also frequently associated with spontaneous resolution, particularly in those patients with early onset of the eruption. For patients in whom pruritus is a significant complaint, the use of antihistamines or ketotifen may be helpful. Adult patients with persistent UP who are distressed by the appearance of the eruption may derive temporary benefit from PUVA photochemotherapy, which can cause fading and partial resolution of the eruption and a reduction in pruritus. Intralesional corticosteroid injection or potent topical corticosteroids (especially under occlusion) may flatten individual lesions, but the usefulness of these approaches for patients with multiple cutaneous lesions is obviously diminished by the associated discomfort, inconvenience, or adverse effects of the cumulative corticosteroid dose. For those patients who find their eruption very distressing, it is important to emphasize that in many individuals the lesions will fade, at least partially, with the passage of time. Treatment of lesions of TMEP for cosmetic improvement has not been studied, but the tunable dye laser may prove a useful therapeutic tool.

Therapy for patients with systemic mast cell disease is individualized, directed at the alleviation of dominant symptoms. For patients with indolent systemic mastocytosis, antihistamines are the mainstay of treatment. H_1 antagonists are helpful in the reduction of flushing, headache, rhinitis, pruritus, urtication, and, to a lesser extent, gastrointestinal symptoms and neuropsychiatric manifestations. H_2 antagonists are principally helpful in the treatment of associated gastrointestinal symptoms, and may be a useful adjunct for relief of cutaneous, neuropsychiatric, and other systemic symptoms in a patient on full doses of H_1 antagonists with only partial relief. The oral administration of cromolyn sodium, an inhibitor of mast cell activation, is remarkably beneficial in the reduction of gastrointestinal symptoms, and has also been demonstrated to improve flushing, pruritus, urtication, headache, and neuropsychiatric manifestations of the illness. Chronic use of aspirin or nonsteroidal anti-inflammatory drugs is useful in some patients with pronounced flushing or episodic vascular collapse unrelieved by antihistamines and cromolyn. These agents should, however, be cautiously introduced in the patient with mastocytosis since vascular collapse may occur acutely at the start of therapy. Development of gastritis or duodenitis may limit utility in many patients. Ketotifen, an orally absorbed mast cell activation inhibitor, has been helpful in some patients with flushing as a prominent feature of their presentation. Newer antimediator agents may in the future play a part in the clinical management of patients with mastocytosis. Obviously, the avoidance of alcohol and other trigger factors including certain foods, extremes of temperature, anxiety, and stress are important parts of the management of this condition.

Cherner JA, Jensen RT, Dubois A, et al.: Gastrointestinal dysfunction in systemic mastocytosis. A prospective study. *Gastroenterology.* 1988;95:657–667.
An excellent prospective study of gastrointestinal functions and their correlation with symptoms in 16 patients with systemic mastocytosis.

Frieri M, Alling DW, Metcalfe DD: Comparison of the therapeutic efficacy of cromolyn sodium with that of combined chlorpheniramine and cimetidine in systemic mastocytosis. Results of a double blind clinical trial. *Am J Med.* 1985;78:9–14.
The effectiveness of cromolyn sodium and combined treatment with chlorpheniramine and cimetidine are compared in patients with systemic mastocytosis. Neither regimen is clearly superior to the other, but cromolyn may be more beneficial in relieving gastrointestinal symptoms, while the combination of chlorpheniramine and cimetidine may be more effective in relief of itch and urtication.

Horan RF, Austen KF: Systemic mastocytosis: Retrospective review of a decade's clinical experience at the Brigham and Women's Hospital. *J Invest Dermatol.* 1991;96:5S–13S.

Kolde G, Frosch PJ, Czarnetzki BM: Response of cutaneous mast cells to PUVA in patients with urticaria pigmentosa: histomorphometric, ultrastructural and biochemical investigations. *J Invest Dermatol.* 1984;83:175–178.
Study of pathologic, ultrastructural, and biochemical changes in lesional skin with PUVA, and eventual reversion of the noted alterations following discontinuation of PUVA.

Metcalfe DD: The treatment of mastocytosis: An overview. *J Invest Dermatol.* 1991;96:55S–56S.

Metcalfe DD: Classification and diagnosis of mastocytosis: Current status. *J Invest Dermatol.* 1991;96:2S–4S.

Parker RI: Hematologic aspects of mastocytosis: I. Bone marrow pathology in adult and pediatric systemic mast cell disease. *J Invest Dermatol.* 1991;96:47S–51S.
The preceding three useful references, along with the Horan article, are from a journal supplement devoted to mast cell disease.

Roberts LJ, Sweetman BJ, Lewis RA, et al.: Increased production of prostaglandin D2 in patients with systemic mastocytosis. *NEJM.* 1980;1400–1404.
Demonstration of marked overproduction of PGD2 in two patients with systemic mastocytosis, and therapeutic response to aspirin in one of these individuals.

Soter N. Austen KF, Wasserman SI: Oral disodium cromoglycate in the treatment of systemic mastocytosis. *NEJM.* 1979;301:465–469.
Demonstration of the efficacy of oral cromolyn in patients with systemic mastocytosis in a double-blind, double-crossover study.

Travis WD, Li C-Y, Bergstralh EJ, et al.: Systemic mast cell disease. Analysis of 58 cases and literature review. *Medicine.* 1988;67:345–368.
A superb retrospective study of systemic mast cell disease and its natural history, clinical manifestations, laboratory findings, and histopathology.

59. ATOPIC DERMATITIS
Arthur K. F. Tong and Michael E. Bigby

Atopic dermatitis is a noninfectious, inflammatory cutaneous disorder that is usually associated with asthma, hay fever, allergic rhinitis, or increased serum IgE levels either in the same individual or within the family. There is no single pathognomonic feature of atopic dermatitis, and the diagnosis is based on a combination of historical, clinical, and histologic features.

The accuracy of **epidemiologic studies** is limited by the lack of definitive diagnostic criteria for atopic dermatitis; however, a recent national screening survey estimated the prevalence of atopic dermatitis to be 7 to 24 per 1000. The highest prevalence was in children. A community survey in Bristol, England, showed a prevalence of 3.1% in children under the age of 5. In a prospective study of 1753 infants, 4.3% developed atopic dermatitis by age 7. One-third of children with a personal or family history of allergic rhinitis or asthma also have atopic dermatitis. The onset of the disease was in the first year of life in approximately 60% of patients and before the age of 5 in 85% of patients. Long-term follow-up studies indicate that the disease resolves in about 40% of patients by adulthood. Patients with severe diseases are more likely to have a persistent course.

The **clinical features** of atopic dermatitis include a wide constellation of morphologic findings. In acute stages, patients have pruritic, poorly demarcated erythematous plaques composed of papules, vesicles, and erosions. The vesicles frequently rupture, producing exudate and honey-colored crusts. In chronic stages, lichenification, scaling, and hyperpigmentation or hypopigmentation are common. The face and extremities are the most commonly affected sites in infancy and early childhood. The diaper area, perioral area, and periorbital areas are often spared. In atopic adults, the disease tends to be located on the neck and in the antecubital and popliteal fossae. Other associated cutaneous features include hyperlinear palms, extra infraorbital skin folds (Dennie-Morgan sign), geographic tongue, pitted keratolysis of the palmar creases, and ichthyosis vulgaris.

Atopic dermatitis tends to wax and wane, with acute flares superimposed on chronic disease. Periods of complete inactivity may alternate with generalized disease. Erythroderma with total skin involvement can occur. A majority of patients improve during the summer and deteriorate during the fall and winter. The improvement in summer may be related to higher humidity and sun exposure. In winter, low humidity, indoor heating, and irritation from woolen clothes may aggravate the condition.

Patients with active atopic dermatitis may develop widespread infection with herpes simplex virus (eczema herpeticum). Colonization or superinfection of the skin by *Staphylococcus aureus* is common. Patients may also be predisposed to dermatophyte infection or to viral processes such as warts or molluscum contagiosum either because of the disease itself or because of its treatment.

Immunologic abnormalities have been documented in patients with atopic dermatitis, although their role in the pathogenesis of the disease is unknown. Serum IgE levels are elevated in 40% to 80% of patients. The degree of elevation tends to parallel the extent and severity of the disease. Abnormalities in cytokine production and variations in the proportions of subpopulations of T cells have been reported in small subsets of patients. Atopic patients have a relative increase in the number of CD4-positive T cells that secrete IL-4, and a relative decrease in the number of CD4-positive T cells that secrete IL-2 and gamma-interferon. Of note, IL-4 (BCSF1) stimulates B cells to secrete IgE. A relative decrease in the number of CD8-positive cells has also been reported.

Defects in cell-mediated immunity have been noted in up to 80% of patients with atopic dermatitis. Reported defects include increased susceptibility to viral infections (herpes simplex, vaccinia, coxsackie A16); decreased susceptibility to contact allergy (poison ivy, poison oak, dinitrochlorobenzene [DNCB]); and depressed delayed type hypersensitivity to tuberculin, streptokinase-streptodornase, and *Candida* skin tests. Scratch tests are frequently positive for a wide variety of allergens, including foods and environmental antigens. The relationship between positive scratch tests and the etiology and pathogenesis of the disease is uncertain. Skin disease may sometimes be triggered by food challenges; however, food allergy cannot be demonstrated to be responsible for atopic dermatitis in most patients. A correlation between positive scratch tests to food and positive responses to food challenges has not been established.

Physiologic abnormalities may accompany skin disease in atopic patients. White dermographism, characterized by the development of pale plaques within erythematous lesions in response to stroking, may occur. The reaction is not blocked by procaine or atropine and therefore is probably not under neural influence. Since the same response has been demonstrated in seborrheic dermatitis and contact dermatitis and is absent in uninvolved skin, the reaction may be a nonspecific phenomenon in cutaneous inflammation. Other physiologic changes that have been reported include increased sweating in response to acetylcholine, decreased production of sebaceous-gland-derived lipids, and increased transepidermal water loss through involved skin.

The **histologic features** of atopic dermatitis are not specific and may be similar to those present in a variety of other disorders, including allergic contact dermatitis, acute photoallergic dermatitis, id reactions, vesicular dermatophytosis, and inflammatory pityriasis rosea. The hallmark of acute atopic dermatitis is spongiosis (intercellular edema) of the epidermis, associated with a mononuclear cell infiltrate in the dermis. Exocytosis of lymphoid cells into the epidermis and microvesicle formation may also be seen in acute stages. In older lesions, scale crust may be observed in the stratum corneum. In chronic lesions, there is striking hyperplasia of the epidermis, with elongation of rete ridges and prominent fibrosis beneath rete ridges in a lamellar-like array. Hypercellularity of the dermis occurs, in association with a prominent mononuclear cell infiltrate. Fibrosis around venules and small nerves may also be observed.

Immunohistologic studies reveal that the infiltrate in lesions of both acute and chronic atopic dermatitis is predominantly composed of T cells that are CD3-, CD4,- and Ia-positive. Only a small number of cells in the perivascular infiltrate are CD8-positive. Langerhans' cells identified by staining with monoclonal antibodies OKT6 or Leu6 (anti-CD1) are increased in both acute and chronic lesions.

The **differential diagnosis** of atopic dermatitis includes spongiotic eruptions that occur in several rare genetic disorders. Wiskott-Aldrich syndrome is an X-linked, recessive disorder characterized by an atopic-dermatitis-like cutaneous eruption, abnormal platelet structure and function, and abnormalities in humoral and cellular immunity. Patients with this syndrome have severe, recurrent bacterial infection. In Job's syndrome, an atopic-dermatitis-like eruption is associated with markedly elevated serum IgE levels, defective T-cell functions, recurrent *S. aureus* infection, and recalcitrant candidiasis. Almost half of patients with phenylketonuria have an atopic-dermatitis-like rash during the first year of life. This rash clears with appropriate dietary therapy and reappears with phenylalanine loading.

The **treatment** of atopic dermatitis must be tailored to fit each patient. Adequate hydration of the skin and avoidance of irritants may be all that is necessary in very mild disease. Emollients such as white petrolatum should be applied immediately after each daily bath or shower to trap moisture in the skin. Topical corticosteroids and tar preparations are useful in most cases. In acute, exudative cases, a medium-potency topical corticosteroid lotion or cream should be applied after a bath or shower, or after application of aluminum acetate or saline compresses. For chronic, lichenified lesions, potent topical corticosteroid ointments are best applied immediately after a bath or shower. Soaking or using compresses of water-soluble tar preparations may speed resolution and decrease the need for topical corticosteroid use.

Other agents may also be helpful when added to a regimen of topical care. Adequate doses of antihistamines should be administered to control pruritus and prevent scratching, which acutely causes excoriations and secondary infections and chronically leads to lichenification. Behavioral therapy may be a useful adjunct for some patients. With severe involvement, a short course of systemic corticosteroids may be necessary, although a flare with discontinuation is common. The risks of systemic corticosteroids limit their use in long-term therapy. Oral antibiotics directed against *S. aureus* may help reverse flares even when outright infection cannot be documented. Preliminary data indicate that widespread atopic dermatitis may clear up or improve with administration of systemic gamma-interferon or thymopoetin. Avoidance of some foods has led to improvement in several studies. Favorable responses to cyclosporine have been reported in uncontrolled studies. However, the toxicity of cyclosporine and the chronic nature of atopic dermatitis make it an unattractive candidate for therapy of this disorder. Eczema herpeticum resolves spontaneously without scarring; its severity, complications, and duration may be decreased by systemic acyclovir.

Although there is no known cure for the disease, the long-term **prognosis** for patients with atopic dermatitis is favorable. Several studies suggest that spontaneous remission occurs in 40% to 50% of patients by age 15. A recent prospective study of 2000 children with atopic dermatitis reported that the disease cleared up in almost 90% during a 15-year follow-up period. Predictors of persistent disease include a family history of atopic dermatitis, associated asthma or hay fever, and late onset of severe disease.

Hanifin JM: Atopic dermatitis. *J Am Acad Dermatol.* 1982;6:1–13.
Thorough review of atopic dermatitis by an investigator with extensive clinical and research experience.

Leung DYM, Bhan AK, Schneeberger EE, et al.: Characterization of the mononuclear cell infiltrate in atopic dermatitis using monoclonal antibodies. *J Allergy Clin Immunol.* 1983;71:47–56.
  CD4-positive T cells and CD1-positive Langerhans' cells are prominent.
Recombinant gamma interferon in treatment of patients with atopic dermatitis and elevated IgE levels. *Am J Med.* 1990;88(4):365–370.
  Twenty-two patients with chronic severe atopic dermatitis were treated with gamma interferon. The total clinical severity of atopic dermatitis improved with treatment, without a significant fall in IgE levels.
Ricci M, Del Prete GF, Maygi E, et al.: Advances in understanding of mechanisms of IgE disregulation in atopy by the application of in vitro methods. *J Allergy Clin Immunol.* 1986;78:988–994.
  Discussion of the role of IL-4-secreting T-cells and elevated IgE levels in atopic dermatitis.
Sampson HA, Albergo R: Comparison of results of skin tests, RAST, and double-blind, placebo-controlled food challenges in children with atopic dermatitis. *J Allergy Clin Immunol.* 1984;74:26–33.
  Food allergy may play a significant role in a subset of patients in this study. Statistical correlations between food challenges and diagnostic tests are determined.
Sampson HA: Jerome Glaser Lectureship. The role of food allergy and mediator release in atopic dermatitis. *J Allergy Clin Immunol.* 1988;81:635–645.
  Review of the pathophysiology of atopic dermatitis and the role of food allergy in its pathogenesis.
Sowden JM, et al. Double-blind, controlled, crossover study of cyclosporin in adults with severe refractory atopic dermatitis. *Lancet.* 1991;338:137–140.
  Patients treated with cyclosporine (5 mg/kg per day) for 8 weeks had improvement in the extent and activity of their disease when compared to recipients of placebo. Two-thirds of patients receiving cyclosporine report adverse reactions.
Tong, AKF, Mihm MC: The pathology of atopic dermatitis. *Clin Rev Allergy.* 1986;4:27–42.
  Review of the pathologic features of atopic dermatitis.
Van der Heijden FL, et al.: High frequency of IL-4-producing CD4 + allergen-specific T lymphocytes in atopic dermatitis lesional skin. *Invest. Dermatol.* 1991;97(3):389–394.
  CD4 + T-cell clones isolated from the skin of atopic dermatitis patients who were allergic to house dust mites reacted to mite antigens and induced IL-4 but not gamma interferon or IL-2. Thus, T-cells in atopic dermatitis may be of the Th-2 type.

60. CONTACT DERMATITIS
Edward V. Maytin

Contact dermatitis (CD) is a common problem loosely defined as an inflammatory dermatosis resulting from direct cutaneous contact to an external agent. It accounts for up to 40% of all occupationally acquired illnesses. Estimates of the scope of the problem include an incidence of at least 70,000 new cases per year in the United States, with a prevalence ranging from 2% to 7% in dermatology clinics. The highest rates of disability are seen in an occupational setting. In the general population, hand eczema is a common complaint, affecting 22% of women in one survey.

Contact dermatitis (CD) usually presents as an "eczematous" process, meaning that the eruption has a characteristic clinical and histologic appearance with acute (erythema and vesiculation), subacute (oozing and crusting), and chronic (lichenification) stages. CD can be divided, according to pathogenesis, clinical features, and histology, into five types: irritant, allergic, phototoxic, photoallergic contact dermatitis, and contact urticaria.

Irritant CD is produced by exposure to chemicals that directly damage the epidermis (such as acids, alkalis, and soaps) and is very common. It does not require prior exposure to the chemical nor involvement of immunologic mechanisms. Most people react similarly to contact with the agent in irritant CD, in contrast to allergic CD, which develops only in sensitized individuals. The dermatitis may vary in severity, depending on the strength of the irritant and on local factors such as the degree of hydration of the skin, the thickness of the stratum corneum, occlusion (e.g., urine in a diaper), or the presence of preexisting dermatitis. The eruption is usually sharply demarcated and is characterized by erythema, scaling, and edema. Vesicles are less commonly seen than in allergic CD. As with all eczematous dermatitis, it resolves through a subacute stage and may become chronic with repeated exposure. The hands are frequently affected as discussed in detail in Chap. 54.

Allergic CD is also quite common and holds special interest because of its potential severity and recurrent nature. The terms *allergic contact dermatitis* and *contact dermatitis* are sometimes erroneously used interchangeably. Poison ivy is the classic example. The patient characteristically presents with markedly pruritic erythematous and edematous papules and plaques with prominent vesicle or bulla formation in a distribution consistent with contact from an external source. The dermatitis may also present as, or evolve into, subacute or chronic variants.

Production of allergic CD requires sensitization to an antigen. The initial exposure may not elicit a skin eruption; a susceptible patient will develop hypersensitivity to the substance within 10 to 14 days. Subsequent exposure will elicit an eczematous dermatitis within 12 hours to 2 days. Immunologic events in allergic CD require interaction among antigen, Langerhans' cells, and T lymphocytes. During sensitization, Langerhans' cells (dendritic, macrophage-like cells within the epidermis) bind the antigen and process it, probably through interactions with cell membrane proteins, to render it allergenic. These Langerhans' cells leave the epidermis, travel through local lymphatics to regional lymph nodes, and in an HLA-restricted fashion, present the antigen to T cells that then become primed "memory cells." These primed T cells circulate throughout the body, ready for another encounter with the antigen. A subsequent rechallenge with the antigen begins an elicitation process. Antigen, again bound to an antigen presenting cell, is presented to and recognized by the primed T cells. This interaction triggers a cascade of events, including clonal T-cell expansion, release of soluble mediators, and recruitment of other inflammatory cells. Several hours after the start of the elicitation response, Langerhans' cells appear damaged and decreased in number within the epidermis.

The chemical structure, dose, and route of presentation of an antigen profoundly affect its sensitizing potential. It may be that an antigen, upon first presentation, sets into motion two competing mechanisms: sensitization (formation of T-helper cells) and specific immune tolerance (formation of T-suppressor cells). An antigen applied to the skin may result in sensitization, perhaps because Langerhans' cells in the skin favor the priming of T-helper cells, while the same antigen given intravenously results in tolerance, possibly because splenic macrophages favor T-suppressor cells. Similarly, high doses of antigen applied epicutaneously favor tolerance, perhaps because a large amount of antigen bypasses epidermal Langerhans' cells, acting like a systemic administration. These immunologic events can be further modified by external factors such as topical or systemic glucocorticoid administration, exposure to UV radiation, and a history of atopic dermatitis, all of which cause suppression of one or more steps in the production of contact hypersensitivity.

The most common contact allergens in the United States are plants. Over 90% of the population is known to be sensitized to poison ivy, poison oak, and poison sumac. These plant species, formerly under the genus *Rhus,* now called *Toxicodendron,* share certain features, including an odd number of leaves and sap that turns black when exposed to air. This sap, found in leaves, stems, and roots, contains the oil urushiol, a mixture of highly antigenic 3-pentadecylcatechols. Related antigens are found in the resin of the Japanese lacquer tree (used in Japan as a furniture lacquer), in the shells of the cashew nut, in the dye of the India marking nut (used to color clothing in India), and in the skin of mangoes (causing a common, in Hawaii, dermatitis around the mouth).

Usually within 12 hours to 2 days after exposure to these plants, itching, erythema, and vesiculation begin at the sites of contact. To avoid reaction, the individual may remove urushiol from the skin by washing with soap and water within 10 minutes of contact. Dried urushiol resin stays active indefinitely (on clothes, under fingernails), and the antigen may thus be spread to other parts of the body or to other individuals. Contrary to popular belief, however, blister fluid is not antigenic. Smoke from burning plants can cause severe and widespread dermatitis. Complications of extensive exposure include postinflammatory hyper- or hypopigmentation, superinfection, severe edema leading to mechanical obstructions (such as urinary retention from urethral swelling), and, occasionally, renal damage (from IgG deposition). In addition, a hypersensitivity eruption (e.g., id reaction or erythema multiforme) may develop at sites not exposed to the antigen.

Other common plant groups causing contact allergy are *Primula obconica* (primrose) and members of the Compositae family (chrysanthemums and ragweed). The antigenic molecule in the resin from Compositae plants is a sesquiterpene lactone. Ragweed dermatitis, seen in an airborne distribution on the face and neck, is due not to an allergy to pollen but to bits of plant material containing the resin. Ragweed respiratory allergy (hay fever), on the other hand, is due to the pollen.

For **phototoxic CD** to occur, both topical exposure to plant products or perfumes that contain psoralens (furocoumarins) and exposure to UV radiation are required. Berloque dermatitis (French for "pendant" or "droplike") results from application of perfumes that contain oil of bergamot, a naturally occurring psoralen. After sun exposure, macular hyperpigmentation with sharp margins and streaking appears on the neck or hands at the sites of application. There is little or no erythema. A more severe reaction with painful erythema and bulla formation may result from exposure to certain concentrated plant juices, such as lime juice, followed by light exposure. The dermatitis usually appears 24 hours after sun exposure and peaks at 48 hours. Photochemotherapy or PUVA exploits this process for the treatment of psoriasis.

Photoallergic CD requires prior sensitization to an allergen. Repeat exposure to the antigen and simultaneous exposure to UV light or, rarely, to visible light produces the eruption. Photoallergic and phototoxic reactions may be difficult to distinguish clinically because they can look identical, and many offending agents may cause both types of reactions. Substances implicated in photoallergic CD reactions include musk ambrette in perfumes, para-aminobenzoic acid (PABA) in sunscreens, and tetrachlorosalicylanilide (TGSA), which was used as an antimicrobial in soaps in the 1960s.

Contact urticaria differs from the other four types of CD in that the reaction is immediate, with formation of wheals rather than an eczematous process. Mechanisms can be either nonimmunologic, with direct effects on dermal endothelial permeability (e.g., sodium benzoate or dimethyl sulfoxide), or immunologic, mediated by IgE (e.g., foods, dog/cat saliva).

Contact dermatitis appears in three **histologic patterns,** grouped as (1) irritant/phototoxic, (2) allergic/photoallergic, and (3) contact urticaria. The irritant/phototoxic pattern results from direct damage by the external agent, and appears as epidermal cell ballooning and necrosis, with a perivascular infiltrate in the superficial dermis. The time for development of these changes is variable (many days for mild irritants, a few hours for strong acids, 24–48 hours for phototoxicity). Allergic/photoallergic reactions, on the other hand, are characterized by spongiosis (edema between keratinocytes), edema in the papillary dermis, and a perivascular cell infiltrate. Repeat exposure to the allergen causes these changes to appear in 2 hours, and they become fully developed in 4 to 6 hours. After 2 days, spongiosis disappears and acanthosis, parakeratosis, and exocytosis predominate. A biopsy of contact urticaria shows edema in the papillary dermis within minutes of exposure; no changes in the epidermis are seen.

Evaluation of a patient with CD can be difficult since many of these processes look similar and since many patients may have several mechanisms operating at once. For example, an elderly patient with seborrheic dermatitis can develop an allergic reaction to the cream used to treat the seborrhea. The inflamed skin then becomes irritated by the soap the patient uses. Of primary importance is the identification of the component of the eruption due to an allergic mechanism, since that part of the eruption can be completely prevented by avoidance of the incriminated allergen. Primary uncomplicated allergic CD can look like any eczematous dermatitis (e.g., stasis, nummular, or dyshidrotic eczema), and CD produced by different allergens appears identical; therefore, a test to reproduce the dermatitis with suspected substances can be helpful. Even common allergens often go unsuspected until specifically tested.

Patch testing can identify the specific allergenic ingredients within a known offending cream or mixture. The American Academy of Dermatology produces a standard patch-test kit with 20 allergens of significance in the United States. This roster of substances changes from time to time to reflect changing epidemiologic patterns. A positive reaction to one of these antigens may lead to more-specific testing with individual chemicals (as listed in the appendix of Fisher's *Contact Dermatitis*). Knowing the allergen allows the patient to avoid substances containing it.

Standard patch tests are done under occlusion. Chemicals are dissolved in an appropriate vehicle, most commonly white petrolatum, at concentrations chosen to minimize irritancy. A bead of test material is placed in an aluminum chamber (Finn chamber) and attached to the upper back with hypoallergenic tape (Dermicel or Scanpor). The test sites are examined after 48 hours and again at 72 hours. An evaluation is also done 2 to 3 days later because some test substances, such as neomycin and formalin, give delayed reactions. Response is graded on a scale of 1+ to 3+, based on erythema edema, vesiculation, and bulla formation. It may be very difficult to distinguish irritant responses from allergic responses, although the former tend to be more burnlike with sharp margins, while the latter have vesiculation and edges that tend to spread beyond the areas of contact.

Adverse effects of patch testing are rare, if the testing is done properly. Possible side effects include the "angry back" syndrome (a nonspecific generalized reaction at all patch-test sites), a flare of atopic dermatitis, and hyperpigmentation, infection, or scarring at the patch-test site. Occasionally, patients may become sensitized to a patch-test substance.

Testing for irritants can be difficult. Application of a suspected substance in the antecubital fossa twice daily for 10 days is a fairly sensitive test for irritants as well as weak allergens missed by the patch test. A soap-chamber method for ranking the irritancy of soaps was developed, but has limited utility.

The substances on the standard patch-test tray provided by the American Academy of Dermatology are found in a large variety of natural products, medicaments, and cosmetics. These common sensitizers are discussed in detail below, for application to individual problems and to illustrate the range of problems that can be caused by allergic contact sensitivity. Other substances can, of course, also be sensitizing, even hydrocortisone and fluocinolone without their vehicles. Although sensitization to any agent occurs via a topical route, a few contact allergens cross-react with systemic agents and may therefore exacerbate skin disease.

Benzocaine, a PABA ester, is a weak but ubiquitous sensitizer found in topical anesthetics such as creams and sprays for relief of sunburn, cough drops, ear drops, and suppositories. Benzocaine-sensitive individuals may cross-react to a number of related compounds, including cocaine, procaine, procainamide, sulfonamides, diazides, and PABA, which is found in sunscreens. Alternatives to benzocaine include topical anesthetics containing pramoxine or the amide class of anesthetics such as lidocaine. In general, the sensitizing potential of topical anesthetics is greater than that of injectable anesthetics. Sensitivity to injectable lidocaine (Xylocaine) is quite rare; in those cases, procaine or other amides such as bupivacaine (Marcaine) may be used with careful patient monitoring.

Stabilizers and preservatives in creams, medicaments, and cosmetics are frequent sensitizers. The **parabens** (esters of para-hydroxybenzoic acid) are examples. **Thimerosal** is a preservative in eyedrops, nasal medications, and vaccines. (Alternatives include medicaments containing benzalkonium chloride as the preservative or sterile saline eyedrops requiring no preservative.) **Imidazolidinyl urea and quaternium-15** are often added as gram-negative antiseptics. (Alternatives include parabens or sorbic acid, as preservatives.) **Ethylenediamine** is a potent and frequent sensitizer once or still used as a stabilizer in the following items: (a) antifungal creams such as Mycolog and Tri-Statin (alternatives include ointment forms of Mycolog or Tri-Statin); (b) intravenous aminophylline, which is a mixture of theophylline and ethylenediamine (alternatives include oral theophylline or a preservative-free form of intravenous theophylline, available from Travenol, Deerfield, IL); (c) tincture of Merthiolate (alternatives include Betadine solution or Hibiclens); (d) the antihistamine hydroxyzine (Atarax), an ethylenediamine derivative (alternatives include diphenhydramine and cyproheptadine).

Neomycin is one of the most common topical antibiotics to cause allergic CD. Sensitivity to neomycin occurs in 5% of the general population and in 30% of patients with stasis dermatitis or chronic otitis externa. Neomycin-sensitive patients may also cross-react with gentamycin, streptomycin, or kanamycin (alternatives include topical erythromycin or bacitracin). Bacitracin and erythromycin topical ointments are very rare sensitizers.

Wool alcohols, generally known as **lanolin,** are made from sebaceous gland secretions of sheep. They are used as a base for cosmetics, greases, waxes, soaps, leather finishes, and shoe polishes. (Sensitive individuals should avoid lanolin-containing cosmetics and medications. Patients should consult product labels, *Physicians' Desk Reference,* or the manufacturer.)

Structurally related to benzoic acid derivatives such as PABA and benzocaine, **para-phenylenediamine** is found in permanent-type hair dyes. Cross-reactions can also occur to some semipermanent hair dyes that contain derivatives of para-phenylenediamine, and to the spectrum of cross-reactors seen with benzocaine, as discussed above. (Alternatives include temporary hair tints, or for men, metallic hair dyes.)

Several compounds in rubber can be sensitizers. **Thiurams** are used as accelerators and vulcanizers in neoprene. Antabuse, the drug used in the rehabilitation of alcoholics, is also a thiuram. **Mercaptobenzothiazole** is another rubber accelerator and is also found in antifreezes as a corrosion inhibitor, in fungicides, and in flea powder. **Carbamates** are found in elastic underwear, and only become contact sensitizers after reacting with chlorine in bleach. (Complete avoidance of rubber articles is required for sensitized patients; lists of hypoallergenic brands of shoes, swim goggles, and surgical gloves can be found in Adams and Fisher's article—see references. For patients allergic to rubber or adhesives in the inner soles of shoes, the inner sole can be removed and replaced with foam rubber and Elmer's Glue-All. Patients sensitive to carbamates should avoid using chlorine bleach for their laundry.)

Formaldehyde is used in resins, dyes, textiles, leather tanning, photographic toners, and urinary antiseptics. (Sensitive patients should wear cotton, silk, or 100% synthetic clothing, and avoid treated fabrics such as permanent press, antistatic, or flame-retardant materials. Adding a cup of powdered milk to the laundry may help remove formaldehyde.) Shampoos may contain formaldehyde, or formaldehyde-releasing chemicals. (Alternatives include formaldehyde-free shampoos such as Prell, Neutrogena, Sebulex, and White Rain.) Leather, neoprene, plywood, belts, plastic fingernails, and adhesives in shoes contain **p-tert-butylphenol formaldehyde resin.** (Alternatives for dermatitis to shoes: see above.) **Epoxy resin** is another widely used adhesive. (For an alternative, substitute a resin with a molecular weight >500.) **Rosin,** or colophony, is a resin from the pine tree *Pinus palustris,* used widely for adhesives, sealants, lacquers, varnishes, inks, paints, and on the bows of stringed instruments. The allergens are abietic acids and alcohols. (Sensitized patients should avoid rosin by inspection of product labels.)

Potassium dichromate is an oxidizing agent in dyes, glues, paints, safety matches, and cement. (Avoid, by reading product labels. Cement dermatitis can be prevented by adding sulfates to the cement in order to reduce the chromate from its hexavalent form to a nonsensitizing trivalent form.)

Nickel is ubiquitous and by far the most common contact-sensitizing metal, followed by chromium, mercury, and, in Europe, cobalt. Nickel is abundant in articles encountered daily, such as inexpensive zippers and paper clips. Metal watch bands and costume jewelry are often chrome-plated, but perspiration will cause nickel to leach out through microscopic pores in the plating, leading to "watchband dermatitis." Gold rings more often cause an irritant rather than allergic dermatitis; however, white gold is an alloy that contains up to 17% nickel. (The nickel-sensitive patient should learn to use the Dimethylglyoxime Spot Test available from Allerderm Labs, Mill Valley, CA to identify items that contain nickel. Pierced earrings should have stainless steel posts pretested with the dimethylglyoxime test to avoid elicitation of the eruption. Jewelry dermatitis may be improved by coating the jewelry with nail polish. For very sensitive patients, low-nickel diets and nickel-free utensils may be required.)

Balsam of Peru is a resinous exudate from a tree found in Central America, containing cinnamates, vanillins, and a host of other resins. It serves as a broad screen for allergies to fragrance and flavorings. Balsam of Peru or its components are found in cosmetics, prepared foods (chocolate, baked goods, cola, and soft drinks), citrus peel, spices, cough lozenges, and suppositories. (Fragrance-free cosmetics are made by a variety of cosmetic companies, including Allercreme and Clinique.)

The **treatment** of CD depends on its severity. Mild disease (a few linear papules or patches of vesicles) may be symptomatically improved by Calamine shake lotion, cool compresses, and cold sprays, which relieve itching and dry vesicles. Moderate to severe acute CD (bullae, swelling) will respond somewhat to similar agents, but Burow's compresses (aluminum acetate) on involved skin or cold diluted boric acid on involved eyelids, Aveeno baths, and systemic antipruritics may also be helpful. Potent topical corticosteroids are often used but proof of their efficacy is lacking. Severe acute disease with marked widespread edema may need treatment with systemic corticosteroids. One helpful regimen is prednisone given at 60 mg/d for 4 days, 40 mg/d for 4 days, 20 mg/d for 4 days, and 10 mg/d for 10 days. The importance of a long 3-week taper must be emphasized. A 5- to 7-day regimen with methylprednisolone, as is often used for exacerbations of asthma, is too short a regimen for CD and often results in rebound. Chronic CD is usually treated with regimens similar to those for atopic dermatitis, including hydration, topical corticosteroid ointments, antihistamines, and antibiotics, all of which have variable results.

Prevention of disease is paramount to the well-being of the patient and consists mainly of identification of allergens and irritants followed by avoidance of the toxic or allergenic substances. Chemical barrier creams containing polyamine salt and linoleic acid dimers may be helpful, especially in the workplace. Desensitization, studied extensively for poison ivy, has not been shown to have any clinical relevance.

Adams RM, Fisher AA: Contact allergen alternatives. *J Am Acad Dermatol.* 1986;14:951–969.
A practical discussion of two dozen common allergens found on a standard patch-test tray, with information on the chemical nature of each substance, where they are found, and how to avoid them. Lists of products that contain a particular allergen (e.g., creams containing benzocaine), and safe alternatives (e.g., topical anesthetics unrelated to benzocaine), are especially useful.
Andersen KE, Benezra C, Burrows D, et al.: Contact dermatitis. A review. *Contact Dermatitis.* 1987;16:55–78.
Recent epidemiologic studies on the prevalence of contact dermatitis in Europe are discussed.
Breathnach SM: Immunologic aspects of contact dermatitis. *Clin Dermatol.* 1986; 4:5–17.
Contact dermatitis is a MHC class II, restricted T-cell mediated response controlled by several down regulatory mechanisms.
Cronin E: *Contact Dermatitis.* Edinburgh/New York: Churchill Livingstone; 1980: 1–915.
* *A standard text, more conversational in tone but less exhaustively referenced than Fisher's text. Chemical structures are shown for most substances, a potentially useful feature.*
Dooms-Goossens AE, Debusschere KM, Gevers DM, et al.: Contact dermatitis caused by airborne agents. *J Am Acad Dermatol.* 1986;15:1–10.
A review of the anatomic distribution and differential diagnosis of CD caused by airborne allergens in particle or droplet form. Special emphasis is placed on dermatitis of the face and neck.
Engasser PG: Cosmetics and contact dermatitis. *Dermatol Clin.* 1991;9(1):69–80.

A complete evaluation of most patients with cosmetic-induced contact dermatitis can be accomplished in a dermatologist's office.

Fisher AA (ed.): *Contact Dermatitis,* 3rd ed. Philadelphia, PA: Lea & Febiger; 1986: 1–954.

Undoubtedly the most comprehensive textbook on the subject of contact dermatitis. Important points made in the text are highlighted in boxes, for quick review. An appendix provides patch-test concentrations for over 1000 contact allergens.

Frosch PJ, Kligman AM: The soap chamber test: a new method for assessing the irritancy of soaps. *J Am Acad Dermatol.* 1979;1:35–41.

One of the few systematic methods, other than the "use" test, for assessing irritant contact dermatitis. This study is the basis of recommendations by many dermatologists to use Dove or Aveenobar as nonirritating soaps.

Gollhausen R, Enders F, Przybilla B, et al.: Trends in allergic contact sensitization. *Contact Dermatitis.* 1988;18:147–154.

A report on the frequencies of positive reactions to each of 24 contact allergens in a standard patch-test tray observed over a 7-year period from 1977 to 1983, in nearly 12,000 patients. The frequency of sensitivity to nickel, balsam of Peru, and potassium chromate appears to be increasing.

Guin JD, Gillis WT, Beaman JH: Recognizing the Toxicodendrons (poison ivy, poison oak, and poison sumac). *J Am Acad Dermatol.* 1981;4:99–114.

This article is a field guide, with color photographs, for poison ivy and all its nasty relatives.

Orchard S, Fellman JH, Storrs FJ: Poison ivy/oak dermatitis: Use of polyamine salts of a linoleic acid dimer for topical prophylaxis. *Arch Dermatol.* 1986;122:783–789.

One approach for patients with established contact hypersensitivity may be to use topical agents that provide a chemical barrier between antigens and the skin, to prevent elicitation of the dermatitis. This study identifies several polyamine salts of a linoleic acid dimer, which are effective as topical protectants against poison ivy antigen.

Piguet PF, Grau GE, Hauser C, Vassalli P: Tumor necrosis factor is a critical mediator in hapten induced irritant and contact hypersensitivity reactions. *J Exp Med.* 1991;173 (3):673–679.

The results presented in this study in mice suggest a role for tumor necrosis factor in mediating inflammation in allergic and irritant contact dermatitis.

Soner JG, Rasmussen JE: Plant dermatitis. *J Am Acad Dermatol.* 1983;9:1–15.

A description of the most common plants that cause dermatitis in the United States organized by mechanism into several categories of injury, including mechanical (cactus needles), pharmacologic (nettles), primary irritant (pineapple), allergic (poison ivy, primrose), phytophotodermatitis (limes), and pseudophytophotodermatitis (fungus on celery).

XI. CUTANEOUS MANIFESTATIONS OF SYSTEMIC CONDITIONS

61. ACQUIRED IMMUNODEFICIENCY SYNDROME
Anita M. Grassi

AIDS is a lethal disorder first recognized in 1981; AIDS patients develop a profound depression of CD4 + -T-cell functions and are susceptible to a variety of infections and malignancies. Initially defined clinically by the presence of marker diseases, commonly Kaposi's sarcoma, *Pneumocystis carinii* pneumonia, or candidal esophagitis, AIDS is now known to be caused by a human retrovirus (human immunodeficiency virus I, HIV-1). HIV-1 binds to CD4, a surface antigen found predominantly on helper T lymphocytes. Infection and depletion of CD4 + T cells leads to profound immunodeficiency. The virus is transmitted by sexual or blood-borne contact with infected individuals or by receiving infected blood or blood products. High risk groups include intravenous drug abusers and homosexual men. However, heterosexual transmission is becoming increasingly important. Children born to mothers who are HIV-positive are also at risk for development of the disease.

The clinical signs and symptoms of AIDS are protean and may include generalized lymphadenopathy, weight loss, malaise, lethargy, fever, cough, and chronic diarrhea. Laboratory examination may reveal anemia, lymphopenia, leukopenia, and idiopathic thrombocytopenia. The liver transaminases may be mildly elevated. There is often a hypergammaglobulinemia. The ratio of CD4 + T lymphocytes to CD8 + T cells is decreased to less than 1.5:1 (normal, approximately 2:1). Serum antibodies to HIV-1 proteins can be identified in nearly 100% of patients.

Impairment of cellular immunity in AIDS patients affects several organ systems, including the skin. Most clinical manifestations of AIDS are due to opportunistic infections or to the development of neoplasms. Skin lesions in AIDS patients can be loosely grouped into three categories: malignancies, infectious processes, and miscellaneous dermatoses.

Kaposi's sarcoma (KS) is one of the most common and easily recognized clinical manifestations of AIDS. Some of the initial case reports of AIDS in 1981 described the unusual presentation of KS in young homosexual men. Moritz Kaposi originally described KS in 1872 as a disease consisting of multiple hyperpigmented, hemorrhagic, cutaneous sarcomas seen in elderly men of Mediterranean or Jewish background. Since 1960, however, clinical variants have been recognized, and KS is now classified into four subgroups: classic (sporadic), African (endemic), allograft-associated, and AIDS-associated (epidemic). The cutaneous lesions and course vary. In the classic form, the sarcomas involve the feet and lower extremities, have an indolent benign course, and are often associated with venous stasis or lymphedema. The African form may either resemble the classic type or present as deep, infiltrating tumor masses that can invade underlying structures, including bone. A lymphadenopathic African variant exists in children and adolescents that is highly lethal. Transplant recipients on immunosuppressive therapy may develop rapidly progressive, generalized mucocutaneous lesions with nodal or visceral involvement. Occasionally these tumors will regress when immunosuppressants are withdrawn.

Patients with AIDS-related KS usually present with cutaneous lesions, mucous membrane lesions, or lymph node involvement. At the time of diagnosis, lesions may already be widespread. Early lesions are typically violaceous oval papules or plaques that do not blanch with pressure. They often enlarge rapidly to purple or red nodules or coalesce to form dense plaques and are sometimes surrounded by yellow-brown ecchymosis. They are distributed predominantly over the trunk, head, and neck area, including the oral cavity.

Many patients with AIDS and KS will develop systemic involvement with time. Visceral lesions are common, especially in the gastrointestinal tract and lungs. Gastrointestinal sarcomas are submucosal and therefore usually produce no symptoms. Pulmonary KS, however, is often aggressive, producing dyspnea and pleural effusions. It may be confused with *P. carinii* pneumonia but will have a negative gallium scan. Once pulmonary lesions occur, the prognosis is poor.

Histologically, KS appears as a proliferation of abnormal vascular structures. These irregular vascular slits contain unusually large endothelial cells amid fascicles of spindle cells and extravasated red blood cells. Most authors believe that KS arises from endothelial cells because of the presence of factor-VIII-related antigen, an endothelial cell marker. Kaposi's lesions also express other vascular-associated antigens including E92 and OKM5. However, other studies have demonstrated a strong resemblance between KS cells and normal lymphatic endothelium by the presence of other surface markers including Ia and 5'-nucleotidase, and by lectin binding.

The diagnosis of KS should be confirmed by a tissue biopsy. Radiation therapy may be used for palliation or to treat limited disease. Individual cutaneous lesions may respond well to cryotherapy, intralesional vinblastine injection, or laser therapy. They may also be surgically excised. Chemotherapy has been used to treat widespread disease or visceral involvement. Vincristine, vinblastine, bleomycin, and etoposide (VP-16) are the most commonly employed chemotherapeutic agents. Immune modulators such as recombinant alpha-interferon have also been reported to produce tumor regression.

Other **malignancies** may be seen in AIDS patients. Hodgkin's and non-Hodgkin's lymphomas, and aggressive lymphoid tumors of B-cell origin, occur but with rare cutaneous involvement. Basal cell carcinomas, squamous cell carcinomas, cutaneous T-cell lymphoma, and melanomas have also been reported.

The defect in CD4 + T-cell function in AIDS patients makes them susceptible to a variety of **opportunistic infections** with bacterial, viral, fungal, protozoal, or mycobacterial organisms. Some commonly encountered agents include *P. carinii, Candida, Toxoplasma gondii,* and *Mycobacterium avium-intracellulare.* In addition, AIDS patients may develop severe forms of infections that would otherwise produce limited illness in a normal host.

Infections with cytomegalovirus (CMV), herpes simplex virus (HSV), and varicella-zoster are frequently seen in AIDS patients. CMV may lead to retinitis, pneumonitis, encephalitis, esophagitis, or nonhealing perianal ulcers. HSV may also present as chronic, perianal ulcerations that persist for months and are associated with proctitis. Many AIDS patients similarly develop atypical, chronic HSV ulcerations of the skin or oral, esophageal, and genital mucosae. Antiviral drug therapy with oral or intravenous acyclovir is generally effective, but the lesions may recur after discontinuation of therapy. Herpes zoster, which is generally seen in elderly patients, has been reported to have a sevenfold higher incidence in AIDS patients. It may be an indicator for the presence of AIDS among members of high-risk groups. The distribution is usually localized to a dermatome, but dissemination may occur. Systemic acyclovir is indicated.

Other viral infections that affect normal individuals occur aggressively in patients with AIDS. Particularly extensive, disseminated molluscum contagiosum may be seen, often presenting with large facial papules or nodules in contrast to the small umbilicated papules of the anogenital and truncal regions seen in normal hosts. Condylomata acuminata are common and may enlarge rapidly in AIDS patients. Multiple flat and filiform warts can be seen, especially over the bearded region of the face in men.

Oral thrush is one of the most common clinical signs of AIDS. Development of oral candidiasis in a previously healthy member of a high-risk group may be the presenting sign of the disease. The esophagus may also be involved. Long-term antifungal therapy with nystatin or ketoconazole may be required. AIDS patients may also have extensive eruptions of tinea pedis, tinea cruris, angular cheilitis, or *Pityrosporon* folliculitis.

Unusual skin lesions may be seen with disseminated infections. Cryptococcosis has been reported to present with herpetiform or umbilicated lesions in AIDS patients. Disseminated histoplasmosis may likewise present with a variety of skin lesions including papules with central keratotic plugs, pustules, and papulonecrotic ulcers. Sporotrichosis may also occur as ulcerative papules and nodules. An extensive folliculitis of the back, chest, arms, and perianal area may occur in AIDS patients and may be accompanied by a flare of acne. Though assumed to be infectious, these lesions, when cultured, are often sterile. Patients with AIDS and syphilis may progress rapidly from the primary to tertiary stages and remain seronegative. *M. avium-*

intracellulare and amebiasis have also been reported to produce skin lesions in AIDS patients. Because of this propensity to develop opportunistic cutaneous infections, any skin lesion should be thoroughly evaluated. The evaluation should often include a KOH preparation; a Tzanck preparation; bacterial, viral, and fungal cultures; and a biopsy.

Seborrheic dermatitis has been reported to have a 46% prevalence in patients with AIDS as opposed to a 5% prevalence in the general population. Seborrheic dermatitis in AIDS patients is often a more severe eruption consisting of thick, greasy, hyperkeratotic plaques on the face, chest, and scalp. It can be quite inflammatory and may resemble the malar rash of lupus. Histologically, AIDS-associated seborrheic dermatitis may differ from that seen in the normal population, displaying widespread parakeratosis, necrotic keratinocytes, increased plasma cells, focal leukocytoclasis, and thick-walled dermal vessels. Treatment with topical 2% ketoconazole cream is reported to produce rapid clearing. The histology and response to ketoconazole suggest an etiology related to overgrowth of the yeast *P. ovale*.

Oral "hairy" leukoplakia presents with white plaques on the lateral borders of the tongue in patients with positive HIV-1 serology. The lesions are 2 mm to 3 cm in size and are raised with a verrucous or "hairy" surface. Their histology appears wartlike, with acanthosis, parakeratosis, ballooning degeneration, and extremely fine keratin projections. Epstein-Barr virus and papillomavirus particles have been identified on electron microscopy. It is unclear, however, whether these viruses have an actual etiologic role in this lesion.

Drug eruptions are a common complication of trimethoprim-sulfamethoxazole therapy for *Pneumocystis carinii* pneumonia in AIDS patients, occurring with an incidence of 65–70%. Such drug reactions usually present as generalized, papular exanthems. They usually occur between the eighth and twelfth days of therapy, may be accompanied by gastrointestinal symptoms, and may persist after withdrawal of the drug. After the rash clears, many patients can be successfully retreated with trimethoprim-sulfamethoxazole by starting with a small dose and increasing the dose slowly until therapeutic levels are achieved.

Psoriasis may develop simultaneously with the onset of AIDS or flare after the immunodeficiency syndrome is diagnosed. The psoriasis that occurs in AIDS patients is often widespread, even erythrodermic. It is typically difficult to manage. Some treatments such as methotrexate are also immunosuppressive and may exacerbate other AIDS-associated conditions.

Bacillary epithelioid angiomatosis presents as single or multiple reddish-purple papules that may resemble pyogenic granulomas or lesions of Kaposi's sarcoma. Clumps of pleomorphic coccobacilli may be demonstrated in this condition by War-thin-Starry stain. Since it is potentially fatal, it should be treated with antibiotics, typically erythromycin, 1 to 2 grams per day.

There are many other skin lesions reported in AIDS. Scabies infestation may present with extensive crusted plaques indicative of Norwegian scabies. Eosinophilic pustular folliculitis has been described and may be the result of an immunologic reaction to skin dermatophytes or saprophytes. The lesions of eosinophilic pustular folliculitis are pruritic, erythematous papules or follicular pustules located on the face and trunk. Purpuric lesions due to leukocytoclastic vasculitis have been reported. There is some evidence to suggest that the virus, HIV-1 itself, may be the antigenic source for this immune complex vasculitis. Nail discoloration resembling that seen in the yellow nail syndrome, acquired ichthyosis, xerosis, and a chronic pruritic papular eruption of unclear pathogenesis have also been observed.

Skin manifestations are commonly present in pediatric as well as adult AIDS patients. Cutaneous infections are frequently seen in children, whereas neoplasms are rare. Candidiasis, herpetic infections, dermatophytes, and staphylococcal infections are common. Inflammatory dermatoses may also occur, along with failure to thrive.

Chernosky ME, Finley VK: Yellow nail syndrome in patients with acquired immunodeficiency disease. *J Am Acad Dermatol.* 1985;13:731–736.
A report of four cases of nail discoloration in AIDS patients.

Cockerell CJ: Cutaneous manifestations of HIV infection other than Kaposi's sarcoma: clinical and histologic aspects. *J Am Acad Dermatol.* 1990;22:1260–1269.
An overview of reported skin findings in AIDS.

Coldiron BM, Bergstresser PR: Prevalence and clinical spectrum of skin disease in patients infected with human immunodeficiency virus. *Arch Dermatol.* 1989;125:357–361.
A study of the prevalence of cutaneous disease in 100 patients infected with HIV.

Dover JS, Johnson RA: Cutaneous manifestations of HIV infection. *Arch Dermatol.* 1991:127;1383–1391 (part I), 1549–1558 (part II).
A wide range of common eruptions occurs in AIDS patients.

Fisher BK, Warner LC: Cutaneous manifestations of the acquired immunodeficiency syndrome. *Int J Dermatol.* 1987;26:615–630.
An excellent general review of dermatologic involvement.

Friedman-Kien AE, Saltzman BR: Clinical manifestations of classical, endemic, African, and epidemic AIDS-associated Kaposi's sarcoma. *J Am Acad Dermatol.* 1990;22:1237–1250.
An excellent discussion of the different clinical subtypes of Kaposi's sarcoma.

Gordon FM, Simon GL, Wofsy CB, et al.: Adverse reactions to trimethoprim-sulfamethoxazole in patients with the acquired immunodeficiency syndrome. *Ann Intern Med.* 1984;100:495–499.
A discussion of the high incidence of reactions to trimethoprim-sulfa.

James WD, Redfield RR, Lupton GP, et al.: A papular eruption associated with human T-cell lymphotropic virus type III disease. *J Am Acad Dermatol.* 1985;13:563–566.
A series of four cases of HIV-1–positive patients with similar pruritic truncal eruptions thought to be distinctive for AIDS.

Klein RS, Harris CA, Small CB, et al.: Oral candidiasis in high-risk patients as the initial manifestation of the acquired immunodeficiency syndrome. *N Engl J Med.* 1984;311:354–358.
A study showing that the presence of unexplained oral candidiasis in high-risk groups may be a predictor of AIDS.

Lupton GP, James WD, Redfield RR, et al.: Oral hairy leukoplakia. *Arch Dermatol.* 1987;123:624–628.
A good overview of clinical and histologic features.

Mathes BM, Douglass MC: Seborrheic dermatitis in patients with acquired immunodeficiency syndrome. *J Am Acad Dermatol.* 1985;13:947–951.
A study that demonstrates increased incidence of seborrheic dermatitis in AIDS patients.

Pennys NS, Hicks B: Unusual cutaneous lesions associated with acquired immunodeficiency syndrome. *J Am Acad Dermatol.* 1985;13:845–852.
A description of some unusual presentations of common skin infections.

Straka BF, Whitaker DL, Morrison SH, et al.: Cutaneous manifestations of the acquired immunodeficiency syndrome in children. *J Am Acad Dermatol.* 1988;18:1089–1102.
This article addresses clinical features of pediatric AIDS.

62. MUCOCUTANEOUS COMPLICATIONS OF CHEMOTHERAPY
Andree A. Haas

Cancer chemotherapy is used to treat both solid tumors and hematologic malignancies, often in combination with surgery or radiation therapy or as adjunctive therapy. Dermatologists are frequently asked to evaluate cutaneous problems arising in these patients, who are often quite ill, immunocompromised, and on multiple medications. The drugs used are cytotoxic, and they nonspecifically inhibit rapidly dividing cells—both normal and tumor cells. Many of the complications are directed at rapidly dividing tissue such as skin, bone marrow, gastrointestinal tract, and mucous membranes. Some of the cutaneous lesions associated with these antineoplastic drugs occur in high frequency and may be morphologically distinctive.

Stomatitis may occur in association with many chemotherapeutic agents and usually occurs 4 to 10 days after administration of the drug. The eruption begins with diffuse erythema of the mucosal surface and can progress to ulcers and erosions. If the drug is stopped, the mucosa will heal within 5 to 7 days. The severity of the stomatitis is related to the dosage and frequency of the drug, but reactions have been seen at low doses as well. Stomatitis occurring after administration of a particular drug usually recurs when the drug is readministered. However, lowering the dose or frequency of the drug administration may reduce the severity of the reaction.

The most common drugs associated with stomatitis are bleomycin, cytarabine, dactinomycin, daunorubicin, fluorouracil, and methotrexate. Although rare, stomatitis has also been reported with the use of amsacrine, mercaptopurine, mithramycin, mitomycin, or procarbazine.

Alopecia is a common side effect of chemotherapy. Cytotoxic drugs may produce partial or complete inhibition of mitosis or impairment of metabolic processes in the hair matrix, resulting in a thinned, weakened hair shaft. Alopecia caused by mitotic inhibition affects only actively growing anagen hairs, causing an anagen effluvium. Hair loss is most pronounced on the scalp. Other terminal hairs, such as the beard, brows, lashes, axillary, and pubic hair, are variably affected. Hair loss is usually seen 1 to 2 weeks after chemotherapy but becomes more noticeable 1 to 2 months later. The alopecia is dose-dependent and reversible after the drug is stopped. Hair regrowth may be associated with a change in color or texture.

The drugs most commonly associated with alopecia are bleomycin, cyclophosphamide, dactinomycin, daunomycin, doxorubicin, hydroxyurea, fluorouracil, mechlorethamine, methotrexate, mitomycin, vinblastine, and vincristine.

Intravenous infusion of concentrated antineoplastic medications often causes a local, **chemical phlebitis**. Phlebitis is seen following the administration of carmustine, daunomycin, doxorubicin, fluorouracil, or mechlorethamine.

Extensive **soft tissue necrosis** and cutaneous ulceration may be seen with extravasation of some of the chemotherapeutic drugs. Extravasation in the paravenous space is usually associated with immediate pain and erythema. A delay of symptoms may be seen if the leak is into the dermis or subcutaneous tissue. If a large amount of material is extravasated, extensive necrosis and ulceration can be seen. Local necrosis following extravasation is most frequently seen with doxorubicin, but has also been reported to occur with dactinomycin, daunomycin, mechlorethamine, mithramycin, mitomycin, and vinca alkaloids.

Certain cancer chemotherapeutic agents interact with various wavelengths of **radiation** and produce specific dermatologic reactions, such as radiation recall and enhancement, photosensitivity, and "reactivated" sunburn.

Radiation recall is an inflammatory reaction that may occur in the radiation portal when previously irradiated tissue is exposed to either dactinomycin or doxorubicin. This may occur months to years after completion of radiation therapy, and may be seen in the skin, lung, esophagus, intestine, and heart.

Radiation enhancement occurs when radiotherapy and chemotherapy are given simultaneously. Chemotherapeutic drugs inhibit the repair of sublethal radiation damage to tissue, thus producing a decreased skin tolerance to radiation with resultant erythema, edema, and occasional necrosis and ulceration in the portal area. The drugs most commonly associated with this radiation sensitivity are dactinomycin and doxorubicin, but it has also been seen with bleomycin, fluorouracil, hydroxyurea, and methotrexate.

Photosensitivity has been seen with dacarbazine, fluorouracil, and vinblastine. Methotrexate given in high doses has also been shown to produce a "reactivated" sunburn.

Pigment changes, usually hyperpigmentation, can be seen following administration of various chemotherapeutic drugs. Hyperpigmentation may be generalized or may affect the hair, nails, or mucous membranes.

Generalized hyperpigmentation can be seen following the use of busulfan, cyclophosphamide, fluorouracil, hydroxyurea, or methotrexate. Linear or flagellate streaks of hyperpigmentation have been seen following bleomycin administration, and cannot be reproduced with scratching. A serpiginous hyperpigmentation has been seen over veins used for the infusion of either bleomycin or fluorouracil, and bleomycin can produce hyperpigmentation over pressure points. Doxorubicin has been reported to cause hyperpigmentation of the palmar creases, palms, soles, and the dorsal surface of the knuckles.

Doxorubicin, busulfan, cyclophosphamide, and fluorouracil can cause hyperpigmentation of the oral mucosa. Nail hyperpigmentation, which may be diffuse or in bands, can be seen following the use of cyclophosphamide, daunorubicin, doxorubicin, or fluorouracil. Transverse white bands, which grow distally with the nail, have also been associated with the use of cyclophosphamide. These changes differ from Beau's lines by the lack of nail plate involvement. Horizontal pigmented bands ("flag sign") can be seen in the hair following high-dose methotrexate administration.

Approximately 65% of the patients receiving asparaginase can experience a **type I or IgE-mediated reaction** consisting of urticaria, angioedema, or anaphylaxis. Both serum sickness and chronic urticaria have been reported to occur with the use of asparaginase. Cisplatin can cause an IgE-mediated reaction. Five to ten percent of patients experience flushing, pruritus, erythema, urticaria, dyspnea, bronchospasm, diaphoresis, vomiting, and hypotension shortly after infusion of cisplatin. Other agents that can cause type I reactions are cyclophosphamide, doxorubicin, chlorambucil, daunorubicin, melphalan, methotrexate, and thiotepa.

Urticaria and angioedema have been seen with the administration of procarbazine, and erythema multiforme has been associated with the administration of hydroxyurea or mechlorethamine. Toxic epidermal necrolysis has been reported in two patients who received mithramycin. Vasculitis can occur in patients who have been on hydroxyurea.

Allergic contact dermatitis, or type IV cell-mediated immunity, is commonly seen in patients using topical mechlorethamine for mycosis fungoides. An irritant dermatitis can occur with the use of daunorubicin, doxorubicin, or fluorouracil.

An acneform eruption involving the face and trunk has occurred 5 days after initiation of actinomycin-D therapy. These papulopustules usually resolve within 3 to 5 days and may leave a macular hyperpigmentation.

Bleomycin can produce localized nodules and infiltrated plaques on the extremities and buttocks and acral sclerosis. A biopsy of these infiltrated lesions shows dermal sclerosis and appendageal entrapment as seen in scleroderma. Bleomycin and vinblastine used in combination may produce a Raynaud's phenomenon.

A diffuse erythema of the head and neck, often indicating toxicity, may be seen in 35% of patients receiving mithramycin.

The onset of porphyria cutanea tarda has been observed in patients receiving busulfan therapy. No milia or blisters were seen, but hirsutism, hyperpigmentation, and skin fragility were present. Following intravenous administration of either cytarabine or fluorouracil, inflammation of preexisting actinic keratosis or seborrheic keratosis can occur.

Beau's lines, proximal onycholysis, and increased nail brittleness have been seen following administration of fluorouracil. Onychodystrophy has been reported with hydroxyurea and bleomycin therapy.

There are many cutaneous complications associated with cancer therapy. Because these patients tend to be on multiple medications, it may be very difficult to link a specific drug to a particular cutaneous reaction.

Abel EA: Cutaneous manifestations of immunosuppression in organ transplant recipients. *J Am Acad Dermatol.* 1989;21:167–169.
  Skin disease is an important cause of morbidity in organ transplant recipients. The cutaneous diseases found include drug reactions to immunosuppressive drugs, skin cancers potentiated by these drugs, opportunistic infections, and Kaposi's sarcoma. This review discusses all areas in depth.
Dreno B: Mucocutaneous side effects of chemotherapy. *Biomed Pharmacother.* 1990;44:163–167.

The skin is a frequent target for the side effects of the increasing number of chemotherapeutic agents now being used. The report reviews these manifestations.
Hood AF: Cutaneous side effects of cancer chemotherapy. *Med Clin North Am.* 1986;70:187–209.
  A comprehensive review of cutaneous side effects of cancer chemotherapy organized by cutaneous reaction pattern.

63. THE SKIN AND DIABETES
Martin A. Weinstock

The cutaneous manifestations of diabetes mellitus are many and varied. Clinically normal skin of persons with diabetes differs from nondiabetic skin in several respects. The vasculature is less responsive, as indicated by subnormal histamine-induced vasodilatation and reduced reflex hyperemia. The dermal blood vessels are thicker and have narrower lumina with deposition of extra basement-membrane-like material and other materials, and degeneration of elastic fibers. The collagen in diabetics is nonenzymatically glycosylated, which may render it stiffer, less soluble, and more difficult to degrade. Some abnormalities of diabetic skin may be benign curiosities, but others are fatal in the absence of timely intervention.

Diabetics are predisposed to certain specific bacterial and fungal **infections.** In the setting of hyperglycemia, diabetic leukocytes have been found to be abnormal by several functional assays, but the relevance of this finding to clinical disease remains unclear. *Staphylococcus aureus* appears to colonize the nares with increased frequency in insulin-dependent diabetics. Although colonization has not been definitively linked to more frequent clinical staphylococcal infection, the infections that do occur may be more difficult to manage. *Corynebacterium minutissimum* gives risk to erythrasma, a pruritic, erythematous, and scaly disorder of intertriginous areas, to which diabetics are prone. It is most commonly restricted to inguinal and axillary areas and responds well to treatment with topical or systemic erythromycin. *Pseudomonas aeruginosa* is associated with a malignant form of external otitis in diabetics. This infection is characterized by failure to respond to local therapy, invasion of cartilage and bone, and a high mortality rate. Unlike other forms of external otitis, the malignant form of external otitis requires debridement and aggressive therapy with parenteral antibiotics such as an antipseudomonal beta-lactam agent in combination with an aminoglycoside. Necrotizing fasciitis is an infection with multiple organisms and may manifest as a red, warm, tender subcutaneous plaque that becomes anesthetic and necrotic. This disease and its variants, Fournier's gangrene (perineal phlegmon) and synergistic necrotizing cellulitis, also require prompt aggressive treatment with debridement and broad-spectrum parenteral antibiotics including anaerobic coverage.

Diabetics are also prone to certain fungal infections. Most prominent among these is candidiasis, which, in the form of thrush or balanitis, may be the presenting sign of diabetes. Other cutaneous candidal infections include chronic paronychia, erosio interdigitale blastomycetica (finger web infection), and intertriginous candidiasis. A less common but more serious fungal infection is rhinocerebral mucormycosis. This infection, which typically occurs in the context of acidosis, may present simply as eye irritation or lacrimation, or the patient may have extensive necrotic lesions of the nose or palate. Other presentations include epistaxis, unilateral cellulitis, unilateral headache, perioral numbness, or loss of consciousness. The organisms classically invade from the sinuses into the retro-orbital space and then into the brain, with a strong predisposition to travel along arteries, thereby causing thrombosis and necrosis. Investigation of suspected cases includes culture, examination of scrapings with potassium hydroxide, and biopsy. The characteristic microscopic appearance of the organism is wide hyphae with irregularly spaced perpendicular branching. Amphotericin B is the antifungal agent of choice, but surgery is usually required as well. Even with optimal management, the outcome is often poor.

Diabetics may develop cutaneous **complications of vascular disease and neuropathy.** Diabetic foot ulcers are particularly significant because they are common in chronic diabetes, and they often lead to loss of limb. Preventive measures are of primary importance and include meticulous daily inspection of the feet and shoes, avoidance of trauma, including extremes of temperature, and careful choice of shoes and socks. Diabetic peripheral vascular disease has many other cutaneous signs, including atrophy with loss of hair on extremities, dependent rubor, dystrophic nails, and cold toes and feet. It is thought that the association of diabetes with rubeosis, Terry's nails (a white or light pink nail bed and a distal pink to brown nonblanchable band), and nail bed telangiectasia may be a reflection of microvascular disease.

Diabetic dermopathy is a common asymptomatic disorder of the elderly, particularly men, with long-standing diabetes. The diagnosis is considered when round or oval hyperpigmented atrophic plaques are present on the lower legs with no history of trauma in a diabetic individual. The histologic picture consists of epidermal atrophy with hemosiderin deposition and basal layer hyperpigmentation. This type of lesion has been experimentally produced in diabetics by thermal trauma, and it is suspected that occult injury of this type accounts for many of the cases.

Anhidrosis of the lower body, sometimes with severe associated compensatory hyperhidrosis of the face and upper trunk, is a manifestation of autonomic neuropathy. The induction of severe sweating of the face and upper trunk by certain foods (diabetic gustatory sweating) is thought to be due to vagus neuropathy.

Necrobiosis lipoidica diabeticorum is a distinctive disorder that most commonly affects the pretibial skin of young female diabetics. It occurs, however, in many anatomic locations, in all ages, in both sexes, and may also occur in nondiabetic individuals. Approximately 1 in 300 diabetics is reported to have these lesions, which may cause significant disfiguration and ulceration. They typically appear as asymptomatic red papules or plaques that may spontaneously resolve (approximately one in five do so) or expand and leave in their wake a yellowish, depressed plaque with epidermal and dermal atrophy. One-third of the lesions are said to ulcerate at some time in their course. The distinctive histopathologic picture includes full-thickness involvement of the dermis with palisading granulomas and areas of acellular degenerating ("necrobiotic") collagen. This is associated with impaired collagen production by lesional fibroblasts. Treatment with intralesional steroids may be useful in the early, inflammatory stage.

Scleredema diabeticorum is a thickening of the skin of the back and neck preceded by a subtle erythema. It is insidious in onset and probably irreversible. Occasionally it affects other sites or limits range of motion. The thickening, which is "wooden" by palpation, is primarily due to dermal mucin deposition, although collagen is also increased. There is a separate syndrome of waxy skin associated with limited joint mobility in the fingers; this syndrome typically occurs in children several years after the onset of diabetes. Finally, thickened acral skin and an increased proportion of thick collagen fibers have been reported to be associated with diabetes in the absence of clinical disease.

Acanthosis nigricans is a velvety, hyperpigmented epidermal thickening of skin folds, particularly the posterior neck and axillae, which commonly occurs in noninsulin-dependent diabetes and other hyperinsulinemic states (e.g., obesity), and is rarely associated with antibody-mediated, insulin-resistant diabetes. It is thought to result from direct stimulation of the epidermis by insulin. A subtle bumpiness of the knuckle skin ("finger pebbles"), possibly related to acanthosis nigricans, has also been described in diabetics.

Diabetics are subject to hyperlipidemia, and consequently have an increased frequency of several types of **xanthomas.** Eruptive xanthomas are red-yellow papules that appear in crops, typically on the buttocks or extensor surfaces of the extremities. These papules are associated with marked elevations of triglycerides. Tendinous xanthomas, most characteristically diagnosed by palpation of the Achilles tendon, are associated with hypercholesterolemia. Xanthelasma are soft, yellowish plaques on the eyelids and are associated with hyperlipidemia and apolipoprotein abnormalities. All xanthomas are characterized histopathologically by accumulations of lipid-laden histiocytes.

Bullous pemphigoid and epidermolysis bullosa acquisita are two immunologically mediated **blistering disorders** that have been reported to be more common in diabetes. Even in the absence of these disorders, diabetic skin blisters more easily than nondiabetic skin. Acral blistering in diabetics without a history of antecedent trauma is often classified as bullosis diabeticorum, a poorly characterized disorder that is typically associated with neuropathy. The relationship of this disorder to occult injury and ischemia is unclear.

Diabetics with chronic renal failure are particularly predisposed to **Kyrle's disease,** a disorder characterized by pruritic keratotic papules that most commonly appear on the extremities, buttocks, and sacral region. The lesions may be small, brownish, horny, follicular papules as large as 1 cm and very warty in appearance. Histologically, massive focal hyperkeratosis of the follicular or extrafollicular epidermis is found overlying and within an atrophic epidermis without a granular layer. The keratotic plug may perforate into the dermis, leading to inflammation and formation of foreign-body granuloma. In some patients, some lesions may show epidermal perforation of abnormal collagen (reactive perforating collagenosis) or other follicular wall components (perforating folliculitis). Although Kyrle's disease is known to affect older patients with severe diabetic nephropathy, often end-stage and on hemodialysis, it has also been described in younger, healthy individuals. In either case, it runs a relentless and unpredictable course: individual lesions may enlarge and become painful or undergo spontaneous involution, but the process continues at other sites. Treatment is not often helpful, particularly long-term; but keratolytic agents, topical retinoic acid, and emollients are generally tried first. Eradication of painful lesions by electrocautery, cryotherapy, or surgical excision may afford relief. Etretinate may induce temporary remission if the adverse effects can be tolerated.

There are a variety of other disorders that have been said to be associated with diabetes. Vitiligo appears to be associated with insulin-dependent diabetes mellitus as well as with a variety of other autoimmune disorders. Other possibly associated disorders include granuloma annulare, lichen planus, pruritus (particularly of the scalp and vulva), non-AIDS-associated Kaposi's sarcoma, carotenodermia, pigmentary purpura, and intracutaneous herniation of fat.

Finally, there are a number of systemic disorders that are associated with diabetes and cutaneous manifestations. A partial list includes porphyria cutanea tarda, pancreatic glucagonoma, ataxia-telangiectasia, hemochromatosis, and the syndromes of Achard-Thiers, Buschke-Ollendorff, Cockayne, Fanconi, Lawrence, Seip-Berardinelli, and Werner.

Bernstein JE, Levine LE, Medenica MM, et al.: Reduced threshold to suction-induced blister formation in insulin-dependent diabetics. *J Am Acad Dermatol.* 1983;8:790–791.
  Experimental evaluation of the tendency to blister formation in diabetics.
Edidin DV: Cutaneous manifestations of diabetes mellitus in children. *Pediatr Dermatol.* 1985;2:161–179.
  Review article.
Flier JS: Metabolic importance of acanthosis nigricans. *Arch Dermatol.* 1985;121:193–194.
  Discussion of the pathophysiology of acanthosis nigricans.
Hanna W, Friesen D, Bombardier C, et al.: Pathologic features of diabetic thick skin. *J Am Acad Dermatol.* 1987;16:546–553.
  Discussion of the histopathology of diabetic thick skin.
Huntley AC: The cutaneous manifestations of diabetes mellitus. *J Am Acad Dermatol.* 1982;7:427–455:
  Review article.
Jelinek JE: *The Skin in Diabetes.* Philadelphia, PA: Lea & Febiger; 1986.
  A book-length review of the subject.
Kozak GP, Hoar CS, Rowbotham JL, et al.: *Management of Diabetic Foot Problems.* Philadelphia, PA: W.B. Saunders; 1984.

Detailed discussion of this crucial area, based on the experience of the Joslin Clinic and New England Deaconess Hospital.

Lithner F: Cutaneous reactions of the extremities of diabetics to local thermal trauma. *Acta Med Scand.* 1975;198:319–325.
Description of the sequelae of experimental thermal trauma to the extremities of 35 diabetics and 25 control subjects.

Lowitt MH and Dover JS: Necrobiosis lipoidica. *J Am Acad Dermatol.* 1991:25;735–748.
The pathogenesis of NLD remains unknown and therapy is not uniformly effective.

Parker F: Xanthomas and hyperlipidemias. *J Am Acad Dermatol.* 1985;13:1–30.
Review of the pathophysiology and clinical features of these distinctive cutaneous lesions.

Sibbald RG, Schachter RK: The skin and diabetes mellitus. *Int J Dermatol.* 1984;23:567–584.
Review article.

64. SARCOIDOSIS AND OTHER GRANULOMAS
William Frank

The granulomatous disorders are a diverse group of diseases with a wide variety of etiologies, characterized histologically by focal accumulation and proliferation of histiocytes often arranged in a palisading fashion and by the presence of multinucleated giant cells. Cutaneous granulomas can be caused by sarcoidosis, granuloma annulare, foreign-body reactions, numerous infectious diseases, and by a large group of rare or poorly defined disorders. These disorders may be difficult to distinguish clinically because the cutaneous reaction pattern is often not specific. A tissue biopsy is usually necessary for diagnosis. Although granulomas with specific characteristics appear in some disorders, the histology can also be nonspecific. Fungal and bacterial cultures and stains, special stains, and phase contrast microscopy may be helpful in determining definitive diagnosis.

Sarcoidosis is a systemic disease of unknown etiology and is characterized histologically by the noncaseating granuloma. The estimated incidence is 20 per 100,000 in the general population, but varies depending on the specific population studied. It is most common in Ireland and among black females in the United States. Generally, patients are diagnosed between the ages of 20 and 40.

Cutaneous manifestations are present in 20% to 35% of patients, are often the first sign of disease, and help the clinician make a prompt diagnosis. Lupus pernio is a distinctive form of cutaneous sarcoidosis, consisting of persistent purple papules or plaques. It most commonly occurs on the nose, cheeks, and ears. Individual lesions can range in size from small papules to large, coalescent plaques covering large portions of the face. Cutaneous sarcoidosis can also present as infiltrated papules, nodules, plaques, annular lesions, or hypopigmented macules occurring on the torso or extremities. Violaceous nodules may be found in sites of old scars and appear similar to keloids. Lesions of sarcoid often display a yellow-brown color when viewed through a glass slide pressed over the lesion (diascopy). However, this finding is nonspecific and is typical of cutaneous granulomatous lesions of many causes. Because these skin lesions are not pathognomonic for sarcoidosis, a biopsy is essential for definitive diagnosis.

Other skin lesions not containing granulomas histologically may be seen in sarcoidosis. Erythema nodosum is common, occurring in 15% to 20% of patients, often accompanied by constitutional symptoms such as fever and arthralgias. It usually presents with tender, warm, erythematous nodules on the anterior shins, rarely occurring in other locations. Histopathologically, erythema nodosum is a septal panniculitis. A symmetric nonpruritic macular and papular eruption, often with rapid onset, may also be seen in sarcoidosis. A biopsy is nonspecific, usually indicating a hypersensitivity reaction.

Every major organ system can be involved in sarcoidosis. Pulmonary involvement is present in over 90% of patients and is the most common clinical manifestation. Bilateral hilar adenopathy is the most frequent radiographic sign. A large proportion of patients with isolated hilar adenopathy will have spontaneous resolution of disease. Peripheral lymph nodes are involved in 30% to 75% of patients, and a biopsy can be helpful in diagnosis. Hepatomegaly is present in 20% of cases, but almost 80% will have histopathologic hepatic involvement. Ocular involvement occurs in up to 50% of patients, usually as granulomatous uveitis that occasionally results in glaucoma or blindness. Conjunctival granulomas can be seen. Sarcoidosis in the central nervous system ranges from meningeal involvement to infiltration of the pituitary. Cardiac manifestations include heart block, arrhythmias, and sudden death.

A high index of clinical suspicion and a suggestive biopsy are necessary to make the diagnosis of cutaneous sarcoidosis. The characteristic histopathologic finding is noncaseating granulomas comprised of radially arranged epithelioid cells (modified macrophages). Langhans' giant cells, multinucleated histiocytes with nuclei arranged in an arc around the cell periphery, are often present. Although the presence of granulomas with these morphologic characteristics in a biopsy is suggestive of sarcoidosis, other disorders should be excluded. Fungal infection, mycobacterial infection, foreign-body granuloma, or, rarely, protozoal infection may present with a similar histologic appearance. Cultures and stains for fungi and mycobacteria, as well as microscopic examination of the tissue with polarized light to detect foreign bodies, should be done to rule out these disorders.

The cause of sarcoidosis is unknown. An infectious etiology has been proposed for many years, but numerous efforts have failed to isolate an agent. The claims that sarcoidosis is a hypersensitivity reaction to an exogenous agent such as beryllium are unsubstantiated. Since patients generally have decreased cell-mediated immunity and cutaneous anergy, and large numbers of activated T lymphocytes are recoverable from bronchoalveolar lavage samples, an as-yet-unidentified immunologic mechanism is likely.

Evaluation of a patient with cutaneous sarcoidosis should include a complete history and physical examination, posteroanterior and lateral chest x rays, an ophthalmologic examination utilizing a slit lamp, and an ECG.

The use of systemic steroids is rarely warranted in the treatment of cutaneous sarcoidosis, with the possible exception of ulcerative lesions, extensive lupus pernio, or widespread, scarring lesions. Potent topical corticosteroids and local corticosteroid injection of lesions can be helpful. Systemic administration of antimalarials, allopurinol, methotrexate, and cis-retinoic acid have been reported to be of benefit in some instances.

Granuloma annulare (GA) is an idiopathic asymptomatic dermatosis characterized by papules arranged in an annular configuration. It is an uncommon disorder, identified in less than 0.5% of patients presenting to dermatologists. Females are affected twice as often as males (2.5:1). Although GA can occur at any age, 70% of patients are less than 30 years of age. It is usually self-limited and has a characteristic histology.

The primary lesions of GA are discrete, firm, flesh-colored, erythematous or violaceous 3- to 4-mm papules. There is usually no scaling, and pruritus is uncommon. Roughly half of all cases present with a single cluster of papules in an annular or arciform configuration on one extremity. Most patients have lesions limited to the arms or legs, although GA can be seen on both extremities simultaneously, on the trunk, or, rarely, on the face. About 15% of patients will have generalized and widespread symmetrically distributed papules. Generalized lesions often lack annular configuration.

Two clinical variants of GA may be recognized. Annular erythematous lesions with peripheral scale resembling erythema annulare centrifugation have been rarely reported. The erythema is more prominent than the papular component. As in typical

GA, these rings spread centrifugally. Perforating GA is uncommon. Typical papules of GA develop a yellow hyperkeratotic center that may spontaneously exude a viscous fluid. Transepidermal elimination of collagen is responsible for these clinical features.

The clinical appearance of GA is usually characteristic, but a biopsy is helpful to confirm the diagnosis. Histologic examination shows multiple areas of granulomatous inflammation with central zones of complete or incomplete collagenous degeneration. The histology is quite similar to that of necrobiosis lipoidica diabeticorum (NLD), but in GA the areas of collagen degeneration are smaller and there is much more mucin deposition. Clinically and histologically, the differential diagnosis of GA includes tinea corporis, NLD, sarcoidosis, and annular elastolytic giant cell granuloma.

The association of GA with other diseases is disputed. A relationship between GA and diabetes mellitus was initially postulated (especially generalized GA) because of the histologic similarity of GA to NLD. Studies have not consistently found a higher incidence of elevated fasting blood sugar in patients with GA. Although not understood pathogenetically, lesions of GA may develop in herpes zoster scars, warts, and sites of trauma.

Lesions may persist for less than 1 month or for many years. The disorder will resolve spontaneously within 2 years in 50% of patients. Generalized GA usually lasts 1 to 2 years longer than the localized form. Treatment is not necessary, and often not very helpful. Potent topical steroids can clear selected lesions. Intralesional injection of triamcinolone diacetate, 5–10 mg/ml, is also useful, however care must be taken to avoid atrophy. Since it is an asymptomatic disease involving only the skin, the risks of oral steroids and immunosuppressive agents generally outweigh the benefits.

Chemically induced granulomas represent the response of the body to a substance of low solubility or high immunogenicity. *Foreign-body granuloma* is a term used to describe the reaction to inoculated substances that are poorly eliminated from the dermis because of low solubility. The list of agents that can cause foreign-body granulomas is extremely long. Metal-based dyes used in tattooing, dirt, talc, silicone, amalgam, glass, cactus, thorns, sea urchin spicules, retained insect parts, paraffin, hair, and sutures are but a few of the culprits. A variety of substances also cause similar granulomatous reactions on a presumed immunologic basis. Beryllium, which is used in the aerospace industry, has been clearly demonstrated to cause cutaneous granulomas. Zirconium, in the lactate form, formerly used in deodorants, was a cause of many cases of granulomatous eruptions in the axillae. It was also responsible for eruptions produced by certain topical poison oak preparations that are no longer on the market. Other substances known to cause immunologically mediated granulomas include mercury, chromium, and cobalt.

Chemical granulomas usually present as asymptomatic single or multiple indurated nodules that occasionally ulcerate. Penetrating injury is required to introduce the foreign body into the dermis. However, because the latency period between inoculation and granuloma formation is long, this history is frequently difficult to obtain. The diagnosis of chemical granuloma usually requires a biopsy. Tissue examination reveals granulomatous inflammation in which foreign-body giant cells are prominent. The presence of foreign-body particles is diagnostic. Techniques such as special staining and phase contrast microscopy can help identify specific etiologic agents.

Foreign-body granulomas can be excised, with variable cosmetic success. Silica, zirconium, and other granulomas of the immunogenic type tend to heal spontaneously over a prolonged period of time.

The list of **infectious etiologies** that can result in granulomatous inflammation is long. In general, these diseases are caused by direct inoculation or hematogenous or lymphatic spread. Deep fungal infections such as histoplasmosis, coccidioidomycosis, paracoccidioidomycosis, blastomycosis, sporotrichosis, chromomycosis, and aspergillus can cause granulomatous inflammation. Cutaneous tuberculosis due to *Mycobacterium tuberculosis* or the atypical mycobacteria such as *M. marinum* ("swimming pool granuloma"), *M. kansasaii, M. avium-intracellulare,* and *M. fortuitum* complex should be considered in the differential of infectious granulomas. Leprosy should be considered in any hypoesthetic lesion. Other infectious diseases that can occasionally cause granulomas include brucellosis, tularemia, cat-scratch disease, leishmaniasis, schistosomiasis, secondary syphilis, and scabies. The correct diagnosis depends on clinical suspicion and proper fungal, bacterial, and acid-fast bacterial stains and cultures of tissue specimens, and appropriate serologic testing.

Necrobiosis lipoidica diabeticorum is most commonly a cutaneous manifestation of diabetes mellitus. Half of the patients with NLD have diabetes, and many have a family history of diabetes. The lesions most commonly occur on the shins and consist of yellowish plaques with an erythematous or violaceous border and central atrophy. Most patients are female. The major complication is ulceration of the central region. A biopsy is confirmatory, revealing typical granulomatous inflammation with marked collagenous degeneration; however, biopsy sites are usually very slow to heal. The presence of NLD is not correlated with the severity of the diabetes.

Lymphomatoid granulomatosis is a systemic necrotizing granulomatous vasculitis characterized by pulmonary involvement, neurologic manifestations, and skin lesions. One-third to one-half of patients have cutaneous manifestations such as violaceous papules, plaques, or ulcerated nodules. The lesions may precede systemic involvement. The disease is associated with a poor prognosis. In a study of 148 patients treated with various modalities, the median survival was 18 months. Lymphoma accompanies the vasculitis in 10% to 20% of patients. Other granulomatous vasculitides include Wegener's granulomatosis and the Churg-Strauss syndrome.

Granuloma faciale primarily occurs in middle age and consists of discrete reddish brown, slowly enlarging plaques and nodules on the face. There is no association with systemic illness. A biopsy shows vasculitis as well as a polymorphous dermal infiltrate rich in eosinophils that is separated from the epidermis by a grenz zone. Lesions tend to be persistent. Intralesional corticosteroid injections are sometimes helpful. Excision in toto may be followed by recurrence in the scar. Argon laser surgery has been described as causing lesions to involute.

Annular elastolytic giant cell granuloma appears on the head and neck as annular plaques with raised, erythematous borders and central hypopigmentation. This may represent the same entity as Miescher's granuloma and actinic granuloma. Histology shows granulomatous inflammation, giant cells often with asteroid body formation, and elastic fiber degeneration. Effective treatment has not been described.

In about 10% of cases, **rosacea** can be accompanied by granulomatous infiltration that is thought to be a foreign-body reaction to keratin. The usual treatments for rosacea are effective; however, a prolonged course may be required for improvement to be seen.

Juvenile xanthogranuloma is a benign disorder usually seen in infancy and is characterized by the eruption of one or many reddish yellow nodules that gradually enlarge and then spontaneously regress. A biopsy shows a granulomatous infiltrate with vacuolated histiocytes containing lipid (foam cells). This entity must be distinguished from histiocytosis X, which may be clinically similar.

Granuloma gluteale infantum is characterized by reddish blue, smooth nodules in the diaper region of young infants and, rarely, in the elderly wearing diapers. The eruption usually is preceded by diaper dermatitis. The two factors most often associated with the entity are disposable diapers and the use of topical steroids. In most reported cases, topical steroids had been used prior to the onset of eruption. In a few instances, *Candida albicans* infection has been demonstrated histologically.

Cheilitis granulomatosis (Miescher-Melkersson-Rosenthal syndrome) is a rare condition characterized by chronic, recurrent swelling of one or both lips, occasionally associated with unilateral facial paresis and scrotal tongue. The condition often appears in childhood or adolescence, but may appear at any age. The earliest manifestation is usually sudden diffuse swelling of the upper lip. After repeated attacks, lip swelling becomes persistent. Histology may only reveal edema and a perivascular infiltrate, but in other cases shows granulomatous inflammation.

Granuloma multiforme begins as papules, which enlarge to form annular lesions with defined raised borders and central hypopigmentation. The condition is endemic in eastern Nigeria and must be differentiated from leprosy. Adult women older than

40 are usually affected. The initial lesions are usually papules in exposed areas of the upper trunk. These coalesce to form annular plaques with sharply defined raised borders and hypopigmented centers. The etiology of this condition is unknown.

Dabski K, Winkelmann RK: Generalized granuloma annulare: Clinical and laboratory findings in 100 patients. *J Am Acad Dermatol.* 1989;20:39–47.
  Clinical and laboratory findings in a series of patients seen at the Mayo Clinic over a 20-year period.
Dabski K, Winkelmann RK: Generalized granuloma annulare: Histopathology and immunopathology. *J Am Acad Dermatol.* 1989;20:28–39.
  A systemic review of 100 cases and comparison with localized granuloma annulare.
Hanke WC, Bailen PL, Roenigk HH: Annular elastolytic giant cell granuloma. *J Am Acad Dermatol.* 1979;1:413–421.
  Discusses the clinical and pathologic features and compares them with similar diseases.
Katzenstein AL, Carrington CB, Liebow AA: Lymphomatoid granulomatosis. *Cancer.* 1979;43:360–373.
  A clinicopathologic study of 152 cases.
Kerdel FA, Moschella SL: Sarcoidosis. *J Am Acad Dermatol.* 1984;11:1–19.
  A thorough review of cutaneous sarcoidosis.
Muhlbauer J: Granuloma annulare. *JAAD.* 1980;3(3):217–230.
  A general review of granuloma annulare.
Muller SA, Winkelmann RK: Necrobiosis lipoidica diabeticorum. *Arch Dermatol.* 1966;93:272–281.
  Discusses the clinical and pathologic characteristics of 171 patients with NLD.
Tozman EC: Sarcoidosis: clinical manifestations, epidemiology, therapy, and pathophysiology. *Curr Opin Rheumatol.* 1991;3(1):155–159.
  Opinionated clinical review of sarcoidosis.
Van Gundy K, Sharma OP: Pathogenesis of sarcoidosis. *West J Med.* 1987;147:168–174.
  An updated review of the pathogenesis of sarcoidosis.
Webster GF, et al.: Weekly low-dose methotrexate therapy for cutaneous sarcoidosis. *J Am Acad Dermatol.* 1991;24(3):451–454.
  Three patients responded favorably to weekly, low dose methotrexate therapy. Ulcerated sarcoid lesions and facial granulomas responded best.
Zic JA, et al.: Treatment of cutaneous sarcoidosis with chloroquine. Review of the literature. *Arch Dermatol.* 1991;127(7):1034–1040.
  The cutaneous manifestations of sarcoidosis can often be successfully treated with chloroquine while avoiding retinopathy.

65. CUTANEOUS SIGNS OF INTERNAL MALIGNANCY
Edward V. Maytin

Dermatologic manifestations of malignancy may be roughly classified according to whether the dermatoses result from direct or indirect effects of the tumor. Direct effects result from infiltration of the skin by neoplastic cells, either by local extension or by metastatic spread from other sites. Indirect effects are remote effects unrelated to a site of primary or metastatic tumor involvement and are sometimes called paraneoplastic phenomena. Commonplace examples include icterus or palmar erythema from liver metastases and petechiae or purpura from leukemic bone marrow infiltration, both representing remote effects seen in the skin. However, other more exotic paraneoplastic conditions can be seen. They fulfill two essential criteria: the dermatosis develops coincident with or after the onset of the tumor, and both the dermatosis and the tumor follow a parallel course (i.e., remove the tumor and the dermatosis resolves). In addition to the direct and indirect effects of malignancy on the skin, there are numerous inherited disorders with characteristic cutaneous findings and a predisposition to internal malignancy.

A skin eruption caused by local extension of a tumor is exemplified by **Paget's disease of the nipple,** arising from extension of underlying ductal breast carcinoma. It presents as a sharply demarcated, scaly, erythematous plaque that is indurated to palpation, and usually involves only a portion of one nipple. Pathologic examination of an appropriate biopsy specimen reveals large cells with big nuclei and pale cytoplasm, called Paget cells, in the epidermis and ductal carcinoma cells in the deep dermis. The clinical differential diagnosis includes psoriasis and eczema. The prognosis is favorable following complete surgical excision if no palpable masses are found within the breast. In **extramammary Paget's disease,** large eczematous plaques occur in the vulvar, perianal, and axillary regions. In about 25% of patients, an underlying carcinoma of adnexal origin may be found. The pathogenesis of extramammary Paget's is hotly debated. It may represent a local effect of an underlying tumor or an in situ carcinoma of eccrine sweat gland origin. In both mammary and extramammary forms of Paget's, surgery is the treatment of choice.

Metastases to the skin may appear in a patient with known malignancy or may be the first presenting sign. They are usually pink, red, plum, brownish black, or flesh-colored firm papules and subcutaneous nodules, from 1 mm to several centimeters in size. Such lesions should always be biopsied for histologic confirmation. Metastases to skin are less frequent than to other organs, probably occurring in about 5% of patients with disseminated disease. Carcinomas (lung in men, breast in women) are the most frequent sources, followed by lymphomas and leukemias. The location of the lesions can sometimes help in diagnosis. For example, breast cancer can appear on the anterior chest wall as small nodules, as a cellulitis-like eruption (inflammatory carcinoma), or as sclerosing, leather-like skin (carcinoma en cuirasse). Stomach carcinoma may metastasize to the umbilicus (Sister Joseph nodule). Scalp metastases often arise from renal, lung, or breast carcinoma, resulting in nodules or hair loss with scarring (alopecia neoplastica). Renal and thyroid carcinomas may produce pulsatile metastases with bruits. Lymphomas, especially T-cell lymphomas (mycosis fungoides/Sézary syndrome), can infiltrate the skin as plaques, nodules, or diffuse erythroderma. Involvement with B-cell lymphoma (both Hodgkin's and non-Hodgkin's) occurs, but less commonly. Leukemic cell infiltrates in the skin (leukemia cutis) are most common with chronic leukemias. Gingival involvement may be found with both chronic and acute leukemias, especially those of monocytic origin. A relatively high proportion of monocytic leukemias will exhibit cutaneous metastases, but lymphocytic leukemic infiltrates are seen more often, because of the higher incidence of lymphocytic leukemias. Patients with acute myeloblastic leukemia may have chloromas, cutaneous nodules that turn green when a cut surface is exposed to air. They owe their color to the presence of myeloperoxidases within the tumor cells.

Paraneoplastic cutaneous syndromes may be highly associated with malignancy or may be rather nonspecific. One syndrome always associated with malignancy is **acrokeratosis of Bazex,** an eruption of the extremities, nose, and ears that is associated with cancer of the respiratory tract (lungs, esophagus, tongue) or the gastrointestinal tract. Skin lesions begin on the hands and feet as symmetric, scaling, erythematous plaques, bluer in color than psoriasis lesions. Severe nail involvement with subungual hyperkeratosis, flaking, and shedding of the nail plate is common. Later, the ear, bridge of the nose, elbows, and knees may become involved. Microscopic examination of a biopsy specimen shows nonspecific inflammation. Histologic features of psoriasis are absent. The skin lesions, which can precede the diagnosis of a tumor, predict the presence of malignancy with nearly 100% certainty. They resolve when the tumor is removed. Symptomatic treatment with keratolytics and topical steroids may be attempted.

Erythema gyratum repens, another rare disorder, presents with an eruption that has a distinctive zebra-stripe or wood-grain appearance, and is highly associated with common internal malignancies such as breast, lung, and gastrointestinal carcinomas. Waves of slightly raised, erythematous plaques with a fine collarette of scale move across the cutaneous surface at a rate of about 1 cm per day. Histopathology is nonspecific, but a diagnosis can be made on clinical appearance alone. The diagnosis of erythema gyratum repens should trigger an extensive search for an internal neoplasm. In cases where the tumor can be removed, the dermatosis usually resolves in less than 6 weeks.

Hypertrichosis lanuginosa is an excessive growth of fine, lanugo (fetal type) hairs that appears suddenly in association with various gastrointestinal tract tumors, especially carcinoid and islet cell tumors. Soft hairs cover the face, ears, and, sometimes, the entire body. A painful glossitis, with red papules on the tongue, may be associated. When fully expressed, the hypertrichosis is a fairly specific paraneoplastic marker, although the differential diagnosis also includes anorexia nervosa and adverse effects from drugs such as steroids, phenytoin, penicillamine, streptomycin, and minoxidil.

Acquired ichthyosis of sudden onset may herald the onset of Hodgkin's lymphoma or other hematologic malignancies including non-Hodgkin's lymphoma, mycosis fungoides, or multiple myeloma. A biopsy of an area with grossly visible scaling reveals histologic evidence of thickening of the stratum corneum. It is usually, but not always, a late sign of malignancy. **Pityriasis rotunda,** a localized form of acquired ichthyosis, presents as sharply demarcated, scaly, disklike patches on the trunk, and has been seen with hepatocellular carcinoma in Asians (Japanese) and South African blacks.

Diffuse melanosis is another late sign of malignancy, usually associated with metastatic melanoma. Diffuse gray-brown hyperpigmentation develops, resulting from either circulating free melanin or widespread single-cell metastases. Dark streaks in the nails may be found. Tumors that produce corticotropin or alpha-melanocyte-stimulating hormone may also cause diffuse melanosis. The differential diagnosis includes nonmalignant causes such as adrenal insufficiency, severe malnutrition, and drugs (busulfan, phenothiazines, antimalarials, and arsenic poisoning). Hemochromatosis may cause a similar hyperpigmentation. One helpful differential diagnostic sign is the presence of melanuria: in severe melanosis, the urine is initially clear after voiding, but blackens after several hours of exposure to air because of the oxidation of tyrosine metabolites to form melanin.

Necrolytic migratory erythema, an erosive eruption of the face and intertriginous areas, is a marker for glucagonoma, a glucagon-producing tumor of pancreatic islet cells. Erythema, vesicles, pustules, and erosions appear first on the center of the face and the groin, then progress to involve the shins, ankles, feet, and fingertips. Superficial vesicles often become confluent to form bullae. The differential diagnosis includes atypical psoriasis and mucocutaneous candidiasis. Proposed pathogenetic factors, such as high glucagon levels or low amino acid levels, have not been well substantiated. Glucagonoma is also associated with other cutaneous abnormalities including glossitis, stomatitis, nail dystrophy, and alopecia, as well as with serious systemic problems such as weight loss, anemia, and diabetes. About 70% of glucagonomas have already metastasized at the time of diagnosis. If the disease can be controlled, the dermatitis resolves.

Paraneoplastic pemphigus is a newly described entity, seen mostly in patients with leukemias and lymphomas. Patients present with severe symptoms reminiscent of both pemphigus vulgaris (cutaneous blistering) and of erythema multiforme (painful erosions of the lips, oral cavity, and conjunctiva, and target-like lesions on the palms and soles). Skin biopsies display an overlapping constellation of features as well, including the necrosis of individual keratinocytes typical of erythema multiforme, an intercellular epidermal pattern of immunofluorescence (typical of pemphigus vulgaris), and basement-membrane antibody staining typical of bullous pemphigoid. Symptoms are severe and refractory to treatment, but may resolve after effective treatment of the underlying malignancy.

There are a number of cutaneous signs that may be present in association with malignancy or may occur in its absence. **Acanthosis nigricans** is a gray-brown velvety thickening of the skin, involving axillae, base of the neck, groin, and antecubital fossae symmetrically. Benign causes include obesity and abnormalities of the hypothalamic-pituitary-adrenal axis, such as Addison's disease. When it occurs suddenly and is rapidly progressive, acanthosis nigricans may be associated with intra-abdominal adenocarcinoma, usually carcinoma of the stomach. Skin changes may be secondary to peptide production by the tumor. Similarly, excess adrenal glucocorticoids causing **Cushing's syndrome** can be seen with corticotropin-producing carcinomas of the lung.

Bowen's disease, carcinoma in situ of the epidermis unrelated to sun exposure, was thought to indicate an up to ninefold increased risk of various internal neoplasms. Recent studies, however, have suggested that in some populations, other etiologies such as arsenic exposure are responsible for an increased risk of both Bowen's disease and internal malignancy. Also hotly debated is an apparent association between **dermatomyositis** and common malignancies in the elderly. The association is not a strong one and is nonexistent for polymyositis alone; therefore, screening for the most common malignancies by history, physical examination, stool hemoccult test, and chest x ray is warranted unless other suggestive symptoms are present. **Migratory superficial thrombophlebitis** and **nodular panniculitis** can be seen with cancer of the pancreas. These conditions present similarly, as crops of tender nodules on the lower extremities, resembling erythema nodosum. Nodules on the upper extremities and abdomen may also be found. Both processes are associated with inflammation of blood vessels within fat lobules, although the primary pathophysiologic mechanisms may be different. It is thought that hypercoagulability or deposition of immune complexes causes thrombophlebitis, while in nodular panniculitis, the release of trypsin and lipases from the diseased pancreas injures subcutaneous fat.

Generalized **pruritus,** sudden in onset and not readily explainable by other causes, raises the possibility of polycythemia vera, leukemia, or lymphoma. The pruritus of polycythemia vera typically occurs after baths, and the pruritus of lymphoma is severe and burning and tends to start on the legs, while that of leukemia may be less severe and more generalized. Another marker of leukemia is **Sweet's syndrome,** an acute febrile neutrophilic dermatosis, which presents as painful red plaques and nodules on the face and extremities that expand peripherally with central clearing. A biopsy reveals a dense dermal infiltrate predominantly composed of neutrophils. Although Sweet's syndrome is commonly associated with acute myelocytic and sometimes myelomonocytic leukemia, the neutrophils in the dermis are not necessarily malignant, in keeping with the paraneoplastic nature of the syndrome. Sweet's syndrome may also occur in otherwise healthy individuals, usually middle-aged women, with fever, an elevated white count, and recurrent crops of lesions.

Other common skin lesions are sometimes reported in association with internal tumors: eruptive angiomas, bullous pemphigoid, eruptive seborrheic keratoses (sign of Leser-Trélat), skin tags, and plane xanthomas. Because both the skin conditions and the malignancies are very common, these associations are hard to prove and of little practical help as early markers of malignancy.

A confusing array of rare, genetically determined disorders with associated skin manifestations show an increased predisposition to malignancy. The pathogenetic mechanisms usually incriminated include altered patterns of differentiation in embryologic tissues or faulty genetic repair mechanisms. Among autosomal dominant conditions, **Cowden's disease** produces multiple benign hamartomas (facial trichilemmomas, oral fibromas, and keratotic papules of palms and soles) and is associated with a very high incidence of breast and thyroid carcinoma. **Gardner syndrome** displays a different constellation of benign growths of the skin (epidermal and sebaceous cysts, lipomas, and fibromas), as well as those of bone (osteomas) and the gastrointestinal tract (colonic polyps). In Gardner syndrome the incidence of colon adenocarcinoma is so high that a colectomy is often done prophylactically. **Neurofibromatosis** is a group of disorders with variable associations, usually benign cutaneous neurofibromas, café au lait spots, axillary freckling, and acoustic neuromas. Malignant neurilemmoma occurs in about 5% of patients, and rarely other brain tumors. **Peutz-Jeghers syndrome** consists of pigmented macules of the lips and digits, polyps of the small intestine, and a moderate (2% to 3%) incidence of adenocarcinoma. An autosomal dominant form of **tylosis** (palmar-plantar hyperkeratosis) has been reported in two kindreds, with a 95% incidence of esophageal cancer.

Autosomal recessive disorders with cutaneous signs and increased incidence of malignancy include **Bloom's syndrome,** a disease in which a defect of DNA repair results in photosensitivity and telangiectasias of sun-exposed skin and a high incidence of leukemia. **Ataxia-telangiectasia** is characterized by cerebellar ataxia, telangiectasias of bulbar conjunctiva and flexural skin, and an increase in incidence of leukemia and lymphoma.

An X-linked recessive condition, **dyskeratosis congenita** results in ripplelike hyperpigmentation, oral leukoplakia, nail loss, pancytopenia, and a very high incidence of carcinomas and leukemias. **Wiskott-Aldrich syndrome,** also X-linked recessive in inheritance, is characterized by a combination of eczema, purpura, and recurrent infections and is associated with thrombocytopenia and decreased IgM levels. Leukemia and lymphoma occur in 10% of these patients.

The evaluation of skin signs associated with internal malignancy can be confusing because many of these signs also have several possible benign causes; however, some guidelines are helpful. The highly associated, malignancy-specific dermatoses are always worrisome, especially if the onset is sudden and the dermatosis is severe. Common dermatoses that have a bizarre course or fail to respond to usual therapies are suggestive of malignancy. Severe, generalized pruritus without any cutaneous changes suggests lymphoma or leukemia. Dark red, purple, or brown, firm to hard nodules in clumps should always be biopsied to exclude metastatic disease.

Anhalt GJ, Kim SC, Stanley JR, et al.: Paraneoplastic pemphigus: an autoimmune mucocutaneous disease associated with neoplasia. *N Engl J Med.* 1990:323:1729–1735.
This new entity features severe cutaneous blistering erosions on mucosal surfaces, and a characteristic pattern of autoantibodies that bind to host tissues containing desmosomes (e.g., skin, gut, respiratory, and bladder epithelia). The disease is reproduced in mice by passive transfer of patient serum.

Assaad SN, Carrasco CH, Vassilopoulou-Sellin R, et al.: Glucagonoma syndrome: rapid response following arterial embolization of glucagonoma metastatic to the liver. *Am J Med.* 1987;82:533–535.
Within 10 days after embolization of the arterial supply to an area containing glucagonoma metastases, the patient's rash cleared completely.

Chanda JJ: Extramammary Paget's disease: prognosis and relationship to internal malignancy. *J Am Acad Dermatol.* 1985;13:1009–1014.
The author summarizes 197 cases of this cutaneous adenocarcinoma that occurs in vulvar, scrotal, and perianal regions of older people. The 24% incidence of an underlying glandular (skin appendage) carcinoma is lower than the incidence of underlying breast carcinoma in mammary Paget's, but is still significant. In addition, 12% of cases have other internal malignancies.

DiBisceglie AM, Hodkinson HJ, Berkowitz I, et al.: Pityriasis rotunda: A cutaneous marker of hepatocellular carcinoma in South African blacks. *Arch Dermatol.* 1986;122:802–804.
This rare paraneoplastic condition consists of multiple scaly, round patches and may be a form of localized acquired icthyosis.

Flint GL, Flam M, Soter NA: Acquired ichthyosis: a sign of nonlymphoproliferative malignant disorders. *Arch Dermatol.* 1975;111:1446–1447.
Four patients with carcinomas of the lung, breast, or cervix developed pronounced dryness and scaling. Ichthyotic changes were demonstrated by biopsies.

Giardiello FM, Welsh SB, Hamilton SR, et al.: Increased risk of cancer in the Peutz-Jeghers syndrome. *N Engl J Med.* 1987;316:1511–1514.
A study of 31 patients with this syndrome of GI polyps and pigmented macules of the lips revealed an overall cancer frequency of 48%. The relative risk is 18 times that of the general population.

Jacobsen FK, Abildtrup N, Laursen SO, et al.: Acrokeratosis paraneoplastica (Bazex syndrome). *Arch Dermatol.* 1984;120:502–504.
In this case, the characteristic purplish erythema and scaling of the nose, ears, and distal digits preceded the discovery of a lung carcinoma by 1 year.

Jemec GBE: Hypertrichosis lanuginosa acquisita: report of a case and review of the literature. *Arch Dermatol.* 1986;122:805–808.
The sudden appearance of downy hairs in a previously hairless area can denote widespread dissemination of a variety of internal malignancies.

Kahan RS, Perez-Figaredo RA, Neimanis A: Necrolytic migratory erythema: Distinctive dermatosis of the glucagonoma syndrome. *Arch Dermatol.* 1977;113:792–797.
Two case reports are presented, with clinical histological photographs. In one patient, surgical removal of the glucagonoma led to clearing of the rash within 48 hours.

Kahana M, Levy A, Ronnen M, et al.: Pityriasis rotunda in a white patient: Report of the second case and review of the literature. *J Am Acad Dermatol.* 1986;15:362–365.
Pityriasis rotunda is usually seen in blacks and Orientals.

Langlois JC, Shaw JM, Odland GF: Erythema gyratum repens unassociated with internal malignancy. *J Am Acad Dermatol.* 1985;12:911–913.
The authors were unable to find an underlying malignancy in this case, but conclude that an aggressive search for cancer is still warranted when this distinctive dermatosis is encountered. Good clinical photographs are shown.

McLean DI: Cutaneous paraneoplastic syndromes. *Arch Dermatol.* 1986;122:765–767.
A discussion about the criteria that define a paraneoplastic syndrome.

Shutze WP, Gleysteen JJ: Perianal Paget's disease: classification and review of management: report of two cases. *Dis Colon Rectum.* 1990;33:502–507.
The authors present two typical cases of extramammary Paget's disease, with good photographs, discussion, and review of the literature.

Skolnick M, Mainman ER: Erythema gyratum repens with metastatic adenocarcinoma. *Arch Dermatol.* 1975;111:227–229.
This bizarre scaly eruption, with a wood-grain-like pattern, is very rare (under 30 cases reported). This case report features clinical and histological photographs and a review of the literature.

Thiers BH: Dermatologic manifestations of internal cancer. *CA—A Cancer Journal for Clinicians.* 1986;36(3):130–148.
One of the most readable reviews of this topic, with excellent photographs.

Wagner RF, Nathanson L: Paraneoplastic syndromes, tumor markers, and other unusual features of malignant melanoma. *J Am Acad Dermatol.* 1986;14:249–256.
Few paraneoplastic syndromes or tumor markers have been reported in conjunction with malignant melanoma, perhaps because melanoma remains more fully differentiated than other tumors. The appearance of vitiligo in melanoma patients seems to predict longer survival.

66. RASHES IN PREGNANCY
Sharon J. Littzi

Many changes occur in the skin, hair, and nails of a pregnant woman. Most of them are related to underlying hormonal changes and changes in vascularity, and are thus termed physiologic changes of the skin. In addition, several specific idiopathic dermatoses occur in pregnant women. This chapter will review these physiologic skin changes and specific dermatoses, beginning with the physiologic changes.

Hyperpigmentation may occur in up to 90% of women, especially on the areolae of the breasts, axillae, genitalia, inner thighs, and linea nigra. In addition, freckles, nevi, and scars may darken. Generalized hyperpigmentation is rare and suggests hyperthyroidism. Hyperpigmentation often progresses until delivery and usually regresses postpartum; however, the pigment may not return to the original color, especially in the previously hypermelanotic sites. The cause of the hyperpigmentation is uncertain, but it is postulated that the pigment changes are related to changes in estrogen and progesterone and possibly melanocyte-stimulating hormone (MSH).

Melasma, also known as the mask of pregnancy, is a symmetrical, macular hyperpigmentation that is often blotchy but sharply marginated on the face. It has been reported to occur in 50% to 75% of pregnant women. It is more common in dark-complexioned women and is frequently precipitated or exacerbated by sun exposure. In addition to hormonal factors, a genetic predisposition has been postulated.

Jaundice may occur, especially in the last trimester of pregnancy, secondary to physiologic alterations in hepatic function. Significant hyperbilirubinemia is rarely seen unless other problems occur.

Vascular lesions often appear or increase in size during pregnancy. Vascular spider angiomas appear between the second and fifth months of pregnancy, and 75% of these new lesions fade by the seventh week postpartum. Circulating estrogens are believed to play a major role in the formation of these vascular spiders. Pregnant women may also spontaneously develop superficial or subcutaneous cavernous hemangiomas, which usually appear at the end of the first trimester and enlarge slowly until delivery. Hemangioendotheliomas and glomangiomas are less common.

Palmar erythema reportedly occurs in two-thirds of whites and one-third of blacks, with an onset in the first trimester. Two clinical forms are recognized: (1) erythema of the hypothenar and thenar eminence and the palms near the metacarpal phalangeal junction and (2) cyanosis and pallor of the palms with diffuse mottling. The second type is indistinguishable from that seen in hyperthyroidism or liver disease. Palmar erythema usually resolves within 1 week postpartum, and has been attributed to various etiologies including estrogen, changes in blood volume, and genetic predisposition.

Varicosities often appear in the third month of pregnancy in as many as 40% or more of women, most commonly in the hemorrhoidal veins. There may be some hereditary predisposition to varicose veins as well. Increased blood volume and abdominal pressures are thought to be the inciting factors.

Vasomotor instability induced by estrogen may cause a transient **cutis marmorata** pattern on the legs, but it should disappear postpartum. Persistence requires a search for an underlying hematologic or connective tissue disease.

Purpura may develop during the latter part of pregnancy, especially on the legs, because of increased capillary permeability and fragility. These factors probably also account for the increased incidence of **pitting edema** of dependent areas and the face and eyelids, which is seen in 50% of women.

In up to 2% of all pregnant women, a **pregnancy tumor** (or pyogenic granuloma of pregnancy, granuloma gravidarum, gingivitis gravidarum) appears on the gums during early pregnancy. The lesion, which is friable and bleeds easily, appears as a soft, smooth mass that is shiny, red to purple in color, either pedunculated or sessile, and usually arising from the interdentate papillae. Lesions may also occur on cutaneous sites on the upper body. The tumor usually regresses postpartum, although surgical removal under local anesthesia is often done, with little morbidity, to give the patient a rapid cure. Histologically these lesions are pyogenic granulomas.

Other **tumors** may also occur. Most pregnant women develop numerous skin tags, also called molluscum fibrosum gravidarum, on the face, neck, and anterior chest region. These skin tags generally regress postpartum. Dermatofibromas, neurofibromas, leiomyomas, and keloids may increase in size. Desmoid tumors arising from muscular aponeuroses are also reported. The effect of pregnancy on melanoma is debated. Currently it is felt that pregnancy has no effect on clinical stage I disease, but pregnancy is not recommended for a patient with stage II disease.

Most pregnant women develop **striae** during the sixth and seventh months of pregnancy. There seems to be a familial tendency. Striae are less common in black and Asian women. Many theories regarding the development of striae are available, a combination of hormonal factors and stretching providing the mainstay of these proposals. It is controversial whether or not the application of oils and massage prevents their appearance.

The **activity of glands** in the skin varies. Apocrine gland activity decreases during pregnancy and usually results in improvement of hidradenitis suppurativa and Fox-Fordyce disease; however, postpartum flare is common. Eccrine gland activity progressively increases near the end of the pregnancy, although, paradoxically, palmar sweating is decreased. There may be an increased incidence of miliaria and dyshidrotic eczema as a result of increased eccrine activity. Sebaceous gland activity is unpredictable, but most researchers believe that it increases during the third trimester. The effect of pregnancy on acne is variable. Hypertrophy of the sebaceous glands associated with the lactiferous ducts on the breasts may occur and appear as brown papules, called Montgomery's tubercles.

Hair and nail changes are a common complaint of pregnant women. Hirsutism is commonly seen in pregnant women and is most pronounced on the face, arms, legs, and back. An increased number of anagen hairs may be present secondary to adrenocortical and estrogen effects. When severe hirsutism occurs, androgen-secreting tumors or polycystic ovarian disease should be considered. Immediately postpartum, there is conversion of anagen hairs to telogen hairs (resting phase). Four to twenty weeks later, these resting hairs fall out and alopecia of varying degrees secondary to this telogen effluvium develops, which may take up to 15 months for full recovery. A frontoparietal recession resembling male-pattern baldness may occur in some women, which usually completely resolves but may persist. The **nails** may develop softening, distal onycholysis, and transverse ridging early in pregnancy (sixth week). The etiology is unknown.

Gingivitis is the most common mucous membrane manifestation of pregnancy and occurs in up to 100% of women. It often begins in the first trimester and progressively increases. Clinically, there is inflammation, edema, bleeding, and even ulceration of the gums.

In addition to the physiologic changes seen in the skin during pregnancy, there are four specific dermatologic diseases unique to the pregnant female that have been described. Unfortunately, these entities present a confusing picture to the clinician because several of them have features that are overlapping, and not all of them have firmly defined clinicopathologic criteria. Even more confusing are the multiple names given to several of these diseases. Some of these entities are clearly described with firm clinical, histologic, and laboratory findings: herpes gestationis, pruritus gravidarum, and impetigo herpetiformis. Pruritic urticarial papules and plaques of pregnancy (PUPPP) is also fairly well substantiated; however, it has features in common with poorly described syndromes named papular dermatitis of pregnancy, prurigo of Besnier, toxemic rash of pregnancy, and prurigo annularis.

Herpes gestationis (HG) is a rare bullous disorder with an incidence of about 1 in 5000 pregnancies. Most patients are multiparous when they present with HG, and it usually recurs with subsequent pregnancies or the use of oral contraceptives. The onset is most frequently in the second trimester, but is variable and may occur in the second week until the early postpartum period. The eruption may also wax and wane during the pregnancy. For example, a patient who develops HG in the second trimester may go into remission during the last 6 weeks of pregnancy and then have a flare in the postpartum period, especially premenstrually or with the use of oral contraceptives. The average duration postpartum is 15 months for the urticarial component and 4 weeks for the bullous eruption. The cases that begin early in pregnancy have a better prognosis and terminate soon after delivery. HG is intensely pruritic, and the eruption may begin with pruritus alone or in combination with constitutional symptoms of fever, malaise, chills, headache, and hot and cold sensations.

The early skin lesions consist of erythema and urticarial plaques that coalesce and form bizarre geographic figures. Target lesions may occur as well as vesicles and finally bullae, which are tense. It may take up to 4 weeks for the bullous eruption to appear; therefore, in the early stages the diagnosis may be difficult without histologic and immunofluorescent studies. The lesions most commonly develop around the umbilicus, but may also be generalized or occur on the thighs, palms, and soles. Facial and oral lesions are rare. Once the bullae rupture, they form denuded areas or areas covered with a yellowish or hemorrhagic crust. Scar formation is rare; however, postinflammatory pigmentation is not uncommon.

The histology of the urticarial lesions shows a superficial and deep, dense, perivascular lymphohistiocytic infiltrate with eosinophils. As the plaques become more edematous, the biopsy shows dermal edema, spongiosis, and necrosis of the basal cells at the tips of the dermal papillae. The bullous lesions show subepidermal split identical to that of bullous pemphigoid lesions; at times knowledge of the clinical situation is needed in order to differentiate the two. The bullae in HG usually contain numerous eosinophils.

Immunofluorescent studies performed on fresh frozen tissue demonstrate deposition of C_3 at the basement membrane zone of lesional skin. Less commonly IgA, IgM, C1q, C_4, C_5, and properidin are present. Immunoelectron microscopy studies show a fairly uniform deposition of reaction products throughout the lamina lucida, similar to that of bullous pemphigoid, although some authors report that the reaction products in bullous pemphigoid are more preferentially located around the half-desmosomes. Indirect immunofluorescent studies usually reveal a circulating HG factor composed of an IgG that is capable of fixing complement at the basement membrane zone. This factor may pass through the placenta and be responsible for HG-like skin lesions that occur in approximately 25% of newborns. The titer of HG factor is unrelated to disease activity. Additional laboratory findings in HG may reveal a leukocytosis with eosinophilia. HG is believed to be an autoimmune phenomenon or an immunologic-associated entity.

The major differential diagnosis of HG includes PUPPP, bullous pemphigoid, erythema multiforme, pemphigus vulgaris, pemphigus foliaceus, dermatitis herpetiformis, bullous drug eruption, and scabies.

The treatment consists of topical steroids and antihistamines in mild cases, and prednisone in the more severe cases. There has also been some response in some patients to azathioprine or dapsone.

The prognosis of the infant has been debated, and there may be an increased risk of stillbirth or prematurity. In the presteroid era, an increased maternal morbidity was also reported.

Impetigo herpetiformis (IH) is a very rare, severe pustular dermatosis that usually arises suddenly in a pregnant patient without previous history of psoriasis. It presents most commonly in the last trimester, but may occur as early as the third month. It usually resolves after pregnancy, but recurs with subsequent pregnancies. The pathophysiology of this entity is uncertain, but is may represent a form of acute, pustular psoriasis triggered by a change in metabolic state.

The earliest lesions of IH are erythematous irregular patches usually found in the intertriginous areas. At the margins of the patches, superficial pustules appear, which may be arranged in groups or rings. The eruption progresses by peripheral extension of the active pustular margin. The central areas erode and crust. The eruption may become confluent, sparing the face, hands, and feet. Subungual pustules and painful mucous membrane and esophageal lesions have been reported. The lesions heal without scarring, but may leave residual hyperpigmentation. The histology is identical to that of pustular psoriasis. Laboratory findings consist of a leukocytosis and an elevated sedimentation rate. The pustules are sterile when studied bacteriologically. Hypocalcemia and hyperphosphatemia may be present in some cases as manifestations of hypoparathyroidism.

The differential diagnosis of IH includes pustular psoriasis, subcorneal pustular dermatosis, and infectious impetigo. Dermatitis herpetiformis and HG may occasionally present with pustules.

The treatment of choice is systemic steroids coupled with the use of antibiotics for secondary infection. Responses to gonadotropin and vitamin D along with parenteral calcium have also been described in treatment of this entity. With treatment, maternal mortality is rare; however, placental insufficiency and stillbirth are the usual result of pregnancy, despite adequate control of the disease.

Pruritus gravidarum (PG) has a reported incidence of 0.02% to 2.4% of pregnancies with a much higher incidence in Scandinavia (3%) and Chilean Indians (14%). It is a nonfatal and reversible cholestatic process that occurs in genetically predisposed women. Although characterized by generalized pruritus without primary skin lesions, excoriations secondary to scratching may be seen.

Beginning in the last trimester of pregnancy in two-thirds of cases, mild to severe pruritus may initially be localized but later usually generalizes. Icterus may develop 2 to 4 weeks after the onset of the pruritus. Anicteric forms in which cholestasis has been proven by a liver biopsy do occur. The liver may be enlarged and tender, the urine dark, and the stools clay-colored. Associated symptoms of anorexia, nausea, and vomiting may be present, and all symptoms tend to clear postpartum. Symptoms may recur with subsequent pregnancies.

Laboratory studies may reveal normal or slightly elevated bilirubin. Alkaline phosphatase, 5' nucleotidase, may be elevated. The SGOT, SGPT, and LDH are usually normal. Prothrombin time may be prolonged in severe cases. The skin histology is not relevant, but liver biopsies have revealed nonspecific cholestasis with widely dilated bile canaliculi. The liver parenchyma is otherwise normal.

The pruritus of PG is proportional to the concentration of bile acid in the skin rather than in the serum. Placental estrogens and progestins are believed to interfere with hepatic excretion of bile acids. Progestins may also play a role in the inhibition of hepatic glucuronyl-transferase, thereby reducing the amount of estrogen clearance from the blood. Estrogens may interfere with the normal diffusion of fluid across the membrane of the hepatocyte.

The differential diagnosis for this condition must exclude other causes of jaundice if it is present, and if not, then other causes of pruritus must be excluded, such as scabies, urticaria, drug eruption, atopic dermatitis, neurodermatitis, and candidal and trichomonal infections.

Treatment of PG is usually conservative, with oatmeal baths and antihistamines; however, in some cases more-aggressive therapy is warranted, with cholestyramine (binds bile acids in the gut) and vitamin K. Phenobarbital has also been used as it acts in promoting bile excretion.

Maternal prognosis is excellent. Fetal prognosis is controversial; prematurity and intrauterine asphyxia have been reported, as well as intrauterine death (6 of 56 cases in one study).

Pruritic urticarial papules and plaques of pregnancy (PUPPP) is a very pruritic skin eruption developing over a few days in the third trimester of a primipara. It consists of urticarial papules and plaques initially presenting primarily on the abdominal striae and then spreading to the thighs, buttocks, flanks, and arms; one case report also mentioned the face. The eruption usually clears within 1 or 2 weeks postpartum or sooner. There are usually no abnormal laboratory findings in PUPPP. The histology of PUPPP has been reported to show dermal edema of varying severity and a perivascular (superficial, or superficial and deep) lymphohistiocytic infiltrate with or without eosinophils. These findings may be observed in some urticarial lesions of HG; immunofluorescent studies are crucial to differentiate the two at this stage.

Although a common disorder, estimated to occur in 1 of 300 primigravidas, this eruption was not well described until 1979. It bears some resemblance to previously described dermatoses of pregnancy, including toxemic rash of pregnancy and Nurse's prurigo of pregnancy. The lack of good clinical descriptions and histologic studies in these latter two conditions makes a comparison impossible. PUPPP may develop as a stasis or vascular phenomenon, since women who develop the disorder put on more weight than women who do not.

The differential diagnosis includes drug eruptions, urticaria/angioedema, and early HG. PUPPP has not been associated with any maternal or fetal mortality. Topical steroids have been found to be useful in the management of this entity, as well as antihistamines for itch.

Many cutaneous eruptions with poorly described clinicopathologic correlations have been described as specific to the condition of pregnancy. Autoimmune progesterone dermatitis has been described in one patient who, in two successive pregnancies, developed an acneform eruption on the extremities and buttocks, associated with arthritis and a positive skin test to progesterone. Both pregnancies terminated in spontaneous abortion. Papular dermatitis of pregnancy was described by Spangler in 1962 in a series of patients with a pruritic papular eruption associated with an elevated urinary chorionic gonadotropin level and an increase in fetal mortality. Not only were the calculations of fetal mortality performed incorrectly, the disease has not been reported since. The toxemic rash of pregnancy reported by Bourne in 1962 may be identical to PUPPP. Prurigo gestationis reported by Besnier in 1904 is similar. Zoberman recently reported a pruritic folliculitis in a series of pregnant women; this process may also represent a variant of PUPPP.

Holmes RC, Black MM: The specific dermatoses of pregnancy. *J Am Acad Dermatol.* 1983;8:405–412.

A study of 64 patients and review of the literature emphasizing the classification of the eruptions specific to pregnancy.

Laatikainen T: Effect of cholestyramine and phenobarbital on pruritus and serum bile acid levels in cholestasis of pregnancy. *Am J Obstet Gynecol.* 1978;132:501–506.
Serum bile acid concentrations were followed in 29 patients treated with phenobarbital or cholestyramine. Cholestyramine may provide relief from itch in a few patients.

Lawley TJ, Hertz KC, Wade TR: Pruritic urticarial papules and plaques of pregnancy. *JAMA.* 1979;241:1696–1699.
First report of 12 patients with this characteristic eruption of unknown etiology.

Lotem M, Katzenelson V, Rotem A, et al.: Impetigo herpetiformis: a variant of pustular psoriasis or a separate entity? *J Am Acad Dermatol.* 1989;20:338–341.
This case report and review of the literature suggests that impetigo herpetiformis is a distinct entity.

Morrison LH, Anhalt GJ: Herpes gestationis. *J Autoimmun.* 1991;4:37–45.
This rare, self-limited bullous disease of pregnancy most likely has an immunological basis because of the frequent finding of C3 along the basement membrane zone of perilesional skin, the presence of herpes gestationis factor, increased incidence of HLA-DR3 and HLA-DR4, and association with other autoimmune diseases.

Slingluff CL Jr., Reintgen DS, Vollmer RT, et al.: Malignant melanoma arising during pregnancy. A study of 100 patients. *Ann Surg.* 1990;211:552–557.
In 100 patients who were pregnant at the time of diagnosis of melanoma, compared to 86 age-matched nonpregnant women with melanoma, there was no decrease in survival. However, there were statistically higher metastatic rates, with lymph node metastases occurring earlier.

Winton GB: Skin diseases aggravated by pregnancy. *J Am Acad Dermatol.* 1989;20:1–13.
The pregnant patient may have skin disease not associated with her pregnancy but aggravated by her condition. This paper reviews a wide range of disorders and discusses how each of these diseases is altered by pregnancy and how treatment may differ during gestation.

Wong RC, Ellis CN: Physiologic skin changes in pregnancy. *J Am Acad Dermatol.* 1984;10:929–940.
Authors comprehensively review the long list of common changes occurring in the skin because of pregnancy.

Yancey KB: Herpes gestationis. *Dermatol Clin.* 1990;8:727–735.
This review of the clinical and laboratory findings of the disease emphasizes factors that may be important in pathogenesis.

67. ARTHRITIS AND RASH
Robert H. Shmerling

Diseases presenting with rash and arthritis may be divided into rheumatic, infectious, and miscellaneous categories. Prompt diagnosis is essential as many of these diseases are life-threatening and most are treatable. It should be noted that individually, dermatologic and musculoskeletal symptoms are among the most common problems presenting to primary care practices and their simultaneous occurrence could be due to chance alone. However, true arthritis associated with a skin eruption should be considered to be due to a single disease process until significant evidence suggests otherwise. This chapter will address disorders that cause both rash and arthritis on presentation to a primary care physician or dermatologist.

Rheumatic Diseases Causing Rash and Arthritis

Systemic lupus erythematosus (SLE) is a multisystem disorder characterized by the presence of circulating autoantibodies. Tissue damage is mediated by immune complex deposition. Its cause is unknown and incidence is highest among young women. Diagnosis is guided by 11 criteria established by the American Rheumatism Association: four dermatologic findings (malar rash, discoid lesions, oral ulcers, and photosensitivity), five organ system disorders (arthritis, serositis, renal, neurologic, and hematologic disease), and two criteria based on abnormal autoantibodies (antinuclear antibodies, anti-double-stranded DNA, among others). Dermatologic abnormalities of various types are seen in 85% of patients with SLE, the most common of which are a photosensitive erythematous skin eruption, the distinctive urticarial malar (butterfly) rash sparing the nasolabial folds, a nonspecific morbilliform maculopapular eruption (exanthem) resembling drug hypersensitivity, and a macular erythema of the palms and fingers. Subacute cutaneous lupus erythematosus (SCLE) presents with persistent erythematous, annular lesions with central atrophy and slight scaling. These lesions may resemble psoriasis, cause no scarring, and are thought to correlate with less severe systemic disease. Chronic discoid lupus erythematosus (DLE) lesions, often provoked by sun exposure, are annular with a red, edematous edge, hyperkeratosis, and central atrophic scarring. Although one-fifth of SLE patients experience such lesions, the majority of patients with discoid skin lesions have disease confined to the skin. Typical palpable purpura of cutaneous vasculitis may also be observed in SLE, generally with evidence of active disease elsewhere. The biopsy of a typical skin lesion of SLE often has a distinctive, sometimes diagnostic, histologic appearance: varying degrees of follicular and appendageal plugging, epidermal thinning, thickening of the basement membrane zone, dermal edema and mucin deposition, lymphocytes arranged in perivascular and periappendeal sites, and necrotizing venulitis. When immunofluorescent studies are performed, immunoglobulin and complement deposition are seen at the dermal-epidermal junction, a finding also noted in some patients with rosacea, scleroderma, leprosy, and porphyria cutanea tarda. The skin disease of SLE usually occurs in the context of other systemic manifestations of the disease. The joint disease of SLE is a symmetric, nonerosive polyarthritis commonly involving the small joints of the hands and wrists, as well as the knees, ankles, elbows, and shoulders. Joint pain and morning stiffness are often in excess of joint findings, and the synovial fluid is generally of a mild inflammatory type (white blood cell counts near 3000/mm^3). Evidence of involvement of other major organ systems must be sought rigorously.

Therapeutic options specifically for the skin disease of SLE depend on the type of lesion. For DLE, the use of a potent topical fluorinated corticosteroid or an intralesional injection of corticosteroid is appropriate as these lesions often cause permanent scarring or alopecia if they are left untreated. If such local measures fail, antimalarial agents such as hydroxychloroquine, 200 to 400 mg every day, (along with an ophthalmologic examination at least twice yearly to detect dose-related retinopathy) may be helpful. Quinacrine or dapsone may also prove beneficial for DLE. For SCLE, local measures are generally ineffective, and pharmacologic intervention similar to that used for DLE is indicated. Strict avoidance of sun exposure and conscientious daily use of a sunscreen with a sun protection factor of at least 15 should be strongly advised even in black patients. Antimalarials administered for arthritis or other constitutional symptoms, systemic corticosteroids used to treat neurologic or severe multisystem disease, or immunomodulatory agents such as azathioprine or cyclophosphamide given for nephritis will often suppress the cutaneous manifestations of the disease. Systemic corticosteroids and immunomodulatory agents are rarely required for the patient in whom skin disease is the predominant manifestation since the risks of these medications often outweigh the benefits.

Psoriatic arthritis is common. Approximately 5% to 10% of patients with psoriasis develop an arthropathy that can parallel the skin disease or run its own independent course. In 15% to 20% of cases, the joint disease occurs first. There is little correlation between the severity of the skin disease and the presence or absence of joint disease, although nail disease (including pitting, furrows, hyperkeratosis beneath the distal nail plate, and separation of the nail plate from the nail bed) does occur more often in patients with arthritis, especially in the distal interphalangeal joints. The joint disease is most often an asymmetric and oligoarticular process involving small joints of the hand or other larger joints. Tendon sheath inflammation can lead to "sausage digit." Other manifestations include arthritis mutilans (a severe, deforming arthropathy of the hands or feet), a symmetric polyarthritis resembling rheumatoid arthritis (RA), or sacroiliitis and spine disease similar to ankylosing spondylitis.

Therapy with PUVA, antimetabolites such as methotrexate, or retinoids such as etretinate may improve both the skin disease and the arthritis. Other modalities to treat psoriasis, including topical agents, have no effect on the joints. Similarly, a host of agents have been empirically used to treat the joint disease, including antimalarials, oral or parenteral gold, and penicillamine, but few data exist to suggest a definitive disease-modifying effect for any of these agents. Antimalarials are thought by some to be associated with an increased risk of an exacerbation of the patient's typical psoriasis or the development of exfoliative dermatitis.

Reiter's syndrome, by definition, consists of the clinical triad of nongonococcal urethritis, conjunctivitis, and arthritis, but only one-third of patients present with all three components. The mucocutaneous manifestations (keratoderma blennorrhagica, circinate balanitis, and oral erosions) are so characteristic that some physicians regard the syndrome as a tetrad to include these lesions. Reiter's syndrome may follow venereal (e.g., *Chlamydia*) or dysenteric infections (including some species of *Shigella, Salmonella, Yersinia,* and *Campylobacter*) by 1 to 4 weeks. Keratoderma blennorrhagica is an eruption of the soles and palms, consisting of enlarging papules with a pustular center, marked hyperkeratosis, and crusting. It may also occur on the scalp, elbows, buttocks, and knees and may be indistinguishable from pustular psoriasis both clinically and histopathologically. Circinate balanitis, which can occur independent of urethritis, is a crusted, dry plaque on the glans penis in circumcised men, and a shallow, serpiginous, painless erosion in uncircumcised men. Oral lesions are also shallow, painless erosions and occur on the tongue or hard palate. Nail changes may occur with subungual small, yellow pustules that enlarge and later become hyperkeratotic and scaly, generally without pitting. The joint disease of Reiter's syndrome is typically an oligoarticular, asymmetric polyarthritis commonly involving the knees, ankles, and small joints of the feet. Sausage digits and heel pain are examples of inflammation of tendons and their insertion sites, often seen in this disease. Therapy is indicated primarily for the joint disease and includes nonsteroidal anti-inflammatory drugs, low-dose methotrexate, physical therapy, and occasional corticosteroid injections.

Still's disease refers to a subset of patients with juvenile RA who present with systemic features including fever and rash. Adult-onset Still's disease is characterized by an evanescent, erythematous macular eruption that favors the extremities, trunk, and face and is most prominent during febrile periods. Histologic examination of a skin biopsy shows a relatively nonspecific mild polymorphonuclear infiltrate around blood vessels. The polyarthritis is generally symmetric, with a predilection for wrists, hands, and knees. Fever generally follows a circadian rhythm with highest temperatures in the afternoon. Other systemic features, including pericarditis, adenopathy, and splenomegaly, are commonly observed. Therapy for the skin disease alone is not warranted, although joint inflammation may require therapy with aspirin or other nonsteroidal antiinflammatory drugs, corticosteroids, or other agents used in the treatment of RA (e.g., gold).

Arthritis and vasculitis are commonly associated in a variety of disease states including RA and SLE. In RA, palpable purpura may be associated with ischemic leg ulcers and subcutaneous nodules and tend to occur in patients who have a very high rheumatoid factor and active systemic disease. Polyarteritis nodosa (PAN), cutaneous necrotizing venulitis (hypersensitivity vasculitis), Henoch-Schönlein purpura (HSP), Churg-Strauss disease, cryoglobulinemia, and Wegener's granulomatosis all may present with varying degrees of arthritis and skin manifestations. These disorders differ clinically by the size of the vessel affected (e.g., medium-sized arteries in PAN, smaller vessels in necrotizing venulitis), organs involved (e.g., lungs spared in PAN, involved in Churg-Strauss disease), and, in some cases, histopathology (e.g., granulomatous vasculitis in Wegener's granulomatosis, or IgA deposition in HSP).

Several important issues should be stressed in approaching the patient with palpable purpura and arthritis: (1) infection must be ruled out by thorough evaluation, (2) patients with these disorders may deteriorate rapidly and therefore require close observation, and (3) a coordinated, multidisciplinary evaluation involving a dermatologist, rheumatologist, and other specialists appropriate to the case should help classify the patient's disorder and thereby guide therapy.

Other rheumatic diseases, including **dermatomyositis** (DM), **mixed connective tissue disease (MCTD),** and **scleroderma** may present with joint and dermatologic manifestations. In DM, painless muscle weakness, a purple periorbital discoloration (heliotrope), and a pinkish red, scaly maculopapular rash over the forehead, cheeks, and knuckles (Gottron's sign) are characteristic presenting features. MCTD is a disorder of variable clinical expression including puffy hands, Raynaud's phenomenon, sclerodactyly, serositis, myositis, and arthritis. The skin disease is not specific and may resemble that of SLE or DM. The joint disease resembles that of SLE except that bony erosions may develop. A high-titer antinuclear antibody (ANA) with a speckled pattern and antibodies to ribonucleoprotein (RNP) are helpful diagnostic features. Scleroderma is generally characterized by edema, induration, and atrophy of the skin during various stages of the illness, but occasionally "salt and pepper" hyper- and hypopigmentation or telangiectasia precede skin thickening. A symmetric polyarthritis is occasionally a presenting feature of the disorder and may be mistaken for RA. Treatment is generally directed to the systemic manifestations of these disorders, not the skin disease.

Infectious Causes of Rash and Arthritis

Infectious processes often present with concurrent skin and joint findings, and the features of each can be helpful clues to the diagnosis. As mentioned earlier, patients with new-onset skin lesions and arthritis should be thoroughly evaluated for infection before other diagnoses are assigned.

Bacteremia with or without endocarditis may produce a characteristic array of cutaneous findings, including Osler's nodes (painful digital tuft papules), Janeway lesions (painless papules on the palms or soles), splinter hemorrhages, and petechiae. All of these findings may be due to septic microemboli, though immune-complex deposition and primary perivasculitis have also been hypothesized. Bacteremia with gram-positive organisms (especially *Staphylococcus aureus*) commonly cause pustules, subcutaneous abscesses, or purpura, while *Neisseria meningitidis* is typically associated with small petechial lesions that have indistinct margins and a dark vesicular center. It should also be noted that the portal of entry in bacteremic disease is frequently cutaneous, so these patients should be carefully examined for traumatic skin lesions, carbuncles, or other cutaneous sources of infection.

The joint disease of bacteremia or endocarditis generally has one of two patterns: purulent arthritis in one or occasionally more joints (the knee is the most frequently affected) or a "reactive," sterile oligoarthritis that may be immune complex–mediated. Immunocompromised hosts or those with prior joint disease have an increased risk of septic arthritis in more than one joint.

A septic process causing rash and arthritis is suggested by clinical presentation (acute onset of fever, chills, arthritis, typical skin lesions) and confirmed by blood, skin, or synovial fluid cultures. Occasionally a Gram stain of skin aspirate or synovial fluid or a skin biopsy will suggest a pathogen even before culture results are known. Antibiotic therapy should be directed toward the most likely organism (e.g., *S. aureus* or *Neisseria*) and should not be delayed until culture results are available. A joint with a bacterial infection should be repeatedly drained, with anticipated eradication of infection as documented by negative cultures and declining synovial fluid white blood cell count. If this is not observed, more extensive therapy, such as surgical debridement, may be required.

Gonorrheal infection (*Neisseria gonorrhoeae*) usually causes localized genitourinary infection, but in less than 5% of cases, disseminated disease occurs, causing a rash in two-thirds of affected patients and arthritis in half. The dermatitis of disseminated gonococcal infection (DGI) consists of painful, hemorrhagic or purpuric macules, papules, pustules, vesicles, or even bullae. Fewer than 20 lesions are present, and they usually spare the face, palms, and soles. Cultures of lesions rarely grow organisms, suggesting that they result from immune-complex deposition. A skin biopsy reveals a neutrophilic and mononuclear infiltrate, occasionally with fibrinoid necrosis or subepidermal bullae. The arthritis is generally monoarticular, particularly affecting the knee, wrist, or ankle, but an asymmetric arthritis of two or three joints or a periarthritis is common as well. Fever and chills may accompany the joint and skin disease, yet localized genitourinary symptoms are frequently absent. Thus, suspicion should be high in any sexually active patient with new-onset arthritis or tenosynovitis and the appropriate skin lesions, and in such patients, cultures of the cervix or urethra, rectal area, and pharynx should be performed. A Gram stain of synovial fluid is diagnostic in only one-quarter of patients, and cultures grow gonococci in roughly half. Blood cultures are positive in less than half of the cases with dermatitis but almost never with purulent arthritis. When suspicion of DGI is high, penicillin therapy (4 million units IV/d) should be started without waiting for culture results. Although penicillin resistance is uncommon among strains causing DGI, ceftriaxone should be administered when the incidence of resistance is appreciable (e.g., in many large, urban hospitals). Depending on the progression of disease and severity at the time of presentation, a portion of the 7- to 10-day antibiotic course may be given orally on an outpatient basis. If a large joint effusion persists, repeated aspirations are indicated. Generally, a clinical response to antibiotics is dramatic within a day or two. Erythromycin, tetracycline, or spectinomycin may be used in the patient who is allergic to penicillin.

Viral infections recognized as causing arthritis provoke varied skin reactions. Rubella (and occasionally rubella vaccination) typically causes a morbilliform eruption starting on the face and descending rapidly, lasting 2 or 3 days, and associated with marked lymphadenopathy, especially of the suboccipital group. The arthritis is sudden in onset, involves fingers, wrists, and knees, and usually abates within 2 to 3 weeks. Parvovirus infection, also known as erythema infectiosum, or "fifth disease," is associated with a skin eruption that begins with red cheeks ("slapped cheek") followed by a lacy erythematous rash on the buttocks, arms, and legs that can recur for months. The arthritis has been described as a symmetric polyarthritis resembling RA that often affects hands, wrists, and knees, and is almost always self-limited. Hepatitis B virus infection may be associated with a diffuse urticarial, petechial, or morbilliform maculopapular eruption and symmetric polyarthritis, all of which resolve when clinically apparent liver disease develops. Diagnosis depends on measurement of liver function tests and detection of hepatitis B surface antigen in the blood. Infection with human immunodeficiency virus (HIV) has been associated with psoriatic arthritis, Reiter's syndrome, arthralgia, and cutaneous findings that may mimic SLE. While many other viruses, including arboviruses, smallpox, adenovirus, and herpesviruses, have been associated with arthritis and rash, they are rare causes in North American populations.

Lyme disease is a multisystem disorder characterized by rash, varying neurologic dysfunction, carditis, and arthritis. It is caused by the spirochete *Borrelia burgdorferi*. The deer tick (*Ixodes dammini* and *I. pacificus*) is the vector that harbors this spirochete and accounts for the three geographic regions in the United States where Lyme disease primarily occurs: the Northeastern coast, Wisconsin and Minnesota, and Oregon and California. The disease generally presents from May through November, when exposure to the tick is most common.

The rash, erythema chronicum migrans (ECM), is pathognomonic for this disorder and starts within days at the site of the tick bite as an erythematous macule or papule with gradual expansion, resolving with a flat, partially cleared center. The outer edge may be raised and very erythematous, and the entire lesion can measure up to 60 cm in diameter. The center occasionally appears bright red with induration, vesicles, or necrosis. The lesions occur most often in the axilla, groin, and thigh but may occur anywhere on the body. Secondary lesions appear within a few days in half of patients, and these lesions are similar to the initial lesion except that they are generally smaller and are not related to the site of the tick bite. Lesions last 3 to 4 weeks and may be accompanied by other skin eruptions (malar rash, urticaria, evanescent erythematous blotches) or systemic symptoms (fever, chills, headache, fatigue). Other early clinical features include migratory arthralgia, adenopathy, hepatitis, and meningismus. ECM, secondary lesions, and these other subacute signs and symptoms are considered Stage 1 disease. Several weeks to months later, neurologic or cardiac disease (Stage 2 disease) may develop. The characteristic neurologic dysfunction includes encephalitis, meningitis, cranial nerve palsy, or peripheral neuropathy, which often occur in combination and resolve without sequelae after several months. Cardiac disease, beginning a few weeks after ECM, develops in about 10% of patients and is manifested by atrioventricular conduction block or myopericarditis. Although the process lasts several days to weeks without permanent residua, supportive care, including pacemaker placement, may be required.

The arthritis of Lyme disease (Stage 3 disease) develops in 60% of patients 2 months to 2 years after ECM and typically involves one or two large joints, especially the knee. Effusions may be sizable. A symmetric polyarthritis involving large and small joints rarely develops, and in about 10%, the process is chronic and erosive.

Diagnosis currently depends on documenting serologic evidence of exposure to the spirochete, *B. burgdorferi.* Specific IgM titers are elevated 3 to 6 weeks after ECM, and IgG is generally present by the time arthritis occurs. A biopsy of the center of a lesion of ECM reveals dermal fibrin deposition, vessel ectasia, and edema with an infiltrate of lymphocytes, while in the periphery, an eosinophilic and lymphocytic infiltrate surrounding dermal vessels is seen. These findings are relatively nonspecific unless an organism is documented on silver staining (Warthin-Starry). Antibiotic therapy is effective, especially early in disease. The optimal therapy for early disease appears to be oral tetracycline (250 mg qid for 10 to 20 days); alternatives include penicillin (500 mg qid) or erythromycin (250 mg qid). Parenteral penicillin (20 million units/d for 10 days) or ceftriaxone (2 g/d for 2 weeks) is recommended when the disease is recognized later, particularly in patients with meningitis or neurologic deficits. For arthritis, parenteral ceftriaxone may be more effective than parenteral penicillin.

While the incidence of **rheumatic fever (RF)** seemed to be nearing zero in the 1960s and 1970s, reports of a recrudescence appeared in the mid-1980s, with rash and arthritis prominent presenting features. Erythema marginatum is unique to this disease and consists of a ringed lesion with raised edges that quickly spreads outward in a geographic pattern leaving behind a pale center. The trunk and extremities are favored sites. Generally the eruption follows the onset of arthritis (which itself follows streptococcal exposure by 2 to 3 weeks) and is associated with carditis. A biopsy reveals degenerating perivascular polymorphonuclear cells and debris. RF is also associated with subcutaneous nodules over areas exposed to trauma, such as knuckles, elbows, or other bony protuberances. The arthritis of RF is classically migratory with rapid onset and resolution of individual joints, a pattern that may be promptly interrupted by aspirin therapy. Recent reports have emphasized a more static polyarthritis in adults. Knees and ankles are most often affected. Carditis and chorea are other "major" criteria devised to guide the diagnosis, while fever, previous RF, arthralgia, elevated C-reactive protein, and prolonged P-R interval make up the "minor" criteria. When two major or one major and two minor criteria are present in the setting of documented streptococcal infection (by positive culture or elevated antistreptolysin-0 titer) the diagnosis is likely. Therapy is largely supportive: bed rest and moderate- to high-dose aspirin therapy is the mainstay, while high-dose corticosteroid therapy is reserved for critically ill patients with carditis. Prevention of RF by prompt diagnosis and treatment of streptococcal pharyngitis is the most effective "treatment."

Miscellaneous Disease

Other nonrheumatic, noninfectious diseases may manifest coincident articular and cutaneous lesions. **Inflammatory bowel disease** is associated with peripheral arthritis or spondylitis in 5% to 20% of cases and occasionally erythema nodosum, aphthous stomatitis, and pyoderma gangrenosum are observed. **Intestinal bypass procedures** for treatment of morbid obesity have been complicated weeks to years later by a dermatitis-arthritis syndrome in 15% to 20% of cases. The skin lesions are erythematous macules that become papular and finely pustular, resembling disseminated gonococcal infection, while the joint disease is abrupt in onset, polyarticular, and symmetric. **Amyloidosis,** both primary and secondary, may cause an arthritis of the shoulders, wrists, knees, and fingers as well as skin lesions consisting of waxy or purpuric papules, especially in skin folds. Patients with **sarcoidosis** have erythema nodosum or granulomatous skin lesions in one-third of cases, and knee or ankle arthritis (or periarthritis) is common in acute disease. **Hemochromatosis** is characterized by hyperpigmentation and a degenerative arthropathy, particularly of the hands, knees, and hips, in up to half of cases. Therapy is variably successful in these disorders and is generally directed toward the primary disorder rather than the cutaneous manifestations.

Approach to the Patient with Rash and Arthritis

The evaluation of patients with concurrent rash and arthritis must be individualized. The pace of the work-up depends on the overall status of the patient, the severity of disease, and the diagnoses under consideration. The history should be thorough, with particular attention to temporal relationships (e.g., did rash, arthralgia, or another symptom occur first?), risk factors for infection (e.g., is the patient sexually active or a user of intravenous drugs?), past dermatologic history (e.g., has the patient had psoriasis?), and precipitants of disease (e.g., does sun exposure trigger the rash?). When specific diagnoses are entertained, such as Lyme disease, specific risk factors, such as tick exposure, should be explored. Finally, other organ-system disease and family history are important to note, as in SLE. As in any history, a detailed history of past medical problems, and systems review may prove helpful, especially in patients with suspected rheumatic disease (e.g., is there a history of morning stiffness, Raynaud's phenomenon, or Sicca symptoms?). The physical examination should help to direct a differential diagnosis by the features of the skin eruption, distribution of joint inflammation, and any other organ-system findings.

Ancillary data should be selectively gathered to help confirm or exclude diagnoses suggested by history and physical examination. Particularly useful routine tests include a complete blood cell count with differential, and evaluations of renal and liver function. The erythrocyte sedimentation rate is likely to be elevated in most of the illnesses that cause rash and arthritis and therefore has rather limited clinical utility. When the clinical presentation suggests rheumatic fever and a source of streptococcal infection has not been identified, an antistreptolysin-0 titer should be ordered. The rheumatoid factor is present in 65% to 80% of patients with rheumatoid arthritis, but false-positive tests, especially in low titer, are seen with advancing age and in many of the disorders in this chapter. Therefore, even when there is a reasonable likelihood of RA, the rheumatoid factor is only somewhat helpful. The ANA has higher sensitivity and specificity, especially when titer, pattern, and associated autoantibodies are considered. Depending on the laboratory performing the test, the ANA is positive in at least 95% of patients with SLE, half of which are above 1:640, while over 95% of normal patients are ANA-negative. Other serologic evidence of SLE includes the presence of antibody to double-stranded DNA or Sm antigen, though these occur in a minority. A peripheral pattern is relatively specific for SLE, although speckled patterns are most common. Patients with SCLE are commonly ANA-positive in a speckled pattern with anti-Ro or anti-La antibodies present. In patients with DLE, the ANA is usually negative, but when positive, systemic disease is more likely. Patients with MCTD are almost always ANA and anti-RNP positive. It should be noted that many patients with rheumatic illnesses other than SLE are ANA-positive and that endocarditis and hepatitis, and probably other systemic infections, may cause transient autoantibody formation.

When a joint effusion is apparent, or one joint seems inflamed in excess of others, arthrocentesis should be performed to exclude infection and to classify the articular process. Blood cultures are also appropriate in this setting. The cervix, urethra, and rectum should be cultured when gonorrheal infection is suspected.

A skin biopsy may be helpful when the diagnosis, and therefore the optimal therapy, are not clear. Histopathology can be diagnostic of a type of disease (e.g., small-vessel vasculitis) or a specific disease (e.g., sarcoidosis or DLE); or it may be nonspecific (e.g., Still's disease). Immunofluorescence studies may help to suggest a disease such as SLE or to confirm one such as HSP. Unless organisms are seen or cultured from the lesion, histologic examination of skin biopsies in infectious disorders tends to be less specific.

Arnett FC: Reiter's syndrome. *Johns Hopkins Med J.* 1982;150:39–44.
An authoritative but concise discussion of the illness, based on a case presentation, including historical, clinical, radiographic, and laboratory findings as well as proposed pathogenesis.

Churchill MA, Geraci JE, Hunder GG: Musculoskeletal manifestations of bacterial endocarditis. *Ann Intern Med.* 1977;87:754–759.
In this retrospective study of 192 cases of endocarditis, 44% had musculoskeletal symptoms or signs (including arthralgia, arthritis, low back pain, and myalgias) and 22% had mucocutaneous disease.

Gibson LE. Cutaneous vasculitis: Approach to diagnosis and systemic associations. *Mayo Clin Proc.* 1990;65:221–229.
The roles of examination and biopsy in the classification of cutaneous vasculitis are discussed along with brief descriptions of the most common entities. Unfortunately, most of the photographs are black and white.

Inman RD: Rheumatic manifestations of hepatitis B infection. *Semin Arthritis Rheum.* 1982; 11:406–420.
The extrahepatic manifestations of hepatitis B infection, including arthritis, nephropathy, cryoglobulinemia, and vasculitis, are discussed in the context of a possible pathogenic role for circulating immune complexes.

Kaye BR. Rheumatologic manifestations of infection with human immunodeficiency virus (HIV). *Ann Intern Med.* 1989;111:158–167.
A review of the rheumatic disorders observed in patients infected with HIV, including Reiter's syndrome and psoriatic arthritis. Standard immunosuppressive therapy for these disorders caused significant morbidity.

Larson EB: Adult Still's disease. Evolution of a clinical syndrome and diagnosis, treatment, and follow-up of 17 patients. *Medicine (Baltimore).* 1984;63:82–91.
This article presents a rather detailed review of historical, diagnostic, and important clinical features of adult Still's disease, and includes a review of eight published series as well as the experience of the author with 17 patients. The course of the illness and response to therapy are also reported.

Malane MS, Grant-Kels JM, Feder HM, et al. Diagnosis of Lyme disease based on dermatologic manifestations. *Ann Intern Med.* 1991;114:490–498.
The most characteristic and diagnostic features of cutaneous Lyme disease, as well as the rarer manifestations are reviewed along with color photographs of the lesions. This article should be useful to any practitioner evaluating a potential case of Lyme disease with skin findings.

Masi AT, Eisenstein BI: Disseminated gonococcal infection (DGI) and gonococcal arthritis: II. Clinical manifestations, diagnosis, complications, treatment, and prevention. *Semin Arthritis Rheum.* 1981;10:173–197.
This thorough review of DGI concentrates on clinical and therapeutic issues. The pathology of the skin lesions is covered in Part I, which is written by the same authors and immediately precedes this article.

McCarty GA: Autoantibodies and their relation to rheumatic diseases. *Med Clin North Am.* 1986;70:237–261.
This article would be helpful for any physician attempting to interpret an ANA titer or pattern or deciding which tests to order.

Treatment of Lyme Disease. *Med Lett Drugs Ther.* 1989;31:57–59.
This review of the antibiotic therapy for early and late disease references the best literature on the subject.

Utsinger PD: Systemic immune complex disease following intestinal bypass surgery: bypass disease. *J Am Acad Dermatol.* 1980;2:488–495.
Twenty-one patients with this disorder are described, 17 of whom had circulating cryoproteins, suggesting a pathogenic role for immune complexes. Interestingly, three of six patients tested had anti–E. coli antibody in the cryoprotein.

Veasy LG, Wiedmeier SE, Orsmond GS, et al.: Resurgence of acute rheumatic fever

in the intermountain area of the United States. *N Engl J Med.* 1987;316:421–427.
A remarkable increase in new cases of acute rheumatic fever in several western states (mostly Utah) is described. Only 2 of 74 patients had erythema marginatum, but 91% had carditis.

Watson R. Cutaneous lesions in systemic lupus erythematosus. *Med Clin North Am.* 1989; 73:1091–1111.
The specific and nonspecific skin findings observed in SLE along with histopathologic and serologic correlates are reviewed. This chapter appears with three others that describe chronic cutaneous lupus, subacute cutaneous lupus, and lupus panniculitis.

White DG, Woolf AD, Mortimer PP, et al.: Human parvovirus arthropathy. *Lancet.* 1985;1:419–421.
Nineteen patients, representing 12% of patients seen in an "early synovitis" clinic, had evidence of recent parvovirus infection. Only four patients recalled having had a rash, and only one had the characteristic facial rash of erythema infectiosum. A second article on the same topic follows this one in the same issue.

Wright V, Roberts MC, Hill AGS: Dermatologic manifestations in psoriatic arthritis: a follow-up study. *Acta Derm Venereol (Stockh).* 1979;59:235–240.
A group of 227 patients with psoriasis and rheumatic symptoms is presented with particular emphasis on the temporal sequence of skin and joint disease, nail changes, and the generally favorable course of illness.

68. CALCIUM DEPOSITS
Scott B. Phillips

Calcification of the skin and the subcutaneous tissues occurs when calcium and phosphate ions, normally in a metastable equilibrium in extracellular fluids, form a more stable inorganic solid phase as a result of changes in their concentration or other stimuli. Heterotopic ossification is a similar deposition but in an organized matrix to form true bone. Both processes can be physiologic, e.g., formation of bone and teeth. However, pathologic mineralization of tissues is seen in a wide variety of disorders. Calcium in tissue stains deep blue with hematoxylin and eosin staining and black with the von Kossa stain for calcium.

Calcification as a Result of Hypercalcemia or Hyperphosphatemia
In **renal failure,** the serum phosphorus increases as the kidney's ability to clear it decreases. Serum calcium is low as intestinal absorption is decreased because of insufficient renal production of 1,25-dihydrocholcalciferol. This leads to increased parathyroid hormone secretion resulting in bone resorption, further increasing serum calcium and further elevating serum phosphorus. Skin and subcutaneous calcification (calcinosis cutis) can occur, usually around large joints, and may be small, multiple asymptomatic nodules or, less often, larger lesions that may be disabling because of their size. When a calcified nodule is aspirated, pasty white material is seen. Treatment includes lowering the serum phosphorus level by dialysis or using aluminum hydroxide gels to bind phosphorus in the gastrointestinal tract. The abnormal calcifications can decrease in size or disappear.

The ingestion of large amounts of calcium (e.g., milk) and antacids or calcium carbonate results in hypercalcemia and the **milk alkali syndrome.** This syndrome is usually accompanied by some degree of renal insufficiency, which further increases serum calcium and phosphorus. Calcium deposition then occurs, often around the large joints. Kidney stones containing calcium, calcification of the renal parenchyma, and metabolic alkalosis also result. Discontinuing the ingestion of milk and antacids can result in the resolution of the abnormal calcifications. The diagnosis of the milk alkali syndrome can be made only when the serum calcium level returns to normal on reduction of the excessive calcium intake.

Despite the hypercalcemia characteristic of **hyperparathyroidism**, it is also accompanied by hypophosphatemia and rarely results in metastatic calcification unless complicated by renal failure and subsequent hyperphosphatemia.

Calciphylaxis may be seen following successful renal transplantation. In this setting, secondary or tertiary hyperparathyroidism can occur with severe hyperphosphatemia leading to calcification of arterioles and arteries within the dermis and subcutaneous tissue. The accompanying intimal proliferation results in arterial insufficiency and ischemic tissue necrosis with ulcerations on the fingers, legs, and thighs.

Hypervitaminosis also may cause calcification. Large doses of vitamin D were at one time used in the treatment of diseases such as rheumatoid arthritis. Doses as low as 50,000 IU/d for an extended period of time can result in para-articular calcification. Hypercalcemia and renal insufficiency have been seen as early as 12 days when the dose exceeds 500,000 IU/d. Metastatic calcification usually does not occur unless some hyperphosphatemia is also present.

Tumoral calcinosis is a very rare disorder in which mineralization occurs around degraded collagen, resulting in masses of calcium (calcium phosphate or calcium carbonate) overlying pressure areas and around large joints. Minimal hyperphosphatemia can be present. Most cases are found in younger people, with a 2:1 male predominance. Many patients have been non-white, and some familial occurrences have been reported. Reduction of calcium and phosphorus intake by means of aluminum hydroxide gels to bind intestinal phosphorus helps the calcific masses to disappear. Lesions can also be excised.

In **sarcoidosis,** hypercalcemia occurs in about 10% of patients. This is the result of increased intestinal absorption of calcium caused by an increased sensitivity to vitamin D. Metastatic calcification is possible if the calcium-phosphorus balance in the extracellular fluids is disrupted.

Destruction of bone by **malignancies** with resultant hypercalcemia is rarely associated with skin and subcutaneous calcification. It has, however, been seen when the hypercalcemia has been treated with large doses of phosphate.

Calcification Associated with Normocalcemia and Normophosphatemia

Progressive systemic sclerosis is a systemic disorder of connective tissue, characterized by induration and thickening of the skin (scleroderma), microvascular and large-vessel abnormalities, and fibrotic degenerative changes in various organs of the body. Calcifications (calcium hydroxyapatite) that occur in these patients tend to be small and localized to the hands, feet, knees, and hips, but larger, widely distributed deposits can occur. They are usually, but not always, present in skin involved with the disease. Inflammation around these deposits with ulceration and scarring can also be observed. Secondary hyperparathyroidism (elevated serum parathyroid hormone, low ionized serum calcium, decreased urinary calcium and phosphate) can be detected in scleroderma patients with such calcinosis cutis. There is no effective therapy. Trials of phosphate depletion and the use of diphosphonate or disodium etidronate to inhibit calcification have been unsuccessful.

Polymyositis and dermatomyositis are disorders of inflammation that are part of a spectrum of disorders affecting skin and striated muscle to variable degrees. No known abnormality of calcium or phosphorus metabolism exists. The calcifications, which occur in the muscles, skin, tendons, and subcutaneous tissues, are more extensive and larger than those seen in progressive systemic sclerosis. The buttocks, thighs, arms, and trunk can be severely involved, and ulcerations as well as local inflammatory reactions are common. The face and neck are rarely involved. Spontaneous remission of calcifications can occur. In juvenile forms of the disease, calcifications in subcutaneous and fascial planes can occur as a serious late complication called calcinosis universalis. This can progress to total incapacity despite resolution of the myositis. Contracture of joints, muscle atrophy, and failure of a limb to develop are additional complications of the abnormal calcification.

Besides the characteristic hyperextensibility of the skin in **Ehlers-Danlos syndrome,** easy skin splitting, bruising, and calcified subcutaneous spherules also occur. These spherules are usually less than 6 mm in diameter and most frequently occur in the lower extremities, though sometimes they occur in the arms. They are calcified necrotic fat or fibrocaseous material surrounded by a dense fibrous tissue capsule, which also calcifies. The spherules are radiographically ovoid in shape with a dense outer shell surrounding a more diffuse and less dense central core.

Pseudoxanthoma elasticum is a disorder of the elastic tissue, affecting skin, eyes, and the cardiovascular system. It is characterized by yellow papules and plaques in flexural areas and laxity of skin, as well as calcifications in the walls of blood vessels and, rarely, in the subcutaneous tissues. High calcium intake in adolescence has been correlated with clinical severity.

Miscellaneous Disorders

Dystrophic calcification can be seen in areas of physical or thermal injury to the skin and subcutaneous tissues and resulting scar formation. This is the most common form of abnormal calcification.

Nodular calcified lesions have been found on the heels of infants who as neonates received multiple heel sticks for phlebotomy. The lesions appear as multiple small depressions on the heels with yellow or white specks appearing in them between ages 4 and 12 months. They slowly enlarge to form nodular deposits that migrate to the surface and are extruded with subsequent healing.

Up to 10% of patients with prolonged venous stasis of the lower extremities complicated by stasis dermatitis and recurrent ulceration may have calcification or ossification located in the subcutaneous tissues sparing skin and muscle. Such calcification can be detected radiographically.

Calcinosis circumscripta, i.e., localized calcification, or the widespread calcification known as calcinosis universalis has been reported in the absence of local tissue injury, systemic disease, or metabolic defect. These patients are usually children. The lesions can be papular, nodular, or plaquelike and may be located over the extremities. Ulceration can occur with a discharge of a chalklike, creamy material.

Idiopathic calcinosis of the scrotum consists of multiple asymptomatic calcified nodules of the scrotal skin with or without a surrounding granulomatous foreign-body reaction. They begin to appear in childhood and early adult life, increase in size and number, and sometimes break down with discharge of their chalky contents.

Subepidermal calcified nodules, or cutaneous calculi, usually present as a single small, raised, hard nodule in children. The most common location is the face. Lesions can also be numerous and first appear at a later age. Histologically the calcified material is located in the uppermost dermis, though in larger nodules it may extend into the deeper dermis.

Cutaneous calcinosis can be seen after the administration of calcium gluconate used to treat neonatal hypocalcemia or tetanus. If extravasation into tissue occurs, an acute or subacute reaction characterized by erythema, swelling, or warmth, and induration can occur, with subsequent calcification that resolves over the next 5 to 6 months.

In some parasitic infections, such as with the tapeworm larvae (*Taenia solium*), the female guinea worm (*Dracunculis medinensis*), loiasis, and *Echinococcus* cysts (hydatid disease), dead parasites may become calcified in the skin or subcutaneous tissues and be detected radiographically.

Werner's syndrome is characterized by premature senility, diabetes mellitus, hypogonadism, sclerosis of arteries, and arterial calcification in the lower extremities as well as subcutaneous calcifications of the soft tissues around the knees and ankles.

Abnormal ossification of the skin and subcutaneous tissues is the heterotopic formation of bony structures, including lamellae, lucunae, and occasionally bone marrow, within the skin and subcutaneous tissues. This may sometimes involve the transformation of dermal fibroblasts to osteoblasts.

Ossification, termed osteoma cutis, can be seen in **skin tumors** such as pyogenic granulomas, fibroxanthomas, pilomatrixomas, chondroid syringomas, epidermal inclusion cysts, trichoepitheliomas, hemangiomas, scars, and also with nevi and basal cell carcinomas. It is also seen in folliculitis and, rarely, in lesions of acne vulgaris.

Abnormal calcification of the basal ganglia is seen in **hypoparathyroidism** but usually not when caused by injury to the parathyroid glands. It can occur in idiopathic hypoparathyroidism when the parathyroid glands are either absent or replaced by fat or fibrous tissue. In both cases, hypocalcemia with some amount of hyperphosphatemia is noted. A similar biochemical situation exists in pseudohypoparathyroidism, but the typical patient is short, thickset, round faced, and has shortened metacarpal or metatarsal bones. Calcification of the basal ganglia is seen, and in 60% of patients, subcutaneous ossifications presenting as hard, nontender nodules are observed. Lesions can be located anywhere, but are typically found around large joints. Biopsies reveal the presence of true bone. Parathyroid hormone is present, but there is end organ (bone and kidney) resistance to its action. In pseudo-pseudohypoparathyroidism the patients resemble those with pseudohypoparathyroidism but biochemically are normocalcemic and normophosphatemic. Subcutaneous ossifications are also found in these patients.

With **myositis ossificans,** the formation of bone in muscles may occur locally, secondary to muscle trauma (especially of the flexors of the upper arm and the quadriceps femoris), or systemically, as in myositis ossificans progressiva. Traumatic myositis ossificans starts as a doughy mass a few hours after physical injury, with heterotopic ossification observed within a month. Increases in serum alkaline phosphatase, serum calcium, and phosphorus are seen. The presence of true bone encapsulating an osteoid zone around an undifferentiated area distinguishes traumatic myositis ossificans from true sarcoma, which does not have zones. Myositis ossificans progressiva is a disorder characterized by muscle ossification early in life and associated with congenital abnormalities including microdactylia or adactylia of thumbs or great toes. Serum calcium, phosphorus, and alkaline phosphatase are usually normal.

In some **neurologic disorders,** such as paraplegia, hemiplegia, and head injury, there is deposition of bone around the large joints below the level of the neurologic insult. Tissue around the joints becomes inflamed, with ossification following within a few weeks accompanied by an increase in serum alkaline phosphatase. Radiation therapy and surgery have not been of great benefit.

Bowyer SL, Blane CE, Sullivan CB, Cassidy JT: Childhood dermatomyositis: factors predicting functional outcome and development of dystrophic calcification. *J Pediatr.* 1983;103:882–888.
  This paper is a review of 47 children with dermatomyositis. The authors found that the best predictor of both good functional recovery and minimal calcinosis was early immunosuppressive treatment after the onset of symptoms.
Feingold KR, Elias PM: Endocrine skin interactions. Cutaneous manifestations of pituitary disease, thyroid disease, calcium disorder, and diabetes. *J Am Acad Dermatol.* 1987;17:921–940.
  This is a general review of endocrine-skin interactions including those that lead to altered calcium metabolism and calcium deposition.
Khafif R, DeLima C, Silverberg A, Frankel R: Calciphylaxis and systemic calcinosis. Collective review. *Arch Intern Med.* 1990;150:956–959.
  A review of pathogenesis, clinical course, and treatment of calciphylaxis.
Mendoca LE, Lavery LA, Adam RC: Calcinosis cutis circumscripta. A literature review and case report. *J Am Podiatr Med Assoc.* 1990;80:97–99.
  A current review of the literature and a case report of calcinosis cutis circumscripta are presented.
O'Donnell TF Jr., Geller SA: Primary osteoma cutis. *Arch Dermatol.* 1971;104:325–326.
  A case report and short review of osteoma cutis are presented.
Orlow SJ, Watsky KL, Bolognia JL: Skin and bones. *J Am Acad Dermatol.* 1991;25:205–221, 447–462.
  This review discusses the eight categories of skin disorders in which a radiograph may detect bony changes or abnormalities in calcification.
Roth MJ, Grant-Kels JM, Rothfield NF: Extensive calcinosis cutis with systemic lupus erythematosus. *Arch Dermatol.* 1990;126:1060–1063.
  This paper discusses a case of striking calcinosis cutis in a patient with SLE.

69. AMYLOIDOSIS
Anita M. Grassi

Amyloid is an eosinophilic, extracellular, fibrous protein with unique ultrastructural and biochemical characteristics. By light microscopy, it is a homogenous, amorphous substance that appears pink with hematoxylin and eosin stain. Electron microscopy reveals bundles of linear, nonbranching, aggregated fibrils, 7.5 to 10 nm in diameter, arranged in a beta-pleated sheet conformation. The beta-pleated sheet configuration of the fibrillar components produces the characteristic apple-green birefringence with Congo red stain under polarizing light. The fibrils are relatively insoluble and resist proteolysis, which enables their deposition in tissue with consequent loss of normal architecture and function. Numerous organs may be affected, including kidney, liver, heart, intestine, and skin, creating diverse clinical manifestations.

Amyloid fibrils result from several pathogenic mechanisms that share as a common end point the accumulation of beta-pleated sheet polypeptides. One class of amyloid proteins, called AL, consists of the variable region of intact immunoglobulin light chains or their N-terminal fragments. Enzymatic digestion of certain immunoglobulin light chains in vitro creates beta-pleated sheet polypeptides, suggesting that AL fibrils may be cleaved from protein precursors. AL amyloid occurs in primary systemic amyloidosis. Another class of amyloid fibrils, designated AA, is antigenically related to a circulating serum alpha-globulin called SAA that acts as an acute-phase reactant and is seen in secondary systemic amyloidosis. In localized cutaneous disease, the amyloid fibrils may result from filamentous degeneration of keratinocyte tonofilaments. In addition, a normal serum glycoprotein, the P-component, constitutes 10% of all amyloid.

There is no single classification of amyloidosis, but four major clinical groups are recognized. Primary systemic amyloidosis, or AL type, includes myeloma-associated amyloidosis and has no evidence of any preceding or concurrent disease except multiple myeloma. Secondary systemic amyloidosis, or AA type, coexists with an underlying inflammatory or infectious disorder, such as rheumatoid arthritis or osteomyelitis. Localized or organ-limited amyloidosis involves a single organ without evidence of systemic disease. Hereditofamilial syndromes include amyloid associated with familial Mediterranean fever. Dermatologic manifestations are seen primarily in primary systemic and localized amyloidoses.

Skin involvement is common in **primary systemic amyloidosis,** with an overall prevalence of 21% to 40% depending on the series. The cutaneous lesions are varied and include purpura, papules, plaques, nodules, scleroderma-like changes, alopecia, and macroglossia. Intracutaneous hemorrhage is often one of the most prominent skin findings. The hemorrhage is attributed to infiltration of small vessel walls by amyloid, resulting in increased fragility. However, coagulation defects, particularly Factor X deficiency, have been reported in association with this disease. Petechiae, purpura, and ecchymoses may be distributed diffusely or around body folds such as eyelids, neck, axillae, and anogenital area. Purpura may appear spontaneously or as a result of minor trauma. Such "pinch purpura" has been used as a diagnostic sign. Valsalva such as coughing or straining may likewise cause hemorrhage and is responsible for the characteristic postproctoscopic periorbital purpura.

Papules are another characteristic skin lesion in primary systemic amyloidosis. They are usually a few millimeters in diameter, smooth, shiny, translucent, or waxy. Papules vary from flesh-colored to yellowish, and may have a hemorrhagic component. They are also distributed over eyelids, face, neck, and anogenital region. They are nontender and typically nonpruritic, in contrast to the frequently pruritic papules of lichen amyloidosis.

Nodules, plaques, scleroderma-like changes, and alopecia are less common manifestations of primary systemic amyloidosis. Nodules are discrete and variable in size. They can occur on the mucous membranes and occasionally resemble oral tumors that present with dysphagia. Plaques may be solitary or confluent. Scleroderma-like changes can result from more diffuse skin infiltration of the face, neck, and hands in which the skin becomes tight, thickened, and smooth and has a limited range of motion. The patient may develop a loss of facial wrinkling, a masklike expression, and an inability to smile. Alopecia is most frequently limited to the scalp or pubic area but has been reported to be universal.

Macroglossia is present in 12% to 20% of patients with primary systemic amyloidosis. The tongue may be large enough to prevent complete closure of the mouth and make swallowing solid food difficult. It is often smooth, hard, dry, and sometimes fissured. A common finding is that of indentations where teeth press against the tongue. The differential diagnosis of AL amyloidosis includes other systemic disorders such as scleroderma, dermatomyositis, systemic lupus erythematosus, rheumatoid arthritis, hypothyroidism, senile purpura, Parkinson's disease, and scleredema.

On histopathologic examination of the skin in AL amyloidosis, there is amyloid deposition throughout the dermis, often extending into the subcutaneous fat. The papillary dermis is the primary site of involvement. Subcutaneous tissue may show amyloid deposition around individual fat cells, or "amyloid rings." The epidermis is spared but may be thinned by underlying deposits. Amyloid deposits are seen within and surrounding the walls of small blood vessels, sweat glands, sebaceous glands, and hair follicles. An inflammatory cell response is typically not present. Alopecia results from amyloid deposits in the pilosebaceous unit with atrophy and loss of the hair shaft.

Localized cutaneous amyloidosis can be classified under organ-limited amyloidosis and is a disorder confined to the skin, with no evidence of systemic disease. Three clinical variants have been described: lichen amyloidosis, macular amyloidosis, and nodular amyloidosis. Lichen amyloidosis is typically a persistent, pruritic eruption consisting of dome-shaped papules. The incidence of lichen amyloidosis is not known. It is reported more frequently among Asians and dark-skinned South American populations. The papules are 2 to 3 mm in size, firm, nontender, and range from flesh-tone to yellowish brown in color. They are frequently hyperkeratotic and without associated purpura. The distribution is predominantly over the lower extremities, especially the shins, calves, thighs, and dorsa of the feet, often sparing the knees. Due to severe pruritus, excoriation and lichenification may be seen. The amyloid deposits of lichen amyloidosis, unlike the AL type, are strictly confined to the papillary dermis. Connective tissue, blood vessels, and epidermal appendages of the deeper dermis and subcutaneous tissue are not involved. Demonstration of typical amyloid deposits will differentiate lichen amyloidosis from clinically similar eruptions such as hypertrophic lichen planus, papular mucinosis, and lichen simplex chronicus.

Macular amyloidosis consists of oval, hyperpigmented patches that have a rippled appearance. The macules are typically pruritic and are located on the lower extremities as well as the upper back and arms. They may be mistaken for postinflammatory hyperpigmentation. The pathology of macular amyloidosis is similar to that of the lichenoid type.

The nodular variant of localized cutaneous amyloidosis is far more rare than the preceding two types. These lesions are single or multiple nodules, 1 to 3 cm in diameter, often with central atrophy. They may be located on the trunk, extremities, face, or genital area. On histopathologic examination, there are large masses of amyloid throughout the dermis and extending into subcutaneous fat, similar to that of primary systemic amyloidosis. Likewise, there is infiltration of blood vessels and sweat glands. An inflammatory infiltrate of plasma cells and giant cells is often present at the periphery of amyloid deposits. Although the nodular variant is grouped with localized cutaneous amyloidosis, its true classification is in question. Extracutaneous sites are not involved at presentation; however, with long-term observation, up to 50% of patients with the nodular form are reported to develop evidence of systemic disease.

Secondary systemic amyloidosis (AA type) occurs as a result of chronic inflammatory or infectious diseases including rheumatoid arthritis, chronic osteomyelitis, tuberculosis, leprosy, inflammatory bowel disease, and neoplasms. Rheumatoid arthritis is the most common cause in the United States, with autopsy studies documenting amyloidosis in 10% to 15% of rheumatoid arthritis patients. Systemic amyloid deposition has also been reported to be associated with chronic dermatoses such as decubitus and stasis ulcers, thermal burns, basal cell carcinomas, hidrandenitis suppurativa, and psoriasis.

Cutaneous lesions in secondary systemic amyloidosis are quite rare. If a patient presents with AA amyloidosis and cutaneous disease, the skin lesions are probably not related to the amyloid. Conversely, a patient with skin lesions attributed to amyloid and evidence of a systemic disease is more likely to have AL amyloidosis. In the latter instance the work-up should be directed toward uncovering a possible plasma cell dyscrasia, and an exhaustive work-up for evidence of an inflammatory or infectious disease is not recommended.

The rare **hereditofamilial syndromes,** which are associated with amyloidosis, are mostly inherited as autosomal dominant traits—except for familial Mediterranean fever, which is an autosomal recessive disorder. Clinically these diseases tend to involve primarily one of three organ systems: the nervous system, the kidneys, or the heart. The neuropathic hereditary amyloidoses may have marked involvement of peripheral sensory and motor nerves, producing severe trophic ulcerations. One of the renal hereditary amyloidoses, which is known as the Muckle-Wells syndrome, consists of a triad of urticaria, deafness, and nephropathy. Cutaneous lesions are otherwise not a prominent feature of hereditofamilial amyloidoses.

The **diagnosis of amyloidosis** can be confirmed only by the presence of amyloid bundles on a tissue biopsy. Congo red remains the most specific stain for amyloid, yielding green birefringence under polarized light. Crystal violet may also be used, producing reddish metachromasia. Thioflavin-T causes a yellow-green fluorescence, but false-positive results are common.

The choice of site for a tissue biopsy depends on the clinical situation. A bone marrow biopsy is easily obtained and enables evaluation of plasmacytosis, but is positive in only 30% of patients. A rectal biopsy has a high diagnostic yield of 73% and is relatively free of complications. Organ-specific biopsy sites include kidney, liver, skin, and gingiva. Liver and renal biopsies have a high diagnostic yield but are more invasive procedures. Liver biopsies are particularly prone to hemorrhage. Skin biopsies are simple to perform and may provide valuable diagnostic information. A recent study showed that a punch biopsy from either clinically involved or normal skin reveals amyloid deposits in 50% of patients with systemic amyloidosis. Furthermore, the newer technique of abdominal fat pad aspiration yields positive results in 67% to 90% of patients.

No single laboratory study is diagnostic of amyloidosis. The work-up of patients with suspected systemic involvement might include assessment of renal function, liver function, calcium level, serum and urine protein electrophoresis, and immunoelectrophoresis. Immunoelectrophoresis is particularly important in order to detect monoclonal light chains.

No good **therapy** exists for either systemic or localized amyloidosis. Clinical trials of melphalan and prednisone have shown some symptomatic improvement but no change in overall survival. Colchicine and dimethylsulfoxide have been investigated, with disappointing results. The major therapeutic goal in AA amyloidosis is to treat the underlying focus of inflammation or infection. The lesions of localized cutaneous amyloidosis may persist indefinitely. Antipruritic agents such as antihistamines may provide symptomatic relief from severe itching. Keratolytic agents, topical steroids with occlusion, and local steroid injections have been used with some success. The prognosis for patients with primary systemic amyloidosis is poor. Median survival from the time of diagnosis is about 5 months for patients with multiple myeloma and 13 months for those without myeloma.

Breathnach SM: The cutaneous amyloidoses. *Arch Dermatol.* 1985;121:470–473.
   A summary of recent developments in the pathogenesis of, and therapy for, the cutaneous amyloidoses.

Brownstein MH, Helwig EB: The cutaneous amyloidoses: I. Localized forms. *Arch Dermatol.* 1970;102:8–19.
   A review of 39 examples of localized cutaneous amyloidosis with extensive clinical and pathologic descriptions.

Brownstein MH, Helwig EB: The cutaneous amyloidoses: II. Systemic forms. *Arch Dermatol.* 1970;102:20–28.
Excellent histologic and clinical correlation of 140 cases of primary and secondary amyloidosis with emphasis on clinical findings and differential diagnosis.

Glenner GG: Amyloid deposits and amyloidosis: the Beta-fobroloses. Parts I and II. *N Engl J Med.* 1980;302:1283–1291, 1333–1343.
An excellent review of the characteristics and pathogenesis of amyloid fibrils.

Koch SE: Acquired macular pigmentation. *Arch Dermatol.* 1986;122:463–468.
A case report of macular amyloidosis with a concise discussion of cutaneous amyloidoses.

Kois JM, Sexton FM, Lookingbill DP: Cutaneous manifestations of multiple myeloma. *Arch Dermatol.* 1991;127:69–74.
A retrospective review of the cutaneous findings in 115 patients with multiple myeloma.

Kyle RA, Greipp PR: Amyloidosis (AL): clinical and laboratory features in 229 cases. *Mayo Clin Proc.* 1983;58:665–683.
A thorough review of clinical and laboratory findings in 299 patients with primary systemic amyloidosis seen at the Mayo Clinic from 1970 through 1980.

Slagel AG, Lupton GP: Post-proctoscopic periorbital purpura. *Arch Dermatol.* 1986;122:463–468.
A case report of periorbital purpura in primary systemic amyloidosis with a short summary of systemic amyloidoses.

70. MUCIN DEPOSITS
Scott B. Phillips

There are two types of mucin. Dermal mucin forms the ground substance and consists of acidic mucopolysaccharides, largely hyaluronic acid. Dermal mucin is PAS-negative, but stains with alcian blue at pH 2.5. Epithelial mucin, referred to as sialomucin, contains both neutral and acidic mucopolysaccharides. It is PAS-positive, and also stains with alcian blue. Mucin appears on hematoxylin- and eosin-stained sections of skin as a basophilic stringy material. It also stains with colloidal iron stains and metachromatically with toluidine blue and Giemsa stains.

Cutaneous mucinoses are characterized by abnormal deposits of mucin in the dermis. They can be either primary, with metabolic or idiopathic etiologies, or secondary, as manifestations of other disease processes.

Primary Mucinoses
Lichen myxedematosus (papular mucinosis) is a rare disease characterized by fibroblast proliferation, increased deposition of acid mucopolysaccharides in the skin, and the presence of a paraproteinemia, usually lambda light chain immunoglobulin G. It has been classified into four different clinical types: (1) a generalized lichenoid papular eruption, often termed scleromyxedema, (2) a discrete papular form, (3) lichenoid plaques, either localized or generalized, and (4) urticarial plaques and a nodular eruption that eventually change to the generalized lichenoid form. The etiology is not known. Papular mucinosis usually affects adults between 30 and 50 years of age, and affects males and females equally. It presents as the discrete papular form with 2- to 3-mm-wide papules and has a symmetrical distribution on the dorsal surface of the hands and forearms, upper trunk, face, and neck. The papules may coalesce to form lichenoid plaques. A nodular variant with nodules and cystic lesions can occur.

In the scleromyxedema variant, induration and sclerosis of the skin is present together with the lichenoid papules. Patients complain of stiffness and lack of mobility of the skin, but systemic manifestations are rare, though an elevated erythrocyte sedimentation rate and eosinophilia can sometimes be detected. Histologically, the papillary and upper reticular dermis show deposition of mucopolysaccharides and proliferation of spindle and stellate fibroblasts. The collagen fibers are thinned and separated by the mucin, and there is a decrease in the normal amount of elastic fibers. An inflammatory lymphocytic infiltrate or eosinophilic infiltrate can be seen around the area of abnormality. Treatment of scleromyxedema is unsatisfactory, with little effect from topical or intralesional steroids or intralesional hyaluronidase. Chemotherapeutic agents including mephalen and cyclophosphamide have been used with variable results but are limited by their toxicity.

Generalized myxedema is a manifestation of severe hypothyroidism in which the entire skin becomes puffy with a boggy, nonpitting edema. This results from the dermal accumulation of the mucopolysaccharides chondroitin sulfate and hyaluronic acid. It is most noticeable in acral parts where the lack of subcutaneous tissue makes dermal changes more prominent. Histologically the mucinous deposition appears first in the papillary dermis, most prominently around hair follicles and vessels. There is separation of collagen bundles, and some degeneration of collagen may occur secondarily. Treatment includes thyroid hormone replacement, with the myxedematous changes being reversible.

Pretibial myxedema is part of the triad of Grave's disease, which includes nonnodular goitrous hyperthyroidism, ophthalmopathy, and dermopathy. There is enhanced mucopolysaccharide biosynthesis by fibroblasts, resulting in mucin deposits in the mid and lower dermis. The increased amounts of hyaluronic acid and dermatan sulfate produced result in a thickened dermis. Stellate fibroblasts may be present, or as in most cases, the fibroblast number is unchanged. Clinically the lesions present as sharply circumscribed flesh-colored, pink, or violaceous plaques or nodules that involve the anterolateral aspects of the lower extremities. They are symmetrical, nonpitting, sometimes yellow to brown in color, and waxy in appearance with dilated follicular pores giving the skin a peau d'orange appearance.

Mucopolysaccharidoses are a group of diseases characterized by a deficiency of specific lysosomal enzymes, resulting in inadequate degradation of either mucopolysaccharides or glycosaminoglycans. In all types the normal-appearing or slightly thickened skin stains for mucin within fibroblasts. The mucin is most commonly dermatan sulfate or heparan sulfate. The cutaneous papules, seen only in Hunter's syndrome (deficient iduronate sulfatase), show mucin not only within dermal fibroblasts but also in extracellular deposits between collagen bundles and fibers.

Follicular mucinosis (alopecia mucinosa) presents as grouped follicular papules, sometimes with associated erythema and scaling extending to the interfollicular skin, with loss of hair. Mucin is deposited in the outer root sheath and sebaceous gland areas and can sometimes cause follicular destruction if extensive. Otherwise, the alopecia is reversible. Mycosis fungoides and cutaneous T-cell lymphomas can be associated with this condition in about 10% to 15% of adult cases and must be ruled out by a biopsy. Follicular mucinosis occurs more often in men. There is no effective therapy.

Cutaneous focal mucinosis refers to solitary asymptomatic nodules, papules, and occasionally cystic lesions that occur on the face, trunk, or extremities. They rarely exceed 1.5 cm in diameter and are usually flesh colored or white. A biopsy is necessary for diagnosis as the clinical appearance is not totally diagnostic.

Digital myxoid cysts can be either connected to the synovial lining of the interphalangeal joints or localized to the skin as a focal cutaneous mucinosis. They are easily diagnosed by their typical location on the digits as raised translucent cystic nodules usually less than 2 cm in diameter, with expression of clear viscous material when punctured. They occur more frequently in females.

Treatment of focal mucinosis and myxoid cysts is excision or local destruction. Myxoid cysts can recur. They sometimes disappear spontaneously or respond to intralesional corticosteroids. Histologically the two disorders appear similarly as a nonencapsulated collection of mucinous matrix (hyaluronic acid) in the dermis that compresses and separates the adjacent collagen. Widely spaced spindle and stellate cells are present with small cystic areas that become larger in mucinous cysts.

True myxomatous neoplasms rarely occur in the skin, but when they do they are often seen in a subungual location. The true myxoma is a benign neoplasm composed uniformly of plump stellate cells in a mucinous matrix that is different from that present in mucinous cysts or in mucinous degeneration of the skin.

Cutaneous mucinosis in infancy refers to a case report of an otherwise healthy 16-month-old child who presented with multiple symmetrical 1- to 2-mm papules on the elbows, upper arms, and dorsal surface of hands. No serum paraprotein was detected. The papules were histologically similar to those of cutaneous focal mucinosis but with no fibroblastic proliferation.

Secondary Mucinoses

In **lupus erythematosus,** hyaluronic acid containing mucin deposits is present in the mid and lower dermis, in addition to the typical changes of lupus. Rarely in systemic lupus erythematosus, papular and nodular lesions distinct from the lupus lesions can be observed. Dermal mucin is also present in **dermatomyositis.**

Plaque-like cutaneous mucinosis (PCM) is characterized by asymptomatic persistent (years) erythematous infiltrated papules and plaques on the mid chest and mid upper back. These papules histologically show a perivascular and periappendageal dermal lymphocytic infiltrate with deposition of mucin between the dermal collagen bundles. **Reticular erythematous mucinosis** (REM) is characterized by a persistent (years) erythematous, reticular, slightly infiltrated or urticarial eruption in the same locations with a similar histologic picture, though sometimes accompanied by hydropic degeneration of the basal layer of the epidermis. The mucinous deposition in PCM is alcian blue–positive as well as mucicarmine-positive, while that in REM is only alcian blue–positive. Antimalarial therapy has been reported to be effective in some cases of REM, while antihistamines and steroids are not.

Jessner's lymphocytic infiltrate, Degos' disease, and granuloma annulare may each be associated with the deposition of mucin in the stain.

The dermal mucin deposits seen in psoriatic patients treated with **PUVA therapy** correlate with length of treatment and disappear when PUVA is discontinued. The mucin deposits may be produced by fibroblasts altered by PUVA therapy or may be secreted as part of a repair mechanism for PUVA-induced dermal changes. **UV radiation** has also been reported to exacerbate REM.

Mucin deposits have been associated with **tumors,** including basal cell carcinomas, appendageal tumors, neural tumors, dermatofibrosarcoma protuberans, and pyogenic granulomas.

Cohen PR, Rabinowitz AD, Ruszkowski AM, et al.: Reticular erythematous mucinosis syndrome: A review of the world literature and report of the syndrome in a prepubertal child. *Pediatr Dermatol.* 1990;7:1–10.
   The REM syndrome has possible relationships with altered states of immune function such as diabetes, thyroid disease, and neoplasms. Antimalarial drugs are the most successful approach to management of the photosensitive dermatosis.
Koopman RJ, Happle R: Autosomal dominant transmission of the NAME syndrome (nevi, atrial myxoma, mucinosis of the skin and endocrine overactivity). *Hum Genet.* 1991;86:300–304.
   A family with the NAME syndrome is described, in which there was male-to-male transmission, which supports the concept of the autosomal inheritance of this trait.
Mehregan DA, Gibson LE, Muller SA: Follicular mucinosis: Histopathologic review of 33 cases. *Mayo Clin Proc.* 1991;66:387–390.
   Of thirty-three patients with the histologic diagnosis of follicular mucinosis (alopecia mucinosa), nine had mycosis fungoides, three others had lymphoproliferative disorders, and two had Kaposi's sarcoma. An analysis of the biopsy features is presented. Gene rearrangement studies found three clones in three patients; two had mycosis fungoides, and one was a patient with dermatitis.
Sonnex TS: Digital myxoid cysts: a review. *Cutis.* 1986;37:89–94.
   A review of digital myxoid cysts, their differential diagnosis, natural history, and treatment.
Rongioletti F, Parodi A, Rebora A: Papular and nodular mucinosis as a sign of lupus erythematosus. *Dermatologica* 1990;180:221–223.

In about 80 percent of fifteen cases reported, papular and nodular mucinosis has been associated with systemic lupus with joint and kidney involvement.

Truhan AP, Roenigk HH Jr.: The cutaneous mucinoses. *J Am Acad Dermatol.* 1986;14:1–18.

This review discusses the primary mucinoses and considers current therapy and proposed mechanisms.

Valicenti JM, Fleming MG, Pearson RW, et al.: Papular mucinosis in L-tryptophan-induced eosinophilia-myalgia syndrome. *J Am Acad Dermatol.* 1991;25:54–58.

Flesh-colored papules which on biopsy reveal a focal accumulation of mucin in the upper middermis has been described in several patients with the eosinophilia-myalgia syndrome. The lesions slowly regressed after L-tryptophan was discontinued.

71. PYODERMA GANGRENOSUM
Sewon Kang

Pyoderma gangrenosum is a chronic ulcerative skin condition of unknown etiology and is often associated with a wide variety of systemic diseases. It has been reported in all age groups, although most cases occur between the third and fifth decades. Males and females are affected equally. Despite many attempts, no specific laboratory or histologic findings have been identified. Sixty years after the initial description, the diagnosis of pyoderma gangrenosum is still based on medical history and clinical examination of the patient.

The **primary lesion** of pyoderma gangrenosum is an ulcer. Usually beginning as a pustule or vesiculopustule, it evolves with central necrosis and peripheral extension. An early lesion may appear as a hemorrhagic indurated plaque. An ulcer is produced by sloughing of the necrotic tissue. Borders of the ulcer are well defined with a characteristic undermined edge of 4 to 8 mm that is violaceous and edematous with surrounding erythema. The base of the lesion is usually clean, although some purulence may be noted. The ulcer often extends through subcutaneous fat, revealing fascia or muscle at the base. A single lesion or multiple lesions in varying stages of progression or resolution may be present. When adjacent lesions coalesce, large serpiginous ulcerations develop. Ulcers vary greatly in size from 1 or 2 cm to 40 or 50 cm. Lesions have been described on virtually all parts of the body; however, the most common location is the lower extremities.

Patients frequently complain of pain and tenderness associated with lesions of pyoderma gangrenosum. They generally note that the ulcer arose spontaneously, although in approximately 40% of patients, a history that the lesion developed at a site of trauma can be obtained. This poorly understood pathergic response may occur after venipuncture, a skin biopsy, or any significant insult to the skin. Although it is not pathognomonic for pyoderma gangrenosum, when observed, the diagnosis should be considered.

The **clinical course** of pyoderma gangrenosum varies. In acute disease, pustules erupt and rapidly progress to ulcers that continue to enlarge dramatically over a course of days unless arrested by treatment. A slower progression from pustules to plaques to ulcers over a period of weeks to months may also occur. Regardless of the speed of progression, lesions of pyoderma gangrenosum usually heal spontaneously within months to years, leaving characteristic atrophic, irregular, and often cribiform scars. Recurrent episodes are frequent.

Histologic findings in pyoderma gangrenosum are not specific. A dense neutrophilic infiltrate in the dermis and subcutaneous fat is a consistent finding when an early pustular lesion or an active indurated margin of an expanding lesion is biopsied. Necrosis and extravasation of red blood cells are frequently seen as well. Necrotizing vasculitis has been reported in this entity but is uncommon.

Most patients with pyoderma gangrenosum have an **associated systemic illness.**

Ulcerative colitis is most frequent, followed by Crohn's disease. Almost half the patients with pyoderma gangrenosum have one of these two gastrointestinal diseases. It has also been observed in patients with chronic active hepatitis, sero-positive and sero-negative rheumatoid arthritis, and various hematologic abnormalities including acute lymphoblastic leukemia, multiple myeloma, acute and chronic myelogenous leukemia, and paraproteinemia. Both monoclonal, usually IgA, and polyclonal hypergammaglobulinemia have been observed in patients with pyoderma gangrenosum. In up to 50% of the patients, however, no associated systemic illness can be identified.

Despite numerous investigations into infectious, immunologic, and serologic factors, the **pathogenesis** of pyoderma gangrenosum remains an enigma. Because so many seemingly unrelated systemic illnesses are associated with the skin condition, some authors have suggested that pyoderma gangrenosum may be the common cutaneous end point of a number of different processes.

The **differential diagnosis** of pyoderma gangrenosum includes infection, vasculitis, and several idiopathic disorders. Because the borders of the ulcers often appear serpiginous, chronic herpes simplex infection should be excluded. Other infectious processes warranting consideration include tertiary syphilis and the deep mycoses, particularly blastomycosis and cryptococcosis. Cutaneous amebiasis can present similarly. In the presence of early papulopustular lesions, the diagnoses of folliculitis, furunculosis, and transient acantholytic dermatosis (Grover's disease) are often entertained. Plaquelike lesions may resemble insect bites, cellulitis, erythema nodosum, and panniculitis. Sweet's syndrome, also associated with hematologic malignancy in some cases, is manifested by purple-red plaques that are similar both clinically and histologically to early lesions of pyoderma gangrenosum, but ulceration is not a feature and the lesions heal without scarring. Some acute forms of vasculitis, such as Wegener's granulomatosis or polyarteritis nodosa, may be considered, although the lesions are generally more polymorphous than that of pyoderma gangrenosum. Since there are no pathognomonic clinical or histologic features diagnostic of pyoderma gangrenosum, careful microbiologic and histologic examinations are needed to exclude these disorders. Adequate evaluation generally requires large excisional biopsies that include the base and border of the ulcer and adjacent viable tissue.

Without a clear understanding of the pathogenesis of pyoderma gangrenosum, **therapy** for this disorder has naturally been empiric. Whether or not an underlying associated disease is present, local therapy is important to minimize the risk of secondary infection and trauma. Normal saline compresses or mild whirlpool treatments followed by an application of an antimicrobial cream keep the ulcers clean. Vigorous debridement is usually avoided because of the fear of stimulating a pathergic response. Use of topical corticosteroids is generally not successful, although intralesional triamcinolone acetonide injections have been reported to induce dramatic improvement. Recently reported to be effective is a 2% solution of sodium cromolyn applied topically 3 times a day by means of a compress.

Systemic therapy is often required when the disease progresses despite optimal topical care. Sulfasalazine was the first successfully used systemic agent. Initially used to treat pyoderma gangrenosum associated with ulcerative colitis, it was later found to benefit even those without the bowel disease. Administration of sulfapyridine, the active metabolite, has been effective also. Sulfones, especially dapsone, in doses up to 400 mg/d, are also used routinely, especially for patients with chronic, slowly progressive disease.

The most extensively used drugs in systemic therapy for pyoderma gangrenosum have been the corticosteroids. They can be quite successful in producing swift healing of ulcers and may be the drugs of choice for acute, rapidly progressive disease. Prednisone, 60–120 mg daily, may be required initially to arrest the growth of ulcers, and the drug is then tapered as the course of the illness allows. Intravenous pulse therapy with methylprednisolone sodium succinate (1 g/d for 5 days) is reported to be beneficial in patients who have failed more conventional treatments. This form of therapy requires close patient monitoring as sudden electrolyte shifts may induce cardiac arrhythmias and subsequent cardiac arrest.

Other agents used for pyoderma gangrenosum that has not responded to more standard therapies include clofazimine, used in doses of 300 to 400 mg daily. Minocycline hydrochloride may also be beneficial, probably because tetracyclines have anti-inflammatory properties. Immunosuppressive agents such as azathioprine, melphalan, cyclophosphamide, and cyclosporine A have been used whether or not the pyoderma gangrenosum was associated with an identifiable systemic disorder. They are effective in some patients, providing support for an immunlogic defect as a pathogenic factor.

Treatment of an underlying disorder such as inflammatory bowel disease may be associated with improvement in pyoderma gangrenosum, although the skin condition can pursue a divergent course. Inflammatory bowel disease is often controlled medically with systemic agents similar to those used for pyoderma gangrenosum alone. Surgical therapy, such as protocolectomy, has been reported to be effective in resolving both ulcerative colitis and pyoderma gangrenosum. Immunosuppressive agents are generally the treatments of choice for hematologic and immunologic disorders associated with pyoderma gangrenosum.

Callen JP, Case JD, Sager D: Chlorambucil—an effective corticosteroid-sparing therapy for pyoderma gangrenosum. *J Am Acad Dermatol.* 1989;21:515–519.
A patient who failed to respond to intensive topical care to the ulcer, two attempted skin grafts, oral prednisone, sulfasalazine, dapsone, multiple trials of intralesional triamcinolone acetonide, hyperbaric oxygen, azathioprine, methotrexate, clofazimine, minocycline, and three courses of pulse methylprednisolone therapy healed on treatment with therapy with chlorambucil, 4 mg/day. The use of chlorambucil in pyoderma gangrenosum may be an effective adjunctive steroid-sparing therapy.

Cave DR, Burakoff R: Pyoderma gangrenosum associated with ulcerative colitis: treatment with disodium cromoglycate. *Am J Gastroenterol.* 1987;82:802–804.
Topical cromolyn may be an effective treatment.

Dean SJ, Nieber S, Hickerson WL: The use of cultured epithelial autograft in a patient with idiopathic pyoderma gangrenosum. *Ann Plast Surg.* 1991;26:194–195.
A cultured epithelial autograft was effective therapy in this patient who had not responded to several medical therapies.

Elgart G, Stover P, Larson K, et al.: Treatment of pyoderma gangrenosum with cyclosporine: results in seven patients. *J Am Acad Dermatol.* 1991;24:83–86.
Seven patients who had pyoderma gangrenosum were treated with cyclosporine after their condition proved resistant to conventional therapy. Three patients had a remission, three had an intermediate response, and one did not respond. Cyclosporine is useful in the treatment of patients with refractory pyoderma gangrenosum, and this suggests an immune mechanism in the pathogenesis of this disorder.

Levitt MD, Ritchie JK, Lennard-Jones JE, et al.: Pyoderma gangrenosum in inflammatory bowel disease. *Br J Surg.* 1991;78:676–678.
Of 34 patients with PG, 22 had associated ulcerative colitis and 12 had Crohn's disease. Multiple lesions were present in 71%, and over half were situated below the knees. Two-thirds of cases resolved without intestinal resection. In the 13 patients with active pyoderma gangrenosum at the time of surgery, the pyoderma healed promptly in 6, only with additional therapy in 4, and very slowly or not at all in 5.

Paller AS, Sahn EE, Garen PD, et al.: Pyoderma gangrenosum in pediatric acquired immunodeficiency syndrome. *J Pediatr.* 1990;117:63–66.
The authors describe two children with human immunodeficiency virus infection in whom pyoderma gangrenosum developed. Although pyoderma gangrenosum most commonly occurs in children with inflammatory bowel disease, it has also been described in patients with a variety of immunodeficiencies.

Prystowsky JH, Kahn SN, Lazarus GS: Present status of pyoderma gangrenosum: review of 21 cases. *Arch Dermatol.* 1989;125:57–64.
Summary of high-dose intravenous glucocorticosteroid therapy (pulse therapy) used for severe, refractory cases of pyoderma gangrenosum, with a discussion of associated IgA monoclonal gammopathy.

Ross HJ, Moy LA, Kaplan R, et al.: Bullous pyoderma gangrenosum after granulocyte colony–stimulating factor treatment. *Cancer.* 1991;68:441–443.
This is the first case report of biopsy-proven neutrophilic dermatosis associated with administration of a hematopoietic growth factor: a patient who had bullous pyo-

derma gangrenosum at the site of previous eczema during treatment with granulocyte colony–stimulating factor. The lesions resolved promptly when the drug was discontinued.
Schwaegerle SM, Bergfeld WF, Senitzer D, et al.: Pyoderma gangrenosum: a review. *J Am Acad Dermatol.* 1988;18:559–568.
Excellent review.

72. XANTHOMAS
Richard Gold and Michael E. Bigby

Xanthomas are localized infiltrates, usually in the skin and tendons, characterized by the presence of foam cells. Foam cells are macrophages that are filled with lipid droplets. Xanthomas may result from several processes, including metabolic abnormalities and histocytic proliferation. Xanthomas can be classified into two categories: those associated with hyperlipidemias and normolipidemic xanthomas.

Hyperlipidemic xanthomas can be associated with elevations of plasma lipoproteins: very low density lipoproteins (VLDL), low-density lipoproteins (LDL), and intermediate-density lipoproteins (IDL). The genetic hyperlipidemias have been divided into six large groups: familial hypercholesterolemia, polygenic hypercholesterolemia, familial hypertriglyceridemia, familial combined hyperlipidemia, broad beta disease, and familial lipoprotein lipase deficiency. Four of the genetic hyperlipidemias are frequently associated with xanthomas. Familial hypercholesterolemia is an autosomal dominant LDL receptor defect characterized by early coronary artery disease, hypercholesterolemia, tendon xanthomas and xanthelasma. Broad beta disease is a rare, autosomal dominant disorder characterized by peripheral vascular disease, elevated levels of cholesterol and triglycerides, and tuberous and palmar crease xanthomas. Familial lipoprotein lipase deficiency is a very rare, recessive disorder associated with very high triglyceride levels and eruptive xanthomas. Familial combined hyperlipidemia is a common, autosomal dominant disorder rarely associated with xanthomas. It should be stressed that a specific genetic disease may produce more than one lipoprotein pattern and, conversely, primary and secondary causes of hyperlipidemia may produce similar lipoprotein patterns.

The hyperlipidemic xanthomas are usually divided into five distinct entities. **Xanthelasma** is by far the type most commonly encountered in clinical practice. It consists of slightly raised, soft, yellow-orange plaques localized to the eyelids. Although it is often seen in the elderly in the absence of elevated lipids, its presence in patients under 40 is suggestive of familial hypercholesterolemia. **Tuberous xanthomas** are firm, yellow to orange, lobulated nodules usually located on the extensor aspects of the knees and elbows in patients with broad beta disease. **Tendon xanthomas** are subcutaneous nodules attached to tendons and ligaments, especially the Achilles tendon and extensor tendons of the fingers. The overlying skin is normal. It usually occurs in association with familial hypercholesterolemia. **Plane xanthomas** are yellow, soft, macular or slightly palpable plaques. When localized to the palmar creases, the condition is called xanthoma stratum palmaris and is suggestive of broad beta disease. Plane xanthomas can become generalized and are then termed diffuse planar xanthoma. **Eruptive xanthomas** are small yellow papules with an erythematous halo and usually imply significant hypertriglyceridemia as seen in familial lipoprotein disease deficiency. They occur in crops on the extensor surfaces of the arms, legs, and buttocks.

The secondary cause of hyperlipidemia can also induce xanthoma formation. Secondary hyperlipidemia may be due to obesity, pancreatitis, nephrotic syndrome, hypothyroidism, cholestatic liver disease, and dysglobulinemia. Estrogens, corticosteroids, etretinate, and 13-cis-retinoic acid may also cause hyperlipidemia. It is important to rule out these secondary causes when evaluating patients with xanthomas and hyperlipidemia.

The differential diagnosis of xanthomatous lesions is broad and includes milia, syringomas, mastocytomas, nevus sebaceous, sebaceous hyperplasia, nevus lipomatous, and pseudoxanthoma elasticum. Tendon xanthomas may be confused with rheumatoid nodules and gouty tophi.

Normolipidemic xanthomas are common. Xanthelasma is frequently found in the elderly without hyperlipidemia. The remaining normolipidemic xanthomas are more unusual and their classification complex. It appears that the local tissue metabolic abnormalities play a role in the accumulation of lipid in foam cells.

Several of the normolipidemic xanthomas are important because of their association with systemic disease. **Diffuse planar xanthoma,** a subtype of plane xanthoma, presents as orange-yellow plaques of the periorbital region and upper trunk. It has been reported that 50% of patients will have paraproteinemia, most often multiple myeloma. It can also be seen in patients with erythroderma and atopic eczema.

Xanthoma disseminatum is a rare histiocytic proliferation with secondary xanthoma formation. The lesions are red-yellow papules and plaques that eventually turn brown. They characteristically affect the flexural creases and mucous membranes, and 40% of patients will have diabetes insipidus. **Juvenile xanthogranulomas** are red-yellow papules and nodules, usually occurring on the face. They first appear in the first 6 months of life but can occur in older children and adults. Ocular involvement may occasionally result in glaucoma and blindness. **Necrobiotic xanthogranulomas** are xanthomatous plaques of the periorbital region and trunk. They frequently become ulcerated, atrophic, and scarred. They are associated with paraproteinemia.

The treatment of xanthomas is variable, depending on the type and the underlying cause. Normolipidemic xanthelasma can be treated with trichloracetic acid, surgical excision, or the carbon dioxide laser. Dietary measures and agents that lower plasma lipid levels can be effective therapy for tuberous, tendinous, palmar, and especially eruptive xanthomas. Eruptive xanthomas usually completely resolve with normalization of triglyceride levels. Diffuse planar xanthoma and necrobiotic xanthogranuloma may respond to treatment of the underlying disease. Dermabrasion and electrocoagulation have been used to treat xanthoma disseminatum. Juvenile xanthogranuloma lesions usually involve within several years and require no therapy.

Finan MC, Winkelman RK: Necrobiotic xanthogranuloma with paraproteinemia. *Medicine*. 1986;65:376–388.
  Twenty of 22 patients had paraproteinemia. The periorbital region was a frequent cutaneous site.
Gladstone GJ, Beckman H, Elson LM: CO_2 laser excision of xanthelasma lesions. *Arch Ophthalmol*. 1985;103:440–442.
  Six of nine patients had excellent cosmetic results. Two other patients developed mild hypopigmentation.
Mather-Wiese VL, Marmer EL, Grant-Kels JM: Xanthomas and the inherited hyperlipoproteinemias in children and adolescents. *Pediatr Dermatol*. 1990;7:166–173.
  A useful review of the hyperlipoproteinemias and xanthomas.
Mishkel MA, Cockshott WP, Nazir DJ, et al.: Xanthoma disseminatum: Clinical, metabolic, pathologic and radiologic aspects. *Arch Dermatol*. 1977;113:1094–1100.
  A concise review of this interesting disease.
Parker F: Xanthomas and hyperlipidemias. *J Amer Acad Dermatol*. 1985;13:1–30.
  An excellent review of xanthomas found in primary and secondary hyperlipidemias.
Parker F: Normocholesterolemic xanthomatosis. *Arch Dermatol*. 1986;122:1253–1257.
  Discusses possible mechanisms and proposes a classification scheme.
Vail JT, Adler KR, Rothenberg J: Cutaneous xanthomas associated with chronic myelomonocytic leukemia. *Arch Dermatol*. 1985;121:1318–1320.
  A case of chronic myelomonocytic leukemia with striking cutaneous xanthomas in the absence of elevated plasma lipids.
Yamakawa K, Yanagi H, Saku K, et al: Family studies of the LDL receptor gene of

relatively severe hereditary hypercholesterolemia associated with Achilles tendon xanthomas. *Hum Genet.* 1991;86:445–449.

In this study of seventeen hypercholesterolemic families, most, if not all, of the hypercholesterolemia associated with Achilles tendon xanthomas were caused by a defect of the LDL receptor gene.

73. PSYCHOCUTANEOUS DISORDERS
Thomas G. Cropley

The interplay between cutaneous diseases and emotions is fascinating, but as yet poorly understood. Many primary diseases of the skin may be profoundly influenced by the patient's psychological state: exacerbations of atopic dermatitis and chronic urticaria, in particular, are precipitated by stressful events. Emotion, usually in the form of anxiety attending some life stress, also seems to produce clinical worsening of psoriasis, dyshidrotic eczema, alopecia areata, herpes simplex, generalized pruritus, and warts. Behavioral therapies directed toward stress reduction, such as biofeedback and hypnosis, have proved useful in the management of some of these conditions, especially dyshidrotic eczema. In addition, there are a number of disorders that are primarily psychiatric in nature but whose outward signs and symptoms are referable to the skin. This chapter will focus on these psychocutaneous disorders.

Neurotic excoriations, frequently referred to as neurodermatitis, are the somatic manifestation of an obsessive-compulsive disorder. The typical patient is an older adult whose skin surface is covered with hundreds of linear and stellate excoriations and scars of various ages. The lesions are limited to those areas that the patient can reach; therefore, the central back is spared. Patients may experience pruritus, but this symptom is often surprisingly mild in view of the extent of excoriation. Koblenzer describes these patients as obsessively intolerant of irregularities of the skin surface. Their hands ceaselessly wander, picking off any small papules or crusts. As the crusted erosions resulting from this activity accumulate, they too are removed, thus establishing a vicious cycle.

Supportive psychotherapy, usually by the primary physician, and symptomatic relief of pruritus often suffice to control the compulsive habit. Behavioral techniques have been used successfully in more severely disturbed patients. In those patients in whom pruritus is prominent, conditions that may produce itching, such as hyperbilirubinemia and lymphoma, should be excluded by appropriate studies.

Pruritus does not usually accompany neurotic excoriations. However, itching may be exacerbated by stress; and patients often sublimate anxiety by scratching. Although generalized pruritus is more typically a manifestation of dry skin or metabolic disease such as hypothyroidism, it may on occasion be a somatic complaint in anxious individuals. More commonly, itching due to stress is localized, and the patient's repeated scratching produces lesions of lichen simplex chronicus.

Trichotillomania, like neurotic excoriations or habitual hair plucking, is a compulsive disorder. This condition appears to be relatively common, especially among young children in whom it serves as a relatively harmless outlet for tension. Older patients, predominantly adolescent females, often have an associated obsessive-compulsive disorder in which the pulling of hair may have symbolic meaning. Trichotillomania may occasionally be seen in other psychiatric disorders, particularly schizophrenia, borderline personality disorder, and depression. Regardless of other psychiatric diagnoses, patients almost invariably are markedly anxious.

Clinically, trichotillomania presents as one or more ill-defined, irregularly shaped patches of nonscarring alopecia. Within these areas are broken hairs of variable length, which often are arranged in linear or circular fashion. The frontal and temporoparietal regions are most frequently affected. Microscopic examination of plucked hairs reveals the striking absence of telogen hairs, a feature that has been considered diagnostic of trichotillomania. In doubtful cases, a biopsy of the scalp reveals empty hair follicles, catagen hairs, and trichomalacia (coiled, distorted hair shafts). Many patients with trichotillomania also exhibit nail destruction (onychomalacia) and hair swallowing (trichophagy).

Young children with trichotillomania are usually reacting to some acutely stressful event, such as the birth of a sibling, the divorce of the parents, or the mother's return to full-time employment. Common to all of these situations is anxiety and a sense of loss—of the mother or of the child's status as an only child, for example. In behavioral terms, the loss of hair is less threatening than the precipitating loss, and thus provides a transitional object through which anxiety can safely be dissipated. Koblenzer recommends that the child be provided with a woolly or whiskered toy to substitute for his or her own hair, and that possible precipitating factors be gently explored with the parents.

Older patients present more of a therapeutic challenge. Frequently patients deny their role in producing the alopecia, and derive considerable secondary gain from it. A nonjudgmental, supportive approach, as used in factitious disorders (see below), is most likely to be successful. Concomitant anxiolytic or antidepressant therapy, with the choice of agents determined by the patient's predominant affect, may be needed. Biofeedback and hypnosis have been used successfully in a few patients.

Recent advances in the treatment of obsessive-compulsive disorder with antidepressant drugs have prompted investigators to study the efficacy of this type of therapy in trichotillomania. In a study by Swedo, clomipramine significantly reduced the frequency of obsessive thoughts concerning hair pulling during a 10-week, double-blind crossover study in which subjects received desipramine as a control. Three of four patients studied by Pollard had relapsed at three month follow-up, however, despite significant initial improvement, suggesting that clomipramine may not prove effective in long-term management of trichotillomania. Christenson et al. failed to demonstrate any benefit of fluoxetine therapy in an 18-week study, despite that drug's frequent utility in treatment of obsessive-compulsive disorder.

Factitious disorders are defined as "physical or psychological symptoms that are produced by the individual and are under voluntary control." *Voluntary* in this sense means that these acts are done deliberately, but not necessarily that the acts can be controlled. Factitious disorders are distinguished from malingering in that in the latter case an obvious environmental goal (e.g., avoidance of military service) is recognizable, rather than a psychological motive.

The spectrum of volitionally produced lesions of the skin is limited only by the means at the patient's disposal for producing them. Ulcers, produced by acids, caustics, injected feces, milk, or other substances, constitute one large group of factitia. Also common are round scars produced by cigarette burns, disfiguring linear scars on the face and elsewhere resulting from repeated laceration with the nails or a sharp instrument, and purpuric macules produced by a vacuum cleaner or other suction device. Two clinical features are common to all factitious skin lesions. First, lesions produced by external means have the appearance of an "outside job": the lesions are linear or geometrical in shape, with sharply defined borders, and may be arrayed in grids, straight lines, or in other unnatural ways. Second, patients angrily and vehemently deny their role in the production of the lesions.

Most patients with factitious disease are severely disturbed, and fall somewhere on the continuum from borderline personality disorder to frankly psychotic. Borderline patients are able to form only infantile relationships with others, and have an insatiable need for nurturing. The appearance of factitia in these patients represents a means of insuring attention from family members and health providers. In psychotic patients, the factitious skin lesions are incorporated into their delusional systems.

Therapy is directed toward the underlying emotional disorder. Mildly disturbed patients may be helped by a nonconfrontational approach with cultivation of a good relationship. In most cases, however, the patient is lost to follow-up once he or she is "found out." Psychotic patients are best referred to a psychiatrist. In general, nonpsychotherapeutic measures such as antibiotics and occlusive dressings are doomed to failure so long as the emotional disturbance is not addressed.

One specific factitious skin disorder is worthy of further mention. The psychogenic purpura syndrome, or Gardner-Diamond syndrome, affects women almost exclusively and presents as painful bruising of the skin after trivial trauma. Neurologic symptoms and gastrointestinal bleeding are seen as well. Intradermal injection of the patient's own blood will reproduce the painful bruises. Personality profiles of these patients are remarkably uniform and reveal a masochistic character structure. Patients form overly dependent relationships yet paradoxically harbor intense anger toward those closest to them. The prognosis for these unfortunate individuals is very poor.

Delusions related to the skin are beliefs that are adhered to tenaciously by the patient despite abundant evidence that the belief is incorrect. Because they are evidence of a disordered thought process, delusions are a symptom of psychosis. Dermatologists are familiar with the patient who has an unshakable belief that his or her skin is infested with insects or mites. The patient usually complains of feeling bugs crawling within the skin, and will go to extraordinary lengths to rid herself or himself of them. Frequently these individuals have consulted many physicians and have been unsuccessfully treated multiple times with scabicidal drugs as well as homemade concoctions of commercial insecticides. Often, the patient brings a jar containing the "bugs" (pieces of lint or skin detritus) to the physician's office as "proof" of infestation. This common disorder has been variously called acarophobia, parasitophobia, and the delusion of parasitosis, which is the preferred term. Currently, this disorder is classified as a monosymptomatic hypochondriacal psychosis and thus firmly placed among the psychoses.

Therapy for this disorder has long been problematic, since this type of psychosis does not respond to conventional neuroleptic therapy. Recently, pimozide, a diphenylbutylpiperidine neuroleptic drug used to treat Tourette's disorder, has been reported to effectively control, but not cure, the delusion of parasitosis. The drug is administered in a single daily dose of 2 to 8 mg.

Another monosymptomatic hypochondriacal psychosis occasionally seen in dermatologic practice is the delusion of bromhidrosis. In this condition, the patient is convinced that his or her body odor is profoundly offensive. Affected individuals are frequently adolescents with fastidious habits and no discernible body odor. As a rule, these persons are markedly ambivalent sexually and display a flat affect. The prognosis is extremely poor for these patients, and many eventually develop true schizophrenia. No published data are available regarding treatment of this disorder with pimozide.

It is essential that the physician adopt a nonconfrontational, supportive posture when working with a patient suffering from either form of monosymptomatic hypochondriacal psychosis. Referral to a psychiatric consultant may be helpful. Above all, the physician must avoid reinforcing the delusion with unnecessary or dangerous therapies.

Anogenital pruritus and **glossodynia** may represent a depressive equivalence in some patients. Here, organic disease such as lichen sclerosis et atrophicus and monilial infection must be ruled out. Symptomatic therapy with a cooling, antipruritic regimen should be combined with informal psychotherapy. Often, such discussion will uncover significant heterosexual or homosexual conflicts giving rise to the symptom of itching.

American Psychiatric Association: Factitious Disorders. In: *Diagnostic and Statistical Manual of Mental Disorders*. 3rd ed. Washington, D.C.: APA; 1980;285–290.
    Summary of diagnostic criteria for monosymptomatic delusional states.
Christenson GA, Mackenzie TB, Mitchell JE, et al: A placebo-controlled, double-blind crossover study of fluoxetine in trichotillomania. *Am J Psychiatry*. 1991;148:1566–1571.
    Twenty-one adult, chronic hair pullers were studied in an 18-week placebo-controlled, double-blind crossover study of fluoxetine in doses up to 80 mg/d. No significant drug by period interactions were found in weekly subject ratings of hair pulling, the urge to pull hair, the number of hair-pulling episodes, or the estimated amount of hair pulled per week.
Engels WD: Dermatologic disorders. *Psychosomatics*. 1982;23:1209–1219.
    From the psychiatric literature comes this interesting discussion of these disorders from a psychodynamic viewpoint.

Koblenzer CS: Psychosomatic concepts in dermatology. A dermatologist-psychoanalyst's viewpoint. *Arch Dermatol.* 1983;119:501–512.
Perhaps the best review ever written on the subject. Dr. Koblenzer's dual training as a dermatologist and psychoanalyst uniquely qualifies her to discuss "psychodermatology."

Koo JYM, Pham CT: Psychodermatology: practical guidelines on pharmacotherapy. *Arch Dermatol.* 1992;128.
This review describes the major psychodermatologic disorders and provides management guidelines, including the use of specific psychopharmacologic agents.

Krishnan KR, Davidson JR, Guajardo C: Trichotillomania—a review. *Compr Psychiatry.* 1985;26:123–128.
Short review with good discussion of psychodynamics of trichotillomania.

Lachapelle JM, Pierard GE: Traumatic alopecia in trichotillomania: a pathologic interpretation of histologic lesions in the pilosebaceous unit. *J Cutan Pathol.* 1977;4:51–67.
Trichotillomania is easily recognized with practice. Scalp biopsy may have a role in the evaluation of suspected trichotillomania.

Medansky RS, Handler RM: Dermatopsychosomatics: classification, physiology, and therapeutic approaches. *J Am Acad Dermatol.* 1981;5:125–136.
Comprehensive review, written from the perspective of practicing dermatologists. Emphasis is on therapeutics.

Munro A: Monosymptomatic hypochondriacal psychosis manifesting as delusions of parasitosis. *Arch Dermatol.* 1978;114:940–943.
Not much has been written about this interesting entity. This article describes the typical features.

Oranje AP, Peerboom-Wynia JD, De Raeymaecker DM: Trichotillomania in childhood. *J Am Acad Dermatol.* 1986;15:614–619.
This review focuses on the importance of distinguishing trichotillomania as a reaction to stress from trichotillomania as a symptom of more severe psychiatric disorders.

Pollard CA, Ibe IO, Krojanker DN, et al.: Clomipramine treatment of trichotillomania: a follow-up report on four cases. *J Clin Psychiatry.* 1991;52:128–130.
Three of four patients who initially report dramatic reduction in symptoms on clomipramine therapy relapsed completely at 3-month follow-up, although all four were still taking previously effective levels of the drug. The fourth patient relapsed for about 2 weeks but regained initial treatment benefits.

Swedo SE, Leonard HL, Rapoport JL, et al.: A double-blind comparison of clomipramine and desipramine in the treatment of trichotillomania (hair pulling). *N Engl J Med.* 1989;321:497–501.
Thirteen women with severe trichotillomania completed a 10-week, double-blind crossover trial of clomipramine and desipramine. Treatment with clomipramine resulted in significantly greater improvement in symptoms than desipramine.

XII. PERIORIFICIAL DISORDERS

A rational approach to the differential diagnosis of oral lesions can be made by first dividing them into those that are acute in onset and generally resolve quickly and those that tend toward chronicity. These groups can be further subdivided into those diseases where ulceration occurs and those that do not ulcerate. The acute disorders are generally infectious in nature except for drug-induced mucositis and recurrent aphthous stomatitis. The chronic diseases are frequently immunologic or neoplastic.

Acute Oral Ulcerations

Primary oral infection with **herpes simplex virus** type 1 or 2 is known as herpetic gingivostomatitis. Although primary herpes may occur soon after birth if the child is exposed to maternal herpes simplex during passage through the birth canal, the majority of individuals contract primary herpes simplex during infancy or early childhood. Most primary infections are clinically silent; however, a minority of patients develop acute gingivostomatitis, which may be quite mild, manifesting only as a sore throat and mild fever. Symptomatic cases can, however, present in a more dramatic fashion, with pharyngitis, fever, and numerous 1- to 3-mm-wide painful vesicles throughout the oral cavity. The vesicles coalesce and rupture quickly, leaving wide areas of denuded mucosa often covered with an adherent gray exudative pseudomembrane. The finding of "scalloping" of the borders of denuded areas may aid diagnosis. Recurrent herpes simplex only rarely involves the oral cavity; most cases occur on the lips or perioral facial skin.

Treatment of primary herpetic gingivostomatitis now centers on the use of acyclovir, which may be given intravenously or orally, although many infants with gingivostomatitis are unable to take medications orally. In severe cases, patients may not be able to maintain adequate water intake and therefore require intravenous fluid therapy. Pain can often be managed topically, especially around meal time, with 2% Xylocaine jelly or 0.5% dyclonine (Dyclone) solution, applied as needed. More severe pain is better managed with systemic analgesics. Attention to oral hygiene will reduce bad breath and unpleasant taste sensations, and will gently debride exudate to speed reepithelialization. A 50:50 mixture of hydrogen peroxide and Cepacol mouthwash is an effective mouth rinse.

Herpes zoster may on occasion appear in the distribution of the thyroglossal or lingual nerve. In such cases, an eruption of vesicles on an erythematous background appears, involving either one side of the hard and soft palate and adjacent buccal surface or one side of the tongue. As in herpes zoster elsewhere, the diagnostic feature is the striking unilaterality of the eruption, which respects the midline exactly. Oral analgesic and hygienic measures, as discussed for herpes simplex, are generally helpful. The role of acyclovir in uncomplicated herpes zoster is controversial; however, its use may speed healing and reduce the likelihood of developing postherpetic neuralgia. A recommended dose is at least twice that suggested for herpes simplex.

Coxsackie A16 is an enterovirus that produces a distinctive clinical syndrome known as **hand-foot-and-mouth disease.** The disease occurs in epidemics, affecting children primarily, but with transmission to adults as well. The virus implants in the oral mucosa or intestinal tract, following which a viremic phase lasting 3 to 6 days ensues. After a short prodromal illness consisting of low-grade fever and malaise, fragile vesicles, usually no more than 5 to 10 in number, appear in the mouth, with particular predilection for the tongue, buccal surfaces, and hard palate. The vesicles become grayish pustules and rupture soon after appearing, leaving exquisitely painful superficial ulcers. The ulcers are surrounded by an erythematous halo and are covered with a grayish yellow pseudomembrane, thus mimicking aphthous ulcers exactly. Ulcers resolve without treatment in about 1 week. At the same time that oral vesicles appear, cutaneous lesions develop on the palms, sides, and dorsal surface of the hands and feet. Lesions are erythematous, oval-shaped macules or papules, which become vesicular and then pustular. The pustules have a peculiar gray color that, along with their ovoid shape, makes them fairly distinctive. Unlike the paucity of oral lesions, the cutaneous lesions of hand-foot-and-mouth disease may number in the dozens. Both viral cultures and detection of a rising titer of complement-fixing antibody to Coxsackie A16 have been used to confirm the diagnosis of hand-foot-and-mouth disease. Specimens for viral culture should be taken from vesicle fluid, throat swabs, and stool.

Recurrent aphthous stomatitis (RAS) is an extremely common condition characterized by the periodic eruption of solitary or multiple painful ulcers in the mouth. It is estimated that aphthae affect 20% to 55% of the population, with a slight female preponderance. Onset of RAS is usually in the second decade, and lesions usually continue to appear throughout life. The majority of affected individuals have so-called minor aphthae. Minor aphthae present as one lesion or several, which, after a brief prodrome or erythema and pain or tingling, rapidly ulcerate. The ulcers are surrounded by a zone of erythema and centrally consist of a superficial ulcer covered by a grayish yellow fibrinopurulent exudate. Minor aphthae are particularly prone to developing in the buccal and labial mucosae and their reflections, as well as on the sides and undersurface of the tongue. Those portions of the oral mucosa that are bound to bone (the gingivae and hard palate) are only rarely involved. Minor aphthae heal without treatment in around 7 days. About 10% of patients with RAS have herpetiform aphthae, which are identical to minor aphthae except that they tend to be smaller and more numerous, sometimes appearing by the hundreds throughout the mouth. In this situation, viral culture to distinguish herpetiform aphthae from primary herpetic gingivostomatitis may be necessary. Major aphthae occur in about another 20% of patients. Major aphthae tend to be large, often measuring several centimeters across, and are deep and painful. They also tend to be solitary or few in number. Major aphthae usually will heal in 2 to 3 weeks, which distinguishes them from chronic ulcerations due to lichen planus or lupus erythematosus.

Individuals with Behçet's syndrome develop aphthous ulcers, often of the major type. In addition to the oral cavity, the vaginal and urethral epithelia are frequently involved. These aphthae tend to heal more slowly than others. Oral aphthae also occur in some patients with Crohn's disease and ulcerative colitis, and less commonly in patients with pernicious anemia, iron deficiency anemia, and celiac sprue.

The etiology of RAS is not known. However, it has been demonstrated that 70% to 80% of individuals with RAS have circulating autoantibodies to oral mucosal homogenates, and that RAS patients' lymphocytes are cytotoxic to cultured oral mucosal cells. It has been suggested that the autoantibodies are produced in response to *Streptococcus sanguis,* strain 2A, a common oral cavity inhabitant that shares several antigenic determinants with normal adult mucosa. Thus, an immune etiology for RAS appears likely. There may also be a genetic predisposition to RAS in some individuals. HLA types A2 and B12 are common in RAS patients, and HLA-B12 is also associated with Behçet's syndrome.

Treatment of aphthae should include hygienic measures and topical anesthetics, as already discussed. Tetracycline oral suspension 125 mg (5 ml) swished for 5 minutes 4 times daily and then swallowed may be effective, although this has not been evaluated prospectively. Corticosteroids can be effective, and may be administered as a short systemic course or, less effectively, via intralesional injection or topical application. Dapsone, colchicine, azathioprine, and levamisole, an anthelmintic drug, have all been reported to be effective in anecdotes. Finally, deliberate colonization of the mouth with *Lactobacillus* to eliminate *S. sanguis* has been reported to work well. Regardless of whether aphthae are treated or not, they do resolve with time. Patients should be instructed to avoid trauma such as that produced by sharp bread crusts or hard-bristle toothbrushes, as this may precipitate new ulcers.

Erythema multiforme (EM) is another common condition that produces acute ulceration of the oral mucosa. Usually, oral lesions appear concurrently with the characteristic target-shaped skin lesions of EM. Diagnosis is seldom difficult in this situation. However, about 25% of individuals with EM have involvement only of the oral mucosa. In this case, differentiation from herpetic gingivostomatitis or aphthous stomatitis may be difficult. Severely affected patients (Stevens-Johnson syndrome) have severe involvement of two or more mucosal surfaces with widespread cutaneous lesions and fever. In this setting, oropharyngeal mucositis may extend into the esophagus and trachea. Recurrent EM may occur, and in most cases, is precipitated by recurrent herpes simplex or by repeated exposure to a drug.

Erythema multiforme of the oral cavity characteristically involves the anterior half of the mouth most severely. Patients may have erythematous or dusky grayish red macules or, rarely, intact bullae in the mouth; but typically the labial and anterior buccal surfaces, the gingivae, and the hard palate are more or less diffusely eroded. Multiple pinpoint areas of bleeding, and hemorrhagic crusts at the lip margins are virtually pathognomonic of EM.

Treatment of oral EM is nonspecific. Topical anesthetics and systemic analgesics reduce pain, and hydrogen peroxide and Cepacol rinses maintain hygiene. Oral acyclovir may reduce the frequency of recurrences in individuals predisposed to them, even in the absence of culture-positive recurrent herpes simplex. Topical and systemic corticosteroids have their advocates, but convincing evidence of their efficacy in oral EM is lacking.

Acute necrotizing ulcerative gingivitis (ANUG), or trench mouth, occurs primarily in young adults. It appears to be a synergistic bacterial gangrene of the interdental papillae, caused by the normal bacterial flora of the mouth and presenting as a gingivitis. The patient complains of marked pain and bleeding of the gums after eating or brushing. Fetid breath and a metallic taste in the mouth are often noted. At first, the interdental papillae are tender and red. Very soon, however, punched-out ulcerations appear on the papillae, and entire papillae may slough. Like acute herpetic gingivostomatitis, it presents with fever, lymphadenopathy, and painful ulcerations in the mouth; however, ANUG generally affects an older age group and is limited to the interdental papillae. Referral to a dentist is of paramount importance, because the necrotic tissue must be debrided. Penicillin is usually administered for 10 days.

Drug-induced stomatitis presents as acute inflammation and ulceration of the oral mucosa and occurs via one of three mechanisms. Hypersensitivity reactions such as EM and fixed drug eruption may occur but are relatively uncommon. Direct irritation of the oral mucosa by a medication may cause ulceration—for example, an "aspirin ulcer," a painful, solitary ulcer produced by allowing an aspirin tablet to dissolve in the mouth (a folk remedy for toothache). Most commonly, however, drug-induced oral mucosal erosions result from administration of antineoplastic drugs. Most chemotherapeutic drugs can produce mucosal necrosis and sloughing. Methotrexate, fluorouracil, bleomycin, and daunorubicin are common offenders.

Chemotherapy-induced mucositis is generally diffuse. A period of tenderness and erythema precedes the ulcerative slough by several days. Hemorrhagic crusts and bleeding, similar to that seen in EM, may occur, especially in the presence of thrombocytopenia. Secondary infection with *Candida albicans* is common and may prolong the ulceration. Reepithelialization occurs once the course of chemotherapy is completed. The measures already discussed to reduce pain and maintain oral hygiene should be instituted. *Candida* superinfection usually responds to topical antifungal agents, but it may require systemic therapy in the setting of immunosuppression, fever, or invasive infection.

Syphilitic chancre can be difficult to diagnose when it appears in the oral cavity. Like chancre occurring elsewhere, chancre in the mouth presents as an ulcer with firm, indurated borders, present most commonly on the upper and lower lips and on the tongue. It is usually painless or only minimally uncomfortable, and the ipsilateral, cervical or submental lymph nodes are enlarged. The dark-field examination, used to diagnose primary genital syphilis, is of no help in oral syphilis, because of the normal presence of spirochetes in the mouth. Also, serologic tests for syphilis may not yield a positive result when a chancre is present. Thus, the clinician must be suspicious when evaluating indurated ulcers of the mouth. A biopsy is a helpful diagnostic procedure if the VDRL yields a negative result, especially since it excludes squamous cell carcinoma, the major differential diagnosis for chancre when the lesion's age is uncertain.

Acute, Nonulcerative, Symptomatic Lesions

Candida albicans is a normal inhabitant of the colon. Under appropriate conditions, such as diabetes mellitus, neutropenia, immunosuppression, or chronic antibiotic therapy, *Candida* may colonize or invade the oral mucosa. Candidiasis may be manifested only by erythema and mucosal discomfort, but more typically it produces white, curdlike patches that can be scraped off the mucosa with a tongue blade. The scraped surface may bleed slightly. Severely neutropenic patients may have more invasive candidiasis, in which case true ulcers of the oral cavity may appear. Odynophagia due to esophageal involvement may be present. A potassium hydroxide mount of scraped material will reveal budding yeast and pseudohyphae.

Treatment of oral candidiasis is easily accomplished in nonimmunosuppressed individuals, through the use of Mycostatin oral suspension or clotrimazole troches 4 times daily. Patients with invasive candidiasis usually require treatment with systemic ketoconazole.

Candidiasis, like oral hairy leukoplakia, appears to be a poor prognostic sign in HIV-seropositive individuals, many of whom develop AIDS within a relatively short period of time.

The oral lesions of **secondary syphilis,** called mucous patches, are highly infectious white or grayish pink papules and plaques on mucosal surfaces, almost never occurring in the absence of skin lesions. They may reappear over several years if untreated. The VDRL almost always gives a positive result. As in the case of primary syphilis of the oral cavity, dark-field examination of mucous patches is of no use diagnostically, because of the nontreponemal spirochetes that normally inhabit the mouth.

Chronic Oral Ulcerations

Lichen planus is an idiopathic disorder of skin and mucous membranes. The cutaneous lesions classically are violaceous, polygonal, flat-topped papules with a predilection for the wrists, lower legs, and genitalia. Oral lichen planus is found in association with cutaneous disease in two-thirds of individuals; it occurs in the absence of lesions outside the oral cavity in about one-fourth of cases. The oral lesions are identical in these two situations: either asymptomatic violaceous or erythematous papules and plaques covered with lacelike white lines (Wickham's striae), or painful, chronic ulcerations arising in similar plaques. The buccal mucosa is the most common site of involvement, followed by the tongue and lips. The papillae are effaced in involved areas of the tongue, giving it a shiny, grayish pink atrophic appearance.

Although squamous cell carcinoma may arise in lesions of chronic oral lichen planus, the disease is often self-limited and thus need only be treated if symptomatic. Ulcerative lesions are very persistent, sometimes lasting months or even years. The ulcers tend to be painful and may be disabling. Systemic corticosteroid therapy may be of some benefit, but the most reliable means of treating ulcerative lichen planus is with intralesional steroid injection, which may need to be repeated at intervals. Potent topical steroids such as betamethasone dipropionate and clobetasol propionate may be tried, but the medication must be applied very frequently (every hour or so). Recently, use of topical tretinoin (Retin-A) has also been advocated.

All three forms of **lupus erythematosus,** discoid, subacute cutaneous, and systemic, may be associated with oral lesions. Oral lesions in discoid and subacute cutaneous lupus erythematosus resemble those of oral lichen planus. Typically one chronic ulcer or more are present, which have Wickham's striaelike lines radiating outward from the ulcer edge. Oral involvement in systemic lupus erythematosus, analogous to the cutaneous lesions, tends to consist of diffuse erythema and edema, sometimes with palatal petechiae. Ulcers are rare in systemic lupus erythematosus.

Bullous pemphigoid is an immune-mediated blistering disease of the skin, which occurs primarily in the elderly. About one-third of patients have oral lesions at some point in the course of their disease; only uncommonly do oral lesions occur without obvious cutaneous plaques or blisters. The typical oral lesion of bullous pemphigoid is a tense blister, which may be unnoticed by the patient. Although the blister roof is thicker and therefore less fragile than the delicate blisters of pemphigus, most oral pemphigoid blisters eventually rupture, leaving an erosion that heals very slowly.

Cicatricial pemphigoid, or mucous membrane pemphigoid, is a rare variant of bullous pemphigoid and is characterized by oral, genital, and conjunctival blisters and erosions, usually without significant skin involvement. Unlike the lesions in most cases of bullous pemphigoid, the lesions of cicatricial pemphigoid often heal with significant scarring, leading to blindness in the case of ocular lesions. Cicatricial pemphigoid may present with fragility, pain, and easy bleeding of the gingivae, so-called desquamative gingivitis.

Bullous pemphigoid and cicatricial pemphigoid have similar histology, characterized by submucosal blister formation and inflammation. Direct immunofluorescence of perilesional mucosa is diagnostic, revealing C3 and, often, immunoglobulins in a linear pattern along the basement membrane zone. A biopsy of chronic oral erosions and ulcerations is often necessary to distinguish bullous and cicatricial pemphigoid from pemphigus vulgaris and lichen planus.

Treatment of both bullous and cicatricial pemphigoid often requires high doses of systemic corticosteroids and immunosuppressive agents such as cyclophosphamide or azathioprine. Topical and intralesional steroids seem to be less effective than in oral lichen planus, but are worth trying. Dapsone has been reported to be effective in some cases of cicatricial pemphigoid.

Pemphigus vulgaris is another immune-mediated blistering disease of skin and mucous membranes. It tends to occur in a younger age group than bullous pemphigoid. Patients are frequently of Ashkenazi Jewish heritage. Unlike bullous pemphigoid, where oral lesions occur only in a minority of affected individuals, pemphigus involves the oral mucosa frequently. Oral involvement may, in fact, precede any other manifestations of pemphigus by several years. It usually presents in the oral cavity as desquamative gingivitis (as described for cicatricial pemphigoid, above) or as fragile blisters and erosions. The erosions have a tendency to enlarge and coalesce, so that much of the oral cavity may be denuded. Hoarseness from laryngeal involvement and dysphagia from deep pharyngeal erosions may be present.

A biopsy of perilesional mucosa reveals acantholysis and suprabasilar cleft formation identical to that seen in cutaneous lesions. Likewise, direct immunofluorescence reveals intercellular deposition of immunoglobulin. Indirect immunofluorescent examination of the patient's serum may be positive as well.

Systemic therapy for pemphigus is usually necessary and often requires high doses of corticosteroids and immunosuppressives to control the disease. This may not be necessary in patients whose disease is limited to the oral cavity, however, as potent topical steroids and intralesional steroid injections may suffice in some cases. Topical anesthetics and hygienic measures are often helpful as well.

Squamous cell carcinoma of the lips and oral cavity is, unfortunately, a common problem, accounting for 4% of cancers in men and 2% in women. Cigarette smoking, chewing tobacco, snuff use, and alcohol use all are risk factors. Lip cancer is more common in urban areas, intraoral carcinoma in rural areas. A recent disturbing rise in the incidence of oral cancer in young men has been attributed to increasing use of smokeless tobacco.

Most intraoral squamous cell carcinomas arise from the floor of the mouth or the ventral and lateral surfaces of the tongue, suggesting that pooling of soluble carcinogens may play a role. Whether arising from the lip or intraorally, most carcinomas present as a painless nodule. With time, the nodule enlarges and ulcerates, at which point it becomes painful. Regional lymph node enlargement may be noted at first examination, especially if the tumor arises from the floor of the mouth. A biopsy of the nodule is mandatory to confirm the diagnosis, and should be deep enough to allow the extent of invasion to be determined. Patients with lip carcinoma have the best prognosis, both because the tumor is usually well differentiated and because most lip cancers can be resected easily. Five-year survival of over 90% is the rule. Patients with carcinomas of the tongue or of the floor of the mouth have a less favorable prognosis, with 5-year survival rates on the order of 50%. Radiation therapy is usually combined with surgical resection in these cases.

Chronic, Nonulcerative Mouth Sores

Both candidiasis and secondary syphilis, described as acute conditions, may in fact produce lesions that persist for protracted periods. In addition to these diseases, another entity, **geographic tongue,** produces symptomatic oral lesions that tend toward chronicity. Geographic tongue is a common, idiopathic disorder that occurs in adults. Although lingual lesions are typical, it may also involve the adjacent mucosa.

The primary lesion of geographic tongue is an area that is shiny, red, and devoid of papillae, bordered by a second zone that appears white because of elongation of the papillae. These lesions move about on the surface of the tongue from one day to the next, creating bizarre patterns. Patients may not notice any unusual sensation in the affected area, but commonly they report tingling, burning, and hypersensitivity.

Although the etiology of geographic tongue is unknown, it occasionally occurs in association with generalized pustular psoriasis. Some authors have suggested that geographic tongue may be a mucosal variant of psoriasis, but most dispute this theory. Therapy is symptomatic, though good results have been claimed with brief applications of keratolytic agents.

Ahmed AR: Pemphigus: current concepts. *Ann Intern Med.* 1980;92:396–405.
Therapeutically oriented review article.

Anhalt GJ: Pemphigoid. Bullous and cicatricial. *Dermatol Clin.* 1990;8:701–716.
Bullous pemphigoid antigen has been identified by Stanley J, et al., as an approximately 230 kD protein. The protein has been cloned and is being sequenced.

Birt D, From L, Main L: Diagnosis and management of longstanding benign oral ulceration. *Laryngoscope.* 1980;90:758–768.
Emphasis is on adequate examination and a low threshold for obtaining biopsies.

Burgess JA, Johnson BD, Sommers E: Pharmacological management of recurrent oral mucosal ulceration. *Drugs* 1990;39:54–65.
Nice discussion of topical and systemic therapy of a variety of ulcerative and erosive conditions in the mouth.

Conklin RJ, Blasberg B: Common inflammatory disorders of the mouth. *Int J Dermatol.* 1991;30:323–335.
A recent review of stomatology for the dermatologist, with emphasis on ulcerative conditions.

Flint S: Oral mucosa. *Practitioner* 1991;235:56–63.
Reviews common oral neoplasms as well as oral ulcers.

Kaplan B, Barnes L: Oral lichen planus and squamous carcinoma. Case report and update of the literature. *Arch Otolaryngol.* 1985;111:543–547.
A reminder that chronic ulcerative conditions of the mouth, including lichen planus, may develop into carcinoma.

Lennette EH, Magoffin RL: Virologic and immunologic aspects of major oral ulcerations. *J Am Dent Assoc.* 1973;87:1055–1073.
Thorough discussion of virology of herpes simplex, herpes zoster, and Coxsackie A16, among others. Dated, but recommended highly.

Scully C, Porter S: Recurrent aphthous stomatitis: Current concepts of etiology, pathogenesis, and management. *J Oral Pathol Med.* 1989;18:21–27.
A reasonably comprehensive, recent review.

Sloberg K, Hersle K, Mobacken H, et al.: Topical tretinoin therapy and oral lichen planus. *Arch Dermatol.* 1979;115:716–718.
Seventy-one percent of treated patients, vs. 29% of placebo-treated controls, improved with topical tretinoin in an adhesive base.

Stokes RW, Koprince D: Recurrent aphthous stomatitis. Review of the literature. *J Am Osteopath Assoc.* 1982;81:776–782.
Nice discussion of pathogenesis and treatment.

Weathers DR, Baker G, Archard HO, et al.: Psoriasiform lesions of the oral mucosa (with emphasis on "ectopic geographic tongue"). *Oral Surg.* 1974;37:872–888.
Geographic tonguelike lesions occur elsewhere in the oral cavity and may be confused with lichen planus or leukoplakia.

75. CHEILITIS
Joop M. Grevelink

The term *cheilitis* is used to describe any acute or chronic inflammation of the lips. Diseases of the lip can be limited to the lip or can be associated with other cutaneous or mucous membrane processes.

Exposure to solar irradiation produces both acute and chronic inflammation, known as **actinic cheilitis.** The acute form, a sunburn of the lip, is characterized by painful erosions with edema, vesiculation, and ulceration. With excessive long-term exposure, chronic changes occur, predominantly involving the lower lip, and include diffuse atrophy, a silver gray color, and an ill-defined vermilion border. Poorly demarcated white keratotic plaques may be present. Erosions that heal slowly or are persistent and dryness are also common patient complaints. Histopathologic examination of a biopsy specimen shows ortho- and parakeratosis with areas of hyperplasia, atrophy, and dysplasia.

Acute and chronic actinic cheilitis may be prevented with use of lipsticks containing sunscreens and avoidance of sun exposure during peak hours. Treatment is not always easy. The application of 5% fluorouracil cream 3 to 4 times daily for 2 weeks or liquid nitrogen cryotherapy may be effective. Vaporization with the carbon dioxide laser is the treatment of choice. Sometimes a vermilionectomy with mucosal advancement is performed, especially in severe cases.

Commonly occurring in areas of chronic actinic cheilitis, squamous cell carcinoma of the lip is usually first seen as a white hyperkeratotic plaque, which may quickly grow into a crusted nodule. Areas suggestive of squamous cell carcinoma warrant an immediate biopsy. If confirmed, excision is the treatment of choice. Squamous cell carcinoma of the lip has a metastatic rate of 10% to 20%.

Allergic contact dermatitis involving the lips is relatively uncommon. **Allergic cheilitis** presents as an eczematous dermatitis of the lips. Lesions consist of erythematous plaques made up of papules, vesicles, and occasionally bullae. Plaques may become lichenified, and hyperpigmentation is common. Among the agents causing allergic contact dermatitis of the lips are various metallic salts, mouthwashes, and anesthetics used by dentists. Denture adhesives, chewing gum, and lipstick may also be incriminated.

Some substances cause an irritant contact dermatitis that looks similar to allergic reactions. The most common lip irritant is saliva. Many people bite or lick their lips as a tic, a habit, or in obsessive-compulsive disorders. Therapy is best directed at correcting the behavior.

Cheilitis exfoliativa is an idiopathic disorder characterized by persistent scaling and crusting of the lips in patients where other causes such as allergic or irritant cheilitis have been excluded. The exfoliative process is localized to the mucocutaneous junction. In severe cases, large sheets of epithelium desquamate and leave an erythematous and tender surface. The process repeats in cycles of 7 to 10 days. The etiology is unknown and topical corticosteroids are sometimes effective.

Oral **lichen planus** may have a variety of morphologies: reticulated white plaques, vesicles or bullae, atrophy, and erosions. Although lesions are typically found on the buccal mucosa, tongue, and gingivae, they can also be observed on the vermilion border of the lips. The lesions are usually asymptomatic, and spontaneous remissions occur in about half of the patients. Frequently, there is evidence of lichen planus on the skin. Smoking or other trauma may play a role in initiating oral lichen planus. The histology of the white keratotic lesions shows hyper- and parakeratosis, a bandlike lymphocytic infiltrate in the upper dermis, and liquefaction degeneration of the stratum germinativum. Malignant transformation of oral lichen planus to carcinoma has been reported. Oral lichen planus is difficult to control. Treatment with topical, injectable, or systemic corticosteroids may be effective. Topical tretinoin (Retin-A) and, most recently, cyclosporine mouth rinse, have also been used with some success.

Leukoplakia (leukokeratosis) literally means "white plaque," and the term is used to describe white mucosal lesions that cannot be characterized clinically or histologically as signs of any other specific disease (e.g., lichen planus or candidiasis). Leukoplakia is common in smokers and is often called smoker's patch. The majority of cases appear between the fourth and seventh decades. Leukoplakia has considerable malignant potential, and a biopsy with microscopic evaluation is necessary to exclude malignancy. Typical pathologic features in leukoplakia are hyper- or parakeratosis, acanthosis, and a mononuclear cell infiltrate. Some degree of epithelial dysplasia is found in approximately 25% of biopsies of lip leukoplakia, indicating the possibility of development into squamous cell carcinoma. Surgical excision or ablation of involved areas is indicated.

Discoid lupus erythematosus may affect the vermilion border of the lips. Mild disease is characterized by a diffuse or localized erythema with a few telangiectases. Adherent, indurated, keratotic scaling may develop. Late lesions show minute white spots correlating with atrophy. Histologically in discoid lupus erythematosus, orthokeratosis with keratotic plugging, atrophy of the rete processes, interface and periadnexal lymphocytic inflammation, and liquefaction degeneration of the basal layer are found. It is difficult to distinguish these lesions, on clinical or histologic grounds, from those of lichen planus or leukoplakia. The presence of other cutaneous or systemic disease, or immunofluorescence studies on a lip specimen, may help to distinguish the underlying process. The oral lesions of lupus erythematosus tend to follow a chronic course and are relatively resistant to treatment. Topical or injectable corticosteroids are often used at first. The antimalarials may also be administered systemically and are the first choice for widespread or recalcitrant cutaneous disease. Avoidance of sun exposure is mandatory.

Cheilitis angularis (rhagades, perlèche) is characterized by lateral lip fissures radiating from the angles of the mouth. Redness, superficial ulceration, and crusting occur at the angles of the mouth and adjacent skin surface but usually not on the buccal mucosa. The causes of cheilitis angularis are many. Loss of the vertical dimension of the intramaxillary space (caused by aging, loss of teeth, ill-fitting dentures, or various facial paralyses) results in overclosure of the bite. Drooling and maceration predispose an individual for infection, as a localized dermatitis develops in the deep wrinkles at the labial angles. *Staphylococcus aureus* and *Candida albicans* are commonly found organisms. An intraoral *C. albicans* infection may be associated. Infections can be treated with topical antibiotics or topical antifungal agents. The associated irritant dermatitis may require intermittent application of a low-potency steroid cream. Correction (if possible) of the vertical dimension will often resolve the problem. Implantation of filling substances such as collagen or Fibrel to correct deep folds has been reportedly successful in carefully selected patients.

The differential diagnosis of cheilitis angularis includes nutritional deficiencies such as ariboflavinosis (vitamin B_{12} deficiency), kwashiorkor, and iron deficiency. Protein malnutrition disease (kwashiorkor) can show angular cheilitis as one of its symptoms as well. A thin vermilion border and angular cheilitis are seen in sideropenic dysphagia (Paterson-Brown-Kelly syndrome or Plummer-Vinson syndrome), an iron-deficiency disease in middle-aged women. In secondary syphilis, so-called split papules (condylomata lata) can be found at the angles of the mouth. These papules may be seen simultaneously with mucous patches on the buccal mucosa— slightly raised, grayish white lesions surrounded by a red halo. Diagnosis is made by serologic testing or skin biopsy.

Herpes labialis, also known as a fever blister or cold sore, is caused by the herpes simplex virus. It presents as a recurring vesicular eruption of the skin adjacent to or on the vermilion border. The eruption may be accompanied by fever, lymphadenopathy, and painful intraoral vesicles and erosions in the first outbreak. After resolution in 10 to 14 days, the virus remains dormant in sensory nerve ganglia until stimulation by sunlight, viral upper respiratory illness, stress, or other (sometimes unclear) factors. Prodromal symptoms, such as itching or neuralgia, are commonly reported by patients. For patients with frequently recurring lesions, oral acyclovir may reduce the frequency of attacks and shorten the viral shedding time. The topical use of acyclovir probably has no effect on the course of the disease.

Cheilitis glandularis apostematosa (myxadenitis labialis) is a rare condition that particularly involves the lower lip, causing diffuse enlargement and sometimes eversion. Salivary glands and ducts are enlarged, producing firm nodules that express a viscous mucinous substance on palpation. Patients complain of the lips' sticking together with long mucinous strands, especially in the morning. Histologic examination of a biopsy specimen taken from the buccal mucosa shows hyperplasia of the mucous glands, enlargement of ducts, and infiltration with plasma cells and lymphocytes. The etiology is unknown, but heredity and exposure to irritants such as wind, sun, dust, and tobacco have been implicated. It has been reported to occur more frequently in males and whites. Degeneration to epidermoid carcinoma has been reported but is quite rare. Electrocoagulation of ducts and glands or surgical extirpation of redundant tissue may provide some relief.

The **Melkersson-Rosenthal syndrome** (cheilitis granulomatosa of Miescher) consists of a triad of symptoms: recurrent or persistent diffuse swelling of both lips, recurrent facial nerve paralysis, and a "scrotal tongue" (lingua scrotalis). The cheilitis may occur alone, thought to be a mild or oligosymptomatic form of the syndrome. Clinically, the lips are massively swollen, so that patients are described as having a tapir snout. Superficial scaling and fissuring usually accompany the swelling. Histologic examination of an appropriate specimen reveals a granulomatous reaction with noncaseating areas of epithelioid and giant cells and a perivascular accumulation of plasma cells, lymphocytes, and histiocytes. The disease is of unknown etiology and runs a chronic course with remissions and exacerbations. Injections of steroids have been reported to be moderately successful, although therapy is generally unsatisfactory.

Cheilitis plasmacellularis is characterized by a sharply outlined, infiltrated, dark red plaque that has a lacquerlike glazing of the surface on the lower lip. Pathologic features include psoriasiform epidermal hyperplasia and diffuse dermal infiltration with plasma cells. A similar histologic picture can be seen in Zoon's balanitis. No effective treatment has been identified.

Some other cutaneous diseases also have lip involvement on occasion. Oral lesions in psoriasis are extremely unusual and are commonly associated with the pustular and exfoliative forms of the disease. In atopic eczema, diffuse redness with scaling of the lips is seen infrequently. Treatment of either process is difficult. Topical steroids may be useful.

In summary, cheilitis may be acute or chronic with a limited number of morphologies but a large number of causes. When one is evaluating a patient with swelling, redness, or scaling of the lips, careful history taking, a full mouth exam, and a total body skin exam may give clues to the right diagnosis.

Aiba S, Tagami H: Immunoglobulin-producing cells in plasma cell orificial mucositis. *J Cut Pathol.* 1989;16:207–210.
  Plasma cell orificial mucositis is a benign idiopathic condition of orificial mucous membranes characterized histologically by a dense, bandlike plasmocytic infiltrate. Eight cases were studied and the polyclonal plasma cell infiltrate was found, composed of IgG- and IgA-producing cells, which was consistent with the pattern observed in the inflammatory infiltrate around certain epidermal neoplasms, such as actinic keratosis, Bowen's disease, squamous cell carcinoma, and syringocystadenoma papilliferum.
Allen CM, Camisa C, Hamzeh S, et al.: Cheilitis granulomatosa: report of 6 cases and review of the literature. *J Am Acad Dermatol.* 1990;23:444–450.
  The occurrence of nontender swollen lips that on biopsy reveal noncaseating granulomas in the lamina propria is diagnostic for granulomatous cheilitis. Granulomatous cheilitis occurs in the Melkersson-Rosenthal syndrome, which includes unilateral facial paralysis, facial (and lip) swelling, and fissured tongue. One of six patients was treated with hydroxychloroquine sulfate, which stabilized the process.
Beacham BE, Kurgansky D, Gould WM: Circumoral dermatitis and cheilitis caused by tartar control dentifrices. *J Am Acad Dermatol.* 1990;22:1029–1032.
  Twenty women had burning and itching around the corners of the mouth, followed by pruritic perioral patches of erythema 4 to 14 days later. All patients had begun using tartar control toothpaste one to two weeks before onset, and on discontinuation of toothpaste, marked improvement was seen within 1 to 6 weeks.

Crotty CP, Dicken CM: Factitious lip crusting. *Arch Dermatol.* 1981;117:338–340.
Four patients with factitious lip crusting are presented. All patients had personality disturbances and had bizarre hemorrhagic or keratotic crusts on the lips.

Feigal DW, Katz MH, Greenspan D, et al.: The prevalence of oral lesions in HIV-infected homosexual and bisexual men: three San Francisco epidemiological cohorts. *AIDS.* 1991;5:519–525.
Hairy leukoplakia, pseudomembranous and erythematous candidiasis, angular cheilitis, Kaposi's sarcoma, and oral ulcers were more common in HIV-infected subjects than in HIV-negative subjects. Among HIV-infected individuals, hairy leukoplakia was the most common lesion.

Robinson JK: Actinic cheilitis: a prospective study comparing four treatment methods. *Arch Otolaryngol Head Neck Surg.* 1989;115:848–852.
Forty patients with actinic cheilitis were treated with one of four modalities: topical fluorouracil, chemical peel with trichloroacetic acid, lip shave, or carbon dioxide laser ablation of the vermilion. Patients treated with carbon dioxide laser ablation had no recurrence of the problem during a 4-year period.

Swerlick RA, Cooper PM: Cheilitis glandularis: a re-evaluation. *J Am Acad Dermatol.* 1984;10:466–472.
A review of five cases of clinically diagnosed cheilitis glandularis and of 48 cases of cheilitis glandularis published in the literature indicated that the salivary glands were normal in appearance in almost all cases. The authors conclude that many cases believed to be cheilitis glandularis are actually actinic cheilitis, chronic irritant cheilitis, or factitial cheilitis.

Warnakulasuriya KA, Samaranyake LP, Peiris JS: Angular cheilitis in a group of Sri Lankan adults: a clinical and microbiologic study. *J Oral Pathol Med.* 1991;20:172–175.
Among 49 patients examined clinically and microbiologically, 5 were full denture wearers, 18 had low hemoglobins, and pathogenic organisms were isolated from 59% of the lesions, Candida *spp. in 24 patients, and* S. aureus *in 11 patients. A positive relationship between commissural leukoplakia and an infective etiology of angles was noted.*

Williams PM, Greenberg MS: Management of cheilitis granulomatosa. *Oral Surg Med Pathol.* 1991;72:436–439.
A patient with 8 months' duration of granulomatous labial enlargement of the lower lip was successfully managed with intralesional steroid injections.

Zelickson BD, Roenigk RK: Actinic cheilitis. Treatment with the carbon dioxide laser. *Cancer.* 1990;15:1301–1311.
Forty-three patients with biopsy-proven actinic cheilitis were treated with the carbon dioxide laser. After at least 10 months, 26 patients thought that the lip was improved or had not changed. Complications were few and included only mild hypertrophic scarring.

76. URETHRITIS
William Frank

Urethritis is defined as "inflammation of the urethra." It can be caused by infectious agents such as *Neisseria gonorrhoeae* or *Chlamydia* and in some cases by noninfectious agents. Reiter's syndrome is closely related to infectious urethritis.

Gonococcal urethritis is caused by the gram-negative diplococcus *N. gonorrhoeae.* In almost all cases it is a sexually transmitted disease. The incidence is highest in persons aged 18 to 24 years and is more common in the unmarried, black, poor, and urban. There was a dramatic increase in the incidence of gonorrhea between the mid 1960s and mid 1970s. This increase has been attributed to the increased number of young adults engaging in sexual intercourse, to the widespread use of oral contraceptives in place of barrier methods, and to the increase in the 18- to 24-year-old age group during this time. The incidence has been slowly declining since 1975. The disease often occurs in those persons with a past history of sexually transmitted diseases.

The symptoms of dysuria and urethral discharge often begin abruptly. Seventy-five percent of patients have symptoms within 5 days of exposure and 90% within 2 weeks. Most patients have dysuria and a majority (75%) will have a frankly purulent discharge. Meatal erythema is common.

Because the symptoms of gonococcal and nongonococcal urethritis are often indistinguishable, the diagnosis should be made by a Gram stain of urethral discharge. Highest yield in the male is obtained by expression of the discharge from the penis before the first morning voiding. The presence of four or more polymorphonuclear leukocytes per oil immersion field confirms the diagnosis of urethritis. A Gram stain of discharge showing gram-negative intracellular diplococci in symptomatic males is 98% sensitive and 98% specific for gonococcal urethritis. If the Gram stain is negative, a culture on selective media such as Thayer-Martin should be done. Diagnosis in the female patient is made by culture.

Treatment includes adequate coverage of agents causing nongonococcal urethritis as well as gonococcal urethritis since many patients have concurrent disease. Plasmid-mediated beta-lactamase production by *N. gonorrhoeae* has become a major problem. These strains still account for less than 5% of isolates in the United States, but they are endemic in Asia and Africa. In certain regions of the United States, these strains are becoming more widespread. In areas without resistant strains, ampicillin 3.5 g or amoxicillin 3.0 g given orally with 1 g of probenecid orally plus tetracycline 500 mg PO qid for 7 days is effective. Doxycycline 100 mg PO bid for 7 days may be used instead of tetracycline. In areas endemic for resistant strains, ceftriaxone 250 mg IM plus 7 days of tetracycline is recommended.

Nongonococcal urethritis (NGU) is inflammation of the urethra caused by any agent other than *N. gonorrhoeae*. It is estimated that 75% to 80% of all cases are due to *Chlamydia* and possibly *Ureaplasma urealyticus*. Although NGU has not been a reportable disease in the United States, it is in Great Britain, where its incidence is reported to be twice that of gonorrhea. Most incidence reports on sexually transmitted diseases come from venereal disease clinics. It is therefore very likely that NGU is more prevalent than thought, because NGU is more prevalent than gonococcal urethritis in the higher socioeconomic groups, and these patients less often attend venereal disease clinics. NGU is most common in young adults, those of lower socioeconomic status, and people who live in urban settings. It is associated with multiple sexual partners and lack of use of barrier methods of contraception. NGU and gonococcal urethritis often occur together. It is estimated that 20% to 30% of men with gonococcal urethritis and 25% to 30% of women with gonococcal cervicitis or urethritis have concurrent *Chlamydia* infection. One-third of women treated only for gonococcal cervicitis will develop postgonococcal urethritis.

Chlamydia trachomatis accounts for 40% to 60% of all cases of NGU. It is an obligate intracellular organism that characteristically produces intracellular inclusion bodies in infected cells. The isolation of the organism in large studies of patients with urethritis, seroconversion of patients with NGU, and the presence of the organism in many patients with postgonococcal urethritis all strongly support the etiologic role of *Chlamydia*. *Ureaplasma urealyticus* has been implicated as a causative agent in NGU. At present the evidence is circumstantial. Although the organism can be cultured from many patients with NGU, its presence in a large number of asymptomatic persons makes the association with NGU difficult to assess. However, many feel that *Ureaplasma* is responsible for a significant number of cases of NGU. In 20% of patients neither *Chlamydia* nor *Ureaplasma* is identified. Uncommon causes of urethritis include herpes simplex, *Candida, Trichomonas vaginalis,* periurethral abscess, and intraurethral condyloma. Other noninfectious causes are local trauma, chemical irritation, foreign body, noninfectious ulceration, chemical contraceptive agents, and calculous gravel.

The symptoms of NGU are usually mild and insidious, in contrast to the symptoms of gonorrhea, which are often severe and abrupt. However, the overlap in symptoms is significant, and the diagnosis should never be made on clinical grounds alone. The average incubation time is 2 weeks, somewhat longer than in gonococcal urethritis. Symptoms include mild dysuria, scanty to moderate whitish discharge, and urgency. The discharge is frankly purulent in 11% to 33% of cases. *Chlamydia* can be recovered from the endocervix in 45% to 90% of female partners of infected men. Both men and women can be asymptomatic carriers.

The **diagnosis** of NGU is made in a patient with urethritis after gonococcal urethritis has been excluded. If the Gram stain of the urethral discharge fails to show intracellular diplococci, then the presumptive diagnosis of NGU is made. A culture should be performed to confirm the negative Gram stain. *Chlamydia* culture is 80% to 95% sensitive and 100% specific, and is considered the gold standard. However, it is expensive and technically difficult. Direct immunofluorescence of urethral smears using monoclonal antibodies is 78% to 92% sensitive and 97% specific. The ELISA test has similar accuracy. Culture of *Ureaplasma* can be performed only at reference laboratories and is expensive.

Treatment of NGU can be initiated without knowledge of the specific etiologic agent. NGU can smoulder for many months, but the risks of transmission and complication necessitate treatment in all cases. The antibiotic of choice is tetracycline 500 mg PO qid for 7 days. Alternate therapies are erythromycin 500 mg PO qid for 7 days and doxycycline 100 mg PO bid for 7 days. Erythromycin ethylsuccinate 400 mg PO qid for 1 week is recommended for pregnant women. Both patient and sexual contacts need to be treated, since there is a high incidence of asymptomatic *Chlamydia* carriage, both in males and females. Treatment failure may be due to patient noncompliance, reinfection, or the presence of another causative agent.

Complications of NGU can be severe. Transmission of *Chlamydia* to the female can result in cervicitis, which can cause pelvic perihepatitis or subsequent ectopic pregnancy. Urethral strictures, acute epididymitis, Reiter's syndrome, inclusion conjunctivitis, and neonatal pneumonia in children born to mothers with cervical *Chlamydia* are other complications.

The classic clinical triad of **Reiter's syndrome** consists of arthritis, urethritis, and ocular inflammation. The association of arthritis affecting young males after recent sexual exposure has been noted numerous times over the past 500 years, but it was not until 1942 that Bauer and Engleman proposed the clinical syndrome. Reiter's case report in 1916 described a soldier who had bloody diarrhea followed by purulent conjunctivitis, urethritis, and polyarthritis. Many patients do not fulfill the clinical triad of Reiter's syndrome but have many of the features. More recently, *Reiter's syndrome* has been defined as "an episode of arthropathy occurring within 1 month of an episode of urethritis or cervicitis."

The cause of Reiter's syndrome is unknown. The relationship between infection and subsequent arthritis is well documented; however, the underlying pathophysiology remains unknown. Reiter's syndrome occurs in association with nongonococcal urethritis; enteric infection due to *Shigella, Salmonella,* and *Yersinia;* and possibly other infections. Sixty to eighty percent of patients with Reiter's syndrome are HLA-B27 antigen positive.

Reiter's syndrome occurs throughout the world. The incidence is higher in Navajo Indians and in certain Greenland populations. Arthritis occurs in about 1% of males with nongonococcal urethritis and in 2% to 3% of patients with selected causes of diarrhea. Reiter's syndrome is much more common in men, especially when associated with NGU. The male-female ratio in these cases is roughly 30:1. In a study from the Mayo Clinic, the incidence in Rochester, Minnesota, over a 30-year period was 3.5 per 100,000. The cases were males, and all but one followed an episode of urethritis.

The arthritis of Reiter's syndrome is an oligoarthritis affecting the ankles, feet, or knees. The period of time between infection and the onset of joint symptoms is less than 1 month in 80% to 90% of patients. The Mayo Clinic study showed a 63% incidence of persistent symptoms of symptomatic recurrence. Ocular lesions predominantly seen in reactive arthritis are conjunctivitis and uveitis and occur in about half of patients. Keratoderma blennorrhagica consists of hyperkeratotic and crusting plaques on the palms and soles. It is seen in 10% to 25% of patients. Circinate balanitis usually presents as hyperkeratotic penile plaques and occasionally as mostly painless ulcers. It occurs in 10% to 40% of patients.

Behçet's syndrome is a chronic, relapsing systemic disease of unknown etiology, characterized by oral and genital ulcerations and ocular abnormalities. It is five times more common in males, with a peak incidence in the 20- to 30-year-old age group. It occurs worldwide but is more common in Japan, where there has been a large increase in incidence in the past 30 years.

The major criteria used to diagnose Behçet's include recurrent oral aphthous ulcers, eye lesions, genital ulcerations, and skin lesions. Minor criteria are the findings of arthritis, gastrointestinal lesions, epididymitis, and CNS involvement. The diagnosis of complete Behçet's requires all four major criteria. Incomplete Behçet's requires three major criteria or ocular manifestations.

The oral lesions are almost always present (90%) and are similar to those of aphthous stomatitis. The ulcers are superficial, sharply demarcated, and have an erythematous border. They are painful and recurrent, and can be found anywhere on the oral mucosa. Genital ulcers are also painful, often scar, and occur in the majority of patients (60% to 90%). Uveitis is present in 70% to 90% of patients and can result in permanent loss of vision. Skin manifestations other than oral and genital ulcers are common. These manifestations include erythema nodosum and pyoderma, as well as diffuse eruptions. Other features include arthritis, neurologic symptoms, superficial thrombophlebitis, arterial thrombosis, aneurysms, and an increased skin reactivity to minor trauma ("pathergy"). Patients with CNS and cardiovascular involvement have a poor prognosis. The common pathologic lesion appears to be a vasculitis, particularly of venules.

Oral ulcerations can be treated with triamcinolone 0.1% cream in Orabase, viscous lidocaine, or tetracycline rinses (250 mg in 5 ml of water and rinsed for 2 minutes). Oral corticosteroids are the mainstay of systemic therapy for severe disease with widespread involvement or ocular involvement. Azathioprine, cyclophosphamide, chlorambucil, cyclosporine, colchicine, and nonsteroidal anti-inflammatory agents have all been used with variable success.

Arbesfield SJ, Kurban AK: Behçet's disease. *J Am Acad Dermatol.* 1988;19:767–779.
  This recent review article emphasizes the current understanding of diagnosis, pathogenesis, and treatment.
Bowie WR: Approach to men with urethritis and urologic complications of sexually transmitted diseases. *Med Clin North Am.* 1990;74:1543–1547.
  A useful in-depth review that discusses urethritis and epididymitis in younger men, as well as prostatitis, epididymitis, and other problems of older men.
Felman VM, Nikitas JA: Nongonococcal urethritis. A clinical review. *JAMA.* 1981;245:381–386.
  A general review of the clinical manifestations and etiology of nongonococcal urethritis.
Hook EW, Holmes KK: Gonococcal infections. *Ann Intern Med.* 1985;102:229–243.
  The clinical spectrum of the disease and its treatment are presented.
Keat A: Reiter's syndrome and reactive arthritis in perspective. *N Engl J Med.* 1983;309:1606–1615.
  The author reviews his data and experience in the relationship of nongonococcal urethritis and Reiter's syndrome.
Michet CJ, Machado EB, Ballard DJ, et al.: Epidemiology of Reiter's syndrome in Rochester, Minnesota: 1950–1980. *Arthritis Rheum.* 1988;31:428–431.
  The age-adjusted annual incidence rate for males was 3.5 per 100,000. No female cases were identified. More than 63% of patients had prolonged or recurrent disease.
Mitchell SA, Shukla SR, Thin RN: Aetiology of non-gonococcal urethritis: a possible relation to other infections. *Int J STD AIDS.* 1990;1:429–431.
  Chlamydia trachomatis can be identified in up to 60% of cases of NGU. This paper reports a role for other genitourinary infections, such as candidiasis, warts, and herpes simplex, in the causation of NGU.
Treatment of sexually transmitted disease. *Med Lett Drugs Ther* 1988;30:5–10.
  Current guidelines for treatment of gonorrhea.

77. VULVAR DISEASES
Paul B. Googe

The vulva may be involved in a plethora of diseases that vary greatly in etiology but produce surprisingly similar symptoms. Itching and burning, rash, or vaginal discharge, accompanied by anxious discomfort, are typical complaints, and a specific diagnosis is made only by a careful medical history, physical examination, and laboratory evaluation. The physician must be tactfully diligent and gather all possible pertinent historical facts without bias or embarrassment concerning the personal or sexual behavior of the patient. Identifiable disease processes include infections by bacteria, fungi, viruses, and parasites, noninfectious inflammatory or bullous dermatoses, and neoplastic conditions. At times, the symptoms outweigh objective signs, and the patient must be followed regularly to ultimately determine the etiology of her problems. A complete pelvic and speculum examination of the lower genital tract with appropriate cultures is recommended in all patients. Microscopic examination of KOH, Gram's stain, and Tzanck preparations of scale or discharge from the area and examination with Wood's lamp are important maneuvers to correctly identify any infectious pathogen and allow specific therapy. Routine examination of the total skin surface may also provide important clues since the vulvar complaints may represent a more generalized disease process. Often, more than one process is causing the symptoms and eruption: for example, an eczematous dermatitis in the perineum may be secondarily infected by bacteria or *Candida*. In particular, a patient with sexually transmitted disease is at risk for several infections at one time, and the physician must always be suspicious of multiple agents being present.

There are several infectious diseases or infestations that may be localized to the vulva.

Erythrasma presents as asymptomatic, reddish brown scaly plaques in the crural folds. Similar lesions may be present in the axillae or web spaces of the feet. Wood's lamp examination in a darkened room demonstrates a coral red fluorescence to the lesions. Erythrasma is usually caused by *Corynebacterium minutissimum,* which responds to oral erythromycin and various topical antibiotics. Recurrences may be prevented by intensified local hygiene.

Dermatophyte infections are uncommon in the vulvar and inguinal areas of women. Typical lesions are erythematous scaly plaques with well-demarcated, red, scaly "active" borders. The edges are sometimes scalloped with an "advancing front." A scraping of the lesion prepared with KOH and examined microscopically demonstrates hyphae. If the lesions are small and do not involve hairy skin, topical antifungal creams applied twice daily are effective. The treatment should be continued for 7 to 14 days after clinical clearing, to prevent rapid relapse. If large areas or hairy areas are involved, orally administered griseofulvin may be necessary to clear the rash and delay recurrence.

Candidal infection involving the vulvar skin produces pruritus, maceration, erosions, and erythema with satellite lesions consisting of thin-walled 1-mm-diameter pustules. Vaginal candidiasis is often coexistent and should be treated concurrently. It presents with itching, burning, and sometimes dyspareunia and dysuria. A profuse, thick, white vaginal discharge and varying amounts of erythema and edema are seen. KOH preparation of scrapings from the skin lesions or of the vaginal discharge demonstrates budding yeast forms of *Candida* microscopically. Miconazole or clotrimazole vaginal suppositories (100 mg for 7 days or 200 mg for 3 days intravaginally at bedtime) are effective in the management of vaginitis. Miconazole or clotrimazole vaginal creams are alternatives. Nystatin (100,000 units intravaginally at bedtime for 14 days) may be less effective. Cutaneous lesions respond to topical imidazoles or nystatin used twice daily. Predisposing conditions such as pregnancy, diabetes mellitus, or broad-spectrum antibiotic or oral contraceptive therapy should be documented and managed appropriately.

Hidradenitis suppurativa is a chronic suppurative inflammatory disease involving the apocrine sweat glands. The vulva, perineum, and perianal skin may be involved with or without axillary skin involvement. Abscesses and fistulas may form with subsequent induration and scarring of the regions involved. Pain, redness, and swelling are typical. Although the disease is not a primarily infectious process, chronic broad-spectrum antibiotic therapy such as tetracycline or erythromycin is usually helpful in controlling the development of new lesions. In difficult cases, control may be achieved only with antibiotic treatment specifically directed against flora found in rigorous aerobic and anaerobic cultures of abscess contents. Acute painful lesions may require incision and drainage. Surgical extirpation of large involved areas may be necessary and is often curative.

Pediculosis pubis is a sexually transmitted infestation by the blood-sucking louse *Phthirius pubis*. Transmission may also uncommonly occur via clothing or bedding. The prevalence among patients seen in sexually transmitted disease clinics is 2.5% to 5%. About one-third of these patients have another venereal disease. The main symptom is itching. Signs of infestation are the presence of lice, nits attached to hairs, blue-gray macules (maculae caeruleae), or the presence of excreta. While the anogenital region is almost always involved, the axillae, scalp, trunk, thighs, or eyelashes may be infested as well. One percent lindane shampoo (Kwell) or 1% permethrin cream (Nix) applied to affected areas for 4 and 10 minutes, respectively, are equally effective. Contaminated clothing and linen may be disinfected by laundering in hot water or by sealing in plastic bags for 10 days. Sexual partners must be evaluated and treated if also infested. Treatment failures should be retreated, and possible sources of reexposure investigated.

Scabies, while typically producing lesions on the male genitalia, uncommonly cause pruritic papules or nodules on the vulva. Characteristic skin lesions elsewhere with a positive scraping for mites allows definitive diagnosis and therapy.

Larva currens is a parasitic infection that produces rapidly evolving, urticarial, pruritic, serpentine lesions in the perianal skin. The lesions occur in patients with chronic intestinal strongyloidiasis, and the diagnosis is established by identification of the organism in skin biopsies or by identification of larvae in stool specimens. Cutaneous lesions may be a sign of massive infection. Oral thiabendazole is the treatment of choice.

Vaginitis alone or with vaginal itching, dysuria, odoriferous discharge, and reddened edematous mucosa may be caused by infections with *Trichomonas vaginalis* or *Gardnerella vaginalis*. Trichomonads are flagellate, pear-shaped organisms and can be demonstrated in wet preparations of vaginal fluid or spun urine examined microscopically. Metronidazole (250 mg PO tid for 5 to 7 days or 2 g PO once) is an effective agent. Pregnant women may be treated with clotrimazole vaginal suppositories (100 mg at bedtime for 7 days). The *Gardnerella* pathogen may be cultured or detected by the presence of "clue cells" (epithelial cells coated with bacteria) in a wet preparation of the discharge. Amoxicillin or a cephalosporin (500 mg PO tid for 7 days) is an alternative to metronidazole. Both sexual partners should be treated.

Primary herpetic vulvovaginitis may appear 1 to 7 days after exposure to herpes simplex. Localized pain or paresthesias in the vulva, vagina, perineum, buttocks, or thighs are followed by grouped vesicles or blisters on erythematous bases within 24 to 30 hours. The lesions may become widespread with increasing severity of pain. Ulcerations, swelling, fever, malaise, regional lymphadenitis, and urinary retention may occur. When begun early in the disease, acyclovir (200 mg PO 5 times daily for 10 days) is effective in decreasing the duration of pain, the amount of viral shedding, and the severity of the primary eruption. Recurrent episodes of herpes are generally more localized and without systemic manifestations. They may be improved with oral acyclovir (200 mg PO 5 times daily) if instigated at the first evidence of a prodrome (itch or pain at the site) and continued for 5 days. Continuous therapy with acyclovir (200 mg 2–4 times daily) may suppress recurrences in patients with frequent episodes.

Pinworm infection caused by *Enterobius vermicularis* classically presents with perineal and perianal itching. It may occasionally secondarily involve the vulva and vagina when larvae hatch from perianal deposits of eggs and migrate erroneously into the genital tract. Intense pruritus and occasionally a serous discharge are present. The diagnosis should be considered when there is anal pruritus. Microscopic examination of transparent, plastic adhesive tape that has been applied to the perianal region may detect eggs. Wet preparations of vaginal discharge may also be diagnostic. Treatment consists of a single dose of pyrantel pamoate or mebendazole, repeated once 2 weeks later.

Venereal diseases such as gonococcal and *Chlamydia* infections must, of course, be considered in the differential diagnosis of vaginal discharge. With these pathogens, vulvar involvement is usually minimal, and signs and symptoms of cervicitis or pelvic inflammatory disease may be evident. Diagnosis depends on microbiologic identification of the pathogen. Ulcerations of the genitalia are commonly caused by sexually transmitted disease but may also be due to dermatoses, neoplasia, trauma, or systemic illness. Evaluation of genital ulcers of an infectious nature has been covered in another chapter (see chap. 38).

Alterations of the skin of the mons pubis, inguinal folds, perineum, and labia may be present in **inflammatory skin conditions** with or without involvement of other cutaneous or mucosal surfaces. The exclusion of infectious agents by microscopic examination of skin scrapings or by culture is always important. Also, secondary infection of inflammatory conditions must always be considered in these locations. A biopsy should be performed when the clinical appearance is unusual, if lesions fail to respond or if they progress during therapy, or if malignancy is suspected.

Psoriasis of the vulva appears as well-defined, raised, red plaques with fine silvery scales. When plaques are located on mucosal or macerated areas, the scale may not be obvious. The presence of the Auspitz sign (pinpoint bleeding after removal of scale) may confirm the clinical impression. Pustular psoriasis involving the vulva has been described and may be difficult to differentiate from pustular candidiasis. Typical plaques of psoriasis elsewhere are helpful in diagnosis. Maceration will improve with compresses of normal saline or an aluminum salt solution (Burow's solution) applied 4 times a day for 15 minutes. Low-potency topical steroids are used for short periods without occlusion. Prolonged application of high-potency topical steroids should be avoided because of their potential for inducing atrophy and striae in this area. The failure of topical steroid therapy should raise questions about the diagnosis, and a biopsy may be necessary to exclude a neoplastic condition such as squamous cell carcinoma in situ or Paget's disease.

Lichen planus of the vulva produces polygonal, violaceous flat-topped or conical papules with a delicate scale. The papules may coalesce into small plaques. Lesions typically have a reticulated, delicate white scale, which is called Wickham's striae. Mucosal lesions, labial or vaginal, may appear only with Wickham's striae or erosions. Bullae may also occur. The vulva and vagina may be involved primarily or as part of a more generalized eruption. A biopsy is often needed to make the diagnosis, which may be associated with varying degrees of hyperplasia and atypia. Low-potency topical steroids may be helpful, although lesions of lichen planus are usually persistent. Thickened chronic lesions should be biopsied on an annual basis to exclude the development of a squamous cell carcinoma, a rare but well-documented occurrence.

Lichen sclerosus et atrophicus occurs as red or white plaques with loss of skin markings in the inguinal folds, perineum, or inner aspects of the vulva. The labia minora, vestibule, and clitoris are commonly affected, sometimes with constriction of the introitus. The early lesions may be only millimeters in diameter with gradual confluence and enlargement. Well-developed plaques are translucent to stark white with depression and wrinkling similar to cigarette paper. Telangiectases, erosions, blisters, or focal areas of thickening and scale may be present. Extensive areas of thickening or ulceration should be biopsied to exclude neoplasia. The lesions may occur at any age. Itching is common and often severe, although some patients are asymptomatic or complain only of dyspareunia. Extragenital lesions occur occasionally. Therapy includes topical testosterone, topical steroids, and surgical excision. Chronic lesions should be followed carefully for the rare development of squamous cell carcinoma.

Lichen simplex chronicus appears as hyperpigmented and erythematous, poorly demarcated areas of thickened skin with a characteristic accentuation of normal skin markings (lichenification). Lesions on mucosal surfaces are pale or white but without lichenification, and a biopsy is usually necessary to differentiate this dermatosis from other processes. These alterations are secondary to chronic rubbing or scratching, and therapy must be directed toward breaking this behavior. Antihistamines and topical steroids are helpful in diminishing the itch. Irritants, other dermatoses, and neoplasia must be excluded as instigators of chronic scratching behavior.

Seborrheic dermatitis occurs mainly in the pubic area but may extend to the vulva. Pruritus and erythema with scale accumulated around follicles are evident. Often the patient also has seborrheic dermatitis in more typical locations such as the scalp and eyebrows. Low-potency topical steroids or topical ketoconazole may be used for effective control of the process.

Contact dermatitis of the vulva may occur with exposure to agents that are primary irritants or that produce an allergic reaction. Vulvar skin is more sensitive than either vaginal mucosa or the adjacent skin of the extremities or trunk, thus vaginal preparations may cause vulvar dermatitis without an apparent vaginitis. Mild reactions present only with erythema, which is difficult to see on vulvar skin since it typically is pigmented; and accompanying pruritus may be falsely labeled neurogenic. Severe reactions present with intense erythema, watery exudate, and sometimes vesicles. Components of feminine hygiene preparations, spermicides, topical medications, lubricants, condoms, and depilatories are some of the possible causes of contact dermatitis in this area. Detailed historical information is critical, to identify an etiologic agent that can be avoided to prevent recurrence. Avoidance of the offending agent in addition to the use of saline or aluminum salt compresses, low-potency topical steroids, and oral antihistamines is helpful. Oral prednisone may be indicated in severe, well-documented contact reactions.

Primary **blistering diseases** of the skin may present in the vulva or may involve the vulva as part of a generalized eruption. Intact blisters or erosions occur in pemphigus vulgaris, bullous pemphigoid, cicatricial pemphigoid, and epidermolysis bullosa acquisita. Inflammatory dermatoses including erythema multiforme, toxic epidermal necrolysis, lichen planus, lichen sclerosus et atrophicus, and fixed drug eruption may also present with vulvar blisters or erosions. Recognition of typical generalized eruptions and a biopsy are often necessary for correct diagnosis.

Neoplastic conditions, benign and malignant, are common in the vulva and may arise in any location or from any cell type normally present. A large variety of tumors have been reported, although common tumors belong to a relatively small group. They may appear as nodules, exophytic protrusions from the skin surface, thickening of the skin, or endophytic, ulcerating processes. Excision or biopsy may be necessary to differentiate neoplastic from inflammatory or infectious processes.

Condyloma acuminata are warty tumors caused by sexually transmitted human papillomaviruses. The lesions are typically rounded papules with a cobblestoned, pebbly, or verrucous surface. They may be millimeters or centimeters in size and are often multiple. The presence of one condyloma should prompt a search for other lesions on the cervix, vagina, urethral meatus, vulva, perineum, anus, buttocks, and thighs. Sexual partners must be examined and treated. The differential diagnosis includes condyloma lata, a manifestation of secondary syphilis. Therapeutic modalities include cryosurgery with liquid nitrogen, electrocautery, carbon dioxide laser surgery, topical application of podophyllin or fluorouracil, and intralesional injection of interferon. A quick response is unusual; therapy is often prolonged and frustrating. Some sexually transmitted human papillomaviruses, particularly HPV 16 and 18, have been associated with squamous cell carcinoma in situ and with invasive squamous cell carcinomas of the vulva, anus, and cervix. Thus the need for thorough evaluation of the patient and her sexual partners and for application of acetic acid and examination under $10 \times$ magnification (colposcopy) cannot be understated.

Squamous cell carcinoma of the vulva is thought to pass through an in situ phase of relatively long duration before becoming invasive with ominous growth characteristics. In situ lesions are often solitary, scaly white plaques with a predilection for the labia, fourchette, and clitoris, or they may be single or multiple pink-gray patches or papules, quite innocuous in appearance. A black color or a granular texture is observed occasionally. Ulceration is uncommon. Itching may be present. The mean age is in the fifth decade, although a wide range may be affected. Multiple lesions in a young woman suggest bowenoid papulosis, a human papillomavirus–

associated condition that resembles squamous cell carcinoma in situ histologically. Its biologic behavior has not yet been definitely determined. The relationship of vulvar squamous cell carcinoma to human papillomavirus infection is uncertain, although some tumors have been found to contain viral components when studied appropriately. The presence of ulceration, exophytic masses, nodules, or adenopathy implies invasive carcinoma. Any persistent thickening of the skin or lesions that progress despite therapy should be biopsied to exclude carcinoma.

The histopathologic diagnosis of squamous cell carcinoma of the vulva can be difficult, and the terms used by pathologists are often confusing. Hyperplastic lesions—whether they occur de novo, or are associated with a chronic dermatitis such as lichen planus or lichen sclerosus et atrophicus, or are caused by human papillomaviruses—may exhibit a spectrum of histologic changes ranging from completely benign epidermal hyperplasia to various degrees of cytological atypia (dysplasia) to squamous carcinoma in situ to invasive squamous cell carcinoma. The term *vulvar dystrophy* is nonspecific, used by some pathologists to denote these inflammatory and neoplastic processes with or without atypia of the keratinocytes. The pathological diagnosis of squamous atypia or dysplasia is based on the presence of cytological abnormalities of the keratinocytes, the lack of proper epidermal maturation, and the extent of these changes within the epidermis. Such changes are typically reported as dysplasia or as vulvar intraepithelial neoplasia (VIN). The degree of atypia is usually graded and reported as mild dysplasia (VIN I), moderate dysplasia (VIN II), or severe dysplasia or carcinoma in situ (VIN III). Many authorities believe there may be a stepwise progression from dysplasia to carcinoma in situ to invasive carcinoma.

Patients with atypical or dysplastic squamous lesions of the vulva require close follow-up and therapy to prevent the possible occurrence of invasive squamous cell carcinoma. Treatment for atypical squamous lesions of the vulva includes surgical excision, cryotherapy, and carbon dioxide laser vaporization. Mild dysplasia may resolve with repeated application of fluorouracil cream. Squamous cell carcinoma invasive in the skin alone is treated by similar procedures. The goal of therapy is to ablate the lesion with preservation of surrounding normal tissues and function. Deeply invasive disease or disease metastatic to regional lymph nodes requires more radical surgery. Because dysplasia is often associated with human papillomavirus, many patients have multiple lesions, and their sexual partners are at risk for similar disease. Patients are therefore often referred to physicians or clinics performing specialized care.

Extramammary Paget's disease of the vulva is most commonly a malignancy of cutaneous epithelial cells of apocrine origin that spreads superficially but extensively within the epidermis. Less commonly, a urogenital glandular malignancy that metastasized to the vulvar skin is identified. Both processes produce one or more patches or plaques of thickened epidermis, often with a pink, white, or scaly appearance. Microscopic spreading of tumor cells beyond the clinically visible borders of the lesion is common. A nodule in such a plaque indicates an area of tumor invasion within the dermis. Paget's disease limited to the epidermis may be cured by complete excision. Clear margins should be confirmed pathologically. Invasive disease may be followed by local and systemic metastases. Careful clinical and pathological evaluation of patients with vulvar Paget's disease is required to exclude extension into urogenital tissues and to exclude an underlying urogenital malignancy.

Pigmented lesions of the vulva are present in up to 20% of the general population and are usually benign. They may be of melanocytic or squamous cell origin. Flat, dark brown lesions may represent lentigenes or simple hyperpigmentation. Raised dark lesions may be nevi, bowenoid papulosis, condyloma, seborrheic keratoses, or squamous cell carcinoma. Melanomas are rare in the genital tract and represent 5% of all melanomas occurring in women. Prognosis is generally poor even with extensive surgery. Pigmented lesions of uncertain nature or of increasing size should be biopsied or excised. Lesions left intact should be photographed or charted and followed by the physician and the patient. Any change in the lesion should prompt a biopsy. Because of the location, changing lesions may go unnoticed unless a concerted effort is made to follow them closely.

Tumefactive processes in the labia are common and may present as cysts, abscesses, or tumors. Epidermal inclusion cysts arise in the hairy portion of the labia majora. Bartholin's gland cysts are commonly present in the posterior labia majora. Excision or marsupialization is usually curative. Abscesses may occur in the Bartholin's gland, requiring antibiotic therapy and marsupialization. Any tissue removed should always be examined histologically, as benign or malignant tumors may arise in the labia and be mistaken for a Bartholin's gland cyst or abscess. Small, unchanging cysts may be followed conservatively.

Molluscum contagiosum may involve genital skin and is caused by a pox virus of the same name. The lesions are painless, dome-shaped, pink-gray papules with central umbilication. They may be multiple or solitary and range from millimeters to 1 to 2 cm in size. A central white core may be plucked out and examined microscopically with a toluidine blue, safranin, or rose bengal stain to detect the diagnostic intracellular inclusions, or molluscum bodies. Lesions may be treated by curettage, cryosurgery, electrodesiccation, or topical agents such as salicylic acid preparations. Molluscum contagiosum may occur as a sexually transmitted disease, and sexual partners should be examined.

The variety of identifiable conditions that produce vulvar disease is impressive. Nonetheless, there are some cases of vulvar discomfort that have no apparent diagnostic identity or etiology, but may be chronic, debilitating conditions in which pain, dyspareunia, burning, emotional distress, and sexual dysfunction seem out of proportion to clinical findings. These cases have been termed **vulvodynia**, or vulvar vestibular syndrome. The clinician must be diligent in excluding contact dermatitis as well as other dermatologic or systemic illnesses. Inability to diagnose and treat effectively is not an indication for dismissal of the patient's symptoms as depressive or anxiety equivalents. Complete dermatologic, gynecologic, and psychiatric evaluation and support are in the patient's best interest.

Barnhill RL, Albert LS, Shama SK, et al.: Genital lentiginosis: a clinical and histopathologic study. *J Am Acad Dermatol.* 1990;22:453–460.
Ten melanotic macules of the penis and vulva were evaluated. The lesions were relatively large (up to 2 cm), multifocal, irregular in outline, and had variegated pigmentation. Most were regarded as clinically atypical in appearance. Histologic examination showed slight melanocytic hyperplasia, stromal melanophages, and no cytologic atypia of melanocytes. It is not yet possible to predict the natural history of genital lentiginosis or its relation to mucocutaneous melanoma.

Dalziel KL, Millard PR, Wojnarowska F: The treatment of vulval lichen sclerosus with a very potent topical steroid (clobetasol propionate 0.05%) cream. *Br J Dermatol.* 1991;124:461–464.
All 13 patients who completed a 12-week course of twice daily topical applications of clobetasol propionate 0.05% cream showed marked clinical improvement. Histologic measurements of skin biopsies taken before and after treatment showed a significant reduction in the characteristic features of lichen sclerosus. Two patients went into complete clinical and histologic remission.

Degefu S, O'Quinn AG, Dhurandhur HN: Paget's disease of the vulva and urogenital malignancies: a case report and review of the literature. *Gynecol Oncol.* 1986;25:347–354.
Report of a case associated with an underlying urogenital malignancy.

Edwards L: Vulvar lichen planus. *Arch Dermatol.* 1989;125:1677–1680.
The presentation of lichen planus of the vulva varies from subtle, fine, reticulate papules to severe erosive disease accompanied by scarring and loss of the normal vulvar architecture. In most patients with vulvar lichen planus, cutaneous lesions are usually absent, and oral disease may be asymptomatic.

Helm KF, Gibson LE, Muller SA: Lichen sclerosus et atrophicus in children and young adults. *Pediatr Dermatol.* 1991;8:97–101.
A retrospective study of 52 children and young adults revealed that in 56% of patients the eruption was still present after a follow-up of 7.5 years. Younger patients were most likely to show improvement. On average, the condition resolved during adolescence.

Hording U, Daugaard S, Iversen AK, et al.: Human papillomavirus type 16 in vulvar carcinoma, vulvar intraepithelial neoplasia, and associated cervical neoplasia. *Gynecol Oncol.* 1991;42:22–26.

Using polymerase chain reaction to examine vulvar and cervical biopsies from 43 patients with vulvar neoplasia for HPV type 16, DNA sequences were found in 14 of 24 (58%) vulvar squamous cell carcinomas and in 15 of 19 (79%) VIN lesions. Nine patients (21%) had associated cervical neoplasia and six of these harbored HPV 16 in both lesions.

McKay M: Vulvodynia. A multifactorial clinical problem. *Arch Dermatol.* 1989;125:256–262.

Symptomatic vulvar burning (vulvodynia) in the absence of abnormal physical findings may be classified into five sign-symptom complexes: (1) vulvar dermatoses, (2) cyclic vulvitis, (3) vulvar papillomatosis, (4) vulvar vestibulitis, and (5) essential vulvodynia. Remission or exacerbation of symptoms may occur when treatment for one condition affects the onset of another.

Ridley CM: Lichen sclerosus et atrophicus. *Arch Dermatol.* 1988;123:457–460.

Epidemiologic and prognostic information on lichen sclerosus et atrophicus and a synopsis of a classification scheme for vulvar disorders.

Sanchez NP, Mihm MC Jr.: Reactive and neoplastic epithelial alterations of the vulva. *J Am Acad Dermatol.* 1982;6:378–388.

A concise clinicopathologic review of noninfectious vulvar conditions.

78. GINGIVAL HYPERPLASIA
Joop M. Grevelink

The periodontium holds the tooth in place in the jaw. It consists of a mucosal surface (the gingiva), the periodontal ligament, cementum, and the alveolar bone. The gingiva is firmly attached to the alveolar tooth socket as well as to the tooth itself and fills the interdental spaces. The portion that covers the teeth is called the free gingival margin. The gingival mucosa is continuous with the alveolar mucosa, which is continuous with the buccal or labial mucosa. The gingiva may be hyperplastic because of inflammation, tumor, fibroblast proliferation, or mucosal thickening.

Gingivitis, also called periodontitis when it involves the other structures of the periodontium, is a chronic inflammatory process characterized by erythema, swelling, and hypertrophy. It can be generalized, involving the entire gingiva, or localized around one tooth or more, mimicking a nodule. Gingivitis is seen most often in the presence of bacterial plaque, which consists primarily of calcium salts (tartar) in the saliva that are deposited on the teeth. Plaque formation depends on an interplay between mouth flora, saliva, and the normal or diseased local anatomy. Accumulation of plaque leads to gingival inflammation and hypertrophy. Local factors, including irritation, can alter the host's reaction to plaque and to the bacteria that collect around plaque. When gingivitis is allowed to progress to periodontitis, the teeth loosen and eventually fall out. Good oral hygiene consisting of daily brushing of the teeth and flossing of the interdental spaces, as well as regular visits to a dental hygienist, keeps plaque to a minimum.

Systemic **hematologic and immunologic disorders** may be associated with gingivitis. However, even when pronounced hyperplastic gingivitis is seen in conjunction with systemic abnormalities, bacterial plaque is thought to be the inciting factor. Patients with neutrophil dysfunction, neutropenia, or immunodeficiency often have severe gingivitis, periodontal disease, and loss of alveolar bone, suggesting that the immune system plays a protective role in reducing periodontal disease. Gingival hypertrophy occurs more often in acute leukemias than in chronic leukemias (approximately 35% vs. 10%) and in nonlymphocytic leukemia more often than in lymphocytic leukemia. Massive gingival hyperplasia obscuring the teeth, gingival bleeding, and loss of alveolar bone are characteristic of acute monocytic and myelomonocytic leukemias. This severe gingivitis is often caused by disease-associated neutropenia and thrombocytopenia, but in some patients, it may also be due to a true infiltration of leukemic cells. Infiltration of abnormal cells into alveolar bone, producing gingival inflammation, also occurs in Letterer-Siwe disease, a histiocytic proliferative disease that presents with cutaneous, visceral, hematologic, and bony involvement. Gingival engorgement has been described in polycythemia vera and idiopathic thrombocytopenic purpura. Immunologic disorders are also associated with gingival hyperplasia. Selective IgA deficiency is a relatively common immunoglobulin deficiency (prevalence of 1 in 600 in the general population), manifested by gingival hyperplasia, sinopulmonary infections, autoimmune disease, oral ulceration, herpes labialis, and tonsillar hyperplasia. Chediak-Higashi syndrome is a rare autosomal recessive disorder in which the function of the neutrophil is impaired. It is characterized by oculocutaneous albinism, recurrent infections, hematologic and neurologic abnormalities, and death in the early teens. Gingival hyperplasia is frequently present.

Drugs cause gingival hyperplasia by inducing neutropenia and immunosuppression or by altering fibroblast proliferation and metabolism. Cyclosporin-A is known to affect both the immune system and the fibroblast. Gingival hyperplasia related to its use is most often confined to the free gingival margin and the interdental papilla. It is often associated with bleeding of the gums and persists as long as the patient is on the drug. Calcium channel-blocking agents, particularly nifedipine, have been reported to cause either a nodular or a diffuse gingival hyperplasia. Both altered calcium metabolism and increased fibroblasts that contain mucopolysaccharides have been implicated. Proliferation of fibroblasts containing sulfated mucopolysaccharides has also been observed in phenytoin-induced gingival hyperplasia, which occurs in approximately 50% of patients on the drug. The hyperplasia disappears slowly after discontinuation of the drug.

Benign and malignant primary **tumors** of the gingiva can produce solitary or multiple nodules of the gingiva. Gingival nodules require a biopsy and a histologic examination for adequate diagnosis. Benign tumors that have been reported in the gingiva include odontoma, congenital myoblastoma, giant-cell epulis, epulis gravidarum, pyogenic granuloma, hemangioendothelioma, and leiomyoma. Multiple benign fibromas occur in Cowden's syndrome, an autosomal dominant disorder of multiple hamartomas and internal malignancies, and give a cobblestone appearance to the surface of the mucosa. A similar clinical picture may be seen with multiple neuromas in patients with the syndrome of multiple endocrine neoplasia; with multiple angiofibromas seen in tuberous sclerosis; and with abnormal mucosal keratinization associated with Darier-White disease. Malignant tumors that present as gingival nodules include squamous cell carcinoma, melanoma, ameloblastoma, granular cell tumor, and leiomyosarcoma. Squamous cell carcinoma (epidermoid carcinoma) is the most common. It may appear as a white plaque (leukoplakia) or as an inflammatory nodule with ulceration, often misdiagnosed in patients wearing dentures as traumatic hypertrophy. Primary melanomas usually affect the upper gingiva. The presenting complaint may be hyperpigmentation, nodule, or pain. The prognosis is very poor for patients with gingival melanomas, even after radical therapy. Although rare, metastases to the gingiva also occur and have been most frequently reported from adenocarcinoma and melanoma.

A broad spectrum of oral lesions (glossitis, cheilitis, stomatitis, gingivitis) is often attributed to **vitamin deficiency,** despite the lack of well-controlled studies. Best substantiated clinically is the association of gingivitis with the lack of either niacin or vitamin C. In particular, a severe gingivitis with hemorrhage, ulceration, and purpura occurs in patients with other manifestations of scurvy (vitamin C deficiency). Adequate oral hygiene by itself seems sufficient to reverse the gingivitis.

Gingival hyperplasia occurs as a component of several **genetic syndromes.** Papillon-Lefèvre syndrome is inherited as an autosomal recessive trait and is manifested by redness and diffuse hyperkeratosis of the palms and soles and by psoriasiform lesions on the knees and elbows. Characteristic of this syndrome is premature loss of deciduous and permanent teeth, preceded by gingival inflammation and hyperkeratosis that are usually apparent within the first few years of life. Patients with Down's syndrome, when compared with other retarded individuals, have more severe periodontal disease present at a younger age. Increased pocket formation at the free gingival margin and alveolar bone loss lead to early loss of teeth. Mucolipidosis II (I-cell disease), a rare autosomal recessive disorder, is characterized by severe psychomotor retardation, shortness of stature, Hurler-like facial features, and gingival enlargement, often associated with hypocalcification of the dental enamel. Gingival fibromatoses are a group of congenital disorders that share gingival fibromatosis (GF) but are distinguished by other features. These disorders include

GF without hypertrichosis (autosomal dominant)
GF with hypertrichosis or epilepsy (autosomal dominant)
GF with cartilage defects, absent nails, hepatosplenomegaly (autosomal dominant; Zimmerman-Laband syndrome)
GF with microphthalmia, mental retardation, athetosis and hypopigmentation of the skin (autosomal recessive; Cross syndrome)
GF with progressive deafness (autosomal dominant)
GF with mental deficiency, aggressive behavior, corneal opacities, dental root resorption, dentigerous cysts (autosomal dominant; Rutherfurd syndrome)
GF with multiple hyaline fibromas in the skin, painful flexion contractures, generalized osteoporosis, osteolysis of terminal phalanges, recurrent infections (autosomal recessive; Murray-Puretic-Drescher syndrome).

Gingival hyperplasia may be associated with **endocrinologic disorders.** Although no good studies are available at present that conclusively link diabetes to periodontal disease, there seems to be general agreement that in diabetes a susceptibility to dental plaque formation and subsequent gingival hyperplasia is increased, probably because of a defect in polymorphonuclear cell chemotaxis. In pregnancy, gingivitis is a commonly observed phenomenon, especially toward the end of the first trimester. It may also be seen with the use of oral contraceptives. Papillomatous enlargement of the gingiva can be seen in acanthosis nigricans, with either inherited or noninherited forms, or when it is associated with other endocrinologic diseases. Accompanying the oral lesions is a velvety hyperpigmentation of the skin in flexural areas.

Other rare processes may be associated with gingivitis. Granulomatous inflammation of the gingiva may mimic multiple pyogenic granulomas. It is most often seen in **Wegener's granulomatosis,** a necrotizing vasculitis predominantly localized to the upper respiratory tract and kidneys. Destruction of underlying alveolar bone may be associated. Congenital exposure to **polychlorinated biphenyl** (PCB) is characterized by intrauterine growth retardation, open fontanelles, overgrowth of the gingiva, and brown staining of teeth, skin, and mucous membranes.

Evaluation of a patient with gingival hyperplasia and inflammation includes a comprehensive medical history and a complete physical examination with the clinician looking for evidence of local or systemic factors associated with gingivitis. As noted above, the differential diagnosis in children includes primarily genetic disorders and drugs, while in adults an altered immune system, endocrinologic disorders, drugs, neoplasia, and paraneoplastic phenomena should be considered. **Treatment** is directed both toward management of the primary illness and toward control of dental plaque formation, since in many of these processes, plaque and the host's reaction to plaque play a definitive role in eliciting and maintaining the hyperplasia of the gingiva. Effective oral hygiene by itself may be sufficient to reverse gingivitis. If the gingivitis fails to improve or if it is marked by one nodule or more or an atypical appearance, a biopsy is necessary to exclude malignant tumors.

Bartkowski SB, Panas M, Wilczanska H, et al.: Primary malignant melanoma of the oral cavity. A review of 20 cases. *Am J Surg.* 1984;148:362–366.
    The first symptom in 50% of patients was hyperpigmentation of the mucosa; other presenting complaints were tumor and pain. Radical surgery was ineffective in 12 of 13 patients.
Brown RS, Beaver WT, Bottomley WK. On the mechanism of drug-induced gingival hyperplasia. *J Oral Pathol Med.* 1991;20:201–209.
    The multiple proposed mechanisms causing drug-induced gingival hyperplasia are reviewed. They include hypotheses with regard to inflammation from bacterial plaque,

increased sulfated glycosaminoglycans, immunoglobulins, gingival fibroblast phenotype population differences, epithelial growth factor, pharmacokinetics and tissue-binding, collagenase activation, and disruption of fibroblast cellular sodium/calcium flux.

Butler RT, Kalkwarf KL, Kaldahl WB: Drug-induced gingival hyperplasia: phenytoin, cyclosporine, and nifedipine. *J Am Dent Assoc.* 1987;114:56–60.

After summarizing observations and results of laboratory and clinical studies of gingival hyperplasia associated with these drugs, the authors report that the primary preventative measure is to maintain a high standard of oral hygiene and to eliminate gingival irritation.

Seymour RA: Calcium channel blockers and gingival overgrowth. *Br Dent J.* 1991;25:376–379.

All classes of calcium channel blockers have been implicated in causing gingival overgrowth. This review discusses the prevalence, clinical features, histopathology, and management of this side effect.

van der Bijl P, Dreyer WP, Radomsky JB: Drug-induced gingival hyperplasia. Selective review of the literature and a photometric assessment technique. *Ann Dent.* 1989;48:16–21, 46.

This article reviews possible mechanisms for the causation of gingival overgrowth and also describes a photometric technique for assessing this problem.

XIII. PRINCIPLES OF THERAPY

79. COSMETICS
Christopher R. Shea

The fields of cosmetology and dermatology maintain an uneasy alliance for several reasons. First, a number of cosmetic manufacturers have promoted their products with fanciful, pseudomedical claims to "rejuvenate" skin, "encourage" hair growth, and the like; the reader is referred to the chapter on cutaneous quackery for further discussion. Second, the greatest disability from many skin diseases stems from their effects on personal appearance and body image rather than from pain, itching, or loss of function; a concern for cosmesis thus embraces an affirmative concept of the health of the skin as more than the absence of disease. Finally, many cosmetic and toiletry products can induce adverse reactions in the skin, such as contact dermatitis, folliculitis, and so forth. The distinction between cosmetology and normal skin care is difficult to delineate, and the proliferation of cosmetic products and their numerous ingredients can be bewildering.

Products for styling, grooming, and coloring hair are numerous. Hair sprays contain film polymers that set the hair in its groomed configuration. As with all the cosmetics to be discussed, the active ingredient (in this case, the polymer) is only one of many, including solvent, propellant, perfume, and so on. Such additional ingredients can be very important causes of adverse reactions, as discussed below. Bleaches usually have hydrogen peroxide as their active ingredient, which oxidizes the melanin within the hair shaft. Most hair dyes (so-called permanent dyes) also contain hydrogen peroxide, which serves both to bleach the natural hair color and to oxidize a color intermediate into its pigmented form; the color intermediates are typically diamines such as p-phenylenediamine. Other classes of hair dyes include vegetable dyes, such as henna, and "hair restorers" that darken the hair gradually by the formation of sulfides of lead or bismuth. Permanent wave products contain an alkaline (pH 8–10) solution of thioglycolate, which breaks disulfide bonds of keratin by reduction, allowing the hair to be set in a curled position; in a second step, the thioglycolate is quenched by acid and the thioglycolate bonds are reformed by action of hydrogen peroxide. Hair relaxers contain a similar thioglycolate solution, or else sodium bisulfite or sodium hydroxide; the neutralizer employed depends on the particular reducing agent. Depilatories are a more extreme example of a similar kind of formulation: a thioglycolate, sulfide, or sodium stannite is applied with strong alkali (pH 12.5), which is then rinsed and neutralized. *Epilation,* in contrast to *depilation,* denotes the removal of hair below the skin surface; epilation can be effected by the application of heated, liquid waxes (such as beeswax) in colophony, which harden upon cooling and pull out the hair when removed.

Perfumes are found in a huge variety of products, not only in colognes, aftershave lotions, and perfumes as such. For example, many detergents, toothpastes, fabric softeners, and topical medications contain fragrance products. Even cosmetics labeled "unscented" may contain a masking perfume, such as ethylene brassylate (musk T). The dermatologic importance of perfumes resides in their ability to provoke contact dermatitis.

Bleaching creams are intended to lighten dark skin, whether diffusely or focally, for conditions such as melasma or lentigo. In the past, components such as mercurials were used and sometimes caused severe reactions (e.g., nephrotoxicity, neurotoxicity) from systemic absorption. Present formulations contain hydroquinone, which is generally safe except for irritant reactions (which can eventuate in hyperpigmentation) and rare instances of nail pigmentation and cutaneous pseudoochronosis. The effect of hydroquinone is temporary and often less than satisfactory; the use of bleaching creams should always be combined with adequate protection from UV radiation.

Most **facial makeup** products have similar pigment mixtures, which are formulated in different vehicles to make powders, creams, and fluids. The pigments themselves include iron oxide, a large assortment of organic red dyes, micas, and others. Eye makeup pigments are similar, although the variety of desired shades requires the use of a larger assortment of pigments for green (chrome oxides), blue (ferric ferrocyanide), orange (tartrazine), and so forth. Again, the vehicle determines the final form, whether a powder, stick, or fluid. Lipsticks are largely lipid (carnauba wax or beeswax) with appropriate solvents, pigments, and antioxidants.

Nail lacquers contain film polymers and polymer resins, together with pigments similar to those used in facial cosmetics, dissolved in organic solvents such as toluene. Artificial nails can be affixed with acrylate-type glues or applied as acryl-type polymers. Nail lacquer removers are mostly organic solvents such as acetone.

Corrective cosmetics are products used to disguise a frank deformity. Ugliness, like beauty, is in the eye of the beholder, and therefore whether one decides to go to some trouble to cover up a lesion depends greatly on one's personality, as well as on the social climate in which one lives. In some societies, for example, vitiligo is a disease with disastrous consequences for marriage and employment. Corrective makeup is valuable not only for this disorder but also for disguising scars, hyperpigmentation, vascular lesions, healing incisions, and ecchymoses. Artful use of cosmetics can also minimize physical traits that are normal but are considered unbecoming.

The sheerness or translucency of most normal cosmetics, currently considered a desirable property, is a detriment for disguising major defects such as extensive vitiligo or port-wine stains. A higher concentration of pigments, especially of light-scattering ingredients such as titanium dioxide and iron oxides, is therefore added to corrective cosmetics. After the makeup cream is applied, sealing powders may be dusted on to waterproof the application. It is not easy to find or blend the right color (which must be done in appropriate lighting), to apply the makeup evenly, or to keep it from smudging during the day. Some manufacturers have "clinics" that teach the appropriate skills; in the right hands, corrective makeup can produce magnificent results. Sometimes, optical tricks such as using a green-tinged makeup to disguise a red lesion are helpful. Another type of corrective cosmetic, used almost exclusively to mask vitiligo, contains dihydroxyacetone. Such products tend to stay on the skin longer and are therefore less trouble to use; unfortunately, however, the match between the stain and the patient's natural skin color can be poor. Vitiligo patients using such products should also use broad-spectrum sunscreens, both because vitiliginous skin is not adequately protected by the stain and because tanning of the adjacent, normal skin will enhance the contrast.

It is well established that numerous chemicals can be **comedogenic** when applied to human skin. Chief among these chemicals are coal tar products and aromatic hydrocarbons. Compared to these agents, cosmetics appear to be only mildly comedogenic. *Pomade acne* was introduced in 1970 to describe an eruption of comedones, and rarely inflammatory lesions, in black men who had used hair oils daily for a year or more. Subsequently, the concept of acne cosmetica was advanced to explain a low-grade facial acne in women using a variety of facial cosmetics. In order to screen cosmetics for this effect, as well as to quantify the degree of comedogenicity, the rabbit ear model is often used. In this assay, the inner skin of the external ear canal of a rabbit is painted with the substance to be tested, generally 5 times a week for 2 weeks, and the development of comedones is then assessed. Histopathologically, the follicular plugging produced in this model is very similar to that seen in acne vulgaris in human skin. The chief advantage of the model is that the rabbit ear is much more sensitive than human skin; for this reason, compounds that are not comedogenic in the rabbit ear model may be considered noncomedogenic in human skin. The model has been criticized in view of the subjectivity involved in assessing the degree of comedogenicity and also because of discrepancies between different laboratories in assessing certain products. Modified rabbit ear models, employing histologic as well as noninvasive techniques to quantify the changes more accurately, have been proposed in recent years. Despite some controversy, the rabbit ear model is widely accepted.

According to results of the rabbit ear model, a wide variety of cosmetics have been declared comedogenic. There is no clear chemical similarity among all classes of comedogenic cosmetics, and the pathophysiologic basis of this effect is unclear. It is not true, as is often supposed by patients, that all oils are intrinsically bad for acne; furthermore, a number of non-oil products, including blush and rouge compounds, are comedogenic according to this assay. It is difficult for the practicing dermatologist to keep abreast of all the potential comedogenic risks of cosmetics; the formulation of products is often changed without notification, and particular lines of cosmetics include products that have markedly different degrees of comedogenicity. It appears that acne cosmetica occurs more frequently in women who have a history of acne in the past, although it can arise de novo. If acne cosmetica is suspected, an attempt at elimination of at least some facial cosmetics may be warranted.

It is difficult to assess the true incidence of **contact reactions** to cosmetics because the majority are undoubtedly not reported, the patient simply changing to a different type of cosmetic. Several surveys in the United States and abroad have been performed, but the results are quite discordant with respect to both the overall incidence of adverse cosmetic reactions and the relative risk of various products. One of the largest studies in recent years, that of Adams and Maibach, found that allergic contact dermatitis was far more frequent than irritant, photoallergic, or phototoxic reactions. The most frequent causes of cutaneous reactions were found to be fragrances, preservatives and p-phenylenediamine, in that order. The particular fragrances responsible were not always discovered, as it is common practice to patch-test for fragrance allergy with a mix of ingredients. The most frequent preservative found to cause cutaneous reactions was quaternium-15. The most frequent body site affected was the face, and this finding reflects both the frequency of cosmetic use on facial skin and the intrinsic sensitivity of facial skin to contact dermatitis. It is notable that facial eruptions can be caused by nail lacquers, for example, while periungual dermatitis from these products is unusual. In a study by de Groot et al., the preservative Kathon CG was by far the most common allergen in cosmetics; however, Kathon CG is not commonly used by American cosmetic manufacturers. The dermatologist must maintain a high index of suspicion of cosmetic reactions when confronted with a case of dermatitis of unknown cause. In half the patients studied by Adams and Maibach, cosmetics were not initially suspected, by either the physician or the patient, to have caused dermatitis that was later proved by patch testing to be due to cosmetics. Cosmetic reactions may present with a distinctive distribution of lesions, as with aerosol reactions to hair sprays. Similarly, the pattern in a phototoxic or photoallergic reaction may be clinically distinctive. Numerous ingredients have been demonstrated as capable of causing photoreactions—including musk ambrette, which can cause photoallergic and persistent light reactions, and bergapten (5-methoxypsoralen), previously used in perfumes such as Shalimar.

As in other cases of suspected contact dermatitis, patch testing can be useful when a cosmetic reaction is suspected. The problem of nonspecific, irritant reactions must be considered, and appropriate dilutions of products, especially when the natural solvent is volatile, may be necessary. Positive reactions to balsam of Peru or fragrance mix may indicate the possibility of cross-reactions to a wide variety of chemicals, including cinnamates in toothpastes, tincture of benzoin, and so forth. It is said that p-phenylenediamine, when fully oxidized to dye in hair, is nonallergenic, although this point is controversial. Finally, the dermatologist who suspects a cosmetic reaction must not narrow his diagnostic focus too much; there are well-documented cases of reactions to rubber sponges and other cosmetic applicators rather than to the cosmetic itself.

Adams RM, Maibach HI: A five-year study of cosmetic reactions. *J Am Acad Dermatol*. 1985;13:1062–1069.

Impressive study of 713 patients with cosmetic dermatitis out of a total of 281,000 patients seen by 12 dermatologists over 5 years. In half the cases, it was not initially suspected that cosmetics were responsible. Fragrances, preservatives, p-phenylenediamine, and glycerol monothioglycolate were the most frequent allergic sensitizers.

Bergfeld WF, Elder RL, Schroeter AL: The cosmetic ingredient review self-regulatory safety program. *Dermatol Clin*. 1991;105–122.

The CIR is a system of documentation, review, and analysis of cosmetic ingredients. To date, 310 ingredients have been evaluated.

de Groot AC, Bruynzeel DP, Bos JD, et al.: The allergens in cosmetics. *Arch Dermatol*.

1988;124:1525–1529.

In this prospective study of 119 European patients, preservatives (especially Kathon AG) were the most common allergens, followed by fragrances and emulsifiers.

Dooms-Goossens A: Reducing sensitizing potential by pharmaceutical and cosmetic design. *J Am Acad Dermatol.* 1984;10:547–553.

There are various ways to reduce the risk of allergic contact dermatitis, including changes in solvent, chemical modification, and addition of antioxidants, sequestering agents, diluents, or neutralizing agents.

Draelos ZK: *Cosmetics in Dermatology.* New York, NY: Churchill Livingstone; 1989.

Short, inexpensive, and authoritative paperback covering most aspects of cosmetics.

Engasser PG, Maibach HI: Cosmetics and dermatology: bleaching creams. *J Am Acad Dermatol.* 1981;5:143–147.

This brief review concludes that hydroquinone is generally safe but relatively ineffective at lightening skin.

Fulton JE Jr., Pay SR, Fulton JE III: Comedogenicity of current therapeutic products, cosmetics, and ingredients in the rabbit ear. *J Am Acad Dermatol.* 1984;10:96–105.

Good review, with product names, of cosmetic testing in the rabbit ear model.

Larsen WG: Perfume dermatitis. *J Am Acad Dermatol.* 1985;12:1–12.

Fragrance materials are the most common cause of allergic contact dermatitis to cosmetics. Fragrances are present in many types of cosmetic and noncosmetic products, not just in perfumes. Patch testing with the fragrance mix can be used for screening, but irritant false-positive reactions are not uncommon; the author therefore recommends testing individual components instead.

Mills OH, Kligman AM: Comedogenicity of sunscreens. *Arch Dermatol.* 1982;118:417–419.

The vehicles rather than the active ingredients appear to be responsible for comedogenicity. Coconut oil and cocoa butter are culprits. Comedogenicity of some products was enhanced by exposure of the rabbit ear to UV radiation.

Nater JP, DeGroot AC: *Unwanted Effects of Cosmetics and Drugs Used in Dermatology.* 2nd ed. New York, NY: Elsevier; 1985.

Not a cozy bedside read, this encyclopedic text exhaustively lists ingredients in cosmetics and discusses their hazards, especially with regard to contact dermatitis. Extraordinarily complete bibliography.

O'Donoghue MN, ed.: *Dermatol Clin.* 1991;9.

This issue contains 17 useful reviews on topics related to cosmetics and cosmetic surgery.

Plewig G, Fulton JE, Kligman AM: Pomade acne. *Arch Dermatol.* 1970;101:580–584.

Even products of relatively low comedogenic potential, such as mineral oil, can cause acne after prolonged daily use.

Seidel L, Copeland I: *The Art of Corrective Makeup.* Garden City, NY: Doubleday; 1984.

The text understandably includes a good deal of self-promotion for the Seidel brand of cosmetics, but it also gives valuable advice on methods of application.

Tucker SB, Flannigan SA, Dunbar M, et al.: Development of an objective comedogenicity assay. *Arch Dermatol.* 1986;122:660–665.

In the rabbit ear model, planimetry of follicular orifices, from either biopsy specimens or silastic casts, permitted more precise quantification of comedogenicity.

80. TOPICAL THERAPY

R. Rox Anderson

The skin and eyes are exposed organs available for direct application of drugs and other compounds. When the target organ for drug therapy is the skin itself, topical application can often achieve higher levels in the epidermis and upper dermis than systemic administration of the same drug, yet with less systemic toxicity. Many safe topical agents would be toxic or lethal if oral or systemic routes were used to achieve effective drug levels in the skin. Drugs with otherwise poor bioavailability or rapid metabolic degradation may be excellent therapeutic agents when administered topically. With topical therapy, drug levels are highest in the stratum corneum, decreasing rapidly with depth because of removal and metabolism. Topical therapy is therefore ideally suited for delivery of compounds to the stratum corneum, epidermis, and papillary dermis, and is generally less appropriate for the treatment of deep cutaneous disorders.

For target organs other than skin, the skin sometimes offers a useful route of administration. The impressive barrier function of skin can be viewed as both an impediment and an advantage for topical administration of systemic drugs. Large or charged molecules are either excluded or penetrate very slowly into normal skin. On the other hand, the skin can act as a reservoir and slow-release system, a particularly useful function when one is administering drugs that are rapidly metabolized. At present, cardiac nitrates, scopolamine, clonidine, nicotine, and estradiol are available as transcutaneous systemic drugs. Further scientific development of transcutaneous drug delivery holds great promise.

The stratum corneum provides the major barrier to entrance of substances into the skin and to passive loss of water from the skin. It is specifically adapted for its function as a barrier. Eight to fifteen lamellae of flattened, 1-μm-thick, keratin-laden corneocytes are tightly stacked and attached by lipophilic cement substances. The alternation of hydrophilic and hydrophobic planes provides a diffusion barrier for most molecules that rivals or exceeds the best plastic food wrappings. There is no bulk transport through the stratum corneum, and sweat ducts play little or no role in drug penetration. Even in hairy skin, follicular penetration represents a minor contribution to percutaneous absorption of most drugs, although it may yield more rapid penetration for low-molecular-weight hydrophilic drugs. By far, the most important route for topical drug penetration is passive diffusion through the complex structures of the stratum corneum. Removal of stratum corneum by stripping with tape increases permeability and water loss by one or more orders of magnitude.

In general, percutaneous absorption is greatest for low-molecular-weight and lipophilic (nonpolar) compounds. Free ions, large polymers, and the various proteins and nucleic acids, often found in cosmetics and claimed to have specific benefits, have essentially no uptake into the skin. For any given substance, Fick's law of diffusion is obeyed, such that the steady-state flux through the skin is directly proportional to (1) the concentration of the applied substance, (2) its diffusion coefficient in the stratum corneum, and (3) its partition coefficient between the externally applied vehicle and the stratum corneum. In addition, diffusion is inversely proportional to the thickness of the stratum corneum. These four primary factors determine the uptake of various compounds.

Many practical issues affect percutaneous absorption. Hydration of the stratum corneum either by soaking or occlusion increases the diffusion of most compounds through it by an order of magnitude over otherwise similar nonoccluded applications. Vehicles strongly affect partitioning of drug between the external surface and the stratum corneum; therefore, the same concentration of the same drug usually has different potencies when applied in different vehicles. Varying the vehicle is a frequent cause for relative ineffectiveness of generic topical formulations. Body site is another major factor, related primarily to thickness of the stratum corneum. The penetration of hydrocortisone is 40 times higher in scrotal skin than in forearm skin, and 7 times higher in forearm skin than in plantar skin. Nail plates have much greater permeability per unit thickness than stratum corneum, especially when hydrated with water and occlusion. The age of the patient also affects diffusion, best studied in children. The skin of premature infants generally has decreased barrier function. Full-term infants and children appear to have skin with normal barrier function for hydrophilic compounds, but moderately increased permeability for lipophilic compounds. In addition, the surface area to body mass ratio is much higher in childhood, so that systemic side effects of topical therapy are more likely.

The stratum corneum may be stripped to improve diffusion. The usual method is to apply adhesive tape and then pull off quickly. More exotic means such as an excimer laser have been proposed theoretically. Parakeratotic dermatoses and open lesions have abnormal or absent stratum corneum, with increased or highly variable permeability. "Penetrants" and lipid solvents have also been used to enhance the penetration of drugs into skin. The most studied and controversial penetrant is dimethyl sulfoxide (DMSO), a solvent that is restricted in the United States because of potential toxicity. DMSO appears to replace water in the stratum corneum, leading to partially reversible enhanced pathways for diffusion. Other solvents such as acetone and alcohols extract some of the intercellular and intracellular lipids that limit hydrophilic compound diffusion. Frequently found in topical preparations, they are added mainly for their ability to solubilize drugs or vehicle components.

One major goal of topical therapy, namely the alteration of the physical condition of the skin, has little to do with a specific therapeutic agent; it is generally the result of the vehicle in which the drug has been mixed in order for it to be administered topically. The appearance and feel of the skin may be changed by increasing or decreasing the moisture content of the stratum corneum, removing scale, and debriding, precipitating or drying exudates, as well as cooling the surface to produce vasoconstriction. The rationale for choosing among vehicles such as ointments, creams, lotions, and powders depends on which specific physical effects are desired. The vehicle in topical therapy is, therefore, as much an "active" ingredient as any drug, and is frequently the major beneficial component. The vehicle may also adversely affect treatment. A drying vehicle used to treat a dry, fissured dermatitis can exacerbate the eruption or an ingredient in the vehicle may superimpose an irritant or allergic contact dermatitis. The popular adage If the skin is wet, dry it, or if the skin is dry, wet it is both a useful and deceptively simple statement about one of the functions of a vehicle. For example, the most effective way to "wet" the skin is to apply greasy ointments, water-in-oil ointments, or occlusive wrappings, preferably to moistened skin. Rubbed-in applications of oils or simple ointments such as petrolatum after bathing are the mainstay of treating xerosis and chronic eczematous or papulosquamous disorders. Conversely, the most effective way to "dry" skin that is involved with acute, exudative dermatoses is to periodically apply cool, wet compresses with or without astringents, followed by open air or absorbent powders. Therefore, for this use, lotions (aqueous solutions) or gels are the vehicles of choice rather than ointments. Such treatments are antipruritic, vasoconstricting, drying, and debriding. Often patient preference, cosmetic considerations, or other practical issues ultimately determine what type of preparation will be used, and it is wise to have patients test both the type of preparation and its recommended application before they leave the office. The range of topical preparations is wide.

Wet dressings are water- or saline-soaked cotton gauze or cloth compresses used for oozing, weeping, crusted, bullous, eroded, or ulcerated skin. They are usually applied for 10 to 30 minutes 3 to 4 times daily. Evaporation from the dressing soothes and dries by cooling the skin surface and causing vasoconstriction. Wet compresses also facilitate the removal of crusts and exudate atraumatically. If the compress is allowed to dry, its removal debrides the skin ("wet-to-dry" dressing), but may create more trauma than necessary. If the dressing is applied and then covered (a closed wet dressing), maceration and heating occur, neither of which are useful in treating skin disease. Agents frequently used in wet dressings are compounds that precipitate protein and thereby decrease exudation (astringents), such as aluminum acetate in weak aqueous solution (Burow's solution, Domeboro or Blu-Boro). Also added to wet dressings in some situations are antimicrobial agents such as silver nitrate, acetic acid, povidone-iodine, chlorhexidine, and neomycin. Additives, especially neomycin, may be associated with allergic contact sensitivity, which must be suspected if an acute eczematous condition continues despite therapy.

Lotions are usually aqueous solutions that contain some oil, fragrance, preservatives, stabilizers, and often a high percentage of alcohols. **Gels** are similar aqueous or alcoholic solutions to which a gel-state polymer has been added. They are solids at room temperature but melt at skin temperature. They are easier to apply than lotions, but on contact with the skin, a gel behaves much like a lotion. Evaporation of the aqueous phase cools and dries, and is often soothing. Lotions and gels are best used for oozing and weeping acute dermatoses. Common therapeutic agents added to lotions and gels include antibiotics (e.g., in the treatment of acne) and corticosteroids (for the treatment of inflammatory dermatoses). Lotions and gels are particularly useful in hairy areas in whites, for whom greasy hair is seldom cosmetically acceptable; however, blacks and other individuals with kinky hair frequently prefer ointments or oily creams, which enhance the ability to comb and care for hair.

Creams are oil-in-water suspensions or emulsions, in which microscopic droplets of lipid phase material are suspended in an external, continuous hydrophilic phase. Creams also contain stabilizers, preservatives, and usually some alcohols. Oil-in-water creams are therefore easily mixed with, and washed away by, water. After application, creams seem to disappear with evaporation of the aqueous phase ("vanishing creams"), leaving a nearly imperceptible deposition of the less volatile phase. As with lotions and gels, evaporation produces a drying effect. Creams are therefore not generally useful in the treatment of dermatoses associated with dry skin. Drugs in creams may partition to either the hydrophobic or hydrophilic compartments. Creams are useful vehicles for administering antibiotics and corticosteroids.

Ointments employ lipophilic bases. They are occlusive and promote hydration, both of which facilitate delivery of many drugs, including corticosteroids. Ointments are therefore generally more effective vehicles than creams and lotions, in addition to their promotion of a softer, smoother skin surface. An ointment is the vehicle of choice in the treatment of any dry dermatosis. Water-soluble ointments contain inert oils that are miscible with water, such as polyethylene glycols (carbowaxes), and are useful, rarely irritating skin lubricants. Water-in-oil ointments ("cold creams") are not washable or miscible with water, since the external phase is hydrophobic. They will, however, take up water in significant amounts. Water-in-oil ointments contain emulsifiers and look grossly like creams, but failure to simply wash them from the fingers with water can easily identify the difference. Absorbable ointments such as hydrophilic petrolatum, or Aquaphor, are in essence water-in-oil ointments without the water but with the added emulsifiers. They take up water from the environment and are difficult to wash off. Water-repellent ointments are simple hydrophobic ointments such as petrolatum. They are very stable and in general do not require additives, so that irritant or allergic contact dermatitis is exceedingly rare with their use. Of all the vehicles, they are the most occlusive and therefore the most effective. Unfortunately, they are often the least cosmetically acceptable to patients, a problem sometimes overcome by showing the patient that "rubbing in" a sparing application does not lead to greasy, shiny skin.

Powders are dry solids that are useful to promote drying by supplying a large surface area for evaporation, a property which also reduces friction. Thus, they are usually used in intertriginous areas. Talc, a mineral powder, is nonabsorbent and well tolerated. In contrast, starch or cellulose powders may absorb water and form an irritating paste. Starch powders may also exacerbate or promote yeast infections since *Candida albicans* can readily metabolize glycogen. Many powder formulations are available with antibacterial, antimonilial, or antifungal agents. Powders may also be suspended in an ointment to form a **paste**, which is somewhat less occlusive than an ointment. Pastes have been popular in the past, but they are difficult to compound and generally leave a visible residue, so they are now used relatively infrequently.

As already mentioned, vehicles frequently contain **other ingredients.** Emulsifiers are used to stabilize the phase separations in creams and absorbable ointments. The most familiar emulsifiers are soaps and detergents or anionic surfactants such as sodium lauryl sulfate and quaternary ammonium compounds. Some neutral emulsifiers are available, including polysorbates, lanolin (wool fats), and carbowaxes. Stabilizers and preservatives are used to prevent oxidation and microbial growth. Parabens, esters of *p*-hydroxybenzoic acid, are especially common additives and, unfortunately, may also cause allergic sensitization. Solvents such as alcohols, acetone, and propylene glycol are present in most vehicles and may irritate the skin if present in high concentrations or if applied to already inflamed skin with an altered chemical barrier function.

Table 80-1 Topical steroid agents and potencies

1 (most potent)	Betamethasone dipropionate cream, ointment 0.05% (optimized vehicle) (Diprolene) Clobetasol propionate cream, ointment 0.05% (Temovate) Diflorasone diacetate ointment 0.05% (optimized vehicle) (Psorcon) Halobetasol propionate cream, ointment 0.05% (Ultravate)
2	Amcinonide ointment 0.1% (Cyclocort) Betamethasone dipropionate ointment 0.05% (Diprosone) Desoximethasone cream, ointment 0.25%, gel 0.05% (Topicort) Diflorasone diacetate ointment 0.05% (Florone, Maxiflor) Fluocinonide cream, ointment, gel 0.05% (Lidex, Lidex-E) Halcinonide cream 0.1% (Halog)
3	Betamethasone benzoate gel 0.025% (Benisone, Uticort) Betamethasone dipropionate cream 0.025% (Diprosone) Betamethasone valerate ointment 0.1% (Valisone) Diflorasone diacetate cream 0.05% (Florone, Maxiflor) Triamcinolone acetate ointment 0.1% (Aristocort A), cream 0.5% (Aristocort-HP)
4	Amcinonide cream 0.1% (Cyclocort) Betamethasone benzoate ointment 0.025% (Benisone, Uticort) Betamethasone valerate lotion 0.1% (Valisone) Desoximethasone cream 0.05% (Topicort-LP) Fluocinolone acetonide cream 0.2% (Synalar-HP), ointment 0.025% (Synalar) Flurandrenolide ointment 0.05% (Cordran) Hydrocortisone valerate ointment 0.2% (Westcort) Triamcinolone acetonide ointment 0.1% (Aristocort, Kenalog)
5	Betamethasone benzoate cream 0.025% (Benisone, Uticort) Betamethasone dipropionate lotion 0.02% (Diprosone) Betamethasone valerate cream, lotion 0.1% (Valisone) Clocortolone cream 0.1% (Cloderm) Fluocinolone acetonide cream 0.025% (Fluonid, Synalar) Flurandrenolide cream 0.05% (Cordran) Hydrocortisone butyrate cream 0.1% (Locoid) Hydrocortisone valerate cream 0.2% (Westcort) Triamcinolone acetonide cream, lotion 1% (Kenalog), cream 0.025% (Aristocort)
6	Aclomethasone dipropionate cream 0.05% (Aclovate) Betamethasone valerate lotion 0.05% (Valisone) Desonide cream 0.05% (Tridesilon) Fluocinolone acetonide solution 0.01% (Synalar)
7 (least potent)	Dexamethasone 0.1% (Decadron Phosphate) Hydrocortisone 0.5%, 1.0%, 2.5% (generic, Hytone, others) Methylprednisolone 1% (Medrol)

Source: Modified from Cornell and Stoughton (1985) and Stoughton and Cornell (1987).

Over 30 years ago, the development of the first topical fluorinated **corticosteroid** revolutionized dermatologic therapy. More potent compounds have been developed continually ever since (Table 80-1). Physiologically, corticosteroids interact with cells via intracytoplasmic receptors that directly regulate new protein synthesis at the genetic level. **Pharmacologic effects** of corticosteroids are primarily anti-inflammatory by many mechanisms: they produce vasoconstriction, interfere with leukotriene pathways, decrease DNA synthesis and mitotic rate in the epidermis, suppress mast cells, interfere with epidermal Langerhans' cell antigen presentation and keratinocyte interleukin-1 expression, suppress fibroblast activity, and alter dermal ground substance. These widespread effects are the basis for both the therapeutic benefits and the adverse reactions associated with topical corticosteroid administration.

Although the majority of experimental data indicates that the **potency** of topical corticosteroids is not restricted to any one of their specific biologic effects, potency has traditionally been measured with a cutaneous vasoconstriction assay. Clinical trials support the potency ranking of topical corticosteroids by this assay for treatment of psoriasis. Potency is determined by (1) chemical structure, (2) concentration, (3) vehicle, with ointments being most potent, and (4) application techniques (e.g., occlusion may greatly enhance the effect). Frequency of application is less important than many patients and clinicians assume. Good evidence suggests that the stratum corneum is a significant reservoir for topical hydrocortisone, releasing the agent for over 1 week after a single application. Once-daily applications are as effective in psoriasis treatment as thrice-daily applications, provided the same amount of drug is applied daily. The effectiveness of topical corticosteroids both clinically and in vasoconstrictor assays often decreases after approximately 1 week of use, a pharmacologic event known as tachyphylaxis. Steroid-induced suppression of epidermal DNA synthesis and mitosis also occurs transiently, with rebound after 48 hours. These findings suggest that application every 2 days may be a preferred regimen. When tachyphylaxis occurs, a change to another corticosteroid preparation may be warranted.

The **risks** of topical corticosteroid use include production of cutaneous atrophy and systemic suppression of adrenal function. Atrophy is of particular concern on the face and intertriginous skin, sites where percutaneous penetration is facilitated. It has been clearly shown that topical preparations applied to one part of the body are transferred by casual behavior to many other sites on the body, especially the face and genitalia, in a 24-hour period. Thus, chronic application of high-potency steroids on any body site may lead to atrophy elsewhere. HPA axis suppression and hypercortisolism with fasting hyperglycemia, insulin resistance, and polymorphonuclear leukocytosis occurs rapidly with use of potent compounds over 40% to 50% of the body surface in psoriatic patients. In general, halogenated compounds should be avoided on the face, and very potent compounds should not be used under occlusion or for prolonged periods without careful monitoring and warnings. Infants and children have an increased risk of developing adverse effects and are best served by the use of topical corticosteroids with relatively low potency.

Some cutaneous processes may be masked or exacerbated by the use of topical corticosteroid preparations. Infections and infestations, particularly candidiasis, impetigo, and scabies, may be promoted or masked. Rosacea and perioral dermatitis are exacerbated by topical corticosteroids. Reappraisal of initial diagnosis and longitudinal follow-up of patients using topical corticosteroids are therefore important.

Arndt KA; Treatment principles. In: *Manual of Dermatologic Therapeutics*. Boston, MA: Little, Brown; 1989:193–200.

> *A detailed, practical review of types of topical medications, the amount to dispense, and principles of the use of vehicles and other additives.*

Barry B; *Dermatological Formulations—Percutaneous Absorption*. New York, NY: Dekker; 1983.

> *A detailed and authoritative presentation of percutaneous absorption mechanisms and topical therapy agents.*

Cornell RC, Stoughton RB: Correlation of vasoconstrictor assay and clinical activity in psoriasis. *Arch Dermatol*. 1985;121:63–67.

Good evidence that the classical vasoconstriction assay correlates with efficacy, at least for treatment of psoriasis.

du Vivier A: Tachyphylaxis to topically applied steroids. *Arch Dermatol.* 1976;112: 1245–1248.

An interesting study, showing that epidermal proliferation and DNA synthesis in the hairless mouse is suppressed for approximately 100 hours after corticosteroid applications, but subsequently recovers and shows resistance to further applications.

Fredericksson T, Lassus, A, Bleeker J: Treatment of psoriasis and atopic dermatitis with halcinonide cream applied one and three times daily. *Br J Dermatol.* 1980; 102:575–577.

Once-daily application without occlusion was as effective as 3 times daily, in a double-blind, multicenter trial in 95 patients. Both regimens were superior to applications of the vehicle alone.

Garden JM, Freinkel RK: Systemic absorption of topical steroids. Metabolic effects as an index of mild hypercortisolism. *Arch Dermatol.* 1986;122:1007–1010.

A clear demonstration that class II topical steroids applied to roughly half the body surface rapidly induce metabolic adrenal suppression and hypercortisolism.

Johnson R, Nusbaum BP, Horwitz SN, et al.: Transfer of topically applied tetracycline in various vehicles. *Arch Dermatol.* 1983;119:660–663.

In a study of 50 patients, topical tetracycline applied to one site was easily transferred to other, sometimes remote sites.

Senter TP: Topical fluocinonide and tachyphylaxis. *Arch Dermatol.* 1983;119: 363–364.

An interesting brief report of a double-blind randomized study of 52 male psoriatic patients, comparing once-daily application with occlusion to thrice-daily application with occlusion. There was no significant difference between the two groups.

Stoughton RB, Cornell RC: Review of super-potent topical corticosteroids. *Semin Dermatol.* 1987; 6:72–76.

The development of super-potent topical corticosteroids has allowed effective treatment of otherwise recalcitrant disorders. Pharmacology is reviewed.

Stoughton RB: Are generic formulations equivalent to trade name topical glucocorticoids? *Arch Dermatol.* 1987;123:1312–1314.

The answer to the title question is no, based on the vasoconstriction assays presented in this paper. Aside from major differences in vehicles and compounding, generic corticosteroids also more frequently contain common sensitizers.

Tan PL, Barnett GL, Flowers FP, Araujo OE: Current topical corticosteroid preparations. *J Am Acad Dermatol.* 1986;14:79–93.

A practical review and guide to topical corticosteroid formulations.

Yohn JJ, Weston WL: Topical glucocorticosteroids. *Curr Probl Dermatol.* 1990; 11: 2, 31–63.

This review discusses in depth all aspects of glucocorticoids—pharmacology, absorption, mechanism, and adverse reactions.

81. PHOTOTHERAPY
Jeffrey S. Dover

Phototherapy is the treatment of skin disease by means of non-ionizing electromagnetic radiation, usually visible or UV light, with or without the addition of photoactive drugs. Visible light includes wavelengths of light from 400 to 700 nm. The UV spectrum is arbitrarily divided into three segments—UVA, UVB, and UVC. UVA is defined as 320 to 400 nm, UVB as 290 to 320 nm, and UVC as 200 to 290 nm. UVC does not reach the earth's surface because of absorption in the ozone layer. Both UVA and UVB reach the earth's surface, are erythemogenic (cause burning) and are melanogenic (cause tanning). The amount of energy required for UVA to induce these effects is approximately one thousand times greater than for UVB despite the fact that it penetrates to a greater depth in skin. Once absorbed, energy in the UV and visible portions of the electromagnetic spectrum causes specific molecules to attain states of electronic excitation. In these states, molecules are capable of undergoing chemical reactions. It is this photochemistry that is the basis for most therapies using UV radiation and visible light.

Visible light is used in phototherapy for neonatal hyperbilirubinemia. Glucuronyl transferase, the hepatic enzyme that facilitates the conjugation of bilirubin to its more water soluble form for gut excretion, is not maximally active at birth. In newborns, especially prematures, unconjugated bilirubin may accumulate in the skin and in neonatal brain tissue, causing jaundice and irreversible brain damage. Exposure of the skin to blue light (450 nm) decreases free bilirubin in the blood and skin and decreases the incidence of toxic CNS accumulation. Blue light is thought to degrade bilirubin by photo-oxidative processes and to isomerize unconjugated bilirubin into a more water soluble form that passes directly into the bile for elimination through the gastrointestinal tract.

Ultraviolet B phototherapy is a common and effective treatment for a variety of skin disorders. Two types of light sources with substantial UVB output are currently available: medium pressure hot quartz mercury vapor lamps and phosphor-containing fluorescent tubes. In addition to UVB, both sources emit considerable amounts of UVA and variable amounts of visible light and infrared radiation. They have been shown to be clinically effective and practical for use in outpatient settings. Delivery units employ an average of 16 bulbs arranged vertically in a metal box the size of a small closet in which the patient stands during the treatment. The bulbs may also be arranged horizontally above and below a Plexiglas (clear) table so that elderly or ill individuals may lie down. Factory-made units are supplied with timing mechanisms, dosimetry monitors, and ventilation fans. These units can also be made available for home use, although devices with four vertically aligned bulbs that can be affixed to a door are more commonly used for home UVB phototherapy. Bulbs require regular calibration to prevent underexposure, causing ineffective control of disease, or overexposure, causing burning.

Psoriasis is the most common disorder treated by UVB phototherapy. Postulated mechanisms for UVB-induced clearing of psoriasis include effects on dermal blood vessels, preferential killing of abnormal cells, effects on the epidermal or dermal immune systems, and inhibition of recruitment of basal cells from the resting phase. Because of marked variability in phototherapy equipment and treatment regimens, it is somewhat difficult to evaluate the efficacy of UVB phototherapy for psoriasis. However, in general, most patients with mild to moderately severe psoriasis of recent onset obtain substantial improvement or clear completely after 18 to 30 UVB treatments in an outpatient facility. Small patches of skin are tested first with varying amounts of UVB radiation to determine the minimal erythema dose (MED), which is the minimum dose of energy required to produce minimally perceptible erythema in skin 24 hours after irradiation. The first dose of UVB radiation and the incremental doses depend on the patient's skin type, as reflected by the MED, and the time interval between treatments. The first dose of total body exposure to UVB should be 80% to 90% of the MED. Subsequent treatments are given 3 times weekly, with a 10% to 15% increase in the dose of UVB light given at each treatment. The first several treatments last less than 1 minute; as exposures are increased, the duration of treatment may be as long as 10 to 15 minutes. The schedule is tailored to the individual patient according to the acute side effects of burning and discomfort. After the psoriasis has cleared, a maintenance schedule may be helpful; in one study, continuing UVB phototherapy approximately once weekly after clearing increased the duration of remission by 30% compared to patients who received no maintenance therapy.

Several topical compounds have been combined with UVB phototherapy in attempts to maximize its efficacy. Tar was initially used for its phototoxic effects in the so-called Goeckerman regimen. Although it is effective, the mechanism of action is unclear since it has been shown that the effective wavelengths for tar photosensitization are in the UVA range. Tar may have an antipsoriatic effect that is independent of UV light and additive when used with low-dose UVB exposures. Emollient bases such as petrolatum (Vaseline) alone are as effective as tar when combined with erythemogenic doses of UVB. Emollients increase the amount of UV light absorbed by psoriatic plaques by filling the multiple skin interfaces present in thickened stratum corneum of the plaques and reducing scatter of the UVB light. They also lessen the pruritus and dryness of psoriasis. The use of topical corticosteroids in conjunction with UVB may accelerate the response of psoriasis especially in the early phase of clearing. They do not appear to lead to an earlier relapse after stopping treatment. In stubborn cases of psoriasis, systemic agents such as methotrexate, etretinate or hydroxyurea may be combined with phototherapy to improve the response.

Although psoriasis is the most common disorder treated with UVB phototherapy, it is also used to treat uremic pruritus, atopic dermatitis, pityriasis lichenoides, pityriasis rosea, pustular psoriasis, parapsoriasis, and cutaneous T-cell lymphoma (mycosis fungoides). One-half to two-thirds of patients with uremic pruritus respond to UVB phototherapy 3 times a week within 4 weeks. Other dermatoses are treated like psoriasis with responses that may not be as rapid or as complete and with relapses after treatment is discontinued. Low doses of UVB light with very small increments have been used to induce tolerance in patients with photosensitive disorders such as polymorphous light eruption.

Patients with photoexacerbated diseases such as lupus erythematosus should be excluded from UVB phototherapy. Although UVB phototherapy is not absolutely contraindicated in pregnancy, its use is not routinely recommended. Long-term side effects of UVB phototherapy include premature photoaging and carcinogenesis with an increased incidence of wrinkling, actinic keratoses, lentigines, telangiectasia, and basal cell and squamous cell carcinomas. Radiation received from UVB phototherapy is cumulative with chronic sun exposure. Use of this therapy should therefore be judicious, with minimal doses delivered to the face, genitalia, and large unaffected areas of the body. These areas are often covered for some or all of the exposure time. It is advisable to avoid treating young children who are not bothered by the cosmetic appearance of their rash, regardless of how extensive it is. Individuals treated with UVB need to be adequately informed of the risks, so that they will limit future nontherapeutic sun exposure and obtain evaluation of any lesions that may appear subsequently. The decision to treat patients who have had skin cancers, melanoma, or dysplastic nevi or a history of exposure to ionizing radiation (including grenz rays), topical mechlorethamine, or arsenic should be carefully weighed against the possibility of inducing further photocarcinogenesis.

Photochemotherapy is the use of non-ionizing electromagnetic radiation following administration of a photosensitizing chemical to achieve a therapeutic benefit. In the doses used, the radiation alone or the chemical alone would have no significant biologic effect. The most commonly used form of photochemotherapy is psoralen-UVA (PUVA) therapy, which was discovered thousands of years ago but only became clinically practical in the mid-1970s. PUVA therapy consists of oral or topical administration of a psoralen (a furocoumarin found in certain plants such as lemons, limes, and celery) and subsequent irradiation of the skin with UVA light. The most widely used psoralen in the United States is 8-methoxypsoralen (8-MOP), administered in an oral dose of 0.4–0.6 mg/kg followed in 1 hour by exposure to UVA.

Most UVA treatment units are equipped with fluorescent bulbs that produce high-intensity UVA light with maximum emission at a wavelength of 360 nm. These bulbs may be arranged in a stand-up unit, a Plexiglas table unit, or in a hand-and-foot unit designed for adequate exposure of the palms and soles. Full-body units usually employ 48 high-energy UVA bulbs. These units have timing devices and dosimetry monitors, although periodic external monitoring of power output is also required. The bulbs may be arranged in tandem with UVB-emitting bulbs to produce a single unit with dual capabilities. Tanning parlors use high-intensity broadband fluorescent UVA bulbs that are similar to those used in PUVA therapy. High-intensity UVA can produce a deep brownish gray tan, but without psoralen it is ineffective at clearing most dermatoses.

The mechanism of action of PUVA therapy is not fully known. At least one of its effects is the light-mediated addition of psoralen to DNA by linkage with pyrimidine bases. The formation of psoralen-DNA cross-links leads to a decrease in the rate of

DNA synthesis, one possible explanation for the therapeutic benefit of PUVA in those dermatologic disorders characterized by excessively rapid cell replication, such as psoriasis. It may also inhibit immune events such as the migration of inflammatory cells to the skin or their replication.

PUVA therapy is highly effective in the management of psoriasis: it clears psoriasis in nearly 90% of treated patients. Treatments are administered either 2 or 3 times weekly until clearing. An average of 20 treatments over 6 to 10 weeks is required to achieve clearing in psoriasis. Initial UVA exposure doses are determined in two ways. They may be chosen in a fairly arbitrary fashion based on skin type or by calculating the minimal phototoxic dose (MPD). In patients with psoriasis the initial UVA exposure doses for types I (always burn, never tan), II (usually burn, tan with difficulty), III (sometimes burn, tan average), IV (rarely burn, tan with ease), and V (never burn) skin are 1.0, 2.0, 2.5, 3.0, and 4.0 Joule/cm^2 respectively. These empirically determined UVA doses are calculated to produce just less than one MPD, an exposure sufficient to induce uniform mild erythema. Alternatively, the patient's MPD may be precisely determined in a fashion similar to that for determining a patient's MED for UVB therapy except that in this case 8-MOP is ingested 1 hour before exposing several small areas of buttock skin to varying doses of UVA radiation. The dose that induces uniform mild erythema in the exposed area at 72 hours is considered the MPD. PUVA therapy is initiated at the MPD dose and subsequent exposures are increased by 1.0 Joule/cm^2 if burning and discomfort are minimal. For optimal results, the 8-MOP tablets should be taken exactly 1 hour prior to PUVA therapy to coincide with the peak blood level of 8-MOP in most individuals. Chronically sun-exposed areas such as the face and hands and sensitive areas such as the genitalia and nipples should be covered during treatment unless they are involved, in which case they should be exposed for one-quarter to half of the total body exposure time. Maintenance treatments weekly or biweekly are usually necessary to prevent exacerbation of the disease. In difficult cases of psoriasis, UVB phototherapy or systemic agents such as methotrexate and etretinate may be added in an effort to improve outcome.

PUVA may also be used in the treatment of pustular and other variants of psoriasis, cutaneous T-cell lymphomas, atopic dermatitis, lichen planus, and vitiligo. Regimens for treating the first four processes are similar to those used in the treatment of psoriasis, though improvement may not be as rapid or as complete. The dose of light used and the number of treatments given vary individually, depending on the response of the disease. Seventy percent of vitiligo patients improve when treated twice weekly for more than 1 year with either 8-MOP or 4,5,8-trimethylpsoralen in conjunction with exposure to UVA. On average, a course of treatment consists of at least 150 PUVA exposures, although improvement may be seen after 50 treatments. Total repigmentation is rare; small patches on the trunk of recent onset respond best, while lips and hands respond poorly. A full 30% of patients do not respond at all. PUVA treatment for vitiligo should be limited to highly motivated patients over 12 years of age with extensive disease. PUVA therapy may also induce tolerance to sun exposure in patients with polymorphous light eruption (PMLE) or other photosensitivity disorders. A short course of PUVA, 2 or 3 times a week for 3 or 4 weeks, using a psoralen and low doses of UVA will prevent development of PMLE lesions upon subsequent exposure to sunlight. PUVA may be effective by producing a protective tan or perhaps by inducing immune tolerance.

The risks associated with PUVA therapy are both acute and chronic. Acutely, sunburnlike painful erythema may occur, occasionally producing bullous lesions. Psoralen alone may produce pruritus and nausea in a small number of patients. These adverse effects can usually be prevented by careful individual assessment of appropriate dosimetry or managed with suitable topical or systemic therapy. They present no absolute contraindication to the use of PUVA therapy. The chronic long-term toxicity of this modality remains to be determined. PUVA is known to be both mutagenic and carcinogenic in experimental systems. Hyperpigmentation secondary to increased melanogenesis occurs in most patients. Lentigines and pigmentary mottling occur in some patients. The prevalence of premature aging of the skin, actinic keratoses, Bowen's disease, and squamous cell carcinoma is increased. Prior skin cancer, previous exposure to ionizing radiation, arsenic ingestion, and possibly the previous use of topical tar preparations increase the likelihood of neoplasia in these patients. Another potential toxicity of PUVA is cataract formation. Animals treated with psoralens in high doses and exposed to UV light develop cataracts. Although only a few cases of premature cataracts have been described in patients treated with PUVA without eye protection, use of UVA opaque glasses (e.g., UV 400) is recommended. The glasses must be worn immediately following ingestion of 8-MOP and for the rest of the day. While in the PUVA chamber, the eyes must be totally covered with UVA opaque goggles that are provided by the PUVA technician. Patients with cataracts may be treated with PUVA as long as proper ocular protection is used. Pregnant women and patients with sun-sensitive disorders such as lupus erythematosus should not receive PUVA therapy.

Abel E: *Photochemotherapy in Dermatology.* New York, NY: Igaku-Shoin; 1992.
  An up-to-date in-depth discussion of photochemotherapy.
Anderson TF, Waldinger TP, Voorhees JJ: UVB phototherapy: an overview. *Arch Dermatol.* 1984;120:1502–1507.
  A well-referenced review of the uses of UVB phototherapy.
Dover JS, McEvoy MT, and Rosen CF, et al.: Are topical corticosteroids useful in phototherapy for psoriasis? *J Am Acad Dermatol.* 1989; 20:748–754.
  This prospective, randomized, double-blind, placebo-controlled trial studied 52 patients to assess the effect of a potent topical corticosteroid cream used in conjunction with UVB phototherapy on psoriasis. Although there was a trend toward a slightly more rapid response in the topical corticosteroid-treated group, there was no significant difference in patients' early response to therapy, number of treatments, and UVB dose required to achieve clearing. For most patients, the use of potent topical corticosteroids appeared to produce, at most, a modest beneficial effect.
Harber LC, Bickers DR: Photosensitivity diseases. In: *Principles of Diagnosis and Treatment.* 22nd ed. Toronto: B.C. Decker, Inc., 1989:58–109.
  An excellent section on therapeutic effects of light with individual chapters on UVB, PUVA, phototherapy for infants, and combined therapies using UV light.
Gupta AK, Anderson TF: Psoralen photochemotherapy. *J Am Acad Dermatol.* 1987;17:703–704.
  A detailed, up-to-date review of PUVA; basic and practical concepts.
Lindelof B, Sigurgeirsson B, Tegner E, et al.: PUVA and cancer: a large-scale epidemiological study. *Lancet.* 1991;338:91–93.
  This study of 4799 Swedish patients who received PUVA between 1974 and 1985 identified a dose-dependent increase in the risk of squamous cell cancer of the skin. Male patients who had received more than 200 treatments had over 30 times the incidence of squamous cell cancer found in the general population.
Morison WL: *Phototherapy and Photochemotherapy of Skin Disease.* 2nd ed. New York, NY: Raven Press; 1991.
  An excellent practical small text helpful to physicians using phototherapy and photochemotherapy.
Saurat JH, Geiger JM, Amblard P, et al.: Randomized double-blind multicenter study comparing acitretin-PUVA, etretinate-PUVA, and placebo-PUVA in the treatment of severe psoriasis. *Dermatologica.* 1988;177:218–214.
  Acitretin-PUVA treatment was significantly superior to placebo-PUVA with respect to decrease in lesional scores after 6 weeks of therapy, number of PUVA exposures, and total dose of UVA until remission.
Stern RS, Lange R: Non-melanoma skin cancer occurring in patients treated with PUVA five to ten years after first treatment. *J Invest Dermatol.* 1988;91:120–124.
  This report reviewed findings after 10 years of a prospective study of 1380 patients enrolled in the PUVA study and demonstrated a strong association between cumulative exposure to PUVA and an increased risk of squamous cell carcinoma of the skin. There was also a modest dose-dependent increase in the risk for the development of basal cell carcinoma for patients who received an excess of 200 treatments compared to patients who had received fewer than 160 treatments within the same time period.

Stern RS, Members of the Photochemotherapy Follow-up Study: Genital tumors among men with psoriasis exposed to psoralens and ultraviolet A radiation (PUVA) and ultraviolet B radiation. *N Engl J Med.* 1990;322:1093–1097.

In patients exposed to high levels of PUVA, the incidence of invasive squamous cell carcinoma was 286 times that in the general population and 16.3 times that in patients exposed to low levels. Patients exposed to high levels of UVB radiation had a risk of genital tumors 4.6 times higher than that in other patients.

Stern RS, Zierler S, Parrish JA: Skin carcinoma in patients with psoriasis treated with topical tar and artificial ultraviolet radiation. *Lancet.* 1980;5:732–735.

A retrospective analysis of the risk of developing squamous cell carcinoma from the use of tar and phototherapy.

82. RETINOIDS
Jay A. Levin

Retinoids are naturally occurring or synthetic derivatives of vitamin A. They have diverse biologic effects, including regulation of epithelial differentiation, stimulation of collagen synthesis, enhancement of wound repair, alteration of cell membrane structure, and inhibition of tumor promotion. These actions are most clearly expressed in the skin, and dermatologists have been pioneers in the research concerning their clinical utility. Today retinoids are widely used in therapy for recalcitrant acne, psoriasis, disorders of keratinization, chemoprevention of skin cancer, and the reversal of photoaging.

During the early part of this century, scientists demonstrated that vitamin A is a necessary dietary nutrient for vision, growth, reproduction, and the maintenance and differentiation of epithelial tissue. Its major natural sources are the beta-carotenes found in yellow and green leafy vegetables and the long-chain retinyl esters found in some animal fats and fish oils. Vitamin A (retinol) is transported through the circulation via chylomicrons to the liver, where storage in the ester form represents greater than 90% of the body's total reserves. When needed, retinol is complexed to a transport protein called serum retinol binding protein (RBP) and then released into the circulation. Only this retinol-RBP complex is able to bind to the specific membrane receptors of target cells and be transported intracellularly. It is currently felt that many retinol functions may be mediated through intracellular receptor proteins that affect expression of genes involved with differentiation and proliferation, similar to steroid and thyroid hormone interactions. Because vitamin A is stored in hepatic fat stores, plasma levels remain relatively stable despite dietary fluctuations. Toxicity is felt to reflect excess soluble retinol, that which is not bound to RBP. Synthetic retinoids bind differently, and toxicity occurs in a more direct relationship to administered amounts.

Vitamin A deficiency provides a model for understanding how retinoids serve as therapy for such a wide range of dermatologic conditions. In vitamin A deficiency there is inhibition of epithelial proliferation, growth, and differentiation. Squamous metaplasia occurs, characterized by increased cell proliferation and hyperkeratosis. The earliest clinical effects of vitamin A deficiency are found in the eyes, with xerophthalmia (dry eyes), night blindness, corneal ulceration, and keratomalacia. Cutaneous manifestations of vitamin A deficiency include dryness, fine scaling, and follicular hyperkeratosis. Low levels of vitamin A were therefore thought to be related to skin conditions involving abnormally increased cell proliferation and hyperkeratosis. Experimental trials were undertaken with oral vitamin A taken in megadoses and demonstrated that improvement could be seen in diseases such as Darier's disease and pityriasis rubra pilaris in which follicular hyperkeratosis resembled the lesions of vitamin A deficiency. Subsequently, vitamin A was used with some success in treatment of acne, psoriasis, and disorders of keratinization. Unfortunately, side effects associated with hypervitaminosis A limited both compliance and effectiveness. For this reason, the aim of pharmacologic research has been to produce synthetic retinoids that provide a better therapeutic index (improved efficacy with less toxicity). In 1963, Stuttgen in Berlin reported the retinol metabolite retinoic acid could improve ichthyosis, but unfortunately, systemic use of this agent, tretinoin, was limited by its extensive adverse effects. In 1972, Peck at the National Institutes of Health showed that an isomer of tretinoin, isotretinoin, taken systemically, produced excellent results in severe acne. Subsequent investigation produced an aromatic form of tretinoin, etretinate, with a better therapeutic index for psoriasis and some disorders of keratinization. Other derivatives are being studied. Available in the United States today are topical tretinoin (Retin-A), oral isotretinoin (Accutane), and oral etretinate (Tegison).

Topical tretinoin has been used since 1969 for **acne vulgaris** and is now considered standard therapy. Tretinoin acts independent of irritancy as a keratolytic agent by increasing the rate of follicular proliferation and producing greater epidermal cell turnover and faster elimination of comedones. It is therefore used primarily in patients with numerous comedones in combination with agents such as antibiotics or benzoyl peroxide. A clinical response is not seen for 2 to 3 months and may require 6 to 12 months for maximal improvement. Toxicologic data have shown that topical tretinoin is safe. Although tretinoin penetrates the skin and accumulates in the upper dermis, it is absorbed in very small amounts by blood and lymph vessels. Tretinoin is available as a gel, cream, or liquid; typical side effects are dryness, irritation, and photosensitivity. Fair-skinned individuals are particularly prone to develop dryness, peeling, and irritation, and very dark-skinned patients may develop postinflammatory hyperpigmentation. Patients are therefore first given a low-dose cream (0.025%) or gel (0.01%) to use in small amounts nightly or every other night. The concentration can be increased as the patient tolerates the drug. The patient should also be instructed to use oil-free moisturizers and sunscreen daily. In the years since its introduction, topical tretinoin has also been used with varying success to treat flat warts, molluscum contagiosum, oral lichen planus, linear verrucous nevi, ichthyoses, epidermal pigmentary disorders, and other premalignant and malignant skin conditions.

The use of topical tretinoin for **photoaging** was suggested when some postadolescent females using tretinoin for acne described smoother, less wrinkled skin. Previous studies had demonstrated that the agent enhanced repair of UV-damaged skin in hairless mice. In 1988, a double-blind, vehicle-controlled study was published, describing subtle improvement in the wrinkling, sallowness, roughness, and mottled pigmentation that characterize sun-damaged skin. The most impressive improvement occurred in fine wrinkling. These promising results have been questioned, although open studies have also noted an improvement in photoaging. Histologic studies confirm a replacement of atrophic epidermis by hyperplasia, elimination of dysplasia and atypia, new collagen formation in the papillary dermis, uniform dispersion of melanin granules, and eradication of microscopic actinic keratoses. The regimen used is similar to acne treatment, with particular attention to protection from any further sun exposure. Maximum improvement may require use of tretinoin for 12 months with prolonged use for maintenance.

Oral isotretinoin has been used to treat **acne** since the late 1970s. While it is effective in treating acne vulgaris, the associated toxicity and teratogenicity justify its use only for severe disfiguring cystic acne unresponsive to aggressive standard therapy. Isotretinoin may also be effective in the treatment of gram-negative folliculitis, acne fulminans, acne conglobata, dissecting cellulitis of the scalp, and acne rosacea. Rare cases of hidradenitis suppurativa also respond. Improvement in these disorders is felt to result principally from inhibition of sebum production vital for acne lesion formation (sebaceous glands atrophy during treatment). Without sebum, secondary bacterial growth is suppressed. In addition, isotretinoin alters keratinization of the follicle and inflammatory response. Currently it is recommended that the drug be given at 1 mg/kg/d for 4 or 5 months as an initial course of therapy. After treatment is stopped, the condition may continue to improve for at least 2 months, although quantitative sebum production slowly returns toward pretreatment levels. Only about one-third of acne patients require a second course, which should be administered only after a 6-month hiatus and may require higher doses, up to 1.5–2.0 mg/kg/d.

Psoriasis is the other principal disease for which synthetic retinoids are useful. Etretinate is more effective than isotretinoin, particularly for pustular and erythrodermic variants. Unlike acne, psoriasis requires long-term administration of retinoids, and relapses occur if therapy is discontinued. Because of the toxicity associated with long-term retinoid therapy, etretinate should be reserved for recalcitrant psoriasis in males and in postmenopausal females. An effective dose of etretinate is usually 0.75–1.0 mg/kg/d. Initial therapy for erythrodermic psoriasis begins at 25 mg/d and increases to 50 mg/d after several weeks. While chronic psoriasis vulgaris may respond to 50 mg/d, pustular psoriasis may require higher initial doses of 75 mg/d.

Etretinate may be used alone or in combination with conventional psoriasis therapies such as topical corticosteroids, tars, anthralin, phototherapy with UV radiation (UVB, 280–320 nm), and methotrexate. The combination of etretinate with photochemotherapy using oral psoralens and long-wave UV radiation (PUVA) is a regimen now widely employed in Europe for extensive psoriasis. This combined therapy, called RE-PUVA, has the dual advantage of less cumulative UVA exposure and reduced dose and duration of etretinate therapy.

Patients with recalcitrant **disorders of keratinization** such as Darier's disease and pityriasis rubra pilaris have improved with systemic retinoid therapy. Lamellar ichthyosis also clears, but caution is advised in long-term administration of retinoids to children because of concerns with adverse effects on the skeletal system. For these disorders, similar results have been recorded with either isotretinoin and etretinate. There have also been some unusual responses with etretinate in which patients with palmoplantar hyperkeratosis have noted blistering and patients with blistering disorders have worsened.

Retinoids may have a role in the **chemotherapy or chemoprevention** of epithelial carcinomas. Epidemiologic studies suggest that low serum retinol levels are associated with an increased risk of cancer, although the relationship is best established for the retinol precursor, beta-carotene. The profound effects of retinoids on cell differentiation and proliferation have been noted in both normal and neoplastic cells. Studies in animals have shown that retinoids can act directly on non-neoplastic cells to suppress the process of malignant transformation induced by carcinogens, radiation, or transforming growth factors. Administration of retinoids to malignant cells in vitro is able to convert these cells from a neoplastic phenotype to a differentiated, non-neoplastic type. Because synthetic retinoids may thus suppress hyperplasia and squamous metaplasia induced by carcinogens and restore a more normal pattern of epithelial differentiation, they have been used in humans in the treatment and prevention of basal cell carcinoma, squamous carcinoma, actinic keratoses, nevoid basal cell carcinoma syndrome, xeroderma pigmentosum, multiple keratoacanthomas, porokeratosis of Mibelli with malignant degeneration, epidermodysplasia verruciformis, oral leukoplakia, cutaneous metastases of malignant melanoma, and cutaneous T-cell lymphoma. A variety of clinical studies are underway concerning prevention of cancer of the bladder, breast, and skin. Low-dose retinoids appear to be of particular value in preventing new tumors in patients with immunosuppression or basal cell nevus syndrome as long as therapy is maintained. Studies investigating the use of retinoids in treatment of established cancer have demonstrated a 50% to 70% "objective response rate" or "partial remission" of basal cell carcinomas and have noted remissions in patients with metastatic or widespread squamous cell carcinomas of the head and neck. In one study of 40 patients equally divided into isolated or multiple basal cell carcinomas, the response rate to retinoid therapy was similar, but the relapse rate at 1 year differed significantly, with 86% of multiple and 10% of isolated carcinomas recurring. Other studies have suggested that retinoids are better employed against in situ squamous cell carcinoma (Bowen's disease) than against invasive disease. The role of retinoids for chemoprevention and chemotherapy remains unclear.

The major **adverse reactions** associated with the administration of synthetic retinoids reflect the toxic effects of vitamin A.

The greatest risk in the use of synthetic retinoids is the potential for **teratogenicity.** Both isotretinoin and etretinate produce birth defects in humans, commonly involving head, ear, thymus, heart, endocrine, and skeletal systems. Facial dysmorphia, hydrocephalus, and spontaneous abortions are commonly reported. While isotretinoin is a potent teratogen, it is rapidly eliminated, with a half-life of 1 day. Therefore, after only 1 month off therapy and the completion of 1 full menstrual cycle, women may become pregnant safely. It must be emphasized that patient understanding of this risk and compliance with effective contraception beginning at least 1 month prior to initiating therapy and continuing until at least 1 month after cessation of therapy are necessary to prevent unplanned pregnancies. Etretinate is lipophilic, preferentially stored in fat cells, and has a half-life of 120 days. It has been detected in serum even 2 years after one course of therapy. Etretinate is such a potent teratogen that women of childbearing potential who receive this drug must avoid pregnancy for an as yet undetermined period of time after treatment. Acitretin, the principal metabolite of etretinate, may soon be approved for use. While similar in efficacy and toxicity to etretinate, acitretin has a reported half-life of only 50 hours. Three weeks after discontinuation of treatment, acitretin was not detected in the serum in one study. However, the manufacturer of acitretin voluntarily withdrew it from European markets and reintroduced it with new warnings about the necessity for extended contraception after therapy is discontinued. Therefore, like etretinate, acitretin should not be used in women of childbearing potential except in rare and carefully considered circumstances.

The predominant symptoms of acute toxicity of the synthetic retinoids involve the skin and mucous membranes, principally mucocutaneous drying and chapping. Commonly observed are cheilitis, facial dermatitis, conjunctivitis, xerosis with itching, dryness of the nasal mucosa with minor nosebleeds, dry mouth with thirst, excessive palmoplantar desquamation, and skin fragility with peeling after minor trauma. On initiation of therapy with isotretinoin, acne may flare. Some patients with very active cystic lesions may note the formation of pyogenic granuloma–like lesions on the trunk or extremities; such lesions often respond to therapy with topical or systemic corticosteroids. Colonization of the dry nares by *Staphylococcus aureus* may lead to a bacterial folliculitis for which systemic antibiotics are necessary. Other adverse effects include arthralgias with pain and tenderness of the bone and joints, muscle pain after exertion, and increased photosensitivity. Mental depression, hair loss, and difficulty wearing contact lenses have also been described. Rarely, a patient may develop pseudotumor cerebri with headache, papilledema, and visual changes, the risk of which increases with concomitant tetracycline-derivative administration.

Isotretinoin is usually administered for acne for a course of several months, but etretinate is administered for lengthy periods when one is treating psoriasis and disorders of keratinization, and the problems of chronic retinoid usage become more apparent. The most worrisome of these involves changes in the bony skeleton, resembling diffuse idiopathic skeletal hyperostosis. Radiographically the skeletal changes consist of calcification of the anterior spinal ligament and bony bridging in the feet and ankles. In children, premature closure of epiphyses has been noted, and older patients may have modeling defects with enhanced bone resorption. In addition, there have been reports of acute hepatotoxic reactions in patients taking etretinate, probably due to an idiosyncratic allergic hypersensitivity reaction since patients with preexisting liver disease have undergone continuous therapy with etretinate for up to 6 years without the onset of chronic hepatotoxicity. Hair loss, also more of a problem with etretinate, becomes more noticeable after 1 to 2 months of therapy.

Abnormal laboratory test results seen with retinoids are common. Transient minor elevations in liver function tests occur in approximately 15% of patients, but return to normal after less than 1 month, and then remain normal despite continued therapy. Most commonly affected are the transaminases. Dose-dependent elevations of triglycerides and hyperlipidemia of mainly very low density lipoproteins are also seen. Patients should be monitored for acute pancreatitis and therapy discontinued if triglyceride levels reach 800 mg/dl. Hypertriglyceridemia is more common in patients who have predisposing conditions such as obesity, high alcohol intake, diabetes, and pretreatment hyperlipidemias.

More than 2000 retinoids have now been synthesized, each with distinct cellular effects. Studies are being undertaken to evaluate possible new drugs and ascertain their unique spectra of clinical efficacy and adverse effects. Some retinoids will work better in some disease processes than others. Differences in relative toxicity could influence retinoid selection in diseases where therapeutic effects are comparable. Because of their profound effects on epithelial growth and differentiation, retinoids will be particularly pertinent in the treatment of skin disease.

Ellis CN, Voorhees JJ: Etretinate therapy. *J Am Acad Dermatol.* 1987;16:267–291.
  Discussion of the uses and adverse effects of oral etretinate administered for the treatment of psoriasis and other dermatoses.
Garewal HS: Potential role of beta-carotene in prevention of oral cancer. *Am J Clin Nutr.* 1991 Jan;53(1 Suppl):294S–297S.
  The demonstrated ability of retinoids to reverse oral leukoplakia suggests a role for retinoids in preventing oral cancer.
Goldfarb MT, Ellis CN, Voorhees JJ: Retinoids in dermatology. *Mayo Clin Proc.* 1987;62:1161–1164.
  Short and easily readable summary of therapeutic uses of the retinoids.
Goodman DS: Vitamin A and retinoids in health and disease. *N Engl J Med.* 1984;310:1023–1031.
  Sophisticated discussion of the role of vitamin A and its synthetic relatives in regulation of cutaneous and systemic processes.
Kligman AM, Grove GL, Hirose R, et al.: Topical tretinoin for photoaged skin. *J Am Acad Dermatol.* 1986;15:836–859.
  Comparative study of 0.05% tretinoin cream and its vehicle, concluding that tretinoin is capable of at least partly reversing the histologic and clinical effects of excessive sunlight exposure.
Lippman SM, Chimm OS, Meyskews FL, Jr.: Nonsurgical treatments for skin cancer: Retinoids and alpha-interferon. *J Dermatol Surg Oncol.* 1988;14:862–869.
  Review of retinoid activity against premalignant disorders and established cancers of the skin.
Lotan R, Clifford JL: Nuclear receptors for retinoids: mediators of retinoid effects on normal and malignant cells. *Biomed Pharmacother.* 1991;45(4–5):145–156.
  Retinoids exert their effects through nuclear receptors that regulate transcription.
Lotan R: Retinoids as modulators of tumor cells invasion and metastasis. *Semin Cancer Biol.* 1991; 2(3):197–208.
  The author reviews the mechanisms responsible for the ability of retinoids to modulate tumor growth and metastasis.
Orfanos CE, Ehlert R, Gollnick H: The retinoids, a review of their clinical pharmacology and therapeutic use. *Drugs.* 1987;34:459–503.
  Detailed and extensive review of clinical pharmacology, mechanisms of action, and therapeutic uses of synthetic retinoids.
Stuttgen G: Historical perspective of tretinoin. *J Am Acad Dermatol.* 1986;15:735–740.
  Chronologic review of the development and use of synthetic retinoids to treat skin disease.
Weiss JS, Ellis CN, Headington JT, et al.: Topical tretinoin improves photoaged skin. A double-blind, vehicle-controlled study. *J Am Med Assoc.* 1988;259:527–532.
  A 16-week study of 30 patients who treated their faces and forearms, demonstrating statistically significant but controversial clinical and histologic improvement.

83. SULFONES
Anita M. Grassi

Sulfones are antibacterial agents that are chemically related to sulfonamides and have specific applications in dermatology. Sulfapyridine, a sulfanilamide derivative, is likewise an effective treatment for several cutaneous disorders. Both sulfones and sulfapyridine were recognized initially for their antistreptococcal activity. The sulfones were subsequently shown to have activity against acid-fast bacterial infections. Today, they are the primary mode of therapy for infectious and inflammatory diseases such as leprosy and dermatitis herpetiformis.

The most commonly used sulfone is 4,4′-diaminodiphenyl-sulfone, or **dapsone**. Most other sulfones taken orally are metabolized in the stomach to dapsone. Dapsone is readily absorbed from the gastrointestinal tract. It undergoes acetylation (deactivation) as well as simultaneous deacetylation in the liver, achieving an equilibrium state. It is conjugated in the liver with glucuronic acid. Ninety percent of the drug is excreted by the kidneys as a glucuronide and 10% is excreted in bile. Dapsone is highly protein-bound, contributing to a long half-life with detectable serum levels up to 35 days after cessation of treatment. Dapsone is available in 25- and 100-mg tablets. In general, there is a dose-related increase in side effects with dosages greater than 100 mg/d. Side effects discussed below include hemolysis, methemoglobinemia, and agranulocytosis.

Sulfapyridine is less water-soluble than dapsone and is therefore absorbed through the gastrointestinal tract more erratically. It is similarly acetylated in the liver, conjugated with glucuronic acid, and excreted by the kidneys. However, unlike dapsone, it does not undergo deacetylation. Studies have suggested that patients who have a slow acetylation genetic phenotype may have increased serum concentration of the drug, hence increased toxicity. Up to 20% of sulfapyridine is protein-bound. This can displace other drugs, e.g., coumadin, tolbutamide, and methotrexate, augmenting their effects. The low solubility of sulfapyridine can also result in crystalluria and renal damage. Sulfapyridine is available in 500-mg tablets, and the suggested therapeutic range is 2–6 g/d. Like dapsone, side effects are largely dose-related.

The **mechanism of action** of dapsone and sulfapyridine has been extensively studied. It is known that both drugs competitively inhibit incorporation of para-aminobenzoic acid into folic acid by bacteria. They are bacteriostatic agents that may be bactericidal in high concentration. Their efficacy in inflammatory and bullous diseases is less well understood. Most of the disorders for which dapsone is an effective treatment have prominent infiltration by neutrophils on histology, e.g., dermatitis herpetiformis, subcorneal pustular dermatosis, and pyoderma gangrenosum, suggesting that sulfones may interfere with neutrophil function. Studies have shown that dapsone does not inhibit in vitro chemotaxis, mobility, release of lysozymes, or phagocytosis of neutrophils. Moreover, evidence suggests that sulfones do not affect complement activation or deposition of immunoglobulins in dermatitis herpetiformis. Recent studies reveal that sulfones inhibit neutrophil myeloperoxidase-mediated iodination and cytotoxicity. Polymorphonuclear leukocytes release myeloperoxidase and hydrogen peroxide when they phagocytize bacteria, killing the organisms. This process requires iodination, forming I_2 from NaI. Both dapsone and sulfapyridine have been shown to prevent iodination, thereby perhaps reducing inflammation.

The **indications** for the use of dapsone in the treatment of dermatologic conditions include dermatitis herpetiformis, leprosy, subcorneal pustular dermatosis, bullous diseases, pyoderma gangrenosum, and erythema elevatum diutinum. Of these, dapsone is particularly effective as a primary agent in the first three disorders. It is used as an alternative or adjunctive agent for the rest. Dapsone in conjunction with a gluten-free diet is the primary mode of therapy for dermatitis herpetiformis. Eighty percent of patients with dermatitis herpetiformis may be controlled with dietary restriction alone, but compliance is difficult and improvement can take months to years. Eighty percent of patients will respond to dapsone in a dosage of 50 to 100 mg daily. Almost all patients will improve with up to 300 mg/d but with increased risk of toxicity. Suggested treatment regimens start with dapsone at 100 mg/d and increase by 50 to 100 mg/d per week if no change occurs in 1 week. Once the lesions are cleared, the dose can be decreased by 25 mg/d per week until stable maintenance doses are reached. With adequate dosage, patients improve quite rapidly, often within 1 week. Dapsone is considered more effective than sulfapyridine in dermatitis herpetiformis.

The introduction of sulfones in the 1950s had a dramatic impact on the treatment of leprosy. Dapsone was the first safe, effective drug available for leprosy. It not only arrested the disease but eliminated the need for isolation of afflicted individuals. It remains the mainstay of leprosy therapy today, although resistance to the drug is becoming more widespread and it is now used in conjunction with other agents. Current World Health Organization recommendations for treatment of patients with intermediate, tuberculoid, and borderline-tuberculoid infections consist of rifampin 600 mg once a month with dapsone 100 mg/d for 6 months. Annual follow-up is necessary to evaluate the patient for relapse. When on rifampin, patients become noninfectious in 1 to 2 weeks. Treatment guidelines for borderline, borderline-lepromatous, and lepromatous leprosy include rifampin 600 mg once a month, dapsone 100 mg/d, and clofazimine 50 mg/d with an additional 300-mg dose once a month for at least 2 years and until skin smears are negative. These WHO recommendations differ somewhat from current U.S. treatment regimens and are subject to ongoing evaluation because of the emergence of drug resistance.

Subcorneal pustular dermatosis, or Sneddon-Wilkinson disease, is a chronic pustular eruption with a relapsing course that affects mostly women over 40 years old. The pathology shows subcorneal pustules of polymorphonuclear leukocytes that can also be seen migrating from dermal capillaries and as a perivascular infiltrate. Most cases will respond to dapsone with rapid clearing. Maintenance dapsone may be required to prevent recurrence. Some patients, often men, may respond poorly to dapsone or sulfapyridine.

Dapsone has been shown to be beneficial in several other dermatologic conditions but with less consistency. For example, dapsone may be helpful in other bullous conditions such as IgA linear bullous dermatosis, chronic bullous dermatosis of childhood, bullous pemphigoid, epidermolysis bullosa acquisita, and pemphigus. It can be used as a sole agent, but often requires high doses, increasing the chances of toxicity. It is perhaps best used as a steroid-sparing agent, allowing lower doses of both dapsone and prednisone.

Specifically, linear IgA disease may be initially controlled with dapsone at 100–200 mg/d, tapered slowly with the addition of prednisone if exacerbation occurs during the taper. It may be possible to control these patients on an every-other-day regimen of each drug. Chronic bullous dermatosis of childhood, similar to linear IgA disease of adults, has been reported to respond to sulfapyridine 65 mg/d, tapered to 40–50 mg/d. The required doses of either sulfapyridine or dapsone may be so high as to preclude treatment, however. Epidermolysis bullosa acquisita typically does not respond to corticosteroids, but some investigators have had good results with dapsone and suggest it as an alternative to immunosuppressive agents. Up to 15% of patients with bullous pemphigoid may completely clear with sulfapyridine or dapsone alone in doses similar to those for dermatitis herpetiformis. These patients often have more neutrophils than eosinophils on their histology. Pemphigus vulgaris is preferentially treated with high-dose prednisone, but dapsone has been reported as an effective steroid-sparing agent for long-term therapy. In addition to bullous diseases, there are several reports of the efficacy of dapsone in other disorders that involve neutrophil infiltration, including pyoderma gangrenosum, acne conglobata, erythema elevatum diutinum, and leukocytoclastic vasculitis.

The **adverse effects** of dapsone tend to be dose-related and in general are uncommon on doses less than 200 mg/d. Concerns over the safety of dapsone may have been exaggerated by the high doses used in early studies. Numerous cases of agranulocytosis seen among military troops in Vietnam who were receiving low-dose dapsone as malaria prophylaxis may have been precipitated by concurrent use of other antimalarials such as chloroquine. It should be noted that millions of patients have been successfully treated with dapsone for years with a relatively low rate of toxic side effects. In general, dapsone is considered a relatively safe medication at low dosage with proper monitoring.

The most common toxic effects of dapsone are hemolysis and methemoglobinemia. Nearly all patients receiving doses of 200 mg/d of dapsone will experience some degree of hemolysis while those on 300 mg/d may have a 25% decrease in their hematocrit. Patients with G-6-PD deficiency are less tolerant of the drug, with hemolysis occurring at doses of 50 mg/d. Studies have shown that dapsone does not interfere with the enzymatic activity of G-6-PD, however. Rather, it appears that a toxic hydroxylamine metabolite of dapsone formed in the liver makes the red blood cells more susceptible to oxidation. This leads to precipitation of hemoglobin as Heinz bodies, causing destruction of the red cell in the spleen or by osmotic lysis. The degree of hemolysis varies with the serum concentration of the drug. Hemolysis may not occur for a month in normal individuals, but it may occur sooner in G-6-PD–deficient patients. Sulfapyridine can cause hemolysis by similar mechanisms.

Some degree of methemoglobinemia will occur in any patient taking at least 100 mg/d of dapsone. A toxic hydroxylamine derivative of dapsone and sulfapyridine also appears to facilitate oxidation of iron from the ferrous to ferric state, producing methemoglobin. A patient with fifteen percent methemoglobinemia will have clinical cyanosis with bluish lips and nailbeds; thirty to forty percent methemoglobinemia can create dizziness, headache, and dyspnea. The symptoms may be well tolerated, but can precipitate angina in patients with cardiac disease.

Agranulocytosis occurs in 0.1% of patients on sulfapyridine. It also can occur with dapsone, usually with doses of greater than 100 mg/d. As previously mentioned, there was an outbreak of agranulocytosis among military personnel given dapsone at 25 mg/d for malaria prophylaxis, perhaps due to interaction with chloroquine taken simultaneously. It is considered an idiosyncratic reaction that occurs early in therapy. Mild leukopenia can also occur.

Neurologic effects of dapsone include peripheral neuropathy and psychosis. Both are thought to be dose related. The neuropathy is usually motor in nature, causing weakness in distal muscles of the hands and feet. This effect is reversible but may take months to years. Patients with a history of psychiatric illness may be more prone to develop psychosis while on dapsone.

Several other toxic side effects have been reported with dapsone. These include cholestasis, a mononucleosis-like syndrome, hepatitis, and nephrotic syndrome. These side effects are generally considered hypersensitivity reactions and are not dose related. Cutaneous reactions include morbilliform eruptions, erythema multiforme, erythema nodosum, and toxic epidermal necrolysis.

Patients on dapsone or sulfapyridine should be closely followed for possible adverse effects. Initially a CBC and differential should be performed weekly. If they show no changes, then the frequency can be decreased to every other week for several weeks, then monthly, and finally to every 3 months. Tests of kidney and liver function should be done every other week at first, less often once a stable dose is achieved. During sulfapyridine therapy, urinalysis should be obtained to rule out precipitation in the kidneys. Tests for methemoglobin and G-6-PD levels should precede the start of therapy but do not need to be repeated unless clinically indicated.

Basset N, Guillot B, Michel B, et al.: Dapsone as the initial treatment in superficial pemphigus. *Arch Dermatol.* 1987;123:783–785.
A collection of nine cases of superficial pemphigus treated with dapsone.
Bernstein JE, Lorincz A: Sulfonamides and sulfones in dermatologic therapy. *Int J Dermatol.* 1981;20:81–88.
An excellent overall review of dermatologic uses of sulfones.
Fredenberg MF, Malkinson FD: Sulfone therapy in the treatment of leukocytoclastic vasculitis. *J Am Acad Dermatol.* 1987;16:772–778.
A report of three cases of vasculitis successfully treated with dapsone.
Jablonska S, Chorzelski T: When and how to use sulfones in bullous diseases. *Int J Dermatol.* 1981;20:103–105.
A concise summary of the efficacy of sulfones in bullous diseases from dermatitis herpetiformis to pemphigus foliaceous.

Jacobson R: The face of leprosy in the United States today. *Arch Dermatol.* 1990;126:1627–1630.
An editorial discussion of Hansen's cases in the United States with particular emphasis on treatment regimens and the emergence of drug resistance.
Johnson DA, Cattau EL, Kuritsky JN, et al.: Liver involvement in the sulfone syndrome. *Arch Intern Med.* 1986;146:875–877.
A discussion of dapsone hypersensitivity and report of a case.
Lang PG: Sulfones and sulfonamides in dermatology today. *J Am Acad Dermatol.* 1979;1:479–492.
A comprehensive review of sulfones, including detailed discussion of pharmacology, doses, mechanisms of action, and adverse effects.
Manfredi G, DePanfilis G, Zampetti M, et al.: Studies on dapsone induced haemolytic anemia. *Br J Dermatol.* 1979;100:427–432.
A study showing that hemolysis induced by dapsone is not related to functional impairment of G-6-PD.
Millikan LE: The sulfones: safety and efficacy. *Int J Dermatol.* 1981;20:102–103.
An editorial perspective on the relative safety of sulfones.
Potter MN, Yates P, Slade R, et al.: Agranulocytosis caused by dapsone therapy for granuloma annulare. *J Am Acad Dermatol.* 1989;20:87–88.
A concise discussion of this adverse effect of dapsone and a report of a case.
Sneddon IB, Wilkinson DS: Subcorneal pustular dermatosis. *Br J Dermatol.* 1979;100:61–68.
Clinical cases and discussion of this disorder with confirmation of the usefulness of dapsone.
Wozel G; The story of sulfones in tropical medicine and dermatology. *Int J Dermatol.* 1989;28:17–21.
A good historical perspective on the use of dapsone.

84. ANTIMALARIALS
Ethan A. Lerner

Three antimalarials are used in dermatology: chloroquine (Aralen), hydroxychloroquine (Plaquenil), and quinacrine (Atabrine, Mepacrine). The indications include systemic lupus erythematosus (SLE), discoid lupus erythematosus (DLE), polymorphous light eruption (PMLE), solar urticaria, porphyria cutanea tarda (PCT), granuloma annulare, and sarcoidosis. This chapter highlights the history, chemistry, potential mechanism of action, clinical indications, dosages, and side effects of these compounds.

Antimalarials have been used primarily to treat malaria. Their use dates to the 1600s when the Countess of Chinchon, wife of the viceroy of Peru, was apparently cured of malaria by the bark of a tree. The tree, cinchona, now bears her name. The active ingredient, quinine, proved difficult to synthesize. In search of other antimalarials, quinacrine was synthesized in 1932. As antimalarials were urgently needed during the campaigns of World War II, and quinacrine was felt to be too toxic, hundreds of thousands of compounds were made and chloroquine was developed by the French in 1943. After the war it was found that German chemists had synthesized chloroquine in 1934.

Quinine was first used in the treatment of DLE in 1894, and quinacrine (Atabrine) was used successfully for DLE in 1940. However, it was a report in 1951 on the effectiveness of quinacrine in patients with DLE and also in patients with SLE and associated rheumatoid arthritis that popularized the use of antimalarials in dermatology.

Between 1951 and the mid-1960s, most dermatologists used antimalarials for a variety of cutaneous diseases and systemic diseases with cutaneous manifestations.

In 1955, the first cases of chloroquine-induced retinopathy were reported. By the mid-1960s, a large number of apparently confirmatory reports appeared, and the use of antimalarials in dermatology was virtually abandoned in favor of "safer" drugs such as nonsteroidal anti-inflammatory drugs (NSAIDs), systemic corticosteroids, gold, and cytotoxic agents. Since 1982 it has been known that the ophthalmologic complications of antimalarials have been overstated. With appropriate monitoring for potential side effects, the antimalarials serve an important role in dermatologic therapeutics.

The parent chemical structure of both chloroquine and hydroxychloroquine is the 4-aminoquinolone nucleus. Quinacrine has an additional benzene ring attached to this structure and is therefore an acridine rather than an aminoquinolone compound. All three of these bitter-tasting compounds are well absorbed from the gastrointestinal tract, even in the presence of diarrhea. They have an affinity for tissues including skin, white blood cells, liver, spleen, adrenals, and especially the retinal pigment epithelium. As a result of this tissue affinity, it takes 3 to 4 weeks to reach a plasma-tissue equilibrium for the chloroquines and up to 3 months for quinacrine.

All of the antimalarials are slowly excreted in the urine. A small amount of hepatic clearing takes place. Chloroquine is not removed effectively from the body during either renal or peritoneal dialysis, so doses must be cut by at least one-half in such patients.

The primary effect of antimalarials is the altering of the pH, and thus the function, of acid vesicles (lysosomes). This single important event may explain the large variety of purported **mechanisms of action** of chloroquine. These include interactions with DNA and RNA, suppression of lymphocyte transformation, inhibition of complement-mediated hemolysis, inhibition of hydrolytic enzymes, stabilization of (lysosomal) membranes, alteration in arachidonic acid metabolism, and inhibition of chemotaxis. The chloroquines also bind to porphyrins, forming a complex that leads to porphyrinuria, thus explaining their usefulness in the treatment of PCT.

Antimalarials are useful in the **management** of many dermatologic diseases. However, it should be noted that rheumatoid arthritis is the only disease for which the effectiveness of antimalarials has been demonstrated by double-blind studies.

Antimalarials are useful for treating the cutaneous lesions of both DLE and SLE and are most effective when lesions are tumid and scaly rather than atrophic. Antimalarials should be used after topical or intralesional steroids have been tried. Decreasing the dose of antimalarials should be done only after the disease is clearly under control, as treatment failures may occur otherwise. Sunscreens (or avoidance of sun exposure) should be used concurrently. Good responses are usually obtained in 4 to 12 weeks, and treatment will typically have to be maintained for months, with weaning from the medication sometimes possible during the winter. Typical doses are 200 mg bid for hydroxychloroquine (Plaquenil) or 500 mg daily for chloroquine phosphate (300 mg chloroquine base). Doubling these doses may be necessary in some patients. The effects and side effects of these two drugs are apparently identical and additive; therefore, nothing is gained by using them together. For reasons of tradition, dermatologists seem to prefer to prescribe Plaquenil. Quinacrine (Atabrine) is as useful and can be used alone or in combination with the chloroquines. Its propensity to turn skin a lemon yellow color limits its use in whites. The starting dose is 100 mg tid, decreased to a maintenance dose of 100 mg/d as the disease comes under control.

The dosage schedules noted above for the chloroquines are used in the treatment of solar urticaria and PMLE. Treatment is continued only while the disease is active and should otherwise be tapered off because potential side effects of the drugs usually outweigh the difficulty of the clinical problem being treated. Fifty percent of patients will relapse within 6 months.

PCT can be treated with chloroquine because the drug-porphyrin complex is excreted in the urine, leading to a reduction in porphyrin levels. The gastrointestinal side effects noted in years past with doses of 250–1000 mg/d of chloroquine can be avoided with an equally effective regimen using 125 mg 2 to 3 times a week for 6 to 18 months. If phlebotomy is performed concurrently, a dose of 250 mg a week can be used.

The chloroquines, at the doses used in the treatment of lupus erythematosus, have also been reported to be effective in the treatment of sarcoidosis and granuloma annulare. Chloroquine has been used to treat psoriasis in photosensitive patients. Quinine sulfate, at a dose of 260 mg daily, is sometimes used in the treatment of nocturnal leg cramps. Anecdotal reports suggest that quinine may also be useful in the treatment of granuloma annulare. One report suggests that chloroquine may temporarily clear lichen planus of the nails.

Before treatment with any of the antimalarials is begun, a number of tests should be performed. These tests include a complete blood count along with BUN, creatinine, and liver function tests, ophthalmologic examination, and, if clinically indicated, 24-hour urine for uroporphyrins and coproporphyrins to rule out underlying PCT. The package inserts on the drugs recommend obtaining a G-6-PD level, but there is no pathophysiologic reason for these drugs to induce hemolysis. Hemolysis can occur with other antimalarials, such as primaquine. Eye examinations should be repeated every 6 months.

Antimalarials have a number of potential **side effects.** The chloroquines are known to induce black or purple patches, particularly on the shins or hard palate. Transverse pigment bands may occur in the nails. Pathologically, the drug forms a complex with melanin, resulting in the deposition of yellow-brown granules in the dermis. Atabrine causes diffuse lemon yellow coloring with yellow-brown nonmelanin granules in macrophages in the dermis. The change in eye color that occurs with the use of Atabrine is identical to that seen in jaundice (but otherwise unrelated). Chloroquine has been reported to bleach hair in blonds and redheads.

The chloroquines can cause a lichenoid dermatitis, exfoliative erythroderma, centrifugal annular erythema, urticaria, or exacerbation of psoriasis. Chloroquine can be beneficial in the treatment of psoriasis in patients who are photosensitive. There is a report that some Australian soldiers who took quinacrine for malaria prophylaxis during World War I developed squamous cell cancers of the hands.

Reversible asymptomatic corneal deposits have been noted in SLE patients treated with chloroquines and are not a contraindication to continued use. Difficulty with accommodation secondary to muscle relaxation may occur, but it resolves after a few weeks of treatment. The "dangers" previously reported involved the fundus. These included pigment changes in the macular region with loss of central vision and impaired dark adaptation when total doses exceeded 100 to 300 g. None of the reports was adequately controlled. Recent reports show no visual problems with doses in the kilogram range of chloroquines. Nevertheless, it is prudent to have eye examinations performed every 6 months and to try to limit doses to 4.4 mg/kg for chloroquine and 7.7 mg/kg for hydroxychloroquine.

All of the antimalarials can cause a leukopenia that is reversible. Quinacrine has caused aplastic anemia. Hemolysis secondary to G-6-PD deficiency does not occur with these drugs.

A rare, idiosyncratic myasthenia gravis–like reaction has been reported with chloroquine. A temporary muscle relaxant effect (as noted above with regard to visual accommodation) can cause a mild ileus. All of the antimalarials have been associated with psychoses and seizures when used at very high doses. Quinacrine is contraindicated in psychotic patients.

Nausea, vomiting, diarrhea, headaches, pruritus, and sweating are reported side effects of the antimalarials. These problems can usually be controlled by decreasing the dose, switching the drug, or waiting them out. Side effects have been reported with chloroquine more often than with hydroxychloroquine, but this observation can be attributed to the wider use of chloroquine.

Large numbers of women with malaria have received antimalarials. While there are no reports of fetal malformations from the chloroquines, they do cross the placenta. Deafness, mental retardation, and convulsions have been reported in infants of women who received chloroquine during pregnancy. There is one report of multiple anomalies in a baby whose mother took quinacrine (100 mg/d) during the first trimester. Chloroquine is not secreted in breast milk.

The increased use of chloroquines has led to chloroquine poisoning in both infants who find pills and adults who attempt suicide. Five grams is a fatal dose in adults.

Treatment of overdoses must be rapidly instituted because of irreversible damage to the myocardium within 3 hours. Treatment is best accomplished with mechanical ventilation, diazepam, and epinephrine.

Fitch CD: Antimalarial schizonticides: ferriprotoporphyrin IX interaction hypothesis. *Parasitology Today.* 1986;2:330–331.
A parasitologist's view on the interaction of antimalarials with porphyrins.

Koranda FC: Antimalarials. *J Am Acad Dermatol.* 1981;4:650–655.
An excellent overall review.

Krogstad DJ, Schlesinger PH: Acid-vesicle function, intracellular pathogens, and the action of chloroquine against plasmodium falciparum. *N Engl J Med.* 1987; 317:542–549.
Up-to-date theory on the mechanism of action of chloroquine.

Lycka BA: Misconceptions about antimalarials. *Int J Dermatol.* 1989;28(10):648–649.
The retinal toxicity of the antimalarials may be overestimated.

Olansky AJ: Antimalarials and ophthalmologic safety. *J Am Acad Dermatol.* 1982;6:19–23.
Provides an in-depth rebuttal to alleged concerns about retinal toxicity induced by antimalarials.

Public Health Laboratory Service, Malaria Reference Laboratory: Prevention of malaria in pregnancy and early childhood. *Br Med J.* 1984;289:1296–1297.
Discusses antimalarials and their use during pregnancy and notes that the higher doses used in the treatment of collagen vascular disease, compared to that for malaria prophylaxis, may not be safe.

Riou B, Barriot P, Rimailho A, et al.: Treatment of severe chloroquine poisoning. *N Engl J Med.* 1988;318:1–6.
Provides an aggressive treatment regimen for chloroquine poisoning.

Weiss JS: Antimalarial medications in dermatology. A review. *Dermatol Clin.* 1991;9(2):377–385.
The antimalarials have a wider margin of safety than previously appreciated.

85. TOPICAL AND SYSTEMIC ANTIBIOTICS
Richard J. Sharpe

The dermatologist treats a wide variety of cutaneous infections as well as primary skin conditions that are exacerbated by microbial colonization or secondary infection. In addition, dermatologists have historically played an important role in diagnosing and treating sexually transmitted diseases. Dermatologic research has shown that certain antibiotics, notably tetracyclines and erythromycin, have weak anti-inflammatory properties, which probably account for their utility in many dermatologic conditions. For example, this anti-inflammatory effect is probably important in explaining the effectiveness of these drugs in acne vulgaris.

Dermatologists have pioneered the development and use of topical antimicrobials. Topical use of these agents can minimize or eliminate potential side effects. Certain antibiotics, such as bacitracin, neomycin, and polymyxin B, although too toxic to be used systemically, are safe when used topically.

Penicillin is an organic acid originally obtained from cultures of *Penicillium* mold. Penicillin G can be considered the prototype penicillin and is active against most gram-positive aerobic bacteria and a variety of anaerobes. Various derivatives of penicillin have extended spectrums due to such properties as resistance to beta-lactamases or improved binding to penicillin-binding proteins (PBPs) on cell walls. The absorption of penicillin G from the gastrointestinal tract is variable and incomplete. Several penicillin derivatives have improved stability in the low pH stomach environment and more consistent absorption.

The antibiotic activity of penicillins involves initial binding of these drugs to PBPs with subsequent inhibition of cell wall synthesis. These PBPs are actually the enzymes involved in synthesis of the bacterial cell wall. Penicillins irreversibly bind these transpeptidases, carboxypeptidases, and endopeptidases at their active sites and hence abolish their activity. Autolysins, present in most bacterial cell walls, are necessary for penicillin to be bactericidal and not simply bacteriostatic. Penicillin resistance can be due to many mechanisms, including altered or decreased PBPs, bacterial beta-lactamases, and decreased autolysins to name a few.

Penicillins are minimally toxic in animals, and the limited toxicity in many animals, including humans, is due to the companion cation. Unfortunately in humans, allergic reactions to penicillin are not uncommon. These reactions range from IgE-mediated immediate hypersensitivity, including potentially fatal anaphylaxis, to serum sickness reactions. Hypersensitivity of one type or another to penicillin probably occurs in about 1% to 2% of the general population.

If the appropriate penicillin is chosen, then most skin and skin structure, bone, joint, respiratory, genitourinary tract and CNS infections can be treated. In certain severe gram-positive infections, such as endocarditis or enterococcal bacteremia, the appropriate penicillin should be used in conjunction with an aminoglycoside. Aminoglycosides are synergistic with penicillins in treating certain gram-positive and gram-negative infections.

Penicillin G is the prototype penicillin. It is active against most nonpenicillinase-producing gram-positive cocci, including most strains of enterococci, and also gram-negative diplococci. Anaerobic bacteria are also susceptible to penicillin G, with the noted exception of many anaerobes found in the intestine and in pelvic infections, particularly *Bacteroides fragilis*. In general, oral or lung anaerobic infections can be adequately treated with penicillin G. Penicillin G should be used only parenterally. Penicillin V has essentially the same spectrum of action as penicillin G but is more efficiently and less erratically absorbed after oral administration than is penicillin G.

Dicloxacillin, cloxacillin, oxacillin, nafcillin, and methicillin are all beta-lactamase-resistant penicillins. They all have essentially the same spectrum as penicillin G but are also active against penicillinase-resistant strains. Of the group, nafcillin has slightly better tissue penetration and tends to be more active on a weight basis than the others. For non-beta-lactamase-producing organisms, penicillin G is usually more active than the beta-lactamase-resistant penicillins. In clinical practice, however, the advantage of penicillin G in these situations is usually insignificant except when one is treating enterococcal infections due to non-penicillinase-producing strains of this organism.

Ampicillin has the same spectrum of activity as penicillin G, but it also covers many non-beta-lactamase-producing gram-negative organisms. However, ampicillin is not effective against *Pseudomonas* species. Amoxicillin has the same spectrum of action as ampicillin and has the advantage of better and more consistent absorption after oral administration. Carbenicillin is active against organisms covered by ampicillin, but also is effective against many species of *Pseudomonas* and other gram-negative organisms not covered by ampicillin. Ticarcillin, pipracillin, mezlocillin, and other related semisynthetic penicillins show even greater activity against non-beta-lactamase-producing gram-negative organisms and *Pseudomonas* species.

If a beta-lactamase inhibitor is administered concurrently with a non-beta-lactamase-resistant penicillin, then the spectrum of activity of the penicillin can be extended. Examples of this include amoxicillin-clavulanic acid (Augmentin) and ampicillin-sublactam (Unisyn). Augmentin is particularly useful for treating outpatient respiratory tract infections but is also useful for skin structure infections.

The **fluoroquinolones** are structurally related to nalidixic acid, an antimicrobial agent first synthesized in 1962. Nalidixic acid, though active against many gram-negative bacteria in vitro, has many limitations. Among the problems that limit the clinical utility of nalidixic acid are rapid emergence of resistance, frequent superinfections, and many side effects, including drug eruptions, gastrointestinal upset, and multiple CNS effects.

Certain fluorinated derivatives of nalidixic acid, the so-called fluoroquinolones, have greater clinical utility as antimicrobials. This class of antibiotics has a broader spectrum of activity and is active against most gram-positive and gram-negative aerobes, including most species of *Pseudomonas*. In addition, several of the fluoroquinolones are active against *Mycoplasma, Chlamydia, Legionella,* and certain atypical mycobacteria. Anaerobic organisms are relatively resistant to currently available fluoroquinolones.

Fluoroquinolones act by inhibiting the prokaryotic enzyme, DNA gyrase, which is necessary for supercoiling of DNA. These agents are bactericidal and exhibit synergistic activity with certain beta-lactam antibiotics. However, they exhibit antagonism with rifampin and chloramphenicol.

Fluoroquinolones are readily absorbed after oral administration and, because of their low molecular weight and minimal protein binding, enter most tissue compartments. They are useful for treating many types of infections because of their excellent penetration and broad spectrum, including soft tissue infections and gonococcal and nongonococcal urethritis. Most multiple drug-resistant isolates of *Pseudomonas* are susceptible to these agents, as are many strains of methicillin-resistant *Staphylococcus aureus*. However, currently available fluoroquinolones have no significant activity against anaerobes and only borderline activity against streptococcal species.

The side effect profile of the fluoroquinolones is favorable, and the frequency of side effects in most studies has been equivalent to or lower than that of comparison drugs such as trimethoprim-sulfamethoxazole, cephalosporins, ampicillin, and aminoglycosides. Gastrointestinal upset, lightheadedness, headache, and drowsiness are rare but are the most commonly encountered side effects in most studies; photosensitivity can rarely occur. However, fluoroquinolones are contraindicated in children and adolescents because of possible toxic effects on developing cartilage.

Of the presently available fluoroquinolones, norfloxacin should be used only for treating urinary tract infections, while ciprofloxacin, ofloxacin, enoxacin, pefloxacin, fleroxacin, lomefloxacin, and several other compounds under development are potentially useful for treating skin and skin structure, bone, joint, respiratory, and genitourinary infections plus infectious diarrhea.

The **cephalosporins** were originally isolated from a *Cephalosporium* mold. The drugs in this class are beta-lactam antibiotics with the same mechanism of action as the penicillins.

The first-generation cephalosporins such as cefazolin, cephalexin, and cephalothin have an antibiotic spectrum that is similar to that of beta-lactamase-resistant penicillins, but are also effective against certain gram-negative organisms. In general, first-generation cephalosporins are ineffective against *Hemophilus influenzae, Pseudomonas,* and enterococci.

Second-generation cephalosporins such as cefuroxime have greater activity against gram-negative organisms, including *Hemophilus influenzae*. However, they are not effective against *Pseudomonas* species.

Third-generation cephalosporins have even greater gram-negative coverage, including activity against many species of *Pseudomonas*. Ceftriaxone is a third-generation cephalosporin that can be administered IM or IV, has a long serum half-life, and can be administered once daily. A single dose is effective against uncomplicated gonorrhea due to both penicillinase- and non-penicillinase-producing isolates. Ceftriaxone has excellent activity against *Borrelia burgdorferi*.

Erythromycin is a macrolide antibiotic isolated from *Streptomyces erythreus*. Erythromycin inhibits protein synthesis in susceptible microorganisms by binding to the 50 S ribosomal subunit in these organisms.

Erythromycin is effective against most gram-positive cocci and bacilli, including streptococci, *Staphylococcus aureus, Corynebacterium* species, and anaerobes such as *Propionibacterium acnes*. Most strains of gonococci are sensitive, as are atypical organisms including *Chlamydia* and *Mycoplasma* species and spirochetes as well as *B. burgdorferi*.

Erythromycin is well tolerated, but gastrointestinal upset may limit its use in certain individuals. Macrolides structurally related to erythromycin are under development; they are more acid stable than erythromycin, show better oral absorption, and have more favorable pharmacokinetics. As with the tetracyclines, some evidence suggests that erythromycins may exert a mild anti-inflammatory effect. The recently approved macrolide clarithromycin is particularly useful for treating respiratory tract pathogens.

The **tetracyclines** were discovered while screening microorganisms from soil samples for antibiotic activity. Since isolation of the parent compound, a number of derivatives have been found to be useful.

The tetracyclines are bacteriostatic for a wide range of microorganisms and function by blocking the interaction of aminoacyl transfer RNA with messenger RNA. They thus inhibit protein synthesis. They are active against a wide range of microorganisms including *Mycoplasma, Chlamydia, Rickettsia, Legionella,* and spirochetes including *Borrelia.* Tetracyclines are also effective against certain gram-positive and gram-negative aerobes and anaerobes. In addition to exerting their antibiotic effect, the tetracyclines also exert a mild anti-inflammatory effect, which contributes to their utility in certain conditions such as acne vulgaris.

Tetracycline is the most commonly used member of the tetracycline family. Doxycycline and minocycline have longer serum half-lives and require less frequent dosing. These derivatives also are more reliably absorbed. All tetracyclines are potentially photosensitizing, but minocycline has the lowest potential for this effect. Vertigo occasionally occurs with minocycline. As with all broad-spectrum antibiotics, superinfection with resistant organisms is a potential problem.

The **aminoglycoside** antibiotics are broad-spectrum bactericidal drugs with excellent activity against most aerobic gram-negative bacilli. Most *Staphylococcus* species and enterococci are also sensitive to the aminoglycosides. Drugs in this class are synergistic with beta-lactam antibiotics for many organisms including *Pseudomonas* species.

Gentamicin and tobramycin can be used either topically or systemically. Neomycin is useful only topically, because of its systemic toxicity. Amikacin is useful systemically and has greater activity against *Pseudomonas* than the other antibiotics in this group. Topical use of aminoglycosides, particularly neomycin, is associated with a high rate of contact hypersensitivity. All aminoglycosides are nephrotoxic and can cause partial or complete kidney failure.

The **monobactams,** of which aztreonam is the first available agent, have a monocyclic beta-lactam nucleus that is structurally different from that of the classical beta-lactams (e.g., penicillin, cephalosporins, etc.). They have excellent activity against a wide range of gram-negative organisms, including multiresistant isolates. They have an excellent toxicity profile and exert synergistic activity, similar to that of classical beta-lactams against most *Pseudomonas* strains, with aminoglycosides.

Clindamycin, like erythromycin, binds the 50 S subunit of bacterial ribosomes and suppresses protein synthesis. Many gram-positive cocci, with the exception of enterococci, are sensitive to clindamycin. Clindamycin has excellent activity against most anaerobic bacteria, including *Propionibacterium acnes.* It is an excellent agent against *Staphylococcus aureus* and streptococcal species.

Clindamycin can be administered topically, orally, or parenterally. Pseudomembranous colitis has been linked to all routes of administration; however, it is rare in an outpatient setting.

Metronidazole was originally developed because of its utility in treating trichomonal infections. Subsequently, it was shown that metronidazole has efficacy in treating anaerobic infections.

Metronidazole can be administered orally or parenterally. Recently, topical metronidazole has been used successfully in the treatment of rosacea.

A disulfuram-like reaction is common with metronidazole. Metronidazole and several of its metabolites are mutagenic. These data and metronidazole's carcinogenicity in rodents suggest that this drug should be used prudently when administered systemically, but available data suggests that topical metronidazole is very safe.

Rifamycins are a group of macrocyclic antibiotics produced by *Streptomyces mediterranei.* Rifampin is a derivative of one of these antibiotics.

Rifampin inhibits protein synthesis in a wide range of gram-positive and gram-negative bacteria and mycobacteria. After oral administration rifampin is found in all body fluids. This property and the exquisite sensitivity of most strains of *Staphylococcus aureus* and meningococci make rifampin useful for eliminating carrier states of these organisms. Long-term use of rifampin as a single agent is associated with the emergence of resistant strains in many instances.

Rifampin can induce hepatic toxicity, especially if used in conjunction with other hepatotoxic agents.

Vancomycin is an antibiotic isolated from the culture broth of *Streptomyces orientalis*. Vancomycin inhibits cell wall synthesis in susceptible bacteria.

Most gram-positive cocci, including enterococci, are sensitive to vancomycin. It is the drug of choice for life-threatening infections caused by gram-positive aerobic cocci. Vancomycin is poorly absorbed after oral administration, and this property coupled with its activity against *Clostridium difficile* makes it useful for treating pseudomembranous colitis.

Systemic administration of vancomycin can result in hypersensitivity reactions, ototoxicity, nephrotoxicity, and occasionally a shocklike state. Most of these side effects can be minimized if serum concentrations are monitored and dosages adjusted.

The **bacitracins** are a group of polypeptide antibiotics produced by *Bacillus subtilis*. Most commercial preparations contain a mixture of bacitracins, but bacitracin A predominates.

Bacitracin inhibits cell wall synthesis in a variety of gram-positive cocci and bacilli and in several gram-negative organisms. *Pseudomonas* species are resistant.

Bacitracin is safe topically, but causes serious nephrotoxicity if administered systemically. Contact hypersensitivity rarely occurs secondary to topical use.

The **polymyxins** are antibiotics isolated from *Bacillus polymyxa*. They are cationic detergents that interact with cell membranes. These agents disrupt the cell membranes of susceptible bacteria. Polymyxin B is the most useful member of this class of antibiotics. It is active against many gram-negative bacteria, including *Pseudomonas* species.

Polymyxin B is no longer used systemically, because of its toxicity and because of the availability of other agents. Topical use of polymyxin B is well tolerated and is rarely associated with untoward side effects.

Mupirocin is an antibiotic produced by *Pseudomonas fluorescens*. This agent inhibits bacterial protein synthesis by binding to isoleucyl transfer RNA synthetase. It is primarily active against aerobic gram-positive cocci including *Staphylococcus* species and *Streptococcus pyogenes*. It is approved for topical use in the treatment of impetigo, and data demonstrates that it is at least as effective as orally administered erythromycin in treating this condition. Mupirocin might also be useful either alone or in combination with systemic antibiotics in clearing *S. aureus* nasal carrier states. Burning, stinging, or pain at the site of application occasionally occurs. Contact dermatitis is rare.

Spectinomycin, an antibiotic produced by *Streptomyces spectabilis*, binds to the 30 S ribosomal subunit of susceptible bacteria. This drug is effective against a number of gram-negative organisms. The primary use of spectinomycin today is for the treatment of uncomplicated gonococcal infections in penicillin-allergic individuals. It is also useful against beta-lactamase-producing strains of gonococci. Rarely, urticaria, chills, and fever occur secondary to spectinomycin treatment.

The **sulfonamides** were the first agents that became useful for treating a wide range of systemic bacterial infections. They remain an important part of our armamentarium, despite the availability of a wide range of antibiotics. The utility of sulfonamides has been expanded with the introduction of the combination trimethoprim-sulfamethoxazole, which is a synergistic combination of antimicrobial agents. Sulfonamides act by inhibiting the utilization of para-aminobenzoic acid in the synthesis of folic acid. Trimethoprim inhibits dihydrofolate reductase. The combination is synergistic in inhibiting folate synthesis.

The sulfonamides are effective against many gram-positive and gram-negative organisms as well as *Actinomyces, Nocardia,* and *Pneumocystis carinii*. The sulfonamides have poor activity against most streptococcal isolates and most anaerobes. Silver sulfadiazine is a topical sulfonamide primarily used for treating burns and ulcers.

Sulfonamides as well as the combination of trimethoprim and sulfamethoxazole have been reported to produce blood dyscrasias and crystalluria. Hypersensitivity reactions, including Stevens-Johnson syndrome, can be fatal.

The selection of the appropriate antibiotic requires a correct diagnosis and is aided by certain diagnostic tests, such as Gram's stain and culture. In many instances, an empiric antibiotic can be chosen and the clinical response to treatment can then be observed. Certain infectious conditions will resolve without antibiotic therapy. For example, hot tub folliculitis, although caused by *Pseudomonas* species, is usually self-limited. In this case the potential risks of antibiotic therapy outweigh the benefits in most instances. If the patient is immunocompromised, however, the clinician might consider the use of systemic antibiotics. Therefore, the choice of antibiotics, as well as whether to use them at all, depends on the clinical setting in many instances. Indiscriminate use of broad-spectrum antibiotics also poses the hazard of accelerating the emergence of resistant bacteria.

In the ultimate decision involving the use of antimicrobials in selected conditions encountered by the physician, the current *Physicians' Desk Reference* and other current sources should be consulted prior to instituting therapy. As with all interventions, the risks and benefits of therapy must be carefully weighed. For example, it would be inappropriate to treat a self-limited infection such as hot tub folliculitis with a highly toxic antibiotic such as an aminoglycoside and risk irreversible organ damage (i.e., kidney failure).

Bleicher PA, Charles JH, Sober AJ: Topical metronidazole therapy for rosacea. *Arch Dermatol.* 1987;123:609–614.
A well-designed and executed study that documents the effectiveness of topical metronidazole in rosacea.

Dattwyler RJ, Volkman DJ, Conaty SM, Platkin SP, Luft BJ: Amoxicillin plus probenecid versus doxycycline for treatment of erythema migrans borreliosis. *Lancet.* 1990;336:1404–1406.
This study demonstrates equal efficacy of amoxicillin 500 mg PO tid plus probenicid 500 mg PO tid versus doxycycline 100 mg PO tid both for 21 days in the treatment of erythema migrans. No patients (N = 72) needed further antibiotic treatment.

Eady EA, Holland KT, Cunliffe WJ: Topical antibiotics in acne therapy. *J Am Acad Dermatol.* 1981;5:455–459.
Discusses the approach and rationale to the use of topical antibiotics in acne therapy.

Hirschmann JV: Topical antibiotics in dermatology. *Arch Dermatol.* 1988;124:1691–1700.
An excellent synopsis covering the rationale and use of topical antibiotics in dermatology.

Ramirez-Ronda CH, Saavedra S, Rivera-Vasquez CR: Comparative, double blind study of oral ciprofloxacin and intravenous cefotaxime in skin and skin structure infections. *Am J Med.* 1987;82(suppl. 4A):220–223.
This study illustrates the efficacy of oral ciprofloxacin in the treatment of skin structure infections.

Hooper DE, Wolfson JS: Fluoroquinolone antimicrobial agents. *N Engl J Med.* 1991;324:384–394.
This review provides a concise and up-to-date summary of the fluoroquinolones, ranging from their mechanisms of action to clinical uses and side effects.

Sanders WE Jr.: Efficacy, safety and potential economic benefits of oral ciprofloxacin in the treatment of infections. *Rev Infect Dis.* 1988;10:528–543.
This review concisely discusses the points described in the title. It is recommended reading for anyone who prescribes fluoroquinolones.

86. DERMATOLOGIC SURGERY
Suzanne M. Olbricht

A wide range of physical modalities may be employed to remove or destroy benign and malignant skin lesions. Cryosurgery, curettage, application of acids, electrosurgery, and standard surgical techniques such as fusiform excision and primary repair are commonly used by most dermatologists. Some dermatologists perform more specialized procedures, including Mohs micrographic surgery, complicated repairs with flaps and grafts, implantation of soft tissue filling substances, hair transplantation, dermabrasion or chemical peeling, blepharoplasty, and laser surgery. All of these procedures may be accomplished in the physician's office, although some may require office modifications, specialized equipment, and trained assistants.

The standard agent used for **cryosurgery** is liquid nitrogen at $-195.6°C$. It must be kept in a metal container, but it is inexpensive, noncombustible, and readily available from medical and industrial sources. Techniques used to destroy a wide array of benign and malignant skin lesions are generally simple and fast, and yield rewarding results. The liquid nitrogen may be applied to the skin with a cotton-tipped applicator, or it may be delivered via a spray from a commercially available hand-held instrument consisting of a reservoir and an arm with an aperture that can be varied in size (e.g., a Cryospray unit). The exact mechanism of injury is unclear but may include mechanical damage to the cells by intracellular and extracellular ice formation, osmotic changes related to dehydration of cells during ice crystal formation, thermal shock, denaturation of proteins, and vascular stasis with resulting necrosis of tissue. For benign lesions, a loosely wrapped cotton-tipped applicator is dipped into the liquid nitrogen and promptly placed onto the cutaneous lesion without pressure. The lesion becomes white as it freezes, accompanied by a stinging or burning sensation that subsides within several minutes of thawing. A 5- to 30-second application is adequate for small and superficial lesions and generally does not require local anesthesia. Some practice is required for the physician to discover the technique that allows adequate freezing of the lesion and produces good results. The degree of injury is roughly proportional to the intensity of the freezing. Dressings are not required after treatment. The area can be washed twice a day with mild soap and water and an antibiotic ointment applied. Most lesions are red and scaly for several weeks before crumbling to leave a smooth surface. A blister may form, and the patient may be mildly uncomfortable. Generally, light freezing does not produce scarring. Lesions that may be treated in this fashion include lentigines, seborrheic keratoses, actinic keratoses, warts, and molluscum contagiosum. Some lesions may require more than one treatment, generally spaced 3 weeks apart. Complications of treatment can include hypopigmentation or scarring.

A malignant lesion such as basal cell carcinoma or squamous cell carcinoma may be treated with aggressive cryosurgery. Cure rates reported average 95%. Liquid nitrogen is delivered via a spray to effect complete freezing of a field that includes the tumor and its margins, both circumferential and deep. Appropriate lethal destruction is determined either by measuring the depth of freeze with thermocouple-tipped needles placed in the tumor or by standardized timing of the freeze-and-thaw cycle. Rapid cooling and slow thawing produce the most damage, and repeated freeze-thaw cycles are more damaging than a single freeze. Under local anesthesia, the site is therefore sprayed vigorously for 20 to 30 seconds and then allowed to thaw. Adequate destruction is achieved with a thaw time of more than 90 seconds for each of two freeze-thaw cycles. The result of aggressive cryosurgery is a local frostbite reaction with swelling, pain, and bullae formation for 1 to 2 days, followed by an ulcer covered by a crust that separates in 2 to 6 weeks. Erythema may persist at the site for months. The mature scar, cosmetically acceptable to selected patients in some locations, is hypopigmented, flat or somewhat depressed, and sclerotic. It softens and elevates with time but never regains normal aging lines or skin folds. Sensory loss may be produced in areas where the nerves lie superficially. Large lesions, difficult tumors such as morpheaform basal cell carcinomas, or tumors in sites of developmental fusion planes have a high rate of recurrence and are best treated by excision with microscopic evaluation of margins rather than destruction.

Curettage is the use of a curet (a cutting instrument with a circular or oval-shaped cutting edge and a handle) to remove diseased tissue. It is not sharp, but it will remove friable tissue without difficulty. Used primarily for treating benign lesions such as warts, molluscum, milia, seborrheic keratoses, and actinic keratoses, it may also be used in conjunction with cryosurgery, electrosurgery or excision in the treatment of basal cell carcinomas or squamous cell carcinomas. Local anesthesia may be necessary in the treatment of large lesions. A curet is chosen with a diameter appropriate for the size of the lesion and the purpose of the procedure. Large curets (over 4 mm) are generally used to remove large lesions quickly, but smaller curets (2 to 4 mm in size) may clean the base of the wound or treat a small lesion more easily. The tissue is removed with a firm, quick, downward scoop, and the base and margins of the wound are scraped. Normal epidermis and dermis are generally not affected. Hemostasis may be achieved by a hemostatic agent or electrodesiccation.

Trichloracetic acid is commonly found in the dermatologist's office, in concentrations of 30% to 80%. Used in weak concentration as a hemostatic agent, it is applied with a lightly moistened cotton-tip swab to the wound after clearing away as much blood as possible with dry gauze. A 50% solution may be applied with a lightly moistened wooden stick or cotton-tip swab to skin tags, seborrheic keratoses, and molluscum contagiosum. A concentrated solution of trichloracetic acid or monochloracetic acid may be painted cautiously on warts or xanthelasma. Treatment is accompanied by a burning sensation, which is followed by evidence of a chemical burn and then by healing with resolution of the lesion. Care must be taken to insure that the acid does not drip or spread onto any skin or mucosal surface not intended to be treated.

Electrosurgery may be used alone or with curettage for simple and effective removal of both benign and malignant cutaneous lesions. The small electrosurgical units most often found in physicians' offices are versatile and useful tools. They deliver a high-frequency alternating current, producing an electrical field around the treatment electrode, usually a needlelike tip. The electric current causes both mechanical disruption of cells and heat. *Electrodesiccation* is a term used to describe very superficial destruction achieved primarily by dehydration of cells. The patient is not incorporated into the electrical circuit. The tip is either held in contact with the tissue or kept a short distance away, and the current is transmitted through a spark. Electrocoagulation produces more severe destruction, primarily by heat. The patient is grounded by being placed on a large indifferent electrode. The treatment tip, placed in or on the tissue, develops an intensely hot current and literally boils or coagulates the lesion. In contrast to electrodesiccation, electrocoagulation produces wider and deeper tissue destruction, better hemostasis, and more scarring. With either technique, sterilized or single-use needle electrodes should be used, since hepatitis B has been spread from patient to patient with the use of reusable nonsterilized electrosurgical electrode tips. The use of high energy current can also deactivate a pacemaker, so special precautions should be used for these patients.

Very superficial lesions treated with good results by light electrodesiccation include telangiectasias and spider angiomas. Local anesthesia is not required. The vessels are traced with brief pulses of current. As they disappear, the area becomes red and swollen. On the day after treatment, the patient develops small crusts that separate in 2 to 5 days with good wound care. Warts, actinic keratoses, molluscum contagiosum, skin tags, and seborrheic keratoses are generally treated more vigorously, depending on the size of the lesion. Local anesthesia may be required for patient comfort and cooperation. An effective technique for treating large lesions is to deliver the current directly to the surface of the lesion until char is visible. The char is then removed with a curet, and any residual lesion is retreated. The wound produced by electrosurgery is left to heal by secondary intention. Good wound care including washing twice a day with soap and water and then applying an antibiotic ointment may facilitate reepithelialization and healing. Healing time depends on the size of the lesion and the amount and depth of tissue destruction.

A malignant skin lesion such as basal cell carcinoma or squamous cell carcinoma may be treated successfully by electrosurgery; however, a standardized protocol is required to achieve an adequate cure rate. Under local anesthesia, a curet is used to debulk the tumor and scrape the sides and base of the resulting defect. Electrocoagulation is then used to char the base and sides of the wound. A second curettage is immediately performed, followed by a second electrocoagulation. Postoperative wound care should be stressed. Healing may require 2 to 6 weeks, resulting in a flat white or hypertrophic scar. In a study of basal cell carcinomas treated first by curettage and electrocoagulation repeated three times in rapid succession followed by excision of the wound by shave technique, residual tumor was found in 8.3% of lesions treated on the trunk and extremities and in 46% of lesions on the face. It may therefore be best to reserve this treatment for tumors of the trunk and extremities.

Standard surgical techniques may be used to remove a variety of dermal and epidermal benign lesions as well as malignant lesions. Planning of the surgery must take into account desired margins of apparently normal skin needed to be removed for an adequate cure rate. For a benign nevus or a sebaceous cyst, no normal tissue needs to be sacrificed; however, for treatment of a dysplastic nevus, basal cell carcinoma, or squamous cell carcinoma, a margin of 2 to 4 mm is generally required. Margins for melanoma are debated; however, 1-cm margins are probably adequate for thin, early lesions and as much as 3 cm may be advisable for thick, late lesions. Five-centimeter margins with excision of a thin layer of underlying muscle is standard therapy for dermatofibrosarcoma protruberans. Surgical excision is performed under local anesthesia. Lesions such as dermal nevi may be adequately removed by shaving with a No. 15 blade. Pedunculated nevi or fibroepithelial polyps may be clipped with a sharp scissors such as a gradle. Hemostasis is then obtained by a styptic (aluminum sulfate or ferric subsulfate solution) or electrodesiccation. Healing is by secondary intention, facilitated by good wound care. Alternatively, a lesion may be excised with a fusiform design into upper subcutaneous fat and repaired primarily. Undermining is often required to facilitate closure of the wound edges. Hemostasis may be achieved with spot electrodesiccation. Absorbable sutures are often placed subcutaneously to effect obliteration of dead space and eversion of the wound edges. Skin sutures oppose the epidermal edges and stabilize the wound. A dressing is applied to the wound postoperatively. Sutures are removed in 5 to 21 days, depending on the site and size of the wound. Sometimes a lesion and its normal skin margins are removed as a disk. In some circumstances, this wound may be left to heal by secondary intention. If it is repaired, the long axis of the wound is determined after undermining. Standing cutaneous cones (dog ears) are excised as dictated by the site and mobility of the patient's skin. Closure then proceeds as before. Large wounds may require a graft or the movement of tissue as flaps.

A specific surgical procedure was developed in 1936 by an American dermatologist, Frederick Mohs, to deal with difficult and recurrent basal cell carcinomas. He performed a staged procedure in which he removed small amounts of accurately mapped tissue under local anesthesia after fixing the skin in vivo with zinc chloride. He then microscopically examined a horizontal section of the inferior margin immediately, and reexcised as necessary until the tissue removed had a completely tumor-free margin. He allowed the wound to heal by secondary intention. As practiced today, **Mohs microscopically controlled surgery** is a fresh tissue technique used for the excision of basal cell carcinomas, squamous cell carcinomas, and a wide variety of other, rarer skin cancers. Under local anesthesia, the tumor is assessed and debulked by curettage. The defect is then excised by saucerization of 1 to 2 mm of tissue. Hemostasis is achieved by electrodesiccation or a styptic. The saucerized tissue is mapped, flattened, and frozen, then cut in horizontal section. The entire undersurface of the lateral and inferior margin is systematically reviewed for the presence of tumor. This microscopic review differs from the usual vertical frozen sections of the pathologist, and allows for evaluation of all the margins rather than a sampling. Repeated saucerizations are performed the same day until the margins are clear. The wound may be allowed to heal by secondary intention, or closed immediately. Large defects may require major reconstructive procedures. The advantages of the Mohs micrographic procedure include maximal preservation of normal tissue and precise delineation of the tract of the tumor. Indications for the procedure, therefore, are recurrent tumors (recurrence rate for the use of other modalities to treat recurrent tumors is 20% to 50% vs. 4% to 9% for Mohs surgery); primary tumors known to have high recurrence rates; and primary lesions where maximal preservation of tissue is necessary, such as the eyelid, nose, finger, genitalia, and areas around the major facial nerves.

Some dermatologists and many plastic surgeons practice cosmetic procedures designed to improve the patient's appearance. Substances available to fill dermal defects, such as wrinkles, scars, or deep "laugh lines" include Zyderm, Zyplast, and Fibrel. These agents are prepackaged by their respective manufacturers and implanted into the defect via a small-gauge needle. The effects are temporary but may ameliorate depressions with little risk. Persistent dermatitis occurs rarely. The instillation of silicone or autologous fat obtained from liposuction may give comparable and longer-lasting results, but their use is controversial. The changing of surface contour and texture may also be achieved by dermabrasion or chemical peeling. A dermabrader consists of a wheel with a granular surface and a motor that spins the wheel rapidly. The spinning wheel is used to grind off the surface epidermis. Alternatively, solutions containing phenol or trichloracetic acid may be used to effect sloughing of the epidermis. Both procedures require skill on the part of the physician and wound care on the part of the patient. Scarring is the major complication of either procedure. Hair transplantation is generally performed in two parts: a surgical scalp reduction procedure and movement of small hair-bearing plugs of skin from the inferior scalp to bald areas. It is most effective in men, for whom results may be striking.

Cottel WI, Proper S: Mohs surgery, fresh tissue technique. *J Dermatol Surg Oncol.* 1982;8:576–587.
   This presentation of a modified method of the fresh tissue technique includes a discussion of the developmental background and advantages of Mohs surgery.
Pollack SV: *Electrosurgery of the Skin.* New York: Churchill Livingstone; 1991.
   Information necessary to make the physician a "compleat" electrosurgeon is presented in an informative and readable style.
Stegman SJ, Tromovitch TA, Glogan RG: *Basics of Dermatologic Surgery.* Chicago, IL: Year Book Medical Publishers, Inc.; 1982.
   This relatively short, handbook-style text discusses practical issues including instruments, sterilization and preoperative preparation, hemostasis, suture material, biopsy techniques, planning and designing a surgical excision, dressings, and complications.
Swanson NA: *Atlas of Cutaneous Surgery.* Boston, MA: Little, Brown and Company; 1987.
   Excellent drawings and suggested exercises accompany this workbook-style text, which directs the physician through simple surgical procedures and some advanced procedures.
Torre D: Cryosurgery of basal cell carcinoma. *J Am Acad Dermatol.* 1986;15:917–926.
   The treatment of basal cell carcinoma by cryosurgery is approached practically, with discussion of indications, equipment, methods, and results.

87. LASERS IN DERMATOLOGY
Jeffrey S. Dover

Atoms and molecules are normally found in a stable state of energy termed the resting state. Light energy can be absorbed by atoms, causing the transition of electrons from the resting state into an excited state. Because this excited state is not stable, the electrons spontaneously emit the absorbed energy and return to the resting state. The energy released by this process, termed spontaneous emission, may be emitted as light that travels in packets known as photons. If the atom in its excited state is irradiated with energy of the same wavelength or frequency that was previously absorbed, the atom returns to its resting state and yields two waves of light energy of the same wavelength and frequency traveling in the same direction in perfect spatial and temporal phase. If this phenomenon, termed stimulated emission of radiation, occurs repeatedly, laser (light amplification by stimulated emission of radiation) light is produced.

Laser light behaves differently from all other sources of electromagnetic radiation. It is monochromatic (one wavelength) and coherent (highly ordered and directional). These properties allow selective absorption of energy by specific light-absorbing compounds and the ability to tightly focus and aim the beam. Laser light can therefore produce thermal injury with a high degree of selectivity in a nonspecific highly controlled manner. For this reason lasers have become routinely used therapeutic tools in dermatology.

The characteristics of each laser depend on the active medium and the power supply. The active medium—which may be a gas (e.g., carbon dioxide), solid crystal (e.g., Nd-YAG) or liquid (e.g., fluorescent dye)—determines the wavelength; and the power supply determines the wave type, which is usually either continuous (e.g., electrical) or pulsed (e.g., flashlamp pumped). Laser light may be transmitted to the target by mirrored tubes (e.g., carbon dioxide laser) or by flexible optical fibers (e.g., argon or dye lasers), depending on the laser wavelength. Carbon dioxide, argon, a dye, copper vapor, and ruby lasers are currently the most commonly used lasers in dermatology.

The **carbon dioxide laser** emits infrared light at a wavelength of 10,600 nm. Since infrared radiation is invisible, a low-powered, helium-neon laser producing red light is aligned with the carbon dioxide beam for directional guidance. Carbon dioxide laser light is absorbed by water and penetrates to a limited extent (about 0.1 mm) into skin independent of tissue color. The absorbed energy is converted to heat, causing thermal tissue damage. When a tissue temperature of 100° C is reached, tissue is vaporized into a plume of smoke. The vaporized area is surrounded by a narrow zone of irreversible thermal denaturation, which appears clinically as black char, which in turn is surrounded by reversible thermal damage. The beam can be delivered with a large spot size and low power to vaporize tissue superficially. Alternatively, it can be focused tightly to a small spot, resulting in a very high power density to cut tissue while coagulating small blood vessels, thus providing a relatively bloodless field.

Used as a cutting instrument, the carbon dioxide laser has several advantages including limited thermal damage adjacent to the target site, allowing for preservation of margins for histologic evaluation; noncontact surgery, reducing potential transfer of infectious agents and malignant cells; sterilization of the vaporized area; and especially sealing of small blood vessels, which provides a relatively bloodless surgical field. Cutting with the carbon dioxide laser is especially useful for patients with bleeding disorders or on anticoagulants; for those with pacemakers or electronic monitoring devices, which limit electrosurgery; and for those with vascular lesions or lesions in highly vascular sites such as the scalp.

To cut tissue, a focused, relatively high power beam (15–30 W) is drawn across the skin at a smooth steady rate of approximately 0.25 cm/second. The initial incision produces a slightly charred, cut surface. Char, serum, blood, or any surface moisture will absorb the carbon dioxide laser beam, limiting further cutting. The skin is wiped with a gauze sponge, moistened with normal saline, and patted with a dry sponge before further cutting is done as required to complete the incision.

The carbon dioxide laser is also used to vaporize superficial lesions. Although the indications for use of the carbon dioxide laser are relative rather than absolute, this laser is often preferred for treatment of recalcitrant, widespread, painful or hyperkeratotic warts, widespread condyloma acuminata, lymphangiomas, actinic cheilitis, tattoos, rhinophyma, and small benign facial skin tumors such as multiple appendageal tumors.

Because thermal tissue damage is painful, local anesthesia is required for these procedures. When the clinician is treating a superficial skin lesion such as a recalcitrant plantar wart, the carbon dioxide laser beam is defocused and drawn back and forth across the wart until the surface is vaporized and charred. The char is wiped away with a saline-moistened gauze, the area is patted dry, and the next layer of tissue is vaporized and charred. This process is continued until the full thickness of the wart is removed. After treatment, a white lifeless-appearing ulcer remains, which requires 2 to 8 weeks to heal.

Wounds from superficial vaporization are usually allowed to heal by secondary intention, while laser incisions are usually closed primarily. During the early phase of wound healing, the tensile strength of carbon dioxide laser incisions may be less than that of a scalpel wound as a result of thermal damage at the wound edge. Sutures are kept in place several days longer to insure proper healing. Complications of carbon dioxide laser surgery include bleeding, infection, and scarring; all of them may be minimized with proper technique and wound care.

The **argon laser** emits at six different wavelengths in the blue-green portion of the visible spectrum, with the majority of the light emitted at two wavelengths: 488 nm and 514 nm. Argon laser light, which is delivered to skin via optical fibers as a continuous or shuttered beam, can penetrate up to 1 mm into the skin. Melanin pigment and hemoglobin are the primary tissue absorbers of the argon light; therefore, the argon laser is used to treat cutaneous vascular anomalies and benign cutaneous pigmented lesions. It is very effective in treating mature, purple, slightly hypertrophic port-wine stains; facial telangiectasias; small hemangiomas; other small vascular lesions and pigmented epidermal lesions.

Although argon laser light is selectively absorbed by hemoglobin in vessels and by melanin pigment, heat deposited in these locations diffuses out into adjacent tissue, resulting in nonselective thermal damage to neighboring structures. The potential for nonselective thermal damage with secondary tissue alteration and potential resultant scarring is the major limitation of argon laser surgery.

Local anesthesia is required when one is treating port-wine stains with the argon laser. A test area of 1 to 2 cm in diameter is treated. Crusts, lasting 7 to 10 days, require appropriate wound care. The test area is evaluated 4 months later to serve as an indicator of treatment outcome. If there is lightening without textural or pigmentary change, the rest of the port-wine stain may be treated. Port-wine stains less than 5 by 5 cm can be treated in one session. Larger lesions require several treatment sessions separated by at least 6 weeks to ensure complete healing of the previously treated site. Telangiectasias are treated without anesthesia by tracing out each individual vessel with a spot size the diameter of the vessels. Only minimal crusting occurs posttreatment, and little wound care is required.

Organic fluorescent compounds dissolved in solvents are the active media in **dye lasers.** By choosing different dyes, the clinician can produce laser light of virtually any color (wavelength) in the visible spectrum. Dye lasers are designed as either continuous or pulsed sources.

Selective thermal damage can be induced in tissue targets that absorb well at the emitted wavelength when the pulse duration or exposure time is shorter than the cooling time or thermal relaxation time of the target. For example, selective thermal damage can be confined to a blood vessel without damage to the surrounding connective tissue if the clinician chooses a wavelength that is well absorbed by hemoglobin, such as 577 or 585 nm, as long as the laser pulse duration is shorter than the thermal relaxation time of a small cutaneous vessel. These physical requirements are met by the pulsed dye laser.

With the 577- to 585-nm pulsed dye laser, most patients experience only a very brief stinging sensation with each pulse, so the need for local anesthesia is limited. Young children are sometimes intolerant of the procedure and may require either local or general anesthesia. A test area is first treated with three or four pulses of laser light at two or three different energies to determine optimal treatment parameters. After evaluation of the test area 4 weeks later, the rest of the port-wine stain is treated. A blue-gray discoloration is the only change induced in the treated skin. Because crusting does not develop, wound care is limited. An average of six treatment sessions of each individual site is required to obtain maximal lightening. Port-wine stains, especially light pink to red, flat or slightly raised lesions, lighten substantially after pulsed dye laser treatment at 585 nm. Excellent responses in light-colored, flat port-wine stains and the very low risk of scarring make the pulsed dye laser the treatment of choice for port-wine stains in infants and children. Telangiectasias, especially on the face, also respond well.

Continuous beam dye laser treatment at 577 to 585 nm, performed in a similar fashion to argon treatment, produces results similar to those obtained with the argon laser, with the attendant risk of scarring due to diffusion of heat energy into tissues adjacent to the vessels. Newly developed scanning devices that shutter the continuous wave laser sources and potentially reduce the scarring risk are being investigated. These devices make the energy delivered more like that of the pulsed dye laser and clinical results may be similar. Comparative trials are under way.

The **neodymium-yttrium aluminum garnet crystal laser** (Nd-YAG laser) emits energy with a wavelength of 1060 nm in the infrared portion of the electromagnetic spectrum. Like the carbon dioxide laser, the Nd-YAG laser produces light that is invisible and therefore requires a helium-neon beam for directional guidance. Poor absorption of Nd-YAG laser light by biologic tissues such as skin permits it to penetrate deeply (4 to 6 mm) into the skin with wide diffusion. This absorption pattern makes the Nd-YAG laser theoretically useful for treatment of large, thick lesions when diffuse nonspecific damage is desired. The laser is, however, not versatile; unlike the carbon dioxide laser, it cannot be limited to superficial absorption, nor directed to small vessels as with the argon laser, nor absorbed specifically by a single light-absorbing compound such as melanin or hemoglobin as with the dye laser. The Nd-YAG laser is rarely used to treat large, boggy vascular lesions such as mature, hypertrophic port-wine stains, hemangiomas, and vascular tumors of mucosal surfaces, and information regarding treatment outcome is still somewhat preliminary. Because of its ability to penetrate deeply and diffuse widely through skin, the Nd-YAG laser can produce substantial thermal coagulation with little vaporization or char, hence little surface change. Profound thermal damage can therefore be produced unknowingly, making the Nd-YAG laser a potentially dangerous tool.

Other lasers and techniques used for treatment of cutaneous disease include copper vapor, Q-switched ruby, Q-switched Nd-YAG, and pulsed 504-nm dye lasers, and photodynamic therapy. The **copper vapor laser,** which emits light in a train of pulses at 578.2 nm, providing good oxyhemoglobin absorption, produces results in port-wine stain treatment that are similar to those achieved with the argon and continuous wave dye lasers. Comparison with the pulsed dye laser has not yet been reported. It is also effective in the treatment of some benign pigmented lesions. The **ruby laser,** which emits at 694 nm, was the first laser used, and as a Q-switched laser, has recently been rediscovered for the treatment of benign cutaneous pigmented lesions and tattoos. This wavelength is well absorbed by melanin and blue-black tattoo pigment. Q-switching is a manipulation of the beam such that a pulse of extremely short duration but high peak intensity is produced. Heat diffusion to tissues surrounding targeting molecules is therefore limited, and scarring is theoretically minimized. Recent studies have documented that the Q-switched ruby laser clears epidermal pigmented lesions (e.g., lentigines, café au lait macules), dermal pigmented lesions (e.g., nevus of Ota) and tattoos with little if any scarring. Given these findings, several other lasers have been developed that use pulsed light to selectively remove epidermal pigment (pulsed 504-nm dye and Q-switched Nd-YAG lasers), dermal pigment, and tattoos (Q-switched Nd-YAG and alexandrite lasers).

The 630-nm dye and 628-nm gold vapor lasers are also used as sources of red light for **photodynamic therapy** for tumors. The patient ingests a red-absorbing photosensitive dye (hematoporphyrin derivative), which is preferentially taken up by rapidly proliferating cells. The laser beam is then directed toward the tumor, and the intense red light is absorbed by the hematoporphyrin derivative, creating heat and relatively selective thermal damage. The primary indication for photodynamic therapy is widespread or multifocal nonmelanoma skin cancer.

Apfelberg DB, ed.: Special Issue: Cutaneous laser surgery: clinical and laboratory investigations. *Laser Surg Med.* 1986;6:2–99.

A special issue of this multidisciplinary laser journal dedicated to skin uses, with an excellent section on argon laser treatment of port-wine stains and hemangiomas.

Arndt KA, Noe JM, Northam DBC, et al.: Laser therapy: Basic concepts and nomenclature. *J Am Acad Dermatol.* 1981;5:649–654.
Dermatologists and physicists explain basic laser physics.

Ashinoff R, Geronemus RG: Capillary hemangiomas and treatment with the flashlamp-pumped pulsed dye laser. *Arch Dermatol.* 1991;127:202–205.
Ten patients aged 7 weeks to 5.5 years underwent an average of three laser treatments with 70% regression of lesions. All lesions regressed to some extent.

Dover JS, Arndt KA, Geronemus R, et al.: *Illustrated Cutaneous Laser Surgery: A Practitioner's Atlas.* E. Norwalk, CT: Appleton & Lange; 1989.
A hands-on guide to laser surgery of skin disorders, written with a "cookbook" approach and extensively illustrated in color and black-and-white. A detailed section on laser fundamentals is complemented by individual chapters on carbon dioxide, argon, dye, and Nd-YAG lasers and photodynamic therapy.

Garden JM, Polla LL, Tan OT: The treatment of port-wine stains by the pulsed dye laser. Analysis of pulse duration and long-term therapy. *Arch Dermatol.* 1988;124:889–896.
Use of the pulsed dye laser in the treatment of vascular malformations in adults.

Landthaler M, Haina D, Brunner R, et al.: Neodymium-YAG laser therapy for vascular lesions. *J Am Acad Dermatol.* 1986;14:107–117.
The results of Nd-YAG laser treatment of nodular port-wine stains and hemangiomas are discussed, with accompanying excellent color photographs.

Olbricht SM, Arndt KA: Laser in Cutaneous Surgery. In: Fuller TA, ed. *Surgical Lasers: A Clinical Guide.* New York, NY: Macmillan Publishing Co.; 1987:113–145.
A comprehensive, well-referenced chapter on the use of the argon and the carbon dioxide lasers in skin surgery.

Olbricht SM, Stern RS, Tang SV, et al.: Complications of cutaneous laser surgery. *Arch Dermatol.* 1987;123:345–349.
A survey on complications of cutaneous laser surgery.

Tan OT, Sherwood K, Gilchrest BA: Treatment of children with port-wine stains using the flashlamp pulsed tunable dye laser. *N Engl J Med.* 1988;320:416–421.
Excellent results with a very low incidence of scarring in pulsed dye laser treatment of port-wine stains in children.

Taylor CR, Gange RW, Dover JS, et al: Treatment of tattoos by Q-switched ruby laser. A dose-response study. *Arch Dermatol.* 1990;126:893–899.
Fifty-seven blue-black tattoos were irradiated with the Q-switched ruby laser, yielding substantial lightening or total clearing in 78% of amateur tattoos and 23% of professional tattoos.

Wheeland RC: *Lasers in Skin Disease.* New York, NY: Thieme Medical Publishers, Inc.; 1988:1–142.
A practical text with quality black-and-white illustrations.

88. CUTANEOUS QUACKERY
Christopher R. Shea

Dermatology and medical charlatanism have long been associated; the term *quack* is short for *quacksalver,* meaning one who quacks like a duck in promoting his salves. People with skin diseases may be especially vulnerable to quackery, as they usually are acutely aware of their afflictions, unlike many patients with hypertension, diabetes mellitus, and other silent maladies. People also notice the skin conditions of others and may, therfore, ridicule or shun the sufferers "like lepers"; this social dimension of dermatologic illness may lead to a self-consciousness and preoccupation with the skin that can encourage false hope in untested, irrational, or even dangerous remedies. Furthermore, the emphasis on youthful beauty in our society supports a huge cosmetics industry that often disingenuously promotes its wares with pseudoscientific claims.

Quackery is easy to criticize but not always easy to define, except in its most flamboyant forms. Strictly, the term implies an intent to deceive for profit, the hawking of wares known to be useless. Many of the fringe forms of healing and hygiene commonly labeled quackery, however, may be practiced by true believers who simply do not share the basic assumptions and methods of scientific medicine. Similarly, there are numerous folk remedies based neither on holistic metaphysics nor on reductionist science but on empiricism and tradition. Do such heterodox practices qualify as quackery? It may be better to avoid such an inflammatory term, and instead discuss a number of questionable health practices and products related to the skin that fall outside the validated practice of scientific dermatology.

It is ironic that the proliferation of **tanning salons,** i.e., emporia dispensing UV radiation, has come at a time of heightened public awareness of the hazards of sun exposure. This awareness is in large measure the result of a vigorous educational campaign by the American Academy of Dermatology; now such terms as *UVA* and *UVB,* once the arcana of specialists, are common coin of the realm. The public has also been widely informed about the danger to the earth's ecology posed by the depletion of the ozone layer. Finally, the publicity attendant to the excision of basal cell carcinomas from prominent public figures has also served to reinforce the link between skin cancer and open-air activities. In the public mind, however, a suntan still signifies leisure, youth, and robust good looks.

Most tanning salons have UVA (320–400 nm) units, catering to the widespread notion that UVB (290-320 nm) is the "bad" UV, while UVA is the "good" UV that permits one to tan without getting a burn. This concept, however, is an oversimplification. UVA is much less efficient than UVB at inducing erythema, skin cancer, and tanning; the effect of UVA on aging of skin is less well characterized. The degree to which one can enjoy the benefits (tan) of UVA without detriments is not completely clear at present, especially since the commercial UVA sources are not entirely free of UVB. Furthermore, it is almost inevitable that such exposure will be combined with ambient solar radiation, possibly leading to cocarcinogenic or other interactions. In addition, there is now evidence that the pigmentation induced by UVA is not highly protective against UVB-induced damage, so persons depending on their UVA-tans instead of a sunscreen may be at greater risk. One need not go to a tanning salon to partake of this fallacy. Various beach umbrellas, articles of clothing, and sunshields made of material allowing penetration of UVA but not of UVB are now commercially available, again catering to the desire on the part of the phototropic public to get a tan for free. The oral use of the carotenoid canthaxanthin to induce a pseudotan may be dangerous; evidence of retinal injury has been reported.

Among the most mendacious products are those cosmetic preparations said to accelerate tanning by supplying the skin with exogenous tyrosine, the amino acid at the beginning of the metabolic pathway for melanin biosynthesis. Clearly, such products would be expected to work only if the tyrosine concentration within melanocytes were the rate-limiting factor in the process, for which there is no evidence in humans. Study of these products in the laboratory has not shown efficacy.

Many advertisements advance claims for **cosmetic and topical remedies** unsupported by scientific evidence. A product line containing sphingolipids was promoted on the basis that it retarded aging of the skin. A renowned cardiac surgeon led this venture; the advertisements quoted him to the effect that in this enterprise, as in his medical career, he was motivated by the quest for a better quality of life. Nor was he alone in his altruism. Numerous other pseudoscientific cosmetic products contain collagen, which the public now knows to be an important component of the dermis; how efficiently the collagen in these creams can traverse the stratum corneum and viable layers of the epidermis, or its biologic fate in the event of doing so, is not stated, nor is it explained why the dermis should require an exogenous and foreign source of this protein. More recently, a variety of "anti-aging" creams containing antioxidants and free-radical quenchers have been vigorously promoted for their largely unproved or unprovable benefits; likewise, "life serum," said to smooth out wrinkles, is touted to improve the sagging physiognomies of the nation.

The appeal of these products lies in their scientific mystique: biochemistry as the way to better living. An aura of improbable quantification radiates from the advertising copy in such phrases as "41% reduction in wrinkles," without, of course, anything as mundane as a standard deviation, or an explanation of how wrinkles can be measured so precisely. Because such advertisements imply that the products affect the physiology of the consumer, they appear to be making medical claims; some, indeed, seem to be at the threshold of false advertising, a prosecutable offense. The Food and Drug Administration has announced that it will carefully scrutinize all advertising copy for cosmetic products, and will no longer tolerate such health claims. When advertising copy merely states, however, that the skin will "look young," "be rejuvenated," or "feel terrific," the claims are so calculatedly vague that it is hard to say whether they are true or false.

In contrast to the pseudoscience of the advertising copy, there is another school of cosmetic commercialism that is linked to folk medicine and organic living—the many shampoos containing wheat-germ oil and honey, the ointments containing vitamin E (a common contact sensitizer), and especially the aloe products. The juice and gel of *Aloe vera,* a succulent plant, provide a common folk remedy for cuts, thermal injuries, sunburn, and the like; scientific study of the medicinal properties of aloe is scant, however. Several reports have indicated possible benefits in the treatment of frostbite, leg ulcers, and radiation dermatitis, while contact hypersensitivity to aloe has been demonstrated by patch testing in one case.

The theory that overgrowth of intestinal *Candida albicans* is related to myriad modern maladies has gained wide popularity because of Dr. W. G. Crook's bestseller, *The Yeast Connection.* In the dermatologic sphere, the **yeast connection** is invoked as a possible link to psoriasis and eczema; furthermore, a number of dermatologic remedies, such as the use of antibiotics and corticosteroids, are held to put patients at risk of developing yeast-related premenstrual syndrome, arthritis, headaches, poor mental performance, and the like. In his book Crook refers to "reports" (actually anecdotal letters to the editor) in the *New England Journal of Medicine* and *Archives of Dermatology* claiming a response of psoriatic patients to oral nystatin therapy; no well-controlled study of this approach has been performed. Diagnosis of yeast-related illness is based on a global assessment of the patient's life style, diet, and mental and somatic complaints, and by the response to therapy; such an approach assures that the diagnosis will always be accurate, as patients who do not respond can simply be defined as not having the illness. A double-blind, placebo-controlled study of oral nystatin in women with putative candidiasis hypersensitivity syndrome showed no benefit in the relief of systemic or psychologic symptoms, beyond the strong placebo effect. Apart from the obvious problem of the placebo effect, it is improper to make a diagnosis according to the response to treatment, as medicines can have more than one pharmacologic action. Cases resistant to the standard regimen of dietary manipulation, purging, exercise, prayer, and nystatin need not be forsaken; other antimycotic therapy, such as amphotericin-B and ketoconazole, is at hand. While acknowledging that such remedies have a potential for toxicity, Crook argues that the risk of not treating resistant cases may be greater still. He quotes, without demurral, statements by another physician that the use of ketoconazole is cost-effective and that in hundreds of cases treated no serious adverse reactions to ketoconazole were seen. Since severe, idiosyncratic hepatotoxicity may be induced by ketoconazole in 1 per 10,000 cases, this apparent safety is not surprising; but if, as is proposed, a great part of the American public is afflicted with the yeast connection, the potential for toxicity from unbridled antimycotic therapy is considerable indeed.

Laser biostimulation is the use of low-irradiance laser light on diseased tissue; this is said to exert a "stimulatory" influence. Clinical efficacy has been claimed for relief of chronic pain (arthritis, postherpetic neuralgia, etc.) and for promotion of wound healing (from thermal injury, stasis ulcers, etc.). Usually red light, as from a helium-neon laser, is used because of its relatively deep optical penetration. The irradiance is such that little or no heating is perceived subjectively. It is claimed that lasers have unique properties for biostimulation, compared to noncoherent light sources of the same wavelength; such a distinction, however, is hard to rationalize, since the turbidity of tissues (other than the eye) will render the laser radiation noncoherent at its presumed site of action.

Much of the positive work on biostimulation has been performed in Russia and Hungary, and the literature on this topic is therefore not readily accessible; attempts to replicate these positive results by groups in the United States and West Germany have not generally been successful. An interesting finding, however, is that low-irradiance laser treatment of fibroblasts can modulate collagen biosynthesis in vitro; and in vivo this method has reportedly been applied successfully in some cases of keloids. Clearly, much more work in this area is in order. There are also many basic studies, again mainly from Russia, on a variety of low-irradiance laser effects in unicellular organisms. The results, which typically show conflicting biochemical and physiologic effects depending on the particular wavelength and irradiance employed, have not led to an intellectually satisfying or coherent rationalization of why biostimulation should work clinically. For this reason, and because much of the clinical research in this area is poorly controlled, many are reluctant to credit the positive results claimed for this technique. This is not to say that all biostimulation is quackery. Some of the spinoffs of biostimulation research, however, including laser-based acupuncture and laser facelifts, lack even a pretense of attention to scientific method.

While the above discussion has concentrated on treatments without any proven efficacy, there is another dimension to cutaneous quackery, the **abuse of accepted treatments.** Many treatments clearly have a role in a particular disease but may still be inappropriate in a given case. Prime among these in dermatology is topical minoxidil for treatment of male-pattern alopecia. Use of minoxidil is most likely to yield cosmetically significant hair growth in men with recent onset of mild alopecia of the vertex. Unscrupulous practitioners, however, are prescribing this expensive treatment for men who are as bald as a billiard ball—a new twist in the manufacturer's use of mass advertising to the lay public, urging patients with hair loss to ask their doctors about minoxidil, and offering a discount coupon redeemable towards the cost of the visit. Minoxidil is not the only "cosmeceutical" that is redefining the practice of dermatology. The reports of reversal of photoaging by topical tretinoin (Retin-A) caused a boom in its sales, followed by the inevitable boomerang as its potential irritancy became manifest. Another related medication that has even greater potential for abuse is isotretinoin: it is approved for the treatment of severe acne, but is too often prescribed for mild acne or even oily skin. In view of the potentially severe side effects of isotretinoin, such as formation of bone spurs, elevation of serum lipids, hepatotoxicity, and horrendous teratogenicity, the use of this drug for trivial indications is irresponsible.

In his pungent 1927 book on quackery, *The New Medical Follies,* Dr. Morris Fishbein discusses many treatments of his age. It is instructive, and a little depressing, to see how many of these practices (chiropractic, astral healing, iridodiagnosis, etc.) have persisted unchanged. In one respect, however, the medical-social climate of over 60 years ago seems quaint: Fishbein relates the case of a lady who had been disfigured by a chemical peel performed by an incompetent practitioner, but "because of the prominence of her social position the woman could not go into court to seek financial reparations for the injury done to her body." In the crowded and aggressive medical marketplace of today, there are ever more dermatologists moving into cosmetic and surgical areas, sometimes on the strength of training taken at a weekend course. Whether the present legal climate will truly serve the public by restraining the abuse of cosmetic dermatology, while allowing its benefits to continue, remains to be seen.

As part of the business sensibility of contemporary medicine, there is a growing amount of **commercial promotion,** and this trend seems especially strong in dermatology. The advertisements for PUVA therapy in the *New York Times* proclaiming, "Vitiligo/Psoriasis: Why Suffer?" have no apparent counterpart in gastroenterology, for example, "Buy one upper endoscopy, get one colonoscopy for free." In Fishbein's time, such commercialism would have been taken as prima facie evidence of quackery, but recent court decisions have considered restrictions on physicians' advertising as illegal restraint of trade. Another aspect of commercialism, however, is now under legal attack: a growing movement in Congress seeks to restrict the right of physicians to dispense prescription drugs for profit. The rationale is that physicians may abuse their patients' vulnerability by overcharging or overprescribing; the proposed legislation, however, would not affect the ability of dermatologists to sell topical medications or nonprescription products such as emollients, shampoos, and cosmetics. Such practices may represent a service to patients, but in the wrong hands, may amount to the promotion of overpriced nostrums by exploiting patients' trust.

Since the basis of a charge of quackery is the lack of scientific proof of safety and efficacy, **biomedical research fraud** is the ultimate quackery. It is surprising that most of the classic works on quackery do not mention this topic. This deficiency, however, is now amply met by the frequent revelations in the lay and scientific press of outrageous acts of scientific malfeasance in the most prestigious research institutes and universities of the United States. In dermatology, the most infamous and pathetic is the Summerlin affair, in which the chief of dermatology at the Memorial Sloan-Kettering Cancer Center was discovered to have crudely faked experiments involving the abrogation of graft rejection by maintaining donor tissue in culture prior to transplantation. More recent major scandals in biomedical research have involved cardiology, immunology, and psychiatry, but in the increasingly interrelated world of biomedical sciences, fundamental findings (or frauds) in any area can affect many distant areas of investigation. Some have found, in the apparent proliferation of research fraud, reason to indict the peer-review system of refereed publication. Optimists, in contrast, will aver that research fraud has always existed and that its more frequent unmasking nowadays signifies the success of the present system. In any case, the increasing competition for diminishing research funds ensures that we will see more examples of the ultimate quackery in the years ahead.

Abergel RP, Meeker CA, Lam TS, et al.: Biostimulation of wound healing by lasers: experimental approaches in animal models and in fibroblast cultures. *J Dermatol Surg Oncol.* 1987;13:127–133.
Interesting review of this group's research on modulation of collagen metabolism by low-irradiance laser irradiation.
Barrett S, Knight G: *The Health Robbers.* Philadelphia, PA: Stickley; 1976.
Historical survey of quackery.
Basford JR: Low-energy laser treatment of pain and wounds: hype, hope, or hokum? *Mayo Clin Proc.* 1986;61:671–675.
Nice review with key references.
Blonz ER: Is there an epidemic of chronic candidiasis in our midst? *JAMA.* 1986;256:3138–3139.
An even-handed commentary, with references, on the "yeast connection."
Cotterill JA: Alternative medicine and dermatology. In: Champion RM, ed. *Recent Advances in Dermatology.* New York: Churchill Livingstone; 1986:251–263.
This is a well-written and reasoned discussion of homeopathy, hypnosis, acupuncture, herbalism and biofeedback as related to skin disease.
Diffey BL: Use of UV-A sunbeds for cosmetic tanning. *Br J Dermatol.* 1986;115:67–76.
Not only pigmentation but also erythema can result from exposure to commercial UVA sources. Itching is a common side effect. The long-term sequelae of such UVA exposure are unknown.
Dismukes WE, Wade JS, Lee JY, et al: A randomized, double-blind trial of nystatin therapy for the candidiasis hypersensitivity syndrome. *N Engl J Med.* 1990;323:1717–1723.
A strong placebo effect was documented. See also the accompanying editorial.
Epstein JH: Suntan salons and the American skin. *South Med J.* 1981;74:837–840.
"In conclusion, tanning for cosmetic purposes is not innocuous."
Fishbein M: *The New Medical Follies.* New York, NY: Boni and Liveright; 1927.
A delightful survey of "cultism and quackery in these United States, with essays on the cult of beauty, the craze for reduction, rejuvenation, eclecticism, bread and dietary fads," etc. Sound familiar?

Fitzgerald FT: Science and scam: alternative thought patterns in alternative health care. *N Engl J Med.* 1983;309:1066–1067.
Some alternative health practitioners are motivated by a mystic credo, others by greed. The public's poor understanding of scientific methods is one reason for the appeal of "magicians and quacks."

Grindley D, Reynoids T: The *Aloe vera* phenomenon: a review of the properties and modern uses of the leaf parenchyma gel. *J Ethnopharmacol.* 1986;16:117–151.
Thorough review, including more recent research on possible actions on arachidonate metabolism.

Hixson J: *The Patchwork Mouse.* Garden City, NY: Anchor Press/Doubleday; 1976.
Cautionary tale of research hanky-panky in dermatology.

Jaworsky C, Ratz JL, Dijkstra JW: Efficacy of tan accelerators. *J Am Acad Dermatol.* 1987;16:769–771.
This study concludes that tan accelerators are worthless. However, interpretation is difficult since the authors used a discontinuous-spectrum UV source, and a single exposure dose instead of a range, and had no quantitative, objective standard for assessing pigmentation.

Lober CW: Canthaxanthin—the "tanning pill." *J Am Acad Dermatol.* 1985;13:660.
Canthaxanthin, a carotenoid promoted to cause "an absolutely safe, deep, gold tan," may cause retinopathy.

Nightingale SL: The FDA challenges "antiaging" creams. *JAMA.* 1987;258:1289.
Cosmetics manufacturers have been notified that improper drug claims will no longer be tolerated.

Spoerke DG, Elkins BR: Aloe vera—fact or quackery. *Vet Hum Toxicol.* 1980;22:418–424.
Aloe may have some pharmacologic actions, but there is little well-controlled research.

Index

The Little, Brown **Spiral**® Manual Series
The Little, Brown Handbook Series
AVAILABLE AT YOUR BOOKSTORE

- ☐ **MANUAL OF ACUTE BACTERIAL INFECTIONS,** 2nd Edition – Gardner & Provine (#303895)
- ☐ **MANUAL OF ACUTE ORTHOPAEDIC THERAPEUTICS,** 3rd Edition – Iversen & Clawson (#434329)
- ☐ **MANUAL OF ACUTE RESPIRATORY CARE** – Zagelbaum & Pare (#984671)
- ☐ **MANUAL OF ALLERGY AND IMMUNOLOGY,** 2nd Edition – Lawlor & Fischer (#516686)
- ☐ **MANUAL OF ANESTHESIA,** 2nd Edition – Snow (#802220)
- ☐ **MANUAL OF CLINICAL EVALUATION** – Aronson & Delbanco (#052108)
- ☐ **MANUAL OF CLINICAL ONCOLOGY,** 2nd Edition – Casciato & Lowitz (#130672)
- ☐ **MANUAL OF CARDIAC ARRHYTHMIAS** – Vlay (#904767)
- ☐ **MANUAL OF CARDIOVASCULAR DIAGNOSIS AND THERAPY,** 3rd Edition – Alpert & Rippe (#035203)
- ☐ **MANUAL OF CLINICAL HEMATOLOGY** – Mazza (#552178)
- ☐ **MANUAL OF CORONARY CARE,** 4th Edition – Alpert & Francis (#035130)
- ☐ **MANUAL OF DERMATOLOGIC THERAPEUTICS,** 4th Edition – Arndt (#051829)
- ☐ **MANUAL OF ELECTROCARDIOGRAPHY,** 2nd Edition – Mudge (#589187)
- ☐ **MANUAL OF EMERGENCY AND OUTPATIENT TECHNIQUES** – Washington University Department of Surgery: Klippel & Anderson (#498688)
- ☐ **MANUAL OF EMERGENCY MEDICINE,** 2nd Edition – Jenkins & Loscalzo (#460559)
- ☐ **MANUAL OF ENDOCRINOLOGY AND METABOLISM** – Lavin (#516503)
- ☐ **MANUAL OF GASTROENTEROLOGY** – Eastwood & Avunduk (#203971)
- ☐ **MANUAL OF GYNECOLOGIC ONCOLOGY AND GYNECOLOGY** – Piver (#709360)
- ☐ **MANUAL OF INTENSIVE CARE MEDICINE,** 2nd Edition – Rippe (#747122)
- ☐ **MANUAL OF INTRODUCTORY CLINICAL MEDICINE,** 2nd Edition – Macklis, Mendelsohn, & Mudge (#542474)
- ☐ **MANUAL OF MEDICAL CARE OF THE SURGICAL PATIENT,** 4th Edition – Coussons, McKee, & Williams (#774936)
- ☐ **MANUAL OF MEDICAL THERAPEUTICS,** 26th Edition – Washington University Department of Medicine: Dunagan & Ridner (#924008)
- ☐ **MANUAL OF NEONATAL CARE,** 3rd Edition – Cloherty & Stark (#147621)
- ☐ **MANUAL OF NEPHROLOGY,** 3rd Edition – Schrier (#774863)
- ☐ **MANUAL OF NEUROLOGY,** 4th Edition – Samuels (#769940)
- ☐ **MANUAL OF NUTRITIONAL THERAPEUTICS,** 2nd Edition – Alpers, Clouse, & Stenson (#035122)
- ☐ **MANUAL OF OBSTETRICS,** 4th Edition – Niswander (#611735)
- ☐ **MANUAL OF OCULAR DIAGNOSIS AND THERAPY,** 3rd Edition – Pavan-Langston (#695475)

- ☐ **MANUAL OF OUTPATIENT GYNECOLOGY,** 2nd Edition – Havens, Sullivan, & Tilton (#350982)
- ☐ **MANUAL OF PEDIATRIC THERAPEUTICS,** 4th Edition – The Children's Hospital Department of Medicine, Boston: Graef (#138886)
- ☐ **MANUAL OF PSYCHIATRIC EMERGENCIES,** 2nd Edition – Hyman (#387193)
- ☐ **MANUAL OF PSYCHIATRIC THERAPEUTICS** – Shader (#782203)
- ☐ **MANUAL OF RHEUMATOLOGY AND OUTPATIENT ORTHOPEDIC DISORDERS,** 2nd Edition – Beary, Christian, & Johanson (#085766)
- ☐ **MANUAL OF SURGICAL INFECTIONS** – Gorbach, Bartlett, & Nichols (#320706)
- ☐ **MANUAL OF SURGICAL THERAPEUTICS,** 7th Edition – Condon & Nyhus (#152617)
- ☐ **MANUAL OF UROLOGY** – Siroky & Krane (#792969)
- ☐ **PROBLEM-ORIENTED MEDICAL DIAGNOSIS,** 5th Edition – Friedman (#293873)
- ☐ **PROBLEM-ORIENTED PEDIATRIC DIAGNOSIS** – Barkin (#081027)
- ☐ **MANUAL OF CLINICAL PROBLEMS IN ADULT AMBULATORY CARE** – Dornbrand, Hoole, Fletcher, & Pickard (#190160)
- ☐ **MANUAL OF CLINICAL PROBLEMS IN CARDIOLOGY,** 3rd Edition – Hillis, Furth, Winniford, & Willerson (#364029)
- ☐ **MANUAL OF DIAGNOSTIC IMAGING,** 2nd Edition – Straub (#818593)
- ☐ **MANUAL OF CLINICAL PROBLEMS IN GASTROENTEROLOGY** – Chobanian & Van Ness (#138975)
- ☐ **MANUAL OF CLINICAL PROBLEMS IN INFECTIOUS DISEASE,** 2nd Edition – Gantz, Gleckman, Brown, & Esposito (#303526)
- ☐ **MANUAL OF CLINICAL PROBLEMS IN INTERNAL MEDICINE,** 4th Edition – Spivak & Barnes (#807389)
- ☐ **MANUAL OF CLINICAL PROBLEMS IN NEPHROLOGY** – Rose & Black (#756377)
- ☐ **MANUAL OF CLINICAL PROBLEMS IN NEUROLOGY,** 2nd Edition – Mohr (#577480)
- ☐ **MANUAL OF CLINICAL PROBLEMS IN OBSTETRICS AND GYNECOLOGY,** 3rd Edition – Rivlin, Morrison, & Bates (#747742)
- ☐ **MANUAL OF CLINICAL PROBLEMS IN ONCOLOGY,** 2nd Edition – Portlock & Goffinet (#714259)
- ☐ **MANUAL OF CLINICAL PROBLEMS IN OPHTHALMOLOGY** – Gittinger & Asdourian (#314714)
- ☐ **MANUAL OF CLINICAL PROBLEMS IN PEDIATRICS,** 3rd Edition – Roberts (#750026)
- ☐ **MANUAL OF CLINICAL PROBLEMS IN PSYCHIATRY** – Hyman (#387223)
- ☐ **MANUAL OF CLINICAL PROBLEMS IN PULMONARY MEDICINE,** 3rd Edition – Bordow & Moser (#102725)
- ☐ **MANUAL OF CLINICAL PROBLEMS IN SURGERY** – Cutler, Dodson, Silva, & Vander Salm (#165751)
- ☐ **MANUAL OF CLINICAL PROBLEMS IN UROLOGY** – Resnick (#740543)

THE LITTLE, BROWN HANDBOOK SERIES